MARCUS AND NARCISSA WHITMAN AND THE OPENING OF OLD OREGON

VOLUME 2

NARCISSA PRENTISS WHITMAN
A painting by Drury Haight based on a Paul Kane sketch believed to be, by strong circumstantial evidence, an authentic likeness of Mrs. Whitman.

Marcus and Narcissa Whitman and the Opening of Old Oregon
By Clifford M. Drury in Two Volumes
Volume 2

Copyright © 1986, 1994, 2014
Discover Your Northwest
New Edition 2014

Published by
Discover Your Northwest
164 South Jackson Street, Seattle WA 98104
DiscoverNW.org

ISBN 978-0-914019-68-8
Two Volume Set ISBN 978-0-914019-66-4
Printed in the USA

All rights reserved. No part of this publication may be reproduced or transmitted in any form or by any means, electronic or mechanical, including photocopy, recording, digital reproduction, or any information storage and retrieval system, without permission in writing from the publisher.

On September 15, 1985, Robert M. Drury, son of the author, signed an agreement to relinquish all rights, privileges, and investment in the books, together with all rights and privileges of the copyright, to Discover Your Northwest (formerly the Pacific Northwest National Parks and Forests Association). We continue to acknowledge and thank Mr. Drury for this lasting and important contribution to the history of the Northwest.

Discover Your Northwest is a 501$_c$3 nonprofit corporation. Our purpose is to provide for the enhanced enjoyment and understanding of visitors to public lands in our areas of operation in Washington, Oregon, Montana, Idaho, and California.

Book and Cover Design by Ben Nechanicky
Portraits on front cover:
Tomahas by Paul Kane; *Narcissa Prentiss Whitman, Dr. Marcus Whitman* by Drury Haight from Paul Kane sketches; *Tiloukaikt* by Paul Kane
Painting on back cover: *Barlow Cutoff* by William Henry Jackson, courtesy William Henry Jackson Collection, Oregon Trail Museum at Scotts Bluff National Monument

MARCUS AND NARCISSA WHITMAN AND THE OPENING OF OLD OREGON

VOLUME 2

CLIFFORD M. DRURY

DISCOVER YOUR NORTHWEST
SEATTLE, WASHINGTON

CONTENTS OF VOLUME II

XVII. NARCISSA'S LONELY YEAR, 1842–1843 1
    ATTEMPTED ASSAULT ON NARCISSA; NARCISSA GOES TO WASKOPUM; LAWS OF THE NEZ PERCES; ELLIS MADE FIRST HEAD CHIEF; RESTLESSNESS AMONG THE CAYUSES; WHITE'S RETURN VISIT; CAYUSES ACCEPT THE LAWS.

XVIII. WHITMAN RIDES, 1842–1843 31
    CROSSING THE ROCKIES IN SEVERE WINTER; PROMOTES OREGON EMIGRATION; WHITMAN IN WASHINGTON; IN NEW YORK AND BOSTON; BOARD RESCINDS FATEFUL ORDER; WHITMAN PLANS FOR THE MISSION'S FUTURE.

XIX. "WESTWARD HO!" 1843 61
    WHITMAN'S VISIT WITH RELATIVES; PERRIN WHITMAN; "MY PLANS REQUIRE TIME AND DISTANCE"; EMIGRANTS GATHER; "TRAVEL, TRAVEL, TRAVEL"; OPENING THE WAGON ROAD TO THE COLUMBIA; AN APPRAISAL OF WHITMAN'S RIDE; REACTION OF THE HUDSON'S BAY COMPANY.

XX. A CHANGING OREGON, 1843–1846 101
    NARCISSA SICK AND DISCOURAGED; CONTINUED ACTIVITIES AT WAIILATPU; MORE NATIVE CONVERTS; INDIANS BECOMING UNEASY; 1844-1845; ARRIVAL OF THE SAGER ORPHANS; GOSPEL OF MATTHEW IN NEZ PERCE; 1845-1846; EMIGRATION OF 1845; ANDREW RODGERS; REMINISCENCES OF THE SAGER GIRLS; WHITMAN CONSIDERS LEAVING WAIILATPU; VISIT OF TOM HILL; INTERNATIONAL BOUNDARY SETTLED.

XXI. PRELUDE TO TRAGEDY, SEPTEMBER 1846 TO NOVEMBER 1847 177
    THE EMIGRATION OF 1846; SEVERE WINTER; METHODISTS GIVE WASKOPUM TO THE AMERICAN BOARD; HINMANS AND PERRIN WHITMAN MOVE TO WASKOPUM; ARTISTS KANE AND STANLEY VISIT WAIILATPU; INTRODUCTION OF MEASLES; CATHOLICS ESTABLISH TWO MISSIONS NEAR WAIILATPU; OREGON EMIGRATION OF 1847; LAST WHITMAN LETTERS; CROWDED WAIILATPU; JOE LEWIS, CHIEF VILLAIN; ROLL-CALL AT WAIILATPU.

XXII. THE WHITMAN MASSACRE 229
    THE MEASLES EPIDEMIC; WHITMAN ACCUSED OF POISONING THE INDIANS; CONSPIRATORS IDENTIFIED; SERVING OREGON THROUGH DEATH; RIDE TO THE UMATILLA; THE MASSACRE; SOME WERE WEEPING; HUDSON'S BAY COMPANY INFORMED; THOSE WHO ESCAPED; FATHER BROUILLET VISITS WAIILATPU; SUMMARY OF THE FATE OF THOSE AT WAIILATPU.

XXIII. CONGRESS ESTABLISHES OREGON AS A TERRITORY 299
   HUDSON'S BAY COMPANY ACTS PROMPTLY; EXPERIENCES OF THE CAPTIVES; OGDEN SECURES THEIR RELEASE; LAPWAI MISSION ABANDONED; DISCOVERY OF STANLEY'S PORTRAITS; IN PURSUIT OF THE MURDERERS; WAIILATPU BURNED; JOE MEEK GOES EAST; END OF THE OREGON MISSION; TERRITORIAL STATUS.

XXIV. EPILOGUE 361
   APPREHENSION OF FIVE ALLEGED MURDERERS; THEIR TRIAL AND EXECUTION; WAIILATPU INVENTORY; MONUMENTS, MEMORIALS, AND ANNIVERSARY OCCASIONS; MYSTERY OF THE SKULLS; WHITMAN LITERATURE; WHITMAN MISSION NATIONAL HISTORIC SITE; CONTINUING FIRST PRESBYTERIAN CHURCH OF OREGON; I BAPTIZE YOU MARCUS WHITMAN.

APPENDICES

   1. INDEX OF THE LETTERS OF THE WHITMANS 415
   2. FINANCIAL REPORTS OF THE AMERICAN BOARD 429
   3. EVOLUTION OF THE WHITMAN-SAVED-OREGON STORY 431
   4. LITERATURE OF THE WHITMAN CONTROVERSY 441
   5. ACCOUNTS OF THE MASSACRE AND THE CAPTIVITY 447
   6. LETTER FROM H. K. W. PERKINS TO JANE PRENTISS 451
   7. WHITMAN'S PROPOSED BILL FOR OREGON 459

BIBLIOGRAPHY 471
INDEX 477

Illustrations in Volume II

Narcissa Prentiss Whitman	inside front
Sketch of Tomahas by Kane	224
Painting of Tomahas by Kane	225
Tiloukaikt by Kane	226
Kane's Sketch of Marcus Whitman	227
Kane's Sketch of Narcissa Whitman	227
Wai-e-cat by Stanley	296
Shu-ma-hici by Stanley	297
Whitman Mission Historical Site	404
The Great Grave at Waiilatpu	405
The Great Grave Dedication	406
The Sager Sisters	407
The Whitman Monument at Waiilatpu	408
Statue of Marcus Whitman	409

[CHAPTER SEVENTEEN]

NARCISSA'S LONELY YEAR, 1842–1843

Narcissa was so deeply concerned with the turn of events which caused her husband on so short notice to leave for the East that at first she did not think of herself. Her hours of loneliness came later. Her immediate concerns were for the safety and comfort of her husband. Aps returned to Waiilatpu on October 4 with a note from Marcus. Narcissa that same day began a letter to her husband which she addressed in care of her parents evidently with the hope that somehow it might reach him before he started back to Oregon. She wrote: "The line you sent me to-day did me great good. I thought I was cheerful and happy before it came; but on the perusal of it, I found that it increased my happiness four-fold. I believe the Lord will preserve me from being anxious about you and I was glad to hear you say with so much confidence that you trusted in Him for safety. He will protect you, I firmly believe. Night and day shall my prayer ascend to Him in your behalf and the cause in which you have sacrificed the endearments of home, at the risk of your life, to see advancing, more to the honor and glory of God. Mr. G[ray] and family did not leave until this morn;[1] they spent the night here, which was a great relief to me. I am sorry we forgot your pencil, comb, and journal."

The next day, Narcissa added the following to her letter: "In arranging the cupboard to-day, I found that you had not taken the compass as you designed to. I fear you will suffer for the want of it; wish I could send it to you with the other things you have forgotten. I intended to have spoken to you about purchasing one or two pair of spectacles. Perhaps you will think of it." Among the Whitman relics at Whitman College is a compass, which may be the one he had forgotten to take. At the close of her entry for October 5, Narcissa wrote: "Where are you to-night, precious husband? I hope you have been prosperous to-day and are sleeping sweetly. Good night, my loved one." According to one of Lovejoy's accounts, he and Whitman camped that night in the snow in the Blue Mountains.

Attempted Assault on Narcissa

After Gray and his family left for Fort Walla Walla on October 4, Narcissa was the only white person at Waiilatpu. John, the Hawaiian, slept in a room in the Whitman home. Late in the night of the 6th, Narcissa had a terrifying experience of which she wrote the next morning to her husband: "My Dear Husband. I got dreadfully frightened last night. About midnight I was awakened by some one trying to open my bed-room door. At first I did not know what to understand by it. I raised my head and listened awhile and then lay down again. Soon the latch was raised and the door opened a little. I sprang from the bed in a moment and closed the door again, but the ruffian pushed and pushed and tried to unlatch it, but could not succeed; finally he gained upon me until he opened the door again and, as I supposed disengaged his blanket (at the same time I was calling John) and ran as for his life. The east dining room door was open. I thought it was locked, but it appears that it was not. I fastened the door, lit a candle and went to bed trembling and cold, but could not rest until I had called John to bring his bed and sleep in the kitchen...had the ruffian persisted I do not know what I should have done." Evidently the Whitmans had an Indian war club, perhaps a souvenir in their bedroom. Of this she wrote: "I did not think of the war club, but I thought of the poker. [There was a fireplace in the bedroom.] Thanks be to our Heavenly Father. He mercifully 'delivered me from the hand of a savage man.'" The quotation which Narcissa used is reminiscent of some verses of the Psalms.

Writing to Mary Walker on November 5, about a month later, Narcissa told of the incident: "...that week husband left, a saucy Indian got into the house about midnight & tried to force himself into my bedroom. John, Mr. McKinlay's man, was sleeping in the house but not very near. But I made a great noise & called as loud as I could & he took to his heels & ran." Elijah White, in a report submitted to the Indian Bureau in Washington, has given us more details of the incident: "He [i.e., Whitman] had hardly left for the States last fall when shocking to relate, at the hour of midnight, a large Indian Chief managed to get into the house, came to the door of Mrs. Whitman's bedchamber and had succeeded in getting it partly open before she reached it. A white man [sic] sleeping in an adjoining apartment saved her from violence and ruin. The villain escaped. There was but one thing worse in this matter on the part of Doctor W.; and that was a great error, leaving his excellent lady thus unprotected in the midst of savages."[2]

Mungo Mevway, the half-Indian and half-Hawaiian lad, who had lived with the Whitmans from 1837 to the fall of 1841 and who then went to live with the missionaries at Tshimakain, unexpectedly arrived at Waiilatpu sometime during the night of October 6. Evidently he spent the night away from the mission house for he did not learn of the attempted assault on Narcissa until the next day. He was the first, besides John, to whom Narcissa spoke of her terrifying experience. Narcissa was haunted with the knowledge that the unknown Indian who had tried to force his way into her bedroom was living on or near the mission premises, no doubt he was from Tiloukaikt's camp. Would he return? Who was there to protect her? Since the intruder had not spoken, she could not identify his voice.

Narcissa sent Mungo to Fort Walla Walla to notify McKinlay of the incident and to ask for someone to come and stay with her. She even suggested that possibly Mrs. McKinlay might be able to do so. Mungo, who was then seventeen or eighteen years old, realized the seriousness of the situation and left early on Friday morning, the 7th, for the Fort. He found the Grays still there and also Tom McKay. The two men with McKinlay agreed that Narcissa would have to be removed to Fort Walla Walla as soon as possible. Both McKinlay and Gray wrote letters to Narcissa informing her of their decision. McKay promised to go to Waiilatpu the next day and stay with her until she could be taken to the

Fort. Mungo was able to make the return trip the same afternoon, which meant that he made a round trip of at least fifty miles that day.

The best information available as to the identity of the intruder is found in Cannon's *Waiilatpu*; he wrote that "the Indian who attempted the assault upon Mrs. Whitman was a second chief of Tilaukait's village named Tamsucky." [3] Cannon also identified Tamsucky as Feathercap. McKay arrived at Waiilatpu on Saturday and, after talking with Narcissa, got in touch with Tiloukaikt and members of his band. Of this Narcissa wrote to her husband: "In talking to Mr. McKay and Feathercap about it, I told them I should leave and go below [probably a reference to the Willamette Valley]—I could not stay and be treated so. I told them I came near beating him with the war club; they said it would have been good if I had done so and laid him flat so that they all might see who he was." If indeed Feathercap (alias Tamsucky) was the guilty party, he showed amazing effrontery; he pretended innocence and gave assurances to Narcissa that "there will be no further danger."

Narcissa's letter to Marcus, which she had started on October 4, became a journal with almost daily entries. On Saturday evening, the 8th, she noted: "The Indians say more Americans are coming." Here is evidence that the increasing Oregon immigration was beginning to give the Cayuses concern. On Sunday, Narcissa tried to carry on with some of the usual religious duties. Ellis from the Nez Perces happened to be at Waiilatpu that day, and since he had been a student at the Red River Mission school and had a fair knowledge of the main doctrines of Christianity, Narcissa asked him to take charge of the usual Sunday service for that day. That evening Narcissa wrote in her journal-letter: "Ellis ...was their minister today. This afternoon I had a Bible class in English with him, John, and Mungo, besides the time I spent with the children. He [Ellis] read and appeared to understand very well."

Narcissa was not in good health when Marcus left for the East; we find a number of references in her letters to this fact. Following the strain of the confrontation which had taken place with the natives in September, the Special Mission meeting, the departure of her husband for the East, and then the frightening experience of the attempted assault, Narcissa suffered a nervous relapse. McKinlay had learned from Mungo that she should not be able to make the trip to Fort Walla Walla on horseback: so he put a "trundlebed" in a wagon when he drove out to

Waiilatpu on the following Monday to get her [Letter 118]. Narcissa, with the three half-breed children, made the trip to the Fort the next day. On the evening of Wednesday, October 12, Narcissa added a note in her letter to Marcus: "The Indians did not like my leaving very well—seemed to regret the cause. I felt strongly to prefer to stay there if it could be considered prudent, but the care and anxiety was wearing upon me too much. Good night, beloved husband."

Although McKinlay provided the best accommodations possible at the Fort, Narcissa suffered for want of the conveniences and comforts of her home at Waiilatpu, primitive as it was when judged by modern standards. Her room was cold, as it had no stove, and the bedding was damp. A week passed before a stove was made available; it is possible that this was brought in from Waiilatpu. On the 14th, a second letter arrived from Marcus and on the 17th, Narcissa added the following to her journal-letter: "I undertook to write to you last Friday, but was too sick to do it and had to give it up. Took a powder of quinine and calomel that night—the next day and yesterday could scarcely go or lie in bed. I suffered much from the lack of conveniences of our dear home, ...for I have been sick ever since I have been here."

On October 22 Narcissa began another letter to her husband in the hope that somehow it could be carried East in time to reach him before he started back to Oregon. In this she wrote: "Almost three long weeks have passed since we exchanged the parting kiss, and many, very many, long weeks are yet to come before we shall be permitted, if ever in this world, to greet each other again ...I follow you night and day, and shall through the whole journey, in my imagination and prayers." Here we see revealed Narcissa's growing sense of loneliness. Stage by stage, she retraced the Oregon Trail in her mind —the Blue Mountains, Fort Boise, Fort Hall, South Pass, Fort Laramie, the Platte River, and finally Westport. She worked out what she felt would be his schedule, only to learn months later how wrong she had been. Finally, in her imagination, she pictured him back in the homes of their loved ones in New York State. "How will you feel, dear husband," she wrote, "when you seat yourself in Sister Julia's house, or with our mothers, and not see the windows filled with Indians, and the doors also; will you not feel lost?"

In this letter of October 22, she made the following reference to the motive which had taken Marcus from her side: "Stay as long as it is necessary to accomplish all your heart's desire respecting the interest of this country, so dear to us both—our home ...Read this letter, my husband, and then give it to my mother—perhaps she would like once more to peep into one of the sacred chambers of her daughter's heart—it may comfort her, seeing she can not see her face again in the flesh." This letter, and that begun on October 4, had to go by sea around Cape Horn and hence did not reach their destination until long after Whitman had left for Oregon.[4] We can only imagine the alarm that members of their families felt when they read of the attempted assault on Narcissa and of her ill health.

THE SPALDINGS IN TROUBLE WITH THE INDIANS

Before Whitman left for Boston, he sent word to Spalding asking him to take care of a number of items at Waiilatpu. This Spalding promised to do [Letter 122]. In Narcissa's letter of October 22 to her husband, she wrote that Spalding had experienced "considerable trouble with the Indians which prevented his coming last week." Although Narcissa did not give details, Dr. White in his report, to which reference has been made, wrote that Mrs. Spalding had been "grossly insulted," and that a disgruntled Indian had "presented his loaded gun, cocked at the breast of Mr. Spalding, abused and menaced as far as possible without shooting him."

Spalding finally was able to leave Lapwai and arrived at Fort Walla Walla on October 21 where he saw Narcissa. He then rode out to Waiilatpu. About a week later, a messenger arrived from Lapwai with a note from his wife, written in a trembling hand. She told of having suffered a severe hemorrhage. The realization that she was alone and ill, without anyone to help her except some friendly Nez Perces, caused Spalding to faint before he had finished reading the note. After recovering, he made immediate preparations to leave for Lapwai. He gave some hasty directions regarding matters at Waiilatpu, selected four of his strongest horses, and with an Indian companion set out for his home. The two left Waiilatpu about nine o'clock at night when it was raining. They stopped once during the night to give their horses a short rest and by daybreak found that they had covered sixty-five miles. They arrived at Lapwai before sundown on the second day of their journey having made the 120 mile trip in nineteen hours.[5] This set a record in the annals of the Oregon Mission. To Spalding's great relief, he found Eliza alive and resting as comfortably as could be expected.

Narcissa at Waskopum

When the Rev, and Mrs. H. K. W. Perkins, Methodist missionaries stationed as Waskopum, also known as The Dalles, learned of Narcissa's situation, they extended an urgent invitation for her to spend the winter with them. After making arrangements to leave David Maim with Mrs. McKinlay, Narcissa and the two little girls left Walla Walla on a Hudson's Bay boat on October 27. The trip down the Columbia to Waskopum took two days. She was warmly greeted by the Perkins couple and also by the Rev, and Mrs. Daniel Lee and Mr. and Mrs. Henry B. Brewer, who were also stationed there [Letter 122]. The Methodist mission at Waskopum was the first branch to be established by the Oregon Methodists outside of the Willamette Valley. The buildings were located about one mile from the south bank of the Columbia River.[6]

In a letter to Mary Walker dated November 5, 1842, from Waskopum, Narcissa wrote: "Since I have been here, it has been difficult for me some of the time to walk & even to move my limbs without groaning. With quiet & rest I expect to be better. Without it I shall be worse. We both felt I was in a way to be better when the Doct. left but I have had so much to excite me, besides care & exposure, that I have not gained but failed since." Writing to her parents on February 7 of the following year, Narcissa returned to the subject of her illness: "My health is very poor; this increases the trial, because, in consequence I have too many gloomy and depressing hours, and evil forebodings, in which I have not strength of mind to rise above." One of her difficulties was her failing eyesight. "My eyes are almost gone," she wrote, "my poor health affects them materially and writing is very injurious to me. I can neither read, write or sew without spectacles, and most of the time, and sometimes with them, I suffer considerable pain."

This letter of February 1843 contains a sad note: the lack of home mail. "September 1840 is my last date from home," Narcissa wrote. "I am expecting to hear soon when the ship comes in." Probably she was here referring to the expected arrival of one of the Company's ships at Fort Vancouver. We know from Narcissa's extant letters that she was most faithful in writing to members of her family. We cannot understand why they did not write more often to her in return.

The Gristmill Burned at Waiilatpu

During the latter part of November 1842, Narcissa received a letter from McKinlay which told of the burning of the gristmill at Waiilatpu together with about two hundred bushels of wheat and corn, and also some lumber and flour [Letters 121 & 124]. McKinlay felt that the fire had been deliberately set. Perhaps some later information reached Narcissa for in her letter of March 4, 1843, she intimated that the fire had been accidentally caused by a son of Feathercap (Tamsucky). She wrote: "Wap-tash-tak-mahl[7] [Feathercap] says his heart is very sore. He does not know how you will think of him when you come to hear of the burning of the Mill—after leaving him in charge of the property. He weeps like a child about it ...He has beat his son severely." Two references in this quotation are worthy of comment. The first relates to Feathercap weeping. Other references in Whitman letters also reveal this Indian as being highly emotional, often subject to weeping. The second reference is to the son who was beaten, evidently because he had caused the fire. A son of Tamsucky, called Waie-Cat, figures in the Whitman massacre. Possibly he is the one involved in the fire incident. If so, he would have been then about fifteen years old.

According to a letter Narcissa wrote on February 7, 1843, her husband had intended to enclose the mill with adobes before he had to leave for the East, but was unable to do so. The part that was burned consisted of the platform which supported the machinery, the frame, the roof, and some nearby granaries. "The sensible part of the Cayuses feel the loss deeply," she wrote, "and they will feel it still more when they want their wheat ground next fall. We hope it will be a good lesson to them and be the one means of making them a better people."

On November 1, 1842, Mr. and Mrs. Littlejohn and William Geiger, Jr., arrived at Waskopum en route to Waiilatpu. Their services had been secured by Gray. Littlejohn had become disillusioned with the possibility of carrying on any independent missionary work in Old Oregon. Therefore, he and his wife had decided to make the overland trip back to the States in the spring of 1843 if they could find some party going that way. On the basis of that hope, they were willing to spend the winter at Waiilatpu. Geiger, whom Narcissa had known at Angelica, New York, and who had arrived in Oregon in the fall of 1839, agreed to take charge of the mission premises at Waiilatpu until Whitman returned. He proved to be a faithful man.

The Laws of the Nez Perces

When Dr. White learned of the attempted assault on Mrs. Whitman and of how Spalding's life had been threatened, he felt that it was his duty to go at once to Waiilatpu and to Lapwai to see what steps could be taken to give the missionaries greater protection. White was aware of the wording of the passports given by the Secretary of War to the missionaries when they went out to Old Oregon in 1836. These documents not only granted them permission to dwell in the Indian country but also called upon "officers of the Army of the United States" and "Indian Agents" to give such protection to them as circumstances might require. White made reference to this when he wrote his official report: "...their passport signed by the Secretary of War made it my imperative duty to protect them in their persons at least from outrage."[8] White felt that this gave him the legal right to take whatever action he felt necessary to protect the lives and property of American citizens in territory which still came under the provisions of the Joint Occupation Treaty of 1818.

Since the Hudson's Bay Company declined to provide river transportation to Fort Walla Walla, White had to make his own arrangements. He hired six men to go with him who "were armed in the best manner, a sufficient number to command respect and secure the object of our undertaking." Perhaps these six also served as boatmen. White also secured the services of Tom McKay, who happened to be in the Willamette Valley at the time, and Cornelius Rogers, both of whom could serve as interpreters. Included in the party, perhaps as one of the armed men, was the half-breed, Baptiste Dorion, son of the Iowa Indian woman who figures as a heroine in Washington Irving's *Astoria*.[9] White and his party of eight or nine met set out for Fort Walla Walla on November 15. Buffeted by strong winds, they were unable to reach The Dalles before November 24. The weather was rainy and bitterly cold. McKay called their experience a "voyage of misery."[10]

Dr. White found Narcissa at the Methodist mission at The Dalles. Of his visit with her, he wrote: "Her noble and intellectual mind and spirit were much depressed and her health suffering ...Our visit encouraged me." Since travel by boat had been so difficult, White decided to continue his journey by land. Having secured horses, the party rode to Fort Walla Walla where they arrived on the 30th. Littlejohn and Geiger, who were still at The Dalles when White arrived, accompanied him to the Fort and then on to Waiilatpu. Mrs. Littlejohn remained at the Methodist mission.

In company with McKinlay, the White party rode out to Waiilatpu on December 1, where White was "shocked and pained at beholding the sad work of savage destruction." His reference was to the burned mill and granary. Even though the premises had remained unprotected for several weeks, except for the possible presence of John, the Hawaiian, there appeared to have been no looting of the mission houses. To White's disappointment, only a few Cayuses were in the vicinity of Waiilatpu when he arrived. Evidently embarrassed over the burning of the mill, most of Tiloukaikt's band had fled. White left word that he would return to Waiilatpu after his visit to Lapwai, at which time he wanted to meet with the chiefs of the whole Cayuse tribe.

Spalding was delighted when he heard that White intended visiting Lapwai. He summoned all of the principal men of the tribe who lived within easy riding distance of the mission to assemble at Lapwai. White wrote: "Seldom was a visit of an Indian Agt. more desired and proper." White had to wait two days after arriving at Lapwai before the Nez Perce chiefs could assemble. During this interval, White inspected the mission premises. Regarding the school, he wrote that he "was happily surprised and greatly interested at seeing such numbers so far advanced and so eagerly pursuing after knowledge." He visited the farms being cultivated by the natives and again was deeply impressed with the progress the Nez Perces were making. Among the twenty-two chiefs who assembled at Lapwai was the venerable Hohots Ilppilp (literally Red Grizzly Bear), also known as Bloody Chief, who was at least ninety years old and who remembered Lewis and Clark. Also present was Five Crows from the Cayuse tribe.

After many speeches by White, McKinlay, McKay, Rogers, and Spalding on the one hand and Bloody Chief, Five Crows, and others, including perhaps Timothy and Joseph, on the other, the Nez Perces were ready to accept White's suggestions. The first related to the adoption of the following code of eleven Articles which White, no doubt with Spalding's collaboration, had compiled:

Art. 1. Whoever wilfully takes life shall be hung.

Art. 2. Whoever burns a dwelling-house shall be hung.

Art. 3. Whoever burns an out-building shall be imprisoned six months, receive fifty lashes, and pay all damages.

Art. 4. Whoever carelessly burns a house, or any property, shall pay damages.

Art. 5. If anyone enter a dwelling, without permission of the occupant, the chiefs shall punish him as they think proper. Public rooms are excepted.

Art. 6. If any one steal he shall pay back twofold; and if it be the value of a beaver skin or less, he shall receive twenty-five lashes; and if the value is over a beaver skin, he shall pay back twofold, and receive fifty lashes.

Art. 7. If any one take a horse and ride it, without permission, or take any article and use it, without liberty, he shall pay for the use of it, and receive from twenty to fifty lashes, as the chief shall direct.

Art. 8. If any one enter a field, and injure the crops, or throw down the fence, so that cattle or horses go in and do damage, he shall pay all damages, and receive twenty-five lashes for every offense.

Art. 9. Those only may keep dogs who travel or live among the game; if a dog kill a lamb, calf, or any domestic animal, the owner shall pay the damage, and kill the dog.

Art. 10. If an Indian raise a gun or other weapon against a white man, it shall be reported to the chiefs, and they shall punish him. If a white person do the same to an Indian, it shall be reported to Dr. White, and he shall redress it.

Art. 11. If any Indian break these laws, he shall be punished by his chiefs, if a white man break them, he shall be reported to the agent, and be punished at his instance."

Each of these laws proposed by Dr. White grew out of definite situations previously faced by either the Whitmans or the Spaldings or by both. The burning of the mill and granaries at Waiilatpu is reflected in Articles 2, 3, and 4. A reaction to the attempted assault on Mrs.

Whitman is seen in Article 5. The confrontation between Whitman and the Cayuses which took place at Waiilatpu in September 1841, when some of Gray's horses were taken without his permission and turned into Whitman's gardens, may have inspired Articles 7 and 8. According to White's report, the Indians at the Lapwai council themselves suggested Article 9 which referred to the keeping of dogs which killed domestic animals. Since the lives of both Whitman and Spalding had been threatened, Articles 1 and 10 were logical.

White stated that the suggested laws were presented "one by one, leaving them as free to reject as accept." It should be pointed out, however, that this code of laws had not been requested by the natives. It was urged upon them by the show of authority by Dr. White, acting as the first United States Indian Agent for Oregon, and with the enthusiastic endorsement of Spalding. No doubt the presence of a Hudson's Bay official, Archibald McKinlay, who evidently supported the proposed code of laws, carried great weight. As has been stated, Simpson had advised McLoughlin to notify all "gentlemen" in charge of the various Company's posts in Oregon to have nothing to do with Dr. White. The very fact that McKinlay, Chief Trader at Fort Walla Walla, was willing to accompany Dr. White to Lapwai indicates that his concern about the increasing lawlessness among the Indians was greater than his fear of incurring the censure of his superiors. Evidently McKinlay felt that this plan of White's to introduce a code of laws among the natives was worth trying. Also present at the Lapwai meeting were Tom McKay and Cornelius Rogers, both of whom spoke in favor of the Nez Perces adopting the laws. Since each was held in high regard by the Indians, their words carried weight.

In an atmosphere of good fellowship, the Nez Perce chiefs agreed to accept the laws. This was the first time that any tribe in Old Oregon voluntarily agreed to accept the white man's system of jurisprudence. The experiment, however, was doomed to failure from the very beginning, as a great gulf separated the white man's concept of a sovereign state and the red man's primitive tribal structure. The code of laws called for sanctions. Here was a glaring weakness, for there were no courts, no police, and no law enforcement agencies among the Indians. Article 3 called for imprisonment, but there were no jails. Hanging was not an Indian method of punishment, and the fact that this was mentioned in Articles 1 and 2 leaves the impression that Dr. White wanted to warn the Indians that this might be the penalty which could be inflicted by white men if circumstances warranted it. Article 11 gives the semblance of impartiality in claiming that the laws applied to the white men as well as to the red. This was impossible of fulfillment, as Dr. White had no authority whatever over the white American population of Oregon. The only sanction stated in the code which could have been used was the lash, as the Indians had already accepted this as a form of punishment.

Ellis Made First High Chief of the Nez Perces

After the chiefs agreed to accept the code of laws, Dr. White requested that one of their number be selected as Head or High Chief. This was an innovation, for the Nez Perces never had had a chief who exercised authority over other chiefs. Asa B. Smith, in his letter to Greene of February 6, 1840, explained that the Nez Perces had three kinds of chiefs: (1) the war chiefs who won their rank through prowess in battle; (2) chiefs who attained a position of influence through "making feasts & feeding the people;" and (3) the "tobacco chiefs" who won followers by distributing tobacco which they had gotten from the white men. Smith summarized: "The power of the chiefs amounts to very little & the people do that which is right in their own eyes."[12]

When Dr. White insisted that the Nez Perces have a High Chief, the first reaction of the council was that he should appoint one of their number. This he refused to do; he called on them to make their own selection. He pointed out the importance of some one having central authority who would act as a spokesman and an intermediary for the tribe. Dr. White gave the chiefs two hours to make their decision; meanwhile he and the other white men withdrew from the council. Describing the meeting in his report to the Indian Bureau, White wrote: "They seemed some puzzled and wished to know if it were proper to counsel with Messrs. McKay & Rogers." White granted this request. After several hours of deliberation, the choice was narrowed to two—Apashwakaikt, also known as Meiway or Looking Glass, and Ellis. The former had been a leader in opposing Smith at Kamiah in October 1840. The latter was a grandson of Bloody Chief and had the distinction of having been a student at the Red River Mission school for about four years, 1830–34. Of him White wrote: "...a sensible man of thirty-two, reading, speaking & writing the English language tolerably well; has a fine small plantation, a few sheep some neat [cattle] stock and no less than eleven hundred head of horses." Ellis was chosen to the great displeasure of Apashwakaikt [Letter 122]. The fact that Ellis could speak English and was sympathetic to the missionaries, even though he had not openly professed Christianity, made him the evident choice by both White and Spalding.

After the conclusion of all business came the festivities. Dr. White paid for an ox which was butchered and the meat barbecued. Of the feast, White wrote: "Our ox was fat, and cooked and served up in a manner reminding me of the days of yore; we ate beef, corn, and peas to our fill, and in good cheer took the pipe, when Rev. Mr. Spalding, Messrs. McKinlay, Rogers, and McKay, wished a song from our boatmen; it was no sooner given than returned by the Indians and repeated again, again & again in high cheer."

After spending about sixteen days at Lapwai, the White party started back to Waiilatpu on December 20. There they met some, but not all, of the Cayuse chiefs. White wrote: "Learning what the Nez Perces had done, gave them great concern and anxiety." Even though one of their number, Five Crows, had been at Lapwai and evidently approved of what the Nez Perces had done, the other chiefs were hesitant to accept the code of laws. White agreed to return in the spring and resume negotiations, when he hoped that all of the Cayuse chiefs would be present. Favored with good traveling conditions on their return trip, White and his party reached Waskopum on December 25.

While at Waiilatpu, either before going to Lapwai or afterwards, the half-breed Dorion spread rumors of a coming large emigration of Americans. No doubt he had overheard some of Dr. White's conversations.

In a letter to her husband dated March 4, 1843, Narcissa wrote: "They [i.e., the Cayuses] say they have been told by Dorion that the Kaiuses are all to be cut off. They do not like such threats. It is also said that they have heard that you have gone home and are coming back next fall with fifty men to fight them." A few days later, Narcissa touched on this same subject when writing to a brother: "They have heard many unwise remarks which have been made by designing persons, especially a half-breed that came up with the agent last fall. Such as troops are coming into the river [i.e., the Columbia] this spring and are coming up with Dr. White to fight them [Letter 126].

The Cayuses had reason to be fearful and suspicious. The Oregon Trail cut across their homeland. They had heard of the probability of a large immigration of white people entering Oregon in 1843. Why had Dr. Whitman gone East so suddenly? Was he more interested in the white man's welfare than he was in theirs? With such fears and suspicions in their minds, it was easy for them to believe the wild rumors spread abroad by Baptiste Dorion, who could always claim that he had overheard some remarks made by Dr. White. In February 1876, more than thirty years after he had crossed the Rockies with Whitman in the winter of 1842–43, Lovejoy, looking back on the events which led up to the massacre, said: "The Indians were very hostile to the Doctor for leaving them, and without doubt, owing to his absence, the seeds of assassination were sown by those haughty Cayuse Indians."

Following the departure of Dr. White and his party, Spalding immediately made preparations for the printing of the *Laws of the Nez Perces* on the mission press. An eight-page booklet appeared with the imprint date of 1842, the fifth item to be printed at Lapwai.[13] Dr. White's name was phonetically spelled as "Taka Hwait." Spalding's great satisfaction in having such a code of laws adopted by the Nez Perces is reflected in a letter he wrote to Greene on February 26, 1843: "Thus far the laws promise much good to the nation and an important aid to the Mission. I have printed the laws & introduced them into the school. They were soon committed to memory by hundreds. I send you a copy." When I first had opportunity to examine the files of the Oregon Mission of the American Board in Boston in 1935, I had the thrill of finding that rare Lapwai item attached to Spalding's letter.

THE WINTER OF 1842–43

Narcissa spent the winter of 1842–43 with her new Methodist friends at Waskopum. Her few letters written during those months bear frequent references to her continued ill health. Sometimes she was confined to her room, unable even to wait upon herself. In one letter she referred to having a "blister" put on her side and being bled [Letter 129a]. A sidelight into the religious customs of that day is found in Narcissa's letter of April 11, 1843 to Mary Walker: "I did attend the Christmas party, a week longer [i.e., later] than was expected. It became a New Years party and a very pleasant one it was." This is the only reference to Christmas found in any of the Whitman letters. The Congregationalists and Presbyterians of that generation, true to the Puritan aspect of their heritage, did not observe Christmas which they considered to be a Roman Catholic custom. The Methodists, on the other hand, who had come out of the Anglican Church, celebrated the day. Thus the Methodist missionaries at The Dalles observed the day, which was a new experience for Narcissa. An examination of the diaries and letters of the members of the Oregon Mission of the American Board show that they occasionally observed Thanksgiving, which was not then a national holiday but just a New England custom, and also New Years and the Fourth of July.[14]

A tragic accident took place on February 1, 1843: a canoe carrying Cornelius Rogers, his wife, and four others was swept over Willamette Falls at what is now Oregon City. All were drowned. George Abernethy, a member of the Methodist Mission who later served as the first Governor of Oregon, 1845–49, sent word of the accident to Narcissa in a letter dated February 4. She forwarded the letter to her husband in care of Secretary Greene with the instruction that if he had started back by the time the letter arrived, it should then be forwarded to Augustus Whitman [Letter 122]. Greene, perhaps knowing that the letter would not reach Marcus at his brother's home, kept it in the Board's files. In all probability Whitman did not learn of the tragedy until he returned to Oregon. Rogers' death was a great loss not only to the missionary work in Oregon but also to the general public, as he had become proficient in the Nez Perce language and his services as an interpreter were increasingly in demand.

Narcissa's letter to Mary Walker of April 11, 1843, told of the drowning of Leverett, the twenty-two-month old son of the Littlejohns in the millrace at Lapwai on March 29. The Littlejohns had gone to Lapwai the previous January where Littlejohn was employed by Spalding. Although the Spaldings had built a fence around their house, the little boy managed to find a hole through which he crawled. Unobserved, he scampered across the field to the millrace where he was drowned. Spalding conducted the funeral service, taking the text used for the service held for Alice Clarissa on Jane 26, 1839. The similarity between the loss of the Littlejohn boy and her own daughter, both very near the same age at the time of death, struck home to Narcissa. "How easy it is for the Lord to take away our comforts," she wrote to Mary, "yes, and our lives too."

In this letter to Mary Walker, Narcissa passed on some news she had received from McKinlay. The Cayuses continued to be aroused by the rumors originating with Dorion that the white men intended to wage war on them. According to McKinlay, the Cayuses believed that Dr. White was to visit them that spring "with an armed force to take away their lands & compel them to adopt & enforce laws to regulate their own people & redress the wrongs of the Whites." Tom McKay had attended a meeting of some of the Cayuse chiefs when they reacted in anger to the implication that "If you do not protect the white, we will compel you to [do so]." Narcissa commented: "They call it threatening language & say that war is declared & they are making preparations accordingly." She told that Five Crows took some of Spalding's booklets giving the code of laws and gave them to the Cayuses. Of this Narcissa wrote: "A few received them while others threw them away with disdain."

RESTLESSNESS AMONG THE CAYUSES

Narcissa wrote a long letter to her husband on March 29, 1843, in which she reviewed the excitement which stirred the Cayuses. The letter, sent in care of the American Board, arrived long after Dr. Whitman had left for Old Oregon, thus he never got to read it. The fact that the Nez Perces had adopted the code of laws and had selected a Head Chief while the Cayuses had not, had become a focal point of trouble. Narcissa explained: "The principal cause of the excitement is; the Kayuses do not wish to be *forced* to adopt the laws recommended by the Agent. They say the laws in themselves are good, they do not object to them—but do not wish to be compelled to adopt (and) enforce them." The Cayuses had come to believe that the white man was trying to force the laws upon them in order to subjugate them. This, the Cayuses believed, was "a deep-laid scheme ...to destroy them and take possession of their country." [15] They accused the Nez Perces of being too willing to accept the laws. The absence of Whitman at that critical time left the Cayuses with no one to whom they could turn for advice. The Nez Perces had Spalding; without his enthusiastic endorsement, perhaps they would not have adopted the laws. We can only speculate what Whitman's attitude would have been had he been present, but in all probability he would have urged the Cayuses to follow the example of the Nez Perces.

Narcissa in her letter of March 29 to her husband told of the seriousness of the excitement. She wrote: "Mr. Geiger writes me that 'the Indians are constantly talking about going to war with the Americans and will not believe anything else but that *you* have gone home for men to fight them.' This last is most trying to me... They have never heard a lisp from me of the object of your visit to the States, no more than what you told them before you left & one would think they had seen enough of you to know that you had not the least desire of that kind toward them. Poor creatures, they know not what to do nor whither they are hastening." The ambiguity of Narcissa's reference to "the object of your visit to the States," implies that there was some motive for his journey beyond mission business.

H. K. W. Perkins, who knew of the reports that Geiger had passed on to Narcissa, wrote to Dr. White about the same time that Narcissa was writing to Marcus and informed him of the restlessness existing among the Cayuses. Perkins stated that the Cayuses were making an effort to form a coalition of Indian tribes to fight the white men, and even a proposal to attack the 1843 Oregon immigration was being discussed. Perkins, speaking for the Methodist missionaries stationed at The Dalles, urged White to return to the upper Columbia country as soon as he could and quiet the fears of the natives.

Looking forward to Dr. White's return visit that spring, Narcissa in her letter to her husband wrote: "I have some fears as to the consequences. But perhaps you will say that they are womanish fears. I grant it. Yet I cannot help feeling a great desire that you should be present at the transaction of so important business to the people among whom we are called to spend our lives. I am requested by the Agent to be there." In this same letter, after expressing her concern, she wrote: "There are redeeming qualities in the character of the Kaiuses notwithstanding they are insolent, proud, domineering, arrogant, and ferocious."

Responding to the request of Dr. White, Narcissa with her two girls left Waskopum on Monday, April 3, and arrived at Fort Walla Walla the following Saturday noon. They stayed at the fort until April 24 before going out to Waiilatpu. Narcissa was pleased to find everything peaceful at the mission. Geiger had done exceedingly well with his farm work in anticipation of a heavy demand for farm produce when the 1843 immigration would arrive. Narcissa was also pleased to see so many of the Cayuses at work on their small acreages. They too anticipated selling such farm products as potatoes to the incoming whites. The one disturbing feature which grieved Narcissa was the blackened ruin of the mill.

Sometime during the spring of 1843, a chief of the Walla Walla Indians, Peu-peu-mox-mox, also known as Yellow Serpent, went to Fort Vancouver to see Dr. McLoughlin.[16] He wanted to know what the Hudson's Bay Company would do if the Americans made war on his people and on the Cayuses. Dr. McLoughlin tried to quiet the chief's fears by telling him that there was absolutely no evidence that the Americans intended to wage such a war and that, should this be the case, the Company would remain neutral. Yellow Serpent's report did much to quiet the fears of the Cayuses.

McLoughlin was displeased when he learned that McKinlay had attended the Indian council held under Dr. White's auspices at Lapwai in December 1842. When he learned that Dr. White was planning to return to the upper country to meet with the Cayuses, he wrote McKinlay warning him that until the boundary question was settled, the Hudson's Bay Company could not "recognize Dr. White as an Indian agent." McKinlay was to treat White only as a private individual. "You cannot permit his holding Council with Indians in the Fort," he wrote, and then added a postscript: "To avoid any misapprehension, you will attend no Indian Council with Dr. White."[17]

Dr. White Returns to Waiilatpu

Sometime during the early part of April 1843, such alarming reports of the situation in the upper Columbia country reached Dr. White at Oregon City that he decided to leave as soon as possible for a return visit to the Cayuses. He now had no Cornelius Rogers to serve as interpreter. He turned to the Rev. Gustavus Hines,[18] a member of the Methodist reenforcement which went out to Oregon on the *Lausanne* in 1838–39. Although Hines did not know the Nez Perce language spoken by the Cayuses, he did have some knowledge of the Chinook jargon which some of the Cayuses understood. Possibly White also expected Mrs. Whitman to help as an interpreter.

Judging by the excitement aroused by Dr. White's first visit to the upper Columbia country, Narcissa was skeptical of any good coming out of a second visit. Writing to a brother on April 14, she said: "The agent is quite ignorant of Indian character and especially of the character of the Kaiuses. Husband's presence is needed very much at this juncture. A great loss is sustained by his going to the States, I mean a present loss to the station and Indians, but hope and expect a greater good will be accomplished by it. There was no other way for us to do. We felt that we could not remain as we were without more help, and we are so far off that to send by letter and get returns was too slow a way for the present emergency." Here Narcissa indicated that her husband's primary motive for his journey East was to strengthen the mission.

On his first visit to the upper Columbia country, White had had a bodyguard of six men. For his second visit, he hired twice as many, "mostly French Canadians," according to Hines. Evidently the rumor-spreading Dorion was not included. White, Hines, and the twelve men left for Waiilatpu in at least two canoes on April 29. Some Indians were hired to help paddle the canoes. The party arrived at The Dalles on May 4; here, evidently for the first time, Dr. White was made aware of the main weakness inherent in his code of laws—that of enforcement. When White had visited the Methodist mission at Waskopum during the previous December, he had persuaded the natives to accept the code of laws and to select a High Chief. After trying to live according to the laws for four months, the chiefs found that offenders condemned to be whipped often resisted even to the point of using a knife. The chiefs did not know what to do in such situations and asked White for advice. He had no good answer for their problem.

Perkins joined the White party when it left The Dalles for the overland trip to Waiilatpu. When White arrived at the mission station on May 9, he was given a cordial welcome by Mrs. Whitman and Geiger. However, he found the Cayuses still in a state of excitement. In his report to the Secretary of War dated November 15, 1843, White wrote: "The Indians flocked around me, and inquired after my party, and could not be persuaded for some time but that I had a large party concealed somewhere near, and only waited to get them convened to open a fire upon them, and cut them all off at a blow. On convincing them of my defenceless condition and pacific intentions, they were quite astounded ...I actually found them suffering more from fear of war from the whites, than the whites from the Indians." [19]

When White asked the chiefs to assemble, they asked for a delay, saying that they wanted Ellis and some of the Nez Perces to be present for the council. While waiting for the Nez Perces to arrive, White and his party visited the fields being cultivated by the Cayuses. Hines estimated that "about sixty of the Kayuses had commenced cultivating the ground." Some had even erected fences around their fields. Feathercap (Tamsucky) acted as guide for the white men and of him Hines wrote: "Of all the Indians I have seen, he has a countenance the most savage." [20]

WHITE'S RETURN VISIT TO LAPWAI

Finding that nothing could be accomplished at Waiilatpu for the time being, White decided to go to Lapwai. He hoped to see Ellis, whose cooperation was needed in persuading the Cayuses to adopt the laws. White and his party arrived at Lapwai on Saturday, May 13, and again Spalding was delighted to welcome the Indian Agent.

Spalding at once decided to take advantage of the presence of Dr. White and the Rev. Gustavus Hines to receive nine Nez Perces into the membership of the First Presbyterian Church of Oregon. Spalding had wanted to do this as early as December 1841, but at that time Dr. Whitman had objected, not because the natives were not ready for church membership but because of personal pique Whitman bore toward Spalding.[21] Now, Dr. Whitman was not present, nor was there an A. B. Smith or a W. H. Gray to object. Nine Nez Perces, four men and five women, were made members of the Mission Church on Sunday, May 14, including Asenath, wife of Joseph, and Tamar, wife of Timothy. This brought the total membership to eleven. After listing the names of the converts, Spalding wrote in the record book: "The Lord's Supper was administered. Rev. Mr. Hines of the Methodist Mission assisted the pastor. Present also Rev. Mr. Perkins ...Elijah White, M.D... & Mr. Littlejohn & wife & Mrs. Spalding." Spalding's joy overflowed. "The Lord be thanked," he wrote. "To him be all the praise for these trophies of his victorious grace. Truly this is a glorious day..."

In a report regarding his work which Spalding submitted to Dr. White, he claimed that during the winter of 1842–43 and the following spring, his Sunday congregations numbered between two and five hundred.[22] Of all the Protestant missionaries who served in Old Oregon, no one had greater success in evangelizing and civilizing the natives than Henry H. Spalding.

On May 18, during the absence of Dr. White and his party, Narcissa wrote a long letter to her husband in which she brought him up-to-date regarding developments at Waiilatpu. The excitement among the natives had subsided after Dr. White had assured them that the United States had no intention of waging war against them. Narcissa bemoaned the fact that such important decisions had to be made by the natives during her husband's absence. "They seem to be and to feel 'like sheep without a shepherd'," she wrote. Narcissa also reported that in the expectation of a large immigration coming in the fall of 1843, Spalding and Geiger had made arrangements to send a pack train to Fort Hall with about 1,000 pounds of flour and other provisions which could be sold to those in need. No doubt this flour had been ground in Spalding's mill. The pack train was placed in care of some trusted Nez Perces. Narcissa took advantage of its departure to send this letter of May 18 with the hope that her husband would get it at Fort Hall. Either the original or a copy was sent to the American Board in Boston.

THE CAYUSES FINALLY ACCEPT THE LAWS

Dr. White and his party returned to Waiilatpu on Friday, May 19, together with Chief Ellis and some four or five hundred Nez Perces. Ellis may have served as the interpreter for the council. The big day came when the Cayuses and the Walla Wallas were present, as Dr. White described the meeting, "in mass." One by one the laws were read and explained. Hines gives the following account: "Yellow Serpent then rose and said: 'I have a message to you. Where are these laws from? Are they from God or from the earth? ...I think they are from the earth because, from what I know of white men, they do not honor these laws." In answer, White explained that all laws establishing a moral order in society came from God and were binding on all men. "Yellow Serpent was pleased with the explanation," wrote Hines, "and said that it was according to the instructions he had received from others, and he was very glad to learn that it was so, because many of his people had been angry with him when he had whipped them for crime, and had told him that God would send him to hell for it, and he was glad to know that it was pleasing to God." [23]

After the council had met for five or six days, the Cayuses and Walla Wallas finally agreed to follow the example of the Nez Perces and accept the code of laws. Five Crows was made Head Chief of the Cayuses.

The meeting was followed by a great feast; Dr. White paid for two oxen which were butchered for the occasion. Contrary to Indian tradition, White invited the native women to join in the feasting. This, no doubt, was to their joy.[24] Having successfully accomplished his objectives, Dr. White started back to the Willamette Valley on Saturday, May 17. With the adoption of the white man's laws, a new era had begun for the Nez Perces and the Cayuses, but troubled days lay ahead. The adoption of the laws by the Indians was tantamount to the surrender of their independence. A realization of this basic fact is one reason why the Cayuses had been so suspicious and so hesitant to give their consent.

Following the selection of Five Crows as Head Chief of the Cayuse nation, Spalding took steps to receive him into the Mission church. Again, there was no one to object. The record books carries the following entry: "June 16, 1843, on profession of his faith in Jesus Christ, Hezekiah [Five Crows] was admitted to the First Presbyterian Church of Oregon, having been examined as to the grounds of his hope some 18 months before ...Has spent two winters in our school at this place." Spalding's exultation on this important addition to the church's membership is seen in what he then wrote: "Go on thou King Immanuel, conquering & to conquer till all these kings & queens shall become nursing fathers & mothers in this little church which is now in the wilderness."[25] Years later when Spalding returned to the Nez Perces in his old age, he used that same record book to list the names of his new converts. Also at that time, he went back to the earlier entries and added certain notes. After Hezekiah's name, he wrote: "Now dead, 1872." Of the twenty-one natives who became members of the Mission church during the years 1838–47, Hezekiah or Five Crows was the only Cayuse. He will enter our story again.

THE SUMMER OF 1843

Although Narcissa was in better health during the spring of 1843 than she had been during the previous winter, Dr. White, as a physician, strongly advised her to go to Fort Vancouver and place herself under the care of Dr. Forbes Barclay, the Company's physician. This she decided to do. Leaving Mary Ann Bridger and David Malin with Mrs. Littlejohn at Lapwai, Narcissa with Helen Mar Meek left Fort Walla Walla on June 1 for Vancouver. Undoubtedly the reason she took Helen with her was that she knew that the child's father, Joe Meek, was then in the Willamette Valley and felt that perhaps they could get together.

Narcissa made the trip down the Columbia in one of the boats of the Hudson's Bay Company's brigade. Of that experience, she wrote: "I had a very fatiguing journey down; came near drowning in the portage once. One of the boats upset, but no lives lost. The boat I was in just escaped capsizing. We arrived here just before sunset, Sabbath [June 4]; displeased with myself and every one around me because of the profanation of the holy day of the Lord" [Letter 137]. This was the first time that Narcissa had been to Fort Vancouver since the mission party left in the late fall of 1836. After an examination of her physical condition, Dr. Barclay advised her to remain under his care for at least a month. We can rest assured that Dr. McLoughlin urged her to stay. There is no evidence of any lack of cordiality between either Marcus or Narcissa Whitman and Dr. McLoughlin after he joined the Roman Catholic Church in November 1842; however, Narcissa no longer made such kindly references to him as when they first met.

In a letter to her father dated April 12, 1844, Narcissa said that Dr. Barclay had "discovered an enlargement of the right ovary," for which he prescribed "iodine to remove it." Although Narcissa did not then know it, she was suffering from "a tumor near the umbilicus" which her husband discovered when he returned in the fall of 1843. In telling her father of her condition, Narcissa wrote that she felt her health was much improved by Dr. Barclay's treatment but "had it not been for the other difficulty of the aorta which was not at that time discovered although it existed, I might have recovered my health. But the medicine I took to cure one tumor was an injury to the other."

Narcissa remained at Fort Vancouver for about two months, or until the end of July, when she accepted an invitation to be a guest in the home of Mr. and Mrs. George Abernethy of Oregon City. She also spent some time with the Rev. and Mrs. Alvin F. Waller and was delighted to discover that Mr. Waller had once ridden a Methodist circuit out of Friendship in Allegany County, New York, and had met her father. A dispute between Dr. McLoughlin and the Methodist Mission, in which Waller was a central figure, was then in its early stages.

Shortly before Narcissa arrived at Oregon City, the Methodists had conducted a camp meeting, at Tualatin Plains, about thirty-five miles distant, with Jason Lee, Gustavus Hines, and H. K. W. Perkins in charge. On Sunday, July 16, Jason Lee led a revival service; nineteen professed conversion, among whom was Joe Meek. In an emotional outburst, Joe cried out: "Tell everybody you see that Joseph Meek, that old Rocky Mountain sinner, has turned to the Lord." [26] There is evidence that although he may have become a Christian, he did not give up his drinking.

Although Narcissa was not present for the July camp meeting, she did attend one held in August which she described as being "a precious season" for her soul. The experience brought back memories of her youth in the church at Prattsburg. In her letter to her father, she wrote: "To witness again the anxious tear and hear the deep-felt inquiry, 'What must I do to be saved?' as I once used to, filled me with joy inexpressible." It is possible that she saw Meek at this August meeting and that he was then able to see his little girl, Helen Mar.

After spending about three weeks with the Abernethys and the Wallers, Narcissa went to Fort George, the former Astoria, to say good-by to the Rev, and Mrs. Daniel Lee and some other Methodist missionaries who were about to sail for the States. The Methodist Mission in Oregon was gradually being dissolved. While at the Fort, Narcissa was entertained in the home of James Birnie, resident trader in charge of the Hudson's Bay Company's post located there. On Sunday, August 13, Narcissa attended a religious service in which both of the Lees, Jason and Daniel, took part. This was the last of many services in which uncle and nephew had joined. Narcissa had the unique pleasure of spending several nights aboard the ship, *Diamond*, on which passage had been booked for the departing missionaries, before she sailed. In her letter to her father, Narcissa reported: "I went down to the mouth of the Columbia river to see them depart and to get a view of the Pacific ocean" [Letter 149].

After the ship sailed on August 15, Narcissa returned to the Willamette Valley. She then spent several weeks in the home of Mr. and Mrs. W. H. Gray, who were living at Oregon City. Sometime during the middle of September, the welcome news reached her of the coming that fall of a large party of immigrants who had with them about 140 wagons. She learned that her husband was with that party and the very thought of seeing him soon caused her great joy. Narcissa made immediate plans to return to Waiilatpu. She and Helen Mar Meek left Oregon City during the last week of September in company with Jason Lee, who was bound for Waskopum. The trip up the river was most uncomfortable, for it rained. As a result of exposure, Narcissa caught a severe cold. They reached Waskopum on Saturday evening, October 7. To Narcissa's great disappointment, Marcus was not there, even though most of the 1843 immigration had already passed on their way down the river.

Narcissa later learned that her husband had been called to Lapwai because the Spaldings were seriously ill with scarlet fever. After returning to Waiilatpu, he then had to leave for Tshimakain to attend Mrs. Eells, who was expecting her second child. As a result, Whitman was unable to go to Waskopum for his wife until the latter part of October. In her letter of April 12, 1844, to her father, Narcissa wrote: "It was a joyful and happy meeting and caused our hearts to overflow with love and gratitude to the Author of all our mercies, for permitting us to see each other's faces again in the flesh." By October 28, the Whitmans were at Fort Walla Walla on their way back to Waiilatpu. Days and weeks passed before each had opportunity to learn of all the experiences which had come to the other during the year of separation. It is easy to imagine Narcissa eagerly inquiring: "Now tell me, dear husband, all that has happened to you."

"Adapted to a Different Destiny"

Although Narcissa was overjoyed to be with Marcus again, the prospect of going back to the isolation of Waiilatpu filled her with dread. In her letter of April 12, 1844, to her father, she wrote: "I turned my face with my husband toward this dark spot, and dark, indeed, it seemed to be to me when compared with the scenes, social and religious which I had so recently been enjoying with so much zest."

Nearly two years after Marcus and Narcissa Whitman had lost their lives in the massacre of November 1847, Jane Prentiss wrote to the Rev. H. K. W. Perkins and asked why the Indians had committed the atrocity. Perkins replied on October 19, 1849, and in a kindly and sympathetic manner tried to explain the background of the massacre from the Indians' point of view. Although, as explained in my introduction to the Perkins letter [Appendix 6], we cannot accept the explanation that Perkins gives as being the real cause for the massacre, his letter does throw light on the Whitman's relationships with the natives.

Perkins, relying on his memories of Narcissa when she was living with the Methodist missionaries at Waskopum, described her as being ill, lonely, and discouraged. He wrote: "Mrs. Whitman was not adapted to savage but *civilized* life. She would have done honor to her sex in a polished & exalted sphere, but never in the low drudgery of Indian toil. The natives esteemed her as proud, haughty, as *far above them*. No doubt she really seemed so. It was her *misfortune*, not her *fault*. She was adapted to a different destiny. She wanted something exalted—communion with *mind*. She longed for society, refined society... I think her stay with us including her visit to the Willamette the pleasantest portion of her Oregon life ...She loved company, society, excitement & ought always to have enjoyed it. The self-denial that took her away from it was suicidal." [27]

Before accepting the opinions of Perkins, it is well to point out some qualifying circumstances. Perkins never met Narcissa during the first six years of her residence at Waiilatpu, and he could not, therefore, judge her attitude towards the natives during that time. No doubt Narcissa did crave the companionship of the Americans in the Willamette Valley, both missionary and non-missionary. Yet the fact that she was willing to return to Waiilatpu with her husband, when her heart cried out for a different environment, is to her everlasting credit.

With the gradual improvement of her health, with a household which grew to nearly twenty, and an ever increasing number of immigrants living for varying periods of time on the mission premises, Waiilatpu no longer was the "dark spot" in Narcissa's thinking, but a hub of activity. As will be told, Narcissa regained her love for Waiilatpu.

Chapter 17 Endnotes

[1] E. C. Ross, Myron Eells, and W. H. Gray, *The Whitman Controversy* (Pamphlet), Portland, 1885, p. 36, states that Gray left Waiilatpu on Oct. 15. Gray was mistaken in his recollection of the date.

[2] Allen, *Ten Years in Oregon*, p. 177. All references in this chapter to Dr. White's reports concerning his visits to Waiilatpu and Lapwai in 1843 are from this book.

[3] *Op. cit.*, p. 67. One of the survivors of the Whitman massacre told Cannon that the Indian who attempted the assault was Tamsucky.

[4] The original letters which Narcissa wrote to her husband, and which he never saw, were later sent to the Oregon Historical Society. See Appendix I. Letter 119, once in Coll. O., is now in Coll. Y.

[5] Drury, *Spalding*, p. 291.

[6] A painting of the Methodist Mission at Waskopum by W. H. Tappan, 1849, is in Coll. O. A reproduction is in Drury, *F.W.W.*, I:168.

[7] See Chap. Eleven, fn. 29. Wap-tash-tak-mahl is mentioned in Whitman letters 100 & 112. See also, Bagley, *Early Catholic Missions*, p. 120.

[8] See Chapter Eight, "Official Government Permit to Reside in Oregon." Allen, *Ten Years in Oregon*, p. 177.

[9] See Chapter Eleven, "Madame Dorion."

[10] Allen, *Ten Years in Oregon*, p. 179.

[11] *Ibid.*, pp. 189–90, but Art. 4 is there omitted. Gray, *Oregon*, p. 228.

[12] Drury, *Spalding and Smith*, p. 139.

[13] See Howard M. Ballou, "History of the Oregon Mission Press," *O.H.Q.*, XXIII (1922):39–52; 95–110.

[14] Cyrus Walker, in his reminiscences published in the *Pacific Homestead*, December 21, 1911, said: "As for me in earlier years, I knew no Christmas ...as I remember, Christmas was not once named." See index to Drury, *F.W.W.*, II, for further references to the non-observance of the day by the American Board missionaries.

[15] Hines, *Wild Life in Oregon*, p. 143.

[16] *Ibid.*, p. 165. L. V. McWhorter, *Hear Ye My Chiefs*, Caldwell, Idaho, 1952, p. 94, claims that "Peopeo Moxmox" should be translated "Yellow Bird." Oliver Frank, a full-blooded Nez Perce from Kamiah, Idaho, has informed me that Peopeo is difficult to translate into English. The meaning is nebulous but in general refers to something that is threatening such as a serpent or a large bird. Moxmox means yellow. Contemporary documents call this chief Yellow Serpent.

[17] *McLoughlin's Fort Vancouver Letters, 2nd Series, 1839–1844*, II:261.

[18] Hines, *Wild Life in Oregon*, supplements White's account of the adoption of the code of laws by the Nez Perces and Cayuses as found in Allen, *Ten Years in Oregon*.

[19] Allen, *Ten Years in Oregon*, p. 214.

[20] Hines, *Wild Life in Oregon*, p. 166.

[21] See Chapter Sixteen, "More Disagreements Within the Mission."

[22] Allen, *Ten Years in Oregon*, p. 203. Spalding's report to Dr. White was written during Whitman's absence in the East. The report shows Spalding's ignorance of the native religion. He does not understand that a "wakin" (p. 207) or "wayakin" is an individual's guardian spirit obtained by a young person in his spirit quest.

[23] Hines, *Wild Life in Oregon*, pp. 177 ff.

[24] Allen, *Ten Years in Oregon*, p. 215.

[25] *Minutes of the Synod of Washington*, 1936, p. 291. According to Spalding's records, he welcomed a Nez Perce into the church on May 14, 1843, who was also called Hezekiah. The Cayuse Hezekiah was received about a month later.

[26] *O.H.Q.*, XXIII (1922):326.

[27] The words italicized are underlined in the original in Coll. W.

[CHAPTER EIGHTEEN]

WHITMAN RIDES
1842–1843

Whitman and Lovejoy left Waiilatpu for the States on Monday morning, October 3, 1842. Considerable detail regarding their experiences during the three months before they arrived at Bent's Fort, in what is now southeastern Colorado, is to be found in the three accounts that Lovejoy wrote, to which reference has been made. Lovejoy's reminiscences harmonize with statements that Whitman made about the journey and add many details that Whitman never mentioned. The two men followed the usual trial eastward to Fort Hall which, according to Lovejoy, was reached in eleven days. Several times Lovejoy mentioned the fact that Whitman refrained from Sunday travel, with but one exception. If Lovejoy meant eleven days of travel, then the two men arrived at Fort Hall on Friday, October 14. Since the distance between Waiilatpu and Fort Hall was about 530 miles, this meant that they averaged about forty-eight miles a day. It had taken the Whitman-Spalding party a month to cover that distance going westward in 1836.

At Fort Hall the two men met Richard Grant, the Hudson's Bay trader then in charge of that post. Grant advised the two not to follow the usual route east through South Pass. Lovejoy explains: "He said it was just perfect folly. The Indians had been up there and murdered the Snake Indians that very season. He told us not to do it. So then

Whitman changed his course and goes by way of [Fort] Uinta, away out to Taos. And around to Santa Fe[1]—away round that way. We were all winter. We made terrible work of it. When we got to Fort Hall, we took men from the Fort, a half breed from St. Louis by the name of Rogers" [L-3]. According to another report, Whitman secured the services of Black Harris, also known as Moses Harris, as a guide at Fort Hall.[2]

There had long been a trail connecting Taos and Santa Fe, in what was then Mexico, with the headwaters of the Platte River. In 1776, the Franciscan explorer, Fray Vélez de Escalante, lead an expedition from Santa Fe into the Great Salt Lake Basin, thus opening the way for trappers and traders. Antoine Robidoux seems to have been in the Uinta Basin, in what is now northeastern Utah, as early as 1831.[3] Robidoux established several trading posts along this old Spanish Trail, including Fort Uncompahgre at the mouth of the river by that name at what is now Delta, Colorado, and another on the Uinta River where it flows from the Uinta Mountains near present-day White Rocks, Utah. These two trading posts were about 150 miles apart.

When Marcus Whitman saw Horace Greeley in New York on March 28, 1843, he told him that his route from Fort Hall went by "Soda Springs, Brown's Hole,[4] Colorado of the West [i.e., Colorado River],[5] the Wina [i.e., Fort Uinta], and the waters of the del Norte [i.e., the Rio Grande]."[6] When Whitman and Lovejoy discussed with Grant at Fort Hall the route to be followed, Grant had considerable reliable information at hand on which to base his recommendations. T. J. Farnham had traveled over the Brown's Hole route in 1839 as had Joe Meek. In all probability, Whitman, Lovejoy, and their guide left Fort Hall on Monday, October 17, for Fort Uinta having decided to take the southern route through what was then a part of Mexico in order to flank the Indian hazard.[7]

An early winter storm struck the area through which Whitman and Lovejoy were traveling shortly after they left Fort Hall. Lovejoy refers to it as "terribly severe weather" [L-2]. This was but a foretaste of much worse weather which they were to encounter. Somewhere along their route in what is now Utah, perhaps at Fort Uinta, Whitman met Miles Goodyear. As a red-haired, nineteen-year-old youth, Goodyear had joined the 1836 mission party in its trek from the Missouri frontier to Fort Hall. Now after an interval of six years, Whitman and Goodyear met again. Goodyear had become an independent trapper. He is reputed to have been the first white settler in what is now the State of Utah. Goodyear wrote a letter dated "Frontier of Mexico, Rocky Mountains, November 1, 1842," which he gave to Whitman to carry to the States.[8] The date of this letter possibly indicates the time that Whitman and Lovejoy were at Fort Uinta.

Whitman hired a new guide at Fort Uinta, of whom Lovejoy wrote: "I think it was an Iroquois Indian and he went on with us. Then came on a big snow storm. We thought we were lost altogether. And this fellow could not go any further. But old Dr. Whitman was a man of great energy.[9] He was going on to the States, he said. We got lost there, got snowed in, the snow buried us & we had to stay there until the storm was over" [L-3]. Lovejoy stated that they were "snowed in for some three or four days," and that when the storm subsided, the weather became "intensely cold" [L-1].

Lovejoy's reference to the cold weather is confirmed in a letter Spalding wrote to A. T. Smith on December 15, 1842, in which he said that the week beginning November 14 was the coldest he had experienced in the country. For three days the mercury was from six to fifteen degrees below zero.[10] This is indeed a low reading for that early in the season for the Clearwater Valley near Lewiston, Idaho, which today is called the "banana belt" of the Inland Empire. Reference has already been made to the cold weather that Dr. White and his party experienced when they left the Willamette Valley on November 15 for Waiilatpu.

The trail that Whitman and Lovejoy followed after leaving Fort Uinta, led down the Uinta River to the Green River. After crossing the Green, the men followed the White River to a tributary which brought them out on the crest of Book Cliffs in what is now east central Utah. The trail then led them over a watershed which divides the flow of the Green from that of the Colorado. They traveled, at what Lovejoy called "a snail's pace," through deep snow to what is now Grand Junction, Colorado. Lovejoy gave no dates for this part of their journey, but it appears that it took them at least two weeks to go from Fort Uinta to the Colorado River.

Crossing the Colorado River

When Whitman, Lovejoy, and their guide arrived at the Grand or Colorado River, they found that it was frozen about one-third of the way across on either side. Only the central part was open and that was because the current was so rapid that the water could not freeze, although, as Lovejoy wrote, "the weather was intensely cold." Lovejoy's account of their hazardous experience in crossing the river follows: "This stream was some one hundred and fifty, or two hundred yards wide, and looked upon by our guide as very dangerous to cross in its present condition. But the Doctor, nothing daunted, was the first to take the water. He mounted his horse, and the guide and myself pushed them off the ice into the boiling, foaming stream. Away they went completely under water —horse and all; but directly came up, and after buffeting the waves and foaming current, he made to the ice on the opposite side, a long way down the stream —leaped from his horse upon the ice, and soon had his noble animal by his side. The guide and myself forced in the pack animals; followed the doctor's example, and were soon drying our frozen clothes by a comfortable fire" [L-1].

On July 4, 1917, the Mt. Garfield Chapter and the Grand Junction Chapter of the Daughters of the American Revolution dedicated Whitman Park in Grand Junction. This is an inner-city community park of one square bock. A large glacial granite boulder, which measures about 6 x 4½ x 3 feet, was placed in the park bearing a plaque with the following inscription:

> WHITMAN PARK
>
> In Honor of
>
> MARCUS WHITMAN
>
> Who Swam the Grand River near this Site
>
> On his Heroic Trans-Continental Ride
>
> Mid-Winter, 1842–43
>
> Which Saved the Great Northwest to the United States

The last line of the inscription shows that those responsible for the wording had accepted the Whitman-Saved-Oregon legend.[11]

After crossing the Colorado River, the men followed the Gunnison River, which empties into the Colorado at Grand Junction, to the mouth of the Uncompahgre River where the Fort by that name was located. This is now the site of Delta, Colorado. There Whitman and Lovejoy remained for three or four days, resting, and obtaining some fresh supplies. Lovejoy stated that a new guide, a Spaniard, was hired to take them to Taos.

Crossing the Continental Divide

The journey from Fort Uncompahgre to Taos took them over the Continental Divide. This proved to be the most dangerous part of their travels. Shortly after leaving the fort, the men encountered a severe snowstorm. Lovejoy, looking back on their terrible experiences, wrote: "After spending several days wandering round in the snow without making much headway, and greatly fatiguing our animals to little or no purpose, our guide informed us that the deep snows had so changed the fact of the country, that he was completely lost, and could take us no further" [L-1].[12]

Although greatly disappointed, Whitman was determined not to give up. "We at once agreed," wrote Lovejoy, "that the Doctor should take the guide and make his way back to the fort, and procure a new guide, and that I should remain in camp with the animals until his return, which was on the seventh day,... With our new guide, traveling slowly on, we reach Taos in about thirty days." The men ran out of provisions. One by one the pack mules were slain and eaten, and even the dog was not spared.

Just at the critical time when the three men were facing the possibility of famishing for want of food, they met a hunting party. "I shall never forget that time," Lovejoy told Bancroft. "I know the old Dr. ate so much it liked to have killed him. We were nearly starved to death though. They told us where to go and put us on the track so that we soon reached Taos" [L-3].

The trail the men followed after leaving Fort Uncompahgre went along the river of that name past the present-day sites of Montrose and Ouray, Colorado. It then swung around the west side of the San Juan Mountains[13] the ridge of which is part of the Continental Divide. The trail crossed the present-day Colorado-New Mexico border before turning eastward to go over the Divide. Although Lovejoy is not definite in giving dates, it seems that they arrived in Taos about the middle of

December 1842. It had taken Whitman and Lovejoy over two months to travel from Waiilatpu to Taos.

From Taos to St. Louis

According to Lovejoy, he and Whitman remained in Taos for "some twelve or fifteen days" [L-1]. They secured fresh animals, bought clothing and other supplies. Lovejoy wrote: "There the Dr. gave us a new outfit." Whitman drew upon the treasurer of the American Board for expenses incurred along the way. This caused some dismay at the Board's offices when the drafts were received in Boston and had to be paid. If Whitman bought a new suit for himself at Taos, it must have been the buckskin he was wearing when he arrived in the East, and which attracted so much attention.

Whitman's next objective on his eastward journey was Bent's Fort, founded in 1833 near what is now Las Animas in southeastern Colorado, by several of the Bent brothers who were engaged in the caravan trade with Santa Fe. Located on the Arkansas River, it became an important station on the trail connecting Taos with Westport, Missouri. The trail from Taos crossed the Sangre de Cristo Mountains, east of Taos, and then angled off in a northeasterly direction towards the Arkansas River. Bent's Fort was about 150 miles, as the crow flies, from Taos.

A detailed account of their travel experiences from Taos to Bent's Fort was given by Lovejoy in his interview with Bancroft in 1878. In reading this report, we get the impression that Bancroft's secretary, Amos Bowman, was taking down in shorthand all that Lovejoy was saying. One can almost hear Lovejoy chuckling as he recalled memories of his travels with Whitman made some thirty-five years and more earlier. "We got a new outfit," Lovejoy said, "and then when we started, that was the wildest chase in the world." He recalled the difficulties they encountered shortly after leaving Taos. "The snow looked just as hard as this floor and about two feet deep." But in places the snow was deeper and the surface crust was not strong enough to bear the weight of the pack animals. "The first thing you saw," Lovejoy said, "the mule would go out of sight & [you] would see nothing but her ears. Some days we would not travel out of sight of the smoke where we had slept. We had a Spaniard from Taos to guide us & nobody else.[14] We used to lift out the mules & start them on again. Like as not they could not go over ten rods before they went into another ditch. We could not see; there was no sign in the world. I think we were from 15 to 20 days traveling what ought to have taken two or three."

When Whitman and Lovejoy were out from Taos about fifteen days, they met George Bent, one of the partners in charge of the fort, who gave Whitman the important news that a party of traders was about to leave Bent's Fort for St. Louis. Whitman, who was impatient over the delays already encountered, decided to push on ahead of Lovejoy with the hope of joining the St. Louis party. Since Lovejoy was planning to return to Oregon with the 1843 emigration, tentative plans were made for the two to meet, perhaps at Fort Laramie. Lovejoy explained that Whitman "taking the best animal, with some bedding and a small allowance of provision, started alone, hoping, by rapid travel, to reach the fort in time to join the St. Louis party, but to do so he would have to travel on the Sabbath, something we had not done before" [L-2].

When Whitman, traveling alone, arrived at the Arkansas River, he believed that he was below Bent's Fort and made the mistake of turning left and went upstream when he should have turned right and gone downstream. When Lovejoy arrived at Bent's Fort on Tuesday, January 3,[15] he discovered to his alarm that Whitman was not there. No one had seen him. The St. Louis party had already left and was encamped about forty miles below Bent's Fort. At Lovejoy's insistence, a messenger was hastily sent to the captain of the caravan asking him to tarry until the Doctor could be found.

Lovejoy's account continues: "Being furnished by the gentlemen of the fort with a suitable guide, I started in search of the Doctor, and traveled up the river about one hundred miles. I learned from the Indians that a man had been there, who was lost, and was trying to find Bent's Fort... I knew from their description that it was Dr. Whitman. I returned to the fort as rapidly as possible but found that the Doctor had not arrived. We had all become very anxious about him. Late in the afternoon, he came in very much fatigued and desponding; said that he knew God had bewildered him to punish him for traveling on the Sabbath. During the whole trip, he was very regular in his morning and evening devotions, and that was the only time I ever knew him to travel on the Sabbath" [L-2]. No doubt Whitman felt it wise to follow the curves of the river while Lovejoy and his guide might have cut across the country at times. This would explain why Lovejoy passed Whitman twice, once while going up the river and again while returning, without them seeing each other.

Whitman remained at the fort overnight and on the following morning, Saturday, January 7, said good-by to Lovejoy and hastened on to join the St. Louis party. Before leaving the fort, Whitman signed an order on January 6, 1843, on the American Board for $301.25 which Bent and Company cashed.[16] With these funds, Whitman paid off his Spanish guide and covered other expenses.

Not a single reference has been found relating to the 400-mile trip that Whitman made with the caravan from Bent's Fort to Westport. We learn from a letter that he wrote to Greene on April 4, 1843, that he arrived at Westport on February 15. Ever since Narcissa bade her husband good-by on October 3, 1842, she had been following in her imagination his progress across the country. By the time Marcus arrived at Westport, Narcissa figured that he was then with her relatives, for on February 7 she wrote to her parents: "I speak as if you were enjoying the society of my dear husband at this time." Months passed before she learned of the long detour that he had been obliged to take in what has been called one of the worst winters of our history.

Whitman remained in Westport for about a week. This we know from a letter in the archives of Whitman College dated from Westport, February 22, 1843, and addressed to C. W. Boyers of Independence. The letter reads: "Dr. Sir. Allow me to introduce to you the bearer, Doctor Whitman, Suprintd. of American Boards Missions Oregon and of the Presbyterian order. Your attention to him will be duly acknowledged by your friend & Obt. Svt. A. G. Boone." The identity of Boone is not known, but Boyers was an elder in the Presbyterian Church of Independence and the town's postmaster. According to Perrin Whitman, his uncle left his animals with Boyers until his return in the late spring.[17]

The next documented date which traces Whitman's progress across the country is found in a letter from B. Clapp to Pierre Chouteau, Jr., dated at St. Louis on March 7, 1843. After referring to the draft for $301.25 which Whitman had cashed at Bent's Fort, Clapp wrote: "Doctor Whitman brought the dft. himself from Bent & Co on his way from the Columbia, where he is established as a mission, being now [On] a visit to Boston. He left to day via the Ohio."[18] According to this, Whitman was planning to go by river steamer up the Ohio, perhaps to Pittsburgh, and then overland to Washington.

As has been stated, Whitman carried several letters written by his wife to some of her relatives, including one to her sister and brother, Jane and Edward. Narcissa had hoped that Marcus would be able to deliver the letter in person at Quincy, Illinois, where they lived. The long detour to Taos, however, had caused such a delay that Whitman felt it imperative to hasten on to Washington; Narcissa's letter to Jane and Edward was mailed in St. Louis. A notation on the back of the letter in Whitman's handwriting reads: "Narcissa Whitman, Rocky Mountains, March 9:43." The postmark bears the stamp of the St. Louis office for that date. Evidently there was a delay of at least two days after Clapp wrote before Whitman left St. Louis.

Whitman, a Guest of Dr. Edward Hale

During his stay of two or three days in St. Louis, Whitman was a guest in the home of Dr. Edward Hale, a dentist, with whom he also stayed on his return journey to Oregon. On July 19, 1871, when Hale was seventy years old, he wrote to H. H. Spalding: "I had the pleasure of entertaining Dr. Whitman at St. Louis on his last visit eastward to confer with the President & heads of departments in relation to the settlement of the N.W. boundary question with Gr. Britain by bartering away for a song the whole N.W. Pacific Territory." [19] Hale's comments regarding the political purpose of Whitman's ride reflect, almost literally, some of the exaggerated statements that Spalding was making in his promotion of the Whitman-Saved-Oregon theory. Spalding's *Senate Document* was ordered to be printed on February 9, 1871; possibly Hale had this item on his desk when he wrote during the following July. Certainly, in view of the circumstances, we cannot take seriously Hale's testimony regarding the political motives involved in Whitman's ride.

Living in the Hale home at the time of Whitman's visit, was a twenty-eight-year-old schoolteacher, William Barrows, who, forty years later, published his *Oregon: The Struggle for Possession*. "On his arrival in St. Louis," wrote Barrows, "it was my good fortune that he should be quartered, as a guest, under the same roof, and at the same table with me... Marcus Whitman once seen... was a man not to be forgotten by the writer." Barrows remembered him as being a man of "medium height... large head... covered with stiff iron-grey hair, while his face carried all the moustache and whiskers that four months had been able to put on it."

Although Whitman's buckskin dress did not attract undue attention in St. Louis, we find several commenting on its strangeness as he traveled East. But Barrows, after forty years, had vivid memories and gave us the following description: "His dress would now appear much more peculiar than in those days and in that city. For St. Louis was then no stranger to blanket Indians, and Yellowstone trappers, in buckskin and buffalo [skin]. The Doctor was in coarse fur garments and vesting, and buckskin breeches. He wore a buffalo coat, with a head-hood for emergencies in taking a storm, or a bivouac nap,... heavy fur leggings and boot-moccasins... If memory is not at fault with me, his entire dress on the street did not show one square inch of woven fabric." Barrows then stated that, notwithstanding his fur clothing, "he bore the marks of irresistible cold and merciless storms... His fingers, ears, nose, and feet had been frostbitten, and were giving him much trouble."[20]

Whitman's Promotion of Oregon Emigration

Barrows remembered that the arrival of Whitman in St. Louis from faraway Oregon aroused great interest in a city of about twenty thousand inhabitants. As soon as news of his presence was spread abroad, Whitman was besieged by a flood of visitors, including "Rocky Mountain men, trappers, traders, adventurers, and contractors for military posts"—who asked a multitude of questions regarding the fur trade, Indian wars, the fate of those who had migrated to Oregon in 1842, and the possibilities of the future for Oregon.

According to Barrows, Whitman was more interested in asking questions than in answering. Elijah White had told him about the pending Webster-Ashburton Treaty which, it was hoped, would deal with the Old Oregon boundary, and the Linn bill which promised 640 acres of land to every white male over eighteen years of age who would settle in Oregon. Barrows remembered that Whitman asked: "Was the Ashburton Treaty concluded? Did it cover the Northwest?" He was told that the Treaty had been signed on the preceding August 9 but that it dealt with the Maine boundary and not with the Oregon.

The Linn bill came to a vote in the Senate on February 3, 1843, and passed by a vote of twenty-four to twenty-two. The opposition claimed that the provisions of the bill violated the Treaty of Joint Occupation and that the boundary question had to be settled before the United States could legally extend its jurisdiction over any part of the Oregon territory. After passing the Senate, the bill was sent to the House, where it was lost in the rush of business which usually marks the closing days of any session of Congress. The third session of the Twenty-Seventh Congress had adjourned on March 4, 1843, but due to the slowness of communications of that time, this was not known in St. Louis when Whitman was there. Hoping that he could reach Washington before Congress adjourned, Whitman was eager to be on his way.

The sentiment on the western frontier at the time of Whitman's visit to St. Louis was strongly pro-Oregon. It was generally believed that the Linn bill would eventually pass, and hundreds of men were ready to migrate to Oregon with their families in anticipation of that enactment. The promotion of the 1843 emigration had been started before Whitman arrived in St. Louis. No claim has ever been made, even by the most fervent adherents of the Whitman-Saved-Oregon story, that Whitman was solely responsible for the large number who went to Oregon that year. There would have been an 1843 emigration had Whitman never gone East. On the other hand, we have evidence that Whitman was zealous in encouraging people to go to Oregon. A study of this influence was made by Myron Eells who published in 1883 his findings in a pamphlet under the title *Marcus Whitman, M.D., Proofs of His Work in Saving Oregon, and in Promoting the Immigration of 1843*.

In gathering information for this pamphlet, Eells wrote to all of the 1843 emigrants whom he could locate and made inquiry regarding the motives which inspired each to go to Oregon. Lindsay Applegate wrote that he had inserted a notice in the Booneville, Missouri, *Herald*, about March 1, 1843, announcing that a party would be going to Oregon and calling on those who wished to join such a party to meet at Westport about May 1. Several stated that they were induced to go to Oregon because of personal interviews with Whitman, through newspaper articles he had inspired or written, and two referred to a pamphlet he had published.[21] Perrin Whitman, a nephew of Marcus who went out to Oregon with his uncle in 1843, claimed in 1898 that many of the emigrants of that year "had come as a result of hand-bills which he [i.e., Marcus] distributed on the frontier as he went through [i.e., while en route to the East], saying that he must be back to start with them at the first peep of grass." [22] It is most improbable that Whitman would have had time or opportunity to write and publish a pamphlet while passing through Missouri but he could have issued a handbill stating the advantages of migrating to Oregon, together with some simple directions as to what should be taken for an overland journey. If such a pamphlet was issued, no copy is known to be extant today.

Among those who were induced to go to Oregon by Whitman were the Hobson, Eyres, and Thomas Smith families, and a young lawyer, John Ricard. At the time Whitman was in St. Louis, Eyres owned a shop in the city which was a meeting place for many who were thinking of going to Oregon. It was there that Whitman met John Hobson. Mention will be made later of the two motherless Hobson girls, Emma and Ann, being received into the Whitman home at Waiilatpu. A reference to sheep in a letter that Whitman wrote to his brother-in-law, J. G. Prentiss, from the Missouri frontier on May 28, 1843, provides evidence that on his eastward journey through Missouri, he was giving advice to would-be emigrants. He wrote: "A great many cattle are going, but no sheep, from a mistake of what I said in passing."

Whitman in Washington

Since Whitman planned to be back on the Missouri frontier in early May, he had but two months to make his journey to Washington, Boston, and then to western New York to see his relatives. Time was short, especially when we remember the conditions of travel of that day. The journey from St. Louis to Washington would have taken about two weeks, which would have put him in the capital city about March 21.

Whitman stopped at Cincinnati on his way up the Ohio River, where he called on Dr. George L. Weed, a representative of the American Board who frequently entertained its missionaries in their travels up and down the river. George L. Weed, Jr., in 1897 wrote his reminiscences of Whitman's visit: "Most unexpected was his appearance at my father's in Cincinnati, where he was a welcome visitor when on his journey across the continent, and where he had brought his bride seven years before. We thought him on the banks of the Columbia. It fell to me to receive him at the door. My memory of that morning is still fresh with boyish wonderment. I stared at what seemed an apparition. He was still dressed in his mountain garb. His fur garments, buckskin breeches, fur leggins, boot moccasins, and buffalo overcoat with head hood, had been poor protection from the cold and storms of the fearful ride. His face and hands and feet had been frozen." [23]

When Whitman asked to see the boy's father, he was told that Dr. Weed was attending a prayer meeting at Dr. Lyman Beecher's church. "Thither," wrote George, Junior, "he hastened. His entrance created consternation, while everyone asked: 'Who, what is he?'" According to the son, Dr. Whitman remained in Cincinnati for only a few hours, perhaps just long enough for the river boat to discharge and take on cargo, and then he left.

Whitman's visit to Washington has been a focal point of discussion in the Whitman controversy. The fact that he went to Washington is so well documented that it is no longer questioned by the severest critic of the Whitman-Saved-Oregon story. The strongest evidence of his presence in Washington is found in the following quotation from a letter that Whitman wrote to the Hon. James M. Porter, Secretary of War, which bears the notation of having been received on June 22, 1844: "In compliance with the request you did me the honor to make last Winter, while in Washington..." [Letter 143].

When Whitman was in Washington, he tried to get in touch with William C. McKay, whom he thought to be still studying at the Fairfield Medical College. At the time Whitman wrote, McKay had transferred to a medical school at Willoughby, Ohio. Dr. McKay, writing his recollection of the incident on January 30, 1885, stated that Dr. Whitman had written to him from Washington, but, since the original correspondence had been lost, he could not give the exact date.[24]

The advocates of the Whitman-Saved-Oregon story have stressed the fact, which can easily be documented, that Whitman visited Washington before going to Boston as evidence that his main motive for going East was political. W. I. Marshall, the caustic opponent of that theory, wrote: "It is altogether probable that he went to Washington from Boston, as he seems to have reached his home in Rushville, N.Y., about April 18th." [25] However, the known chronology of Whitman's travels makes Marshall's theory untenable. We know that Whitman was in Boston as late as April 8 and that he left Rushville for the Missouri frontier on the 20th. This twelve-day period is not long enough for him to have gone from Boston to Washington and then to Rushville with a week or more for visiting his relatives. The fact that Whitman went first to Washington and then to Boston neither proves nor disproves any theory as to which motive, the political or mission business, was primary in his thinking. The determining factor was simply that of convenience in a tight time schedule.

There is evidence that Whitman knew the Hon. John C. Spencer, 1778–1855, who was Secretary of War in President Tyler's cabinet from October 1841 to March 1843, when he was made Secretary of the Treasury. Spencer hailed from Canandaigua, New York, the county seat of Ontario County, where he practiced law. Since Rushville is but ten miles from Canandaigua, it is altogether probable that Whitman, as a medical student riding with Dr. Bryant, had had opportunities to meet Spencer. The first entry in Jonathan Pratt's diary, of which mention has been made, dated January 1, 1824, states that Jonathan had been to Canandaigua to hear Spencer speak. If Pratt knew Spencer, it is reasonable that Whitman did likewise.

Since Elijah White had been in Washington in the spring of 1842 and had received his appointment as Indian Agent for Oregon from Spencer, there is reason to believe that White had told Whitman of Spencer's official position. All Indian affairs were then a part of the responsibilities of the Secretary of War. The Oregon Trail went through Indian country, thus the Secretary of War would have been the Government official most interested in the welfare of Oregon emigrants. When Whitman visited Washington, therefore, he had an important contact with a member of the President's cabinet.

After his return to Waiilatpu, Whitman told William Geiger, Jr., about his experiences in the capital city. According to Geiger, Whitman called on Spencer who introduced him to the Hon. James M. Porter, the new Secretary of War, and also to Daniel Webster, then Secretary of State, and even arranged an interview with President Tyler.[26] Another who claimed that Whitman told him that he had seen the President was Lovejoy, who wrote: "He often expressed himself to me about the remainder of his journey [i.e., from Bent's Fort to Washington and Boston]... He had several interviews with President Tyler, Secretary Webster, and a good many members of Congress" [L-2]. Still others who claimed that Whitman told them he had seen President Tyler include Spalding, Gray, Perrin Whitman, and David Lennox.[27] It is inconceivable that so many different people would have deliberately concocted the story of Whitman's interview with President Tyler.

In Spalding's account of Whitman's meeting with Secretary Webster and President Tyler, we come to the very core of his Whitman-Saved-Oregon story. After pointing out that Whitman and Webster came from the same state, Spalding wrote: "Mr. Webster lived too near Cape Cod to see things in the same light with his fellow statesman who had transferred his worldly interest in the Pacific Coast." Possibly, when Whitman told Spalding of his interview with Webster, he told of the latter's desire to obtain for the United States some rights to a cod-fishery off the Newfoundland coast. Writing more than twenty years later, Spalding's memory could have misled him when he tried to recall exactly what Webster had told Whitman, for Spalding wrote that Webster "had about traded it [i.e., Oregon] off with Gov. Simpson to go into the Ashburton Treaty, for a cod fishery."[28] There is no documentary evidence to support this part of Spalding's Whitman-Saved-Oregon story.

Another point brought out by Spalding in his published lectures is the undocumented claim that Governor Simpson deliberately misrepresented the nature of the Oregon country in order to mislead Webster as to its worth and consequently lessen the interest of the United States in that distant territory. Spalding considered such an alleged degradation of Oregon to be part of a diabolical plot of the Hudson's Bay Company to help England get title to Oregon. Regardless of whether or not Webster had heard the alleged misrepresentations, it would have been perfectly logical for Webster to make inquiry of Whitman regarding the potentialities of the Oregon country.

In reviewing the writings of both Whitman and Spalding regarding the extension of United States jurisdiction over Oregon, we find that neither had anything definite to say about the location of the boundary. Whitman's interest seems to have been centered on emigration; he evidently believed that the boundary question was secondary in importance to getting a large American population to settle in the country.

Regarding Whitman's interview with the President, Spalding wrote:

> The Doctor next sought an interview with President Tyler, who at once appreciated his solicitude and his timely representations

of Oregon... He said that, although the Doctor's representations of the character of the country, and the possibility of reaching it by wagon route, were in direct contradiction to those of Gov. Simpson, his frozen limbs were sufficient proof of his sincerity, and his missionary character was sufficient guarantee for his honesty, and he would therefore, as President, rest upon these and not act accordingly; would detail Fremont with a military force to escort the Doctor's caravan through the mountains; and no more action should be had towards trading off Oregon till he could hear the result of the expedition. If the Doctor could establish a wagon route through the mountains to the Columbia River, pronounced impossible by Gov. Simpson and Ashburton, he would use his influence to hold on to Oregon.[29]

As has been stated, there is evidence to indicate that many in England believed that Oregon could never be colonized by overland emigration from the United States;[30] hence this statement of Spalding's as to what Simpson said in this regard may be accepted as factual.

No doubt Government officials, including the President, were delighted to have the opportunity to talk with Whitman about Oregon. Never before had anyone arrived in Washington from that distant territory so well informed, so qualified to speak with authority about its resources, its Indian tribes, travel conditions on the Oregon Trail, and the desires of the American population already there. Elijah White, who had been in the capital city the previous year, had spent only three years in Oregon; Whitman had spent six. White had gone to and from Oregon by sea; Whitman had made the round trip overland. Moreover, Whitman's arrival in Washington was most timely; the Oregon question was becoming increasingly a subject of great popular interest as well as of official concern.

Synopsis of Whitman's Bill

The best indication of the subject of Whitman's interviews with such officials as Porter, Webster, and Tyler is the contents of a bill which he drew up for Congressional consideration, and which he sent to the Secretary of War after he had returned to Waiilatpu.[31] It is possible that Porter or Tyler, after hearing Whitman stress the necessity for the Government to provide protection to the Oregon-bound emigrants, asked

Whitman to put his recommendations in writing. Much that Whitman had to say struck a responsive chord in Tyler's thinking. In his message that he delivered at the opening of the Twenty-Seventh Congress on December 6, 1841, Tyler had endorsed a recommendation made by the then Secretary of War, John C. Spencer, for the establishment of "a chain of military posts from Council Bluffs to some point on the Pacific Ocean within our limits." [32] When Senator Linn introduced a new Oregon bill early in the Congressional session of 1842–43, he included a provision that the Government build "a line of forts from our western frontier to the mouth of the Columbia River." [33]

Whitman in his proposed bill stressed the need for the protection and welfare of the Oregon emigrants. Whereas the Linn bill called for the establishment of "a line of forts," Whitman suggested "a chain of agricultural posts or farming stations." In Section 1 of his proposal, Whitman stated: "Which said posts shall have for their object to set examples of civilized industry to the several Indian tribes, to keep them in proper subjection to the laws of the United States, to suppress violent and lawless acts along the said line of frontier, to facilitate the passage of troops and munitions of war into and out of said territory of Oregon, and the transportation of the mail..."

Section 5 of the proposal outlined the duty of the superintendents of said posts, calling upon each to cultivate up to 640 acres of land in areas where such was possible, in order to raise produce which could be used by the military and the passing emigrants. Whitman in his accompanying letter to Porter was more specific on this point than he was in his bill. He wrote that if produce were raised at these "farming stations," it could be sold to the emigrants, thus "diminishing the original burdens" of the travelers and at the same time helping "to defray the expenses of such posts." Each post was to be equipped with storehouses, blacksmith, gunsmith, and carpenter shops.

Whitman also thought about the transportation of the mails. In his letter to Porter, he wrote: "I need only add that contracts for this purpose will be readily taken at reasonable rates for transporting the mail across from Missouri to the mouth of the Columbia in forty days, with fresh horses at each of the contemplated posts." The Pony Express, which Whitman here proposed, did not become a reality until April 1860, nearly seventeen years later, and then it served California rather than the Pacific Northwest.

There was a political purpose in Whitman's visit to Washington, how else is it possible to explain his presence in the city and the contents of his proposed bill? Even though no treaty affecting the Pacific Northwest was then under consideration, Whitman, as an enthusiastic booster of Oregon, was able to pass on much valuable information to high Government officials. Although we have no evidence that he discussed the possible location of the Old Oregon boundary, we do know that Whitman stressed the importance of promoting Oregon emigration and the necessity of protecting those traveling over the Oregon Trail. Whitman was eager for the extension of the jurisdiction of the United States over Oregon, and he was convinced that this could best be obtained by first establishing a large American colony in that region.

Whitman in New York

Whitman could not have tarried in Washington for more than two or three days, as he was in New York on Saturday, March 25, 1843. He took passage on a ship bound for Boston on Monday evening, the 27th. During his two-day stay in New York, Whitman made two important calls. The first was on Horace Greeley, editor of the New York *Daily Tribune*. When Whitman knocked at the door of Greeley's office, a woman received him. She was so surprised to see a man standing before her clad in such strange garb that, when Whitman asked to see Mr. Greeley, she curtly told him that he was not in. Disappointed, Whitman turned to go away. In the meantime, Greeley inquired regarding the visitor and was probably told that the stranger, dressed worse than a tramp, had been turned away. Greeley hurried to the window and caught a glimpse of Whitman. Greeley, himself none too particular in matters of dress, saw something in Whitman which attracted his attention. He hurried to the door and called Whitman back. After due apologies, the two men had a long visit.

An account of the interview which Greeley had with Whitman appeared in the March 29 issue of the *Daily Tribune*.[34] It was evidently written on the 28th, for Greeley began by writing: "We were most agreeably surprised yesterday by a call from Doctor Whitman from Oregon, a member of the American Presbyterian Mission in that territory. A slight glance at him when he entered our office would convince any one that he had seen all the hardships of a life in the wilderness. He was dressed in an old fur cap, that appears to have seen some ten years of service, faded, and nearly destitute of fur; a vest whose natural color had long since faded, and a shirt—we could not see that he had any—an overcoat, every thread of which could be easily seen, buckskin pants, etc.—the roughest man we have seen this many a day—too poor, in fact, to get any better wardrobe. The doctor is one of those daring and good men who went to Oregon some ten [sic] years ago to teach the Indians religion, agriculture, letters, etc. A noble pioneer we judge him to be, *a man fitted to be a chief in rearing a moral empire among the wild men of the wilderness.*"[35]

Greeley passed on to his readers information that Whitman had brought about those who had gone out to Oregon in the 1842 migration. He outlined the route that Whitman had followed on his hazardous journey, mentioning the fact that he had gone along the western side of the Anahuac [i.e., the San Juan Mountains] before crossing the Continental Divide. Greeley also had the following story to tell of an unhappy experience Whitman had had when he first arrived in New York: "We are sorry to say that his first reception, on arriving in our city, was but slightly calculated to give him a favorable impression of the morals of his kinsmen. He fell into the hands of one of our vampire cabmen, who, in connection with the keeper of a tavern in West Street, three or four doors from the corner near the Battery, fleeced him out of two of the last dollars which the poor man had."

Several critics of the Whitman-Saved-Oregon story have wondered why Greeley's article about Whitman did not mention the latter's desire to promote Oregon emigration. Greeley's silence on this point, however, is understandable as he was opposed to Oregon emigration. Although he is reported to have said, "Go West, young man, go West," he evidently did not advocate that any go as far west as Oregon.[36] When he learned of the large 1843 emigration, he called the men associated with the venture insane.

The second important call that Whitman made while in New York was on Edward R. Ames, secretary in charge of the Oregon Mission of the Methodist Missionary Society. Ames informed Whitman that because of dissension in the Oregon Mission, Jason Lee had been recalled. Among those most critical of Lee was Elijah White who had passed on unfavorable reports to the Missionary Society when he was in the East in the spring of 1842. As will be told later, Whitman was the first to tell Lee of this action by his church.³⁷

WHITMAN IN BOSTON

Whitman secured passage on the steamer, *Narragansett*, which sailed from New York, Monday evening, March 27, for Boston. The vessel met with rough weather in the Sound, which caused the captain to put in at New Haven at midnight. The inclement weather kept the ship in port until Wednesday morning, the 29ᵗʰ, when she was able to continue her voyage. Thus Whitman was not able to arrive in Boston until the late afternoon or evening of that day.

Among the passengers was a man who, attracted by Whitman, wrote the following sketch of his impressions which appeared in the New York *Spectator*, April 5, 1843.³⁸ The unknown reporter signed his article "Civis." Under the caption, "The Rev. Dr. Whitman From Oregon," Civis wrote:

> We also had one who was observed by all—Doctor Whitman, the missionary from Oregon... Rarely have I seen such a spectacle as he represented. His dress should be preserved as a curiosity; it was quite in the style of the old pictures of Philip Quarles and Robinson Crusoe. When he came on board and threw down his traps, one said 'what a loafer!' I made up my mind at a glance that he was either a gentleman traveler, or a missionary; that he was every inch a man and no common one was clear.
>
> The Doctor had been eight years [sic] at the territory; has left his wife there; and started from home on the 1st of October. He has not been in bed since, having made his lodging on buffalo robe and blanket, even on board the boat. He is about thirty-six or seven years of age, I should judge, and has stamped on his brow a great deal of what David Crockett would call 'God Almighty's common sense.' Of course when he reached Boston, he would cast his shell and again stand out a specimen of the 'humans.'
>
> I greatly question whether such a figure ever passed through the Sound since the days of steam navigation. He is richly fraught with information relative to that most interesting piece of country, and I hope will shortly lay it before the good people of Boston

and New York. Could he appear in New York Tabernacle—in his traveling costume—and lecture on the Northwest coast, I think there would be very few standing places. Much of his route was on foot and occasionally on horse or mule back, with a half-breed guide. To avoid the hostile Indians, he had to go off to the Spanish country, and thence to Santa Fe.[39]

Civis then told the story of how Whitman had been victimized by a "rascally hackman" in New York City. The fact that Civis considered Whitman to have been "about thirty-six or seven years of age," when he was forty, speaks well for Whitman's physical appearance. Early on Thursday evening, March 30, 1843, Whitman called on David Greene in the offices of the American Board in Boston. Although the two had exchanged correspondence for nearly nine years, they had never met before. It is easy to imagine Greene's surprise when he first saw his buckskin-clad visitor. If he was shocked at the outlandish dress of the stranger, he was even more so when the visitor introduced himself as Dr. Marcus Whitman from Oregon. "Why did you leave your station?" Greene demanded. Whitman hastily explained that the Board's order dated February 25, 1842, which dismissed Spalding and Gray and which called for the closing of the stations at Waiilatpu and Lapwai, was the reason. He then presented the original copy of the action taken by the Mission at its September 1842 meeting which was signed by Walker, Eells, and Spalding, and which authorized him to go East to confer with the "Committee of the A.B.C.F.M. in regard to the interests of the Mission." On the back of this page, now in the files of the American Board, is the notation in Greene's handwriting that it was received on March 30, 1843. It had taken Whitman six months to travel from Waiilatpu to Boston.

After his return to Waiilatpu, Whitman told Geiger that he had been given a cool reception in Boston. Henry Hill, Treasurer of the Board, was also shocked at his appearance and asked, quite roughly: "What are you here for, leaving your post?" Hill gave Whitman some money and told him: "Go, get some decent clothes."[40]

The next day, Whitman, now properly clad, was back in Greene's office where his reception was more cordial. On this occasion, Greene brought Whitman up-to-date on the actions of the Board regarding its Oregon Mission subsequent to its February 1842 order. Greene showed Whitman a copy of a letter written to him on April 28, 1842, in which

Whitman read: "When the case of your mission came up in February, it seemed to be a perfectly clear case that the Committee should decide upon it as mentioned in my letter to yourself and the mission written about the first of March[41]... But had your letter of 13th of July [Letter 92] and Mr. Spalding's of the same date, 1841, been before the Com., they would almost necessarily [have] decided differently." Greene, in this letter, authorized Whitman "to go on as you were going before those instructions were received."

After telling of this favorable development, Greene explained to Whitman how further correspondence from Oregon had changed the picture again. He referred to Whitman's letter of May 12, 1842, in which Whitman had written that there was "no better understanding with Mr. Spalding." This letter was written a few days before the scheduled Annual Meeting which Spalding at first refused to attend. Greene then told Whitman how he had laid all of this latest information before the Prudential Committee which met on March 21, a little more than a week before he had so unexpectedly arrived in Boston, and how, as a result, the Committee had voted to abide by the fateful order issued in February 1842.

Thus Whitman learned that, had he not gone to Boston, Spalding would have been dismissed, the two southern stations of the Oregon Mission would have had to be closed, and he and Narcissa would have been expected to move to Tshimakain. Whitman pled for the opportunity to appear before the Prudential Committee. He insisted that conditions had changed. Three of the main complaints against Spalding—Smith, Gray, and Rogers—were no longer in the Mission. A new understanding had been established with Spalding which promised to endure. Whitman argued that it was folly to abandon the flourishing fields at Waiilatpu and Lapwai for the Spokane station with its limited agricultural possibilities. No doubt he emphasized the strategic importance of Waiilatpu as the first outpost in the Columbia River Valley on the Oregon Trail. Perhaps Whitman threatened to leave the Mission and move to the Willamette Valley if the Committee continued to insist that he and his wife move to Tshimakain. Greene was sufficiently impressed with the seriousness of the situation that he agreed to call a special meeting of the Prudential Committee for the following Tuesday, April 4, so that Whitman could present his case in person.

Although eager to be on his way as soon as possible in order to visit relatives in western New York State before leaving for the Missouri frontier, Whitman had to be patient. No record remains as to how he spent those days of waiting. Perhaps one of the Board secretaries would have invited him to his home as a guest. We are told that while in Boston Whitman had his silhouette drawn by a Mr. R. K. Cummings. Whitman considered the result so unsatisfactory that he did not even get a copy for his mother.[42] Daguerreotypes were then being made in Boston, but the cheapest, as then advertised in the daily papers, cost $3.50. No doubt Whitman felt that this was more than he could afford.

THE FATEFUL ORDER OF FEBRUARY 1842 REVOKED

The archives of the American Board contain the minutes of the meeting of the Prudential Committee for April 4, 1843. Seven were present including Greene and Hill. Included with the minutes is a document which seems to be a secretary's summary of what Whitman told the Prudential Committee. It states: "Left the Oregon country 3d October 1842, & arrived at Westport Mo. 15 February & in Boston 30 March 1843. Left unexpectedly & brought few letters. The difficulties between Mr. Spalding & the others were apparently healed. Mr. S. promises to pursue a different course. The mission wish to make another trial, with Mr. Smith & Mr. Gray out of the mission."

Whitman succeeded in persuading the Committee to revoke its former action; for it adopted the following: "Resolved, That Doct. Marcus Whitman & the Rev. H. H. Spalding be authorized to continue to occupy the stations at Waiilatpu & Clear Water, as they did previous to the adoption of the resolutions referred to above." Whitman had the great satisfaction of realizing that one of the main purposes of his long journey had been accomplished. He then brought up Gray's case and asked that his request for release be granted. This was a mere formality, for the Grays had already left the Mission; but for the sake of the record, his resignation was officially accepted.

WHITMAN'S PLANS FOR THE FUTURE OF THE OREGON MISSION

According to the unsigned document of April 4, Whitman gave an optimistic report regarding the response of the Indians to the Christian message. He claimed that "half the year from 30 to 100 & the other half from 100 to 300 attend worship [weekly] at Waiilatpu & Clear Water, each—(giving good) attention & advancing somewhat in knowledge—their temporal condition much improved & improving." The reference to "half the year" reflects the custom of both the Cayuses and the Nez Perces to be gone in search of food for the other half of the time.

In the spring of 1838, Whitman and Spalding, moved by Jason Lee's over-optimistic dream of the political and religious future of Oregon, had asked the Board to send out 220 additional workers. Now, five years later, Whitman had a more realistic understanding of the situation as it affected both the work in Oregon and also the resources of the Board. Hence, his requests for a reenforcement were very modest. In his presentation of the needs of the field, he made reference to the "influx of Papist" missionaries and the need to counteract their influence. He also referred to the expected large 1843 Oregon emigration and to ever increasing migrations in the years to come. He pointed out the demands which the incoming whites would make on the Waiilatpu station for supplies and other forms of assistance. Whitman urged the Committee to appoint an ordained man who could be stationed at Waiilatpu and relieve him of his religious duties.

Whitman also had the following practical recommendation to make: "[That] a company of some five or ten men... be found, of piety & intelligence, not to be appointed by the Board or to be immediately connected with it, who will go to the Oregon country as Christian men and who, on some terms to be agreed upon, shall take most of the land which the missions have under cultivation with the mills & shops at the several stations, with most of the stock & utensils, paying the mission in produce, from year to year, in seed to the Indians, & assistance rendered to them..." Whitman felt that if a few Christian laymen could be found who would settle in the vicinity of each of the three mission stations, they could relieve the three ministers and himself of "the great amount of manual labor, which is now necessary for their subsistence, & permit them to devote themselves to appropriate missionary work among the Indians, whose language they now speak." There is no evidence that Whitman gave any consideration to possible Indian reaction to the establishment of colonies of white people in the vicinity of the mission stations, except the assumption that this would be for their benefit. The Prudential Committee gave a lukewarm endorsement to the idea, but stated that the Board could accept no financial responsibility for the plan and that he was to do the recruiting. Since Whitman had less than two weeks before leaving for the Missouri frontier, there was little possibility that he could enlist men to go to Oregon that year on such short notice.

Whitman raised the question of making a claim on the Government for the value of the horses and other property taken by the Sioux Indians from Gray at Ash Hollow in the summer of 1837. Permission was given Whitman to follow up the claim that Gray had submitted on August 7, 1837, for $2,096.45. An examination of the correspondence bearing on Gray's claim, now in the National Archives, shows that the well-known fur trader and Indian Agent, Major Joshua Pilcher, was asked to investigate the merits of the claim. In his report, Pilcher wrote that he was convinced that "the difficulty arose from Mr. Gray's own imprudence and that most of the claim is altogether unfounded." He recommended that nothing be done.

Whitman wrote to the Commissioner of Indian Affairs from Boston on April 8. His request for indemnity was courteously worded: "We do not wish to press the subject, but leave it with your department to do what you deem proper." He pointed out that: "The horses for which an indemnification is asked belonged in part to the Mission and in part were received by the Mission from the Indians to be vested in cattle & cattle were to be given the Indians in return. As the horses were lost, the Mission has had to pay the Indians for them in cows. There was a considerable abridgment of our, at that time, very small stock." The letter closes with the following: "As missionaries of the A.B.C.F.M., we have no private salary or emolument so that neither Mr. Gray nor myself can have any private interest in the indemnity we ask for the Board. The money would enable us, however, to import more stock to the Indians than we have been able thus far to do." There is no evidence that the claim was ever paid.

Whitman was asked by the Prudential Committee at its meeting of April 4 to write an account of his work, the customs of the natives, their superstitions, legends, etc. In response Whitman penned an illuminating report of about 2,500 words dated April 7, which bears a notation by Greene of being received on the 8th [Letter 128]. In his comments on the customs of the Indians, Whitman noted that if an Indian medicine man, a "te-wat," failed to cure a patient, then "very often in cases of this kind, nothing can save the Conjurer but one or more conspire to kill him." Whitman added: "The number & horror of the deaths of this kind that have come under my observation & knowledge have been great." More than four years later, Dr. Whitman, himself as a white "te-wat," who had been unable to check the ravages of a measles epidemic which was taking a heavy toll of life among the Cayuses, was to become a victim of this custom.

Since the motives for Whitman's ride East have been under such scrutiny, it is well to give the Board's explanation as found in its Annual Report which appeared in September 1843: "Early in the autumn of last year, and immediately after receiving instructions of the Prudential Committee to discontinue the southern branch of the Oregon mission, a meeting of the missionaries from all the stations was held to consider the course to be adopted. In their estimation, the circumstances of the mission and its prospects were so far changed, that they should be justified in going forward with the mission as it then was, until the case could be again referred to the Committee; and it was thought expedient that Doct. Whitman should proceed immediately to Boston with the hope that he might return to his labors early in the ensuing spring."

An amplification of the above was given in the September issue of the *Missionary Herald*: "Another object of Doct. Whitman, in making the above mentioned visit, was to procure additional laborers. He desired to induce Christian families to emigrate and settle in the vicinity of the different stations, that they might relieve the missionary of his secular responsibilities, and also contribute directly, in various ways, to the social and moral improvement of the Indians."[43]

As far as the Board was concerned, Whitman went East on mission business. Nothing was said in its printed accounts of his visit to Boston about a prior visit to Washington. Whitman's modest request for an ordained man to be appointed to serve with him at Waiilatpu was never granted. The financial report of the Board for 1843 shows that the expenditures for the Oregon Mission for that year totaled $3,043.33 [See Appendix 2]. The figures, however, do not indicate just how much of this was incurred by Whitman on his Eastern journey.

Another item from the Board's *Annual Report* for 1843 should be mentioned. Whitman had so stressed the importance of location of Waiilatpu that Greene wrote: "In view of the subject, the importance of sustaining the mission becomes much more obvious & great. It is seen to have new, wider and more permanent bearings... They anticipate the wave of white population which is rolling westward." Whitman, during his visit to Boston, had succeeded not only in inducing the Board to revoke its disastrous order of February 1842, but also in having it recognize that its missionaries in Old Oregon had a responsibility to that "wave of population rolling westward."

CHAPTER 18 ENDNOTES

[1] There is no evidence that Whitman and Lovejoy visited Santa Fe beyond this statement by Lovejoy. Whitman in his report to the Board mentioned only Taos. To have gone to Santa Fe would have required a detour of at least two day's duration and there was no reason for making such a trip. Lovejoy's memory was in error.

[2] Alanson Hinman, in an article in *O.H.Q.*, II (1901):268, refers to Black Harris as "the guide who conducted Doctor Whitman across the Rocky Mountains." Hinman taught school at Waiilatpu in 1844–45 and, no doubt, received this information from Whitman.

[3] Although Robidoux was with Fremont in California, Mount Robidoux, near Riverside, was named for his brother, Louis.

[4] Brown's Hole was on or near the 42° parallel near Green River, in what is now southwestern Wyoming.

[5] Whitman evidently believed that the Green River to be the Colorado River and not merely a tributary. Because of another river in Texas, also called the Colorado, the larger river was then designated as "Colorado of the West."

[6] From interview with Horace Greeley, New York *Tribune*, March 29, 1843.

[7] Rufus B. Sage traveled from Fort Uinta to Fort Hall, Oct. 29–Nov. 5, 1842. See his *Rocky Mountain Life*, Boston, 1857. Possibly Sage met Whitman and Lovejoy while making this trip.

[8] Charles Kelly and Maurice L. Howe, *Miles Goodyear*, Salt Lake City, 1937, p. 43, gives the text of Goodyear's letter which Whitman carried.

[9] Actually at the time Whitman was in his fortieth year and Lovejoy was six years younger. Rather strange that Lovejoy should have referred to him as being "old."

[10] Original Spalding letter in Spokane Public Library.

[11] Information supplied by the Rev. J. Frederick Speer in a letter to me dated December 5, 1965, when he was pastor of the First United Presbyterian Church of Grand Junction, Colo.

[12] An embellished and highly dramatic account of Whitman's ride over the Rockies is in Spalding's *Senate Document*, p. 21. No doubt Spalding did receive some information from Whitman about the hardships he had endured on this transcontinental journey.

[13] The San Juan Mountains were first known as the "Sierra de Anahuac." Whitman once referred to the "Anahuac Mountains."

[14] This was the third Spaniard or Mexican that Whitman had hired as a guide. In his letter to Greene of May 30, 1843, he referred to paying "the Spaniard who came in with me from Taos."

[15] Here Lovejoy gives an exact date which can be confirmed from other sources.

[16] My attention was drawn to this order by Erwin N. Thompson, once historian at the Whitman Mission National Historic Site. Original in Chouteau Collection, Folder 1843, Missouri Historical Society, St. Louis.

[17] Perrin Whitman to Myron Eells, Feb. 10, 1882, Coll. W.

[18] Original in Chouteau Coll., Folder 1843.

[19] Original letter in Coll. W.

[20] Barrows, *Oregon*, pp. 174 ff.

21 Eells, *op. cit.*, pp. 27 ff. Eells quotes from letters written by two people who claimed knowledge of a pamphlet that Whitman is alleged to have written. The evidence is doubtful.

22 *W.C.Q.*, II (1898):2:34.

23 *Ladies Home Journal*, Nov. 1897; *Sunday School Times*, Aug. 23, 1903. Drury, *F.W.W.*, II:54, gives an account of Dr. Weed entertaining members of the 1838 reenforcement on their way to Old Oregon. Dr. Weed conducted a bookstore in Cincinnati.

24 *T.O.P.A.*, p. 92.

25 Marshall, *Acquisition of Oregon*, II:68. He also wrote: "The claim that he went to Washington first has not a particle of contemporaneous evidence to support it." Eells, *Marcus Whitman, M.D.* (Pamphlet), p. 20, quotes Mrs. F. F. Victor as writing in 1880: "There still remains the romantic, though unfortunately foundationless story of Dr. Whitman's visit to Washington with a political purpose." Eells also quote the Hon. E. Evans who, in 1881, wrote: "There is no authentic evidence that Dr. Whitman visited Washington City at all during that journey." Today no reputable scholar makes such claims.

26 Eells, *Marcus Whitman, M.D.*, p. 4.

27 *Ibid.*

28 Marshall, *Acquisition of Oregon*, II:65, quoting from one of Spalding's lectures which appeared in the San Francisco *Pacific*, Nov. 9, 1865.

29 San Francisco *Pacific*, Nov. 9, 1865.

30 See Chapter Sixteen, "War, Diplomacy, or Emigration."

31 See Appendix 7 for a copy of Whitman's proposed bill.

32 Marshall, *Acquisition of Oregon*, I:212.

33 Herbert D. Winters, "Congress and the Oregon Question," *Rochester Historical Society*, II (1931):289.

34 Greeley's article was reprinted in *O.H.Q.*, IV (1903):168 ff.; also in Hulbert, *O.P.*, VII:111 ff.

35 Italics are the author's.

36 According to *The Oxford Dictionary of Quotations*, 2nd ed., 1955, p. 506, this quotation first appeared in the Terre Haute, Ind., *Express*, 1851.

37 Jason Lee to the Methodist Missionary Society, Oct. 13, 1843, quoted by Brosnan, *Jason Lee*, p. 213.

38 *O.H.Q.*, IV (1903):169; *O.P.*, VII:114.

39 "Civis" could easily have confused a reference to the Santa Fe Trail to the city of Santa Fe. See ante, fn. 1.

40 Whitman to Greene, April 1, 1847: "I often reflect upon the fact that you told me you were sorry I came."

41 Greene several times referred to the order of Feb. 25, 1842, as having been written "about the first of March."

42 Mary Alice Wisewell to Myron Eells, March 10, 1882, Coll. W. All efforts to locate a copy of this silhouette have failed.

43 *Missionary Herald*, XXXIX (1843):356.

[CHAPTER NINETEEN]

"WESTWARD HO!"
1843

During the spring of 1843, an awakened interest in Old Oregon stirred the United States from Boston to Westport, and from Chicago to New Orleans. This is evidenced by the number and frequency of editorials and articles about Oregon which appeared in the public press. The Boston *Daily Evening Transcript* for April 4, 1843, called it, "the pioneer's land of promise." The editor declared: "Hundreds are already prepared to start thither with the Spring, while hundreds are anxiously awaiting the action of Congress in reference to that country as the signal for their departure... *The Oregon fever has broken out, and is now raging like any other contagion.*"[1] Since Whitman was in Boston at that time, it is possible that the article came as a result of a call he had made on the editor.

The accounts of Oregon found in such books as Samuel Parker's *Journal of an Exploring Tour Beyond the Rocky Mountains* and T. J. Farnham's *Travels in the Great Western Prairies*[2] found avid readers. The Cleveland *Daily Herald* of March 1, 1843, quoted from a letter Dr. Elijah White had written on August 17, 1842, while en route to Oregon. White advised those planning to migrate in 1843 to take strong light wagons and no baggage except their cooking utensils and provisions for four months. In a bombastic editorial, the Cleveland *Plain Dealer* of March 8, 1843, sang the glories of Oregon: "There is enchantment in the word. It signifies a land of pure delight in the woody solitudes of the West... That is a country of the largest liberty, the only known land of equality on the face of the earth... there is the place to build anew the Temple of Democracy."

The Baltimore *Niles National Register* of April 22, 1843, told of "a large meeting" which was held in St. Louis on the previous March 28 "in favor of colonizing Oregon." Among the resolutions adopted was one which stated that the most effective way "to take possession of Oregon" was by colonization and that this was best promoted by "individual enterprise." Had Whitman been present at that meeting and had he been asked to word the resolutions adopted, they could not have reflected his views more accurately.

This westward surge of population was characterized by a restless energy, a longing for something new, and a desire for free land. The phrase, "the Oregon fever," became popular. The Ohio *Statesman*, in its issue for April 26, 1843, stated: "The Oregon fever is raging in almost every part of the Union. Companies are forming in the East, and in several parts of Ohio, which added to those of Illinois, Iowa, and Missouri, will make a pretty formidable army. The larger portions of these will probably join the companies at Fort Independence, Missouri, and proceed together across the mountains. It is reasonable to suppose that there will be at least five thousand Americans west of the Rocky Mountains by next autumn."

The Painesville, Ohio, *Telegraph* carried the following in its May 24 issue:

WESTWARD HO

The tide of emigration flowing westward this season must be overwhelming. Besides the hundreds and thousands that daily throng the steamboats on the Lakes, there is a constant stream of "movers" on land. From ten to fifteen teams have passed through this town every day for the last three weeks, winding their way to Wisconsin and Iowa, and some, we understand, are bound for the "far west" which in these latter days means a country somewhere between the Rocky Mountains and sundown. Those we noticed had the appearance generally of intelligence, respectability and wealth and gave indication of that enterprising and energetic character which alone takes upon itself the hardships and privations incident to the settlement of a new country.

Such newspaper reports reflect a growing interest in Oregon throughout the nation. Along the western frontier, especially in Missouri, the interest was keen. "The Oregon fever" was contagious. It was "Westward Ho" for the most daring and the most courageous. Whitman took note of what was happening and was delighted.

WHITMAN RETURNS TO RUSHVILLE

Whitman was in Boston for about nine days. Since he wanted to be back at Westport on or about May 1, he was eager to be on his way. Under normal traveling conditions of that day, it would have taken him nearly a month to go from Boston to Westport. Every day he spent in Boston meant one day less that he could spend with relatives in western New York State. We cannot be certain when Whitman left Boston. Possibly it was on Saturday, April 8, after he had submitted his report to Greene of that date and after he had written to the Commissioner of Indian Affairs.

Since Whitman submitted his report to Greene on Saturday, April 8, 1843, it does not appear that he was able to leave for Rushville before that morning. By the spring of 1843, a railroad connected Boston and Buffalo, which passed through Albany. The fare from Boston to Albany, a distance of about 20 miles, was $4.00. A train leaving Boston at eight o'clock in the morning would arrive at Albany that evening. Knowing of Whitman's reluctance to travel on Sunday, he may have spent that day in Albany and then continued his rail journey on Monday. The train passed through Canandaigua where Whitman could have taken a stage for Rushville. This would have been Whitman's first experience riding on a train.

According to Perrin Whitman's recollections, his uncle had only three days to visit his mother and relatives before starting back to Oregon on April 20.[3] Perrin, however, may not have included the time Marcus spent with Narcissa's relatives. In May 1842, Judge and Mrs. Prentiss became members of the Presbyterian Church of Cuba, a small community in western Allegany County. All of Narcissa's letters to her parents after February 7, 1843, were directed to Cuba.

A few scattered references tell of Whitman's visit with his relatives in Naples and Rushville. Martha Wisewell, a daughter of Whitman's sister Alice, wrote that the first indication his mother had of the presence of her son in the States was through reading the account of his visit with Horace Greeley.⁴ Perrin claimed that his grandmother gently rebuked her son for going to Boston before visiting her in Rushville and that Marcus replied: "Business before pleasure, mother, but I am here now to visit you." ⁵ According to Whitman's nephew, Frank Wisewell, so great was the pressure of time on him that he "spent only a single night at his sister's home in Naples." ⁶ This town is about fifteen miles from Rushville.

Among the children in the Wisewell home was Martha, then between eleven and twelve years old, whose recollections were published in the *Sunday School Times* for June 10, 1903. Martha wrote: "While he was there, our house was a gathering place for the neighbors and friends, who listened to his narration of his life and work. I well remember that one day he dressed up in his buckskin suit, that they might see his appearance as he journeyed." A Rushville tradition states that Whitman left his heavy buffalo coat there when he left for Westport.⁷ Martha Wisewell's account continues: "I remember standing opposite him in the room when he had a lasso in his hand. This he threw over my head and drew me up to him, to show the manner of catching animals in the West. And I have not forgotten how this frightened me... Dr. Whitman possessed a singularly pleasant and winning manner. Child as I was, I shall never forget his Christian bearing and conversation. Never solemn nor morose, he was always jovial, lighthearted, and happy." Martha remembered how once her father said to Dr. Whitman: "The Indians are so treacherous, I am afraid they will kill you." Whitman dismissed this fear with the remark that his life was in the Lord's hands. While in the Wisewell home, Marcus became acquainted with a namesake, Marcus Whitman Wisewell, who had been born in 1838.

Whitman spoke in the Presbyterian church in Naples about his experiences as a missionary in Oregon. [In May 1938, I had the pleasure of calling on a lady who had been present on that occasion. She was then nine years old and remembered the event clearly. She recalled that the congregation raised $100.00 that evening for the Oregon Mission. This lady, Mrs. Eliza Ann Housel, died October 10, 1938, at the age of 104.⁸]

Whitman also spoke in the Congregational Church of Rushville at which time a seventeen-year-old lad, James Clark Strong, son of the Rev. Henry P. Strong who had served as pastor of the church for about three years before his death in 1835, was present. In later years, J. C.

Strong became a Brigadier General in the U.S. Army and lived for a time as a civilian in the Pacific Northwest. In his autobiography, General Strong gave the following account of Whitman's plea for Oregon: "He described the Indians, the country, and the climate so vividly that when he said he wanted to get as many as he could to go back with him to settle in the country, I asked him to take me, but he said he wanted only married men."[9] At this meeting Whitman, no doubt, expressed his appreciation for the twenty-five plows which had been sent to Waiilatpu by members of the Rushville church in 1840. In his letter to Greene of May 12, 1843, Whitman reported that the church had made a further contribution of $12.00 to the American Board.

From these two instances, we may assume that Whitman was taking advantage of every opportunity to speak in behalf of the Oregon Mission and to urge all who would listen to migrate to Oregon and settle in the vicinity of the mission stations. The time, however, was too short to recruit settlers who could go out with the 1843 emigration.

Long after Whitman had started back to Westport, word reached the Rev. Samuel Parker in Ithaca of his presence in the States. Parker wondered why Whitman had not called on him and wrote to the Board in June 1843: "I had wished to have known something more definite about Doct. Whitman; his object of returning and prospects, etc. I have heard from his brother in Rushville that he is on his way back to the station."[10] Whitman was much too pressed for time to call on Parker.

PERRIN WHITMAN, NEPHEW OF MARCUS

When Marcus Whitman made his horseback ride from Rushville to St. Louis in the spring of 1835, while on his first journey to the Rockies, he stopped to see his brother Samuel and his family who were then living at Danville, Illinois. In the home was a five-year-old boy called Perrin Beza. In September 1841, Samuel returned with his family to Rushville. There his wife died a year later leaving him with four children, of whom the eldest was Perrin. In later years Perrin told of his memories of his uncle's visit to Rushville in the spring of 1843 and of how his uncle's accounts of the midwinter ride over the Rockies had filled him with wonder. "His personality captivated me," wrote Perrin. "He seemed to have drawn me by some power, for he at once began to plead with my father to gain his consent for me to accompany him on his return trip to Oregon." Samuel's problem in raising four motherless children made him responsive to his brother's plea. Looking back on those days, Perrin wrote: "My father reluctantly consented after three days' pleading, that the doctor should adopt me and take me with him if I was willing to go. My boyish instincts were aroused, and with the promise of a gun, a saddle, and a donkey, my consent was not delayed." [11]

Although Perrin stated that adoption papers were drawn up, actually New York State had no adoption laws before 1873. Possibly Samuel and Marcus drew up a contract such as was then used when a boy was hired out as an apprentice. A family tradition states that Samuel gave Marcus $500.00 to be invested for his son. So it was arranged for the thirteen-year-old Perrin to go with his Uncle Marcus to Old Oregon where he was destined to play an important role in the history of the Pacific Northwest.[12]

Last Farewells

At the most, Marcus could not have had more than a week to visit relatives and friends at Rushville, Naples, Prattsburg, and Wheeler. The hour for the last farewells rushed at him. After being away for seven years, it seemed a pity that his visit was to be so short, but the need to be on the frontier in plenty of time to join the emigration gathering there was paramount. Marcus knew that in all probability he would never see his mother and other loved ones again in this world. It was difficult to say good-by.

Writing to his mother on May 27 from the Shawnee Mission near present-day Kansas City, Kansas, Marcus said: "Oh My Dear Mother! —how often have I thought how reluctant you were for me to go to Oregon & how many fears you had for my safety & comfort." He claimed that he was returning to Oregon with no regrets. Outside of the joy of being with relatives and friends, he said that he had seen nothing which made him want to return to New York State. "Oregon has all my attractions," he wrote. "Oregon has the strength of my affections of body & mind."

When Marcus had returned to Rushville as an eighteen-year-old youth in 1820 after spending ten years with relatives in western Massachusetts, he had wanted to enter the ministry. To his deep disappointment, his mother had objected. In Whitman's first letter to the American Board in which he inquired as to the possibility of receiving an appointment as a missionary, he had mentioned that, although his mother "professes a hope," she was not a member of any church. When he was with his mother in April 1843, he found that she still had not joined the church. This troubled him. His letters to her show that he held her in high esteem. She was a good woman, faithful and true as ever a mother could be. Evidently she was a woman of strong and independent ideas; although she attended church, she would not make a public confession of her faith and become a member.

Whitman's letter to his mother written from the Shawnee Mission reveals his concern over her spiritual welfare. "Let me say in conclusion," he wrote, "that I feel most desirous to know that my Dear Mother was determined to live the rest of her days witnessing a good profession of godliness. What keeps you from this? Is it that you are not a sinner, or if not that, is it that there is no Saviour of sinners, or is it that you have too long refused & neglected to love & obey him?" He closed his plea for her to make a public confession of her faith in Christ with these words: "The word & idea of Mother fill me with tenderest emotions for I have a Mother & have buried a Father. While I am about to say Adieu, let me [say] God is our Father. From your Affectionate Son, Marcus."

Whitman's Visit With His Wife's Relatives

According to Perrin Whitman, he and his uncle left Rushville on April 20 for West Almond in the adjoining county of Allegany to visit Narcissa's brother, Jonas Galusha Prentiss, who owned a store there. There is an abundance of evidence to show that Whitman was constantly seeking those who would be willing to go to Oregon. In a letter to Myron Eells, J. G. Prentiss referred to Whitman's eagerness to get him to migrate.[13] Writing to Prentiss from the Shawnee Mission on May 28, Whitman made reference to a Government "secret service fund" which might be at the disposal of Oregon emigrants. It is possible that Dr. White, who had received some aid from such a fund, had told Whitman about it. The occasional references to a "secret service fund" in the correspondence of the missionaries indicate its existence. There is no evidence that Whitman himself ever received any help from this source.

After Marcus and Perrin had made a brief visit in his home, Jonas took them to Cuba, a village about thirty-five miles further west, where they called on Narcissa's parents and on her sisters, Clarissa and Harriet. The former was married to Norman Kinney and the latter to

John Jackson. Whitman did his best to induce each of these two couples to migrate to Oregon. In his letter of May 28, 1843, to J. G. Prentiss, Whitman wrote: "I shall by no means be surprised to see some if not all of you on our side of the Mountains. Jackson talked favourably." Whitman was too sanguine in his hopes, for neither couple went to Oregon. Whitman also called on another sister of his wife's, Mary Ann, who, with her husband, the Rev. Lyman P. Judson, lived somewhere in the vicinity of Cuba. Judson had been a New School Presbyterian minister but had left that denomination when he became enamored with the vagaries of the New England prophet, William Miller, who was preaching the imminent second coming of Christ.

Whitman's visit with Narcissa's relatives was all too short. Writing to Clarissa more than a year later, Narcissa confided: "My husband's visit was very short, too much so to gain all the information I was in hopes he would bring me" [Letter 155]. Whitman delivered in person the letters that Narcissa had written to her relatives and, no doubt, carried letters from them back to Oregon.

"My Plans Require Time and Distance"

William Miller, a New England farmer, began in August 1831 to preach that the second coming of Christ and the end of the world were at hand. At first his prophecies attracted little attention, but as the announced date for the second coming, March 21, 1843, drew near, the excitement became intense. Whitman was either approaching Washington or in the city on Miller's day of doom and was aware of the excitement that reigned in some circles. Estimates of the number of Miller's followers vary from fifty thousand to a million.[14] The fateful day came—and went—and nothing happened. Miller, although deeply disappointed, went back to his Bible and did some refiguring. He claimed that he had made a mistake of one year and set, therefore, a second date for Christ's second coming—March 21, 1844. Strange to say, Miller was able to hold the allegiance of a large number of his followers after this admission of failure, including Lyman P. Judson. The second date passed without the prophecy being fulfilled. A third date, October 22, 1844, was set and it too proved to be false. This ended Miller's efforts to fix an exact date, but the movement he started continued and in time developed into the Seventh-day Adventist denomination.

In the thinking of William Miller and of his followers, including Lyman P. Judson, there was no need to plan for the future. Why do so if the end of the world were at hand?

On November 5, 1846, several years after he had seen his brother-in-law, Whitman wrote to him. After calling attention to the fact that he was in the East when "the famous time came for the end of the world," Whitman stressed the point that he did not permit such a prophecy to prevent him proceeding with his plans. He wrote: "I did conclude that inasmuch as you had adopted such sentiments, you were not prepared for any work calling for time in its execution,... I was content to pass you in silence. For to my mind, *all my work & plans involved time & distance & required confidence in the stability of God's government...* "[15] Here was the reason why the practical-minded Whitman did not try to persuade the visionary Judson to go as a missionary to Old Oregon.

[Mention will be made in the concluding chapter of this work of the monuments and memorials which have been erected to honor the Whitmans. Among these is a statue of Marcus Whitman which has been placed in Statuary Hall of the Capitol in Washington, D.C., which bears on its base the words:

MY PLANS REQUIRE TIME AND DISTANCE

These words were taken from Whitman's letter to Judson, as quoted above, with some changes.]

WESTWARD BOUND

Marcus and Perrin left on or about April 24 from Cuba, New York, for Buffalo where they expected to take passage on a vessel bound for Cleveland. When the two arrived in Buffalo, they found that the harbor was still blocked with masses of floating ice. The winter of 1842–43 had been uncommonly severe throughout the nation. According to a news story which appeared in the Presbyterian *Foreign Missionary* for June 1886, judge James Otis of Chicago stated: "In the month of April 1843, Dr. M. Whitman and myself were at the same hotel in Buffalo, N.Y., waiting for the ice to leave the harbor so that we could take the steamboat to Cleveland, Ohio. After some four days, we took the stage to Dunkirk [N.Y.], and thence went by boat to Cleveland."

Living in Cleveland at that time was one of Whitman's cousins, Freeman Whitman, son of his Uncle Freeman, with whom Marcus had lived during part of the ten years spent at Cummington, Massachusetts, as a boy. In the home was Freeman's son, known only by his initials, B.F., who later wrote his recollections of the visit of Dr. Whitman. B.F. wrote: "He spent a day and a night there, at our home, almost persuading my father to join the new enterprise." [16] B.F.'s reminiscences not only confirms the report that Whitman went through Cleveland on his way back to Westport, it also reflects Whitman's continued eagerness to recruit settlers for Oregon.

From Cleveland, the two Whitmans traveled to Cincinnati by stage, probably arriving there in time to spend Sunday, April 30, in the home of Dr. George Weed. At Cincinnati they boarded a river steamer which carried them to St. Louis, where they disembarked on or about May 6 [Letter 135]. Upon their arrival in this gateway to the West, Whitman learned that the Oregon emigration would not get started before the end of May because of the lateness of the season. Reports had already reached St. Louis of hundreds who planned to go that year to Oregon with thousands of cattle, horses, and mules. The emigrants could not start until the prairie grass was high enough to provide food for the animals. Thus Whitman found that he had some extra time on his hands.

In all probability Marcus and Perrin were guests in the home of the dentist, Dr. Edward Hale, whom Marcus had visited on his eastward journey. Many years later, Perrin told about his uncle having had a tooth filled with gold by Dr. Hale while he watched with fascination the first dentistry he had ever seen. Dr. Hale had no drill to grind out the decayed matter in the tooth, such as modern dentists use, but had to rely on scraping out the cavity with small scalpels. After the tooth was cleaned, thin strips of gold leaf were pounded in, thus filling the cavity.[17]

Whitman Calls on Jane Prentiss

Since he had some free time, Whitman decided to visit Jane and Edward Prentiss at Quincy, Illinois, a little more than one hundred miles up the Mississippi River. Edward happened to be away when Marcus and his nephew arrived, but Jane was there. There were no members of either the Whitman or the Prentiss families whom Marcus and Narcissa were more eager to persuade to go to Oregon than Jane and Edward, with the single exception of Perrin. Neither Jane nor Edward was married. Both Marcus and Narcissa had dreamed of Jane as a teacher in the Mission school and they hoped that Edward, after completing his studies for the ministry, could take charge of the religious duties at Waiilatpu. In a letter written to Edward from the Shawnee Mission on May 27, Marcus expressed regret at not having seen him at Quincy, and then, in a joking manner, wrote: "Tell Jane two or three young lawyers will be in the party for Oregon but I hope this will not deter her from coming if she has an opportunity."

In another letter addressed to the two, written from Waiilatpu on May 15, 1846, Marcus said: "Narcissa wants Jane to come and I want Edward, but it is not for us that you should come but for yourselves and the Lord. Edward would do well to have a wife and then come, and Jane will be agreeable with or without a husband, as suits her best; for if she comes without one, I shall try to convince her of her duty to marry." All of the endeavors and urgings of both Marcus and Narcissa to induce some of their relatives, in addition to Perrin, to migrate to Oregon were in vain. The only other near relative of any member of the Oregon Mission to go to Oregon during the Mission period was Horace Hart, a brother of Eliza Spalding's, who migrated in 1846.

Advice to Emigrants

Whitman was back in St. Louis on May 12. On that date he wrote a short letter to Greene. He reported that he had been unable to find any families who were willing to migrate to Oregon that year. He referred again to a subject which was troubling him, namely, the growing threat of the Roman Catholic missions in Oregon. Somewhere along his line of travel, perhaps in St. Louis, he had purchased for one dollar a copy of Father P. J. De Smet's *Letters and Sketches* which had been published that year in Philadelphia. He called the book to the attention of Greene and added: "It gives a good account of their Mission in Oregon. You will see by that how things are likely to affect us in that country." Whitman reported that De Smet was then in Westport making arrangements for the departure of a Catholic reenforcement destined for the Flathead country, and that De Smet planned to return to Europe that summer for more missionaries.

Whitman was alarmed over this information. He urged Greene to get the book and read it. "I think a carefull consideration of this book, together with these facts & movements, you will realize our feeling that we must look with much interest upon this the only spot on the Pacifick [sic] coast left where Protestants have a present hope of a foot hold. It is requisite that more good, pious men & Ministers go to Oregon without delay, as Citizens or our hope there is greatly clouded if not destroyed." Whitman's concern over De Smet's activities is also found in letters he wrote to his mother on May 27 and to J. G. Prentiss on the 28th. Whitman's failure to find some Protestant families willing to move to Oregon was a source of great disappointment. He was troubled, also, over the apparent lack of concern on the part of Secretary Greene and the Prudential Committee over his proposal to take some positive steps to counteract the Roman Catholics.

A second book which Whitman saw in St. Louis which gave him concern was Philip L. Edwards' *Sketch of the Oregon Territory; or, Emigrants' Guide*, which had been published in 1842 at Liberty, Missouri.[18] Edwards, who had gone out to Old Oregon with the Jason Lee party in 1834, had returned to the States with Lee in 1838, and had settled in Missouri. Since he had made the round trip between the Missouri frontier and Oregon on horseback, his recommendations as to what emigrants should take and how they should travel were received as authoritative. Here was one who could speak from experience.

Whitman was aroused over what he considered to be the disastrous advice which Edwards had given regarding the impracticability of taking wagons all the way through to the Columbia River Valley. Edwards had written: "And were I to join a company of emigrants, I should always prefer horses and mules to any other mode of conveyance; and inconvenient as it may seem, I should always prefer packing the few necessaries of the journey to the encumbrance of wagons. If the latter are employed at all, let them be light but substantial, and drawn by horses and mules. Let it also be understood, that *they are to be abandoned by the way*."[19] Moreover, the St. Louis *New Era* of May 25, 1843, carried an article by Edwards which filled two columns of fine print. Here Edwards repeated his conviction that wagons could not be taken into the Columbia River Valley and recommended that all emigrants who started their journey with them should be prepared to abandon them along the way and complete their travels on horseback.

Whitman knew far more about the possibility of wagons going through to the Columbia River than did Edwards. He realized the supreme importance of taking wagons all the way when so many women and children were to be included in the 1843 emigration. Therefore, Whitman did what he could to counteract Edwards' advice. While in St. Louis, Whitman assisted the Eyres and Hobson families "in purchasing wagons and mules" [20] J. W. Nesmith, a prominent member of the 1843 emigration, testified that: "Dr. Whitman was persistent in his assertion that wagons could proceed as far as the Grand Dalles of the Columbia River, from which point, he asserted, they could be taken down by rafts or batteaux to the Willamette Valley." [21] No doubt Whitman frequently reminded inquirers that he and Spalding had taken their wagon as far west as Fort Hall, and then the two-wheeled cart as far as Fort Boise. He could also have told that some mountain men had taken three wagons over the Blue Mountains in 1840. To Whitman the success of the 1843 Oregon emigration was crucial, and the key to its success was the ability of the emigrants to take their wagons all the way through to the Columbia.

Following the adjournment of the Twenty-Seventh Congress on March 4, 1843, the senior Senator from Missouri, Thomas H. Benton, had returned to his home in St. Louis. Benton was keenly interested in western exploration and thus became intimately associated with John C. Frémont, who had led several such expeditions into the Far West and who had married Jessie, one of Benton's daughters. According to Perrin Whitman, he and his uncle called twice on the distinguished Senator. "I was with him both times," wrote Perrin.[22] Since Frémont was also in St. Louis at the times Whitman called on Senator Benton, it is reasonable to believe that he met Frémont in the Benton home.[23] Whitman, in his letter of May 27 to Edward Prentiss, said: "Lieut. Fremont of the U. States Engineers Corps goes out with about thirty men to explore for the Government and expects to return this fall." Although Whitman may not have previously met Benton and Frémont, their common interest in the political and economic future of the Oregon country would have established an immediate bond of sympathy.

Frémont and his company left St. Louis by river steamer for Westport on Saturday, May 13, and arrived at their destination on the 18th.

Circumstantial evidence indicates that Whitman and his nephew were passengers on the same vessel. Because of the lateness of the season, Whitman found that the emigration was not yet ready to start. In his letter to his mother written on the 27th, he commented: "I regret I did not stay longer at the east as the companies are so slow in starting. I might about as well have been three weeks later but as I could not know before hand, it was better to be safe." Shortly after arriving at Westport, Whitman and his nephew went to Independence where Whitman reclaimed the animals and camping equipment, which he had left with the Presbyterian elder, C. W. Boyers, the previous February. Possibly at this time, Marcus bought a riding animal for Perrin and another pack animal.

The Emigrants Gather

As soon as the prairie grass was high enough to provide pasturage to livestock, the emigrants began to assemble along the Kansas River beginning a few miles out of present-day Kansas City, Kansas. Peter H. Burnett, who was one of the most influential members of the 1843 emigration and who was to become, seven years later, the first Governor of California, arrived at the emigrants' rendezvous on May 17. Burnett states in his journal that a meeting of the emigrants was held on the 18th and that a committee was appointed to consult with Dr. Whitman. Another committee was appointed to inspect wagons and a third to draw up rules and regulations to govern the migration on its trek across the country.[24]

George Wilkes, a young unmarried man who was also a member of the 1843 emigration, gives more details about this meeting in his journal: "A meeting was held... which resulted in appointing a committee to return to Independence, and make inquiries of Doctor Whitman, missionary... respecting the practicabilities of the road, and an adjournment was made to the 20th to Elm Grove, a little distance off, for the purpose of making final arrangements for the regular government of the expedition."[25] Whitman attended the Elm Grove meeting.

Estimates vary as to the number of people in the 1843 emigration. Nesmith claimed that a roll compiled on May 20 listed 295 males over the age of sixteen who were capable of bearing arms.[26] Burnett thought that there were at least 800 in the emigration, while other estimates go up to one thousand with at least 120 wagons.[27] The latter figure is usually accepted. This number would include the latecomers who were not present at the Elm Grove meeting. The officers elected at the organizational gathering on May 20 included Peter H. Burnett, captain; J. W. Nesmith, orderly sergeant. Captain John Gantt, a former Army officer and mountain man, was hired to guide the emigration as far as Fort Hall. A code of rules was adopted which included the proviso that all young men sixteen or older could vote. This was logical; a sixteen-year-old boy was expected to do a man's work in bearing arms, standing guard, and herding the animals. Women were not permitted to vote. For the sake of efficiency, the emigration was divided into companies, each having about forty wagons. On Monday, May 22, the first wagons began rolling westward.

After meeting with the emigrants on Saturday, the 20th, the Whitmans went to the Methodist Mission founded in 1830 at Shawnee, about six miles southwest of present-day Kansas City, Kansas; there they remained until May 31. Some of the original brick buildings of the Mission are still standing. The fact that Whitman and his nephew spent about ten days at the Methodist Mission probably accounts for a few references to him by some emigrants as being a Methodist missionary.

Four letters which Whitman wrote while at the Shawnee Mission, dated May 27 (2), 28, and 30, are extant. Writing to his mother, Marcus said that his health was good, that he had lost about ten pounds since leaving Rushville, and that Perrin "has been a good boy & is happy." In a letter to J. G. Prentiss, Whitman estimated that the emigration contained "over two hundred men, besides women & children." Whitman was enthusiastic over the prospects of such a large emigration. "It is now decided in my mind that Oregon will be occupied by American citizens. Those who go only open the way for more another year. Wagons will go all the way, I have no doubt, this year." In this same letter, Whitman also wrote: "Lieut Fremont is camped about two miles off for the night." Marcus and Perrin spent the night of Thursday, June 1, with Frémont and his party. Theodore Talbot, a member of the Frémont expedition, noted in his journal: "Dr. Whitman, the Baptist [sic] Missionary, established at Wallawalla on the Columbia, was our guest tonight. He is behind the main body of emigrants, but can of course easily overtake them. He expresses much anxiety for their safe journey, and is determined to do all in his power to assist them, a promise of much value, as well from his practical good sense as his general knowledge of the route."[28]

Whitman's Continued Concern about the Catholics

Whitman's continued concern about Roman Catholic activities in Oregon is found in his letter of May 30 written to Greene while he was still at the Shawnee Mission. Whitman again called Greene's attention to the book which Father De Smet had published: "We cannot feel it to be at all just that we do nothing while worldly men & Papists are doing so much. De Smet's business to Europe can be seen, I think, at the top of the 233 page of his Indian Sketches &c. You will see by his book, I think, that the papal effort is designed to convey over the country [i.e., Oregon] to the English." If Greene had secured a copy of De Smet's book and if he had turned to the page indicated by Whitman, he could have read: "In my opinion, it is on this spot [i.e., Old Oregon] that we must seek to establish our holy religion. It is here that we must have a college, convent & schools... Here is the field of battle where we must in the first place gain the victory."

Although De Smet was evidently referring to a spiritual victory, both Whitman and Spalding were suspicious of the political motives of the Roman Catholic missionaries in Oregon. The fact that Fathers Blanchet and Demers came from Canada and that their transportation had been provided by the Hudson's Bay Company gave grounds for such suspicions. There is plenty of evidence that in the early years of the Catholic Mission in Oregon, the sympathies of the priests were closely allied with the Hudson's Bay Company. Spalding, in later years, stressed what he considered to have been the sinister designs of the Catholic missionaries to help the British Government secure title to the Oregon country. This became a major emphasis in his Whitman-Saved-Oregon story. The quotation given above from Whitman's letter to Greene of May 30, 1843, shows that he found political implications in what was evidently a simple statement by Father De Smet of his spiritual objectives.

Whitman was discouraged over the prospects of the future of Protestant missions in Oregon. When he was told by Secretary Ames of the Methodist Missionary Society of the dismissal of Jason Lee, he no doubt was also informed that the Society had appointed the Rev. George Gary as Lee's successor and had instructed Gary to close out the Methodist work in Oregon. Gary was then on his way to Oregon by sea.

When Whitman was in Boston, he learned more of the financial difficulties of the American Board. The dream that he and Spalding had cherished in 1838 of a reenforcement of 220 missionaries was nothing more than a dream. While in Boston, Whitman, with a more realistic understanding of the financial resources of the Board, limited his request for a reenforcement to just one—he wanted a minister to be sent to Waiilatpu—but even this modest request was denied.

Now faced with the possibility of an enlarged Catholic contingent of missionaries to Oregon, Whitman turned to the only possible alternative to counteract their influence—that of encouraging Protestant settlers to migrate to Oregon. He brought up this possibility again in his letter of May 30 to Greene: "We do not ask you to become the patron of emigration to Oregon but we desire you to use your influence that in connection with all the influx into the country there may be a fair proportion of good men of our own denomination... Also that the Ministers should come out as Citizens or under the Home Missionary Society... I think our greatest hope for having Oregon at least part Protestant now lies in encouraging... good men to go there while the country is open." Even though Whitman's proposal made no demands upon the slender financial resources of the Board, his pleas fell on deaf ears; there is no evidence that the Board acted in any way on his recommendations.

"Travel, Travel, Travel"

Whitman and Perrin started their westward journey on Friday morning, June 2, after spending the previous night with Lieut. Frémont. They had but little baggage which was carried by two, possibly three, pack animals. The cynical Peter Waldo, a member of the 1843 emigration wrote: "I fed him the first part of the road. He had nothing to start with but a boiled ham... I reckon he expected that ham to last him and his boy all the way across. After we crossed the Snake River, we had to feed him again. I did not like it much. But he was an energetic man and I liked his perseverance. He had not much judgment but a great deal of perseverance. He expected the emigrants to feed him and they did."[29]

Waldo's statement about Whitman taking only a ham as his total food supply needs some comment. In all probability, unknown to Waldo, Whitman was promised some food supplies when he met with the emigrants at Elm Grove on May 20 in return for the services he could render both as a supplemental guide to Captain Gantt and also as the doctor for the emigration.

The emigration consisted of a fine type of people. The *Liberty Banner* of Clay County, Missouri, described the men as being of "fine intelligence and vigorous and intrepid character, admirably calculated to lay the firm foundation of a future empire." [30] Estimates vary as to the number of cattle driven to Oregon by the 1848 emigration. According to a statement made by one of the emigrants: "There are over 3,000 and perhaps 5,000 head of cattle, mules and horses attached to the company. Captain Applegate has over 200 head, and others over 100 head." [31] The presence of so many cattle became a controversial issue; some of the emigrants did not want to help guard or drive them and wanted to move faster than cattle could travel. After the main body of emigrants had crossed the Big Blue River in what is now northeastern Kansas, those owning cattle formed a separate company which was called the "Cow Column." [32]

At first the emigrants were careless about their food, throwing away portions after each meal which should have been saved, and generously inviting others to eat with them. They soon learned that every scrap of food, even bacon rinds, had to be conserved. Captain Gantt killed an old buffalo bull on June 15. The wanton killing of the majestic shaggy beasts of the prairies by thoughtless white men, who were slaughtering the animals for their hides or for the thrill of killing, was already beginning to decimate the great herds. Because of the lack of buffalo, some of the emigrants were obliged to butcher some of their cattle.

The vanguard of the emigration came to the South Fork of the Platte River about July 1. There wagon boxes were covered with buffalo skins and made into boats which were used in crossing the river. Whitman and his nephew overtook the main body of the emigrants at this place. Here Whitman rendered valiant service in helping the families cross. Because the late spring had delayed the departure of the emigration from the frontier, Whitman repeatedly warned of the necessity of constant travel. Perrin later wrote: "He never allowed them to stay two nights in one place. Kept them moving every day, if it was only for a little way, so as to change grass for the stock." [33] Jesse Applegate stressed the same fact: "From the time he joined us on the Platte until he left us at Fort Hall, his great experience and indomitable energy were of priceless value to the migration column. His constant advice, which we knew was based on a knowledge of the road before us was 'travel, travel, TRAVEL... nothing else will take you to the end of your journey; nothing is wise that does not help you along; nothing is good for you that causes a moment's delay.'" [34]

Comments of Emigrants

One of the 1843 emigrants, J. W. Nesmith, described Whitman in these words: "He was of a powerful physical organization, and possessed a great and good heart, full of charity and courage, and utterly destitute of cant, hypocrisy, shams and effeminacy, and always terribly in earnest." Regarding Whitman's services to the emigrants, Nesmith wrote: "While with us he was clad entirely in buckskin, and rode one of those patient long-eared animals said to be 'without pride of ancestry or hope of posterity.' The Doctor spent much of his time in hunting out the best route for the wagons, and would plunge into streams in search of practical fords, regardless of the depth or temperature of the water, and sometimes after the fatigue of a hard day's march, would spend much of the night in going from one party to another to minister to the sick." [35]

Applegate also commented on Whitman's services to the members of the emigration as a doctor. He tells that one day a wagon swung out of the train and stopped. In it was an expectant mother and Dr. Whitman, who had been riding alongside the wagon for some time. A tent was pitched, a fire kindled, and water put on to boil. The other wagons rolled by, some wondering why one family should drop out of line and make camp at that hour of the day. The long emigrant train moved on leaving the lone covered wagon far in the rear. Here is Applegate's description: "There are anxious watchers for the absent wagon, for there are many matrons who may be afflicted like its inmate before the journey is over... But as the sun goes down, the absent wagon rolls into camp, the bright, speaking [sic] face and cheery look of the doctor, who rides in advance, declare without words that all is well, and both mother and child are comfortable."

The successful delivery of the child firmly established Whitman's reputation and give confidence to the whole emigration. Applegate further commented: "His great authority as a physician and complete success in the case referred to, saved us many prolonged and perhaps ruinous delays for similar causes, and it is no disparagement to others to say, that to no other individual are the emigrants of 1843 so much indebted for the successful conclusion of their journey as to Dr. Marcus Whitman." At the end of the day when the first baby of the 1843 emigration was born, several of the men of the cow column gathered at the tent of the pilot, with whom Whitman lived, "listening, to his wise and energetic counsel." The pilot sat silent at one side, "quietly smoked his pipe for he knows the brave doctor is 'strengthening his hands.'" [36]

Looking back on his experiences in crossing the country, one member of the 1843 emigration came to the conclusion that it was not wise to depend on buffalo or other wild game for food. Writing from Fort Vancouver on November 11, 1843, S. M. Gilmore advised any in the States who were thinking of migrating to Oregon: "You should bring 200 pounds of flour, 100 pounds of bacon, for every member of the family that can eat, besides other provisions. Make no calculation on getting buffalo or other wild meat, for you are only wasting time and killing horses and mules to get it." He also recommended that wagon beds should be so constructed that they could be converted into boats and used in crossing streams. Such wagon beds should be well covered "so they will not leak, or your provisions and clothes will spoil." [37]

The vanguard of the emigration reached Fort Laramie on July 14. There the emigrants were astounded at the high prices being asked for food items and other supplies. According to Burnett, the following prices were charged: "Coffee, $1.50 a pint; brown sugar, the same; flour, unbolted, 25 cents a pound; powder, $1.50 a pound; lead, 75 cents a pound; percussion caps, $1.50 a box; calico, very inferior, $1.00 a yard." [38] As will be noted, some emigrants of 1843 and following years, who found it necessary to buy food supplies at Waiilatpu, criticized Whitman for what they thought were exorbitant prices he asked. Yet Whitman charged only five cents a pound for flour when it sold for twenty-five cents at Fort Laramie.

The Laramie River was high because of the melting snows in the mountains. Since it could not be forded, the wagon boxes again had to be converted into boats. Waldo reported: "No one was willing to risk himself in swimming the river and carrying the line but Dr. Whitman, which he did successfully." [39] A. L. Lovejoy, whom Whitman had left at Bent's Fort the previous January 7, had crossed the country and joined the emigration somewhere in the vicinity of Fort Laramie in order to return with it to Oregon.

Letters from Narcissa

When Whitman was at Fort Laramie or a little west of it, he had the thrill of meeting a messenger who carried a letter for him from Narcissa which had been written at Waiilatpu on May 18, about two months before. This was the first letter he had received from his wife since he left for the East on October 3 the previous fall. For the first time, Whitman learned of the burning of the mill, an event which had taken place more than eight months before. Believing that he had received some of the letters she had sent to him at eastern addresses, Narcissa made only a passing reference to the incident. Her letter dealt mainly with the excitement which stirred the Cayuses because of the rumors of the coming of American soldiers "for their destruction." She told of Dr. White's meeting with the Nez Perces; of the selection of Ellis to be that tribe's first Head Chief; and of the adoption of the code of laws. She wrote of the reluctance of the Cayuses to accept the laws and of how much they needed their missionary. "They seem to be and to feel 'like sheep without a shepard,'" she wrote. "It may be," she added, "that I am addressing the dead instead of the living. I hope that it is otherwise, and may you be preserved to return in peace... for my anxious heart longs to greet you. The mission sends four horse loads of flour to Fort Boise & Fort Hall for you and your Company." This was welcome news indeed.

Having an opportunity to send letters back to the States, Whitman wrote to Greene on July 20 from "Bigbute Creek, 100 miles west of Laramie's Fork."[40] He forwarded his wife's letter. "I am in no way solicitous for the loss of the Mill," he wrote, "or on account of the excitement [among the natives] & hope no change will be made in the Mission & that you will be able to reinforce us next year." The last sentence of this letter drew attention to one of the hazards of wagon train travel; individuals, especially children, would accidentally fall under a moving wagon and be run over. This often resulted in broken bones or in death. Whitman wrote: "We buried a small boy this morning that died from a wagon having passed over the abdomen."

Arrival at Fort Hall

The company with whom Peter Burnett traveled, crossed the Continental Divide during the first week of August. Whitman, who had by this time pushed on ahead, heard of a new cutoff which shortened the distance to Fort Hall. Burnett referred to this when he wrote: "On the 12th of August, we were informed that Doctor Whitman had written a letter stating that the Catholic missionaries had discovered, by the aid of their Flathead Indian pilot, a pass through the mountains by the way of Fort Bridger, which was shorter than the old route."[41] Burnett's party arrived at Fort Bridger, on Black's Fork of the Green River, on August 14, and at Fort Hall on the 27th.

At Fort Hall, Whitman met again Captain Richard Grant, the Hudson's Bay Company's trader in charge, whom he had seen the previous October.[42] Grant had escorted Mrs. Whitman from Waskopum to Fort Walla Walla with the Hudson's Bay express early in April 1843 and thus was able to give Whitman some recent information regarding his wife and the state of affairs at Waiilatpu. Whitman found several Nez Perce Indians waiting for him at Fort Hall with pack animals loaded with flour, which had been sent by Spalding. What Whitman charged for this flour, which he sold to the emigrants, is not known. Nesmith, in his "Diary of the Emigration of 1843," reported that Grant asked "25¢ per pint" for the flour that he sold.[43] Also at Fort Hall were some other Nez Perces and Cayuses who were returning from the buffalo country. Among them was the Cayuse chief, Stickus, to whom reference has already been made. Of him, Nesmith wrote: "He was a faithful old fellow, perfectly familiar with all the trails and topography of the country from Fort Hall to the Dalles."[44] Stickus and his band joined the 1843 emigration at Fort Hall, traveling with Whitman.

Edward H. Lenox, also a member of the emigration, wrote in his reminiscences that Whitman received a letter from his wife at Fort Hall on August 28 which contained the plea: "Do hurry home."[45] Whitman was eager to press on ahead of the emigration but the critical question which arose at Fort Hall in regard to the feasibility of the emigrants taking their wagons further west caused him to delay.

Confrontation with Captain Richard Grant

The members of the Oregon emigration of 1843 faced a crisis when they arrived at Fort Hall with their 120 wagons and large herds of cattle, horses, and mules. Possibly some thought that Fort Hall marked the end of the Oregon Trail as far as wagons were concerned. Captain Gantt, having piloted the emigration to that point according to his agreement, left with a small party bound for California. Since returning to the States was unthinkable, the emigrants had to choose between two alternatives: leave their wagons and continue their journey on horseback, or attempt to take their wagons across the desert and over the Blue Mountains into the Columbia River Valley, something which many said could not be done.

Among those who strongly recommended the first course of action was Captain Grant, who reenforced his arguments by showing the emigrants the wagons left at the fort by members of the 1842 emigration. Grant had traveled the route between Fort Hall and Fort Walla Walla several times on horseback and was probably sincere in the advice that he gave. Adherents of the Whitman-Saved-Oregon story, however, have argued that Grant, realizing that the American claim to Oregon would be immeasurably strengthened if a wagon road to the Columbia were opened, deliberately did what he could to prevent it.

An indication that Captain Grant might have been aware of the political implications of the successful opening of a wagon road to the Columbia is to be found in the following quotation from George Wilkes' *History of Oregon*: "Some of the members [of the Hudson's Bay Company at Fort Hall] told us that they could scarcely believe their eyes when they saw the immense stretch of our [wagon] line, the number of our lowing herds, and the squads of prancing horsemen, and they inquired laughingly *if we had come to conquer Oregon*, or devour it out of hand." [46] Any joking that Captain Grant, or any of his associates, may have made about the intention of the Americans to take over the Oregon country, could have reflected a realization that that was exactly what was happening.

Burnett, in his *Recollections*, wrote: "I consulted Mr. Grant as to his opinion of the practicability of taking our wagons through. He replied that, while he would not say it was impossible for us Americans to make the trip in our wagons, he could not himself see how it could be done."

Some of the emigrants, probably those without small children, heeded Grant's advice, as Nesmith reported: "Part of the company went on pack animals, leaving their wagons." [47]

In 1897, Perrin Whitman stated in an interview: "When we arrived at Fort Hall, I heard the commandant [i.e., Captain Grant] tell the immigrants that Dr. Whitman would starve them all to death in the Green [the reference should have been to the Snake] River country. He said that they could never get their wagons to the Columbia Valley in their lives. I went and told Dr. Whitman about it, and he got the immigrants together and gave them a harangue. He told them he would get them to the Columbia River if he lived; that they had just to stick to their wagons and follow him, he would get them through." [48]

The emigrants had to face some practical problems. How would it have been possible to mount some eight hundred or more people, including about five hundred women and children, and conduct them safely over five hundred miles of deserts and mountains to Fort Walla Walla? How could a young mother, riding side-saddle, providing such were available, carry an infant child for so great a distance? What about the transportation of supplies? Whitman insisted that if Captain Grant's advice were to be followed, the emigration would end in a tragic disaster. He told them again that wagons had been taken over the Blue Mountains and what had been done once could be done again. "Had we followed Grant's advice," wrote Nesmith, "and abandoned the cattle and wagons at Fort Hall, much suffering must have ensued besides, wagons and cattle were indispensable to men expecting to live by farming in a country destitute of such articles." [49]

The majority of the emigrants accepted Whitman's advice and kept their wagons, but evidently upon the condition that he serve as pilot for the remainder of the journey. Whitman was reluctant to accept this responsibility, as he wanted to push on ahead with a small party of single men including Lovejoy. The words of his wife were echoing through his mind: "Do hurry home," but the urgency of seeing the emigration safely through to its destination outweighed personal desires.

In a letter to Greene written from Fort Walla Walla on November 1, 1843, Whitman explained: "My journey across the Mountains was very much prolonged by the necessity for me to pilot the Emigrants. I tried in vain to come ahead at different points but found it would be at the risk of disaster to the emigrants of having to leave their wagons without the possibility of obtaining a sufficient number of horses to take any considerable part of their families & necessary food & clothing."

Opening the Wagon Road to the Columbia

There was no effort to organize the emigration into separate companies after it had reached Fort Hall. No longer were the emigrants faced with the danger of attack from hostile Indians. Individual groups pushed on as fast as they could. Whitman usually was with the vanguard company. The Snake River was crossed at Salmon Falls, where one of the emigrants, Miles Eyres, whom Whitman had met in St. Louis and whom he had encouraged to go to Oregon, was drowned. Eyres had all of his money in a belt around his waist. His body was not recovered; thus his wife and three children were left almost destitute. They spent the winter of 1843–44 with the Whitmans at Waiilatpu, being among the first of many unfortunate victims of the Oregon Trail to seek the hospitality of the mission station.

About September 20, the first of the emigrants arrived at Fort Boise, where they were kindly received by Francis Payette, the Hudson's Bay trader in charge. For the most part, the emigrants had experienced no difficulty in taking their wagons across the Snake River desert. The most difficult part of their route, however, lay before them in the rugged Blue Mountains. Since it was getting late in the season, Whitman urged them not to tarry but to press on with all possible speed. Perhaps he reminded the emigrants that he had encountered snow in the Mountains during the first week of October of the previous year. In his letter of November 1 to Greene, Whitman wrote: "By taking a light horse wagon, I was enabled to come ahead from Fort Boise." Although Whitman and Spalding had left the latter's light wagon at Fort Boise in 1836, it does not appear that this was the wagon which Whitman used in 1843.[50] Possibly he borrowed such a wagon from some member of the emigration and with it pioneered the wagon road over the Blue Mountains.

Whitman was assisted in guiding the long wagon train over the mountains by his Indian friend Stickus. Nesmith wrote that although Stickus knew not a word of English and the Americans knew nothing of the Indian language, yet "he succeeded by pantomime in taking us over the roughest wagon route I ever saw. Stickus was a member of Dr.

Whitman's church, and the only Indian I ever saw that I thought had any conception of and practiced the Christian religion."[51] Actually Stickus never became a member of the Mission church. Since he and his band lived at some distance from Waiilatpu, he could not have attended very often the religious services Whitman conducted. The Whitman letters contain references to Stickus and always with respect. What Timothy was to Spalding, Stickus was to Whitman.

WHITMAN CALLED TO LAPWAI AND TSHIMAKAIN

While in the Grande Ronde Valley, Whitman received a letter written by Elkanah Walker from Lapwai which carried the distressing news that both Henry and Eliza Spalding were critically ill with scarlet fever. Eliza had been stricken first and for two weeks had hovered between life and death. Believing that her end was near, Henry sent word to Geiger at Waiilatpu and to the two couples at Tshimakain to come and attend her funeral. Geiger arrived at Lapwai on September 14 and Walker on the 15th. They found Eliza out of danger but Henry had been stricken and then, a few days later, the children. As soon as Walker arrived at Lapwai, believing that Whitman would be drawing near to his station at that time with the 1843 emigration, he sent an Indian messenger to intercept him with the urgent plea that he go at once to Lapwai.

Whitman responded by turning over the guiding of the emigration to Stickus and hastened to Lapwai, where he arrived on September 25. He found both of the Spaldings out of danger; the children were still sick but not dangerously so. After staying at Lapwai for only one night, he left on Tuesday, the 26th, for Waiilatpu. Naturally, Whitman told Spalding of his successful intercession with the American Board and of the rescinding of the disastrous order of February 1842. In his letter to Greene of November 1, Whitman wrote of Spalding: "He has expressed a much better state of feeling towards the members of the Mission and the Board since his sickness, and the reception of your letter and my return, than ever before." Contemporary documents do not indicate any further friction between Whitman and Spalding during the remaining years of the Mission. The years of dissension within the Mission were over.

Whitman arrived back at Waiilatpu perhaps by Thursday evening, September 28. By that time Narcissa had heard of her husband's return and was either en route to or had arrived at The Dalles, expecting to meet him there. When Geiger was called to Lapwai, he left only an Indian in charge of the premises at Waiilatpu. When Whitman returned to his station, he discovered that the advance party of the emigration, consisting of men on horseback, had arrived during Geiger's absence and had broken open his house and "left it open to the Indians although wheat, corn, potatoes, garden vegetables, hogs & cattle were in abundance outside" [Letter 142]. Whitman was shocked at the irresponsible, even reprehensible, actions of those whom he had helped.

Whitman was home for only one day before an urgent message came from Cushing Eells. His wife was expecting her second child, and the doctor was needed. After giving hasty instructions to Geiger regarding the selling of supplies to the emigrants, Whitman set out on his 140-mile ride to Tshimakain where he arrived sometime during the night of October 1. According to Mary Walker's diary, Whitman was exceedingly restless during the week he was waiting for the Eells baby to be born; on October 6, she wrote: "Dr. W. very uneasy, regrets he came too soon."[52] No doubt he was constantly mindful of the emigrants streaming by Waiilatpu, many of whom were in need of food, medical attention, and advice. Moreover, he had the natural desire to see his wife as soon as possible. A baby boy was born early on the morning of the 7th, who was named Myron.[53]

At noon of the day the baby was born, Whitman started back to Waiilatpu. En route he overtook Walker and five-year-old David Malin, who had started from Tshimakain a day or so before he did. During Narcissa's absence from Waiilatpu, David had spent most, if not all the time with the Walkers at Tshimakain. Whitman found upon his arrival at Waiilatpu, on October 10, that the main body of the emigrants had already passed. Geiger had been there to meet their needs. "All came in their turns," wrote Whitman, "and were supplied with provisions." Somehow Whitman had obtained a pair of small millstones and soon had the mill in operation, "so that the latter part of the emigration got grinding done. My wheat, beef & most of my hogs & corn & many of my potatoes have been furnished them" [Letter 142].

Successful End of the 1843 Emigration

Upon their arrival at The Dalles, most of the emigrants decided to complete their journey to the Willamette Valley by going down the Columbia River with their wagons and equipment on boats or rafts. The herds of cattle, horses, and mules were driven through the heavy forests which cloak the sides of Mt. Hood into the Valley. A few venturesome men took their wagons over the mountains. In places the terrain was so precipitous that large trees had to be cut down and tied to the descending wagons to serve as a brake. Thus the first great emigration to Oregon came to a successful end. The feasibility of taking wagons through, not only over the Blue Mountains to the Columbia River, but also over the Cascades into the Willamette Valley, had been demonstrated. The wagon road to Oregon was opened at last!

Several years before the 1843 emigration arrived in the Valley, the Rev. Josiah L. Parrish, one of the Methodist missionaries, told Dr. McLoughlin: "Before we die, we will see the Yankees coming across the mountains with their teams and families." McLoughlin scoffed at the idea and said that they might as well undertake a trip to the moon. When some of the emigrants arrived in the Valley, the skeptical McLoughlin went to see them. Meeting Parrish, he exclaimed: "God forgive me, Parrish, but the Yankees are here, and the first thing you know they will yoke up their oxen, drive down to the mouth of the Columbia River and come out at Japan." And again he said: "The devil is in the Americans, the devil is in you people."[54]

That which had seemed to Dr. McLoughlin as improbable as going to the moon had actually come to pass [and now, in our generation, even going to the moon has become an actuality].

Whitman Accused of Charging "Exorbitant Prices"

After their arrival in the Willamette Valley, some members of the 1843 immigration criticized Whitman for charging what they claimed were exorbitant prices for food supplies sold to them at Waiilatpu. Dr. Elijah White became the spokesman for the critics in his report of November 15, 1843, sent to his superiors in Washington: "The Presbyterian Mission, however, for the first time have fallen very heavily under censure from the immigrating party this fall, from the fact principally, as I understand, of their exacting most exorbitant prices for supplies of provisions. I have only ex-parte statements, which if but half true, they deserve the just reprobation of mankind."[55]

Nearly two years later, when Whitman was called to Oregon City on business, he met White on the street and demanded an explanation of the criticisms that White had been spreading abroad. B. F. Nichols, an early Oregon immigrant, tells the story of what happened:

> I was present in Oregon City, some time in the month of June 1845, when Dr. Whitman and Dr. White had what you might call a public controversy. Dr. White from a sectarian jealousy, had written a letter to some of the eastern papers, charging Whitman with misusing immigrants. Dr. Whitman came down and happened to meet Dr. White in Oregon City, when they had a dispute. Dr. White proposed to establish what he had said, so a meeting for a public investigation was called at the Red House. Dr. White called Mr. Geiger, who still lives in Oregon City, as his first witness.
>
> When asked to state how Dr. Whitman had treated the immigrants, Mr. Geiger told a very different story than White had counted on. Instead of telling how Dr. Whitman had misused them, he told of his many kindnesses to them, and what a friend he had always been to them. When White saw that the tables were turned against him by his own witnesses, he jumped up and said: "Mr. Geiger, you can take your seat, sir; I will acknowledge that you can outlie me." He failed to prove a single allegation that he had made, so the investigation proved to be a great triumph for Dr. Whitman.[56]

Burnett also came to Whitman's defense by writing: "This foolish, false, and ungrateful charge was based upon the fact that he asked us a dollar a bushel for wheat, and forty cents for potatoes. As our people had been accustomed to sell their wheat at from fifty to sixty cents a bushel, and their potatoes at from twenty to twenty-five cents, in the Western States, they thought the prices demanded by the doctor amounted to something like extortion, not reflecting that he had to pay at least twice as much for his own supplies of merchandise, and could not afford to sell his produce as low as they did theirs at home." [57] According to Burnett, some of the immigrants felt so strongly about the high prices that Whitman was asking that they refused to buy and, as a result, ran out of food before they got to the Willamette Valley and were obliged to borrow from others.

Whitman was also criticized by some because of the terms he was asking for trading fresh, fat oxen for the worn-out cattle of the immigrants. Of this Daniel Waldo wrote in sharp terms: "Whitman lied to me like hell at Waiilatpu. He wanted my cattle and told me the grass was all burnt between his place and the Dalles. I told him I would try it anyhow. The first night I left for the Dalles, I found the finest grass I ever saw, and it was good every night." [58]

Lenox, in a less critical spirit, said: "My father found it necessary to get new oxen, ours were so worn out, so we traded our five oxen for two fresh ones with Mr. Geiger, working our cows to make out a full team." [59] Another immigrant, J. B. McClane wrote of trading two head of worn-out cattle for a fat ox, but made no criticism of what he considered to be a fair transaction made with Whitman.[60] Whitman frequently extended credit and often was never paid. In this respect his experience was similar to that of Dr. McLoughlin and the Hudson's Bay Company at Fort Vancouver, where credit was likewise given to immigrants who later neglected or even refused to settle their accounts. Geiger and Whitman sold so much of the produce of the Waiilatpu fields in the fall of 1843 that Whitman was obliged to call upon Spalding to furnish supplies for the winter [Letter 142].

An Appraisal of the Results of Whitman's Ride

As outlined in an earlier chapter, evidence indicates that Whitman had three motives for making his journey to Washington and Boston in 1842–43, namely: mission business, political interests, and the desire to counteract Roman Catholic influences.[61] We can now ask: To what extent was Whitman successful in the realization of these objectives? Regarding his concern for the future welfare of the Oregon Mission, he succeeded in inducing the Board to rescind its action of February 1842. Spalding was not to be dismissed nor were the stations at Waiilatpu and Lapwai to be closed.

Linked with his concern over the future of the Oregon Mission of the American Board was his desire to counteract the growing influence of the Roman Catholic missionaries in Oregon by persuading the American Board to send out a reenforcement to its Mission in Oregon and also to promote the emigration of Protestant families. In this objective, Whitman failed, for the Board never sent another missionary to Oregon and seemingly did nothing to encourage Protestants to emigrate and settle in the vicinity of the Mission stations. The four couples already under appointment carried on in their respective stations at Waiilatpu, Lapwai, and Tshimakain without additional help.

POLITICAL RESULTS OF WHITMAN'S RIDE

The most far-reaching results of Whitman's ride are to be found in the political realm. Whitman's interests were not centered upon any possible treaty that the United States might sign with Great Britain which would fix the location of the Oregon boundary. Rather, Whitman's emphasis was on emigration. He was tremendously interested in having the United States Government extend its jurisdiction over Oregon, but nowhere in his correspondence does he indicate any opinion as to just where the border was to be located. He evidently reasoned that the boundary question would automatically be settled if enough American citizens could be induced to settle in Oregon. All the efforts of statesmen and diplomats to fix the boundary at some line favorable to the United States would have been fruitless without a large and growing American colony in Oregon.

A new era in Oregon's history began with the arrival of the large 1843 emigration. The wagon road from Fort Hall to the Columbia River was the magic key which unlocked Oregon's doors to the restless thousands on America's western frontiers. The success of the 1843 emigration guaranteed that other large emigrations would follow. The larger the number of Americans in Oregon, the greater would be the pressure on the government to extend its jurisdiction over the territory.

Whitman remembered with glowing pride the part he had played in the opening of the road to the Columbia. Perhaps the most revealing comment, reflecting his appraisal of the importance of the services he rendered for the political future of Oregon, is in the following extract from his letters to Greene dated November 1, 1843:

> I do not regret having visited the States for I feel that this country must either be American or else foreign & mostly Papal. If I never

do more than to have been *one of the first to take white women across the Mountains* & prevent the disaster & reaction which would have occurred by the breaking up of the present Emigration & e*stablishing the first wagon road across to the border of the Columbia River, I am satisfied.* I cannot feel that we can look on & see Papal & Foreign influence making its greatest effort & we hold ourselves as expatriated & neutral. I am determined to exert myself for my country & to procure such regulations & laws as will best secure both the Indian & white man in their transit & settlement [and] intercourse.[62]

Shortly after his return to Waiilatpu in the fall of 1843, Whitman wrote out the draft of his proposed bill for Congressional consideration, the contents of which he had discussed with government officials while in Washington during the previous March.[63] He also wrote a letter to the "Hon. James M. Porter, Secretary of War." On the back of the letter, now on file in the National Archives along with the draft of his bill, is the notation: "Marcus Whitman. Enc. synopsis of a bill with his views in reference to impot. [importance] of the Oregon Terry... Rec. June 22, '44." Whitman's letter to Porter is undated but from internal evidence and from the date of its receipt, we know that it was written sometime in the fall of 1843. Since the letter and the proposed bill are not known to have been published since 1905, both are given in Appendix 7 of this book.

Whitman's letter to Porter is important as it gives a detailed report about the 1843 Oregon emigration and needs to be read carefully. After making reference to "the immense immigration of families to Oregon" which had taken place that year, Whitman wrote: "I have since our interview, been instrumental in piloting across the route described in the accompanying Bill, and which is the only eligible wagon road, no less than... one thousand persons of both sexes with their wagons, amounting in all to more than one hundred and twenty, 698 oxen and 973 loose cattle." He referred to the "incredible hardships" suffered by the immigrants and claimed that their success in taking their wagons and effects through to the Columbia River had "established a durable road from Missouri to Oregon... contrary to all the sinister assertions of those who pretend it to be impossible." Whitman prophesied that larger numbers of people would be going to Oregon in "each succeeding year."

In this letter to Porter, Whitman pointed out the necessity of extending United States jurisdiction to Oregon so that its citizens could execute legal documents. "At present," he wrote, "no person is authorized to administer an oath or legally attest a fact from the western line of Missouri to the Pacific." Such lack of law often meant real economic hardships.

Aware of a provision in a bill before Congress which would have given 640 acres to every white male over sixteen who would settle in Oregon, Whitman began thinking of how he might claim the land at Waiilatpu. Under the proposed law, no provision was made for such institutions and organizations as the American Board to make such a claim for its mission sites. Whitman touched on this subject when he wrote to Greene on April 8, 1844: "Perhaps in some way, as we have so eminently aided the Government by being among the first to cross the mountains, and the first to bring white women over, and last but not least, as I brought the late emigration on to the shores of the Columbia with their wagons contrary to all former assertions of the impossibility of the route, we may be alowed the right of private citizens by taking lands in the country."

In his letter to Greene of July 22, 1844, Whitman repeated his conviction that it was he who had saved the 1843 emigration from disaster: "No one but myself was present to give them the assurance of getting through." In the last letter he wrote Greene, dated October 18, 1847, just six weeks before his death, we find the following:

> Two things, and it is true those which were the most important; were accomplished by my return to the States. By means of the establishment of the wagon road, which is due to that effort alone, the emigration was secured & saved from disaster in the fall of forty-three. *Upon that event the present acquired rights of U. States by her Citizens hung.* And not less certain is it that upon the result of emigration to this country, the present existence of this Mission & of Protestantism in general hung also.[64]

In these various statements Whitman summarizes his conviction that the opening of Oregon to American settlement hinged upon two events: (1) the successful crossing of the Rockies by the two white women in the summer of 1836, and (2) the successful piloting of the 1843 emigration across the Snake River desert and the Blue Mountains to the Columbia

River. The emigrations of 1844 and later years did not take the risks taken by that of 1843. The 1843 emigration had no precedent to give them assurance of success except the knowledge that three wagons had been taken over the Blue Mountains in 1840 and Whitman's conviction that what had once been done could be done again. The strength of America's position at the diplomatic bargaining table when the boundary issue was finally settled in 1846 with Great Britain, was due to the success of American immigration. That part of Old Oregon up to the 49° parallel was won by the United States largely because of the numerical strength of the American colony in that territory, even though most of the immigrants had settled south of the Columbia River.

Reaction of the Hudson's Bay Company

When George Simpson had visited Fort Vancouver in the summer of 1841, he studied the idea of moving the headquarters of the Columbia Department of the Hudson's Bay Company from Fort Vancouver to some point on Vancouver Island. Several reasons dictated the move, one being the proximity of Fort Vancouver to the Americans in the Willamette Valley, whom Simpson profoundly distrusted. On March 1, 1842, McLoughlin was directed to establish a new depot at the southern end of Vancouver Island. A site was selected and the construction of a new post was begun in 1843 at what is now Victoria, British Columbia. The arrival of the 1843 immigration caused the Company to accelerate its plan of transferring its fur trade from Fort Vancouver to Fort Victoria. By 1845 Fort Vancouver had become little more than a mercantile establishment serving the needs of all Oregon settlers who might apply.

The Governor and Committee of the Hudson's Bay Company in London took note of the increased American activities in Oregon and their correspondence with McLoughlin reflects their alarm. In a letter dated September 27, 1843, to McLoughlin, we may read: "We notice the arrival of Dr. White in the Columbia District with a fresh party of emigrants, and we entirely approve of the course you pursued towards that person. No authority emanating from the Government of the United States is to be recognized west of the Rocky Mountains until the boundary question shall have been settled." This was a reasonable stand to take as long as the Treaty of Joint Occupation remained in effect. "There is little doubt," the letter continues, "that this man is an instrument in the hands of that party in the United States who have been for sometime past urging the Government of that country to take military possession of the Oregon Territory."

The writer of this letter may have known of the large emigration of that year when he wrote: "To their misrepresentations respecting the fertility of the soil and other natural advantages of the valley of the Walamet may be attributed the great influx of Americans to that quarter of late, it being their policy to give the American interests an apparent superiority over the British and *thus to strengthen the claim of the United States to the disputed territory.*" [65] This was precisely the position which had been taken by Marcus Whitman.

On June 21, 1843, before he had heard of the successful American emigration of that year, Simpson wrote to McLoughlin from Red River. Regarding the diplomatic negotiations involving the Oregon border, Simpson optimistically commented: "I am very much of the opinion that the negotiations in regard to it will be brought to a close in the course of this year. The impression on my mind, from all that has reached me, is that the Columbia River from its outlet to its source in the mountains by the Southern branch or Lewis & Clark's route will become the boundary." [66] Simpson evidently knew that Lord Ashburton had been in Washington in the preceding summer and optimistically assumed that the British diplomat would insist upon the location of the border at the Columbia River, which had long been advocated by officials of the Hudson's Bay Company.

The full effect of the successful emigration of 1843 was not felt until 1845, as it took time for the news to get back to the States. The emigration of 1844 numbered only about 1,500 people, whereas that of 1845 totaled nearer three thousand. With the immigrants pouring into Oregon by the thousands, James Douglas, one of the Chief Factors at Fort Vancouver, in a letter to Simpson dated March 5, 1845, pointed out the consequences of continued delay in settling the boundary question: "I am sorry to hear that the settlement of the Boundary question is likely to drag on, from year to year, without being settled, *as the Americans will soon leave nothing to settle.* The people of the West are crowding into the country by sea and land as fast as they can come. Every vessel from the Sandwich Islands brings some addition to their number, and about 1,500 persons arrived last autumn overland from St. Louis, bringing with them nearly

200 wagons and upwards of 1,000 head of cattle. They are branching out into every direction, and settling wherever fancy leads them." [67]

Some students of Northwest history have claimed that since only a few Americans settled north of the Columbia River before 1846, the presence of so many in the Willamette Valley could not have had much influence on the willingness of the British Government to abandon its claim to the disputed territory north of the River when the boundary was fixed at the 49° parallel that year. However, a letter from Douglas dated October 8, 1845, to Sir George F. Seymour of H.M.S. *Collingwood*, gives a different picture. After urging the Admiral to send a vessel to the Columbia "for the support of British influence and the protection of British interests and property in the Columbia River," Douglas explained: "The reasons for this opinion are principally founded on the great and increasing American population who are settling without any regard to the claims of Great Britain in every part of the Territory, *North and South of the Columbia River*. These people not being under the control of any government, and having no generally acknowledged code of laws, and being animated with a spirit exceedingly hostile to Great Britain may, as they have already done, attempt to intrude upon the improvements and invade the property of the British subjects settled in the country." [68]

How different would have been the history of the Pacific Northwest had Great Britain, instead of the United States, been able to send thousands of her citizens to that territory during those crucial years, 1843–45.

CHAPTER 19 ENDNOTES

[1] Italics are the author's.

[2] See Bibliography for data about these two works.

[3] Eells, *Marcus Whitman, M.D.* (Pamphlet), p. 13.

[4] *Sunday School Times*, Jan. 10, 1903.

[5] Perrin Whitman interview, Portland *Oregonian*, Jan. 29, 1899.

[6] Naples, New York, *Record*, Sept. 19, 1913.

[7] *Centennial Celebration* booklet, p. 36, Rushville Congregational Church, 1902.

[8] Information by kindness of Miss Caroline Housel of Naples.

[9] James Clark Strong, *Biographical Sketch*, Los Gatos, Calif., 1910, p. 4.

[10] From copy in possession of the late L. Alexander Mack, grandson of Parker.

[11] *W.C.Q.*, II (1898):2: 33ff.; also Spokane, *Spokesman-Review*, Dec. 26, 1895.

[12] Samuel Whitman's notebook (see Chapter Three, fn. 3) has this item: "July, 1868, Perrin B. Whitman came home—to see me, twenty five yrs. gon." Information by courtesy of Robert Moody of Rushville.

[13] Original letter, Nov. 18, 1883, Coll. W.

[14] William W. Sweet, *The Story of Religion in America*, New York, 1950, p. 278.

[15] Italics are the author's.

[16] Cleveland *Plain Dealer*, May 7, 1895. It is not possible to reconstruct with accuracy the chronology of Whitman's journey westward. Judge Otis may have been mistaken when he claimed that he and Whitman spent four days in Buffalo.

[17] *W.C.Q.*, II (1898):3:36. Dr. Hale was one of the first three dentists who practised in St. Louis for any length of time. He retired in 1864.

[18] Only one copy of the original pamphlet is known to exist; it is in Coll. Y. Ye Galleon Press, Fairfield, Wash., brought out a reprint edition, 1971, 20 pp.

[19] Italics are the author's. Most of the emigrants who made the overland journey to Oregon found that oxen, although slower, were more reliable than horses. See George Wilkes, *History of Oregon*, New York, 1845, p. 68.

[20] Eells, *Marcus Whitman, M.D.* (Pamphlet), p. 31.

[21] *T.O.P.A.*, 1875, pp. 42 ff.

[22] Perrin Whitman, ms., Coll. Wn.

[23] Theodore Talbot, *Journals*, Portland, 1931, p. 3, states that Fremont and members of his party left Cincinnati on May 4 and arrived in St. Louis on the 7th.

[24] Peter H. Burnett, *Recollections of an Old Pioneer*, New York, 1880, p. 101.

[25] Wilkes, *History of Oregon*, p. 67.

[26] *T.O.P.A.*, 1875, pp. 48 ff.

[27] Bancroft, *Oregon*, I:895 ff., gives an incomplete list of the male members of the 1843 emigration and also quotes various authorities as to the number of individuals, wagons, and animals in this party.

[28] Talbot, *Journals*, p. 9.

29 Original Waldo ms., Coll. B. Partly reprinted in Bancroft, *Oregon*, I:405.

30 Reprinted in *National Intelligencer*, June 6, 1843, and in Washington *Globe*, June 8, 1848.

31 Iowa *Gazette*, July 8, 1843. Jesse Applegate was a member of the 1843 emigration.

32 *T.O.P.A.*, 1876, with article by Applegate, "A Day with the Cow Column."

33 *W.C.Q.*, II (1898):2:34.

34 See ante, fn. 82, and *O.H.Q.*, I (1900):381 ff.

35 *T.O.P.A.*, 1880, p. 22.

36 *Ibid.*, 1876, p. 63.

37 *O.H.Q.*, IV (1903):282.

38 Peter Burnett, *Recollections of an Old Pioneer*, New York, 1880, p. 112.

39 Quoted by Eells, *Marcus Whitman*, p. 215.

40 There is some question as to the identity of this creek. The late Dale Morgan of Bancroft Library, Berkeley, in a letter to me dated June 2, 1970, wrote: "It is evidently the stream called Squaw Butte Creek in several of the journals of 1843... and the present La Prele Creek, 17 miles east of 'Big Deer Creek'... Apparently the Oregon emigrants of 1843 somewhat overestimated the distance from Fort Laramie." Hulbert, *O.P.*, VII:322, identifies the creek as being "just west of Deer Creek."

41 *O.H.Q.*, V (1904):76.

42 Grant remained in charge of Fort Hall from 1842 until 1851. The Company abandoned the post in 1855.

43 *O.H.Q.*, VII (1906):342.

44 *T.O.P.A.*, 1875, p. 48.

45 *W.C.Q.*, II (1898):2:31.

46 *Op. cit.*, p. 83. Italics are the author's.

47 *T.O.P.A.*, 1875, p. 48.

48 *W.C.Q.*, II (1898):2:35.

49 Eells, *Reply to Bourne*, p. 112.

50 *W.C.Q.*, II (1898):2:34 quoting Perrin Whitman in 1898: "He [i.e. Dr. Whitman] showed me some of the pieces [of the wagon] at Boise seven years after he had brought it out ...It had just laid there by an old adobe building until it had rotted and sunk into the ground."

51 *T.O.P.A.*, 1875, p. 48.

52 Drury, *F.W.W.*, II:259.

53 Myron Eells in later years was to become one of the foremost champions of the Whitman-Saved-Oregon story. See Appendix 4.

54 *T.O.P.A.*, p. 26. See also account of H. H. Bancroft's interview with Parrish on June 15, 1878. Coll. B.

55 White's original report is in Old Indian Files, National Archives. Miss Allen omitted this from her book, *Ten Years in Oregon*.

56 *W.C.Q.*, II (1898):1:34.

⁵⁷ Burnett, *Recollections of an Old Pioneer*, p. 127.

⁵⁸ Waldo ms., Coll. B.

⁵⁹ Edward Henry Lenox, *Overland to Oregon*, Oakland, Calif., 1904, p. 54.

⁶⁰ McClane ms., Coll. B.

⁶¹ See Chapter Sixteen, "Motives for Whitman's Ride."

⁶² Italics are the author's. See Foreword to this work.

⁶³ See Chapter Eighteen, "Synopsis of Whitman's Bill," and Appendix 7.

⁶⁴ Italics are the author's.

⁶⁵ HBC Arch., B/223/c. Italics are the author's.

⁶⁶ *Ibid.*

⁶⁷ *Ibid.* Italics are the author's.

⁶⁸ *Ibid.* Italics are the author's.

[CHAPTER TWENTY]

A CHANGING OREGON
1843–1846

The success of the large 1843 emigration, followed by ever larger immigrations in each succeeding year, precipitated a cultural conflict for the Indians of the upper Columbia River country. Although none of the immigrants, during the years 1843–47 inclusive, settled on land in the vicinity of Waiilatpu, social and economic changes were introduced among the natives which threatened their mode of life. These were years of transition for both the Indians and the whites in Old Oregon.

Mission activities at Waiilatpu were no longer the same as they had been before Whitman left for Boston. Although Whitman tried to carry on his religious, educational, and agricultural activities as before, things were different. The increasing attention that the Whitmans had to give to the immigrants, especially to those who found it necessary to winter at Waiilatpu, aroused the suspicion and finally the resentment of the Cayuses. Whitman's ride East in 1842–43 was a watershed in the history of the Oregon Mission of the American Board. The first six years were characterized by dissension among the members of the Oregon Mission and by the friendliness of the natives. After Whitman's return, the situation was reversed. The four couples remaining in the Mission worked together in full harmony, but there was growing hostility to the missionaries on the part of the Indians, especially the Cayuses.

When Whitman returned to Waiilatpu in the fall of 1843, he learned that a Provisional Government had been formed at a meeting of Willamette Valley settlers held at Champoeg on May 2, 1843. The restless Americans living in the Valley, tired of waiting for their Government to fill a legal void, decided to take matters into their own hands. A few French Canadians, defying the instructions of their priest and the wishes of the Hudson's Bay Company, voted with the Americans. Until the arrival of the 1843 immigrants, most of the French Canadians and the officials of the Company refrained from giving the Provisional Government their support. After the arrival of the 1843 immigration, some changes were made in the charter of the Provisional Government which made it more acceptable to the French Canadians and, as a result, they voted in the 1844 elections. Dr. McLoughlin also changed his attitude and decided that the Hudson's Bay Company should support the new government in order to secure some degree of protection for the Company's interests. Upon his return to Waiilatpu, Whitman learned that not only had the white settlers in the Willamette Valley adopted a code of laws, but so also had the Cayuses. Whitman soon discovered, however, that the laws which Dr. White had induced the Indians to accept were highly unpopular. In a letter to Greene dated April 8, 1844, Whitman wrote: "It is in vain to urge that the Indians adopted the laws of themselves. The principal chief [i.e., Five Crows] said that they would have preferred their own, if left to their own choice. They have become a mere form as there are none to execute them. They wish mostly to use them to establish complaints against white men rather than punish offenders of their own people."

Whitman was critical of the manner in which Dr. White had forced the Cayuses to accept the laws, yet he realized that the extension of United States jurisdiction over the Indians was both necessary and inevitable. "I have no confidence in two codes of laws for one country," he wrote. "If the Indians are not wise enough to either give laws to their own country, both for themselves and others, or to partake with the whites in the formation of them; they must submit to laws of the immigration that comes among them, as others do. For it is evident that there should be but one code of laws for both the natives and the settlers in the same country." It may be that Dr. White's accusations that Whitman charged exorbitant prices for his produce arose out of White's awareness of Whitman's criticisms of the laws. There is no record that Dr. Whitman ever tried to get any of the Cayuse chiefs to enforce any provisions of the code.

Another new factor which greatly affected missionary life at Waiilatpu after 1843 was the necessity thrust upon the Whitmans to meet the material needs of the annual immigrations. In addition to selling provisions and helping all who were able to travel to continue their journey to the Willamette, special attention had to be given to those who, for various reasons, were unable to go further. Always in the wake of the passing wagon trains was this flotsam of unfortunate people the sick, the weary, the old, the destitute, the widows, and the orphans—who found Waiilatpu a haven of refuge. Out of human kindness and Christian charity, the Whitmans had no choice but to receive these people and to care for them during the winter months or until they were able to continue their travels. The time, attention, and resources they had to give to the immigrants meant a corresponding diminution of activities in behalf of the natives. For instance, the large room called "the Indian room," which had been built in the main mission house for the purpose of being used as a schoolroom or an assembly room for the natives, was turned into an apartment for the immigrants during those months when the Cayuses were most available for instruction.

1843–1844

When Dr. Whitman left the 1843 emigration while in the Grande Ronde Valley in order to go to Lapwai, he entrusted the care of his nephew, Perrin, to someone who promised to take him to Waiilatpu. Perrin arrived at the mission station on September 27,[1] one day before his uncle and Geiger returned from Lapwai. While at Lapwai, Whitman again met the Littlejohns, who, for nearly a year, had been living with the Spaldings. Since Mrs. Littlejohn was expecting to be confined about the first of November, plans were made for the couple to go to Waiilatpu where she would be under the doctor's care.

As has been told, Whitman had gone to Tshimakain the day after his return to Waiilatpu in order to attend Mrs. Eells in her confinement. Upon his return to Waiilatpu on October 10,[2] he found some of the immigrants still streaming by his home, many of whom were in need of provisions. Geiger, eager to return to the Willamette Valley, asked to be relieved of his duties at Waiilatpu. Whitman settled accounts with him by paying him $30.00 for each month he had been at the station. Whitman was well pleased with Geiger's services. "Few could have done better," he wrote [Letter 142]. Littlejohn, who with his wife had by that time arrived at Waiilatpu, was asked to take over Geiger's duties.

Eager to get his wife whom he knew to be at The Dalles, Whitman left for that place about the middle of October. Reference has already been made to the "joyful and happy meeting" of the two after a separation of more than a year. Jason Lee, who had escorted Narcissa to The Dalles, had waited in order to see Whitman. "It was pleasing," wrote Narcissa, "to see the pioneers of the two Missions meet and hold council together" [Letter 149]. While in New York in the spring of 1843, Whitman had called at the offices of the Methodist Missionary Society where he was told that Lee had been dismissed and that a successor, the Rev. George Gary, was already on his way to Oregon to close out the Methodist Mission. Whitman was the first to pass on this distressing news to Lee.[3] "When we parted with Mr. Lee," wrote Narcissa to her father, "we little thought that our first news from him would be that he had set his face toward his native land. But it was, indeed so."

On December 25 of that year, Lee boarded a ship bound for Honolulu on his return voyage to the States. After his arrival in the East, he appeared before the Methodist Society and, after answering the accusations which had been made against him by some dissatisfied associates, including Dr. Elijah White, he was completely exonerated. Lee died on March 12, 1845. According to Spalding, Whitman felt that Lee had been dismissed because of "his stern patriotism and his efforts to Americanize this country."[4] Here is a possible reference to the role that Lee played in inducing the Methodist Society to send out the large reenforcement on the *Lausanne* in the fall of 1839.

NARCISSA, SICK AND DISCOURAGED

The boat trip up the river from The Dalles to Fort Walla Walla was a disagreeable experience for both Marcus and Narcissa. It was rainy and cold. Narcissa was sick, and the exposure increased her suffering. They reached Fort Walla Walla late on Saturday afternoon, October 28 [Letter 141a]. Since Narcissa was too weak to attempt to make the twenty-five mile trip to Waiilatpu on horseback, it was agreed that Marcus would go out to Waiilatpu and return with a wagon. Moreover, Mrs. Littlejohn's time was near, and the doctor felt that he must be there. After writing a letter to Greene dated, November 1, Whitman left for his station. The Littlejohn baby, a girl, was born on the 3rd.[5]

As mentioned in a previous chapter,[6] Narcissa dreaded going back to Waiilatpu. Her feelings were reflected in several letters she wrote at this time, the first of which was to her friends, Mr. and Mrs. George Abernethy of Oregon City, with whom she had spent several weeks during the summer of 1843. After thanking them for their gracious hospitality, she wrote: "Never shall I forget the precious seasons of social and religious enjoyment I have been blessed with in your society. Withdrawing my mind from these pleasing reminiscences, what sounds fall upon my ear and what savage sights do I behold every day around me. Never was I more keenly sensible to the self denials of a missionary life. Even now while I am writing, the drum and the savage yell are sounding in my ears, every sound of which is as far as the east is from the west from vibrating in unison with my feelings. What a contrast with the heavenly music of the Camp Meeting. Dear friends will you not sometime think of me almost alone in the midst of savage darkness" [Letter 141a]. Evidently a band of Indians was holding a war or ritualistic dance of some kind at the Fort near Narcissa's room and within range of her hearing.

Narcissa's ill health contributed to her feeling of despondency. While in the Willamette Valley, she had consulted with three doctors: Dr. Elijah White, Dr. Ira L. Babcock of the Methodist Mission, and Dr. Forbes Barclay at Fort Vancouver, but, because of the lack of medical knowledge of that day, there was little they could do to relieve her sufferings. Whitman, in his letter of November 1 to Greene, reported: "Mrs. Whitman's health has been poor for the last year, having had an enlargement of the Ovarid [ovary?]." In his letter of January 29, 1844, to H. B. Brewer, a member of the Methodist Mission stationed at The Dalles, Whitman was more specific: "Mrs. W's health does not promise to be any better. She is now about [the] house & takes considerable care but she has a throbing tumor near the navel (umbilicus) which I fear is an aneurism of the main artery. Consequently I have little expectation of her ever enjoying health again."

The ballooning of a large artery, referred to as an aneurism, can now be corrected by surgery but such a technique was unknown to that generation. Narcissa described her affliction in a letter to a sister dated

January 30, 1844: "I have not suffered from the disease I took medicine for last summer, but a new and more precarious one has discovered itself, since my return, yet of long standing. It consists of an organic affection of the main artery below the heart, a beating tumor which is liable to burst and extinguish my life at any moment. There is no remedy for it, so I never expect to enjoy better health than I do at present; never do I expect to continue long on the earth."

Several months later, on April 12, Narcissa gave further details about her poor health in a letter to her father: "While I was at Vancouver, I placed myself under Doctor Barclay's care... He discovered that I had an enlargement of the right ovary and gave me iodine to remove it. I was very much improved by his kind attentions for that complaint, and had it not been for the other difficulty of the aorta which was not at that time discovered by Doctor Barclay, although it existed, I might have recovered my health. But the medicine I took for the cure of one tumor was an injury to the other, and for three months after my husband's return, my situation was a source of deepest anxiety to him and he greatly feared that he was about to be bereaved."

Narcissa's despondency appears in both of these letters. In the letter to her sister of January 1844, she wrote: "I felt such a dread to return to this place of moral darkness, after enjoying so much of civilized life and Christian privileges." And in the letter to her father, she repeated the same sentiment: "I turned my face with my husband toward this dark spot, and dark, indeed, it seemed to be to me when compared with the scenes, social and religious, which I had so recently been enjoying with so much zest."

BACK TO WAIILATPU

Among the families whom Whitman met and encouraged to go to Oregon when he passed through St. Louis in the early spring of 1843 was that of John Hobson. Somewhere along the trail, it appears Mrs. Hobson had died, leaving her husband with three girls—one in her mid-teens; Ann, who was thirteen; and Emma, seven. Even as Whitman had felt a responsibility for the wife of Miles Eyres and her children, so in the Hobson case, he promised the distracted father that the three girls could be left at his mission station [Letter 145]. When Narcissa arrived at Fort Walla Walla, she met the Hobson family. By that time the older girl had plans to go to the Willamette Valley with another party. The two younger girls had been hesitant about being left at Waiilatpu, but they quickly changed their minds after meeting Narcissa and begged to be taken into the Whitman home. Narcissa was hesitant. She already had Mary Ann Bridger and Helen Mar Meek. Also at Waiilatpu were David Malin and Perrin Whitman. To her sister, Narcissa wrote: "The girls were so urgent to stop that I could not well refuse them." And so it was arranged that the Whitman household should be increased by two more girls, making six children in all under their care.

On Saturday, November 4, Whitman loaded his family into the wagon, which he had brought in from the mission, and they started the long ride to Waiilatpu. Narcissa, commenting on the difficulties of the ride, wrote: "I was not well when I left W.W., yet I thought I could endure to ride here in one day in a wagon, but it proved too much for me. We were in the evening late before we could reach home, as they [i.e., the animals] had to go slow on my account, and I took cold. For six weeks after, I scarcely left my room and most of the time was confined to my bed [Letter 145]." During December, a combination of complications brought her "very near the gates of death." After passing the crisis, her health slowly but gradually improved, although by the following May, she wrote that she was still weak. Because of her ill health and also because of her enlarged family responsibilities, Narcissa was able to carry on few if any activities for the natives. As far as the Indians were concerned, her main missionary duties were over.

Narcissa's ill health should be remembered when we read H. K. W. Perkins' appraisal of her [Appendix 6]. He never saw her during the first six years of her life at Waiilatpu when she was well and enthusiastic about her work with the natives. Perkins remembered her as being ill, dreading to go back to Waiilatpu. He was correct when he wrote that "her stay with us including the visit to the Willamette, [was] the pleasantest portion of her Oregon life." In view of her physical condition, we can understand why Perkins wrote: "The natives esteemed her as proud, haughty, as *far above them*. No doubt she really seemed so. It was her *misfortune*, not her *fault*. She was adapted to a different destiny." As will be told later, Narcissa's health greatly improved within a few months after her return to Waiilatpu and she became able to carry on her household duties without the handicap of ill health.

"The Foreign Inhabitants of Waiilatpu"

When Narcissa, exhausted from the long, slow wagon trip from Fort Walla Walla, arrived with her husband and the four little girls at Waiilatpu, she found the main mission house and the dwelling that Gray had erected, crowded with emigrants. The Littlejohns with their newborn baby were in the Whitmans' bedroom and for the time being could not be moved. Every room in the two dwellings was occupied except the dining room. There the Whitmans and the two Hobson girls slept for about five weeks. Five emigrant families and four single men were crowded into the other rooms. Jesse Looney, his wife, and six children occupied the Indian room together with a young man by the name of Smith. Mr. and Mrs. John W. East and their four children had the schoolroom east of the kitchen. A French Canadian, whom Narcissa called Alex, a mountain man, and who, she claimed "stops with us without invitation," made his bed in the kitchen, the most used room in the mission house. David Malin and Perrin had their beds in the attic room over the living room, and Helen Mar and Mary Ann slept in the same room with the Littlejohns. This meant that a total of twenty-seven were living in the main mission house of whom fifteen were immigrants and one, a mountain man.

When the Gray house was erected in 1841–42, it was so pretentious, as compared with the dwellings occupied by the other members of the Mission, that it was called at first the "mansion house." This building had six rooms on the first floor and an unknown number on the upper half-story.[7] Possibly the interior of the Gray house was not finished by the fall of 1843, as only twelve emigrants and two "hired men" were living there when the Whitmans returned to Waiilatpu on November 4. Thirty emigrants were being housed in this building at the time of the Whitman massacre. Narcissa does not list the names of all who were living in the Gray house but did mention in her letters a widow with three children, no doubt Mrs. Eyres whose husband had been drowned in the Snake River; a family with four children, and "an aged couple" [Letters 146 & 149]. Writing to her sister Clarissa on May 20, 1844, Narcissa expressed the hope that her parents might migrate to Oregon and live with them at Waiilatpu. She cited the example of the old couple who had gone out to Oregon to be with their children and commented: "They were considerably older than father and mother."

Thus, the total number of white people, whom Narcissa referred to as "the foreign inhabitants of Waiilatpu," living there in the late fall of 1843, was forty-one, of whom thirty were emigrants or mountain men. The immigrants of 1843 set a pattern for the annual migrations which followed, for each year the number of immigrants enjoying the hospitality of the Whitmans varied from thirty to nearly sixty.

Those who had been given shelter in the fall of 1843 also needed food. The occupants of the emigrant house and the Looney family in the Indian room managed to do their own cooking. The others, eighteen in all not counting the Littlejohn baby, ate at the Whitmans' table. In her letter of January 31, 1844, Narcissa described their fare as being scanty, consisting of "potatoes, corn meal, with a little milk occasionally, and cakes from the burnt wheat." She found the diet a great change from "the well furnished tables of Waskopum and Willamette." Writing to Brewer on January 29, Whitman said: "Our entire living has to come from Mr. Spalding's. We live almost entirely without bread, having little flour and prospect of less until harvest. We have nearly consumed three of the largest & fatest oxen already which we got from Mr. Spalding & now have to look to the Indians for more." Sometimes Narcissa felt resentful when she remembered that the best of their produce had been sold to the passing immigrants.

November and December of 1843 were months of great trial for Narcissa. Even though she was a semi-invalid during most of this time, most of the responsibility of running her household fell on her shoulders. Narcissa missed the privacy of her own bedroom during the first weeks after their return, or until December 10 when the Littlejohn family was able to move into new quarters. With twenty-three children on the grounds, there were many annoyances especially on cold or rainy days when the children could not play outside. Of those trying days, Narcissa wrote: "During all this period and for some time after, I was too sick to make any effort at arranging my house or to have the care of my family, and the confusion and noise distressed me exceedingly." She said that the children, including those under her care, "were as wild and uncontrollable as so many wild animals" [Letter 146].

Realizing the imperative need for more living space, Whitman, with the help of some of the emigrant men, added a room to the east end of the main mission house. This later became the schoolroom for white children. The Littlejohns were able to move into it when it was ready. The Looney family of eight moved in December to "the Prince's house up the river" [Letter 146]. Narcissa may here have been referring to the house built by Pambrun for Young Chief in the fall of 1840 on the Umatilla River. The East family with one of the Eyres girls went to live with the Spaldings. This reduced the number of residents at Waiilatpu to twenty-six and made space available for a school to be opened for white children. This was taught by Mrs. Littlejohn who had an enrollment of fifteen. "Now our children are quite tame," wrote Narcissa, "and manageable and we feel that they are all enjoying a great privilege." This marked the beginning of the Waiilatpu school for white children which was continued in following years up to the time of the massacre.

Whitman hired Littlejohn to take care of cultivation on the condition of giving him one-third of the produce which he would be free to sell to the emigrants of 1844. We have no evidence that Whitman asked for or received any compensation from any of the emigrants for the hospitality they enjoyed at Waiilatpu. No doubt the women helped Narcissa in household duties and regarding the men, Whitman wrote: "I intend to give employment by the job in cutting & splitting rails; making fence & breaking new land."

When Narcissa wrote to the Abernethys from Fort Walla Walla on October 31, she stated: "Fremont, the scientific explorer's party have just arrived to-day with ten carts." On his way to the Fort, Frémont had stopped at Waiilatpu, where he had hoped to get some flour but was disappointed to find that none was available. He wrote in his *Narrative* that he had to be satisfied with some "excellent potatoes." Judging by an order drawn on the government dated from "Wascopum, Oregon Territory" on November 24, 1843, payable to Dr. Whitman for $183.31, Frémont got more than potatoes, possibly a beef or some hogs.[8] Narcissa also made reference to a big mule, which Frémont left at Waiilatpu, which the Whitmans called Uncle Sam [Letter 220]. Frémont also left at the mission some extra cannon balls for his howitzer, which fact was remembered by the Indians at the time of the massacre.[9]

The Continuing Activities at Waiilatpu

After reviewing the several references to Narcissa's ill health, it comes as a surprise to learn that Marcus himself was suffering from a disability during the same time which made it difficult for him to carry on his work. Writing to his mother on May 20, 1844, he said: "My whole journey to and from the States seems a dream." He regretted that he had had so little time to spend with his mother and with other relatives and friends. He mentioned the pleasure of seeing "the little growing sprigs under the relation of Nephews; Nieces or Cousins." His mother had been concerned about the dangers and hardships of his return journey. When with her, he laughed off her fears, but, after returning to Waiilatpu, he was ready to admit that the long journey home was "one of fatigue and some danger." Then he added: "But you know Mother, I have long discarded both those as not to be counselled either in matters of duty or pleasure or convenience. I had a lame foot on the road which left me with a tumor on my instep which has given me much solicitude & may give me still much more inconvenience."

Shortly after Marcus and Narcissa arrived at Waiilatpu during the first week of November, an urgent call came from the Walkers at Tshimakain for the doctor to visit them, because Elkanah had come down with scarlet fever. Mary in her diary tells of sending their dependable Indian servant, Solomon, to Waiilatpu on November 13. Solomon returned on the 21st without the doctor but with a note which he had written on the 17th. Whitman explained that his wife's illness and his own affliction made it impossible to respond to the call. He gave some advice: "I think it was favourable that you were bled," he wrote to Elkanah. This is one of the few references in Whitman's correspondence to his approval of the practice, common in that day, of bleeding a patient as a remedy for all manner of diseases, even for scarlet fever. In time Elkanah made a good recovery.

Whitman's foot became so sore in the spring of 1844 that he had to use a crutch. As late as July 22 of that year, he informed Greene that, although his foot was then better, he was still lame and unable "to walk with activity." Summarizing his missionary activities with the natives, Whitman, in his letter to Greene of April 4, 1844, stated: "For the winter we have had few Indians and no school, but were able to hold meetings every Sabbath with a small congregation." Again in the same letter, he reported: "A congregation of from two to three hundred have been in attendance on the Sab.—since some time in Feb.—besides many more who come & go & have more or less opportunity of instruction." The increasing proselytizing activities of the Catholic missionaries in the vicinity of Waiilatpu gave Whitman continued concern. The Indians were quick to take advantage of the rival claims of the Protestants and the Catholics by playing one against the other to see which would give them the largest material benefits. Regarding this Whitman informed Greene that there was an "apparent desire on the part of some to try and make use of the difference between us to enable them to secure some selfish purpose." Whitman believed that the best defense against the Catholics was education. He told Greene that the "gradual increase in knowledge" on the part of the natives would promote a lessened regard for "Papal forms." His difficulty, however, was to find some one able to conduct a school for the Indians as he was far too busy to undertake this responsibility himself. In earlier years, Narcissa had helped in the school but now, because of her ill health and increased household duties, she was unavailable. Whitman tried to hire one of the emigrants to take over the Indian school, but this experiment proved fruitless. So, for the time being, the Indian school was abandoned.

Whitman's work at Waiilatpu was repeatedly interrupted by calls for his professional services by his associates in the Oregon Mission and also by members of the Hudson's Bay Company's residents at Fort Walla Walla. Sometimes these calls entailed days of travel on horseback. During the first week of February 1844, Walker notified him of his wife's expected confinement on or about February 25. A son, their fourth child, came on February 10, earlier than expected and ten days before the doctor arrived. Writing in her diary on February 22, perhaps with some glee, Mary noted: "Dr. W. arrived in the evening. I met him at the door with my babe in my arms."[10] Another confinement case came under Dr. Whitman's care in May 1844 when Mrs. McKinlay, wife of the Hudson's Bay Company's official in charge of Fort Walla Walla, moved to Waiilatpu where she could be under the doctor's care for the birth of her second child. Narcissa explained that "there are no females at the Fort" [Letter 155]. A son was born on May 20.

Profiting by his experience in the fall of 1843 when the immigrants drained him of all provisions except potatoes, a few hogs, and some scorched wheat left in the ruins of the burnt mill, Whitman made every possible effort to be ready for those he expected to arrive in the fall of 1844. In his letter of October 25, 1844, to Greene, he stated that he had from fifteen to seventeen "beeves" which he was selling for six cents a pound. He also planted as many potatoes and garden vegetables as time and cultivated land permitted.

Whitman realized the necessity of getting a suitable gristmill in operation as soon as possible to replace the one which had been destroyed, in order to meet the needs of the residents at Waiilatpu and to be ready for the immigration of 1844. By October 1844, Whitman was able to report to Greene: "Since harvest I have made with the aid of Mr. East a run of fine granite Mill Stones, forty inches across the face & I have got them in good operation so that I shall be able to supply flour & meal which I do at five dollars for unbolted & six for bolted flour per hundred & four for unsifted & five for sifted meal." The mill was placed at the same site as the one that had been burned and another undershot water wheel was made. There is no evidence that the mill at this time was enclosed.

Gradually during the spring and summer of 1844, the immigrants who had wintered at Waiilatpu left for the Willamette Valley. John Hobson sent for his daughter Ann but placed Emma with the Walker family at Tshimakain, where she stayed until May 1845. Most of the immigrants who wintered at Waiilatpu during the years 1843–47 inclusive, moved on the Whitman stage for a few short months and then disappeared into the obscurity of unrecorded history. Not all who made the difficult overland journey were young or middle-aged people. Bancroft in his *Oregon* refers to the death of Jesse Looney on March 25, 1869, at the age of eighty-eight.[11] This means that Looney was sixty-two when he ventured to take his large family over the Oregon Trail to the Pacific Coast.

The Littlejohns left for the Willamette Valley early in the fall of 1844 [Letter 164]. This meant that on the eve of the arrival of the vanguard of the immigration of that year, Waiilatpu was emptied of all its "foreign inhabitants" except the Whitmans, the four children under their care, and perhaps one or two hired men. Writing to his mother on May 20, 1844, Whitman said: "Perrin is a good boy and I think is not homesick." Perrin quickly picked up the Indian language and in this his uncle gave him every encouragement. In his letter to his mother, Whitman wrote that the boy's "articulation will be purely native. No sound is inaccessible to him." Whitman foresaw the day when Perrin would be of great service to the government as an interpreter, as indeed proved to be the case.

More Natives Received into the Mission Church

No missionary who ever served in Old Oregon under either the American Board or the Methodist Society was as successful in his evangelistic and civilizing work with the natives as Henry H. Spalding at Lapwai. Spalding was favored in being located in a larger and more friendly tribe than any other Protestant missionary, and also he was the only Protestant missionary in Oregon who ever returned to his former field after the Whitman massacre. Much of Spalding's success during the years he served under the American Board was due to his strategy in concentrating on winning the chiefs.

As has been noted, Spalding's first converts were Timothy and Old Joseph. During the winter of 1841–42, he conducted a school at Lapwai which enrolled "two hundred and thirty pupils, including most of the chiefs and principal men." [12] In addition to trying to teach a large assemblage of people of all ages, Spalding selected a small group of the most influential men and gave them special attention. On February 14, 1842, Eliza Spalding wrote to her friend, Mrs. A. T. Smith, then in the Willamette Valley, and called the roll of this class: "Joseph, Timothy, Luke, Lawyer, Stephen, Jason, Five Crows (Joseph's brother)..." [13] Of this number, only Five Crows was from the Cayuse tribe. He and Joseph had the same Cayuse mother, but Joseph had a Nez Perce father.

Sometime during the summer of 1841, when on his overland journey around the world, George Simpson met with some of the Cayuses at Fort Walla Walla. "Their chief," wrote Simpson, "who rejoiced in the name of Five Crows, was said to be the richest man in the country, possessing upwards of a thousand horses, a few cattle, many slaves, and various other sources of wealth. Having in addition to all this, the recommendttion of being young, tall, and handsome..." According to Simpson, Five Crows became enamored of the daughter of a Hudson's Bay official, perhaps Maria Pambrun, and after "dismissing his five wives," presented himself at Fort Walla Walla to claim his lady love. "To his dismay," wrote Simpson, "and perhaps also to his astonishment, his suit was rejected." [14]

Polygamy was practiced to a limited extent by the Nez Perces and Cayuses, but it was the firm policy of the missionaries to discourage the custom. Several years after the incident Simpson told about Five Crows, the charge was made in an eastern publication that members of the Oregon Mission of the American Board had received polygamists into the Mission church. When news of this accusation was made known to Spalding, he wrote a vigorous denial to the Board which was published in the *Missionary Herald*. "There is no person now in the church," he declared, "and never has been who has had two wives." [15] Spalding did admit that some of the church members had been polygamists but insisted that they had abandoned the practice on being baptized. The name of Five Crows does not seem to have been mentioned in the published criticism, but the reference may have been to him.

Polygamy posed moral problems for the missionaries and sometimes economic issues for the natives, as can be seen in the following story which has come down through the years. One day a Nez Perce, who had a domineering second wife, approached Spalding and asked if it would be necessary to put away his second wife should he wish to be baptized. "Absolutely," replied Spalding. "Polygamy is a sin. You will have to send your second wife away." The Indian was quiet for a time and then said: "You tell her."

Whitman was called to Lapwai in June 1844 to assist Spalding in examining the Christian faith and experience of several natives who wished to join the Mission Church. Here is evidence that the two men were working together in harmony. Whitman no longer objected, as he had done in December 1841, to the reception of natives into the membership of the church, and Spalding had shown a much more cooperative spirit after Whitman's return from his eastern journey, no doubt being grateful for Whitman's intercession in his behalf. Spalding, as the minister, and Whitman, the elder, constituted the session of the First Presbyterian Church of Oregon which, under Presbyterian polity, was authorized to receive and dismiss members. After due examination, ten were received as members including a French Canadian. Several others who had applied were advised to wait and receive more instruction. "It was an occasion of much interest," Whitman wrote to Greene, "& Joseph, one of the two oldest members, distinguished himself for his discretion & Christian zeal" [Letter 160].

The ten converts were baptized on Sunday, June 23, and publicly welcomed into the membership of the Mission Church. The nine Nez Perces received that day brought the total native membership of the church to twenty-one of whom only Five Crows was a Cayuse. No more natives were received during the remaining three and a half years of the history of the Oregon Mission. If the success of the evangelistic endeavors of the members of the Oregon Mission during its eleven-year history be measured solely by the number of natives who joined the church, then it might be claimed that the Mission was a failure. However, the spiritual results of preaching and teaching the Christian message defy tabulation. The seed had been sown and years later, when Spalding returned to the Nez Perces in his old age, the harvest was reaped when about a thousand Cayuses, Nez Perces, and Spokanes were baptized and received into the First Presbyterian Church of Oregon.

Whitman Comments on Various Issues

Since the Indians had no historian to record their reactions to a number of contemporary events affecting their lives during the 1840s, and since no council was held during that decade with Government officials at which stenographers took down the words of the Indian speakers, we must rely on the correspondence of the missionaries for information about how the natives reacted to the rapidly changing events. How did the Cayuses respond to the thousands of immigrants who each fall crossed their lands? How did they feel about Dr. White's efforts to impose a white man's code of laws upon them? What was the attitude of the land-hungry immigrants towards both the natives and the missionaries? These and many tangent subjects occupied Whitman's attention when he wrote letters during the year under review.

One of the first reactions of the Cayuses to the incoming whites was to profit as much as possible by selling them farm produce or by exchanging fresh horses and cattle for worn-out animals. Whitman, in his letter to Greene of April 8, 1844, said that he thought the Indians had gained much more in these transactions than did the Waiilatpu mission. On May 18, he wrote: "The Indians want settlers among them in hopes to get property from them." Eager to monopolize the market with the immigrants, some of the Cayuses even forbade Whitman "to break a new field as I desired lest I should make money out of their lands by supplying Emigrants" [Letter 148].

Although most of the natives seemed to be eager to make as much money as possible through the sale of provisions to the immigrants, Whitman noted that a few took a long-range view and were "solicitous about so many coming into the Country" [Letter 156]. Even though all of the immigrants of 1844 moved on to the Willamette Valley, Whitman realized that the time was coming when some would want to settle in the Walla Walla Valley. "It will not be long," he wrote, "before there will be settlers among us, when we may look for trouble as the Indians will not like either to respect the interests of the Whites as they ought, nor the Whites to forbear with the Indians."

One of the most penetrating analyses of the developing situation is found in the following taken from Whitman's letter to his mother dated May 16, 1844: "Although the Indians have made and are making rapid advance in religious knowledge and civilization, yet it cannot be hoped that time will be allowed to mature either the work of Christianization or civilization before the white settlers will demand the soil and seek the removal of both the Indians and the Mission. What Americans desire of this kind they always effect, and it is equally useless to oppose or desire it otherwise. To guide, as far as can be done, and direct these tendencies for the best, is evidently the part of wisdom. Indeed, I am fully convinced that when a people refuse or neglect to fill the designs of Providence, they ought not to complain at the results... The Indians have in no case obeyed the command to multiply and replenish the earth, and they cannot stand in the way of others in doing so. A place will be left for them to do this as fully as their ability to obey will permit, and the more we can do for them, the more fully will this be realized. No exclusiveness can be asked for any portion of the human family... The Indians are anxious about the consequences of settlers among them, but I hope there will be no acts of violence on either hand."

In a similar vein Whitman wrote to Greene on May 18, 1844: "Although the Indians are doing much by obtaining stock & cultivating as well as advancing in knowledge, still it cannot be hoped that a settlement [of white people] will be so delayed as to give time for the advance to be made so that they can stand before a white settlement. *For when has it been known that an ignorant, indolent man has stood against money, intelligence & enterprise.*" [16] Whitman was a realist. He saw that the day was inevitably approaching when the Walla Walla Valley would be dotted with the homes and towns of white men. He knew that the natives could never compete with the superior knowledge and the numerical superiority of the incoming Americans. These were critical years of transition for the Indians, and there were none so concerned about helping them as were the missionaries. With the increase of the white population, Whitman also realized that there would be an inevitable shift of emphasis in his missionary work.

In his letter of May 16, 1844, to Narcissa's parents, he wrote: "I have no doubt our greatest work is to be to aid the white settlement of this country and help found its religious institutions." And he added this significant statement: "As I hold the settlement of this country by Americans rather than by an English colony most important, I am happy to have been the means of landing so large an emigration on to the shores of the Columbia, with their wagons, families and stock, all in safety."

Whitman's realistic appraisal of the superiority of the white man's civilization over the primitive culture of the natives, especially in matters referring to future survival, undoubtedly affected his work after his return to Waiilatpu in the fall of 1843. This opinion is reflected in a letter that H. K. W. Perkins wrote on October 19, 1849, when he tried to give reasons why the Cayuses should have killed the Whitmans: "He looked upon them [i.e., the Indians] as an inferior race & doomed at no distant day to give place to a settlement of enterprising Americans. With an eye on this he laid his plans & acted. His American feelings even while engaged in his missionary toils, were unfortunately suffered to predominate. Indeed it might almost be doubted whether he felt half the interest in the natives that he did in the prospective white population. He wanted to see the country settled" [Appendix 6]. This rather harsh criticism of Whitman should be kept in mind as we review his activities with the Indians during the years after his return.

Whitman wanted the Americans to settle in Old Oregon, yet when faced with the possibility of land-hungry immigrants crowding into the Walla Walla Valley, he began to fear the inevitable complications. He expressed this concern in a letter to his brother Augustus dated May 21, 1844. After repeating his conviction that the Indians could never compete with the white men, he turned to what he thought might happen to the Waiilatpu mission: "As soon as we cease to be needed as it were for the benefit of white settlers, for *all other sources have not done so much for the settlement of Oregon as the Missions,* & we become in the way of the interests of the settlers, either by occupying lands they desire or enabling the Indians to hold more firmly to their land by teaching & aiding them to cultivate, *we are sure to become the objects of hatred & efforts will be made to get rid of us...* We must do our duty & be ready to retire at the shortest warning." [17]

Ten days after writing to his brother, or on May 31, Whitman addressed a letter to A. B. Smith, who was then serving under the American Board at a mission station near Honolulu. Whitman, in referring to his journey to Boston, wrote: "I am happy to know that I was enabled if nothing more to reverse the action of the Board in relation to—this Mission." Smith, who was partly responsible for the Board's drastic order of February 1842, could hardly have been pleased with that information. Whitman made mention of the encouragements the government was giving to emigrants, especially in the way of offering free land to all who would settle in Oregon. He then touched on the problem he faced: Was his primary mission to be for the Indian or for the white man? This was the issue he raised when he wrote to Smith: "I do not know how much longer we shall be called to operate for the benefit of the Indians. But be it longer or shorter, it will not diminish the importance of our situation. For if the Indians are to pass away, we want to do what can be done in order to give them the offer of life & then be ready to aid [the immigrants] as indeed we have done & are doing, to found & sustain institutions [of] learning & religion in the Country."

Looking into the future of Oregon, Whitman added: "Could I have staid at home longer, I should have tried to have raised the means of establishing some Academies & Colleges, but I trust to influence others to do so." Here is the first time Whitman mentioned in his letters his dream of founding a college in Oregon. On the following October 25, in a letter to Greene, Whitman returned to this subject by writing: "This is a place most advantageous for the commencement of what may soon be an Academy & College, both on account of its fine & healthy climate & of its eligible situation." Whitman made several references in his later correspondence to this dream of seeing a college established in the Walla Walla Valley; a dream which Cushing Eells was to bring into reality in 1859. This story, however, belongs to a later chapter.

Grounds for Uneasiness among the Indians

Whitman's correspondence for the year following his return in the fall of 1843 reveals his awareness of growing discontent, even hostility in some places, on the part of the Indians to the white men in general and to the Protestant missionaries in particular. A study of Whitman's writings shows that he attributed most of this restlessness to three sources—(1) the agitation of Eastern Indians and half-breeds; (2) the proselytizing efforts of the Roman Catholic missionaries; and (3) the critical attitude of a mountain man, William Craig, who, with his Nez Perce wife, had settled in Lapwai Valley in November 1840, within a few miles of Spalding's mission on the Clearwater.

By the spring of 1844, Whitman had a twofold fear of future developments if the number of Oregon immigrants increased each year, as he fully expected would be the case. The first was from the immigrants themselves. This concern he expressed in a letter to the Methodist missionary, H. B. Brewer located at The Dalles, in a letter dated May 25, 1844: "Immigrants will have this country & Indians & Missionaries must give place as soon as they cease to continue to be necessary stepping stones." However, Whitman felt that the missionaries had more to fear from the Indians than from the white men for he also said in this letter to Brewer: "I have no doubt but the situation of missionaries among Indians will become more & more trying in this country as our work advances & they become more familiar with the whites in general and especially as all the variety of influences operate upon them... To all this may be added the influence of the Shawnees, Delawares & Iroquois & half breeds have in explaining to them the Indian wars on the borders of the States & all resulting in the Indians getting large amounts of money from Americans or whites in general."

The agitation caused by eastern Indians in the employ of the Hudson's Bay Company had become a serious problem for both Whitman and Spalding by the spring of 1844. Whitman explained in a letter to Greene of April 8: "Some most arch grievances were brought against our course which were based on the authority of Tom Hill, a Delaware Indian, who is now in the mountains with the Nez Perces and Flat Head Indians." Hill had settled among the Nez Perces about 1837 and by 1844 had secured for himself a dominant position in the tribe. He was an agnostic and a bitter critic of the way the white men had treated the Indians in the East. Spalding called him a "blasphemous and debased infidel." [18]

Spalding felt the efforts of Tom Hill's anti-missionary agitation more directly than did Whitman, yet the latter was involved, as the Cayuses were receptive to many of the ideas that Hill was spreading abroad. According to Whitman, Hill was friendly with the Catholic priests, thus encouraging distrust of the Protestants. Hill touched sensitive nerves among the natives when he dealt with economic issues. "The Indians say," wrote Whitman to Greene, "they are told that we ought to expend more liberally on them and that it is peculiarly our duty to do so. That we do not give... large prices for all we get of them and break their lands for nothing. These are among their greatest grievances. They complain that they have been obliged to teach us their language and we have not taught them ours in return. They have always caused themselves to be paid for teaching us language and even then a teacher has been hard to obtain and keep." Tom Hill will enter our story again.

Whitman's letters during this year carry frequent references to the negative influences of the Roman Catholic priests on the Protestant work. "The Indians say that they have been told by the Papists not to be afraid we should leave them by their pressing us," Whitman told Greene, "but if we should be vexed to remove, to be calm and see us go off... One of them told me that Mr. Blanchet told him that if they would send me away, he would send a mission among them. I tell them all plainly that I do not refuse to go away if they prefer the Papists to us—and urged them to decide if they wished me to do so, but that I should not go except at the full expression of the people, desiring me so to do."

In addition to the difficulties mentioned above, Whitman and Spalding were both affected by the unfriendly acts and agitation of an ex-mountain man, William Craig, who had settled near Spalding's station. He was the first white settler in what is now the State of Idaho. His wife, a Nez Perce, was the daughter of Old James, the chief whose band lived in that Valley. In order to understand the point of Whitman's comments about Craig, it must be pointed out that Spalding had encouraged such converts as Timothy to cultivate land in the vicinity of the Clearwater station. Old James considered this an intrusion on his rights to the Valley.

Whitman wrote in his letter to Greene of April 8, 1844: "William Craig, a white man from the mountains, whose wife is a native, & a connection of Old James, the reputed owner of the valley in which Mr. Spalding's station is located, is living near the station and has been for several years. He is said both by the Indians & others to be the mover of the measure of the Indians to send Timothy off his land. He is busy in trying to excite the people against the laws as recommended by Doct White and also says much in favour of the Papists, a prediliction of no long standing. The family with whom he is connected say they are determined to obtain a Papal Priest to come among them."

In Summary, 1843–1844

Beginning with Whitman's letter of November 1, 1843, we find that his every letter to the Board carried some reference to the political future of Oregon and to his responsibilities to the incoming white people. He was keenly interested in the importance of the Board encouraging the right kind of people to migrate to Oregon. He never gave up the hope of having "pious laymen" settle in the vicinity of Waiilatpu. His letters during these last years of his life reflect a blending of his missionary ideals with what he considered to be the larger objective of promoting the development of American institutions in Oregon. Whitman referred to the Oregon immigrations as "a part of the onward movement of the world and therefore more to be moulded than to be turned aside" [Letter 157]. The very numerical superiority of the immigrants over the Indian population of Oregon made changes inevitable. There were more people in the 1843 immigration than were in the combined membership if the Cayuse and Walla Walla tribes.

Looking back on the history of the Oregon Mission through the perspective of more than 125 years, we see that most of the factors which precipitated the final tragedy of November 1847 were already present by the fall of 1844 when the Whitmans began their ninth year of residence at Waiilatpu. Indeed, in view of the explosive nature of some of the points of friction, it is surprising that the massacre did not occur at an earlier date.

1844–1845

Profiting by his experience in the fall of 1843, when the immigrants drained him of all provisions excepting potatoes, Whitman made every effort to be ready for those who would arrive in 1844. With the help of one or more hired men and possibly some of the Indians, the harvest was gathered in, the flour mill was put into operation, and cattle and hogs were at hand ready for sale. Narcissa looked forward to the coming of the immigrants with a heavy heart. To her friend, Mrs. Brewer at The Dalles, she wrote on August 5: "We are all of us, I suppose, on the eve of another such scene as last fall—the passing of the emigrants and as it falls the heavier upon my friends at the Dalles, I hope that they have laid in a good stock of strength, patience and every needed grace for the siege."

The Dalles marked the end of the land route of the Oregon Trail for most of the immigrants, as only the most venturesome tried to take their wagons over the Cascade Mountains. The majority preferred completing their journey by going down the river in boats or on rafts. The animals were driven over the mountains. Although the Methodist missionaries at The Dalles were called upon to provide food, we have no evidence that any of the immigrants asked to spend the winter there. Being so close to their destination, they managed somehow to get to the Willamette Valley.

The Indians likewise profited by the previous year's experience. In their eagerness to get American cattle, they rode forth to meet the immigrants and some went as far as Fort Hall, where they traded fresh horses for the travel-worn cattle. Those who were cultivating small acreages eagerly sold or bartered their produce to the incoming whites. This trading the Whitmans welcomed, as they knew that the demand was greater than their ability to supply. The natives would thus be encouraged to do more farming.

The vanguard of the 1844 emigration arrived at Waiilatpu on Tuesday, October 1, having been delayed by a late spring on the Missouri frontier. Among the first to stop at Waiilatpu was a group of young men, and, to the surprise of Dr. Whitman, he found Newton Gilbert of Rushville among them. Years before, Gilbert had been one of his students in both a day school and the Sunday school in Rushville [Letter 178]. Because of the delay in leaving the frontier, many of the immigrants were caught in the snows of the Blue Mountains. Narcissa explained the situation in a postscript dated October 25 to her letter begun on the 9th of that month: "It is now the last of October and they have just begun to arrive with their wagons. The Blue Mountains are covered with snow, and many families, if not half of the party, are back in or beyond the mountains, and what is still worse, destitute of provisions and some of them of clothing. Many are sick, several with children born on the way. One family arrived here night before last, and the next morn a baby was born; another is expected in the same condition... Here we are, one family alone, a way mark, as it were, or center post, about which multitudes will or must gather this winter. And these we must feed and warm to the extent of our powers. Blessed be God that He has given us so abundantly of the fruit of the earth that we may impart to those who are thus famishing."

The 1844 emigration numbered about 1,500.[19] In his letter to Greene of October 25, Whitman said: "The immigrants are passing and must be for some weeks yet, as the season is now so far advanced, and many desire to winter with us. I have given no one any encouragement for staying..." Even though Whitman urged all who could do so to continue their journey, they could not out of Christian charity refuse hospitality to the needy. By October 25, when both Narcissa and Whitman took time to write letters, Waiilatpu was already crowded with immigrant families who wanted to remain through the coming winter, and there were still more to come. In her letter to her parents, Narcissa wrote: "I cannot write any more, I am so thronged and employed that I feel sometimes like being crazy, and my poor husband, if he had a hundred strings tied to him pulling in every direction could not be worse off."

Among the early arrivals who asked to stay at Waiilatpu over the winter was a blacksmith, a hatter, and two Methodist ministers [Letter 164]. A cross section of American life was on the move westward. Among those who paused at Waiilatpu was a young man from New York State, Alanson Hinman, who was induced by Whitman to stay and teach the school for white children. Hinman proved to be a most helpful assistant and played a minor role in the Whitman story during the next three years. He not only taught school; he also helped Narcissa in many household duties, especially in the care of the children. A year later Narcissa wrote: "I feel that I never can be too thankful for the mercies of the Lord in placing such a good young man in our family to do this work for us when my health was so inadequate" [Letter 176]. In her letter of October 9, 1844, to her parents, Narcissa made the following comment: "My health has been improving remarkably through the summer, and one great means has been daily bathing in the river. I was very miserable one year ago now, and was brought very low and poor; now I am better than I have been for some time, and quite fleshy for me. I weigh one hundred and sixty-seven pounds; much higher than ever before in my life. This will make the girls [i.e., her sisters] laugh, I know."

By October 25, the Whitmans learned that "there are more than five hundred souls back in the snow and mountains. Among the number is an orphan family of seven children, the youngest an infant born on the way, whose parents have both died since they left the States." Some concerned persons in the emigration had sent word ahead to the Whitmans asking them to be prepared to receive the children, as they had no relatives or friends to whom they could turn in Oregon. "What we shall do, I cannot say," Narcissa told her parents. "We cannot see them suffer. If the Lord casts them upon us, He will give us His grace and strength to do our duty to them."

The Seven Sager Orphans

When the "Oregon fever" broke out in the western states in 1842 and 1843, Henry Sager was one who caught the contagion. Oregon became for him the promised land. Sager was a restless soul, always dreaming of greener pastures over the western horizon. From the year of his marriage in 1830 to Naomi Carney, to 1839, he and his family lived on a farm in Ohio. He then moved his family to Indiana, then to eastern Missouri, and finally to western Missouri. By the spring of 1844, just before leaving for Oregon, the Sagers had six children—John, age 13; Francisco, better known as Francis, 11; Catherine, 9; Elizabeth Marie, 7; Matilda Jane, 5; and Hannah Louise, 3. Naomi was then expecting her seventh child sometime during the latter part of May.

Sometime in the fall of 1843 Henry sold his farm and blacksmith shop and moved to St. Joseph, Missouri, which was the departure point for many who were planning to leave for Oregon in the spring of 1844. Naomi, remembering her condition, looked upon the journey with deep forebodings. With prophetic insight she declared that she would never live to see Oregon, but Henry remained optimistic and insistent.

The Sager family, with their goods loaded in a large wagon drawn by two yoke of oxen, joined a company of emigrants which met at a point west of St. Joseph, on May 20, to organize. Sager had at least three other oxen and two cows. Following the precedent set by the 1843 emigration, an organization was perfected along military lines for defensive purposes in case of an Indian attack, with Cornelius Gilliam in over-all command. As will be told later, Gilliam figures in the events following the Whitman massacre. Since the emigration was so large, consisting of about 1,500 people, it was broken up into four companies. The one to which the Sager family was assigned was led by William Shaw.

On the evening of May 30, when the Sager family was camped on the Nemaha River in what is now southeastern Nebraska, Naomi gave birth to a daughter who was named Henrietta Naomi.[20] The baby arrived in the midst of a downpour of rain with the mother lying in a damp canvas tent. The birth was difficult, and Naomi was too weak to be moved the next day. The wagon train remained in camp for three days, the resumed the westward trek on Monday, June 2. Naomi and her baby rested on a bed in the springless, jolting wagon. She never fully recovered her strength after her confinement. A series of misfortunes dogged the progress of the Sagers across the country. On July 30, a few days before the wagon train arrived at Fort Laramie, Catherine had the misfortune to fall under the wagon while it was in motion, and one of the back wheels ran over her left leg, breaking it severely. As has been noted, this was a common accident on the Oregon Trail. Although there was a German doctor, known as Dr. Degen,[21] in the emigration, he was not in Captain Shaw's company with which the Sager family was traveling. A messenger was sent to get him. In the meantime, the father set the broken bones to the best of his ability and applied a splint. When the doctor arrived, he declared that the leg had been set as well as he could have done. Catherine was placed in the wagon on a bed near her mother and baby sister. Then the wagon moved on with Dr. Degen now riding alongside.

Captain Shaw's company moved through South Pass on August 23. About this time Henry Sager came down with what was vaguely described as "camp fever." He too was put to bed in the wagon and a young man was hired to drive the oxen. Henry died on August 26, just before the wagon train crossed Green River. Shortly before he died, Henry called Captain Shaw to his side and begged him to see that the family was taken to the Whitman mission. In the meantime, Naomi's health continued to decline. Even though she found lying on her bed in the jolting wagon when the dust stirred up by the many wagon wheels was at times almost stifling, there was no alternative to continuous travel. The Shaw company arrived at Fort Hall on September 1, about a month later than the schedule followed by the mission party of 1836. Five hundred miles of desert and mountains stretched before them before they could reach Waiilatpu.

Catherine, looking back in later years on those trying days, wrote:[22] "Soon after leaving Fort Hall, she [i.e., Naomi] became seriously ill and delirious. She suffered intensely and even was unable to make her wants known. We were traveling over a road so dusty that a cloud of dust covered the train all day, and to screen Mother as much as possible from this, a sheet was hung across the front of the wagon, making the air within close and suffocating. In her delirium she talked continually of her husband, at times addressing him as though present, and beseeching him in pitiful tones to relieve her suffering." On September 11, only sixteen days after her husband had died, Naomi Sager followed him in death.[23] The Shaw company was then camped on the south bank of the Snake River near present-day Twin Falls, Idaho. Shortly before she died, Naomi expressed her wish that her children could be kept together. Her last words were: "Oh, Henry! If you only knew how we have suffered."

Sager Orphans Taken to Waiilatpu

Following the death of Naomi Sager, sympathetic members of the wagon train came forward and took care of the seven orphans. A woman, possibly one who was nursing her own baby, assumed the responsibility of caring for the Sager infant. Catherine wrote: "The rest of us [were] kindly cared for by everybody in the train; in fact, we were literally adopted and everyone... was ready to do us a favor." [24] Dr. Degen continued to drive the oxen and serve as temporary foster father for the seven children. Somewhere along the line of march, the wagon was reduced to a two-wheeled cart. This was all that was needed to carry the meager possessions of the children. Since Dr. Degen succeeded in taking through to Waiilatpu six oxen and one cow that Henry Sager had owned, it may be assumed that the two Sager boys were given the responsibility of driving the animals not needed to pull the cart. Added to the miseries of cold weather and snow in the Blue Mountains was the lack of food. Their flour supply was exhausted and, during the last days of travel, Dr. Degen and the children had nothing more to eat than dried meat.

Arrival at Waiilatpu

The exact date of the arrival of the Sager children is not fixed; we know that it was sometime after October 25 and before the end of the month [Letters 187 & 191]. Catherine never forgot her thrill when, as a nine-year-old girl, she first saw Waiilatpu and met Marcus and Narcissa Whitman. She wrote in her reminiscences: "We arrived at the station between ten and eleven o'clock. For weeks this place had been our talk by day and formed our dreams at night. We expected to see log houses occupied by Indians and such folk as we had seen about the forts [i.e., Forts Laramie, Hall, and Boise]. Instead we saw a large white house surrounded by a palisade." [25] After commenting briefly on the buildings, the gardens, and the irrigation ditches, Catherine wrote: "We drove up and halted near a large ditch. Captain Shaw was in the house conversing with Mrs. Whitman. Glancing through the window he saw us and turned to her and said, 'Your children have come. Will you go out and see them?' He then came out and told the boys to help the girls out and get their bonnets. Alas! It was easier to talk about bonnets than to find them. After much searching one or two were found. By this time Mrs. Whitman had come out.

"Here was a perfect scene," wrote Catherine, "for the pen of an artist. Foremost stood the little cart with the tired oxen lying down. Sitting in the front end of the cart was John, bitterly weeping. On the opposite side stood Francis, with his arms resting upon the wheel and his head in his arms, sobbing aloud. On the near side the little girls stood huddled together, bareheaded and barefooted, looking first at the boys and then at the house, dreading we knew not what! Nearby stood the Doctor and the Captain watching the scene with suppressed emotion. It was thus that Mrs. Whitman found us."

Catherine described Narcissa as being "a large, well-formed woman with beautiful auburn hair, a rather large nose, and a large pair of grey eyes. She wore a dark calico dress and a gingham sunbonnet, and we thought, as we shyly looked at her, that she was the prettiest woman we had ever seen. As she came towards us, she spoke kindly to us; but like frightened rabbits, we ran behind the cart and peeped shyly at her. She then addressed the boys, adding, 'Poor boys, no wonder you weep.'" Seven-year-old Helen Mar Meek, wearing a "green dress, white apron and neat sunbonnet," then joined the group. The personal belongings of the children were carried into the house. "As we neared the steps," remembered Catherine, "Captain Shaw asked if she had any children of her own. Pointing to a grave at the foot of a nearby hill, she said, 'The only child I ever had sleeps there.' She remarked that it was a great pleasure [i.e., comfort] to be able to see the grave from the house." Since the Oregon Trail passed on the north side of the mission house, there was no obstruction cutting off the view of the hill and the little cemetery. Inside the house, the Sager children met Mary Ann Bridger "about nine years old washing the dishes."

Although Captain Shaw and Dr. Degen had fulfilled their promise to the dying Henry Sager that his family would be taken to the Whitman mission, the first reaction of both Marcus and Narcissa was that the responsibility of rearing the seven children was far heavier than they should accept. Several days were spent in debating the problem. Dr. Whitman even suggested sending the boys to Tshimakain to be under the care of the Walkers and the Eellses [Letter 164a]. Captain Shaw, however, reminded the Whitmans of the deceased father's wish that the children be kept together. Whitman raised the question of what the reaction of the American Board might be. He had been sent to Oregon to minister to the Indians and therefore the Board might not wish to allow any money to be spent for the support of white children. "To this," wrote Catherine, "the Captain argued that as the Doctor had been sent out as a missionary that whatever came under that head was his duty, whether natives or whites, and we certainly were objects for missionary charity."

Three days after the older six Sagers had arrived at Waiilatpu, the Sager baby came. Of this Narcissa wrote: "She arrived here in the hands of an old filthy woman, sick, emaciated and but just alive... She was five months old when she was brought here—had suffered for the want of proper nourishment until she was nearly starved. Husband thought we could get along with all but the baby—he did not see how we could take that; but I felt that if I must take any, I wanted her as a charm to bind the rest to me. So we took her, a poor, distressed little object, not larger than a babe three weeks old. Had she been taken past at this season, death would have been her portion, and that in a few days" [Letter 192].

On November 6, 1844, Captain Shaw and Dr. Whitman signed a paper which stated that the seven children were placed in the charge of the latter together with the property of the deceased Henry Sager consisting of "three yoke of oxen, one wagon, one cow and one old steer and several articles of clothing..."[26] The document also stated that if Walker and Eells did not wish to take the boys and if the Whitmans did not want the responsibility of keeping all seven, then Whitman could take all of the children to Oregon City where Captain Shaw would care for them. A few days after Captain Shaw had left, Marcus and Narcissa decided that they would keep all seven. According to Catherine's reminiscences, Dr. Whitman mounted his horse and rode after Shaw, catching up with him just before he reached The Dalles. Whitman gave Shaw the assurance that he and his wife would keep the children and that the Captain should feel no further concern about them.

In the spring of 1845, Whitman visited the Willamette Valley and while there appeared before Judge J. W. Nesmith of the Probate Court and on June 3 was made the legal guardian of the Sager children.[27] The estate of the late Henry Sager was valued at $262.50, which Whitman held in trust for the family. The Whitmans considered adopting the children, thus having them take the name of Whitman, but Captain Shaw advised against it.

The Sager Myth

Among the myths and legends, which have developed around the name of Marcus Whitman, is the completely unhistorical story spun from the imagination of Mrs. Honoré Willsie Morrow. According to this imaginative tale, the thirteen-year-old John took charge of his younger brother and sisters after the death of their mother and escorted them alone over the Oregon Trail nearly five hundred miles to the Whitman mission. They had only one horse and a cow. According to the novelist, there had to be a cow to supply milk for the baby. Perhaps the horse was needed to carry their baggage. Mrs. Morrow gave no explanation as to how the children got food and shelter during the days when they would have been traveling through the snow of the Blue Mountains. She described in vivid imagery how John staggered into the Whitman mission carrying the five-month-old baby and leading the emaciated cow on whose back "were perched a sister aged eight, with a broken leg, and a sister of five who helped support the leg... A sister of three and one of seven walked, besides his eleven-year-old brother, Francis." This incredible story first appeared in the January 1926 issue of *Cosmopolitan*; was reprinted in the

December 1940 *Reader's Digest*; again in the August 1960 issue of the *Digest* under the caption, "Child Pioneer," and with an introduction by Mark O. Hatfield, then Governor of Oregon! Descendants of the Sager children have found great offense in the myth. Protests from historians to the editors of *Reader's Digest* brought no retraction, only the assurance that it would not be published again.

The true story of the Sager orphans is obtainable from the reminiscences of the three Sager girls, Catherine, Elizabeth, and Matilda; from the writings of the Whitmans; and also from the published recollections of members of the 1844 emigration. The documented story of the Sager children is so dramatic, it needs no embellishment by writers of fiction.

WINTER OF 1844–1845 AT WAIILATPU

By November 11, 1844, Whitman was able to tell Walker that all of the immigration had passed Waiilatpu with the exception of seven wagons still to come [Letter 164a]. Writing to Greene on April 4, 1845, Whitman stated that: "After supplying all that came with provisions and urging all to go on that could, twelve families wintered with us." A school for white children was conducted through the winter months with Alanson Hinman as the teacher. Twenty-six were enrolled including sixteen from the immigrant families and ten from the Whitman household. Living with the Whitmans was seven-year-old Eliza Spalding who, according to Catherine Sager, had made the 120-mile trip from Lapwai "accompanied only by an Indian woman" in order to attend the school. Although Whitman did not indicate in his letter to Greene the exact number of immigrants who had wintered at Waiilatpu, the total must have been over fifty-five. This would have included the adults in the twelve families, possibly some single or older people, the sixteen school children and an unknown number of pre-school children. The Whitman household, including Hinman and the Sager children, numbered at least fourteen. Thus the total white population, including the three half-breed children, at Waiilatpu would have been about seventy. Again the mission buildings must have been crowded and, perhaps, even the blacksmith shop was used as a dwelling.

Whitman was responsible for supplying food for this large company for a period of four or five months, or until the immigrants found it possible to continue their journey to the Willamette Valley. In his letter to Walker of November 11, 1844, Whitman reported that after providing supplies to the immigrants who had already passed, he still had "a hundred bushels of wheat, two or more [hundred] of corn left yet & more than a thousand bushels of potatoes & plenty of beef & hogs." Whitman, however, underestimated the amount of food that seventy people could eat over a period of four or five months. In his letter to Greene written during the following April, he reported that he was then drawing on Spalding for additional food supplies and added: "I had to do the same last year."

Catherine Sager remembered that from twenty to twenty-five people ate at the Whitman table during the first winter she lived there. Other kitchens on the grounds served the other people. Alanson Hinman in his published reminiscences stated, with perhaps some exaggeration, that the Whitman family "had nothing in the way of meats for their own use but the necks of the beef which were made eatable by boiling, while the better parts were distributed among the immigrants. Mrs. Whitman was not always so long-suffering as her husband, and would sometimes protest that it was not fair that the immigrants should get all of the best parts, while only the leavings were available for the family. To these protests Dr. Whitman would reply in a jesting tone, that he could stand the scoldings of his wife far better than the complaints of the immigrants, and so it went on through the winter." [28]

No documentary evidence remains to indicate how much Whitman was able to collect from the immigrants for the accommodations provided, but it is evident that some were able to pay something. In Whitman's report to Greene of April 8, 1845, he stated that he had been able to pay in cash for all supplies received from the Hudson's Bay Company besides satisfying a claim for £50/4/4 made by Dr. White and wages due Littlejohn amounting to $128.36. Dr. White's claim may have covered expenses of the meeting held with the Cayuses in the spring of 1843. In addition Whitman reported that he had accepted over $500.00 in notes from the immigrants who had been unable to pay in cash and also "some ten or twelve oxen." He stressed the fact that he did not want to make money out of the sale of provisions to the immigrants, but did want to meet expenses. "It is impossible for us to refuse those who are hungry," he wrote, "even although they cannot pay us and in some cases cannot ever secure payment. Situated as we are, necessity compels us to become supplyers to immigrants and we may as well make the best of it we can."

Greene was not pleased with these developments. Writing to Whitman on April 6, 1846, in reply to Whitman's letters of the fall of 1844 and spring of 1845, Greene said: "We are glad to hear of your prosperity in secular matters, and that you may be able, by means of your grain and your stock, to defray a large part of your expenses. All this is well. Still we are not quite sure that you ought to devote so much time and thought to feeding the emigrants, and thus make your station a great *restaurant* for the weary pilgrims on their way to their promised land. Such a work is very humane & good work; but the work of guiding men to Christ is a better one and coincides better with the vocation of a missionary laborer... We fear the effect of this on your own mind & heart—that you will become too exclusively a man of business: —and upon the Indians, that they will have their thoughts engrossed about improving their outward condition, while they will be led to think their spiritual interests are of little consequence... There is danger also that your mission, like that of the Methodists, will get the name and character of a trading or money making establishment, and thus bring discredit not only on your own station, or mission; but on the missionary work generally..." [29]

Secretary Greene's letters to the Board's Oregon missionaries reflect the wise advice of a man of great experience, yet in this instance, he failed to appreciate Whitman's position. What other course could Whitman have followed as long as he remained at Waiilatpu? If he had not fed the hungry, ministered to the sick, and sheltered the needy, he would have been severely criticized. Whitman brought out this point when on April 1, 1847, he replied to Greene's letter of April 1846 by writing: "If we are not legally, religiously nor morally bound to relieve the passing immigrants, we are necessarily; for the sick and hungry cannot be sent away however pennyless."

The total cost to the American Board of its Oregon Mission for the fiscal year ending March 29, 1845, amounted to $1,822.62. This covered all expenses of the four families, or on the average of a little more than $450.00 for each. As has been stated, none of the missionaries received a salary [Appendix 2]. Through the efforts of Whitman and Spalding, the Mission was becoming increasingly self-supporting. The total expense for the fiscal year ending in March 1847 was only $584.39.

Erection of a Sawmill

On April 8, 1845, in another letter to Greene, Whitman told of the fulfillment of another dream that he had had for his mission. A sawmill had been erected. He wrote: "Partly in order to give employment to those who wintered with us, but more from the necessity of having boards and timber for the use of the Station and [to] supply the Indians—last but not least to prepare fencing for ourselves & the Indians, I have been building a saw mill—which is now in a state of forwardness & which I hope to start soon after planting is over. I have mostly paid for the work as I went along in provisions. The Mill is about twenty miles off in the Blue Mountains where we have an abundance of timber—and a fine seat [i.e., location] with a good road to reach it. We had most of the irons on hand."

The mill was located on a creek, later called Mill Creek, almost directly east of Waiilatpu. As has been stated, Whitman had chosen the confluence of Mill Creek and the Walla Walla River as his mission site. The present city of Walla Walla is about six miles upstream on Mill Creek; the mill site is further upstream. Whitman obtained his sawmill machinery from the dismantled mill which Spalding had erected at Lapwai in the winter of 1889-40. Spalding claimed that he had gotten the irons from Fort Vancouver.[30] In his letter to Greene, Whitman indicated his need for lumber to build a shelter over his gristmill, to place new roofs on his buildings, and to provide the natives with boards. A power driven saw was a great advance over the laborious method of whipsawing which had been his only means to get boards. Looking into the future, Whitman wrote: "In this way the mill will be ready for future use—for ourselves, the Indians, and perhaps a settlement. I do not think it will detract from my ability to meet my expenses as most of [those] whom I employ would owe me and not be able to pay" [Letter 168]. Whitman also managed to have a log cabin erected at the mill where, in later years, some of the immigrants, who were wintering at the mission, were able to stay.

Whitman took advantage of the presence of a millwright among the 1844 immigrants to rebuild his gristmill. Large millstones were shaped and placed, and by April 8, 1845, Whitman was able to write: "I have since had a new set of cogs put in, and the mill does well."[31] This was the third gristmill that Whitman had erected at Waiilatpu.

ACTIVITIES WITH AND FOR THE INDIANS

The presence of so many immigrants at Waiilatpu during the winter of 1844–45, the building of the sawmill and the rebuilding of the gristmill, together with other responsibilities, left Whitman little time to devote to the natives. On April 8, 1845, he reported: "We have had no native school—nor is it likely we can have [one] before next winter." In the earlier years at Waiilatpu, Narcissa had sometimes helped in the school, but this she was unable to do in the fall of 1843 and the following winter. Her failing health and many household duties prevented her sharing in what she had once enjoyed doing. Moreover, the enthusiasm that the Cayuses had at first manifested in the school had waned. The novelty of having missionaries living in their midst had worn off. It also appears that fewer Cayuses were living in the vicinity of Waiilatpu after Whitman's return than had been the case in previous years. This made it difficult to carry on religious instruction for them.

THE GOSPEL OF MATTHEW IN NEZ PERCE

One of the greatest accomplishments of the missionaries working with the Nez Perce and Cayuse Indians during the eleven-year history of the Oregon Mission was the printing at Lapwai in 1845 of the *Gospel of Matthew in Nez Perce*. After Smith and Rogers had left the Mission, the main responsibility of preparing items in the Nez Perce language, such as primers, fell on Spalding. According to a notation in his diary, he began on December 20, 1841, to translate the Gospel of Matthew into the Nez Perce tongue. He sent some of his work to Waiilatpu for Whitman and Gray to review early in 1842, but, the manuscript was returned in April without any corrections having been made. Gray was too poor in the language to make any constructive criticism, and by this time Spalding was so far ahead of Whitman that the latter did not feel qualified to make changes.

Writing to Walker on January 27, 1845, Whitman said: "We have hired a printer who has been printing a book of Nez Perces & English and now is going to print Matthew's gospel. I am going up to see to its preparation but shall not stay long as I have to go again in March." On March 5, he wrote again to Walker: "I suppose the Gospel of Matthew is now printed & we look every day for an arrival from Mr. Spalding when the Printer will come to go to Willamette." Whitman was then expecting to go to Lapwai during the latter part of that month to be present when Mrs. Spalding expected to be confined for the third time. A daughter, Martha, was born on March 20.

The printer to whom Whitman referred was a young French Canadian, Medare G. Foisy, who had accompanied Father Joseph Joset into the Flathead country and who was hired by Spalding and Whitman in the fall of 1844 to assist in operating the Mission press at Lapwai.

Although no exact figure is found in the contemporary writings of Whitman and Spalding as to the number of the Gospels printed, we can estimate the total to be not more than 450. Evidently only a few copies were actually distributed among the Nez Perces and Cayuses, as only a few were sufficiently advanced in learning to be able to read much of the book. After the Whitman massacre, Spalding listed in the inventory of the property lost or destroyed at Lapwai "400 copies of Gospel of Matthew not bound."[32] Today this volume is exceedingly rare, fewer than six copies are known to be extant.[33] Educated Nez Perces, who know their native language, say that Spalding's translation is inaccurate. Even so, to reduce a language to writing, to make a translation, and then to print it was a major achievement. Whitman's part in the project was small. The major credit goes to Spalding.

Continuing Agricultural Activities

Whitman never ceased to encourage the Cayuses to cultivate the soil. In his letter to Greene of April 8, 1845, he wrote: "Some of the Indians are hiring land broken for them by those [i.e., the immigrants] who are here still, which is done at the rate of from three to five acres for an inferior horse. Ploughs are in great demand. I have sold even my last cast plough from the States—as they are the ones preferred by the Indians." Whitman asked Greene to send out fifty more plows, explaining: "A horse is given for a plough and the horses are sold for from ten to fifteen dollars to meet expenses."

The success that the Cayuses had of selling produce to the immigrants in the fall of 1845 gave them further encouragement to do more in the way of farming. Writing to Greene on May 15, 1846, Whitman asked for another shipment of twenty plows, and in a letter to Walker dated July 20, he wrote: "An improved spirit of agriculture is manifested among the Indians this year which bids well for the future. For the first time this year, they have fenced so that I do not have to guard my cattle." The Indians had held Whitman responsible if any of his livestock strayed into their fields and ate their crops. Now this problem was solved by the erection of fences, possibly made from boards brought from the sawmill.

THE SAGER CHILDREN IN THE WHITMAN HOME

The unpublished and published reminiscences of the three Sager girls—Catherine, Elizabeth, and Matilda—open many windows through which we can look into the Whitman home.[34] Elizabeth Sager recalled how, shortly before their arrival at the Whitman mission, her older sister, Catherine, then only nine and a half years old, had washed their clothes so that all would look respectable— "but when I saw little Helen Meek with such pretty clothes, I thought our clothes didn't amount to much." Regarding Mrs. Whitman, Elizabeth wrote: "People who didn't like her, said she was stuck up, said she had red hair; but she was not stuck up, and she didn't have red hair. She was rather reserved, and her hair was a copper gold." [35]

Catherine recalled how hungry she, her brothers, and sisters were when they arrived at Waiilatpu. "It required all the attention of the Doctor and his wife to keep us from overeating and endangering our health," she wrote. Extra attention had to be given to the baby who was dangerously undernourished when she arrived. Matilda wrote that after being fed: "The first thing Mrs. Whitman did was to cut our hair, wash and scrub us." [36] The problem of discipline became an immediate issue. "The Whitmans were New England people," Matilda explained, "and we were taken into their home and they began the routine of teaching and disciplining us in the old Puritan way of raising and training children—very different from the way of the plains." Of this Catherine also wrote: "We had been so long without restraint as to become very unruly and hard to manage. The Doctor and his wife were strict disciplinarians and held the reins of household government with steady hands, and while any deviation of the laid down rules met with instant and severe punishment, every effort made to win their approval was rewarded with their smiles." In her letter of August 9, 1845, to Mrs. Brewer, Narcissa confessed that the children "were said to be very bad when they were left; but there was a reason for that. Left without restraint in such a journey, it could not be expected otherwise." She added, however, that they were not difficult children to manage and that she did not have to use the "rod" very often.

According to Elizabeth, Mrs. Whitman did most of the disciplining: "Dr. Whitman was a very jolly, kindly man. He loved to romp with us children. We didn't feel at all in awe of him as we did of Mrs. Whitman. She enforced all the discipline in the family. Elizabeth gave the following revealing touch in regard to Whitman when she wrote: "He never strolled or walked slowly—he always walked as if he was going somewhere and was on his way." [37] Matilda gave further details about her foster mother: "Mrs. Whitman had the New England idea of discipline. There was no danger of any of us becoming spoiled. She would point to one of us, then point to the dishes or the broom, and we would instantly get busy with our assigned tasks. She didn't scold much, but we dreaded that accusing finger pointed at us. The way we jumped when it was levelled at us, you would have thought her forefinger was a gun and was likely to go off." [38]

The five older Sager children were enrolled in the school taught by Alanson Hinman. Although Marcus reported that Hinman kept an "excellent school" and Narcissa wrote praising him as "a good and faithful disciplinarian" [Letters 168 & 176], the older Sager girls never forgot his harshness in meting out punishment. Catherine wrote: "He was a small-souled tyrant of a man [who] took delight in torturing helpless children... He certainly bestowed on my brothers some of the most cruel whippings it was ever the lot of boys to endure." Catherine remembered that she and others "were too timid and bashful to complain" but that some of the immigrant families "took the matter up and at one time there was indication of trouble." The one who resented such treatment the most was Francis Sager. He became a rebel.

Oregon Mission Meeting, May 1845

No meeting of the Oregon Mission was held after Whitman's return in the fall of 1843 until that held at Waiilatpu beginning May 8, 1845. The Walkers with their four children, ranging in ages from one to seven years, and the Eellses with their two sons, one and four years old, made the 140-mile trip on horseback from Tshimakain. Mrs. Spalding was the only adult member of the Mission not present. She remained at Lapwai with her little boy and two-months old baby girl. The meeting continued until May 14. Reporting on events in his letter of May 20 to Greene, Whitman wrote: "The meeting was eminently one of the utmost harmony of views, interest, and feeling. This state... has been apparent ever since my return from the States." A business meeting of the Mission church was held on Sunday, the 11th. Among the actions taken was the following: "Dr. Whitman was appointed a comt. to inquire after Compo now on the Wallamette." Since Whitman had been commissioned by the Mission to visit the Willamette Valley to take care of some other matters, this request to inquire about Compo was logical.[39]

Disturbing reports had been received about James Conner who had been baptized and received into the church on November 17, 1839, along with Joseph and Timothy. Conner had moved to the Willamette Valley, where he was accused of operating a distillery. In January 1844 his case was brought to the attention of Indian Agent White who ordered the confiscated equipment to be destroyed. Conner then challenged White to a duel. Conner was taken before the circuit court of the Provisional Government, fined $500, and disenfranchised for life.[40] After becoming informed of these developments, the members of the First Presbyterian Church of Oregon voted to excommunicate Conner for such "crimes" as "Sabbath breaking, fighting, neglect of worship, to which he has added polygamy & intent to fight a duel, & liquor vending."[41]

Sunday was always an important day during the Annual Meetings of the Oregon Mission, for then the missionaries could meet together in worship and observe the sacrament of the Lord's Supper. Walker was the preacher for Sunday, May 11. Before the Lord's Supper was served, Spalding baptized Alanson Hinman, the five Sager girls, and Mary Ann Bridger.[42] Hinman was then received into the membership of the church. The two Sager boys were not baptized. The explanation given by Catherine in her reminiscences is that her brothers did not wish to be baptized except by immersion, because their mother had been a Baptist. They had no objection, however, to their sisters being baptized. Narcissa wrote: "We felt it our duty to have them baptized, as many as were willing to be, and according we did so, the girls only consenting" [Letter 176]. Possibly the fact that Hinman was baptized and made a member of the church reacted unfavorably on both of the Sager boys, who may have felt that he was hypocritical in claiming to be a Christian when he had been so harsh in disciplining them. Mary Walker noted in her diary for the following day: "Mr. Hinman had fits in the evening, occasioned probably by excitement on the sabbath." It is possible that he was afflicted with epilepsy.

Francis Sager Runs Away

As soon as the Mission meeting closed, Dr. Whitman made preparations for his trip to the Willamette Valley. Emma Hobson, who had been returned to Waiilatpu by the Walkers when they came to Waiilatpu, was to accompany Dr. Whitman as was also Alanson Hinman. The three left Waiilatpu on Monday, May 26. One of the last, if not the last of the immigrant families to leave for the Willamette Valley was the Perkins family, who evidently left one week after Whitman's departure. It appears that Perkins[43] sympathized with the Sager boys in their resentment against Hinman and urged them to go with him to the lower valley. John refused, but Francis eagerly accepted the invitation.

According to Catherine, Francis told her late on the Sunday evening after Dr. Whitman left that he was planning to leave the next day. "I did not put much faith in his assertions," she wrote, "as I did not think he would go away and leave us. His reason for going was that he thought the discipline was too strict." Evidently John, who learned of his brother's intentions, told Mrs. Whitman, who wept on hearing the news. Catherine's account continues: "Monday morning when I came down to breakfast, I read in the tearful faces of Mrs. Whitman and John the truth of his assertions. Dr. Whitman was not at home, having gone below earlier... When breakfast was ready, Mrs. Whitman sent one of the children to call Francis to breakfast. He refused to come and she then went after him herself and he returned with her, sat down at the table and ate in silence. No one mentioned the subject that filled the minds of all.

Francis arose from the table, took his hat and started for the door. Mrs. Whitman arose from her seat and said in a loud but firm voice, 'Francis, you must not go. You must stay with me.' He replied: 'I must go, I cannot stay.' She motioned to John to bolt the door but before he could do so Francis ran out, mounted a horse and left." He rode away from the mission and later joined the Perkins family and went with them to the Willamette Valley.

While passing through The Dalles, the Perkins family and Francis called on the Brewers at the Methodist Mission. In a letter to Narcissa,

Mrs. Brewer passed on some of the criticisms made by Perkins of the situation in the Whitman home. Replying on August 9, Narcissa wrote: "I read your letter to John; he seemed quite hurt about Mr. P's charges and said that he [Mr. P.] asked him several times if he did not wish to go to the Willamette... I endeavour in all things to act towards the children as if they were my own." Narcissa was deeply hurt over the incident. Catherine wrote: "[She] mourned long over this affair and said it seemed as though someone in the family had died."

Narcissa was left alone at Waiilatpu with the ten children after the departure of the Perkins family. The two fourteen-year-old boys, Perrin and John, had the responsibility of looking after the livestock and milking the cows. Narcissa felt that if only her husband had been home, Francis would not have gone. She wrote to Marcus and told him what had happened, no doubt with the hope that he would find Francis and bring him back. On June 29, while at Fort Vancouver, Marcus in a letter to his sister Alice wrote: "Narcissa has written me since I left home and says she will not allow me to leave home again without she goes with me. She is not in strong health and her spirits flag when I am from home and so much care comes upon her."

It was on this trip to the Willamette Valley that Whitman had his confrontation with White.[44] He also appeared in the Probate Court at Oregon City on June 3 and was appointed the legal guardian of the Sager children. Whitman was able to meet Francis. Of this Catherine wrote: "[He] did not urge him to return as he wanted him thoroughly satisfied with his visit below." After Whitman had returned to Waiilatpu, about July 1, in time for the wheat harvest, he talked with John. Whitman assured John that he would be willing to give some cattle and horses to each of the boys so as to put them "in the way of acquiring property." John wrote of this arrangement to Francis and urged him to return. According to Catherine, "a horse was dispatched for him and soon after harvest, we had the pleasure of welcoming Francis home." Possibly the fact that the court had made Dr. Whitman the legal guardian of the Sager children had some influence on the boy. Certain adjustments in personal relationships were evidently made in the Whitman home, as we hear of no further difficulties. The time came when the older Sager children, along with the younger, were calling Marcus and Narcissa father and mother.

"A Cause of Much Anxiety"

Whitman's letters to Greene of April 8 and May 20, 1845, refer to four potentials for future trouble. The first of these involved the Indians' superstitions regarding their "tewats" [medicine men]. Whitman explained this situation in his letter of April 8: "*A cause of much anxiety*[45] has arisen in connection with... the death of a young man of apoplexy. It is the custom of the Canadians—who are as superstitious as the Indians themselves—to awe them through their superstition of sorcery—by telling them that such and such white men are [more] largely endowed with supernatural power than even their own Tewats." Such reports planted in the minds of the natives gave the idea that Dr. Whitman was a tewat with superior magical powers. As a result, wrote Whitman, "they have been saying I caused the death of the young man who died of apoplexy." Whitman saw the danger to himself if such rumors continued to circulate. He wrote: "An impression of this kind among them if strengthened by such circumstances and by the countenance of such men as the Canadians—and perhaps by the Priests—would make my stay among them useless & dangerous—and might induce me to leave at once." Whereas the illiterate and superstitious Canadians might have ascribed such powers to Whitman, it is inconceivable that any of the Catholic priests would have been guilty of such gross accusations.

Whitman gave Greene a second example of this superstition. During the terminal illness of a local chief: "His son came to me as he was dying and in a passion told me 'I had killed his Father and that it would not be a difficult matter for me to be killed.' You are aware already of their habit to kill their own Medicine Men... when an excuse offers by the death of some of their friends." Whitman knew of the danger which threatened him if one of his Indian patients should die.

The second issue which caused "much anxiety" to Whitman was the possibility of the Roman Catholics opening a mission in the vicinity of Waiilatpu. Whitman informed Greene that Father De Smet had made an appointment to meet the Indians at Fort Walla Walla sometime during the month of April 1844. On March 5, Whitman informed Walker: "The Indians are all notified to meet De Smet at Walla Walla when the grass is about five or six inches long." The height of the grass was a primitive method of indicating time.

After Father De Smet had come and gone, Whitman on May 20 wrote to Greene: "He was seeking an invitation to locate a station among these Indians but I do not know as any one gave him any. I have little doubt, however, but he will manage to obtain his wishes in this respect." Whitman explained that some of the Cayuses thought that having Catholic missionaries settle among them would "create competition" in making available "such supplies as the Mission is wont to furnish them."

There is no evidence that the Roman Catholic missionaries ever made any promises to the natives to give them material rewards for favors received, but the property-conscious natives were hopeful. After explaining this problem to Greene, Whitman wrote: "I do not think I could be induced to come to such a people were it to be done again with the present experience—but it is quite different when the question is of continuance or abandonment. I look upon our situation here as having done enough for the cause of Christianity & Civilization to more than compensate for all the labours & expense incurred..."

In similar words, Whitman wrote to Walker: "I should not feel to stay among the Indians in itself considered, but as we are here now, I do not see how we can leave without exposing the cause of religion to reproach" [Letter 167a].

The third source of trouble which Whitman faced was the anti-American and anti-missionary agitation of the Delaware half-breed, Tom Hill, who had a Nez Perce wife and was living with her people. Whitman wrote that he was a person of "considerable talent," who was exerting "a strong influence against all whites—but most especially against us as missionaries" [46] [Letters 173 & 180a].

The fourth "cause of much anxiety" involved the murder of a Walla Walla Indian, Elijah Hedding, son of Chief Peu-peu-mox-mox [Yellow Serpent] at Sutter's Fort in California by an American in the late fall of 1844. Elijah had spent several years in the Methodist Mission school on the Willamette and had been named after a prominent Methodist bishop. All of the Indians of the upper Columbia River Valley were eager to get cattle by 1844. Knowing about the successful cattle drive sponsored by some of the white settlers of the Willamette Valley in 1837 when about 630 head were driven into Oregon from California, a number of Cayuse, Walla Walla, and Spokane Indians decided to go to California and exchange some of their furs and horses for Spanish cattle. In the party was Elijah Hedding.

At first all went well when the Indians arrived at Sutter's Fort. They were given a cordial welcome and arrangements were made for trading. A serious difficulty arose when the Oregon Indians in a skirmish with local Indians captured twenty-two horses and mules from them. These animals were driven to Sutter's Fort where some of the Americans claimed them as their property saying that they had been stolen. In the argument which ensued, an American, Grover Cook, known for his anti-Indian attitude, killed Elijah Hedding in cold blood while within the Fort. Whitman in his letter of May 20, 1845, to Greene, stated: "It was indeed a barbarous act if we may credit the report of the Indians— which alone we have—for even if they had done any wrong—they were in the fort & might easily have been humbled without resort to capital punishment."

Following the murder, the Oregon Indians hastily left for their homes. They were angry and burning with the desire for revenge. Upon their return, Ellis, as Head Chief of the Nez Perces, was asked to call on Indian Agent White to see what he could do about the outrage. No doubt Ellis referred to the provision in the Tenth Article of the code of laws which White had persuaded the Nez Perces and Cayuses to accept, which contained the provision that if a white man raised a gun against an Indian, "it shall be reported to Dr. White and he shall redress it." The incident must have been most embarrassing to White, as it had occurred in Mexican territory over which the United States had no jurisdiction. All that he could do was to promise to write to the Mexican authorities asking them to redress the wrong. He also sought to appease the Indians by promising them many benefits, including the establishment of a boarding school for Indian youth in the upper Columbia country. Dr. White returned to the States in the fall of 1845, leaving no one to redeem the promises he had made. The whole incident reveals how unrealistic was the White code of laws.

In Whitman's letter of May 20, 1845, to Greene, he stated: "While most of the Indians have been for peace in these parts, some have urged that, as Elijah [Hedding] was educated and was a leader in religious worship and learning... so in revenge one of the same grade must be killed of the Americans." Whitman then reported that both he and Spalding were "proposed as suitable victims." The uncertainty as to what the aroused Indians would do gave Whitman deep concern.

The troubled situation which threatened the peace and effectiveness of the Oregon Mission was discussed by the missionaries at their Annual Meeting held at Waiilatpu in May 1845. Looking back on that gathering, Mary Walker noted in her diary that both Mr. and Mrs. Spalding were "discouraged," and that "Dr. Whitman [was] entertaining fears that his people intend taking his life." [47] Whitman informed Greene that some Indians at Lapwai had ordered Spalding to leave "as soon as he was done planting." After reviewing the darkening situation, Whitman concluded: "Notwithstanding all these discouragements, we do not think we are in danger so as to warrant us to leave our post at present" [Letter 173].

When Whitman was at Fort Vancouver in the latter part of June 1845, he discussed with Dr. McLoughlin the threats that had been made against his life. Dr. McLoughlin had heard about one Indian, supposedly in the employ of the Hudson's Bay Company, who had threatened to kill Whitman. "Do you know about it?" asked Dr. McLoughlin. "Yes," replied Whitman, "I have known it for two years." "You have known it for two years and you told me nothing!" exclaimed Dr. McLoughlin, 'Tray tell me his name." Whitman replied: "His name is Thomas Hill." After thinking for a few moments, Dr. McLoughlin said: "We have no man by that name in the service of the Hudson's Bay Company." [48]

Another reference to a warning given Whitman by Dr. McLoughlin is found in the reminiscences of Judge Nesmith: "I know that Dr. Whitman had cause to dread the vengeance of the Indians long before it overtook him. I heard him, in the spring of 1845, express his apprehension on that subject to Dr. McLoughlin, at Oregon City, and the latter agreed with him upon the danger of his situation, and advised him to come to the Willamette Valley." [49]

1845-1846

Since it took about a year for reports to reach the States of the success of the 1843 emigrants in taking wagons over the Blue Mountains, this achievement had little direct effect on the size of the emigration which started for Oregon in the spring of 1844. Since no news of any disaster had filtered back to the States, the assumption was that the 1843 emigration had been successful. As has been indicated, about 1,500 migrated to Oregon in 1844. By the spring of 1845, however, it was well known throughout the States that the wagon road to the Columbia River had been opened. As a result about three thousand joined the Oregon emigration of that year, three times the number who had gone west in 1843. The arrival of the 1845 immigration in the Willamette Valley doubled the previous American population of Oregon.

The success of these emigrations greatly strengthened the position of the United States Government in its negotiations with Great Britain over the location of the boundary. If there had ever been a serious question in informed British circles about the ability of large numbers of Americans to cross the Rockies and the Blue Mountains with their families, their wagons, and their herds of livestock, such must have been answered when they learned of the success of the 1843 and 1844 emigrations. After 1843 there are no further known references in the writings of Hudson's Bay Company officials or British diplomats to making the Columbia River the boundary; still there was a reluctance on the part of the British Government to accept the 49° parallel.

Frederick Merk has characterized the Oregon section of President Polk's message to Congress of December 2, 1845, as being "tough." [50] Although Polk had shown sympathy to the popular demand to have the boundary fixed at 54°40', he expressed a willingness to draw the dividing line at the 49th parallel. According to Merk, Polk reported that "the British had rejected it out of hand." Polk then withdrew the offer and Congress was asked "to serve notice on England of intention to terminate the 1827 agreement of joint occupation." [51] Congress was also asked to pass laws to authorize the granting of land in Oregon to settlers and emigrants regardless of what England might say or do.

The great public interest in Oregon emigration, especially manifest on the western frontier, provided the background for the letter that Greene wrote to Whitman on February 25, 1846, which contains what one writer calls a delightful bit of "exceedingly typical Atlantic anti-expansion sarcasm." [52] Greene wrote: "Relative to Oregon affairs, there is no great change, in fact, though an increasing interest, especially in our western states, in obtaining immediate possession of it. The population of the Mississippi Valley—that little strip of bottom land!—are all in a panic lest they should be pressed to death, if some outlet cannot be found for the surplus beyond the Rocky Mountains... The probability now is that measures will be adopted before Congress rises, to terminate the joint occupancy [treaty], preparatory for our taking possession of all as high as the 49th parallel."

The Emigration of 1845

The emigration of 1845, having enjoyed favorable weather conditions, arrived in Oregon about a month earlier than that of the previous year. Consequently fewer immigrants arrived at Waiilatpu in a destitute condition. Writing to Walker on September 29, 1845, Whitman reported: "Few of the immigrants call on us. Four hundred and fifty wagons passed Fort Hall but from seventy to one hundred went to California."

Somewhere along the Snake River, Dr. Elijah White and his small party, eastward bound, met the westward emigration. Some asked White if they could obtain supplies at the Whitman station. Although assuring them that they could,[53] White recommended they by-pass both Waiilatpu and Fort Walla Walla by following, after crossing the Blue Mountains, the Umatilla instead of the Walla Walla River to the Columbia. This recommendation reflects White's antipathy to Whitman which was evident at the confrontation the two men had at Oregon City the previous May. To Walker, Whitman explained: "Doc. White told them how plenty & cheap provisions would be at the Dalles."

White was not the only one who gave advice to members of the 1845 immigration. When the immigrants arrived at Malheur River, some two hundred families were induced by Stephen H. L. Meek, an elder brother of Joseph L. Meek, to take a new cut-off which would shorten the distance into the Willamette Valley. Under Meek's guidance, this party followed a trail that led around the southern end of the Blue Mountains and then headed across barren desert land to the Deschutes River. Both grass and water were extremely scarce. The feet of the oxen became so sore because of the rocky soil that some animals refused to travel. At least twenty immigrants are reported to have died during this ordeal, and still others died later from exposure.[54] Meek's life was threatened. He was saved by a friendly immigrant who concealed him in a wagon. It may be that White's enthusiasm for such a cut-off was largely responsible for the venture, but Meek got all the blame. After reaching the Deschutes River, this party followed it to the Columbia, where they rejoined the Oregon Trail.

WHITMAN SAVES SOME IMMIGRANTS FROM AN INDIAN ATTACK

According to an account given by Sarah J. Cummins, who was the seventeen-year-old wife of one of the 1845 immigrants, Whitman was instrumental in saving a party of immigrants from an Indian attack while they were in the Blue Mountains.[55] Being told by some friendly Indians that a party of Cayuse and Walla Walla Indians intended to attack the immigrants while they were in the mountains, Whitman hastened to ride forth to meet them. He met the immigrants in the Powder River Valley during the first week of September. The confrontation with the hostile Indians came in the Grande Ronde Valley. The war party was surprised to discover that the immigrants had been forewarned and that Whitman and some friendly Nez Perces were with them. Sarah Cummins has given us the following account: "Ere the twilight faded, and as it was apparent that great numbers of the Indians were gathering within range, Dr. Whitman began to talk to the chief of the Walla Walla's. The chief of the Cayuses now spoke vehemently in the style of true Indian eloquence. The Doctor spoke again and again, and the chief replied, still defying us to go on. Then Doctor Whitman rose to almost super-human height and, in a stern voice, told them in emphatic terms that the Great Father of the 'Bostons'[56] would send men to defend these travelers, and that ship loads of soldiers and guns would arrive to kill all the Indians who molested his people on their way to the distant valley."

Fearful of an attack during the night Whitman succeeded in keeping the Cayuse chief in the immigrant camp as a hostage. Once when the chief tried to escape, Whitman sternly told him: "Move and my man shoot you like a dog." Sarah Cummins remembered that this warning had its desired effect, but she added: "It was a night of terror to all, not a breath of sleep except the younger children." The next day a party of friendly Nez Perces arrived, having been sent by Spalding, and this greatly-relieved the strain of the situation. The immigrants then continued their march without further threats.

Although Sarah did not name any of the chiefs, in all probability the Walla Walla chief was Peu-peu-mox-mox, father of the slain Elijah Hedding. Several Cayuse chiefs could have been involved including

Tiloukaikt, Tomahas, and Tamsucky. Possibly the Nez Perce chief was Timothy. In this incident we see the evidence of growing hostility of the Indians living in the vicinity of Waiilatpu.

Loss of Sales at Waiilatpu

Most of the 1845 immigrants, after crossing the Blue Mountains, followed White's advice and went down the Umatilla River past present-day Pendleton, Oregon, to the Columbia River. This route shortened the distance to the Columbia and was, therefore, a logical road to follow. White was mistaken, however, in telling the immigrants that they could get all the supplies they needed at less cost at The Dalles than they could at Waiilatpu.

Learning that most of the immigrants would be taking the Umatilla route, Whitman loaded his wagon with flour and other supplies and rode to the Umatilla to meet them. John Ewing Howell, one of the immigrants of that year, wrote in his diary on September 17, 1845: "...camped on the Umatallow river... Dr. Whitman and lady visited our camp this morning and travelled with us and camped with us. He had a wagon-load of flour alone, not bolted, $8 pr. 100 lbs."[57]

Whitman was greatly disappointed in the small amount of sales he was able to make to the immigrants. "I had much less call from them than last year," he wrote to Greene on October 26. "The money I took from them was less than one hundred and fifty dollars and about fifteen dollars trust—three cows and two small steers." Although Whitman sold flour at $5.00 per hundredweight at his station, he charged an extra $3.00 if he had to carry it the twenty-five or more miles to the Umatilla.

In Whitman's letter of April 13, 1846, to Greene, he again blamed White for his loss of sales. "I wrote you in the fall about my dealings with the immigrants," he said, "& told you I had not much call from them. This was owing to Doct. White's telling them they could get a full supply of flour at the Dalls [sic]. The result was that they would not buy of me at five dollars a hundred, but they had to give eight and ten at the Dalls & what was worse it was not there to supply them, & in consequence there was much suffering." Whitman felt that the lack of supplies at The Dalles added "to the deaths that were induced by a wild attempt at a southern route from Boise to the Dalls."

Whitman warned Greene: "I would desire you to keep a lookout for Doct. White's course in the States and especially that he does not take up a self constituted Agency to collect funds to establish a manual labor school among the Nez Perces, which I have no doubt was a favorite plan of his. He went so far as to promise it to the Indians in such a way as to commit this Mission for its fulfilment or to involve us in its failure" [Letter 179]. Here is evidence of one of White's proposals to appease the Indians of the upper Columbia River country following the murder of Elijah Hedding. Nothing further is heard of this project, and Dr. White no longer figures in the Whitman story.

IMMIGRANTS AT WAIILATPU, WINTER 1845–1846

Life was easier for the Whitmans during the winter of 1845–1846 than it had been the previous year because there were fewer immigrants wintering at their station and also because there was a surplus of food supplies. Moreover, Narcissa was enjoying better health.

In his letter of April 13, 1846, to Greene, Whitman wrote: "A few families wintered with us. Three were Mechanics which I hired, one as a mill wright, another a chair maker and wheel maker, and the other as a Black Smith." Whitman commented on the difficulties involved in obtaining much benefit from strangers whose skills were unknown to him and who usually wanted to leave for the Willamette as soon as possible in the spring. The shortness of the days and the inclement weather during the winter also militated against the immigrants doing much useful work.

Among those who spent the winter at Waiilatpu was a gunsmith. Whitman, when writing to Walker on October 29, 1845, made it clear that he would have nothing to do with the "armory business." Whitman was a pacifist by conviction and consistently refused to use force when meeting with angry natives in some tense confrontation. As has been stated, once when slapped by Tiloukaikt, he literally turned the other cheek.

The only known recorded incident in which Whitman is reported to have threatened to use force is the story given to us by Sarah Cummins quoted above. Mrs. Cummins' account was published in 1914, nearly seventy years after the reported incident is supposed to have occurred. She might have been mistaken in her recollections of the event. The frightened immigrant holding the gun could have been the one who threatened to shoot the Cayuse chief if he tried to flee.

Shortly after the A. B. Smiths were forced to leave Kamiah, the natives of that place began to ask Whitman and Spalding to send another missionary to them. On April 8, 1844, Whitman referred to this in his letter to Greene: "The Indian with whom Mr. Smith had the difficulty at Kamiah... has showed both here and at Lapwai how much he regrets his leaving... and that ever since his heart has wept." Among the early arrivals of the 1845 immigrant at Waiilatpu was a young man, Jacob Rynearson, whom Whitman hired to go to Kamiah to open a school for the purpose of teaching the English language to any who might be interested. At first Rynearson met with success as Whitman reported that "about twenty-five [were enrolled] among which were two Delawares & Ellis, the principal Chief" [Letter 191].

Rynearson, however, found the project too difficult and returned to Waiilatpu after spending only a month at Kamiah. He then left for the Willamette Valley [Letter 182]. Thus ended all efforts of the Oregon Mission to carry on educational work for the natives at Kamiah.

One of the most welcomed immigrants to spend the winter of 1845–46 at Waiilatpu was the millwright, Josiah Osborn [or Osborne].[58] He had with him his wife and three children—Nancy, five and a half years old; John, two; and a baby boy who might have been born after the family arrived at Waiilatpu. Osborn repaired the gristmill at Waiilatpu and put it in good running condition. By the end of February 1846, the dam at the sawmill in the mountains was completed and the mill ready for operation [Letter 183b]. Osborn succeeded in attaching a lathe to the water wheel and, as a result, Whitman was able to tell Walker: "Mr. Osborne is at work at chairs & spinning wheels with his lathe... A dozen chairs for each of your families besides an arm chair and an arm rocking chair for sick people are under way." In their primitive situation, even a rocking chair was considered a luxury.

In his letter to Greene of April 13, Whitman wrote: "I could not think to live without the Mill as my house wants a new roof, never having had any but dirt roofs, & besides my Flour Mill has no house over it & I am in want of all the means to thresh & secure our grain, having no barn threshing floor or granary. I hope to do much with the Mill for the Indians also." Whitman used the slabs left over from the logs for fences.

The archives of Whitman College contain an account book of Josiah Osborn which throws light upon the prices Whitman was receiving for supplies. The records began on August 21, 1845, and continued to the following March 7. Whitman was then paying Osborn $1.50 per day, which was given in produce. The following entries are typical:

25 lbs flour at 5 cts per pound	$1.25
1 bushel beets	40
1 bushel potatoes	40
69 lbs. beef	3.79½
8 squashes	1.00
20 lbs. pork	1.40
1 lb. sugar	20
51 lbs. meal	2.04
6 ft. tobacco	60

The tobacco, which came in twisted strands and was sold by the foot, was used in trading with the Indians. The prices here listed give a refutation, if such be needed, to the accusations that Whitman was charging exorbitant prices for his supplies. The Osborn family moved to the Willamette Valley in the spring of 1846, but returned, on Whitman's urging, in the fall of 1847.

Introducing Andrew Rodgers

Traveling with the Osborn family was a sandy-haired, gentle-spirited young man by the name of Andrew Rodgers, who also decided to spend the winter at Waiilatpu. Whitman was delighted to learn that Rodgers was willing to teach the school for white children. He was hired forthwith, and thus another problem that Whitman faced was solved. "We have the best prospects for a good school for the children," Whitman wrote to Walker on October 29. "The teacher is mild but I have no doubt of his faithfulness and integrity. He was well recommended." The Walkers sent their eldest son, Cyrus, to the school, and the Spaldings sent their daughter, Eliza. Three of the children of the immigrants were also enrolled, which brought the total in the school to fourteen.

Also traveling with the Osborns was their cousin, Joseph Finley, who had ventured to make the long journey to Oregon for health reasons. Narcissa wrote: "His disease was consumption, and deep-seated when he left the States" [Letter 186]. Catherine Sager remembered how the friendship between Rodgers and Finley "was like unto that of Jonathan and David." The two men took up quarters in the emigrant house.

In her recollections of Rodgers, Catherine wrote: "He was a well educated man of deep piety... his modest and gentlemanly manner completely won Dr. and Mrs. Whitman. Mrs. Whitman was especially attracted to him by his beautiful voice and his knowledge of singing."

Rodgers had carried his violin with him on his long trek to Oregon. To Narcissa's great enjoyment, he joined her in singing familiar church hymns. Rodgers had been a member of the small Associate Presbyterian Church, one of the branches of the Scottish Covenanter movement that traced its roots back to the early years of the eighteenth century. A principal characteristic of this denomination was its refusal to sing "man-made" hymns but, instead, only paraphrases of the Psalms. Rodgers had been excommunicated by his church "for using Watts Psalms & Hymns." [59]

As has been mentioned, Marcus could not sing. Narcissa had tried to teach him certain tunes on their honeymoon journey across the country without much success. Now there came into her life at Waiilatpu, which must have been very dull at times, a talented and friendly person who could sing and also play the violin. Narcissa was delighted. Rodgers became a welcome member of the Whitman household. Catherine remembered his keen sense of humor.

Despite his hopes regarding the possible beneficial effects of a change of climate and the fervent prayers of those who ministered at his bedside, Finley found that his health was steadily declining. About the middle of January 1846, the Whitmans moved the sick man into their own bedroom and made arrangements to sleep elsewhere. Narcissa wrote about how the sick man, when he realized that death was near, began to ask questions on religious subjects. "He was without a well-grounded hope when he came here," she wrote on April 2, 1846, "and the Lord was pleased to bless our efforts for his salvation." Finley expressed a desire to be baptized and be received into the Mission church. Spalding was sent for. According to the minute book of the church, both Finley and Rodgers were examined as to their faith on February 27, 1846, and after Finley was baptized, both were received into the membership of the church. These were the last persons to join the First Presbyterian Church of Oregon during the mission period.

"Being in my family," wrote Narcissa to Jane, "I was very much with him and read and prayed with him almost daily towards the close of his life. He grew in grace steadily and felt that he was over-privileged to die in such a quiet place, where he could have the society of those who cared for his soul" [Letter 187]. Finley died on March 28, 1846, in his thirty-second year, and was buried in the little cemetery at the base of the hill near the Whitman home. Spalding again rode to Waiilatpu in order to conduct the funeral. Catherine Sager noted that Finley was "the first white man buried there;" the other two adults were a Black and an Hawaiian.

Rodgers Studies for the Ministry

After joining the Mission church, Rodgers decided to study for the ministry. The Mission appointed Elkanah Walker to supervise his studies, and on May 15, 1846, Whitman wrote to Greene and ordered eleven text books. Six of this number were for Hebrew and Greek studies. On November 2, 1846, Narcissa wrote to Mrs. Spalding saying: "Mr. Rodgers acts as our minister and maintains the station with considerable ministerial dignity. He bids fair to be a useful man." Thus to Andrew Rodgers belongs the distinction of being the first candidate for the Protestant ministry on the Pacific Slope of what is now the United States.

Rodgers received at least part if not all of the books ordered. Among them was "Robinsons Greek Lex[icon] of N.T."[60] When those who were held captive at Waiilatpu following the Whitman massacre were evacuated, they were able to take with them most of their personal belongings. Someone took some of the items that Rodgers had owned. After the arrival of the former captives in the Willamette Valley, a question arose as to who should receive the possessions of Rodgers. Since he had no relatives, it was decided that the items should be given to the Rev. Wilson Blain, a pioneer Associate-Reformed Presbyterian minister, who was then living in the Valley. This was a logical decision since Rodgers had once been a member of the Associate Church.

About 1940, I learned that Blain's grandson was living in San Leandro, California. I then knew nothing of any connection Blain had had with the property of Andrew Rodgers. I did know that Blain had served as editor of Oregon's first newspaper, the *Oregon Spectator*. Hoping to find some copies of that pioneer publication, I called on the grandson. Although he had no copies of the *Spectator*, he did give me a box of old books from his late grandfather's library. I found among them Robinson's Greek Lexicon with the signature of Andrew Rodgers on a flyleaf page. This volume is now in the museum of the Whitman Mission National Historic Site.

ACTIVITIES AT WAIILATPU, 1845-1846

Among the 1845 immigrants who visited Waiilatpu that fall was Joel Palmer, who returned to the States the following spring to get his family. Palmer in his published *Journal* tells of the call that Dr. and Mrs. Whitman had paid on the party of immigrants with whom he was traveling while they were encamped in the Grande Ronde Valley on September 17: "They came in a two horse wagon, bringing with them a plentiful supply of flour, meal, and potatoes."

Palmer spent a few days at Waiilatpu and had high praise for what the Whitmans had accomplished. "Their privations and trials have been great," he wrote. "The fruits of their devotion are now manifest and if any class of people deserve well of their country, or are entitled to the thanks of a Christian community, it is the missionaries."[61] Whitman told Palmer that he had found it necessary to butcher thirty-two horses for his table before he was able to turn to his stock of cattle and hogs for meat. Palmer later played an important role in the political life of Oregon, serving as a general in the Cayuse War of 1848.

Whitman's activities with and in behalf of the natives, during the months under review, continued according to established patterns. The excitement which stirred the Indians when they learned of the death of Elijah Hedding at Sutter's Fort died down when they heard that there had been an uprising in California against the Mexican Government and that Captain Sutter had been captured and imprisoned. This was an incident of the Mexican War of 1846. The Cayuse and Walla Walla Indians looked upon the imprisonment of Sutter, which proved to have been only temporary, as a kind of retribution for their own personal grievances. As a result, Whitman was able to write to Greene on October 26, 1845: "They have taken a course most favourable to a good understanding with the whites." But, as will be told, the Cayuses had not forgotten; the murder of Elijah Hedding continued to be a cause of dissatisfaction.

Whitman and Spalding never equated civilization with Christianity, although they were convinced that the two could not be separated. Shortly after their arrival on their mission fields, their letters show that they foresaw an inevitable clash between the Indian culture and that of the white man. Spalding especially stressed his conviction that if the Indians were to survive, they would have to abandon their manner of life and settle down and become farmers and herdsmen. Whitman shared this opinion. As far as the Indians were concerned, there was no alternative. Moreover, the missionaries realized that they could not educate or evangelize a people who were, as Spalding said, "always on the wing." Therefore, both men did all that they could to encourage the natives to farm and to raise cattle, sheep, and hogs. Whitman and Spalding were following the pattern set by government agents working with Indian tribes in the States.

In order to improve his breed of sheep, Whitman ordered "one Merino & one Leicester buck" from the Hudson's Bay Company in April 1846 [Letter 191]. In his letter of April 13 to Greene, Whitman reported that he then had one hundred ewes in his flock which he expected would drop "200 or more lambs in the course of the coming year as they give two sets a year." In his letter of May 15 to Greene, he asked for six sheep shears. The sheep that Whitman and Spalding together owned produced far more wool than could have been used on the few spinning wheels at the two stations and on Spalding's loom. What was done with the excess is not known. Possibly it was sold or traded with the Hudson's Bay Company.

As a boy Whitman had tended a carding machine which processed wool for spinning and weaving [Letter 191]. Because of this experience, Whitman asked Greene to send a complete set of irons for a carding machine and also requested that some person skilled in the manufacture of woolens be sent to Oregon to run the proposed project. Whitman's dream of establishing a woolen industry in Oregon did not receive

Greene's approval. On November 13, 1846, Greene answered four of Whitman's letters including his letter of April 13, 1846, in which he had asked for carding irons. Greene's reply may have been received by Whitman before his death; if so it was the last letter from the Board that Whitman read. In it Greene wrote: "We do not send the mechanist or the manufacturers which you mention as desirable, partly because we do not know where to find them,... and partly, because as a missionary society, we do not think it advisable for us to have much to do with such matters." [62] Thus ended Whitman's attempt to initiate the manufacture of woolens in Oregon.

The old debatable question as to the advisability of teaching English to the natives faced Whitman again in 1846. Writing to Brewer on February 6 of that year, Whitman said: "I do not know when we can hit upon a plan to educate the Indian children. Their own language does not satisfy them and they have not perseverance enough to learn English." Whitman agreed with Dr. White's idea that the only solution to the problem would be to take the children from their parents and put them in a boarding school. Such a project, however, would be expensive and the Mission had neither the funds nor the personnel for such an undertaking.

In his letter of April 13 to Greene, Whitman wrote: "Situated as I am alone, I am not able to give the regular attendance upon school teaching that is requisite for success. No one can teach English to any effect but one that has the medium of both languages for communication." Whitman's experience in sending a man to Kamiah in the fall of 1845, who did not know the Nez Perce language, and expecting him to teach the natives English, proved his point. Whitman added in his letter to Greene that Perrin, then sixteen years old, had made such progress in mastering the Indian language that he would "soon be able to teach." Perrin later became an interpreter for the government.

In addition to the multitude of duties which fell on his shoulders, Whitman found that practically all religious instruction given to the Cayuses devolved upon him. He was as conscientious as circumstances permitted in conducting Sunday devotions for the natives. In his letter of July 20, 1846, to Walker, he commented: "A general good attention is given by the Indians to religions instruction. Gambling, however, is the besetting sin of many especially of the young." Other members of the Oregon Mission made references in their letters to this tendency of the natives to gamble.

Regarding the possibility of a Roman Catholic mission being established near Waiilatpu, Whitman told Walker: "We are to pass at least another year without a Roman Catholick [sic] Station among us. The influence of Ellis is against it & the Indians in general also. Still the Jesuits could obtain what would be to them an invitation to locate among them." Both Whitman and Spalding were inclined to refer to all of the Roman Catholic missionaries as belonging to the Jesuit order when in fact the only one in the area that did belong was Father De Smet.

In the midst of his many cares and responsibilities, Whitman had the misfortune during the first part of December 1845 to suffer a severely bruised left knee as the result of his horse falling on him. For over two months, he had to use a crutch. During the latter part of the following January, Whitman received a call from the Walkers asking him to attend Mrs. Walker when she expected to be confined about the middle of February. Whitman replied on February 3 and explained that he was unable to make the horseback ride because of his injured knee. "Mrs. Walker has the best reason to hope and trust for a safe delivary from her former experience," he wrote. "Let nature have its unobstructive course... Remember that delivery is a natural process" [Letter 183b]. A son, named Jeremiah, their fifth child, was born on March 7.

From Narcissa's Letters

Narcissa's letters written during the spring of 1846 give us some of her thoughts and feelings on a variety of subjects. To her father she wrote on April 10: "I have received no letters from father, mother or any of the sisters or brothers in Allegheny county since husband returned. I wonder why, sometimes, and feel a little like complaining." Again, it is hard to explain either the failure of her relatives to write or the possible loss of letters in transit. On November 3 of that year, Narcissa in a letter to her mother wrote: "Mothers dated Mar. 26, 1846, was sent from Boston to Westport and reached me in about five months after it was mailed. This brings me very near home. Indeed it is the first I have received since those sent by Husband." In other words, this was the first letter from her "home" that she had received for three years!

Narcissa repeatedly urged members of her family, especially Jane and Edward, to migrate to Oregon. In her letter of April 10, 1846, to her father, she even suggested that he had her mother make the overland journey. "If my dear father and mother were here," she wrote, "I think they would be very well contented, for we could give them a comfortable home and enough to eat and do, and if the distance were not so great, I should hope they would come and finish their days with us." Narcissa, however, confessed: "But it is a dreadful journey to perform to get here, and I ought not to ask such a sacrifice of them for my comfort merely... It is not so difficult to get here now as when I came, for families come in wagons all the way. The fatigue is great, however, and the dust from Fort Hall here is very afflicting; aside from that, with food enough and teams enough, no loading except necessary clothing, it would not be difficult."

After mentioning the physical hardships of the overland journey, Narcissa turned to the spiritual effects. "The greatest affliction," she wrote, "would be to the pious soul—it is continually vexed with the ungodly conversation and profanity of the wicked, and is so often brought into straitened circumstances with regard to his own duty in obeying the commands of God, such as keeping the Sabbath, etc., that he often is wounded to that degree that it requires many months, if not years, before he is restored to his wonted health again... I do not say that the journey cannot be performed and the Christian enjoy his peace of mind and continued communion with God all the way. But this I know, that the experience of all proves it to be exceedingly difficult, if not impossible. *It is often said that every Christian gets so that he can swear before the journey is completed.*" [63]

In her letter of April 2, 1846, to Edward, Narcissa again pleaded for him and Jane to write. "I cannot see how it should be difficult for you or the girls to write me, and should you think you might write me five or six times a year instead of once in two or more years." And then Narcissa gave the following description of what was taking place around her as she was writing: "Think of me now while I am attempting to write—half a dozen children making a noise around me, and to put on the climax, the doctor must come in, and taking a paper sit down and read aloud or talk to Mr. Rodgers who is sitting in the room; then in comes an Indian woman or two to sell some dry berries, and I must stop to attend to them, until I am quite lost and scarcely know what I am thinking about, especially when I have nearly twenty letters to write, and but little time to accomplish it in."

Narcissa thanked her brother for sending a box of incidental articles. "I was in hopes," she wrote, "of finding one little article more, that is needed more than most any other because it cannot be obtained here; namely a pi-la-ain, as the Indians call it (louse trap). You will understand me, I suppose—the finest fine combs cannot be obtained here, for that reason I was in hopes of finding one in the box." The lodges of the Indians were always infested with various kinds of vermin which often made life miserable for the white people who came in close contact with the natives.

REMINISCENCES OF THE SAGER GIRLS

The reminiscences of the three Sager girls—Catherine, Elizabeth, and Matilda—give us many intimate glimpses into the Whitman home during those years 1844–47. Through their reminiscences, we learn, not only many details of life at Waiilatpu, but also much about the Whitmans themselves. Here we see Marcus and Narcissa in their lighter moments when they laughed, played, and sang with the children.

Catherine, as the eldest of the three girls, has given us the longest and the most reliable account of life in the Whitman home. Here is one of her recollections:

> Some... may be curious to know how this washing was done for so large a family. About four o'clock in the morning, all hands were called into the kitchen by Mrs. Whitman. Tubs and all necessary paraphernalia were produced. The men and boys with long aprons tied around them brought water and plied the pounders, while the women did the rubbing. With much joking, all went off in good humor and by school time, which was nine o'clock, the clothes were on the line.[64]

Regarding their religious training, Catherine wrote: "On Sabbath morning each child was reminded that it was the Sabbath and each one was admonished to keep quiet." Those who could read were encouraged to do so. Sunday school was held at eleven o'clock. A worship service for the white residents of Waiilatpu was held at three o'clock. Dr. Whitman or Andrew Rodgers usually "read the sermon." The religious instruction of the children continued through the week, with emphasis on memorizing Bible verses. Catherine remembered that: "Prayer meeting was held on Thursday evening during the winter for adults."

Elizabeth recalled many memories of her life at Waiilatpu in her old age when she granted an interview with a newspaper reporter. Among the immigrants of 1846 was a young woman in her late teens, Mary Johnson, who was hired by Dr. Whitman to assist his wife in the house. According to Elizabeth, one day Mary put on Narcissa's "wrapper" while working in the kitchen. While standing at the stove with her back to the door, Dr. Whitman entered and saw her. Pretending that he mistook her for his wife, the doctor tiptoed up to her and suddenly threw his arms around her and gave her a big hug. "She was greatly embarrassed and scandalized," said Elizabeth, while "the Doctor was as solemn as an owl and protested he thought she was his wife." Elizabeth added: "I could tell by the way his eyes twinkled, he was playing a joke on her."[65]

Each of the three Sager girls remembered Narcissa's love for flowers and how she encouraged each to cultivate a small garden each spring. They also recalled how she would take them on walks or horseback rides, especially on Saturday afternoons. Both Catherine and Elizabeth remembered a picnic held in the fall of 1847 when Mrs. Whitman led the children to a site about a mile and a half from their home. Francis pulled a small hand wagon which contained the food and dishes. The most exciting event of the excursion happened when Elizabeth and Helen threw clods of dirt at a wasps' nest which resulted in both Helen and Mrs. Whitman being stung. For punishment the two girls were sent to bed that evening without their supper.

Narcissa took delight in teaching the children to sing. Catherine wrote: "It was the custom for Mrs. Whitman, when she had company, to show off what she called her 'family stairway'... All the children were called and placed in a line standing according to height. After being formally introduced, we entertained the company by singing, accomanied by Rodger's violin. During these exercises the Doctor and his wife looked on, their eyes sparkling with pleasure."

Writing to her sister Harriet on April 13, 1846, Narcissa said: "Every one of my girls goes to the river all summer long for bathing every day before dinner, and they love it so well that they would as soon do without dinner as without that." Since their main meal was served at noon, the bathing took place late in the morning. A secluded spot was used where the girls could bathe in the nude, always with Narcissa or some other woman watching. When the annual Mission meeting was held at Waiilatpu in May 1845, Mrs. Eells took the girls to the river. At that time eight-year-old Emma Hobson nearly drowned. Seeing the little girl struggling in the water, Mrs. Eells frantically screamed for help. Elizabeth wrote of the incident: "An Indian got Emma out and, as she had no clothes on, he took off his blanket, wrapped her up in it, brought her back and handed her gravely to Mrs. Eells." After that a safer place for the girls to bathe was selected.[66]

The children went barefooted in the summer and wore moccasins in the winter. Mrs. Whitman made dresses for the girls out of "hickory shirting" purchased from the Hudson's Bay Company. The Whitman family often slept out-of-doors during the summer months. Catherine commented on the food: "The Doctor ignored fine flour and used unbolted flour or corn meal. As a matter of economy, tea or coffee came to the table only on rare occasions, such delicacies being very hard to procure in Oregon at that time. The country abounded in wild fruits of all kinds which were purchased from the natives. Our good garden supplied the vegetables. Cakes and pastry were served only on holidays. Add to the list, plenty of milk, butter and cheese and you have our diet." Matilda remembered that their most common dish for supper was "corn meal mush and milk." Matilda also recalled how the children would cut watermelons in half and string them together and put them in the river as little boats, playing with them by the hour.

Mrs. Whitman was opposed to the girls associating with the Indian children; thus the Sager girls did not learn the native language. Eliza Spalding at Lapwai had more freedom in this regard and, as a result, she could speak Nez Perce; this proved of great importance to the captives at the time of the Whitman massacre. On the whole, the three Sager girls looked back with appreciation on their three years at Waiilatpu and were generous in praising their foster parents.

On April 10, 1846, in a letter to her father, Narcissa wrote: "I am sometimes about ready to sink under the weight of responsibility resting upon me, and would, were it not that an Almighty hand sustains me. Bringing up a family of children in a heathen land, where every influence tends to degrade rather than elevate, requires no small measure of faith and patience, as well as great care and prayerfulness watchfulness." The refusal of Mrs. Whitman to permit the girls to play with Indian children may have been one reason why the Indians considered her to be "haughty." [67]

WHITMAN CONSIDERS LEAVING WAIILATPU

Several alarming confrontations with the natives which occurred in the fall of 1845 caused Whitman seriously to consider the advisability of moving his family to the Willamette Valley. Catherine Sager has given us the following account of the first incident: "It was the Doctor's custom to grind grain for the natives at his mill, those coming first having their grain ground first. One day Tomahas came to the mill and wanted his corn ground.[68] Not getting it done as soon as he thought he would, and being a fractious fellow, he became enraged. While eating dinner, we heard the mill making a strange sound. The miller, followed by the Doctor, ran to the mill where he was knocked down by Tomahas. He then struck at the Doctor but was seized around the waist by Tiloukaikt. Tomahas roared and foamed like an enraged lion but Tiloukaikt held him fast. He finally promised to leave if released. Then he mounted his horse and rode away and was not seen about for a long time." [69] Catherine explained that Tomahas, impatient because he had not been given prompt service, had put sticks into the hopper of the mill which caused the strange sounds which in turn alerted Whitman and the miller.

Catherine told of another incident which involved Tomahas. She wrote:

> One day while the Doctor was engaged in his field, Tomahas... rode up to the fence in a very preemptory manner and ordered Dr. Whitman to go and grind some corn for him. The Doctor replied that he was not in the habit of doing things for people unless they asked in a proper manner. He [i.e., Tomahas] started off around the field but as he had to go around, the Doctor was able to reach the mill first by cutting across the field, and soon fixed the mill so that it could not be operated.
>
> The Doctor then took an iron bar in his hand, retired a short distance and awaited the coming of Tomahas. He soon ar-

rived and after trying in vain to start the mill, he rushed at Dr. Whitman with his club but seeing that he was armed, he stopped and ordered the Doctor to put down his weapon. To this the Doctor calmly replied that he would put his down when the Indian put his own down.

Tomahas dropped his club but as soon as the Doctor put down his bar of iron, the Indian rushed at him with his club. The Doctor picked up his iron bar and was able to ward off the blow. Tomahas told him to leave the country, that he did not want him there. To this the Doctor replied that if all the Indians wanted him to leave, he would gladly do so, but he could not leave, just because one Indian wanted him to go. He also told him that if he would behave himself, he would do his grinding for him. To this he agreed and they parted in a friendly spirit.

The Doctor, exhausted in body and spirit, came into the house and threw himself on a couch, relating the whole affair, saying that if the Indians would say so, he would gladly leave as he was tried almost beyond endurance.[70]

Confrontation with Young Chief

A situation, more ominous than the threats of physical violence by the excitable Tomahas, faced Whitman on November 24, 1845, when he experienced a frightening confrontation with Young Chief. Tomahas was only a subchief in Tiloukaikt's band; Young Chief, on the other hand, was one of the most influential of the Cayuse chiefs and when he rehearsed all the complaints that the Indians had against the white men in general, and the missionaries in particular, Whitman was deeply disturbed.

The next day Whitman in a long letter to Walker summarized what had happened. He began his letter by saying: "I have given the Indians from now to next spring to consider whether I shall leave them or not. My reasons for doing so arise out of a talk I had yesterday with the Young Chief." Whitman had approached Young Chief regarding the possibility of opening a school for the Indian children. Even before this project could be discussed, Whitman was confronted with "a long list of counts" which Young Chief brought up. Although some of the criticisms made by Young Chief were of an incidental nature, three were in his mind very important. Each of these became a factor in the growing unrest among the Cayuses which came to a tragic climax two years later. In this letter to Walker, Whitman's report of what Young Chief said gives the Indians' side of their conflict with the white men.

Young Chief began by referring to the death of his nephew, Cayuse Halket, at the Red River Mission school. The school's records show that the young man was buried on February 1, 1837. Young Chief maintained that his nephew "was killed at Red River," and said that the white men were responsible for his death. The notation about his death and burial in the school's records gives no hint that Cayuse Halket met a violent death. Young Chief then referred to the killing of Elijah Hedding by Americans at Sutter's Fort in California. Since both of these young men had been educated in a white man's school and had been killed, Young Chief said that he could not be expected to send any more of the Cayuse children to a mission school.

Young Chief then turned to a more serious problem the Indians were facing. Whitman wrote: "He spoke of the Americans as having a design to obtain their country & property." Three great immigrations, totaling about five thousand people, had already passed through the Cayuse country on their way to the Willamette Valley and the Indians had a reason to be afraid of this great influx of white people.

Young Chief had been told by Eastern Indians who had drifted into the Oregon country, such as Tom Hill, what had happened to the Indian lands of eastern United States. Tom Hill had warned the Nez Perces and the Cayuses of their coming fate if white men continued to arrive in Oregon.

It is not known to what extent Young Chief was aware of Whitman's activity in promoting Oregon emigration. For him it was enough to know that Whitman was a "Boston man"; that he had helped guide the immigration of 1843 west of Fort Hall; and that he had given shelter and assistance to scores of immigrants who had passed by his station or who had spent the winter there.

A third complaint had more sinister overtones. Whitman wrote: "He also alluded to the death of a friend of his last year who died of Dysentery with two of his children as the result of diseases which Americans placed among them." Here was a fact that Whitman could not deny. The white man had introduced new diseases among the native tribes of Oregon.

"As he advanced in his remarks," wrote Whitman, *"he made me responsible for or conniving at these things or as having all these agents at my disposal."* [71]

Here Young Chief touched on what was perhaps the most important single reason for the Whitman massacre. The whole point of Young Chief's accusation was that the white men were prepared "with poison and infection" to kill off the Indians in order to gain possession of their lands and horses. Young Chief even accused Whitman of having poison "to kill the people with." He even expressed his fear of eating with white people for fear of being poisoned with the food. Whitman vehemently denied being responsible for the spread of disease and that he was not "accountable for such base things as they might have been told." Young Chief cynically replied: "It is not expected that you would confess it even were it true." Whitman was deeply troubled because of what Young Chief said, for he saw the connection between the Indians' fears and superstitions and his own practice of medicine among them.

Whitman warned Young Chief that such inflammatory language might "remove all restraint from the reckless and that I would have no assurance but that I might be killed on the most slight or sudden occasion." Whitman threatened to leave the field. Young Chief replied that he did not want him to go just then but that if they did decide to go, it must be on their own initiative. "That is," explained Whitman to Walker, "he insists not to let the Indians have the responsibility of sending me off but only agitate enough to get us to go as it were of ourselves."

Although Whitman did not write to Walker until the next day, the recollection of what Young Chief had said was so alarming that he wrote with a quivering pen. Whitman confessed: "I am so nervous that I cannot govern my hand." The original letter, now in the Coe Collection in Yale University library, gives evidence of Whitman's shaky handwriting. Whitman entrusted the letter to Mungo, the half-Hawaiian and half-Indian servant, and told him to carry it to Tshimakain. The Walkers received the letter on Tuesday evening, December 2. Mary noted in her diary that it was of "a disheartening character," and that Dr. Whitman "fears he must leave his people."

When Whitman had the confrontation with Tiloukaikt and Tomahas four years earlier, in September 1841, he reported the incident to McKinlay at Fort Walla Walla, who then issued a stern warning to the two chiefs. This quieted the Cayuses for the time being. There is no indication that Whitman informed McKinlay of these later developments. Although faced with these ominous threats of violence, Whitman felt that there was nothing to do at that time but to stay on and continue with his work. He knew that he had the support of many of the Cayuses including Stickus and Five Crows. Whitman also felt a responsibility to the immigrant families who were wintering at Waiilatpu. The season was too far advanced for all to make the journey to the Willamette Valley.

The only extant letter of Narcissa's written during the fall of 1845 or the following winter is one dated November 28 and addressed to Mrs. Brewer at Waskopum. After referring to the fact that the last of the immigrants not planning to spend the winter at Waiilatpu, had left for the Willamette Valley, she wrote: "I feel greatly worn out both physically and mentally... For the poor Indians' sake and the relief of future travelers to this country, I could wish to stay here longer if we could do it in peace. We fear, sometimes, as if our quietness was past for this country, at least for a season. It may be that you are suffering under the same commotions that affect us, and perhaps more so."

Writing at the same time to Mr. Brewer, Whitman said: "I have lately told the Indians we should leave them in the spring unless they treat us better and hold forth a very different sort of language to us." By the following February 6, Whitman was able to write to Brewer: "I have not brought the question of our leaving before any meeting of the Indians but what is as good or better is that a full & free expression from the most important men has been given me showing a desire for us to stay. I am not preparing to go but am going on the same as before." Thus another crisis was passed.

THE VISITS OF TOM HILL TO WAIILATPU

It so happened that both Ellis and Tom Hill from the Nez Perce country called on Whitman on the evening of the day that he had the unpleasant talk with Young Chief. Ellis was friendly and said that, although he knew that some at Lapwai and at Waiilatpu were in favor of the Whitmans leaving, such was not his recommendation.

Hill, the agnostic, was always critical of missionaries trying to convert the natives to Christianity. He argued that "religion was too sacred a thing for fallible beings to practice and, in as much as they could not keep its holy requirements as not to come short and sin, it was better to have nothing to do with it." Hill was much more impressed by Whitman than he had been by Spalding. After conversing with the natives at Waiilatpu and observing at first-hand what Whitman had been able to accomplish, Hill frankly told Whitman that he had been deceived by false reports. He now had a better opinion of Whitman [Letter 181b].

Hill returned to Waiilatpu about the middle of February 1846 when Whitman invited him and some of his Nez Perce friends to a feast. Catherine Sager had vivid memories of that event. Here is her description:

> Tom Hill... was a finely formed man, being, I should judge, nearly six feet tall and spoke English and the Cayuse [i.e., the Nez Perce] language well... [The feast] was held in the Indian room... A fire was kindled in the yard and a large kettle holding nearly twenty gallons of water was suspended over it. This was to prepare the mush, an indispensible article for an Indian's table... The mush cooked, the kettle was carried in and placed on the floor near the upper end of the room and a small stand covered with a white cloth was placed near it.
>
> A tea tray filled with food was placed on this stand. The Doctor's chair was placed near it, and on one side of the room was a bench for his family. The hour having arrived for the feast, the Doctor having distributed plates and spoons among them, he took his place as master of ceremonies. The chiefs sat around the kettle and the others filed in according to their rank or standing. While the Doctor and the chiefs dipped their food out of the kettle, the others were served out of vessels which they held in their hand. Meat, bread, and other food were handed to them by those serving as waiters. In honor of the occasion, Mrs. Whitman served them tea sweetened with sugar. This she poured into bowls and cups in the dining room and the waiters distributed it from there. We laughed heartily to see how lavish the Indians were to the use of sugar, wanting their tea as sweet as sugar itself and watching them scoop up bits of mush from the floor and eating it.
>
> The feast was held after night, and the room was well lighted with candles and was densely crowded, and when the Indians became overheated, they would go into the open air to cool off.

They all ate quietly in the fashion of Indians with the silence broken only by the supping noises of eating or a remark made by Dr. Whitman... Tom Hill was the orator of the evening. He spoke for two or three hours. Dr. Whitman, his wife, and Mr. Rodgers all spoke very highly of this speech but unfortunately I could not understand him.

Tom was richly and gorgeously dressed on this occasion in full Indian costume. His hunting shirt was of deerskin dyed red and cut full of holes and fringed. This was worn over a striped shirt. His pants were of the same material as his hunting shirt and fringed down the side. On his feet he wore moccasins decorated with porcupine quills, and his long hair hung about his shoulders. During the feast our risibilities had often gotten beyond control, and Mrs. Whitman had to send us outside to indulge our mirth, and here I would like to say that during all the time we lived with her, she never permitted us to show any disrespect or in any way to be discourteous to the Indians... Mrs. Whitman set us the example by always treating them politely and thanking them for any favor that they did.[72]

The gala event did much to create a better feeling between Whitman and the natives and, perhaps, influenced Hill to modify some of his apprehensions. According to a report given by Father Brouillet, when Tom Hill returned to the Lapwai Valley after his visit with Dr. Whitman, William Craig asked him "how he and the Doctor got along." Hill replied: "He was a heap better man that Spalding; he had asked him into his house sometimes." Craig added, however: "After that the Doctor told me that Tom had done some mischief with the Indians in that place."[73]

After the reception of some natives into the membership of the Mission church in June 1844, no further converts were won during the remaining three and a half years of the Mission's history. Surely part of this failure can be traced to Hill's negative influence. Marshall, in his *Acquisition of Oregon* (II:257), stated that Hill "could get much closer to the heart of the Indians than any white missionary ever could do, and influence them vastly more to discard all the white man's words and works and cling to their ancient ways and superstitions." Marshall makes the pointed judgment: "It is doubtful if any other one influence was as potent as Tom Hill in promoting the decadence of the Spalding-Whitman-Eells Mission, and so bringing on the Whitman massacre."

After the feast Whitman gave Hill and his friends, we find no further mention of Hill in the Whitman correspondence. Writing on February 27, undoubtedly after the feast had been held, Whitman stated: "I have & am receiving more assurances of kindness, confidence, good will & affection from the Indians than at any former time. Individual expression has been full & free for me not to leave them. No sympathy has been shown for the remarks of Tautai [Young Chief] which he made last fall." [74] And Narcissa, writing to her friend Mrs. Brewer on July 17, 1846, echoed her husband's judgment: "The Indians are very quiet now and never more friendly."

The International Boundary Settled

The negotiations which the diplomats of the United States and Great Britain had carried on for years, regarding the location of the international boundary in Old Oregon, came to an end on June 15, 1846, when a treaty was signed which fixed the dividing line at the 49° parallel. The United States thus gained the Puget Sound area which Lieutenant Slacum in 1837 had recognized as being of such great strategic importance for the country's naval and commercial interests. Great Britain secured title to all of Vancouver Island, including that part which lay south of the 49° parallel.

The United States Senate ratified the treaty on June 17, too late for the news to be carried overland to Oregon by the emigration of that year. The news was sent across Mexico to Hawaii and from there to the Willamette Valley, where it was received sometime in November.[75] Although the boundary question was settled, the Provisional Government in Oregon carried on for more than two years before Congress authorized a Territorial Government.

The first indication that Whitman knew of the boundary settlement is found in his letter to Greene of April 1, 1847. After referring to his hazardous journey across the country during the winter of 1842–43, he wrote: "I often reflect upon the fact that you were sorry that I came. I did not at that time nor has it since changed my views… American interests acquired in the Country, which the *success of the Immigration of '43 alone have &*

could have secured, have become the foundation and cause of the late treaty with England & the U. States in regard to Oregon." [76] This statement together with others previously given, reveals the great significance Whitman saw in the role he had played in opening a wagon road to the Columbia River in 1843.

Following the retirement of Dr. McLoughlin early in 1846, the administration of the Columbia Department of the Hudson's Bay Company devolved upon Chief Factors Peter Skene Ogden, 1794-1854, and James Douglas, 1803–1877. Following the establishment by the Company of Fort Camosun, later called Victoria, on Vancouver Island in 1843, the fur trade was gradually transferred to that post. Fort Vancouver on the Columbia River became little more than a mercantile establishment for the benefit of American immigrants until a detachment of the United States Army occupied the site in 1849.

CHAPTER 20 ENDNOTES

[1] Perrin Whitman to his father, Sept. 27, 1868: "It is just 25 years to-day since I arrived at Uncle's place." Original in private hands; copy in Coll. W.

[2] Whitman, in his letter 142, stated that he arrived on "Tuesday, the ninth." That particular Tuesday in October 1843 was the 10th. Without the convenience of modern printed calendars, the missionaries often erred in identifying the days of the week.

[3] Brosnan, *Jason Lee*, p. 213, quoting from Lee's letter to his Missionary Society of October 27, 1843.

[4] Warren, *Memoirs of the West*, p. 118.

[5] *O.H.Q.*, XXXIX (1938), p. 19, article by Drury, "The Columbia Maternal Association."

[6] Chapter Seventeen, section, "Adapted to a Different Destiny."

[7] Chapter Sixteen, section, "Activities of W. H. Gray."

[8] John C. Fremont, *Narrative of the Exploring Expedition to the Rocky Mountains in the year 1842*. Syracuse, 1848, p. 219. The original Fremont order is in Southwest Museum, Los Angeles.

[9] Eells ms., Coll. W., bearing date of October 1865. H. B. Brewer, in a letter dated Nov. 7, 1843, to L. L. Giddings, stated: "Lieu. Fremont of the U.S. Army arrived here [i.e., The Dalles] three days ago... He left the States with 40 men armed & well equiped besides 1 cannon & two Howitzers, a part of his men have not yet arrived. One Howitzer & his carriage is with this part of his company—but what surprises us most is he shall take his carriage no further but leaves it for our use." Original in Coll. W.S.H.S.

[10] Drury, *F.W.W.*, II:265. This boy, named Joseph Elkanah, went as a missionary to China under the American Board in 1872, where he served for about fifty years.

[11] *Op. cit.*, I:421.

[12] Drury, *Spalding*, p. 272.

[13] *Ibid.*, p. 273.

[14] Simpson, *An Overland Journey*, p. 101. [See Chapter Sixteen, fn. 20.] Simpson's reference to Five Crows owning slaves recalls a reference in the record book of the Mission church which states that on May 14, 1843, "a middle aged man, Joseph's companion of Snake origin, having been taken a slave when young" was among those received into the membership of the church. He was named Lyman. Italics are the author's.

[15] *Op. cit.*, 1848, p. 104.

[16] Italics are the author's.

[17] Italics are the author's.

[18] Spalding to Greene, Jan. 24, 1846. Coll. A. See also Chapter Sixteen, section, "Agitation by Half-Breeds."

[19] Bancroft, *Oregon*, I:338, estimated the number of immigrants for that year at 1,475.

[20] Pringle ms., p. 3. (For reference to Pringle ms., see "Manuscript Sources" under Bibliography). Catherine Sager states that the baby was born on May 22, but contemporary accounts, as found in the journals of other members of the 1844 emigration, give May 30. See Thompson, *Shallow Grave*, p. 13.

21 Dr. Degen's name is also spelled as Dagon or Dagen. On Nov. 9, 1844, he signed his name on a receipt as "Theophilos Degen, Md [sic], Doctor." Original in Oregon State Archives, Salem, Oregon.

22 Pringle ms., p. 6.

23 Capt. Shaw, in his manuscript, "Mississippi & Columbia River Pioneer Life Compared," Coll. B., p. 13, stated that Naomi Sager died "about 16 days after" her husband.

24 Pringle ms., p. 6.

25 A board fence consisting of slabs of wood set upright was called a "palisade" by Catherine.

26 Thompson, *Shallow Grave*, pp. 41-2, quoting from the original document in the Oregon State Archives. A postscript dated June 22, 1845, added: "One old cow, blind in one eye, recovered from the Indians at five and a half dollars expense."

27 Pringle ms., p. 9; and *O.H.Q.*, XI (1910):312 ff.

28 *O.H.Q.*, II (1901):268 ff. B. F. Nichols in *W.C.Q.*, I (1897):3:20 gives a fine description of Mrs. Whitman's appearance. He also wrote: "I have heard her pray, and she could offer up the finest petition to the Throne of Grace of any person I have ever heard in my life. She was always gentle and kind to the Indians, as she was to every one else." This view contradicts the opinion of H. K. W. Perkins [see Appendix 6].

29 Hulbert, *O.P.*, VIII:165. A few of Greene's letters to members of the Oregon Mission are included in this series.

30 *W.C.Q.*, II (1898):2:34 gives account of interview with Perrin Whitman, April 27, 1898, who then claimed that the sawmill machinery was carried to Oregon in a wagon in 1843. No contemporary account verifies this claim. Spalding, in the inventory he compiled for his station following the Whitman massacre, stated that he got the sawmill irons from Fort Vancouver and that they were later "taken to Waiilatpu." Drury, *Spalding and Smith*, p. 361.

31 According to a letter from Larry J. Waldron, Chief Park Interpreter, Whitman Mission National Historic Site, to the author on March 28, 1972, the museum there has a millstone 18 inches in diameter and that another millstone, 40 inches in diameter is buried near the site of the original mill. This later may be the millstone mentioned in Drury, *Whitman*, p. 352, fn. 6, as then being in the garden of a resident of Yamhill, Oregon. Waldron claims that this larger stone was obtained in January 1961 from Mrs. F. L. Trullinger of Portland, Ore. These large granite stones may have been secured from the same quarry near Lapwai where Spalding got his.

32 Drury, *Spalding and Smith*, p. 365.

33 Copies are in Colls. O. & Y. In 1934 I received a copy, bound in elk hide, from John Frank, a Nez Perce Indian who lived at Kamiah, Idaho. This is now in the Presbyterian Historical Society, Philadelphia. The American Bible Society reprinted the 1845 edition in 1871.

34 Since Catherine was the eldest of the three, she had the clearest recollections of life with the Whitmans and of the massacre.

35 Lockley, *Oregon Trail Blazers*, p. 328.

36 Delaney, *A Survivor's Recollections*, p. 8.

37 Lockley, *op. cit.*, p. 330.

38 Ibid., p. 345.

39 See my article on Charles Compo in Hafen, *Mountain Men*, VIII:87 ff. Following the publication of this book, I learned that Compo returned to the Catholic Church and had his children baptized by a priest, one on June 28, 1848, and others on later dates. See St. Louis Register of Baptisms, St. Louis, Ore. Information received through kindness of Mrs. Harriet D. Munnick, West Linn, Ore.

40 Bancroft, *Oregon*, I:281.

41 Minutes of the *Synod of Washington*, 1936, p. 292.

42 Presumably Perrin Whitman had already been baptized. Why Helen Mar Meek and David Malin were not baptized with the other children is not known.

43 Possibly Joel Perkins, a founder of the city of Milwaukie, Oregon.

44 See Chapter Nineteen, section "Whitman Accused of Charging Exorbitant Prices."

45 Italics are the author's.

46 According to a statement made by Dr. McLoughlin in *T.O.P.A.*, 1880, p. 36, Tom Hill "had been educated at Dartmouth College." In reply to an inquiry, the librarian of Dartmouth in a letter to me stated that the college had no record of any Indian by that name having studied there.

47 Drury, *F.W.W.*, II:282.

48 *T.O.P.A.*, 1880, p. 36.

49 Ibid., p. 23.

50 Frederick Merk, *The Monroe Doctrine and American Expansion*, 1843-1849, p. 23.

51 Ibid., p. 78.

52 Hulbert, *O.P.*, VIII:161.

53 Lockley, *Oregon Trail Blazers*, p. 352.

54 Bancroft, *Oregon*, I:511 ff.; Keith Clark and Lowell Fuller, *Terrible Trail*, Carton, 1966.

55 Sarah J. Cummins, Autobiography and Reminiscences, La Grande, Ore. (1914?), Chapter VIII.

56 The Indians of Old Oregon called the Americans "Boston men," since the first Americans they met were sailors who came from Boston. Englishmen were referred to as "King George's men."

57 *W.H.Q.*, I (1907):151.

58 See Appendix 5 for list of writings of Josiah Osborn and of his daughter Nancy Osborn Jacobs.

59 Minutes of the *Synod of Washington*, 1936, p. 292.

60 A full list of the textbooks ordered by Whitman is in Hulbert, *O.P.*, VIII:181.

61 Joel Palmer, *Journal of Travels over the Rocky Mountains*, Cincinnati, 1847, p. 57. Bancroft, *Oregon*, I:522, called this work "one of the best of its kind."

62 Hulbert, *O.P.*, VIII:206.

63 Italics are the author's.

64 Pringle ms., p. 12.

65 From undated clipping, now in Eastern Washington State Historical Society, from Portland *Journal* containing an article by Fred Lockley about Elizabeth.

66 Delaney, *A Survivor's Recollections*, p. 9.

67 See Appendix 6.

68 See Chapter Sixteen, fn. 27.

69 Pringle ms., p. 15.

70 *Ibid.*, p. 18.

71 Italics are the author's.

72 Pringle ms., pp. 16-7.

73 Brouillet, *House Document*, p. 25.

74 Whitman Letter 184, with postscript dated Feb. 27.

75 The news was published in the Nov. 12, 1846, issue of the Oregon *Spectator*, under the heading "HIGHLY IMPORTANT NEWS."

76 Italics are the author's.

[CHAPTER TWENTY-ONE]

PRELUDE TO TRAGEDY, SEPTEMBER 1846–NOVEMBER 1847

The Whitmans began their tenth year of residence at Waiilatpu in the fall of 1846 under favorable circumstances. In his letter to Greene of September 6, Whitman wrote: "I think we have at no time been as much in the affections of the people as now. A much kinder disposition is manifested toward us, now more than at any former period,—exhibiting the feeling that they could not do without us." On November 3, he wrote again to Greene: "I have never felt more contented in my work and that I was usefully employed than for the last year and at present."

Narcissa expressed similar views in her letter of February 8, 1847, to Mrs. Alvin T. Smith: "We some times talk about going to the Willamette ourselves to live—not that we wish to leave the Indians so long as they will let us stay among them—but if the necessity should come that we must leave them, then we shall find it pleasant to seek some quiet spot among the society of our friends where we may enjoy something of the foretaste of our eternal rest... As it regards the Indians at this station, we feel that our influence for good was never greater among them, than now." And on the following May 19, Whitman in another letter to Greene wrote: "We think the affairs of this Station in regard to the Indians [are] in a very favorable state, such as gives promise of still continued prosperity."

But this was the lull before the storm; the prelude to the final tragedy.

It should be remembered that these favorable conditions prevailed after Dr. McLoughlin, Nesmith, and others had advised Whitman in the spring of 1845 to move from Waiilatpu. The fact that he had weathered several crises gave Whitman a false feeling of security. He relied too much on the goodwill of the natives.

An unfavorable development for the safety of the Whitmans at Waiilatpu came in the summer of 1846 when Archibald McKinlay, who had been so influential in restraining the violence of the Cayuses, was succeeded by William McBean as Chief Trader in charge of Fort Walla Walla. In 1832 Simpson had written the following appraisal of McBean: "...a half breed—about 25 years of age—4 years in the service, writes a fair hand and understands common accounts which is the extent of his education—neither bright nor useful and as yet being equal to the charge of a small Post." [1] McBean had been given charge of a small post at Fraser's Lake, New Caledonia, in 1841, where, evidently, he had made good or he would not have been given the responsibility of being placed in charge of Fort Walla Walla. Whitman informed Greene of the change of command in his letter of September 8, 1847, and stated that McBean was a "papist." McBean did not have the force of character of McKinlay and thus was unable to control the impetuous Cayuses. Being a Roman Catholic, he was sympathetic to the plans of the priests when, in the fall of 1847, they attempted to establish two missions in the vicinity of Waiilatpu. Of this, more will be said later.

Another change in the affairs of the Hudson's Bay Company in Oregon is worthy of note. Dr. McLoughlin retired in the spring of 1846 and moved to Oregon City where, in 1849, he took out American citizenship. McLoughlin ruled, as some have said, as the "uncrowned king of Oregon" for twenty-two years, 1824–1846. So great was his influence over the Indian tribes of Oregon during those years that none dared make war against the whites. It appears to be more than a coincidence that, within eighteen months of his retirement, the Cayuse Indians attacked Waiilatpu. It may be that these Indians had become aware of the declining influence of the Hudson's Bay Company and, therefore, felt free of former restraints.

The Emigration of 1846

The emigration of 1846 was smaller than that of the preceding year. Bancroft estimated that about 2,500 left the Missouri frontier that year, of whom 1,500 or 1,600 went to Oregon, the others going to California.[2] A new route to the Willamette Valley, which branched off the Old Oregon Trail below Fort Hall, had been explored and opened by Jesse and Lindsay Applegate. It followed the Humboldt River, crossed some mountains to the Pit River, then by way of the Klamath Lakes, it finally reached the Willamette. With the opening of the road along the Umatilla in 1845, and this new southern route across the Cascades in 1846, the Whitman mission no longer enjoyed a favored position on the Oregon Trail. It was now on a side road, and only those in urgent need of provisions, the sick, or the weary took the longer route past Waiilatpu. To Whitman's disappointment, these new developments meant that he was unable to sell sufficient provisions to the immigrants to bring his station to a self-supporting basis.

In his letter to Greene of September 8, Whitman said that the immigration had arrived in Oregon much earlier than had been the case in previous years and that: "Thus far no calls have been made upon me for provisions." He also reported: "Mrs. Spalding has a brother who arrived here this morning and is on his way to the station [i.e., to Lapwai]." Horace Hart, a younger brother of Eliza, remained with the Spaldings for more than a year until the family was forced to leave Lapwai after the Whitman massacre. He was the only near relative of any member of the Oregon Mission who went out to Oregon during the mission period. To Narcissa's keen disappointment, no member of her family was among the 1846 immigrants.

Among those who called at Waiilatpu that fall was Anson Sterling Cone, who in later years told how he and his brother Aaron had arrived at the mission about the middle of October and, being in need of a pack horse, proposed to Whitman that they be allowed to work out the price of a horse. "Boys," replied Whitman, "you had better take 'Bob' there and all the provisions you need and go at once. At the end of the season, there will be those coming who will have to stay here anyhow and I had better have work for them." So the Cone brothers took the horse, a trusty white Cayuse pony, and the next summer paid Whitman $25.00 for it and for the provisions received.[3] Anson Cone remembered the doctor as being "sociable and a good joker." Later he served on the jury which convicted the five Cayuses for their part in the Whitman massacre.

From previous experience, Whitman knew that he could expect some needy families of the immigration to stop over at Waiilatpu. Such was the case in the fall of 1846. On November 3, Whitman reported to Greene: "...a party came this way and as is usual with the last of the [immigration]... some among [them] were in very needy circumstances, their teams being very much reduced and quite unfit to proceed. A number also were sick and stopped to winter with us. Six families and some young men remain. The families do not expect to go on until they can pass the Cascade Mountains in June. I shall try to employ them to the advantage of the Mission and the Indians, so as to give them a living, but not to call for funds from the Board. I wish much to have the Indians aided in fencing and ploughing their land." Among those who remained at Waiilatpu to work for Whitman was Joseph Stanfield.[4]

In Whitman's letter to Greene of April 1, 1847, we find more details regarding the 1846 immigration. He wrote: "Of those who stopped, four were very sick. Two or three must have died in all probability if they had not stopped & obtained Medical aid & rest. Three births have occurred also among those who stopped: —the expectation of that event caused them to stop with us for the winter. In all six families besides eight young men wintered with us."

By the time Whitman wrote this letter, he had learned of the great suffering endured by the part of the immigration which had taken the Applegate cut-off. This news caused him to write: "The disaster was great again last year to those who left the track which I made for them in 1843 as it has been in every attempt to improve it. Not that it cannot be improved but it shows what it requires to complete a safe passage and may not fail to demonstrate what I did in making my way to the States in the winter of 42 and 43 after the third of October. It was to open a practical route & safe passage and [make] a favourable report of the journey... which, in connection with other objects caused me to leave my family & brave the toils & dangers of the journey... In connection with this let me say the other great object for which I went was to have the Mission from being broken up just then which it must have been as you will see by a reference to the doing of [the Prudential] Committee which confirmed the recall of Mr. Spalding only two weeks before my arrival in Boston."

Here again Whitman commented on the reasons for his journey East in 1842–43: to promote Oregon emigration and to save his Mission.

THE WINTER OF 1846–1847

Although exact figures are lacking it appears that between forty-five and fifty white people were living at the Whitman mission during the winter of 1846–47. This number would have included the three families and the five single men who were living at the sawmill [Letter 210]. The fact that Whitman sent eight men to the mill is evidence of the importance he placed on getting rails split for fences and lumber sawed for buildings.

By the fall of 1846 Whitman realized that no real progress could be made in inducing the Indians to cultivate until their fields could be fenced. When away on expeditions for food they had to leave their fields unattended with the result that their crops were often destroyed by wandering horses or cattle. Sometimes the offending animals belonged to Whitman with the result that he was blamed for the damage.

Commenting on his work with the natives Whitman wrote to Greene on April 1 1847: "The Indians continue to give the same degree of attention to religious instruction as formerly. I have made large preparation to aid them in cultivating by getting near 20 thousand rails split for them & I hope to plough additional prairie for them as much as they can fence." On the following May 19, he reported having men plowing with "two large ploughs with strong ox teams for three weeks, and shall continue for about two weeks more" [Letter 215].

Whitman's great desire to see the Indians settled never abated. He firmly believed that they would have to abandon their age-old habits of going hither and yon in search of food and settle down and be farmers before they could be educated and Christianized. As has been stated, this was exactly the policy of the United States Government in its dealings with the eastern Indians, except that the government was not especially interested in Christianizing but rather in civilizing them.

As the Whitmans entered upon their tenth year of residence at Waiilatpu, Marcus was able to tell Greene that his wife's health was "better than in some former years" [Letter 200]. Certainly her letters written during these months reflect a happy, contented spirit. On November 3, in a letter to her mother, Narcissa wrote: "We set the table for more than twenty every day three times—and it is a pleasing sight." Nineteen-year-old Mary Johnson, a daughter of one of the immigrant families, was hired for $1.50 a week to assist Narcissa. The services of a kindhearted, motherly woman by the name of Mrs. Pugh were also secured. Of her Whitman wrote to Walker: "We have a fine, pious old lady, fifty-seven years old, who does work for her board but keeps her own sugar & coffee. It is sewing that she does mostly" [Letter 209a]. With better health and reliable help in the home, Narcissa was able to write on November 2: "I never have been more comfortably situated for the winter than I am now."

Whitman was called to Lapwai during the first part of December to attend Mrs. Spalding, who gave birth to a daughter on December 12. She was called Amelia and was the last of the four Spalding children. In addition to three babies born to immigrant women at Waiilatpu that fall, Whitman was also called to Fort Walla Walla on an obstetrical case before the end of the year.

Since Andrew Rodgers was concentrating on his ministerial studies and at the same time trying to master the Nez Perce language, the Whitmans hired William Geiger to teach the school for white children. Geiger, who had taken care of the Whitman station during most of the time Whitman was away in 1842–43, had gone to the Willamette Valley in the fall of 1843. He was a reliable person whom the Whitmans were delighted to welcome back to Waiilatpu.

In her letter to Mary Walker dated November 6, 1846, Narcissa said: "Mr. Geiger is one of the best teachers and managers of children I ever saw. He has concluded to stay until Feb." Whitman wrote to the Methodist missionaries at The Dalles and offered to provide room and board to any of their children whom they might wish to send to the school for $1.25 per week [Letter 199]. The Spaldings sent their two eldest children, Eliza and Henry, and six or seven from the immigrant families attended. The total enrollment, therefore, was about eighteen.

The Whitmans, especially Narcissa, continued to enjoy the fellowship of Andrew Rodgers. She felt that he would have made a good husband for her sister Jane and was instrumental in getting the two to exchange a few letters. Writing to Jane on April 15, 1847, she said: "I can assure you it is no small comfort to have some one to sing with who knows how to sing, for it is true, Jane, I love to sing just as well as ever.

From what I have heard of Edward, it would be pleasant to hear him again; as for you, kala tilapsa kunku⁵ (I am longing for you continually to sing with), and it may be, put us all together, with the violin which Mr. Rodgers plays, we should make music such as would cause the Indians to stare." And in this same letter, she wrote: "We talk, sing, labour, and study together; indeed, he is the best associate I ever had, Marcus excepted, and better than I ever expect to get again, unless you and Edward come and live with me." Rodgers was able to relieve Whitman in taking over much of the responsibility for the Sunday worship services for white residents at Waiilatpu. Often a sermon by the well-known Presbyterian minister, the Rev. Albert Barnes of Philadelphia, would be read. Occasionally Rodgers would read "a discourse of his own composition in the form of a dissertation," as a part of his theological course [Letter 208].

SEVERITY OF THE WINTER WEATHER

The severity of the winter of 1846–47 in the Old Oregon country has sometimes been listed as one of the causes contributing to the restlessness of the natives. Catherine Sager wrote: "This was the coldest winter ever known in this country. Snow lay three feet deep on the ground for several weeks and the winter was bitterly cold. The mill stream was so frozen that no grinding could be done for some time, and so we lived on boiled wheat and corn in the meantime."⁶

Spalding reported that the winter was "the severest winter as to snow, cold weather, & want of grass ever known by the oldest Indians in the region."⁷ On the 16th and 17th of January, the thermometer at Lapwai dipped to 30° below zero. The Indians in their skin or woven mat lodges were ill-prepared for such severe cold weather. Spalding estimated that the Nez Perces lost about one half of their horses and cattle. Wild game likewise suffered, which in turn meant less food from the hunt. The diaries of Elkanah and Mary Walker tell of the great loss of horses and cattle suffered by the Hudson's Bay Company and the Indians of their area. On March 1, 1847, Walker noted that only twenty horses had survived from the Company's herd of 220 at Fort Colville and on April 6, he wrote that one of the chiefs of the Spokane Indians had only two head of cattle left out of a band of fifty. Walker and Eells were able to save most of their animals because they had laid up a supply of grain and fodder, but even so they were obliged to cut down trees in order to give their horses and cattle a chance to eat the pine needles and the tree moss.

Since Waiilatpu was located in a more southerly zone, the loss of animals was not as great there as further north; nevertheless Whitman, in his letter to Greene of April 1, 1847, wrote: "At our station we have had a heavy loss in sheep, calves, and some cattle (old cows), colts & horses." Since Whitman had not been able to sell much, if any, corn and wheat to the immigrants of 1846, he had a supply on hand to feed his livestock. His reference to a "heavy loss" was to that suffered by the natives. The Indians in the vicinity of Waiilatpu did not lose as many horses and cattle as did the Nez Perces and the Spokanes, yet the severe winter seems to have contributed to their restlessness. Catherine Sager wrote: "The natives blamed the white people for bringing the cold."

TROUBLE AT LAPWAI

Although the attitude of the natives at Waiilatpu remained friendly during the winter of 1846–47, such was not the case at Lapwai. On February 3, 1847, Spalding wrote a long letter of twenty-seven foolscap pages to Greene in which he gave a gloomy picture of the situation he faced. A rough element among the Nez Perces, inspired by Old James, the medicine man and chief who lived in the Lapwai Valley, had so terrorized those who wanted to continue in the mission school that it had to be closed. Windows were broken, property stolen or destroyed, and the lives of the Spaldings threatened.[8] "What heart have I to replace the windows and repair the roof to the meeting house," wrote Spalding, "when it is almost certain that the windows will be immediately broken out again. If I build a good fence, it is with the probability that it will be burnt up by those who may camp near it... We are now called upon to pay for the water we use, the wood we burn, the trails we travel in, and the air we breathe."

When Whitman heard of the harassments which the Spaldings were experiencing, he became increasingly concerned about what might happen at Waiilatpu. If a small band of unruly Nez Perces could cause so much trouble, what might the more volatile Cayuses do if they got stirred up. Whitman found it necessary to go to Fort Vancouver for supplies in the early spring of 1847. In a letter written at the Fort on April 1, he said: "...we live at all times in a most precarious state not knowing whether to stay or go nor at what time nor how soon. Whether it may be demanded by the Indians or the Board, I think in the course of the ensuing summer I shall locate claim for land in this lower Country to be ready in case of retirement."

THE METHODISTS GIVE WASKOPUM TO THE AMERICAN BOARD

A surprising development came in 1847: the Methodists gave their Waskopum station to the American Board. Seven years earlier, some members of the Oregon Mission of the American Board, especially A. B. Smith, had been considering giving their work in Oregon to the Methodists. Now the very opposite happened.

Here is the background of events. The Rev. George Gary who succeeded Jason Lee as superintendent of the Methodist Mission in Oregon, arrived in the Willamette Valley on June 1, 1844, with instructions to liquidate the Mission property as soon as possible. The last station to remain in Methodist hands was Waskopum at The Dalles where the Rev. A. F. Waller was in charge, assisted by the layman, H. B. Brewer. It is possible that Gary had written to Whitman sometime before September 1846 suggesting that the American Board assume the responsibility for Waskopum. In his letter to Greene of September 8, Whitman brought up the subject: "The Methodists have been upon the point of relinquishing their last station at the Dalls [sic]. A most important point to be kept. This would make a good addition to us." Whitman appreciated the strategic location of Waskopum on the road linking upper Oregon with the Willamette settlements.

Whitman was most receptive to the suggestion that the American Board take over the Methodist work at The Dalles, for this possibility dovetailed into another plan which Whitman had in mind. He had repeatedly urged Greene to send a minister to assist him at Waiilatpu. On February 25, 1846, Greene wrote to Whitman: "I am aware that you are alone—that your profession is not that of a preacher—and that if you give a larger share of your time to the spiritual concerns of the Indians, not a little of what you are now doing must be neglected, or at least attended to imperfectly. And it is in view of your destitution of helpers that I suggested in one of my letters whether Messrs. Eells and Walker should not abandon or suspend their operations at Tshimakain and remove one of them to your station, and the other to some point –perhaps Kamiah." [9] Greene's suggestion that Tshimakain be closed and its ministers reassigned suggested the possibility that one of them might go to Waskopum.

Of the three stations of the Oregon Mission, that among the Spokanes was always the least promising. The field did not offer the same agricultural possibilities as the Clearwater and Walla Walla Valleys. Spokane Garry, who had spent several years at the Red River Mission school, and from whom so much was expected, had failed to cooperate. His refusal to give up polygamy may have been a reason for his attitude.

The two missionary couples lived at Tshimakain for eight years without having the joy of seeing a single Spokane Indian convert join the Mission church. Greene's suggestion, therefore, that Tshimakain be abandoned was reasonable. A serious objection, however, lay in the fact that the two couples had learned the Spokane and not the Nez Perce language. This meant that if they were transferred, they would have to use interpreters or set themselves to the laborious task of learning another language.

We do not know when Whitman received Greene's letter of February 25, 1846; circumstantial evidence indicates that he had received it before he called on Superintendent Gary of the Methodist Mission at Oregon City in March 1847. When Gary asked Whitman whether the American Board was interested in taking over Waskopum, the latter replied: "...if they had not taken that station in the spring of 1838, *we should have done so in the fall*" [Letter 215]. Gary and Whitman made no final arrangements at that time for the transfer of the property as Whitman wanted to discuss the proposal with his associates. Undoubtedly Whitman was then considering the possibility of having the Eells family live at Waiilatpu and the Walkers move to The Dalles. A meeting of the Mission was scheduled for Tshimakain during the last week of May or the first of June. Final decisions on this important matter had to be postponed until that time.

When Marcus returned to Waiilatpu and told Narcissa of the possibility that the Oregon Mission might obtain the Methodist station at The Dalles and of the need to have the Mission vote on this proposal at its annual meeting, Narcissa felt that she should attend. Writing to Mary Walker on March 30, she said: "I shall be strongly tempted to go to

Tshimakain... I mean I would go if I could, and shall be tempted to try, or would if I could ride native fashion, but I do not know how, neither do I think I can learn." Narcissa had not been to Tshimakain since the summer of 1841 nor had she left Waiilatpu since the late fall of 1843. Her desire to go overcame her scruples about the impropriety of white women riding astride for, as will be told, she made the trip.

Sometime during the middle of May, Eells arrived at Waiilatpu in order to get supplies which Whitman had brought up the river from Fort Vancouver. This gave Whitman an opportunity to discuss with him the idea of closing Tshimakain and of having the Eells family move to Waiilatpu and the Walkers to Waskopum. Eells was inclined to accept the plan but wanted to discuss it with the Walkers before giving his final decision. After arrangements were made for Mary Johnson to take care of all of the children except Catherine Sager, who was to go, Eells with Mrs. Whitman, Rodgers, and Catherine set out for Tshimakain on May 18. Whitman who was able to travel much faster than the Eells party, remained at Waiilatpu for a few days to help the last immigrants who had wintered there leave for the Willamette Valley.

On May 18, just a few hours before the Eells party left, Whitman received a letter from Waller and Brewer stating that they had been authorized by Gary to give the Waskopum station complete with buildings and improvements "without charge" to the Oregon Mission. Reporting this new development in a letter to Greene dated May 19, Whitman stated that the Methodists wanted to transfer the property during the course of that summer or early fall. Whitman wrote: "This will open a new field for our Mission and one we can by no means fail to occupy. For if we allow the Papists to take this station, we might as well give up this [Waiilatpu] also. Immediate action will be had in the matter at our coming meeting... Your letters to the Mission in regard to Tshimakain Station may have something to do with the taking of the station at the Dalls [sic]."

The Eells party, traveling by easy stages, arrived at Tshimakain on Thursday, May 27. One of the Cayuse Indians who went along to help with the packing and the care of the animals was Frank Escaloom (Ish-ish-kais-kais). Members of the Eells party quickly told the Walkers of the prospective closing of Tshimakain and of their possible transfer to Waskopum. Both Elkanah and Mary were dismayed. Elkanah wrote in his diary on the 29th: "I wished I was out of the mission." Mary showed a more determined spirit when she wrote in her diary the next day: "Our minds are made up, let others do as they may, we will remain where we are at present." Narcissa, who enthusiastically favored the idea of having the Oregon Mission take over the Waskopum station, tried to persuade Mary to agree to the transfer. On June 1, Mary wrote in her diary: "Mrs. W. took dinner & supper with us. In the afternoon we talked over the disagreeable matters." [10]

Whitman and Spalding, coming over separate trails, arrived at Tshimakain on Wednesday evening, June 2. Thus all members of the Mission were present except Mrs. Spalding, in what proved to be their last business meeting. Early Thursday morning, Whitman asked Walker to join him in a walk. "He opened the subject to me of my going to the Dalles," wrote Walker in his diary. "I told him that he should not think of my going there." Whitman outlined the plan to Spalding who at once enthusiastically endorsed the idea. When Eells discovered the opposition of the Walkers, he tried to take a neutral position. On Friday, Walker, after considerable persuasion, finally consented to visit Waskopum and make a first-hand investigation. Mary wrote in her diary that evening: "The Mission expressed a unanimous wish that we should go & Mr. W. concluded to harken... Much feeling was manifested on the occasion. We find it very trying to our feelings to think of separating or of leaving these people." Narcissa, in her last extant letter to her mother dated July 4, 1847, told of the decision and wrote: "All seemed to feel that we had come to an important crisis and that God alone could and must direct us."

The Whitmans and the Spaldings left for their respective homes on Monday, June 7. Walker left two days later. He rode first to Waiilatpu where Whitman joined him in the ride to The Dalles. In spite of all the arguments that Whitman was able to muster in favor of the Walkers moving to Waskopum, Walker was unconvinced. He saw the importance of keeping this station in Protestant hands. He knew that he was the logical choice of his brethren to occupy that strategic place. Yet, the very thought of starting life in another frontier post in the midst of a tribe speaking a different language filled him with dread. After being away from his home for three weeks and after a weary 600-mile horseback ride, Walker returned to Tshimakain on June 30. He found his wife deeply opposed to the suggested move. She was pregnant and was to give birth to her sixth child, a son, on December 31ˢᵗ. On July 2, Walker wrote in his diary: "Mrs. Walker said that my going to the Dalls would be at the peril of her life. That at once decided me." [11]

THE SUMMER OF 1847

On July 4, 1847, Alanson Hinman unexpectedly arrived at Waiilatpu. After serving as a teacher of the school for white children at the Whitman station during the winter of 1844–45, Hinman had gone to the Willamette Valley, where, for a time, he was employed by the Methodists to teach in their Oregon Institute. He had married a young woman, Martha Gerrish, who had gone out to Oregon with her family in 1845, and they had become the parents of a child. Hinman had returned to the upper Columbia country with the idea of borrowing the Mission press "for the purpose of printing another paper in the Willamette" [Letter 217]. Whitman was agreeable to the plan, but asked Hinman to call on the three other men of the Mission to get their consent. All agreed; thus Hinman was able to take the press to The Dalles. Thus it escaped the fate of being lost or destroyed when the Spaldings were obliged to abandon their station.[12]

On July 13, Whitman still had not heard of Walker's decision not to go to The Dalles, for on that day he wrote to Walker and told of the arrival in the Willamette Valley of the Rev. William Roberts, who was the successor to Gary. Roberts, however, was to concentrate on Methodist work for white settlers. He was, therefore, as eager as his predecessor to transfer the Methodist property at Waskopum to the American Board.

Sometime before July 26, Whitman received a letter from Walker stating that he and his wife were unwilling to go to The Dalles; they would remain at Tshimakain with the Eellses. Whitman was deeply disappointed. Narcissa in her letter to her mother, begun on July 4, wrote: "Mr. W. is unwilling to remove with his family this year, on account of Mrs. W. being in a state of pregnancy, which was known at the time of the meeting but not made an objection." [13]

In Whitman's last extant letter to Walker, dated July 26, he expressed his regret that Walker could not act "in accordance with the action of the Mission." On July 30 Mary noted in her diary: "Mr. W. received a rather severe letter from Dr. W." The whole affair caused the Walkers much unhappiness.

Walker's refusal to move with his family to The Dalles placed Whitman in a difficult position. Negotiations with the Methodists had already proceeded to such an extent that he felt he could not honorably withdraw. On August 3, Whitman in a letter to Greene said: "We cannot let this station go into other hands than ours if they [i.e., the Methodists] give it up. Should it fall into other hands, it might at once become a papal station or a petty trading post—if not a grog shop." The season was too late for another Mission meeting to be called. The only course open to Whitman was to hire someone to take temporary possession of Waskopum in the hope that the American Board would send out a qualified missionary to occupy the station. Circumstantial evidence indicates that Whitman was able to see Hinman before the latter left for The Dalles with the mission press and that Hinman expressed his willingness to accept the responsibility of taking charge of the Waskopum property for the time being.

Whitman then thought of his nephew Perrin, who had by that time acquired an excellent command of the Nez Perce language and who had often conducted religious services for the Cayuse Indians "much to their satisfaction." Perrin expressed his willingness to go and spend the winter with the Hinmans at Waskopum. In his letter to Greene of September 13, Whitman explained the arrangements: "The religious instruction of this place will devolve on Perrin B. Whitman, my nephew, who will only be eighteen years old in April. But in many respects he is promising & has had a good degree of experience with me... Neither Mr. Spalding nor myself can at all compare with him in speaking or reading the Nez Perce language." The Indians at The Dalles, however, spoke the language of the Walla Walla Indians which differed from the Nez Perce tongue. Anticipating his new responsibilities, Perrin began a study of the Walla Walla language using some linguistic aids prepared by H. K. W. Perkins before he left Waskopum [Letter 219].

In Whitman's letter to Greene of August 3, he mentioned the fact that the Mission at its June meeting had accepted his proposal to build "houses at this Station, so that the Mothers of the families of this Mission might winter here and send their children to school... I have an abundance of lumber sawed—but recent developments show that the houses will not be required this year for any except it may be for Mrs. Spalding." Whitman's plan was for all of the women of the Mission with their children to spend the winter months at Waiilatpu so that those of school age could attend the Mission school. The inventory of the property left at Waiilatpu after the massacre includes the item: "40,000 feet sawed lumber including timber & boards for two houses (32 x 26), ⅓ drawn to station, 20 miles at $25.00 per thousand. $1,000.00." [14] Whitman's vision of what could be done for the welfare of the Mission families far outran the willingness of his colleagues to accept his practical suggestions. Although the Walkers had two children of school age and the Eellses had one, neither family was willing to enroll them for the term beginning in the fall of 1847. Perhaps this reluctance grew out of a sensitivity engendered by the troubled Waskopum situation.

Whitman was not confining his building plans just to the accommodation of the families of the Mission. In his letter of September 13 to Greene, he wrote: "We must have two schools. One for the children of the Mission, and a boarding school for the natives." Here is evidence of Whitman's plans to expand his work for the natives at Waiilatpu before he learned of the intentions of the Roman Catholics to establish two missions in his vicinity.

THE HINMANS AND PERRIN WHITMAN MOVE TO WASKOPUM

Hinman with the mission press left for The Dalles sometime in August. After leaving the press at the Methodist mission, Hinman continued on to the Willamette Valley to get his family. Whitman and his nephew left for Oregon City about the middle of August, as Whitman needed to see Roberts about the transfer of the Waskopum station to the Oregon Mission. Whitman learned that Waller had come to feel that it was a great mistake for the Methodists to abandon their work at The Dalles. In his letter of September 13 to Greene, Whitman quoted Waller as saying: "He could not bear to have his denomination abandon the heathen of Oregon as it would do if they gave up this Station." Under Methodist polity, however, the superintendent, acting under instructions of the Methodist Missionary Society, could overrule the opinions of local workers. While in the Valley, Whitman made arrangements for a boat to carry the Hinman family and their possessions up the river to The Dalles, and then for the same boat to take the Waller and Brewer families and their possessions down the river.

Whitman, the Hinmans, and Perrin arrived at The Dalles sometime before September 7, as is indicated in the following taken from Whitman's letter of the 13th to Greene: "I write to let you know that our Mission has now taken this Station. Mr. Wallers and Brewers families left here on the 7th. instant when we came into possession according to previous arrangements." Whitman reported that the cost to the Mission was $721.13, which included the value of farming tools, some grain, livestock, household furniture, and moving expenses. The Methodists made no charge for the buildings, material improvements, or for their claim to 640 acres of land. Of this amount, Whitman was able to pay $69.75 which left a balance of $651.38 due to be paid the next year. In this letter, Whitman again urged Greene to send at least "one ordained Minister at the earliest date."

Having made the best possible arrangements for the occupation of Waskopum, Whitman hastened back to Waiilatpu to make such preparations as he could for the coming immigration.

Artist Paul Kane Visits Waiilatpu

During the summer and fall of 1847, two artists visited Waiilatpu and made sketches of natives. The first was Paul Kane, a Canadian, who traveled through the Pacific Northwest that summer sketching and painting pictures, especially of Indians. In his *Wanderings of an Artist*, he tells of his visit to Fort Walla Walla in July. After making an excursion to see Palouse Falls, he rode to Waiilatpu where he arrived on July 18. Kane reported that the day was "intensely hot" and that there was no shelter along the way to give relief from "the scorching rays of the sun." The Whitmans gave Kane a cordial welcome and he remained with them for four days. He was impressed with the material progress he saw at Waiilatpu and wrote of Whitman: "He had brought forty or fifty acres of land... under cultivation, and had a great many heads of domestic cattle, affording greater comfort to his family than one would expect in such an isolated spot."

Whitman took Kane to Tiloukaikt's camp. Kane wrote his impressions as follows: "These Indians, the Kye-use, resemble the Walla-Wallas very much. They are allies in war, and their language and customs are almost identical, except that the Kye-use Indians are far more vicious and ungovernable." It should be noted that Kane published his account of his visit to Waiilatpu after he had learned of the Whitman massacre and had discovered that two of the Cayuses he had sketched were ringleaders in it. This knowledge no doubt colored his description of the tribe and the following account of his experience with Tomahas: "Dr. Whitman took me to the lodge of an Indian called To-ma-kis, that I might take his likeness. We found him in his lodge sitting perfectly naked. (Evidently it was another hot day.) His appearance was the most savage I ever beheld, and his looks, as I afterwards heard, by no means belied his character. He was not aware of what I was doing until I had finished the sketch. He then asked to look at it, and inquired what I intended doing with it, and whether I was not going to give it to the Americans, against whom he bore a strong antipathy... I in vain told him that I should not give it to them; but, not being satisfied with this assurance, he attempted to throw it in the fire, when I seized him by the arm and snatched it from him. He glanced at me like a fiend and appeared greatly enraged, but before he had time to recover from his surprise, I left the lodge and mounted my horse, not without occasionally looking back to see if he might not send an arrow after me." [15]

According to J. Russell Harper, editor of *Paul Kane's Frontier*, Kane often made "minor and sometimes major changes" when he redrew and then painted his drawings.[16] The original sketch of Tomahas shows a benign, peaceful looking individual whereas the painted portrait corresponds with his description: "His appearance was the most savage I ever beheld."[17] [See comparison of Kane's sketch and the later portrait in this volume.] Kane also made two black and white sketches of "Til-au-kite." Although they differ from each other in several features, neither bears any likeness to the portrait, labelled to be that of Tiloukaikt, which is in the Royal Ontario Museum, Toronto, Canada. The sketches show Tiloukaikt to be an old man, and so he was called by Catherine Sager, whereas the painted portrait gives the likeness of a much younger man.[18]

Among the Kane sketches in the Royal Ontario Museum is one labelled "The Whitman Mission." The drawing was made while the artist was looking towards the southwest. The building as sketched appears to be a hodgepodge of rooms, some one story and others higher, without any uniform gable line, yet the location of doors, windows, and chimneys agrees rather closely with the floor plan of the house as drawn under the direction of Elizabeth Sager Helm. [See illustration in volume one.] It should be remembered that Kane was not making a finished drawing. This was nothing more than a rough sketch hastily drawn from which he may have expected to redraw a better picture at a later time. The grove of trees to the right of the house may have been the apple orchard which Whitman had planted in that location. Kane indicated a woodpile outside the central door which is also shown in Elizabeth Sager's outline. The absence of a uniform gable line and the lack of a distinct indication of the "T" shape have made positive identification difficult, yet indications, including the label, point to its being a completely authentic picture.

Possible Sketches of Marcus and Narcissa

In August 1968, Ross Woodbridge, an enthusiastic student of the Whitman story, went from his home near Rochester, New York, to Toronto in order to study a collection of between four and five hundred Kane sketches and paintings in the Royal Ontario Museum in that city. Knowing that Kane had spent several days with the Whitmans, Woodbridge was hoping to find something of interest in addition to the two known pictures labelled Tomahas and Tiloukaikt. Woodbridge was happy to find not only Kane's drawing of the Whitman house, but also two sketches which, although not labelled by Kane, might be of Marcus and Narcissa Whitman. Woodbridge was the first to propose this possibility. This tentative identification is based only on circumstantial evidence, yet, as will be indicated below, this is most convincing.

Before reviewing the evidence, it is well to note Kane's method of working. Drawing paper was scarce in the wilderness of Oregon and, therefore, the artist had to be parsimonious in its use. The Kane sketches in Toronto, of what might be Marcus and Narcissa, are on paper either torn or cut from a notebook or from some larger sheet. The page with the sketch of what might be Narcissa Whitman measures only 4 x 5⅛ inches (Museum No. 946.15.299) and that of what might be Marcus Whitman, 3½ x 4⅞ inches (No. 946.15.293).[19]

The description of Narcissa given by those who knew her harmonize with the Kane sketch thought to be of her.[20] She is reported to have weighed 167 pounds in 1844, and the drawing shows a woman who is rather plump. Gray wrote that her form was "full and round," and the Rev. Levi Fay Waldo mentioned her "well rounded features."

Kane's sketch shows a woman with full breasts. Matilda Sager wrote: "She had reddish colored hair, parted in the middle and combed back and twisted in a knot."[21] Others referred also to her custom of parting her hair in the middle, and this is the way Kane pictured her likeness. Matilda Sager has given us conflicting testimony regarding whether or not Narcissa would have worn a low-necked dress as indicated in Kane's sketch. In Matilda's pamphlet, A Survivor's Recollections, she tells that the half-breed Joe Lewis looted a wooden chest at the time of the massacre, which contained Narcissa's clothing, and gleefully displayed "five nice, fancy gauze kerchiefs of different colors, made to wear with a medium low-necked dress."[22] Yet, according to another account given by Matilda on March 26, 1928, in her eighty-ninth year and just eighteen days before she died, Mrs. Whitman "never had her bare neck exposed."[23] Summer temperatures in the Walla Walla Valley often rise above 100°; when high-necked dresses under those conditions would have been most uncomfortable. Kane, as has been stated, referred to extremely hot weather at the time of his visit to Waiilatpu. It is also possible that he took certain liberties with the neckline of the dress, making it lower than it actually was.

The drawing thought to be of Marcus has much stronger circumstantial evidence to support the identification. Several who knew Whitman commented about his carelessness of dress. In this sketch, Kane pictures a man wearing a buckskin jacket and what might be called a slouch hat. Several of the descriptions of Whitman refer to his prominent aquiline nose. An undated clipping from the Corning, New York, *Leader*, commented on a picture of Samuel Whitman, a younger brother of Marcus, as follows: "There was a marked family resemblance, and the picture shows how Dr. Whitman would have looked had he lived to an old age."[24] When a picture showing the profile of Samuel, taken in his old age (which may have been the one referred to by the editor of the Corning paper), is compared with the sketch made by Kane, a striking similarity can be seen.[25]

The most convincing circumstantial evidence to support the theory that this is an authentic drawing of Marcus Whitman is found in another sketch which, on first glance, appears to be nothing more than some idle doodling by the artist. This sketch is in the lower right hand corner of the drawing. When the page is turned upside down, one sees a sketch of what appears to be a girl with a long pole or rake in her hands standing by a bonfire or a pile of wood. The suggestion has been made that since Kane had been along the Palouse River before going to Waiilatpu, this might be a girl standing by a stream holding the handle of a fish net. However, would the artist put such a sketch on his page before he had drawn the likeness of Whitman?

A more plausible explanation connects this small drawing with an incident related by Matilda Sager Delaney in her pamphlet, *The Whitman Massacre*. Matilda, who was eight years old at the time Kane visited Waiilatpu, wrote: "An artist named Kane was sent out by the British Government. He took [i.e., drew] pictures of the Mission. We children were cleaning up the yard and varying labor by trying to balance the rake [handle] on our fingers. Mrs. Whitman reproved us, saying she did not want that in the picture." [26] This indeed might be a sketch of a Sager girl standing by a bonfire and holding the handle of a rake. If this be true, then the presence of the smaller sketch on the page with the picture of a man gives strong endorsement to the identification of the drawing as being a likeness of Marcus Whitman. [27]

The head of the girl in the original drawing measures only two millimeters in height, thus being too small for the artist to draw a face. However, under the left arm of the man is the face of a white girl. Was Kane planning to redraw this scene after he had returned to his studio and give the girl holding the rake this face? Perhaps so. Another unexplained mystery was the letter "W" which, when Woodbridge first examined the sketch, could be seen to the left of the brim of the hat the man was wearing. Did this letter stand for "Whitman"? [28]

After reviewing the evidence above mentioned, I am convinced that these sketches by Kane are authentic likenesses of Marcus and Narcissa Whitman. In this conviction, I am joined by a number of informed students of the Whitman story who, after making a similar study of the evidences, have come to the same conclusion. A few, however, remain doubtful. At my request, an artist friend of mine, Drury Haight, has redrawn and then painted the Kane sketches. This addition of color surely adds a note of brightness to help the imagination. These paintings have been reproduced as the frontispieces in this work.

Artist John Mix Stanley Visits Waiilatpu

The second artist who made a tour of the Pacific Northwest during the summer and fall of 1847, and who also visited Waiilatpu, was John Mix Stanley. Stanley, who hailed from the States of New York and Ohio, was touring the Great Plains and the Far West painting Indians. When he had completed his project, his portfolio contained pictures of Indians from forty different tribes. Stanley arrived at Fort Walla Walla on Saturday, September 25, where he spent a week or more painting Walla Walla Indians before going out to Waiilatpu where he hoped to meet the Whitmans and paint some Cayuse portraits. Unfortunately, when Stanley arrived at Waiilatpu, he found that both Dr. and Mrs. Whitman had gone to meet the immigrants on the Umatilla.

When Whitman and Perrin left Waiilatpu for the Willamette Valley about the middle of August 1847, they drove teams with two wagons to The Dalles where they left them and proceeded by boat down the Columbia the rest of the way to the Valley. Whitman found goods at Fort Vancouver which had been sent out by the American Board including a corn sheller, valued at $15.00 in the Whitman inventory, and a thresher worth $100.00. Whitman had requested Greene to send these items in his letter of October 25, 1844. It took about three years for them to arrive. On his return trip, Whitman took the machinery and other supplies by boat to The Dalles where they were loaded onto the wagons. Leaving Perrin with the Hinmans at Waskopum, Whitman returned to Waiilatpu with the two wagons having, perhaps, the assistance of an Indian. He arrived at his station about the middle of September.

On his way to The Dalles, Whitman had followed the road taken by the immigrants of previous years. Finding this filled with obstacles, Whitman on his return trip explored a new route. Of this Whitman wrote to Greene in his letter of October 18, which is the last extant letter that he wrote: "By following a small stream & then a dry ravine, I was enabled to avoid most of the hills & heavy obstacles to the old wagon road... After I came home, I went a second time which took me near two weeks and completed the route from the Utilla [i.e., Umatilla] to the place where I struck the old road before... This road takes them [i.e., the immigrants] a much shorter & better route by which they avoid many bad hills as well as all the sands of the Columbia and what is still more desirable, they have grass in abundance..."

A few days after Whitman left to guide the immigrants over the new road he had explored, Spalding arrived at Waiilatpu with a pack train loaded with wheat which he hoped to sell to the immigrants while they were along the Umatilla. Hearing of this, Narcissa decided to take the two Manson boys, John and Stephen[29] and Catherine Sager and go with him to the Umatilla, where she expected to meet her husband on his way back home.

Narcissa had a special reason for wishing to meet the immigrants; she was hoping to find a young woman who would be willing to teach the school for white children at Waiilatpu. Catherine in her reminiscences of the trip recalled that they did meet Dr. Whitman and that on Sunday, October 3, Spalding conducted a religious service for a party of immigrants. Because of the illness of a young man among the immigrants, the Whitmans were obliged to tarry for a few days, while the other members of the party returned to Waiilatpu on Monday, the 4th.

In her reminiscences, Catherine wrote that when they got back, they found "a young man there by the name of Stanley, just arrived from the lower country. He was an artist and was going on a tour through the country. He left next morning for Chimakain." During the absence of the Whitmans from Waiilatpu at the time of his visit, Stanley spent several days painting portraits of at least four Cayuses: Tiloukaikt, Tamsucky, Edward (son of Tiloukaikt whom Stanley called Painted Shirt or Shu-ma-hic-cie), and Waie-cat (son of Tamsucky). Stanley, disappointed in not seeing the Whitmans, promised to return in November, when he hoped to meet them and perhaps paint their portraits.

With the aid of some Indians, Stanley made his way up the Columbia River in a canoe to Fort Okanogan, stopping occasionally to paint. He then went to Tshimakain where, according to Mary Walker's diary, he arrived on Sunday, October 24. Stanley spent about a month at Tshimakain and Fort Colville continuing with his project of painting portraits of the natives. He started a portrait of eight-year-old Abigail Walker but, when she and some of her brothers came down with the measles, he had to lay the picture aside for several days. He went to Fort Colville on October 28 and returned to Tshimakain on November 9, when he completed Abigail's portrait and also painted her father.[30] The fact that the Walker children had measles is evidence that the epidemic, sweeping the Oregon country, had reached the Spokane area.

The Introduction of Measles

During the late summer of 1847 and the following fall and winter, a virulent form of measles and dysentery spread with devastating effects through all of Old Oregon, leaving an appalling harvest of death among the Indian tribes. Evidence of the presence of these diseases in the Walla Walla area before any of the 1847 immigration had arrived is to be found in an account told by the artist, Paul Kane.

A party of about two hundred Cayuse and Walla Walla Indians had left Fort Walla Walla about February 1, 1846, to go to Sutter's Fort in California to avenge the death of Elijah Hedding. After being gone for about eighteen months, many at Walla Walla began to believe that all had been killed. A dramatic incident took place at the fort the day after Kane had returned from his visit to Waiilatpu during the latter part of July, when a son of Peu-peu-mox-mox, a brother of the slain Elijah Hedding, suddenly arrived bearing sad news.

Kane, who was an eyewitness, wrote: "No sooner had he dismounted from his horse than the whole camp, men, women, and children, surrounded him eagerly inquiring after their absent friends, as they had hitherto received no intelligence, beyond a report that the party had been cut off by hostile tribes. His downcast looks and silence confirmed the fears that some dire calamity must have happened, and they set up a tremendous howl, whilst he stood silent and dejected with the tears streaming down his face. At length, after much coaxing and entreaty on their part, he commenced the recital of their misfortunes. After describing the progress of the journey up to the time of the disease (the measles) making its appearance, during which he was listened to in breathless silence, he began to name its victims one after another. On the first name being mentioned, a terrific howl ensued, the women loosening their hair and gesticulating in a most violent manner. When this had subsided, he, after much persuasion, named a second and a third, until he had named upwards of thirty." [31]

Kane became alarmed for the safety of the Whitmans when he learned that the Indians were inclined to blame the Americans for the introduction of the disease. He consulted with McBean who shared his concern. "I, therefore," wrote Kane, "determined to go and warn him [i.e., Whitman] of what had occurred. It was six o'clock in the evening when I started, but I had a good horse, and arrived at his house in three hours. I told him of the arrival of the messenger, and the excitement of the Indians, and advised him strongly to come to the fort, for a while at least, until the Indians had cooled down; but he said he had lived so long amongst them, and had done so much for them, that he did not apprehend they would injure him. I remained with him only an hour, and hastened back to the fort, where I arrived at one o'clock a.m."

Kane was surprised to see how calmly Whitman took the news. Evidently Whitman correctly evaluated the attitude of the Indians at that time. He had been warned repeatedly of the danger of remaining at Waiilatpu, but somehow every crisis had passed. Whitman had a streak of obstinacy in him which also might be called a sense of commitment to his task. In July 1847, when the above incident took place, Whitman was making preparations to meet the needs of another immigration. A high sense of duty, plus a strong faith in the providence of God, kept him at his station.

The deadly effects of the measles and dysentery epidemics, which swept through the Old Oregon country in 1847, were aggravated by the age-old custom of the Indians to use their sweat-house for the treatment of disease. The sweat-house was a low, dome-shaped hut in which the sick person would sit naked while steam would be generated by pouring water over hot stones. After spending some time in the superheated, steam-filled atmosphere, the patient would then rush out and plunge into a cold stream.[32] The shock to the body was often all that was needed to kill a person if, at the time, he had a high fever.

THE ROMAN CATHOLICS BEGIN TWO MISSIONS NEAR WAIILATPU

When Whitman was still at The Dalles in September, the first of the 1847 Oregon immigration began passing. He heard reports of the thousands who were on their way to Oregon and became convinced of the importance of being back at Waiilatpu in order to furnish supplies to those in need. Whitman arrived at Fort Walla Walla on his return trip on September 23 where he found seven Roman Catholic missionaries under the newly appointed Bishop of Walla Walla, the Right Rev. A. M. A. Blanchet, and learned to his dismay that the Catholics were planning to establish a number of stations in the upper Columbia River country, two of which were to be in the vicinity of Fort Walla Walla.

Bishop Blanchet was a younger brother of the Rev. Francis Norbert Blanchet,[33] who was made the first Archbishop of Oregon. As has been stated, Fathers F. N. Blanchet and Modeste Demers were the first Roman Catholic missionaries to arrive in Oregon, having arrived in the fall of 1838. A. M. A. Blanchet was consecrated at Montreal on September 27, 1846, for the newly created missionary diocese of Walla Walla which included the vast territory lying between the Rockies and the Cascade Mountains north of the Mexican border. Bishop Blanchet with several priests and lay workers, including Father Pascal Ricard, a Superior of the Oblates of Mary Immaculate, and Father J. B. A. Brouillet, arrived at Fort Walla Walla on September 5, where they were cordially welcomed by William McBean. According to Father Brouillet, Bishop Blanchet knew that "Towatowe [Young Chief], one of the Cayuse chiefs, had a house which he had destined for the use of the Catholic missionaries, and he intended to go and occupy it without delay."[34] As has been stated, Pambrun built a log cabin for Young Chief on the north bank of the Umatilla River, in the fall of 1840.[35] Since Young Chief was known to be friendly to the Roman Catholics and since he had made his cabin available to the priests, the Catholic missionaries were assured of a base of operations within the Cayuse tribe. Since Young Chief was absent on a hunt when the Catholic missionaries arrived at the Fort, the Bishop and his party were delayed in going to the Umatilla. Hence they were at the Fort when Whitman arrived on the 23rd.

SITE FOR THE SAINT ROSE MISSION SELECTED

While waiting for Young Chief to return, Bishop Blanchet and his associates consulted with Peu-peu-mox-mox about a possible site for a mission among the Walla Walla Indians. According to Father Ricard's journal, this chief was reluctant at first "to receive priests in his territory," but finally offered a location "on the right bank of the Columbia, at the mouth of the Yakima." This site was none other than that which W. H. Gray had selected for the station that he wanted to establish in the fall of 1839 and which was known as Shimnap, "about a day [journey] above Walla Walla."[36] The site is near present-day Richland, Washington.

Father Ricard wrote as follows of his visit to the proposed site: "I... there met several savages who were so well-disposed that, in spite of the poorness of the land and the lack of timber, I decided to establish myself there. I had promised to place the first mission of the Oblates in Oregon under the protection of Saint Rose of Lima. I therefore named the area 'Saint Rose,' and my mission 'Saint Rose Mission.'" [37] Father Ricard moved his few belongings to the site on October 12 after hiring two French Canadians at Fort Walla Walla to help him in the erection of a cabin. His mission work with the natives had barely gotten started before the Whitman massacre occurred, which brought everything to an abrupt end.[38]

WHITMAN MEETS CATHOLIC MISSIONARIES AT THE FORT

For several years before the coming of the Roman Catholic missionaries to Fort Walla Walla, Young Chief had indicated his preference for the Catholics, whereas, his brother, Five Crows was a Protestant. When Dr. White met with the Cayuses in May 1843, for the purpose of persuading them to accept his code of laws and then for them to select one to be High Chief, Young Chief was the first choice of the tribe to be appointed to this position.

Young Chief, however, stepped aside because he favored the Catholics while the majority of the people preferred the Protestants. So his brother, Five Crows, was then chosen.[39] This difference in religious preference may have caused a spirit of rivalry to grow up between the brothers. We know that two of the Chief Traders at Fort Walla Walla, Pierre Pambrun and William McBean, were Catholics and extended favors to both the Catholic priests and to Young Chief. In November 1847, just a few days before the Whitman massacre, Young Chief turned his log cabin over to Bishop Blanchet and Father Brouillet, who named it the Saint Anne Mission.

The following extract from the unpublished journal of Bishop Blanchet tells of his meeting with Dr. Whitman:[40] "September 23 & 24. Mr. Whitman stopped at the Fort on his return from the Dalles. He is very unhappy over the arrival of the Bishop of Walla Walla. He admits that he does not like Catholics as such. He even goes so far as to declare that it is not necessary to be baptized to be a Christian. He attributes the Bishop's appointment to the influence of Tawatoe (the Young Chief). He is going to do all that he can to keep the Indians from becoming Catholics. He accuses the Catholics of always having persecuted the Protestants...

and he has promised to color the catholic ladder with blood to demonstrate the intolerance of the Catholics. This he has already begun to do by saying many harmful things about the priests to Yellow Snake[41] [i.e., Peu-peu-mox-mox], chief of the Walla Wallas."

The reference to the "catholic ladder" needs an explanation. As has been stated, both the Roman Catholics and the Protestant missionaries in Oregon used what was called a "ladder" to present their respective versions of church history. This consisted of a board, perhaps ten feet tall and a foot wide, which had horizontal lines drawn across it to indicate the centuries following the birth of Christ. Pictures were drawn within each segment to illustrate certain aspects of history which either group wished to emphasize. The ladders were mutually uncomplimentary. Whereas the Catholic ladder gave a vivid picture of such "heretics" as Luther and Calvin being cast into a fiery hell, the Protestant ladder showed the victim to be the Pope.[42]

According to Ricard, Whitman was so agitated over the arrival of the Catholic missionaries at Walla Walla that one day, after butchering a steer, he "splashed the animal's blood" over a Catholic ladder and gave it to an Indian, as a symbol of what might happen if the Catholic priests were permitted to remain among the Cayuses.[43] On December 20, following the massacre, when Ogden met with some of the Cayuse chiefs, Edward, a son of Tiloukaikt, gave Ogden one of these blood-smeared ladders, and claimed that Whitman had said: *"You see this blood! It is to show you that now, because you have the priests among you, the country is going to be covered with blood! You will have nothing but blood."* [44]

Bishop Blanchet claimed that Whitman resorted to this dramatic gesture in order to demonstrate "the intolerance of the Catholics." Could it not be conjectured that this act revealed a deep latent fear in Whitman's mind regarding his own safety? Could he not have been afraid that the very presence of the Catholics would unleash forces among the natives, unknown to the Catholic missionaries, which would eventually take his life? If so, the animal's blood on the Catholic ladder would have been a symbol of his own blood.

On September 27, Bishop Blanchet noted: "Mr. McKay just arrived with his group from Vancouver. When he passed through the Dalles, Canassissi [a chieftain of that area] told him that the Indians desired to have some priests... Mr. McKay stated that two miles below the Methodist Mission, there is a wonderful site for a mission.... This same gentleman also said that Dr. Whitman paid 600 dollars for the mission property of the Dalles."

This "Mr. McKay" whom Bishop Blanchet mentioned was none other than Thomas McKay who was at the 1836 Rendezvous, where he first met the Whitmans and the Spaldings. It was he who, when he first realized that white women had crossed the Rockies, had said: "There is something that Dr. McLoughlin cannot ship out of the country so easily." And it was he who consulted with Whitman in the spring of 1838 regarding the education of his three sons when they were traveling to the States with Jason Lee. Although McKay remained friendly with Whitman, he had by the fall of 1847 thrown his sympathy so much toward the Roman Catholic missionaries that he was willing to recommend a site at The Dalles within two miles of the Methodist property which Whitman had just purchased.

George Simpson's "Character Book," in the archives of the Hudson's Bay Company, contains the following appraisal of McKay: "One of the best shots in the country and very cool and resolute among Indians; has always been employed on the most desperate service in the Columbia and the more desperate it is, the better he likes it. He is known to every Indian in that Department and his name alone is a host of strength carrying terror with it as he has sent many of them to their 'long home,' quite a 'blood hound' who must be kept under restraint; possesses little judgment and a confirmed liar but a necessary evil at such a place as Vancouver; has not a particle of feeling or humanity in his composition."

Being fully aware of McKay's reputation among the Indians, Whitman tried to hire him so that he would be at Waiilatpu. Of this McKay, in a statement made September 11, 1848, said: "Last fall, during my stay at Fort Walla Walla... the Doctor asked me to go and pass the winter with him, saying that he was afraid of the Indians. I told him I could not on account of my business... He told me also several times last fall that he would leave certainly in the spring for the Dalles. I am aware, moreover, that the Cayuses have a great many times ill treated Dr. Whitman."[45]

Father Brouillet baptized McKay at Fort Walla Walla on October 29, 1847. Following the example of his illustrious stepfather, Dr. McLoughlin, McKay "made an abjuration of heresy and a public confession of the

Catholic faith."[46] McKay was then forty-seven years old. Bishop Blanchet noted in his journal for Sunday, November 7: "First Communion and Confirmation for Mr. Thomas McKay, the half-breed man, a few days ago became a convert from Anglicanism."

CATHOLICS NEGOTIATE WITH YOUNG CHIEF AND TILOUKAIKT

Bishop Blanchet's journal reveals the fact that he was discussing with both Young Chief and Tiloukaikt the possibility of establishing a mission in the vicinity of Waiilatpu. Whitman was fearful of just such a move and this, no doubt, accounted for his outspoken opposition to the coming of the Catholic missionaries to the vicinity. After having lived with Cayuses for eleven years, he knew that this would mean trouble.

Father Brouillet wrote regarding the conference Whitman had with the priests at Fort Walla Walla on September 23 and 24: "He refused to sell provisions to the bishop, and protested that he would not assist the missionaries unless he saw them in starvation."[47]

Ignoring Whitman's objections to the establishment of a mission in the vicinity of Waiilatpu, and with little knowledgment of the Cayuse character or appreciation of the explosive issues involved, Bishop Blanchet and his clergy went ahead with their plans to establish the desired mission. Bishop Blanchet called Tiloukaikt to the fort on October 2 and asked him if he would have any objection "to Dr. Whitman's selling him some lumber." The very fact that the Bishop sought Tiloukaikt's permission to buy some of the lumber Whitman had on the grounds at Waiilatpu indicates the dictatorial power that Tiloukaikt was then exercising over Whitman. Tiloukaikt gave his consent for the purchase of the lumber, but wanted to consult his brother chiefs regarding the payment. He told the Bishop that "the Indians had prevented Mr. Spalding from building near Dr. Whitman." This evidently refers to the house that Whitman had proposed building for Mrs. Spalding and her children to be used during the school term, but which, for some reason, was not erected.

Bishop Blanchet's entry for October 2 continues: "He [Tiloukaikt] complained that Dr. Whitman had promised them many things but had not made good his promises. He related that he himself had told the Doctor that the Young Chief was master of all of his lands and that he had it in his power to permit the planting of a cross [a Catholic mission] there if he so chose; that the piece of ground where he (the Doctor) resided belonged to him." Here we see evidence that the Cayuses had come to appreciate their rights to land ownership. This had never been raised as an issue when, in 1836, they were eager to have missionaries settle in their midst.

On October 26, Young Chief called on Bishop Blanchet at the Fort. According to the Bishop's journal, when Young Chief was asked whether the Cayuses would welcome Catholic missionaries, he replied: "...that he would welcome them warmly, but suggested that they reside near Dr. Whitman. He said that through his wife he had rights over the land belonging to Tilocate [Tiloukaikt]; that he is willing to turn over some of this land to the Missionaries if Tilocate consents to it and that he would be very happy if the Mission were to be erected at the afore mentioned place."

Bishop Blanchet then sent his interpreter to interview Tiloukaikt about the possibility of getting land for a mission. The evident willingness of Bishop Blanchet to establish a Catholic mission adjacent to the Protestant station at Waiilatpu is astounding. Tiloukaikt sent back word that there was indeed "enough land for the Missionaries to locate on his domains," but added that he wanted to consult with the other chiefs first. He would then call on the Bishop. On Thursday, November 4, Tiloukaikt with several of his subchiefs, including one whom Brouillet called "Toursakay" [possibly Tamsucky] arrived at the Fort. A conference was held with the Bishop in the presence of McKay and, according to Brouillet, "all the persons at the fort who chose to witness it."[48]

Blanchet's account of the interviews is as follows: "Tilocate led the conversation and asked many questions, among others: *whether the Pope was the one who had sent the Bishop; whether he was the one who had told him to ask for land; how did the priest live in the Bishop's homeland*—that is to say, *who supplied them with the necessities of life; whether the priests would give gifts to the Indians; whether they would cultivate their land; whether they would help them build houses; whether they would provide food and clothing for the children*, and many other questions. After hearing what the Bishop had to say, Tiloukaikt stated that "he would give land for the Mission."[49]

Brouillet, in his report of the November 4 meeting at the Fort, wrote that Bishop Blanchet told Tiloukaikt that "he would not make presents to the Indians; that he would give them nothing for the land he asked;

that in case they worked for him, he would pay them for their work, and no more; that he would assist them neither in ploughing their lands nor in building houses, nor would he feed or clothe their children." [50]

The nature of many of the questions Tiloukaikt asked the Bishop reveals his interest in the material advantages which he hoped to receive should he permit the Catholics to build near Waiilatpu. The Bishop's clear statement that he would not pay for the land, nor would he give gifts or assist in ploughing, must have been deeply disappointing to Tiloukaikt. Whitman, Tiloukaikt knew, had helped the Indians plough and fence their fields, and then had built a mill and had ground their grain. Upon reflection, Tiloukaikt had some second thoughts.

On November 8, Bishop Blanchet sent Father Brouillet to inspect the site that Tiloukaikt had tentatively offered to make available for the Catholic mission. After meeting with the chief, Brouillet reported that Tiloukaikt "had changed his mind and refused to show it to me, saying that it was too small. He told me that he had no other place to give me but that of Dr. Whitman's, whom he intended to send away." Could it be that Tiloukaikt even then was planning to kill the Whitmans?

Bishop Blanchet gave a slightly different version of Brouillet's report by writing on November 10 in his journal: "He found that the Cayouse of Dr. Whitman are well disposed toward the [Catholic] missionaries. Tilocate and his young braves want to break away from Dr. Whitman. They have even proposed to Fr. Brouillet that he take up residence near them for the winter and they promised to give him Dr. Whitman's land early enough in the spring for planting. This offer, of course, could not be accepted because the Doctor could then say that the priests are trying to make him leave. Consequently, Fr. Brouillet went to see Tawatoe immediately and found him ready to donate his house and part of his land as he had formerly promised."

SAINT ANNE MISSION ESTABLISHED ON THE UMATILLA

On November 11 Bishop Blanchet sent one of the priests of his party, Father Rousseau "with two men and a wagon to make repairs on the house of Tawatoe." Rousseau returned to the Fort on Friday, November 26, with the report that the house had been renovated and was ready for occupancy. The next day the Bishop, Father Brouillet and Deacon LeClaire left Fort Walla Walla for the Umatilla and arrived at their destination about 3:30 p.m. The Bishop noted in his journal that the roof of the house had been "recovered with sod, the floors sealed, the doors and door-frames squared up and the chimneys rebuilt. Rush mats cover the floor..." Then in his characteristic style, referring to himself in the third person, he wrote: "The Bishop is happy to be able to say, along with his associates, that he is in his own house now, or at least that he has found shelter... This mission foundation among the Cayouse is under the protection of Saint Anne."

The Mission of Saint Anne was destined to have an existence of only a few weeks as the massacre at Waiilatpu began on the Monday following the arrival of the Bishop and his associates at Young Chief's.

AN APPRAISAL OF ROMAN CATHOLIC INVOLVEMENT

After the massacre, the Roman Catholic missionaries were severely criticized for their endeavor to establish a mission among the Cayuses so close to Waiilatpu. They should have realized, said some, that their very presence would have made trouble for the Protestants. In answer to such criticism, Father Brouillet wrote that at the time Bishop Blanchet and his party arrived at Fort Walla Walla, "it was publicly known that he had been for years speaking of leaving the Cayuse country." Brouillet made mention of Whitman's purchase of the Methodist station at The Dalles. "Under such circustances," Brouillet wrote, "it would not have been unnatural to believe that he would have liked to dispose of his property the same as any other individual."[51] Since Bishop Blanchet and his priests were new to Oregon, it could not be expected that they would appreciate the danger to which Whitman and his family were exposed by their proposal to establish a rival mission in the vicinity of Waiilatpu.

As has been stated, Whitman's concern about the activities of the Roman Catholic missionaries in the Oregon country dated back to 1838 when the first two arrived. One of the reasons why Whitman made his ride East in 1842–43 was to induce the American Board to take some steps to counteract the growing Catholic influence in Oregon.[52] His best suggestion was for the Board to sponsor the settlement of some Protestant families near its stations, especially near Waiilatpu.

In his last letter to Greene, dated October 18, 1847, Whitman mentioned hearing a report that the Catholics planned to establish colonies in the Walla Walla area. He then wrote: "I cannot blame myself that the plan I laid down when I was in Boston was not carried out. If we could have good families, say two & three together, to have placed in select spots among the Indians, the present crisis which I feared would not have come." [53]

We have no evidence that either the Cayuse or the Catholic missionaries ever had any suspicion of Whitman's plan to have Protestant families settle in the vicinity of Waiilatpu. If the Board had cooperated in such a plan, surely the Indians would have had added reason to be aroused. It is inconceivable that the presence of some Protestant families in the area would have prevented the massacre. On the other hand, this could well have hastened the tragedy.

The establishment of Saint Rose Mission, about forty miles to the northwest of Waiilatpu, and of Saint Anne Mission, about twenty-five miles to the south, marked the beginning of the end of the Oregon Mission of the American Board. Even had there been no measles epidemic and no subsequent massacre, the Whitmans would undoubtedly have moved to The Dalles in the spring of 1848, after having been flanked on two sides by Catholic missions. In that case, surely the families at Tshimakain and possibly the Spaldings at Lapwai would have been obliged also to leave their fields.

THE OREGON EMIGRATION OF 1847

The Oregon emigration of 1847 was larger than that of any preceding year. The best estimates indicate that over one thousand wagons and between four and five thousand people made the western trek that year. Chief Trader Grant at Fort Hall likened the straggling procession which filed past his post to a "travelling mob." [54] There was no over-all organization. Groups of immigrants banded themselves together for mutual protection. Young single men and small family parties were able to push on ahead of the main body. By August 23, Narcissa was able to write: "For the past two weeks immigrants have been passing, probably 80 or 100 wagons have already passed and 1,000 are said to be on the road" [Postscript to Letter 217].

Never before had the Cayuse Indians who lived along the Oregon Trail or the natives along the south bank of the Columbia River been so inclined to steal and to harass the immigrants as they were that fall. When Whitman was on his way back to Waiilatpu from his trip to The

Dalles for supplies in September, he heard many accounts of the Indians stealing livestock and personal property from the immigrants. In a few instances, Whitman was able to recover the stolen property. After his return to Waiilatpu, Whitman, as has been stated, hastened to the Umatilla to guide the immigrants over a new road to The Dalles. He then did what he could to warn the immigrants to be on their guard. John E. Ross told of meeting Whitman on the Umatilla who advised him to use great caution. Ross and his party later "found four families who had been robbed of their cattle and stripped of their clothing. Six women and some children were left naked." [55]

Another account by a member of the 1847 immigration, who was a child at the time, remembered how Whitman was able to retrieve some items belonging to her family which had been stolen by Cayuse Indians. Elizabeth Ann Coonc, in her old age, wrote: "Upon our robbery being reported to Dr. Whitman, he called the Indians together; they gathered in a half-circle in front of the doctor, wrapped in their blankets, many with their faces painted with war paint, and the doctor began to arraign them about the theft. I looked on, standing beside my father (John Fenn) and holding his hand. As the doctor proceeded and the guilty consciences of the Indians were awakened, from time to time, a knife, fork or frying pan would be dropped by an Indian from beneath his blanket and when Dr. Whitman had finished, most of the stolen property was lying about on the ground at the feet of the Indians. One of the Indians threw down a skillet with considerable force and, as I thought, at the doctor, but father said, 'No, they are mad.'" [56]

WHITMAN MEMORIALIZES CONGRESS

After his return from the Umatilla during the first part of October 1847, Whitman, stirred by what he had seen and heard of the harassments inflicted on the immigrants by the Indians, decided to memorialize Congress in an appeal for government protection. His memorial, dated October 16, was addressed "To the Honorable the Secretary of War, To the Committees on Indian Affairs & Oregon in the Senate & House of Representatives of the United States." [57]

The memorial embodies many of the suggestions he had included in his proposed bill which he had submitted to the Hon. James M. Porter, Secretary of War, following his return from his visit to Washington and

Boston in 1843.[58] Again Whitman pled for the government to establish "a line of posts along the travelled route to Oregon at a distance, of not more than fifty miles [apart]." As in his proposed bill, he stressed the importance of these being "farming stations" where agricultural products could be raised and made available both to the military and to the passing emigrants. The military units attached to such posts would be responsible for keeping the Indians in subjection, suppressing the traffic in "ardent spirits," and facilitating the transportation of the mails. Whitman estimated that "with a change of horses at every fifty miles," the mail could be carried from "one hundred to one hundred & fifty miles in twenty four hours." Here, again, he proposed a pony express.

Stressing the need of protection from marauding Indians, Whitman wrote: "Immigrants now lose horses and other stock by the Indians, commencing from the border of the States to the Willamette. It is much to the praise of our countrymen that they bear so long with the Indians when our Government has done so little to enable them to pass in safety. For one man to lose five or six horses is not a rare occurrence." Whitman mentioned especially the harassment suffered by the immigrants along the Columbia River: "The timid Indians on the Columbia have this year in open day, attacked several parties of wagons from two to seven, & robbed them, being armed with guns, bows & arrows, knives & axes." He referred in particular to a "Mr. Glenday from St. Charles, Mo.,... [who] with Mr. Bear his companion, rescued seven wagons from being plundered & the people from gross insult, rescuing one woman when the Indians were in the act of taking all the clothes from her person. The men were mostly striped of their shirts & pantaloons at the time." The Indians by sudden guerilla attacks would catch the white men unprepared and their assaults were effective even with their primitive weapons. Whitman sent this memorial with his letter of October 18 to Greene with the request that copies be made and sent "to such members of Congress & other influential men as you think will favor the object proposed."

On the same day that Whitman was writing his memorial, Dr. McLoughlin wrote to the U.S. Secretary of War from Oregon City and gave similar recommendations for the protection of Oregon immigrants. He wrote: "I am convinced that the manner in which the Immigrants travel from Fort Hall to his place will lead to trouble unless the Measures

I suggested to Dr. Whitman when he left here to go home are adopted." He advised the government to establish a post at Fort Hall, and in this connection, he recommended the appointment of Robert Newell "as a person well qualified for the office of Agent." [59]

LAST WHITMAN LETTERS

No more convincing proof of the faith that Narcissa and Marcus had in the future of Oregon may be found than that contained in letters that Narcissa wrote to members of her family, especially after her husband's return from his eastern journey in 1843, urging them to migrate thither. Her eagerness, especially for her younger sister Jane to go to Oregon, was echoed over and over again in her letters to Jane written after 1843. She yearned for Jane's companionship. In a postscript dated August 23 to a letter begun on July 4, 1847, Narcissa told her mother: "I am expecting to see Jane and Edward this fall; but from those who have already passed, we can hear nothing from them." Hopefully, Narcissa added: "They may be on the road, for among so many, it is not expected that all will be known to each other."

Matilda Sager remembered: "Mrs. Whitman's sister, Jane Prentiss, was coming out to be a teacher. She planned to be out that fall—the fall of 1847. A few weeks before the Indians killed Dr. and Mrs. Whitman and the others, Mrs. Whitman was cleaning the house very thoroughly. I said to her, 'This isn't spring, mother—why are we cleaning house now?' She said, 'Didn't you know that we are looking for your Aunt Jane to come out soon?'" [60]

Narcissa began a long letter to her mother on July 4, 1847, to which she added a postscript dated August 23, a part of which may have been written in September. She told of the arrival of the two half-breed sons of Donald Manson, a Hudson's Bay employee, who were to be educated by the Whitmans. They were John, age thirteen, and Stephen, eleven. She also reported that the P. B. Littlejohns, one of the independent missionary couples who had gone out to Oregon in 1840, had returned to the States. According to Narcissa, Mrs. Littlejohn "was very unwilling to leave the country, but her husband had become such a hypochondriac that there was no living with him in peace. He wanted to kill himself last winter. It is well for him that he has gone to the States, where he can be taken care of... He seems to be very much like Mr. Munger, the individual we had here that became crazy."

Narcissa's last extant letter, dated October 12, was written to Jane, who was then teaching at Quincy, Illinois, and still unmarried. The whole burden of the letter was an appeal for her to come to Oregon. The last paragraph reads: "Jane, there will be no use in your going home to see ma and pa before you come here—it will only make the matters worse with your heart. I want to see her as much as you. If you will all come here, it will not be long before they will be climbing over the Rocky Mountains to see us. The love of parents for their children is very great. I see already in their movements, indications that they will ere long come this way, for father is becoming quite a traveler. Believe me, dear Jane, and come without fail, when you have so good an opportunity.[61] Farewell. N.W."

Both of the two extant letters that Whitman wrote in the fall of 1847 were sent to the American Board. In his September 13 letter, he wrote: "I have sent to the lower country for a good Mechanic or hired man that wintered with me the year before last." The reference was to Josiah Osborn, who, with his family, had spent the winter of 1845–46 at Waiilatpu. Whitman called on Osborn when in the Willamette Valley in August 1847 and persuaded him to return to Waiilatpu that fall to rebuild the mills. Whitman agreed to pay him $300.00 a year if he would stay for a two-year period. This shows that at that time Whitman had no intention of moving away from Waiilatpu. These plans were made before Whitman had learned of the intentions of the Roman Catholics to establish two stations in his vicinity. Osborn had been working for the Methodist Mission but was attracted by Whitman's offer and agreed to go.[62] As will be told, he came to regret the move. The Osborns with their four children, the eldest being a girl seven and a half years old, arrived at Waiilatpu on October 18 and were quartered in the Indian room of the main mission building. That was just six weeks before a combination of circumstances exploded in tragedy.

Whitman had had the misfortune to injure a knee in the late fall of 1845 when the horse he was riding fell on him. For a time he had to use crutches. Evidently the injury continued to be a handicap, as Whitman in his letter of September 13 written while at Waskopum, said: "I have not been able to work for the last six months from a weakness in my knee joint... I feel as though I must employ more help & not work myself. I now intend to devote my whole time & strength to instruct the people. Indeed I ought to itinerate all the time if I would in any good degree meet the Jesuits." Whitman told Greene of his desire to have two schools at Waiilatpu—"One for the children of the Mission, and a boarding school for the natives."

While at The Dalles Whitman had another opportunity to see the passing immigrants and to realize their need for provisions. He wrote: "There are no provisions here more than the Station needs and at my place I have much poorer crops than usual. But we cannot remove ourselves out of the way & must meet the trial the best we can... The first passers never give us any trouble. The weak teams & needy persons come last as also gradually the sick." With a much larger immigration arriving that fall, Whitman realized with apprehension that there would be more calls that year for shelter and care at Waiilatpu than ever before.

Whitman's last letter to Greene, dated October 18, 1847, was written shortly after he had returned from guiding the immigrants, and after he had met Bishop Blanchet and his clergy at Fort Walla Walla. After seeing hundreds of immigrants and scores of wagons streaming westward, Whitman had the subject of Oregon immigration very much on his mind. This was the reason for writing the memorial to Congress which he mailed to Greene with this letter. Again in this letter, as has been previously stated, Whitman stressed the importance of the service he had been able to accomplish in 1843 when he opened the wagon road to the Columbia. "Upon that event," he wrote, "the present acquired rights of U. States by her Citizens hung." Altogether Whitman had witnessed five large Oregon immigrations, including that of 1843. The total number of people involved was about 13,000, some of whom went to California. From about a hundred wagons taken to Oregon in 1843, Whitman saw the number grow annually until there were over a thousand in 1847. Small wonder that he took pride in the role he had played in opening the Oregon country for American settlement.

In this last letter to Greene, Whitman again urged the Board to do something to induce colonies of church people with their ministers to move to Oregon with the hope that they would settle in the interior, seemingly unaware that this would arouse the enmity of the natives. "The Interior of Oregon is unrivalled," he wrote, "probably by any Country for grazing of stock of which sheep are the best. This interior will now be sought after..." He wanted the very best people to migrate, for this was a work "that needs good men." He argued: "Why will not the best men do good & benefit themselves as readily as worldly minded men? Why will Pastors regret to select their best & worthiest men to do good by their persons & their property & influence? Can a mind be found so narrow as not to be willing to part with a Pastor; or a Pastor not to part with a Church member; simply because they are good men & useful where they are?" Whitman was confident that the interior of Oregon would soon be settled and he wanted Americans instead of "the half breed & French population from the Willamette, as they show a disposition to sell out there & come here."

Here in his last letter to Greene, Whitman returned to his hope of having a college established somewhere in the interior. "I know of no place so eligible as at the Dalls close by our station," he wrote. Whitman never ceased looking into the future and dreaming of things that might be. Although this last letter reveals his continued interests in the political future of Oregon, it also shows his continuing concern for the spiritual welfare of the natives. The last sentence of this last letter to Greene was a plea for a missionary for The Dalles: "I hope the want of a man for Dalls Station will not escape your notice. With Esteem, Yours Truly, Marcus Whitman." No letters from either Marcus or Narcissa remain which might have been written during the last six weeks of their lives. Thus we have no direct evidence of any apprehension they may have felt of the coming tragedy. For the events of those weeks, we must turn to the writings of others.

Last Letter from Greene

Greene answered Whitman's letter of October 18, 1847, on the following March 17. It seems evident that some returning traveler to the States had carried Whitman's letter and his memorial to Congress. Greene wrote that he had forwarded the memorial to the Hon. Roger S. Baldwin, U.S. Senator from Connecticut, with the request that it be given consideration. Nothing further is known of the fate of this memorial. Regarding Whitman's plea that the Board do something to induce colonies of Christian people to migrate to Oregon and settle in the interior, Greene wrote: "I must say that I cannot regard it as my duty to make any efforts at all in any form."

Greene was not happy with all the time and energy that Whitman was giving to the immigrants. Surely if Whitman had lived to receive and read the following in Greene's reply, his heart would have been heavy: "We are aware that you must have many secular cares on your hands—much to occupy your mind & time of things which it seems necessary should be done, and [when] no one else seems disposed to do them, you are inclined to undertake them, and spend strength & time about them, which it would be more appropriate & really better for the community around you, for you to spend on efforts aimed more directly at the spiritual welfare of the people. You are known to be a missionary man in your relations and profession, & the people expect you to be mainly occupied in that which is peculiarly missionary work. We doubt the wisdom, taking an enlarged view of the matter, of your spending much time on exploring routes of travel, making roads, etc.... *Do not feel that all Oregon is on your hands, & that the planning, providing & laboring for all its interests are devolved on you.*" [63]

But the man who was thus being rebuked for an excess of patriotic zeal and social concern was already in his grave when that letter was written.

CROWDED WAIILATPU

Waiilatpu was crowded with seventy-five people, including forty-five children, at the time the massacre began on Monday, November 29, 1847. Of this number, fifty-two had crossed the mountains with the immigration of that year. Regarding them, Narcissa wrote sometime in September: "Poor people—those that are not able to get on, or pay for what they need—are those that will most likely wish to stop here, judging from the past; and connected with this, is a disposition not to work, at any rate, not more than they can help." The Whitmans had learned from previous experience that most of those who sought shelter at Waiilatpu for the winter months were either unable or unwilling to work. Possibly some felt that the missionaries were well subsidized by their mission boards and were, therefore, able to extend free hospitality. Narcissa added in the postscript to her letter: "The poor Indians are amazed at the overwhelming numbers of Americans coming into the country. They seem not to know what to make of it" [Letter 217].

Two of the immigrant families who remained to spend the winter of 1847–48 at Waiilatpu did so because one or more of each family had been employed by Whitman. While Dr. and Mrs. Whitman were on the Umatilla River during the first part of October, they met Judge and Mrs. L. W. Saunders and their five children. The Saunders family belonged to a small company of immigrants which hailed from Oskaloosa, Iowa. They had two wagons, with Isaac Gilliland, a tailor, as the driver of one. Mrs. Saunders in later years wrote her reminiscences of the journey across the country and of her experiences at Waiilatpu during the Whitman massacre and subsequent captivity.[64] Among her interesting stories is the description of their custom of putting the cream from their milk in a churn which would be hung on the back of a wagon. The jiggling of the wagon as it rolled along the trail resulted in "sweet fresh butter" by the end of the day.

"We passed by what the Indians called the Priest's House on the Umatilla River," wrote Mrs. Saunders, "and on the seventh of October we met Dr. Whitman... [who was] looking for a teacher. The Doctor offered such strong inducements that my husband agreed to turn back and go as a teacher to Dr. Whitman's mission." Gilliland consented to stay with the family for a few weeks, as Whitman promised him some work as a tailor. They arrived at Waiilatpu on October 12. Since Saunders had had some legal training, Whitman called on him to help write the memorial to Congress which was dated the 16th. Judge Saunders opened his school on the 19th in a room in the long arm of the T-shaped mission building. The schoolroom must have been crowded as there were thirty-two children at the mission between the ages of four and seventeen, although some of these were sick with the measles and were unable to attend.

According to Mrs. Saunders' reminiscences, Mr. and Mrs. Elam Young and their three grown sons—James, Daniel, and John—arrived at Waiilatpu on the 20th. Whitman succeeded in hiring the four men to work for him at his sawmill and they took up residence in the cabin at the site. A little later, the Joseph Smith family, with five children arrived. They too were sent to the sawmill site, except fifteen-year-old Mary who stayed with the Saunders family in order to attend school. Others who came asking for shelter were Mr. and Mrs. Peter D. Hall and their five children; Mr. and Mrs. Nathan L. Kimball with five children; Walter Marsh, his daughter and grandson; Mrs. Rebecca

Hays, whose husband had died on the trail, and her two little boys;⁶⁵ and a single man, Jacob Hoffman.

Among those who paused briefly at Waiilatpu were Mr. and Mrs. John W. Bewley and their seven children, including a son Crocket, and a daughter, Esther Lorinda, usually called by her second name. Both were in their early twenties. Lorinda noted in her diary that after their arrival at Waiilatpu: "Mrs. Whitman prevailed upon me to stay with her until next spring. She said it was late in the season and as my health was not very good, I consented to stay. My mother thought it would be for the best. My oldest brother Crocket, decided to stay with me." ⁶⁶ Lorinda took the place of Mary Johnson, who had worked for the Whitmans during the winter of 1846–47 and who had gone to Lapwai in the summer of 1847 to help Mrs. Spalding. Amos Sales, a young man who had been traveling with the Bewley family, also decided to stay. Also included in the residents at Waiilatpu on the eve of the massacre were two men whom Whitman had hired, Joseph Stanfield,⁶⁷ a French Canadian, and Nicholas Finley, a half-breed from the Spokane country.⁶⁸

On November 7, the W. D. Canfield family, with five children, from Oskaloosa, Iowa, arrived and begged to be received. This was the fifth family, each with five children, to seek accommodations at Waiilatpu that fall. Since every available room had been taken, the Canfields had to camp out until suitable quarters could be arranged for them in the blacksmith shop. Mrs. Osborn was pregnant when she and her husband returned to Waiilatpu in October 1847. Her baby was born on November 14 and died the same day. One of the Osborn girls died of measles two days later. On Monday, November 22, Spalding arrived at Waiilatpu with his daughter, Eliza, who was to attend school. With her coming, all who were destined to be either among the fourteen victims or the forty-six captives in the final tragedy had assembled.

JOE LEWIS, THE CHIEF VILLAIN

In the last company of immigrants to arrive at Waiilatpu in early November was a half-breed by the name of Joe Lewis. According to an anonymous author, who is believed to have been Peter Skene Ogden, Lewis was "a Spanish Creole." ⁶⁹ Both Spalding and Catherine Sager claimed that Lewis had been born in Canada and educated in Maine.

Spalding wrote: "He was a good scholar and good mechanic, and had the appearance of an eastern half-breed, spoke the English [language] as his native tongue, and was a devoted Catholic."[70]

Father Brouillet stoutly denied that Lewis was a Catholic and pointed out that there were then "no Catholic churches, no priests, nor any means whatever of receiving Catholic instruction" in Maine.[71]

Catherine Sager claimed that Lewis had served with Frémont in the Mexican War and then had drifted to Fort Hall. Captain Grant refused to let Lewis stay at the fort. Lewis then attached himself to a party of emigrants but, according to Catherine, was so "thoroughly disliked" by the time they had arrived at Waiilatpu that they refused to let him continue with them. Mrs. Saunders wrote that Lewis was a Delaware Indian who was "sick and in need of clothing" when he arrived at the Whitman station. She added: "The Doctor clothed him and cared for him until he recovered and sent him away with a family who were going to the Willamette Valey. He returned in three days and refused to leave. It was a case of warming a viper in one's bosom." Joe Lewis moved into the lodge of Nicholas Finley which was located within a few hundred yards of the mission house.

THE ROLL-CALL OF THOSE AT WAIILATPU

The following is a list of the residents at the Whitman mission on that fateful Monday, November 29, 1847. The names of the fourteen victims are in italics. The ages of the children and young adults are given in parentheses.

Main Mission House   Total 23

Dr. and Mrs. Marcus Whitman and their family consisting of the seven Sager children—*John* (17), *Francis* (15), Catherine (13), Elizabeth (10), Matilda (8), Louise (6), and Henrietta (4); five half-breed children—Mary Ann Bridger (11), Helen Mar Meek (10), David Malin (Cortez) (8), John (13) and Stephen (11) Manson; Eliza Spalding (10); and *Andrew Rodgers*.

Also, Mr. and Mrs. Josiah Osborn and their children—Nancy A. (7 1/2), John L. (4), and Alexander (2); *Crocket Bewley*, and Lorinda Bewley (adults).

CHAPTER TWENTY-ONE *Prelude to Tragedy, September 1846–November 1847*

Emigrant House   Total 31

   Judge and Mrs. L. W. Saunders and their children—Helen M. (14), Phoebe (10), Alfred (6), Nancy (4), and Mary A. (2); Mary Smith (15); Mrs. Rebecca Hays and her children—Henry Clay (4), and infant son, Rapolean; *Mr.* and Mrs. Peter D. Hall and their children—Gertrude (10), Mary C. (8), Ann E. (6), Rebecca (3), and Rachel (1); *Mr.* and Mrs. Nathan L. Kimball and their children—Susan M. (16), Nathan, Jr. (12), Byron E. (8), Sarah S. (6), and Nina A. (1); *Walter Marsh* and his daughter, Mary E. (11), and grandson, Alba Lyman (2); *Isaac Gilliland, Jacob Hoffmann,* and Joseph Stanfield.

Blacksmith Shop   Total 8

   Mr. and Mrs. W. D. Canfield and their children—Ellen (16), Oscar (9), Clarissa (7), Sylvia (5), and Albert (3); *Amos Sales.*

Sawmill Cabin   Total 11

   Mr. and Mrs. Elam Young and their sons—*James* (24), Daniel (21), and John Q. (19); Mr. and Mrs. Joseph Smith and their children—Edwin (13), Charles (11), Nelson (6), and Mortimer (4).

In an Indian Lodge   Total 2

   Half-breeds, Nicholas Finley and Joe Lewis.

Grand Total 75

   Not counting themselves, the French Canadian Stanfield and the two half-breeds, the Whitmans found themselves responsible for the welfare of seventy people, of whom sixteen were men, nine were women, and forty-five were children under the age of eighteen. There were nineteen boys and twenty-six girls, including the five half-breed children.[72] Possibly the two older Smith boys, listed above as being at the sawmill cabin, were actually at Waiilatpu so that they could attend school. In addition to Lorinda Bewley, three of the girls were fifteen or sixteen years old, thus making them eligible to being taken as wives by their captors.

Chapter 21 Endnotes

[1] Simpson's "Character Book," HBC Arch.

[2] Bancroft, *Oregon*, I:552.

[3] Walla Walla *Union*, August 12, 1936.

[4] Pringle ms., p. 24, states that Stanfield was in the 1846 immigration.

[5] A rare instance of Mrs. Whitman using Cayuse words in her letters.

[6] Pringle ms., p. 18, where the wording is somewhat different from the author's copy.

[7] Drury, *Spalding*, p. 327.

[8] *Ibid.*, p. 326, quoting from a letter from Spalding to A. T. Smith, Feb. 22, 1847.

[9] Hulbert, *O.P.*, VIII:163.

[10] Drury, *F.W.W.*, II:315.

[11] *Ibid.*, p. 317, fn. 30.

[12] This historic press is now in the Oregon Historical Society's museum, Portland.

[13] From postscript dated August 23.

[14] Richardson, *Whitman Mission*, p. 149.

[15] Kane, *op. cit.*, p. 195.

[16] From letter from Harper to me, October 25, 1971.

[17] Hines, *Wild Life in Oregon*, p. 166, wrote in a similar manner about Feathercap (Tamsucky): "He has a countenance the most savage."

[18] J. Russell Harper (ed.), *Paul Kane's Frontier*, Amon Carter Museum, Fort Worth, Texas, 1971, gives a reproduction of a drawing of "Til-au-kite," p. 232. A second drawing by Kane, also labelled as Tiloukaikt, is reproduced as an illustration in this work. The painting in the Royal Ontario Museum was used in Drury, *F.W.W.*, I, p. 168, and *Whitman*, p. 400, with the painting of Tomahas, but in both instances, the identification was erroneously reversed.

[19] Harper, *Paul Kane's Frontier*, p. 231 gives picture of a drawing Kane made of "Mrs. Whitman's fan" apparently made out of long feathers.

[20] See Chapter Seven, section "Their Personal Appearance."

[21] Matilda Sager Delaney to Mrs. Edmund Bowden, March 26, 1928, Coll. W.

[22] *Op. cit.*, p. 18.

[23] *Ibid., passim.*

[24] From undated clipping, possibly 1905, in Coll. Wn.

[25] Drury, *Whitman*, p. 25 gives pictures of Whitman's sister, Alice, and his three brothers. Copy in Coll. Wn.

[26] *Op. cit.*, p. 12.

[27] Ross Woodbridge was the first to note that the smaller sketch in this Kane drawing could refer to the incident mentioned by Matilda Sager.

[28] The letter "W" appears on the picture of this sketch used as an illustration in this book. After the picture of the sketch was taken, some accidental cleaning of the sketch removed the letter "W." The first publication of the sketches, without a discussion of their possible authenticity, came in Thompson, *Shallow Grave at*

Waiilatpu, p. 38. Ross Woodbridge was the first to publish an article which dealt with the identification of the sketches. See Whitman College *Alumnus*, February 1970.

[29] Half-breed sons, ages 13 and 11, of Donald Manson, a Hudson's Bay employee, who had sent his boys to the Whitman mission early in the fall of 1847 to be educated.

[30] See Drury, *Walker*, frontispiece and p. 203, for reproductions of Stanley's paintings of Elkanah and Abigail Walker.

[31] Kane, *Wanderings of an Artist*, pp. 196-7.

[32] This practice was sometimes followed by women if the sweat-house were in a secluded place.

[33] See Chapter Thirteen, fn. 45, for reference to the four Catholic priests in Old Oregon who had the family name of Blanchet.

[34] Brouillet, *House Document*, p. 33.

[35] See Chapter Fifteen, fn. 47, for reference to Young Chief's house.

[36] See Chapter Fourteen, section "Gray Demands a Station for Himself." Also, Drury, *Spalding and Smith*, pp. 156 and 295.

[37] Correcting statement in Drury, *Whitman*, pp. 423-4. Father Ricard's Journal appeared in *Les Missions de la Congregation des Missionaries Oblats de Marie Immaculee*, Vol. 49 (1912), Nos. 197 & 198. Translation furnished by kindness of the late Father W. L. Davis, S.J., Spokane, Wash.

[38] Because of the Cayuse War which followed the massacre, the work at Saint Rose Mission was abandoned. Many years later a settler, Burwell W. Russell, laid claim to the site. The Catholic Church contested the claim in court but lost; title was granted to Russell on April 10, 1882. Information from U.S. Department of Interior, in a letter to me dated December 30, 1936.

[39] Hines, *Wild Life in Oregon*, p. 183.

[40] Bishop Blanchet's original "Journal of First Trip to Walla Walla" is in the archdiocesan archives, Roman Catholic Church, Seattle. The translation from the French was made for me through the kindness of the Rev. A. L. Morisette, S.J.

[41] See Chapter Seventeen, fn. 16. Josephy, *The Nez Perce Indians*, plate 9, gives a sketch of Peu-peu-mox-mox with the note "Yellow Bird but called Yellow Serpent by the whites."

[42] See Drury, *F.W.W.*, I:218 ff., for a discussion of the Protestant and Catholic ladders and for a picture of Mrs. Spalding's representation. A copy of a Catholic ladder is in *Notices and Voyages of the Famed Quebec Mission*, translated by Carl Landerholm, Oregon Historical Society, 1956, p. 44.

[43] Ricard, Journal, No. 197:78.

[44] Brouillet, *House Document*, p. 44. Italics in the original.

[45] *Ibid.*, p. 22.

[46] From record of "Baptisms, Marriages," St. James Cathedral, Vancouver, Wash., for 1842–56.

[47] Brouillet, *House Document*, p. 33.

[48] *Ibid.*, p. 34.

[49] Italics in the original account by Blanchet. See ante, fn. 40.

[50] Brouillet, *House Document*, pp. 33-4.

⁵¹ *Ibid.*, p. 53.

⁵² See Chapter Sixteen, "To Counteract the Roman Catholics."

⁵³ In this letter Whitman called all the Catholic missionaries in the Blanchet party "Jesuits." This, of course, was not the case. Spalding, Gray, and other Protestants were too ill-informed on the Catholic orders to be accurate.

⁵⁴ HBC Arch., B/223/b/33. Douglas & Grant to Governor & Committee from Fort Vancouver, in a letter dated Sept. 20, 1847, quoting Grant.

⁵⁵ Bancroft, *Oregon*, I:645.

⁵⁶ Reminiscences of Elizabeth Ann Coonc in Walla Walla *Union*, August 12, 1936. Her account was written before 1900.

⁵⁷ Hulbert, *O.P.*, VIII:237 ff., gives the full text of the memorial.

⁵⁸ See Chapter Eighteen, "Synopsis of Whitman's Bill."

⁵⁹ Original McLoughlin letter in Old Indian Bureau files, National Archives.

⁶⁰ Lockley, *Oregon Trail Blazers*, p. 332.

⁶¹ Narcissa's letter to her sister was carried to the States by a Mr. Glenday, who was planning to return to Oregon the following year with a party. Narcissa wanted Jane to travel with this group.

⁶² From Osborn letter, April 7, 1848, Coll. W.

⁶³ Hulbert, *O.P.*, VIII:251 ff. Italics are the author's.

⁶⁴ Only one copy of this excellent pamphlet by Mrs. Mary Saunders, *The Whitman Massacre*, Oakland, Calif., 1916, is known to be extant. This is in the Library of Congress. A typewritten copy is in Coll. B., from which a xerox copy was made for me. Pagination used in footnotes of this book is to this copy and not to her published pamphlet.

⁶⁵ Pringle ms., pp. 24 & 39 mentions two sons of Mrs. Hays, a fact usually overlooked in the various listings of those at Waiilatpu at the time of the massacre. In the Pringle scrapbooks, Coll. W., Catherine named the boys, John and Rapolean (possibly Napoleon). Pringle ms., p. 39 mentions death of the Hays baby.

⁶⁶ Pringle ms., author's copy, contains a postscript giving quotations from Lorinda Bewley's diary from which this quotation is taken.

⁶⁷ See ante, fn. 4, of this chapter.

⁶⁸ A son of Jacques (Jacko) Finley (or Finlay) who helped build Spokane House in 1810. Two of the brothers of Nicholas lived in the vicinity of Tshimakain and figure in the story of Walker and Eells.

⁶⁹ *Traits of American Life*, by a Fur Trader (Peter Skene Ogden?), San Francisco, 1933, p. 54.

⁷⁰ Spalding, *Senate Document*, p. 28.

⁷¹ Brouillet, *House Document*, p. 56.

⁷² For list of residents at Waiilatpu at the time of the massacre, see Spalding, *Senate Document*, p. 27; Cannon, *Waiilatpu*, pp. 106-7; Bancroft, *Oregon*, I:647-8; Eells, *Marcus Whitman*, pp. 287-8; Pringle ms., p. 24. The lists vary in several particulars.

TOMAHAS, WHO KILLED DR. WHITMAN
Both are by Paul Kane who visited Waiilatpu, July 1847. Several years after he drew the sketch at left, he learned that Tomahas was convicted of the murder of Whitman and was hanged at Oregon City, June 3, 1850. He then, using artistic license, painted the picture at the right. In his Wanderings of an Artist (page 195), he wrote as though to justify his second picture: "His appearance was the most savage I ever beheld."
Courtesy, Peabody Museum, Harvard University; Royal Ontario Museum, Toronto

TILOUKAIKT, CHIEF OF THE WAIILATPU CAYUSES
One of three dissimilar portraits by Paul Kane of this chief. Two are in the Amon Carter Museum, Fort Worth, and one is in the Royal Ontario Museum, Toronto. Courtesy, Royal Ontario Museum, Toronto.

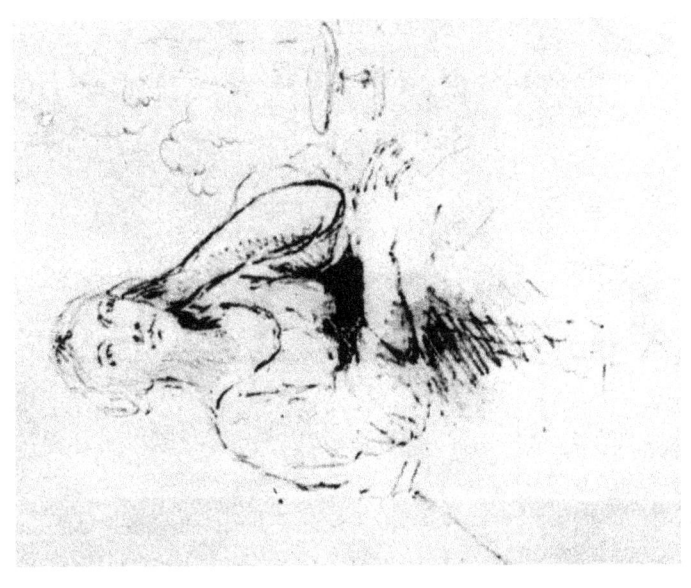

PAUL KANE'S SKETCHES BELIEVED TO BE OF THE WHITMANS

These are possibly authentic sketches of Marcus and Narcissa Whitman drawn in July 1847. For evidence used in verification, see volume two, page 174 ff. On the sketch of Marcus, note the face of a girl below—the left shoulder, the letter "W" before the brim of the hat, and at lower right, inverted, is a figure at a bonfire with the handle of a garden tool. By permission of Royal Ontario Museum, Toronto. Kane sketches 946.15.293 & 946.15.299.

CHAPTER TWENTY-ONE *Prelude to Tragedy, September 1846–November 1847* 227

[CHAPTER TWENTY-TWO]

THE WHITMAN MASSACRE

Both the immigrant's covered wagon and the Indian's lodge or tepee were to be seen at Waiilatpu in late November 1847. How symbolic! The one brought the aggressive white people, skilled in the arts and crafts of their civilization; the other sheltered members of a proud race, still clinging to many of their age-old customs. In between these symbols was the Whitman mission.

Whitman, realizing that the Indians would have to make an adjustment to the encroaching white man's civilization in order to survive, had tried to help the natives bridge the gap from the old to the new. In this, he was only partially successful. Time was too short for such a transition. Even though not a single immigrant had settled in Cayuse territory nor had any member of the tribe been killed by white men passing through their land; yet the very presence of the covered wagons and the tepees at Waiilatpu illustrated the conflict then taking place between the two cultures. The other missions at Lapwai and Tshimakain were too far removed from the Oregon Trail to feel the conflict of cultures focused at Waiilatpu. Only at the Whitman station could a massacre have occurred.

No other member of the Oregon Mission of the American Board was so involved in a conflict of loyalties as Marcus Whitman. As far as the natives were concerned, he continued to do all that was humanly possible to improve their material, educational, and spiritual welfare. His last letters reveal the extensive plans that he was making for their betterment.

At the same time, Whitman could not ignore his responsibilities to meet the needs of the immigrants. Each year, beginning with the fall of 1843, the Whitman mission had been a place of refuge where the hungry were fed, the sick cared for, the orphans given a home, and the destitute clothed. The mission became a hostel for all who, for various reasons, were unable to continue their journey to the Willamette Valley. Here is the basis for the criticism that Whitman was more concerned about the welfare of the white man than the red man; but, located as he was, how could he have done otherwise?

When H. K. W. Perkins tried to explain to Jane Prentiss why the Whitmans were killed [Appendix 6], he commented on the fact that Whitman had lost the confidence of the Indians. Perkins claimed that the Cayuses came to fear rather than to love the Doctor. He wrote: "Dr. Whitman in pursuing his missionary labors never so identified himself with the natives as to make their interests *paramount*. He looked upon them as an inferior race & doomed at no distant day to give place to a settlement of enterprising Americans."

If Whitman felt that the Cayuses were doomed if they did not make a quick adjustment to the white man's civilization, history has shown that he was correct in that judgment. There is no indication of any diminution in Whitman's efforts to help the Cayuses; yet the very fact that he gave aid and comfort to the white people aroused hostility in the minds of the natives. If one accepts the blood feud theory common to primitive people, the Cayuses had a strong case against Whitman. He was the representative of the white race, and therefore shared the guilt of all the wrongs white men had inflicted on the red men. To the Cayuses, whatever aid Whitman gave the immigrants was tantamount to helping their enemies. He thus became the logical target for their hostility.

The Measles Epidemic

Although a variety of factors contributed to the Whitman massacre, the final precipitating cause was the ravages of the measles epidemic. As has been stated in the previous chapter, both measles and dysentery had been taking their toll of native lives during the summer of 1847, and there is evidence that an especially virulent form of measles was introduced into Oregon with the immigration of that year. Unfortunately we have no writings of either of the Whitmans after October 18 to tell what they saw taking place; hence we must rely on the testimony of others.

So many white children at Waiilatpu came down with measles in November that the school, which Judge Saunders had hopefully opened on the 19th of that month, had to be closed. Even some adults were stricken, including Mrs. Osborn who, before she had recovered, gave birth on the 14th to a baby girl. As previously stated, this child died the day she was born. All of the other four Osborn children were ill with measles and on the 24th, six-year-old Salvijane died. Years later Nancy Osborn wrote: "An Indian came into the room where the form of my sister lay. Mrs. Whitman asked leave to show him the dead child. She wanted the Indians to know the measles were killing the white people as well as the Indians and thus hoped to allay the growing distrust of the red men. The Indian looked long at my sister, then cruelly he laughed, to see the paleface dead." [1]

Mrs. Saunders, who has given us one of the most revealing accounts of those tragic days, mentions the death of the Osborn child. She tells of how Narcissa tried to comfort the grief-stricken mother by saying: "Perhaps God thought it for the best that your little child should be called away; it may calm the Indians to see a white child taken as well as so many natives, for otherwise we may all be compelled to leave within two weeks." [2] Spalding also commented: "We hoped that this afflicting providence would show the Indians that the whites in common with themselves were exposed to the ravages of the disease." [3] Matilda Sager recalled that eight of the children of school age in the Whitman household were unable to attend school when Saunders reopened it on the morning of the first day of the massacre, November 29, and that "most of the children of the immigrant families wintering there were [also] unable to attend." [4] The epidemic was severe even among the adult employees of the Hudson's Bay Company. Ogden, in a letter to Simpson dated March 12, 1848, reported that fourteen of the "servants" of the Company had died.[5]

The Dying Cayuse Tribe

A smallpox epidemic, originating in the upper Missouri River country, had swept through Old Oregon to the Pacific Ocean in 1781–82 with devastating effects. A second scourge of "fever and ague," perhaps malaria, ravaged Oregon in 1830–31. Such diseases as tuberculosis, measles, and venereal infections took their frightful toll of lives. Whole tribes, especially along the Pacific Coast, disappeared. Samuel Parker quoted Dr. McLoughlin as saying that nine-tenths of the Indian population of the lower Columbia River region had been swept away.[6] According to another authority, Leslie M. Scott, the white man's diseases had claimed about ninety-five percent of the aboriginal population of the lower Columbia River country before the immigration from the States had begun. Scott wrote: "Without this desolation of the savages, settlement by ox-team pioneers would have been delayed one or two decades, and then would have encountered protracted horrors of savage warfare."[7] Thus in Oregon, history repeated what had happened to the aborigines living in the vicinity of Cape Cod, Massachusetts, just prior to the landing of the Pilgrims in 1620.

Although the tribes in the upper Columbia country were not as seriously affected, they did not escape these epidemics without severe loss. Exact statistics are lacking regarding the number in the Cayuse nation during the year, 1835–47, and estimates made by contemporary writers vary greatly. Parker claimed that they numbered about 2,000,[8] but such an estimate included the Walla Walla tribe, which probably numbered over 1,000. A. B. Smith, with the aid of Cornelius Rogers, was the first to attempt to take a census of those speaking the Nez Perce language. He requested the head of each band to give him a bundle of sticks with each stick representing a person. After collecting and counting the sticks, Smith in a letter to Greene dated February 6, 1840, estimated that there were not more than 3,000 Nez Perces and Cayuses. A year later, he revised his figures downward to 2,400.[9] According to the latter estimate, the Cayuse could not have numbered more than three hundred. Even before the measles epidemic struck in the fall of 1847, the Cayuses were a dying nation.

Following the death of a Cayuse child at Fort Walla Walla during the first week of October 1847, the fatalities grew rapidly.[10] It was hard for the Indians to understand why so many of their number died, both children and adults, when only one white child at Waiilatpu was taken. They knew nothing of immunity. Mrs. Saunders explained in part the reason for the greater mortality among the natives when she wrote: "Dr. Whitman treated the Indian children, but with very little success owing to the ignorance and superstition of their savage parents. They would take the medicine that he gave them, but at the same time, they still clung to their old remedy for all sickness, i.e., a sweating process followed by a plunge into cold water. The inevitable effect of such a treatment was …in almost every case… death. Altho Dr. Whitman explained to them the danger and warned them against it, his words were of no avail, and in their ignorance and superstition they blamed their kind friend for the death of their children and suspected him of trying to kill them off."[11]

Spalding, who arrived at Waiilatpu on Monday, November 22, later wrote of what he saw the next day:[12] "On the 23d three Indians died, including a child. The Doctor, as usual, had coffins made for them and winding sheets prepared, and assisted in burying the dead… It was most distressing to go into a lodge of some ten fires,[13] and count twenty or twenty-five sick with measles, others in the last stages of dysentery, in the midst of every kind of filth, enough of itself to cause sickness, with no suitable means of alleviating their almost incurable suffering, with perhaps one well person to look after the wants of the sick ones." Catherine Sager remembered that just before the massacre: "The Indians all had the measles, and owing to their manner of living, dying by the dozen. I have seen from five to six buried daily."[14]

William McBean, writing from Fort Walla Walla on November 30, 1847, to the "Board of Managers" of the Hudson's Bay Company gave the first account of the massacre. Referring to the Cayuses living in the immediate vicinity of Waiilatpu, he stated: "About thirty souls of the Cayuse tribe died, one after another; who evidently believed the Doctor poisoned them."[15] On July 11, 1848, William Craig made a statement for Father Brouillet in which he claimed that a Cayuse Indian had told him that "one hundred and ninety-seven Indians had died since the immigration commenced passing…"[16] If that number is correct, then the

Cayuses lost more than one-half of their estimated total of 350 during the fall of 1847.

Craig's figures are confirmed by a report made by Dr. Anson Dart, Superintendent of Indian Affairs for Oregon, who made an inspection tour through the upper Columbia River country in the spring and summer of 1851. Dart met with eight Cayuse chiefs at Fort Walla Walla on June 20 and in his report to Washington stated: "We ascertained the whole number of their tribe to be one hundred and twenty six. They were once a numerous and powerful nation, and are still a proud and haughty race, but very superstitious." [17] The Cayuse tribe was indeed dying at the time of the Whitman massacre, and we need not wonder that the chiefs in their desperation and anguish became receptive to the wildest rumors regarding the cause of their misfortunes.

More details regarding the reactions of the natives to the introduction and extent of the measles epidemic are to be found in a letter sent to Sir George Simpson by Ogden and Douglas from Fort Vancouver on March 16, 1848. After referring to the large immigration of 1847 from the States and to the common report that the immigrants had brought the disease with them, the two wrote: "...that highly contagious disease has since extended its ravages over the whole country from Fort Walla Walla to Nisqually, and destroyed one-tenth of the Indian population. That appalling circumstance and the well-known fact that the disease was contracted from the immigrants excited a strong prejudice in the minds of the Indians who believe that the Americans are resolved to destroy them. Such feelings took so firm a hold on the mind of the Cayouses that, in a fit of desperation, they attacked the American Mission at Waiilatpoo near Walla Walla, and murdered Dr. Whitman, his accomplished Lady and 11 other American citizens with a most heartless and revolting barbarity." [18]

WHITMAN ACCUSED OF POISONING THE INDIANS

When scores of the Cayuses were dying of measles and when white children recovered while Indian children and even adults did not, it was only natural for the natives to recall some past events which gave credence to the theory that Dr. Whitman was poisoning them in order to gain possession of their horses, cattle, and land. One incident recalled occurred in 1841 when Gray injected a strong emetic into watermelons to discourage the Indians from stealing them. To the natives, the emetic was "bad medicine" or poison, and they remembered. Archibald McKinlay wrote that they often spoke of the incident and, although Gray was the culprit, Whitman got the blame and was called a *"dangerous medicine man."* [19]

A far more serious reason which made the Indians feel that Whitman was poisoning them arose out of the practice followed by both Whitman and Spalding of poisoning the predatory animals which preyed upon their sheep.[20] When Father Brouillet was collecting material for his *House Document*, he secured the following testimonial from John Young: "I spent the winter of 1846 in Dr. Whitman's employment. I generally worked at the sawmill. During the time I was there, I observed that Dr. Whitman was in the habit of poisoning the wolves. I did not see him put the poison in the baits for the wolves; but two young men of his house, by his order, were poisoning pieces of meat and distributing them in the places where the wolves were in the habit of coming, a short distance around the doctor's establishment.

"The Doctor gave me once some arsenic to poison the wolves that were around the saw-mill. By his order I poisoned some pieces of meat, which I fixed at the end of short sticks about a quarter of mile from the saw-mill. Some Indians who happened to pass there took the meat and ate it; three of them were very sick, and were near dying... Some days afterwards the Doctor told me, laughing, that they would have certainly died if they had not drunk a great quantity of water to excite vomiting. 'I had told them very often,' said he, 'not to eat of that meat which we distributed for the wolves, that it would kill them; they will take care now, I suppose.'" [21]

It is difficult to believe that Whitman would have treated so serious an incident as lightly as John Young claimed, for he surely knew that his own life would have been in danger had any of the Indians died from eating the poisoned meat. If the supposed incident took place in the winter of 1846–47, as claimed, it means that Whitman had probably been using poison to kill predatory animals for eight years. If the Indians actually ate meat containing arsenic poison, it is highly improbable that they would have recovered. The significant fact is that such stories were being circulated among the natives at the time of the measles outbreak.

McBean, in his letter of November 30, 1847, to the officials at Fort Vancouver, repeated what he had learned from the half-breed,

Nicholas Finley, who was the first to carry news of the massacre to Fort Walla Walla. According to Finley, the Indians killed the Whitmans in retaliation, believing that Dr. Whitman was poisoning them in order to get their property. Furthermore, Finley claimed that Andrew Rodgers had told the Indians that he had overheard Whitman and Spalding plotting to poison them. Finley claimed that Rodgers had been induced to tell what he had heard by being promised immunity by the Cayuses. Of this McBean wrote: "It was reported that it was not their intention to kill Mr. Rodgers, in consequence of an avowal to the following effect, which he is said to have made and which nothing but a desire to save his life could have prompted him to do. He said 'I was one evening lying down, and I overheard the Doctor telling Mr. Spalding that it was best you all should be poisoned at once, but that the latter told him it was best to continue slowly and cautiously, and between this and spring not a soul would remain, when they would take possession of your lands, cattle, and horses." Since Rodgers had been killed in spite of the supposed immunity promised him, some explanation of this had to be made, so, according to Finley's report to McBean, it was claimed that: "One of the murderers, not having been made acquainted with the above understanding, shot Mr. Rodgers."

McBean refused to believe such an incredible story. In his report to Fort Vancouver, he wrote: "These are only Indian reports, and no person can believe the Doctor capable of such an action without being as ignorant and brutal as the Indians themselves." [22]

A variation of this story is found in a statement made by a Cayuse Indian to William Craig who, in turn on July 11, 1848, relayed the account to Father Brouillet. Now instead of Andrew Rodgers being the eavesdropper, it was the half-breed Joe Lewis who, strange to say, claimed to have been lying half-asleep on a settee in the Whitmans' private living room. The Cayuse Indian reported: "Joseph Lewis said that Dr. Whitman and Mr. Spalding had been writing for two years to their friends in the east, where Joseph Lewis lived, to send them poison to kill off the Cayuses and Nez Perces; that they had sent them some that was not good, and they wrote for more that would kill them off quick, and that the medicine had come this summer. Joseph Lewis said he was lying on the settee in Dr. Whitman's room, and he heard a conversation between Dr. Whitman, Mrs. Whitman, and Mr. Spalding, in which Mr.

Spalding asked the Doctor why he did not kill the Indians off faster. 'Oh,' said the Doctor, 'they are dying fast enough; the young men will die off this winter, and the old ones next spring...' One of them said, 'That man will hear us,' alluding to Joseph Lewis. 'Oh no,' said another, 'he cannot hear; he is sleeping sound.' They talked rather low, but Joseph Lewis said he could hear all that passed. This Indian messenger stated that Joseph Lewis had made this statement in a council of the Cayuses on the Saturday night previous to the murder, and... [he] told the Cayuses in the council that unless they [the Indians] killed Dr. Whitman and Mr. Spalding quick they would all die." [23]

Spalding, in a letter to Narcissa's parents dated April 6, 1848, claimed that plans for the massacre were made in Finley's lodge several days before the killings began.[24] Since Joe Lewis lived with Finley, he was, therefore, a party to the conspiracy and no doubt inflamed the anger of the Cayuses at that time with his lies about what he claimed to have overheard in the Whitmans' living room. Josiah Osborn, in his account of the massacre dated April 7, 1848, wrote regarding Lewis: "One day he was at work for an Indian named Tamsicky, harrowing in wheat and told him that the Doctor and Mrs. Whitman were scattering poison into the air, and would kill them all off... He then proposed that if they would agree to it, he would help them kill the Doctor and his wife, and all the Americans in their country." [25]

Of all who took part in the massacre, there was no one more active in precipitating the murders than this half-breed with the twisted soul who harbored a deep grudge against Americans in general and the Whitmans in particular. Why was Lewis so eager for revenge? Possibly because Whitman had tried to get rid of him shortly after he had arrived at Waiilatpu. Taking advantage of the accumulated grievances of the Cayuses against the white people, Lewis whipped their anger to the explosive point when they finally decided to kill their benefactors. Several of the contemporary accounts of the massacre by survivors accuse Lewis of playing a leading role in the tragedy. He was the chief villain.

DR. WHITMAN, A WHITE TE-WAT

Another contributory cause of the massacre was the Indians' superstitious faith in the magic power of their medicine men or *te-wats* and the right of the relatives of a deceased person to kill the *te-wat* who had treated the patient. In a letter to Dr. W. F. Tolmie, who had served as physician at Fort Vancouver for a number of years, Archibald McKinlay claimed that the Cayuse and Walla Walla Indians were the most superstitious of any of the Oregon tribes. Regarding the custom of killing unsuccessful *te-wats*, McKinlay wrote: "They shot seven of their own medicine men by the fort during my five years' stay there, and probably over three times that number altogether."[26]

Both Marcus and Narcissa were aware of this practice, and realized the danger when ministering to sick natives [Letter 41]. At times Dr. Whitman refrained from prescribing treatment when he felt that the patient was near death and that he would be blamed if the person died.

As the natives ascribed supernatural powers to their *te-wats*, they believed that Whitman, as a white *te-wat*, also had the ability to cast a magic spell which could cause death. This is illustrated in an incident that took place at The Dalles in September 1847, which was, to the Indians, full proof of such a power. Whitman passing there on his return from the Willamette Valley, had occasion to confront some Cayuse and Walla Walla Indians who had been involved in an altercation with some immigrants which resulted in the death of a man by the name of Shepard. Whitman refused to shake hands with an Indian who had taken part in the killing of the white man. It so happened that this young man choked that night on a piece of dried buffalo meat and died. As a result, many of the Indians believed that the doctor had cast a spell which had caused his death, and was, therefore, more to be feared than any native *te-wat*. Mrs. Whitman gave a feast for the Cayuses in an effort to regain their confidence, but the incident was remembered.[27]

THE CONSPIRATORS IDENTIFIED

The Whitman massacre did not come as the result of the premeditated approval of the leaders of the Cayuse tribe. Perrin Whitman declared in 1897: "Not one-third of them knew a thing about it."[28] Although some members of bands of Young Chief, Five Crows, and Stickus, who lived along the Umatilla River, seem to have known what had been planned, there is no evidence that any from these bands were involved. Father Brouillet probably assessed the situation correctly when he wrote: "It was in Tilokaikt's camp, and by his Indians only, that the Doctor had been killed; then, the Indians of that camp only could be called murderers, and even but a small portion of them, since twelve or thirteen only have been designated as guilty." [29]

Positive identification of the murderers is difficult because their Indian names were spelled in different ways. Some of the Cayuses had been given white people's names. Narcissa, for instance, bestowed the names of members of her family and of friends on several of the young people of the tribe who were among the first to attend classes conducted for their benefit. Some of the adult Cayuses were also known by nicknames such as "Feathercap." Thus it was not unusual for the same person to be known by three or more different names. Before turning to the story of the massacre, it is well to have the culprits identified.

Although we have nineteen eye-witness accounts of the massacre and the subsequent captivity,[30] little help can be gained from such writings in the way of identifying those guilty of participating in the killings. The immigrants had not been at Waiilatpu long enough to get to know many of the Indians by name. Of all the survivors, not counting the half-breeds, only ten-year-old Eliza Spalding knew the native language, and she did not write her reminiscences until her old age. Those of the two older Sager girls, also written in their old age, are helpful.

Our most important source of information as to the identity of the culprits is to be found in two letters written by William McBean, who had taken over the management of Fort Walla Walla following the retirement of Archibald McKinlay in February 1846. Since he was well acquainted with the principal men of the various bands of the Indians living in the vicinity of the fort, there was no one better qualified than he to get accurate information regarding the identity of the guilty.

McBean, in his letter of November 30, 1847, to the Company's officials at Fort Vancouver, gave the names of six Cayuses as being the ringleaders in "the horrible butchery." [31] More than a year later, on January 6, 1850, McBean in a letter addressed to Joseph Lane, Superintendent of Indian Affairs for the Territory of Oregon, gave the names of fourteen whom he thought guilty.[32] This list included four whom he had mentioned in his first letter. Several listed in the second letter were either innocent or had no evidence brought against them. Further identification of the guilty is to be found in the records of the District Court of Oregon which met in Oregon City in May 1850 and which condemned five to be hanged.

Because of the great variation in spelling and the difficulty in keeping unfamiliar Indian names in mind, the following listing has been compiled which gives the variant spellings in the following order: (a) that used in the text of this work, not including quotations; (b) that given by McBean; (c) that found in the court records, here given in italics; and (d) other variants found in the writings of the Whitmans or of the survivors. For the sake of comparison and simplification, the longer Indian names are hyphenated. A few references to sources will be indicated.

1. (a) Tiloukaikt; (b) Teloquoit; (c) *Teloquoit*; (d) Tilkanaiks [Letter 100].
2. (a) Tomahas; (b) Tomah Hash; (c) *Tamahas*; (d) Tau-mau-lish, To-ma-kus.
3. (a) Clokamas; (b) Tlocoomots; (c) *Clokomas*; (d) Klakamas, Klokamas.
4. (a) Ish-ish-kais-kais or Frank Escaloom, a brother of Tomahas; (b) Tsy-ah-yas-tstah-kess; (c) *Isia-ashe-luckas*; (d) Sia-sa-luchus, Tsai-ash-alkis, Isaia-holo-kus, Ish-hol-hol, Isaklome or Wet Wolf. (Victor, Early Indian Wars, p. 104, identifies Frank Escaloom with Tintinmitse.)
5. (a) Kia-ma-sump-kin; (b) Ky-ah-mah-shum-kain; (c) *Kaim-asum-kin*; (d) Qui-ah-may-sun, Quia-ma-shou-skin. Also called Panther's Coat, or Left Hand.
6. (a) Tamsucky or Feathercap; (b) Tomsucky; (d) Tum-suc-kie. Possibly Sakiah or Wap-task-tak-mahl. See fn. 31, Chapter Eleven, and fn. 7, Chapter Seventeen.
7. (a) Wai-e-cat; (b) "Tomsucky's Son."
8. (b) E-you-e-ah-nish, possibly Edward, son of Tiloukaikt, or Shu-ma-hici or Painted Shirt, also called son of Tiloukaikt.

The names of six others whom McBean gave in his letter of January 6, 1850, were not linked with the death of any one person, and, therefore, are not given in the above list. McBean failed to mention the two sons of Tiloukaikt, Edward and Clark, who are known to have helped kill two sick men, unless he gave their Indian names which remain unidentified.

McBean did not mention the chief villain, Joe Lewis, who, as will be stated, had fled long before McBean wrote this second letter.

SERVING OREGON THROUGH DEATH

When Spalding and his daughter arrived at Waiilatpu on Monday, November 22, just a week before the massacre began, they found that the school which Eliza was to attend had been temporarily closed because so many of the children were ill with measles. Spalding had taken with him a pack train of seventeen animals loaded with grain to supplement Whitman's diminishing store. These animals, under the care of a Mr. Jackson, then in Spalding's employ, were sent back to Lapwai on the morning of the ill-fated day, November 29.

Spalding has given the following description of conditions he found at Waiilatpu at the time of his arrival on the 22nd: "All the doctor's family had been sick, but were recovering; three of the children were yet dangerously sick... Mrs. Osborn and three children were dangerously ill; one of their children died during the [following] week. A young man, Mr. Bewley, was also very sick. The doctor's hands were more than full among the Indians; three and sometimes five died in a day. Dear sister Whitman seemed ready to sink under the immense weight of labor and care. But like an angel of mercy, she continued to administer with her ever-ready hand to the wants of all. Late and early, night and day, she was by the bed of the sick, the dying, and the afflicted." [33]

On Thursday, November 25, Spalding and Rodgers rode to Yellow Serpent's lodge near Fort Walla Walla, where they spent the night. Although this chief had rather reluctantly granted the Catholic priests permission to establish Saint Rose Mission in his territory, yet he remained friendly with the Protestants.[34] While in the chief's lodge, a Nez Perce entered and asked: "Is Dr. Whitman killed?" as though he were expecting an affirmative answer. The incident troubled Spalding, as it seemed to indicate that some of the Indians were planning to kill the doctor. On Friday Spalding and Rodgers rode to Fort Walla Walla, where they dined with Bishop Blanchet and some of his clergy. Of this Spalding wrote: "They asked and I cheerfully agreed to furnish them all needed supplies from my station." In this respect, Spalding showed a more tolerant spirit than Whitman had exhibited. At this meeting Spalding argued with the Catholic missionaries over their views regarding the theory of transubstantiation which claimed that the wine and bread in the Mass were changed into the actual blood and body of Christ. Spalding later wrote that he had had "an animated discussion on changing the biscuit into 'God,'" and claimed that: "I showed them plainly they must be deceivers or cannibals." [35] Following the massacre, Spalding became obsessed with the idea that the Catholic priests not only knew about the intentions of the Indians to kill the Whitmans but even gave their tacit approval to the crime. Such a calumny must be rejected in toto. Although the endeavors of the Catholics to establish two missions in the vicinity of Waiilatpu were most untimely, the massacre would have occurred even if they had not been in the vicinity.

WHITMAN WARNED OF THE IMPENDING TRAGEDY

Whitman received several warnings of the hostile intentions of the Cayuse Indians during the summer and fall of 1847. Among the immigrants who spent the winter of 1846–47 at Waiilatpu was the John Settle family. Whitman had hired Settle to work for him and as a result the Settle family was still at Waiilatpu until the late fall of 1847. According to a statement Settle made, some friendly natives approached him in November of that year and urged him "to induce Dr. Whitman to leave the Mission." Settle, being convinced that the Indians did intend to kill Dr. Whitman if he remained, "used every argument possible to get him to leave but Dr. Whitman hardly would listen to him and in fact ridiculed his fear." Settle, convinced that some tragedy was impending, loaded his possessions onto his wagon and with his family and his livestock left Waiilatpu on Friday, November 26, and started for the Willamette Valley.[36] That was only three days before the massacre began.

In trying to understand Whitman's refusal to act on this warning, we must seek to appreciate his situation. Where could he go? He was responsible for the welfare and even the lives of more than seventy men, women, and children, some of whom were seriously ill. The nearest place of refuge was Fort Walla Walla, but the accommodations there were totally inadequate to receive so many even if McBean had been willing to receive them. Moreover, it would have been impossible for all at Waiilatpu to go to the fort without the knowledge of the natives. How would it have been possible to feed so many if they had moved? These and many other problems were involved in any consideration of leaving Waiilatpu. The idea of

Marcus and Narcissa deserting about seventy people while seeking safety only for themselves was unthinkable.

Some critics have wondered why Whitman did not warn the men on the grounds of a possible attack and so put them on their guard. Such a possibility with its suggestion of armed resistance would have brought new perils which Whitman no doubt realized. If the Indians were determined to kill and met resistance, the inevitable outcome would have been a general massacre of all including women and children. It should be remembered that throughout Whitman's eleven-year residence at Waiilatpu, he had consistently followed a policy of non-resistance. Although some of the immigrants at Waiilatpu are known to have had firearms, the only guns that Whitman had were one or two rifles and a pistol which had been used to kill animals to be butchered.

A net of circumstances was closing around the Whitmans during the last days of November 1847 from which there seemed to be no escape. Since to flee was impossible and to resist unthinkable, there seemed to be no alternative except to stay and hope and pray for the best.

THE NIGHT RIDE TO THE UMATILLA

Spalding and Rodgers returned to Waiilatpu on Saturday morning, the 27th. When Whitman told the two of the warning Settle had given and of his departure for the Willamette Valley, Spalding in turn related the account of the Indian who had entered Yellow Serpent's lodge and had asked if the doctor had been killed. All evidence pointed to a plot being hatched by Tiloukaikt and his band.[37] Spalding also passed on the information that Bishop Blanchet, and Fathers Brouillet and LeClaire had left Fort Walla Walla that morning for Young Chief's house on the Umatilla, where they were to open Saint Anne's Mission. Sometime that morning, a messenger arrived from Five Crows and Young Chief with a plea for Dr. Whitman to visit their camps and minister to the sick. Since there were so many dangerously ill in the vicinity of Waiilatpu, among the immigrants and in Whitman's household, it may be doubted if Whitman would have responded to the plea were it not for the fact that a possible solution for the dangerous situation he was facing had entered his mind.

Although Whitman had strongly objected to the coming of the Roman Catholic missionaries to the Walla Walla area, now that they were there, he was considering the possibility of turning over Waiilatpu to them if this were the wish of the Cayuse chiefs. Such a move might have appeased the hostility to him and have permitted him and his family to withdraw from the field in peace. A comment made by Spalding nearly twenty years later supports such a view. Spalding wrote: "Dr. Whitman twice during the last year [i.e., 1847] called the Cayuses together, and told them that if a majority wished, he would leave the country at once... Dr. Whitman held himself ready to sell the Waiilatpu station to the Catholic mission whenever a majority of the Cayuses might wish it."[38]

Knowing that the Bishop and some of his clergy would be at Young Chief's house, Whitman decided to respond to the plea from Five Crows and Young Chief. He could then talk over with the Catholic missionaries the possibility of them taking over the Waiilatpu station. The situation at Waiilatpu had become so threatening that Whitman felt no time should be lost, so he made preparations to leave that Saturday evening. Of this Spalding wrote: "The Doctor requested me to accompany him to the Umatilla, leaving dear Sister Whitman... greatly exhausted with her long and incessant watching with the sick, with three of her own and one of Mrs. Osborne's [children] dangerously ill, to require her constant attention, Mrs. Osborne not yet able to leave her bed..."[39] Narcissa was reluctant to see her husband go. At dusk that Saturday evening, with tears in her eyes, she bade him and Spalding goodby. It was the last time that Spalding was to see Narcissa, the one whom he had loved in his youth.

Spalding's account of their night's ride to the Umatilla is as follows: "The night was dark, and the rain beat furiously upon us. But our intercourse was sweet; we little imagined it would be our last. With feeling of deep emotion we called to mind that eleven years before we had crossed this trail the day before we reached Walla Walla, the end of our seven months journey from New York. We little thought the journey of life was so soon to close. We called to mind the high hopes and thrilling interest which had been awakened in the years that followed; of our successful labors and the constant devotedness of the Indians to improvement... But the principal topic of conversation that dark night was the danger that threatened from another source... We felt that the present sickness among the Indians afforded the Catholics a favorable opportunity to excite them to drive us from the country..."[40]

According to Spalding, as the two rode through the darkness and the lashing rain, Whitman said: "...that unless the Indians requested us to leave, his [Whitman's] days were few—or words to that effect but consoled himself by saying, 'If I am to fall, through the machinations of Papists, *my death may do as much good to Oregon, as my life can*.'" [41] The reference to the Roman Catholics must be viewed in the light of Spalding's later bitter anti-Catholic attitude. As a doctor, Whitman was fully aware of the danger that he faced in ministering to the sick as a white *te-wat*. Yet, what did he mean by saying that he believed his death would do as much good for Oregon as could be accomplished by living? Was he not thinking of the political future of Oregon? Ever since Jason Lee's visit to Waiilatpu in 1838, Whitman had been increasingly eager for the United States to extend its jurisdiction over Oregon as a territory. The draft of the bill which he had submitted for Congressional consideration in the fall of 1843 and the memorial of October 16, 1847, embodied his recommendations for government protection of Oregon emigrants and for the establishment of an orderly government in the Northwest territory. Even though the boundary question had been settled in 1846, only a weak Provisional Government had been established whose influences hardly extended beyond the confines of the Willamette Valley.

Marcus could have heartily endorsed what Narcissa had written to her father on April 10, 1846: "To be in a country among a people of no law, even if they are from a civilized land, is the nearest like a hell on earth of anything I can imagine." Although she was referring to some difficulties with lawless white settlers in the Willamette Valley, her sentiments were especially apropos for those living among the Indians in the interior of Oregon. Literally, the Whitmans and all other white people who were living in the upper Columbia River country in the fall of 1847 were in a land without law, subject to the passions and undisciplined conduct of the natives. Elijah White's efforts to introduce a code of laws in 1843 had ended in failure. How logical for Whitman, when facing the possibility of being killed, to believe that should this happen, the news of his death would reverberate across the nation and move a lethargic Congress to act. Then an official Territorial Government would replace the weak Provisional Government for the benefit of Indians and settlers alike. If such was Whitman's reasoning, then what he said to Spalding is understandable: "I believe my death will do as much for Oregon as my life can."

Warning from Stickus

Whitman and Spalding headed for the lodge of Stickus which evidently was located on the north bank of the Umatilla River near present-day Thornhollow, Oregon. Although Stickus never joined the Mission church, perhaps there was no one among the Cayuses more deserving to be included than he. Catherine Sager stated: "When the Whitman mission was established, he soon became an earnest listener and was really converted to the Christian faith. All his life thereafter he lived as a consistent Christian." As has been stated, it was Stickus who, at Whitman's request, guided the 1843 emigration over the Blue Mountains. There was no member of the Cayuse tribe, not excepting Five Crows, who was more friendly to the whites in general and the missionaries in particular than Stickus. How natural it was, therefore, for Whitman and Spalding to seek the hospitality of this chief after their long night ride from Waiilatpu through wind and rain.

Spalding wrote: "We arrived at the lodge of Stickus thoroughly wet. In coming down the hill to the lodge, my horse fell and rolled partly over me, causing severe pains in my head and one leg during the night and next day. We spread our blankets by a good fire in the lodge and lay by it until morning." On Sunday morning, Stickus conducted his family devotions after which "a good breakfast of potatoes, squash, fresh beef, and wheat bread of his wife's make" was served to his two guests. Spalding commented later on how gratifying it was for them to note the advancement the Cayuses had made by comparing "their present abundance of comfortable living... [with] their wretchedness and starvation when we came among them, eleven years before."

Stickus later testified at the trial of the five accused murderers held in Oregon City in May 1850 that Whitman "was at his lodge on the Umatilla the day before his death, that during the visit... he told him that the Indians about the Mission were talking bad about him... & that he said Whitman was in danger." Stickus warned Whitman especially about the evil intentions of Joe Lewis and reported that Tamsucky had said that "they were going to kill" him.[42] This warning from Stickus, following that so shortly before given by Settle, gave Whitman added reason for consulting with Bishop Blanchet about the advisability of asking the Cayuses to decide whom they wanted to be their missionaries, the Protestants or the Roman Catholics.

After breakfast with Stickus, Whitman left to visit the sick in the camps of Five Crows and Young Chief on the south bank of the Umatilla River. Sometime during the day he returned to the north band and called on the Bishop and his two priests at their newly established Saint Anne Mission in Young Chief's house. Of this Father Brouillet wrote: "...we were visited by Dr. Whitman, who remained but a few minutes at the house, and appeared to be much agitated. Being invited to dine, he refused, saying that he feared it would be too late, as he had 25 miles to go, and wished to reach home before night. On parting, he entreated me not to fail to visit him when I would pass by his mission, which I very cordially promised to do." [43] Although Brouillet gave no details as to what was discussed, his comments support the theory that Whitman had become so alarmed over what Stickus had said that he felt it imperative to return to Waiilatpu that night. The eagerness with which Whitman urged one of the priests to visit him early during the next week indicates that Whitman was ready to withdraw from Waiilatpu should this be the wish of the majority of the chiefs.

Spalding's account of Whitman's meeting with the Catholics confirms this interpretation. He wrote: "About four, the Doctor returned, much fatigued, but said the sickness in his family made it necessary to return. Said he had taken tea with the Bishop and two of his priests... Said he had invited them to come and see him, which they had promised to do in a short time. The Doctor was much pleased with the idea, hoping that we might come to some understanding and bring it before the Indians to say who should be their missionaries." [44]

As Whitman mounted his horse for his lonely ride back to Waiilatpu, Stickus again told him "to be careful for the bad Indians would kill him." [45] In giving this warning, Stickus was risking the possibility of incurring the anger of those of his tribe who were planning the evil deed. Whitman thanked the chief for his warning. Since Spalding was still suffering from his fall, he was unable to return with Whitman. Years later Spalding wrote: "My dear brother bade me good evening and left about sundown, though greatly in need of sleep and rest. My eyes saw him for the last time as he passed at good speed over the hill in the distance..." [46] Their fellowship as co-workers in the Oregon Mission of the American Board, which had begun at Howard, New York, in February 1836, had come to an end.

Monday, November 29, 1847

Since the rain had ceased, Whitman made better time on his return trip than he and Spalding had made going the opposite way during the previous night. He returned to his home about ten o'clock Sunday evening. Narcissa, exhausted with her many cares, had gone to bed, leaving John and Francis Sager to watch over the sick, two of whom, Helen Mar Meek and Louise Sager, were dangerously ill. Catherine Sager, also down with the measles, was sleeping on a settee in the living room. Years later she recalled with vividness the events of that night and the following days.

After the doctor had greeted his wife, he sent the two Sager boys to bed, saying that he would take care of the sick during the remainder of the night. One by one, Whitman examined each patient. "When he came to Helen Meek," wrote Catherine, "he thought her dying; he sat by her and watched her for some time, but she finally revived... I could see that Father [i.e., her foster father] was much troubled about something and I supposed it was about the sick children." After making the rounds, Marcus called Narcissa. She arose and the two sat by the stove in the living room, where they talked in low tones. Catherine wrote: "He related to her what Stickus had told him that day; also that he had learned that the Indians were holding councils every night." After a long talk, Marcus told Narcissa to return to her bed. He promised to call her if he saw any change for the worse in any of the children.

After blowing out the candle, Marcus sat down at the end of the settee on which Catherine lay. "He was apparently deep in thought," she later wrote, "and his manner and portions of their conversation which I had heard kept me awake. Father observed my wakefulness and seemed to understand the reason. He soothed me with kind words until I finally fell asleep and slept until morning."

November 29 dawned cold and foggy. Catherine noted that her father, although "more serious than usual," kept his emotions under control. "We saw nothing of Mother," wrote Catherine. "She did not come out for breakfast. Elizabeth took some food on a plate and a cup of coffee and carried it to her. She was sitting with her face buried in her handkerchief, sobbing bitterly. Taking the food she motioned the child to leave. The food was there, untouched, the next morning." [47]

Mrs. Saunders, in her account of those tragic days, reported that three children of Tiloukaikt's lodge had died of the measles during the night. It may be that one or more of these were his children. Whitman was notified and offered to conduct a burial service. While waiting for the bodies to arrive, Whitman talked with Rodgers about the warning Stickus had given. According to Catherine, after discussing "the trouble that seemed to be brewing; the discontent of the Indians; the Catholics coming in so quickly, and the insinuations of Joe Lewis," the two considered what could be done to improve relations with the natives. Catherine remembered Dr. Whitman as saying: "If things do not clear up by spring, I will make arrangements to move my family to the [Willamette] Valley."

Whitman decided to ask the half-breed, Nicholas Finley, who lived with his Cayuse wife in a lodge about one hundred yards from the Whitman home, what he knew about any supposed plot. Finley was sent for and when he arrived, Whitman asked him: "I understand the Indians are to kill me and Mr. Spalding. Do you know anything about it?" Although Finley was fully aware of what was to happen, since the conspirators had met in his lodge when they agreed on their course of action, he brazenly professed ignorance by replying: "I should know doctor; you have nothing to fear; there is no danger."

In addition to Whitman and Rodgers, ten adult white men, including Joseph Stanfield, were on the premises. Both Bewley and Sales were confined to their beds because of illness. There were also the two Sager boys, John and Francis. All were busy with their appointed tasks. Saunders, the schoolteacher, reopened his school that Monday morning after an interlude of about a week caused by the illness of so many of his pupils. Gilliland, the tailor, was at work on a suit of clothes for Dr. Whitman. He preferred to sit cross-legged on top of a table while plying his needle. Osborn was laying a floor in the former Indian room then being occupied by himself and his family; Hall was busy building an extension to the east end of the stem of the T-shaped mission building. Marsh was grinding wheat at the mill. Stanfield and Francis Sager had been sent to the range to select an animal to be butchered. The animal was shot by Francis and the carcass hung up at a spot between the mill and the blacksmith shop. Hoffman, Kimball, and Canfield were given the task of butchering it.

The bodies of the three Indian children who had died during the previous night arrived at the mission about 11:00 a.m. By this time Narcissa had arisen and without eating her breakfast began to minister to the needs of the sick. Whitman accompanied the dead to the cemetery for burial and was surprised to note that only a few Indians were present, when usually there would be many for such an occasion. He mentioned this to Narcissa on his return and remarked that he thought the butchering of the beef had kept them away. After his return from the cemetery, Narcissa told Marcus that Lorinda Bewley, who was confined to her bed in an upstairs room over the Whitman's parlor, needed his attention. After seeing her, Catherine remembered the doctor saying to his wife: "Poor Lorinda is in trouble and does not know the cause. I found her weeping, and she said that there was a presentiment of evil on her mind that she could not overcome."

THE MASSACRE

Nineteen who survived the massacre and the month's captivity which followed have given us their reminiscences [Appendix 5]. Some were written within a few days of the events described, and others many years later. In addition several people, including Spalding, Brouillet, and McBean, who were not at Waiilatpu at the time of the tragedy but who were involved in contemporary events, have given us their stories. Often these various accounts contradict each other in certain minor details. A conscientious effort has been made to weave these various accounts together to make a single credible narrative.

After the noonday meal on Monday, November 29, 1847, the men returned to their respective tasks and the children went back to school. John Sager went to the kitchen where he continued winding a skein of brown twine preparatory to making a broom. Mary Ann Bridger was in the kitchen washing the noonday dishes. Mrs. Osborn, who had been confined to her bed in the Indian room for about three weeks, ventured to get up and get dressed. She was very weak. She walked into the living room where she saw Dr. Whitman reading and Mrs. Whitman bathing the two older Sager girls. A tub of water had been placed on the floor in the room. Catherine had just been bathed and was dressing; Elizabeth was still in the tub.

The tragic events began when Narcissa went into the kitchen to get milk for some of the sick children. She found the room full of boisterous Indians whose manner alarmed her. One demanded the milk she was carrying. According to Catherine's account: "She told him to wait until she could give her baby some. He followed her to the door of the sitting room and tried to force his way in, but she shut the door in his face and bolted it." [48]

Marcus Whitman, Mortally Wounded

As soon as Narcissa was able to fasten the door, an Indian began pounding on it, calling for the doctor and asking for medicine. Dr. Whitman, laying aside his book, arose and answered the knock. As he unbolted the door, an Indian tried to force his way in, but the doctor succeeded in keeping him out. The Indian demanded medicine, which the doctor promised to get. Whitman closed and locked the door; went to the medicine cabinet located in a closet under the stairway, and got what was needed. As he returned to the kitchen door, he advised Narcissa to lock it after him. It was then about two o'clock in the afternoon.

Catherine tells what then happened: "We could hear loud and angry voices in the kitchen and occasionally Father's soft, mild voice in reply... Suddenly there was a sharp explosion—a rifle shot—in the kitchen, and we all jumped in fright for the outside door." Narcissa's first impulse was to rush into the kitchen to see what had happened, but she quickly controlled herself. Her immediate concern was for the safety of those with her. She called back those who were starting to go out-of-doors. She began dressing Elizabeth who had leaped out of the tub. Turning to Mrs. Osborn, she told her to go to her room and lock the outside door. Mrs. Osborn called her husband to do this. He, not having a hammer handy, used a flatiron to drive a nail over the latch.

Suddenly Mary Ann Bridger, who was the only eyewitness to the attack on Dr. Whitman and John Sager, burst into the living room through the west door. She had fled out of the north door of the kitchen and around the north end of the building. At first the child was so incoherent with fright that she could not speak. Narcissa grabbed her and asked: "Did they kill the doctor?" Mary Ann finally stammered: "Yes." Catherine recalled that Narcissa cried over and over: "My husband is killed and I am left a widow!"

Soon Mary Ann was able to tell what she had seen. She told that the Indians had crowded into the kitchen, including Tiloukaikt and Tomahas, the latter being the one who had demanded the medicine. When Whitman entered the room, he sat down at a table facing Tiloukaikt. According to Spalding's account, who drew upon the child's recollections: "While... [Tiloukaikt] engrossed the doctor's attention, Tomahas stepped behind him, drew a pipe tomahawk[49] from under his blanket, and struck the doctor's head. He fell partly forward. A second blow on the back of the head brought him to the floor."[50] Catherine added more details: "Tiloukaikt chopped the doctor's face so badly that his features could not be recognized." An Indian shot the doctor in the neck, causing profuse bleeding. This was the shot which those in the living room heard. Although fatally wounded, Whitman remained alive for several hours, most of the time unconscious.

As soon as John Sager became aware of the attack on Dr. Whitman, he grabbed a pistol, which might have been the gun he had used to kill the beef then being butchered, and shot twice, wounding two of the Indians.[51] John was then shot by Tamsucky.[52] He received a severe wound in the neck which began to bleed profusely. He had enough consciousness to stuff a part of the scarf he was wearing into the wound to staunch the flow of blood. A sudden commotion outside caused the Indians in the kitchen to rush pell-mell through the south kitchen door to join in the killings taking place there. They left Marcus Whitman and John Sager, both mortally wounded, lying on the floor.

The Attack Out-of-Doors

Following the noon meal on that fateful Monday, Judge Saunders had reassembled his pupils in the schoolroom. The number was smaller than usual because so many of the children were ill. The sudden shooting and the tumult outside naturally brought all activities in the schoolroom to a sudden halt. The half-breed boy, John D. Manson, who was thirteen years old at the time, in his recollections of that tragic day, wrote: "While out at school recess, we saw eighteen or twenty Indians standing around the Mission Premises and they were watching three men dressing a beef. They were clothed with blankets strapped around their waists with belts. When Mr. Saunders, our teacher, rang the bell, we went back to the school room. Very soon a number of shots were fired and Mr. Saunders looked out and saw Mr. Kimball running to the Doctor's house. His arm was hanging limp and bleeding. Mr. Saunders crossed the room and said, 'I must go to my family'... We boys went to the window and saw that the Indians had dropped their blankets and were running about with their weapons in their hands, shooting and shouting." [53]

Pandemonium reigned. It is impossible to give an accurate chronological account of what took place, for the eyewitness accounts differ. Perhaps the first to be killed was Marsh who was operating the gristmill. His death was probably instantaneous as none of the survivors listed him as being among the wounded.

Another killed during the first few minutes of the attack was Hoffman, who was the only one of the victims who was able to offer any effective resistance. Catherine wrote: "Mr. Hoffman was butchering beef and fought manfully with an ax and was seen keeping several Indians at bay. He felled several with powerful blows from his ax, and split one of his assailant's feet before he was finally overpowered. They disemboweled him." [54] No doubt this mutilation was the result of the angry resentment of those whom he had wounded. There is no evidence that the Indians scalped any of their victims.

Catherine Sager, who was standing with Narcissa looking through the upper part of the east door of the living room, which was a window, saw the Indians attack Saunders. Of this she wrote: "Mr. Saunders had commenced school at one o'clock. Hearing the explosion [i.e., the rifle shots] in the kitchen, he ran down to see what caused it. Mother saw him just as he got to the door. She motioned to him to go back. He ran back, and had just got to the stairway [consisting of two or three steps] leading up to the school, when an Indian seized him, but being an active man, the Indian could not master him. I watched the struggle from the window. Sometimes the savage would throw him, but he would bound to his feet again, never losing his hold of the first one. I looked till my heart sickened at the sight. Mr. Saunders wrestling for life with those ruthless murderers, and they with their butcher knives trying to cut his throat. He got loose from them and had got almost to his door... before he was overpowered. His body was pierced with several balls when he fell. They beat his head till it was mashed to pieces."

Elizabeth Sager testified at the Oregon City trial, held in May 1850, that she saw Ish-ish-kais-kais shoot Saunders. Osborn in his testimony given at the same trial said that Tomahas was one of those who took part in the attack. Mrs. Hall, who was watching the horrifying events from a window in the emigrant house, thought that the Indians were attacking Dr. Whitman, and so testified at the trial. She then claimed that Tiloukaikt was one of the assailants. Both Catherine and Elizabeth Sager, however, claimed that Mrs. Hall was mistaken, as Dr. Whitman was never able to leave the kitchen after being struck down. Matilda Sager remembered that after the Indians had killed Saunders, they cut off his head.[55]

Among those who witnessed the attack of the Indians on the three men who were butchering the beef and on the schoolteacher was twelve-year-old Nathan Kimball, Jr. After more than fifty years, Nathan was able to recall with vividness the events of those days. Regarding the mutilation of the bodies of the victims, he wrote: "The bodies, or pieces of them, lay scattered all around, an arm here and a leg there. Some of the men had their breasts torn open and their hearts taken out. I saw two Indians each with a stick and a human heart stuck upon it, which they showed to the women, and told them that they belonged to their husbands, and that they were going to eat them. I don't think they did but I don't know."[56]

Three men, Gilliland, Kimball, and Rodgers, after being seriously wounded managed to find temporary refuge in one of the mission buildings. Gilliland, according to Catherine's account, "was sitting upon his table sewing, (when) an Indian stepped in, and shot him with a pistol."[57] Mrs. Saunders, who was in a room of the emigrant house next to that occupied by Gilliland, ran to see what had, happened after hearing the gunshot. The Indian later identified as Ish-ish-kais-kais, pointed his pistol at Mrs. Saunders.[58] She turned and fled to her room. Gilliland soon followed. In terror, Mrs. Saunders closed the door, shutting out Gilliland, as she thought he was an Indian. Finally, hearing him call: "Let me in, let me in," she opened the door and admitted him. Catherine wrote: "He ran and hid under the bed but soon came out saying, 'It's no use to hide.' He lay down on the bed and died quietly about midnight."

Nathan Kimball, Jr., saw an Indian shooting at his father who was trying to escape. The father had been shot in the arm and the son remembered: "My father had on a white shirt, and I could see that his arm was broken at the elbow, for it was red with blood." [59] The father ran around the south end of the mission house and entered the living room through the west door. Elizabeth Sager remembered that when he burst into the room, holding his bleeding arm he cried out: "The Indians are killing us—I don't know what the damned Indians want to kill me for—I never did anything to them. Get me some water." [60] Since Kimball was a religious man and never swore, the expression "damned Indians" seemed so incongruous to the little girl that she began to giggle. She fully expected Mrs. Whitman to rebuke him "for swearing in the presence of children," but to her surprise nothing was said. Instead, her foster mother hastily got water and began washing the wounded arm.

Rodgers was at the river getting a pail of water when the shooting began. Hidden by the fringe of willows which grew on the banks, he could have escaped detection and fled to Fort Walla Walla for protection. Instead, he rushed back to the mission house. Catherine tells us: "Mother, while ministering to the wounded, went here and there looking out to see what was going on. She had missed Mr. Rodgers from his room and was anxiously watching to see if she could see anything of him. At last she saw him running desperately toward the house, several savages, their knives and tomahawks glinting in the sun, close at his heels. She dashed to the door to open it, but not before he had broken the window with his hand as he sprang against it. As soon as the door closed upon him, the Indians raised a deafening yell and went to find new victims. He was shot through the wrist and tomahawked behind the ear." [61]

Terror In-Doors

Narcissa's immediate concern, after hearing the commotion in the kitchen, was the fate of her husband. After the Indians there had rushed out-of-doors and silence had come to the kitchen, Narcissa ventured to enter. To her horror, she found Marcus lying half-conscious on the floor with his head in a pool of blood. Just at that time, three of the women who were living in the emigrant house—Mrs. Hays, Mrs. Hall, and Mrs. Saunders—burst in through the north kitchen door. With their help, Narcissa half carried and half dragged Marcus into the living room and placed him on a settee. Of the scene that followed, Catherine wrote: "She fastened the door and placed a pillow under his head, and kneeling over him tried to stop the blood that was flowing from a wound in his neck." [62] Narcissa took a towel and some wood ashes from the stove and with these tried to stop the bleeding. She asked him if he knew her. He replied: "Yes," "Are you badly hurt?" "Yes." "Can I do anything to stop this blood?" "No." "Can you speak with me?" "N-no." "Is your mind at peace?" "Yes." He spoke only in monosyllables. Again and again, Narcissa cried out: "That Joe! That Joe! He has done it all. I am a widow!" When Rodgers burst into the room so suddenly, he at once saw the doctor lying on the settee and asked if he were dead. Whitman heard the question and answered with a weak "No." This was the last word he spoke; he then lapsed into unconsciousness.

Several times during those terrifying minutes following the first shootings, Joe Lewis came to the door of the living room and tried to enter. Catherine wrote: "He had a gun in his hand and when Mother would ask, 'What do you want, Joe?,' he would instantly leave." Soon after Rodgers had entered the room, Narcissa went again to the east door to look out through its window. It was then that Ish-ish-kais-kais (Frank Escaloom), who was standing on the steps leading into the schoolroom, raised his gun and shot her. Catherine wrote: "Mother was standing looking out at the window when a ball came through the broken pane, entering her right shoulder.[63] She clapped her hand to the wound saying, 'Oh! Oh!' and fell backwards. She now forgot everything but the poor, helpless children depending on her, and she poured out her soul in prayer for them, 'Lord save these little ones!' was her repeated cry." Catherine also recalled how Narcissa prayed for her parents, saying: "This will kill my poor mother." [64]

Catherine's account of what then happened follows: "The women began now to go upstairs; and Mr. Rogers, too much excited to speak, pushed us upstairs. I said, 'Who will take care of the sick children?' Let me take them up, too; don't leave them here alone." Catherine was thinking of her two sisters, Louise and Henrietta, and Helen Mar Meek, who were probably in beds in the Whitman bedroom. From this time onward, Catherine assumed a responsibility far beyond her years and became a real heroine of those tragic hours. The sick children were carried to the attic room. Altogether thirteen frightened people sought the doubtful safety of the upstairs room. These included two wounded men, Kimball and Rodgers; five women, including Lorinda Bewley who was in her sick bed; and the four Sager and the two half-breed girls.

In the meantime, Osborn, remembering that the floor boards of the Indian room in which he and his family were living, had not been nailed down, lifted several and hastily got his wife, their three children, and himself under the floor. A three-foot space gave them plenty of room to hide. "We lay there listening to the firing," Osborn wrote in a letter dated April 7, 1848, "—the screams of women and children the groans of the dying—not knowing when our turn would come. We were, however, not discovered." [65]

Years later, Nancy Osborn, who was only nine years old at the time, had the following to tell: "In a few minutes our room was full of Indians, talking and laughing as if it were a holiday. The only noise we made was my brother, Alexander, two years old. When the Indians came into the room and were directly over our heads, he said: 'Mother, the Indians are taking all of our things.' Hastily she clapped her hands over his mouth and whispered he must be still." [66]

EXPERIENCES OF THE SCHOOL CHILDREN

As soon as the school children realized what was happening out-of-doors, they quickly shut and locked the door. Francis (also called Frank) Sager suggested that they climb up into a loft which had been built over part of the room for use as a bedroom. Since there was no stairway to the room, nor was a ladder then available, the children moved a table under the door of the loft and piled some books on it. One of the older boys then climbed up and helped the girls to enter. Among them was Matilda Sager, who, many years later, wrote: "Frank told us all to ask God to save us and I can see him now,... as he kneeled and prayed for God to spare us." [67]

Just how long the children remained hidden in the loft is not known, but sometime early in the afternoon Joe Stanfield came calling for the two Manson boys and David Malin. These came down from the loft and were then taken by Stanfield to Finley's lodge which was located to the north of the main mission house. Stanfield assured the boys that since they were part Indian, they would not be harmed. The next day Finley took the three boys to Fort Walla Walla where they were given into the custody of William McBean.

Soon after Stanfield had taken the three half-breed boys to Finley's lodge, Joe Lewis entered the schoolroom looking for Francis Sager in particular. For some reason Joe had a special grudge against Francis and was bent on revenge. After discovering that Francis and the other children were in the loft, Joe demanded that all come down at once. They were then taken out into the yard and lined up to be shot. After the departure of the Manson boys, only Eliza Spalding could understand what was being said by the Indians. She remembered that some of the Indians were opposed to killing the children. Convinced that they would be killed, frightened Eliza covered her face with her apron "so that she would not see them shoot her." [68]

Catherine wrote: "There they stood in a long row, their murderers leaning on their guns, waiting for the word from the chief (possibly Tiloukaikt) to send them into eternity. Pity, however, moved the heart of the chief for, after observing their terror, he said: 'Let us not kill them.'"

The children were then taken into the Indian room. As they passed through the kitchen Francis saw his brother lying mortally wounded on the floor. He leaned over and by some sudden impulse pulled at the scarf which John had stuffed into the wound in his throat. This was the wrong thing to do, as it opened the wound and the blood began to pour out. John tried to speak but could not. He died soon afterwards.

Francis sobbed and said: "I will follow him." Some of the Indians taunted Joe Lewis and said that "if he was on their side, he must kill Francis Sager to prove it." [69] After being thus taunted, Joe grabbed Francis by the nose, jerked him forward, and called him "a bad boy." The Osborns under the floor heard Francis pleading for his life: "O Joe, don't shoot me!" Then came the crack of a gun, "as Lewis proved his loyalty to the red men." Francis fell at the entrance of the north door leading out of the Indian room. At the trial of the five accused murderers held in Oregon City, Clokamus admitted "that he assisted in dispatching young Sager." [70]

MRS. SAUNDERS'S BRAVE INTERCESSION

In the meantime, Mrs. Saunders, not knowing what had happened to her husband or to the Whitmans, and fearing for the safety of all the white women and children, decided to make a desperate appeal for mercy to Chief Tiloukaikt through Nicholas Finley. She bravely ventured to leave the comparative safety of her room in the emigrant house in order to call on Finley in his lodge. John Manson was at the lodge when Mrs. Saunders arrived and has given us the following account of what happened. Since he was able to understand what the Indians were saying, his recollections have special significance.

Soon Mrs. Saunders came up to the lodge where Mrs. Finley [an Indian woman], her sister and several other Indian women were standing. Besides the Cayuse Indian women, there were some Walla Walla Indian men. The women seemed friendly to Mrs. Saunders.

About four hundred feet away from the lodge was a hill that had three Indians on it, looking over the plains. [Possibly looking to see if anyone were approaching.] One of the Indians rode down to kill Mrs. Saunders, but Mrs. Finley expostulated with him and he rode off. Then Chief Tiloukaikt rode down, shaking his hatchet over his head. He threatened Mrs. Saunders with it, but again Mrs. Finley urged him to desist and he rode off. Then Edward Tiloukaikt, the oldest son of the Chief, rode down very rapidly, shaking his tomahawk over his head and that of Mrs. Saunders with fury. She had sunk down on a pile of matting in front of the lodge. But the Indian women shamed him and talked to him. Then he rode off.

Mrs. Saunders then came to me [John Manson] and kneeled down. She begged me to interpret for her to the Chiefs, as she did not understand the language of the natives. She said: "Tell the Chiefs that if the Doctor and men were bad, I did not know it. My heart is good and I want to live. If they will spare my life, I will make caps, coats, and pantaloons for them."

John interpreted for her as she pled with Tiloukaikt for the life of her husband and for the women and children. In all probability her husband by that time had been killed, but of this she was unaware.

"What do they say, John?"

"They are talking about it."

After some consultation, Tiloukaikt and the other chiefs agreed that none of the women and children would be killed. Mrs. Saunders then begged to let all who were in the main mission house go to the emigrant house. Tiloukaikt gave his consent.

Mrs. Saunders then turned to John, while still on her knees, and begged: "John won't you go home with me?" John replied: "I do not dare to go, but I will ask." Tiloukaikt then told Stanfield to take Mrs. Saunders back to her quarters and to get her some meat. John's account continues: "Then Mrs. Saunders rose from her knees and went with Joe Stanfield. The Chiefs and all the natives then left the lodge. They went to Dr. Whitman's house. Very soon, several shots were fired there. Mr. Finley came and told us that three more had been killed. They were Mrs. Whitman, Mr. Rogers, and Francis Sager."

The Deaths of Narcissa Whitman and Andrew Rodgers

The rampaging Indians, after searching the main floor of the Whitman home for Mrs. Whitman and other members of her family, finally came to the door leading to the attic rooms. This had been locked from the inside but the Indians soon smashed it open. "We thought our time had come," wrote Catherine. While the Indians were still breaking down the door, Kimball said that if they only had a gun, they could keep them at bay. Someone remembered that there was the barrel of a broken gun in the attic room. Rodgers got it and held it over the railing of the stairwell. As soon as the Indians, who began ascending the stairs, saw the gun barrel, they hastily retreated.

None of the eyewitness accounts pinpoint the rapidly passing events by giving the time. In all probability all of the events described above, following the firing of the first shot, came within an hour period. Catherine remembered that, following the retreat of the Indians from the stairway, all was quiet before for about half an hour. "We began to think," she wrote, "that the Indians had left, when we heard footsteps in the rooms below, and a voice at the bottom of the stairs called Mr. Rodgers. Mr. R. would not answer for a time. Mother finally prevailed on him to speak, remarking, 'God maybe has raised us up a friend.'" The Indian was Tamsucky. It was he who, according to the best available evidence, was the one who had tried to force his way into Narcissa's bedroom shortly after Marcus had left for the East in October 1842. In a friendly voice, he told Rodgers that he had just arrived on the mission grounds, knew nothing of the terrible events which had taken place, and was then offering his help. Narcissa, eager to grasp at any offer of aid in her hour of desperation, was ready to throw herself upon Tamsucky's promise of aid and deliverance. Catherine, however, had recognized Tamsucky as one of the Indians who had killed Judge Saunders and advised caution. After some consultation, the adults in the upstairs room decided that they should listen to what Tamsucky had to say.

Catherine tells us what then happened: "Mr. Rodgers told him to come upstairs. He replied that he was afraid we had white men there who would kill him. Mr. Rodgers assured him of his safety. He then asked for Mother, and was told that she was badly hurt. Mr. Rodgers finally went to the doorway and talked with him, and succeeded in having him come where we were. He shook hands with us all and seemed very sorry Mother was hurt; condoled with her on what had happened until he won her confidence." When Tamsucky saw the wounded Kimball lying on the floor, he muttered: "Bad Indian. Indian shoot."

Tamsucky then passed on the terrifying information that the Indians were planning to burn the mission house and that Mrs. Whitman and those with her should leave immediately for the lodge of an Indian who lived ten miles away.[71] Narcissa, realizing that she was in no condition to travel and also that it would soon be dark, told him that they could not go at that time. Tamsucky then told her to go to the emigrant house and spend the night there. In reality Tamsucky was scheming to get her and Rodgers out-of-doors where the Indians could complete their bloody designs. Narcissa was completely deceived by his duplicity, but then, what else could she do except to follow his advice? She grasped at his specious promises of protection.

Eager to return to their families in the emigrant house, the three women hastily left. Going with them was Lorinda Bewley who had arisen from her sick bed. Rodgers helped Narcissa go down the stairs. She was so weak from the loss of blood that she had to lie down at once on a settee. With her was Elizabeth Sager, then ten years old, who never forgot how Narcissa averted her face when she saw her husband, still alive but unconscious.[72] The sight of the bloody, mutilated head was too horrible to endure. Kimball decided not to risk leaving the attic room, perhaps suspecting that Tamsucky's promise of safe conduct to the emigrant house did not apply to him. Since no one had been willing or able to carry the sick little girls to the emigrant house, Catherine decided to remain with them. Also in the attic room was Mary Ann Bridger.

Shortly after Narcissa went down stairs, the Indians ordered Rodgers to help Joe Lewis carry her on the settee over to the emigrant house. Even though Rodgers had been wounded in the wrist, he seems to have been able to lift his end of the settee. They moved from the living room through the kitchen and out the north door of the kitchen. Elizabeth, who was following, noted that her brother John's body "was lying across the doorway." As soon as the settee bearing Narcissa had cleared the doorway, some Indians standing near started firing. Elizabeth remembered: "I was still on the sill when a shot from a row of Indians standing there struck Mrs. Whitman on the cheek. I saw the bullet as it hit her. Mr. Rodgers set the settee down on the platform at the doorway saying 'Oh, My God!' and fell." He, too had been struck with bullets. As Elizabeth turned to flee to the upstairs room to rejoin her sister Catherine, she passed through the living room where she slipped in a pool of blood. Upstairs, she stammered out her story of what had happened. "The terror of that moment cannot be expressed," she wrote. "There were no tears, no shrieks." The awfulness of what had happened stunned all, even the younger girls, into silence.[73]

After a volley of bullets had been fired into the bodies of Narcissa and Rodgers, one of the Indians upset the settee and rolled her body into the mud, possibly into an irrigation ditch. With fiendish delight, one Indian lifted up Narcissa's head by grabbing her hair, and lashed her face with his braided leather quirt.[74] Circumstantial evidence indicates that Narcissa died at the time of this attack or shortly thereafter. Rodgers, although mortally wounded, lingered on for several hours in a conscious condition.

"As soon as it became dark," wrote Nancy Osborn, "the Indians left for their lodges... Everything became still. It was the stillness of death." The school children, released by their captors, had fled to the emigrant house where Mrs. Saunders received Matilda. Those in the emigrant house were ignorant of the fate of Kimball and of the four girls who had been left in the attic room, but no one dared go and investigate.

Nancy remembered that while she with the other members of her family were still in hiding under the floor of the Indian room, the stillness which had come to the mission house was broken only by the groans of the dying. Dr. Whitman died about nine o'clock that evening; Rodgers died later. "All we could hear were the dying groans of Mr. Rodgers, who lay within six feet of me," wrote Nancy. "We heard him say, 'Come Lord Jesus, come quickly.' Afterwards he said faintly, 'Sweet Jesus.' Then fainter and fainter came the moans until they ceased all together."

The carnage for the day was over with nine people dead—one woman, six men, and two boys.

Thus ended the earthly life of Narcissa Whitman who, at the time of her death, was approaching her fortieth birthday. And likewise the life of Marcus Whitman who had lived nearly three months beyond his forty-fifth birthday. They were the first Protestants to suffer martyrdom on the Pacific Slope of the United States.[75]

SOME WERE WEEPING

Waiilatpu was a place of contradictions on that bloody Monday afternoon. The violence precipitated a dichotomy of emotions among the Cayuses themselves. Mingled with hideous war cries were pleas of mercy. While some were killing, others were weeping. Again it should be emphasized that only a small minority of the Cayuses took part in the massacre, and they were largely if not exclusively from Tiloukaikt's band. Most of the members of the Cayuse tribe were either unaware of what had been planned or had refused to join in the conspiracy.

Among those who objected to the violence, and who did much to ameliorate the lot of the captives after the massacre, was one whom the survivors called Chief Beardy.[76] Possibly "Beardy" was a nickname bestowed upon him at the time of the massacre by the grateful survivors. No mention of a chief by this name has been found in the writings of the Whitmans nor do we know his Indian name. The Sager girls and Mrs. Saunders make frequent mention of him. He was described as having been one of the most faithful attendants at Whitman's religious services. No doubt the nickname was given because of his hirsute appearance, unusual among the Indians.

Catherine wrote that when Mrs. Saunders went to Finley's lodge, "She saw an Indian at Dr. Whitman's house, talking and gesticulating for some time. He rode toward her, and she saw that *he was weeping*."[77] It was Beardy who was vainly trying to get the other Indians to stop their killings. Mrs. Saunders called to him, and he rode to her and went with her to the lodge. Catherine wrote: "Whether it was her intercession or the speech of the chief [i.e., Beardy] that turned the tide, I know not what, but the chief [Tiloukaikt] heading the murderers said, 'It is enough, no more blood must be shed. The Doctor is dead. The men are all dead. These women and children have not hurt us and they must not be hurt.' "Actually at that time, not all the men had been killed. Four more were to die, but the women and children were spared. Perhaps much of the credit for this act of mercy should go to the influence of Beardy.

Catherine, in summarizing the events of the next day, November 30, noted that some of the Indian women "cried over us and gave us many things." Again and again in the reminiscences of the survivors, we find references to the grief of many of the Cayuses who were shocked by the violence committed by some of their own tribe.

Tuesday, November 30, 1847

Monday night was a night of terror for Catherine Sager, who, although only thirteen years old, was trying to be a mother to her two younger sisters and to the two half-breed girls. Three of the girls in the attic room were very ill. Kimball was in too much pain as the result of his wound to be of any help. No one can read Catherine's account of the massacre and the subsequent captivity without feeling great admiration for the way she tried to measure up to the responsibilities so suddenly thrust upon her.

In Catherine's account of the night of November 9th, we may read: "The Indians seemed to be making preparations to set fire to the house. We heard them ask for fire and splitting up kindlings. We fully expected to perish in the flames but this was more desirable than to be killed by the savages. Night came on. The Indians seemed to have left. We sat on the bed hardly daring to breathe in our fright. I took all the children on one bed. Their clothes were saturated with blood where they had lain on the bed with Mrs. Whitman. I tried to soothe them but they were perishing for water... They cried almost all night." Finally, one by one, the children fell asleep leaving Catherine and Kimball still awake. She remembered hearing "the yowls of the cats" in the room below and the striking of the hours by the clock. No doubt the cats were yowling because of hunger. No one had fed them. "Never shall I forget that awful night," wrote Catherine. "I think of it now with a shudder... I knew not what the new day might bring." Finally, towards morning, out of utter exhaustion, Catherine lapsed into sleep.

When day began to break, Kimball awakened Catherine and said that he was going to try to go to the river for a pail of water. Since everything was quiet in the house, the two felt that perhaps no Indians were around. There is no evidence that the Indians left any guards at Waiilatpu during the night to keep check on its residents. Although Kimball and Catherine talked in low tones, still their conversation awakened the children who at once began to cry for water. Before leaving for the river, Kimball felt it best to have his arm bandaged, as it pained him greatly. He told Catherine to tear up one of the sheets and use that as a bandage. Catherine's initial reaction to the idea of tearing up a good sheet was such that she exclaimed: "Mother would not like to have the sheets torn up." "Child," replied Kimball, "don't you know that your mother is dead, and will never have any use for the sheets?" Reluctantly Catherine tore the sheet into strips and bound up the wounded arm.

Kimball disguised himself the best he could as a blanketed Indian. Taking a pail, he started for the river which he reached in safety. As he was about to return, he noticed that some Indians had arrived on the grounds. Fearful of being detected, Kimball hid in some bushes which grew along the river where he remained all day. About sundown, thinking that the Indians were all gone, Kimball started back to the house. Just as he was climbing over a fence, he was seen by Frank Escaloom[78] who immediately shot him. Catherine wrote: "As he fell the Indian gave a brutal laugh."[79] Evidently death came to Kimball instantly. He thus became the tenth victim of the massacre.

Attracted by the crying of the children early that Tuesday morning, some Indians came to the foot of the stairway leading to the attic and inquired what was the matter. Catherine begged them to get water, which one did and he also got some bread. Since the children cried for more water and the Indian refused to get any more, Catherine decided to go for some herself. Of this she wrote: "I could not bear to hear the piteous calls for water." Going down stairs, she found her shoes where she had left them the day before and went to the river. Upon returning with her pail of water, her life was threatened. She wrote: "Some Indians were sitting upon the fence; one of them pointed his gun at me. I was terribly frightened, but walked on. One sitting near him knocked the gun up and it went off in the air."[80]

As Catherine moved through the lower rooms of the house, she could not have avoided seeing the dead body of Dr. Whitman and one or both of her brothers. She knew from Elizabeth's account that Mrs. Whitman and Rodgers had been killed and that their bodies were lying outside the door of the Indian room. Added to the horror of such sights was the threat to her life. All in all, she had a traumatic experience which found relief in an outburst of weeping after she returned with the water. The other children in the attic room joined her. Of this Catherine wrote: "We were weeping over the slain when Joe Stanfield came in. He told us to stop that noise; that they were dead and it would do them no good, and if the Indians saw us crying, they would be mad." Stanfield told Catherine to take the children to the emigrant house.

Since three of the younger children were too ill to walk, Catherine carried six-year-old Louise, and Elizabeth managed to carry four-year-old Henrietta. These four with Mary Ann started for the emigrant house. Helen Mar Meek had to be left behind but Catherine assured her that she would return and get her. Someone in the emigrant house saw the four children on their way and several rushed out to meet them. "For a few moments," wrote Catherine, "we wept together." Catherine, accompanied by one or more of the women, hastened back to get Helen Mar. "We found her," Catherine wrote, "sitting in the bed, surrounded by Indians and screaming at the top of her voice." [81] She thought she had been deserted.

Sometime during Tuesday, all of the survivors of the massacre were brought into the emigrant house. This included the Canfield family and the two sick men, Crockett Bewley and Amos Sales. As will be told, Hall, Canfield, and the Osborn family had managed to escape. With the exception of the two families still at the sawmill, all of those who were later rescued, numbering over forty, were in the emigrant house. The five Sager girls, now twice orphaned, were together again.

The Hudson's Bay Company Informed of the Massacre

William McBean at Fort Walla Walla first learned of the massacre when Peter D. Hall arrived at the fort about seven o'clock Tuesday morning, November 30. Hall had been busy in carpenter work in the room being added to the east end of the main mission building when the attack began. When the sound of firing in the kitchen was heard by the Indians outside, several rushed to attack Hall, one with a gun which misfired. Hall grappled with the Indian who had the gun and succeeded in getting possession of it. Catherine wrote: "By pointing the gun, he kept them at bay until he reached the river where he plunged boldly in and swam for the opposite shore. His pursuers, seeing him out of reach, yelled defiantly and shot their guns at him without effect."[82]

Shielded by the protecting willows which lined the river banks, Hall cautiously made his way down stream towards Fort Walla Walla. He was able to travel the twenty-five miles during the night and was the first to give McBean the news of the attack at Waiilatpu. His information was fragmentary. He reported that "the doctor and another man were killed," perhaps referring to the death of Marsh at the mill. He could give McBean no details regarding the identity of the murderers nor how the attack originated.[83] In his excited state, he was sure that his wife and children and all white people at Waiilatpu had been slaughtered.

Father Ricard, founder of the Saint Rose Mission, happened to be at Fort Walla Walla on that Tuesday morning and recorded the event in his journal: "I was at the fort with Mr. McBean when, at 7 o'clock, the American brought us the news of the massacre. At 11 o'clock a native Catholic woman arrived, quite breathless, and told us that the Cayuses had resolved to come to the fort and kill all the whites there. At this far from reassuring news everyone in the fort, namely Mr. McBean, Fr. Pandosy, three hired men, and myself, closed the doors, loaded our guns, and prepared to defend ourselves. This was in vain for the Cayuses did not appear. Nevertheless, as a precaution, we kept the doors closed from then on."[84]

Hall was greatly agitated, being fearful that the Indians would seek him out at the fort and kill him. McBean wrote:

> He finally resolved to leave and make for The Dalles. I remarked to him that it was rash and imprudent... The fort being enclosed, doors locked day and night, and fortified with two bastions, he would be safer in it than he would be on the open plain. My arguments had no force. I then asked him if he left a wife and children at the Mission. He replied he had, but supposed them all killed. I observed that it was only a supposition—they might still be living, and that it was wrong to leave them without ascer-

taining their fate. With tears in his eyes, he begged and entreated me to let him go, being sure to reach The Dalles.

Finding he was determined, I provided him with a coat, shirt, provisions and other necessaries for his voyage, and advised him to take the route less frequented by the Indians (across the Columbia river), and to travel only during the night, when he would have a better chance of evading any camp by noticing their fire. I saw him safely across and the last tidings I had of him was that he had safely reached within a few miles of the Deschutes; but unfortunately having taken a canoe from the Indians and being near a rapid, he run down [i.e., attempted to navigate the rapids], and was drowned.[85]

It should be noted that McBean wrote this account some seventeen years after the events described had occurred. In some particulars, his version of his treatment of Hall has been questioned. Hall's body was never found. Although he was not killed at Waiilatpu, Hall is included in the total of fourteen victims because his death is attributable to the events which had taken place at the mission.

McBean was alarmed at the news that Hall had brought to him. Eager to get more information as to what had actually taken place at Waiilatpu, he sent his interpreter, a man by the name of Bushman, on Tuesday morning to make inquiry. In the meantime, Nicholas Finley left the mission with the three half-breed boys that same morning for Fort Walla Walla. Mrs. Saunders, learning from Joe Stanfield that Finley was going to the fort, hastily wrote a note to McBean for Finley to carry in which she listed the names of eleven people she thought had been killed. She included the names of Osborn and Canfield, as she was unaware that both had escaped. Catherine, in her account of what happened on Tuesday, said that when Bushman arrived at Waiilatpu, he was so frightened by what he saw and heard that he "came only to the door and as soon as they assured him that it was so, he left."[86]

Catherine also reported that on Tuesday, Joe Stanfield was busy digging a grave in the mission cemetery "three feet deep and wide enough for all to lie side by side." Stanfield had some help from Beardy and two Walla Walla Indians. From other evidence, it appears that the grave was not as deep as Catherine indicated. It was shallow, and this may have been due to the fact that digging was difficult. Until the bodies were collected on Wednesday morning for burial, they lay where each person had fallen. Some bodies had been covered with blankets.

About two o'clock Tuesday afternoon, the unsuspecting James Young was killed while driving a team of oxen hitched to a wagon loaded with lumber which he had brought down from the sawmill. The murder took place as he was passing an Indian camp a mile or so to the east of Waiilatpu. The name of his assailant is not known. Spalding reported that the Indians, in their frenzied anger against the white men, even killed the two oxen. Later Stanfield buried the body near the place where Young was killed. Hall and Young were the eleventh and twelfth victims. There were still two more to die.

Bushman made the fifty-mile round trip from Fort Walla Walla to Waiilatpu in the same day. On the evening of his return, McBean wrote to the officials of the Hudson's Bay Company at Fort Vancouver, giving them their first news of the massacre. The arrival of this letter at Fort Vancouver on December 6 started the sequence of events which, after about a month, brought about the release of the captives. This story will be told in the next chapter.

Canfield Escapes

Among those who were wounded and who succeeded in finding temporary refuge in one of the mission buildings at the time the attack began, was W. D. Canfield. He and his family, being late comers to Waiilatpu, had to be content with some makeshift accommodations in the blacksmith shop. When the attack began, Canfield was butchering a beef with Hoffman and Kimball. Catherine tells us what happened: "He [i.e., Canfield] saw his family standing in the yard and ran over toward them. As he did so, he was wounded in the side [by a rifle bullet]. Snatching up his youngest child, and calling his family to follow him, he rushed into the house [possibly, the blacksmith shop]. Going upstairs, he concealed himself under some old lumber and rubbish where he lay until night." [87] The Indians did not pursue him into the building. Sometime during the early part of Monday night, Joe Stanfield came and showed him the trail that led to Lapwai. Evidently by this time, Canfield was convinced that the Indians did not intend to kill the women and children; that his life would be in grave danger should he remain on the premises; and that Mrs. Spalding and her family should be warned of their danger. He therefore started out on the 120-mile journey to Lapwai on foot even though he carried a rifle ball under the skin on one side of his body.

Canfield had never been over the trail before, but after being directed to the trail, he followed the well-beaten road which led in a northeasterly direction. Catherine wrote: "After traveling for a day or two, he fell in with an Indian and his boy driving cattle." Evidently they were friendly Nez Perces who had no objection to having a white man accompanying them. Canfield arrived at Lapwai on Saturday, December 4, having taken about four and a half days to make the journey. Mrs. Spalding, Mary Johnson (who had previously worked for Mrs. Whitman) and the three younger Spalding children were in the Spalding home. Horace Hart and Mr. Jackson were temporarily absent. Spalding tells of Canfield's sudden appearance. After being received into the home, he asked: "Has Mr. Spalding yet come?" Mrs. Spalding replied: "No, but we expect him every day." "The stranger replied: 'I have heavy tidings, they are all murdered at the Doct's.' All were silent for a minute. My dear wife simply rose to her feet & with an unfaltering voice said, 'I was not prepared for this, but go on, Sir, let me hear the worst.' 'Mrs. Whitman is murdered & your husband without doubt shared the fate of all the women & children who I expect are butchered.'" [88]

Mrs. Spalding then said that she would inform the Indians at Lapwai as to what had happened. Canfield remonstrated as he feared that they might do what the Cayuses had done, but Mrs. Spalding knew the character of the Nez Perces. She called for Timothy and Eagle and sent a messenger to Craig's home located about eight miles up the valley from Lapwai. Craig, who had a Nez Perce wife, was the only white man who had settled in the vicinity of the Spalding mission. Although at times Craig had given Spalding much trouble, now he willingly offered shelter to Mrs. Spalding and her family. The next day, Sunday, an Indian arrived from Waiilatpu with the report that Spalding had fled on a horse, possibly headed for the Willamette Valley. Although Eliza was relieved to hear that her husband was alive, she remained concerned not only about his safety but also of her daughter who was among the captives being held at Waiilatpu.

When Canfield, Jackson, and Craig urged Mrs. Spalding to move on Sunday to the Craig home, she refused to do so. So strongly did she cling to the Puritan conception of strict Sunday observance that she would not travel eight miles even when grave danger threatened. "We will rest on the Sabbath," she said and then, paraphrasing a Biblical promise, added: "for he that obeyeth the commandment shall be rewarded." The example that Mrs. Spalding set that day in refusing to travel on Sunday was long remembered by the Christian Nez Perces.

On Monday morning, December 6, when Mrs. Spalding and her household were about to leave for the Craig home, a party of dissident Nez Perces from Chief Joseph's band suddenly appeared at Lapwai with evident hostile intentions. As with the Cayuses, these Nez Perces constituted only a small minority of the Nez Perce tribe and, since they lived near the Cayuses, had been adversely influenced by what had taken place at Waiilatpu. They arrived at Lapwai just as Craig and a party of friendly Nez Perces were about ready to escort Mrs. Spalding up the valley. The hostile band, seeing that they were outnumbered, refrained from acts of violence for the time being, but as soon as the Craig party left, they looted the Spalding home. Mrs. Spalding, eager to learn what had happened to her daughter at Waiilatpu, sent two of the most trusted Nez Perces, Timothy and Eagle, to make inquiry.

Artist Stanley's Narrow Escape

Before the story of the escape of the Osborn family from Waiilatpu can be told, it is necessary to review what happened to the artist, John Mix Stanley, for his experiences dovetailed with those of Josiah Osborn. As was told in the previous chapter, Stanley had visited Waiilatpu during the first days of October 1847 but missed seeing the Whitmans as they had gone to meet the immigrants on the Umatilla River. When Stanley left Waiilatpu for Tshimakain on October 4, he promised to return at some later date in order to meet the Whitmans. After spending several weeks at Tshimakain and vicinity, Stanley set out for Waiilatpu on Tuesday, November 28, having with him one of the most faithful of the Spokane Indians for a guide, whom the Walkers had named Solomon. Fortunately for Stanley, Solomon could speak Nez Perce as well as his mother tongue. Stanley and Solomon camped on Tuesday evening, November 30 about twenty miles from Waiilatpu. On Wednesday morning, when within about six miles of Waiilatpu, they met an Indian woman and a boy who gave them the frightening news of the massacre and that the lives of all Americans, or "Boston men" as they were known by the natives, were in danger. The Indian woman warned Stanley that he would surely be killed if he continued on to Waiilatpu.

Heeding the warning, Stanley and Solomon turned their horses towards Fort Walla Walla but they had not proceeded far before they met an armed Cayuse who immediately asked Stanley: "Are you a Boston man?" Solomon, being able to understand what the Cayuse was saying and wishing to protect Stanley, answered for him by telling a lie and saying: "No." The Indian then asked: "What then?" Having come recently from Ohio, Stanley, aware of the danger of saying that he was a "Boston man," replied: "A Buckeye." This was a new nation to the Cayuse who had never heard of the nickname for residents of Ohio. "Oh," said the Indian, "Elysman [English man]," to which Stanley answered: "Yes." After that, according to Stanley's account, "...the villainous wretch suffered me to pass." Commenting on his deception, Stanley added: "Let those laugh who will." [89] For him, the whole terrifying incident was no laughing matter.

Thoroughly alerted by this time as to their danger, Stanley and Solomon left the trail for fear of meeting other Cayuses and spent the rest of that day and the following night in hiding. They reached Fort Walla Walla early on Thursday morning, December 3, where they were given more detailed information from McBean regarding the massacre. Feeling the necessity of informing the Walkers and the Eellses as to what had happened, Stanley, as soon as he was able to do so, addressed a short letter to them. He began by saying: "It is my melancholy duty to inform you of one of the most tragical massacres on record in Oregon." He then gave the names of nine of the victims including Marcus and Narcissa Whitman, Andrew Rodgers, and the two Sager boys. His letter includes the following: "Some attribute the cause to the poisoning of the Indians, although there are many rumors. As I have been here only one-half hour, and hearing so much, and running the gauntlet for two days myself, I am perfectly unnerved and bewildered. Solomon has been faithful to the last; may God bless him! I am informed that a party of Indians started to Mr. Spalding's to complete their horrid butchery, also to the Dalles. Mr. McBean has sent an express to Vancouver requesting them to send up boats for such as may escape." [90]

As soon as the letter was written, Solomon was sent on his way to Tshimakain. He arrived there on Thursday, December 9. The two families were horrified at the news he brought. Walker and Eells questioned Solomon closely to make sure that his story was correct and that it confirmed what Stanley had written. In a letter to Greene, written the next day, Eells stated: "Almost all Natives will exaggerate & distort the truth, but I have confidence to believe that Solomon has endeavored to state to us pretty nearly as he received it from others. He says moreover that all the different individuals gave the same account. Or to give a more literal translation of his expression, 'the speech of all went along in the same track.'"

THE FLIGHT OF THE OSBORNS

The Osborn family had a harrowing experience in their flight from Waiilatpu to Fort Walla Walla. While hiding under the floor of the Indian room, they had heard the shooting of Mrs. Whitman, Andrew Rodgers, and Francis Sager, and had heard the dying groans of Rodgers until late in the evening. Even though Mrs. Osborn had only that day arisen from her sick bed and even though their four-year-old son, John, just recovering from the measles, was too weak to do much walking, the Osborns decided on making the attempt to get to the Fort. There was no other way than to walk the twenty-five miles.

According to Nancy's recollections, they left about ten o'clock that Monday night. Groping their way through the darkness of the Indian room, they searched for some clothing, blankets, and food. "We could find but little," wrote Nancy, "and did not linger long."[91] Osborn wrote: "Taking John Law on my back, and A[lexander] Rogers in my arms, we started. The first step outside was in the blood of an orphan boy [Francis Sager]." According to Nancy, they struck out across the field to the confluence of Mill Creek with the Walla Walla River. The night was dark as a half moon did not rise until about midnight.[92]

Osborn recalled: "We could see no trail and not even the hand before the face. We had to feel out the trail with our feet. My wife almost fainted but staggered along."[93] In addition to carrying his two sons, Osborn also had to carry some of the bedding and some provisions. No doubt the little girl helped, but Mrs. Osborn was too weak to assist.

When they came to the ford across the Walla Walla River, they found the water waist deep and icy cold. Osborn had to cross five times, to take each of the little boys, his nine-year-old daughter, and finally his wife to the other side. Of this last trip, he wrote: "My wife, in her great weakness, came near washing down, but held to my clothes, I bracing myself with a stick." Only the great fear of being killed prompted them to stagger on. After traveling about two miles, Mrs. Osborn fainted. Since they could go no further, they lay down in the mud among some willows. When daylight came, they could hear Indians coming and going on the trail that paralleled the river. The temperature was near freezing. All of Tuesday was spent in hiding and later Osborn wrote: "The day seemed a week."

On Tuesday night, November 30, they continued their slow journey. Now they left the bank of the river with its tangle of willows and shrubbery and ventured to walk on the trail. Several small streams had to be waded. After only a few hours of walking, Mrs. Osborn fainted again. Of their misery that night, Osborn wrote: "[We] crawled into the brush and frozen mud, to shake and suffer from hunger and cold without sleep. The children, too, wet and cold, called incessantly for food, but the shock [i.e., the memory] of groans and yells at first so frightened them that they did not speak loud."

Another day was spent in hiding. When Wednesday night came, Mrs. Osborn was too weak to stand. She urged her husband to take one of the boys and go to the fort for help. They were then at least fifteen miles from their destination. At first Osborn rejected any suggestion of leaving his wife and the children, but she insisted. Finally he agreed to go, as this seemed to be the only possible way all might be saved. Taking John with him, whom he had to carry, Osborn started for Fort Walla Walla. Since Osborn also had had the measles, he found it necessary to rest frequently. He arrived at the fort early Thursday morning, December 2, and to his dismay was given a cool reception by McBean.

In a letter sent to relatives in the States dated the following April 7, when memories were still fresh, Osborn wrote of McBean: "He gave me about a half pint of tea, and two small biscuits. When we had got warm, I asked for assistance to bring in my family, but was unable to procure any." [94] Since McBean had sent his interpreter, Bushman, with news of the massacre to Fort Vancouver, he had only two hired men with him besides the two priests. By Thursday morning, McBean had learned of the dispatch of two bands of Indians—one to Lapwai to kill Spalding if he could be found; the other to The Dalles to inflict a like fate on

Perrin Whitman and others who might be at that mission. Without a doubt, McBean was frightened at the possibility of the Cayuses attacking Fort Walla Walla, especially if they learned that he was harboring one of the Americans and his family who had escaped from Waiilatpu. This seems to be the only rational explanation for McBean's inhospitality to both Hall and Osborn. He was made craven by his fear of an attack by the murdering Cayuses.

Osborn's account continues: "[I] begged Mr. McBean for horses to get my family, for food, blankets and clothing to take to them, and to take care of my little child till I could bring my family to his fort. Mr. Hall had come in on Monday night, but he could not have an American in his fort, and he had put him over the Columbia River; that he could not let me have horses, or anything for my wife and children, and I must go to Umatilla." In other words, McBean was trying to get Osborn and his family to seek refuge with the Catholic missionaries at the newly established Saint Anne Mission.

Osborn's account of his reception by McBean raises serious doubts as to the truthfulness of McBean's account of Hall's disappearance in his letter to the Walla Walla *Statesman* in 1866, to which reference has been made. We have no way of learning how Hall felt about McBean's alleged insistence that he continue his journey to The Dalles. Bancroft, in his *Oregon*, gives this judgment: "McBean was 'below the salt' when compared with other gentlemen in the company."[95]

After McBean's adamant refusal to provide horses and supplies or to receive Osborn and his family if they could have managed to get to the fort, Osborn in his desperation appealed to the priests: "I next begged the priests to show pity, as my wife and children must perish, and the Indians would undoubtedly kill me, but with no better success. I then begged to leave my child, who was now safe in the fort, but they refused." As guests of McBean, the priests found themselves placed in an embarrassing situation. Evidently they agreed with McBean's proposal that Osborn take his family to Saint Anne's Mission on the Umatilla.

At this opportune moment, when Osborn's every plea for help had been rejected, Stanley and Solomon arrived at the fort. No doubt McBean was appalled to have still another American seeking refuge in his undermanned post. There were, however, some extenuating circumstances which made Stanley's presence more acceptable than

Osborn's. Stanley had not fled from troubled Waiilatpu and hence had not been involved in the events which had occurred there. Moreover, he had led a hostile Cayuse to believe that he was an Englishman. Finally, in case of an attack, here was another man who could shoot a gun.

RESCUE OF THE OSBORN FAMILY

As soon as Stanley arrived, Osborn turned to him with his frantic appeal for help. Stanley's response was immediate and sympathetic. After having spent more than a day and a night in hiding in fear for his own safety, he could understand Osborn's concern. Stanley offered the use of his two horses and also gave Osborn some food and clothing. Osborn, greatly relieved, then asked if Solomon could go with him as he felt the need for a guide, and someone to help him. Stanley, however, declined this request as he felt the urgency of sending Solomon back to Tshimakain with word of the massacre as soon as possible in order to put the missionaries there on guard.

McBean, seeing that there was a good probability of Osborn finding his family and bringing them to the fort, then offered to provide a Walla Walla Indian guide with the distinct understanding that if Osborn were able to find them, he should take them to the Umatilla mission. McBean even specified that if he could not find them, then Osborn himself was to go to the Umatilla. Osborn, in his letter of April 7, 1848, said that one of the priests gave him a letter of introduction to Bishop Blanchet. Osborn had no alternative but to accept McBean's terms, as he needed the Indian guide to help him find his family.

Osborn wanted to leave his son, John Law, at the fort and Stanley expressed his willingness to care for the boy, but McBean refused.[96] Fearful of being seen by the watchful Cayuses, Osborn, his son, and the guide did not set out on their search until nightfall that Thursday evening, December 2. Since he had left his family during darkness and since the terrain was strange to him, Osborn had difficulty in locating them. He dared not shout for fearing of being discovered by hostile Indians. The whole night was spent in a fruitless, frustrating search. Friday morning dawned. In desperation Osborn continued looking for his family in the daylight. Early that morning, to the great joy and relief of all, they were found.

Osborn wrote that they had "almost perished with hunger and thirst." While the Walla Walla Indian went for water, Osborn gave them food. As soon as possible, Osborn helped his wife mount one of the horses, and after dividing the children among the three, they started for the Umatilla mission. They had not gone more than a couple of miles before they met an armed Cayuse who threatened to kill Osborn. The Walla Walla Indian shamed the Cayuse by asking if he would "kill an old man that was sick, with a sick wife and children?" The Cayuse put down his gun and allowed them to proceed. He warned Osborn, however, that he would surely be killed if he attempted to go to the Umatilla. Osborn then decided, regardless of the promises he had given to McBean, that he would return to Fort Walla Walla.

Just when the family arrived at this destination is not clear, possibly on Saturday morning, if Osborn had felt it prudent to go into hiding the rest of Friday. When the Osborns arrived at the gate for admission, McBean at first refused to admit them. Mrs. Osborn said that she would "die at the gate, but she would not leave." Reluctantly, McBean admitted them and provided a room where they could stay. Osborn wrote: "We had hardly got warm before McBean came to me and wanted me to leave my family with him, and go down to the valley by myself; but I refused to leave the fort and would not go." It is also reported that McBean provided blankets only after Osborne had signed a promissory note in payment.[97] The Osborns remained at the fort until all the captives were released and then accompanied them down the river to the Willamette Valley during the first week of January. Shortly after their arrival in the Valley, four-year-old John Law died. The exposure he suffered, no doubt, was a contributory cause of his death.

In his letter of April 7, 1848, to which reference has been made, Osborn recounted the terrifying experiences through which he and his family had passed and told of the death of his three children, including the baby who died the day she was born. He ruefully recalled how happy he and his family had been in the Willamette Valley before Dr. Whitman had persuaded him in the late summer of 1847 to accept work at Waiilatpu. "Not being satisfied with doing well," he wrote, "I consented to go."

Events of December 1 to 5

Following the death of the Whitmans, Joe Lewis, Joe Stanfield, and the Indians reveled in looting. Joe Lewis found Narcissa's trunk filled with her most prized possessions, among which were some gauze handkerchiefs which she used to wear with her low-necked dresses. The trunk was soon emptied of its contents.

Joe Stanfield, who appreciated the value of such items as watches and money more than did the Indians, was accused by several of the captives of helping himself to everything of this kind that he saw. Nathan Kimball, Jr., many years later wrote: "There was another brute there by the name of Joe Stanfield. When the massacre commenced, he went through the houses plundering and breaking open trunks and taking whatever he could find of value. Father had a silver watch hung on a nail on the wall. He grabbed it in such a hurry that he left the ring of the watch still on the wall." [98]

Tamsucky helped himself to all of the clothing that had belonged to Judge Saunders. Mrs. Saunders wrote that the Indians broke into all the rooms of the mission buildings and took whatever struck their fancy. "When they had finished," she recalled, "we were left only with what we were wearing and some of our bedding, but we were so glad to have our lives spared that we did not worry over these losses." [99]

Several of the survivors told about the Indians breaking the windows and the doors. Books, papers, and items of no interest to them were left strewn on the floors where members of the Expeditionary Force, sent from the Willamette Valley early in the spring of 1848, found them. Even the kitchen stove, which had been such a treasure for the Whitmans and which the Indians evidently could not use, was maliciously smashed into pieces. The Indian women who looted Narcissa's kitchen quarreled among themselves for the choicest kettles and pans. "The work of destruction went on for some days," wrote Catherine, "...nothing but the walls were left of our once happy home."

Spading had left his best Sunday suit at Waiilatpu when he went with Whitman to the Umatilla. It had a Prince Albert coat, then much in style for ministers.[100] This was stolen, and perhaps Tiloukaikt or some other chief found great pleasure in parading around wearing it. Amid all the confusion and turmoil, now and then something would take place which caused the children to laugh. "One day," wrote Catherine, "a young brave came riding up to the door with a large school map thrown over his saddle, almost covering the small pony. We children were highly amused to see him riding on top of the world." Catherine wrote that Tiloukaikt made the members of his band return many of the things taken. "At another time," she wrote, "one of them came in and gave me a pocket compass belonging to Dr. W., and a bucket of syrup. The squaws would also give us shoes and things they had taken."[101]

FATHER BROUILLET VISITS WAIILATPU

Because of his leg injury, Spalding had tarried two days at the Umatilla after Whitman's departure. On Monday evening, the day the massacre began, Spalding dined with Bishop Blanchet and Father Brouillet. According to the latter, Spalding was most companionable and manifested none of the bitterness towards the Catholics which he displayed after the massacre.[102] Brouillet wrote: "During the conversation, he happened to say that the Doctor was unquiet [i.e., worried]; that the Indians were displeased with him on account of the sickness, and that he had been informed that the murderer (an Indian)[103] intended to kill him." Spalding brushed aside the doctor's fears, and Brouillet added that he "suspected as little as we did what was taking place at the mission of the Doctor." In fact, at the time Spalding was dining with the priests, Dr. Whitman had already been struck down by the tomahawk of Tomahas, the Murderer, and was lying unconscious on a settee in his living room.

During the evening's visit, Spalding told Brouillet that he intended to start back to Waiilatpu on Wednesday morning. As will be told, this information later saved Spalding's life. Brouillet left Saint Anne Mission on Tuesday morning, after he had baptized some sick Indian children who were near death.[104] He arrived at Tiloukaikt's camp early in the evening of that day, November 30. "It is impossible to conceive my surprise and consternation," he wrote, "when, upon my arrival, I learned that the Indians the day before had massacred the Doctor and his wife, with the greater part of the Americans at the mission. I passed the night scarcely closing my eyes. Early in the morning, I baptized three sick children, two of whom died soon after."[105]

Later Spalding severely criticized Brouillet for baptizing the "blood stained children of these bloody murderers."[106] Spalding's criticism arose out of his ignorance of Roman Catholic doctrine regarding the importance of administering the sacrament of baptism to a dying person who had never previously been baptized. According to Protestant doctrine, baptism is an initiatory rite for church membership. To the Roman Catholics, however, baptism is necessary for salvation. Brouillet was only doing his duty, as he had been taught by his church, when he baptized the sick and dying Cayuse children. Spalding was in error when he interpreted such acts as an indication of Brouillet's supposed sympathy for the murderers.

Early on Wednesday morning, Brouillet "hastened to the scene of death to offer to the widows and orphans all the assistance" in his power. He found six women and more than thirty children in the emigrant house in a situation which he reported as "deplorable beyond description." The massacre had suddenly deprived the immigrant colony at Waiilatpu of all male leadership, for the men, with the exception of two who were confined to their sick beds, were either killed or forced to flee. In this emergency, Mrs. Saunders stepped forward and assumed responsibility. No other person at Waiilatpu played such a heroic role as Mrs. Saunders during those days when the Indians were still seeking out their victims and during the month's captivity which followed the massacre.

She was the one who, on Monday, risked her life when she made a desperate appeal for mercy for the women and children to Tiloukaikt. It was she who, after learning that Finley was to take the three half-breed boys to Fort Walla Walla, wrote an account of what had happened in a letter to McBean. It was she who took the initiative on Tuesday morning to get the five children, who were in hiding in the upstairs room of the main mission house, moved over to the emigrant house. Elizabeth wrote how she, twice bereft of a mother, was welcomed: "Mrs. Saunders, who until she saw me had not known if any of us were alive, met me with tears and kisses and said, 'Your dear mother is dead! I will be a mother to you,' and most sacredly did she fulfill that promise."[107] And it was Mrs. Saunders who, taking bed sheets and a bolt of muslin cloth she somehow located, mustered the help of the other women and the older girls and made shrouds for each of the ten dead bodies.

When Father Brouillet arrived on the grounds Wednesday morning, Mrs. Saunders gave him breakfast and solicited his aid in giving the dead a Christian burial. This took place on that same morning. Joe Stanfield had dug a shallow grave and also had washed the bodies before they were wrapped in their shrouds. He then hitched a yoke of oxen to a wagon on which he and the priest placed the dead.

Catherine remembered a gruesome incident which occurred: the oxen became frightened and ran away, upsetting the wagon and dumping the bodies out on the ground. After the animals were caught and quieted, the wagon was reloaded and the improvised hearse, followed by the mourning women and children, made its way to the cemetery. Among the women were two who witnessed the burial of the bodies of their husbands and two who had not learned the fate of their husbands who had fled. According to the recollections of Elizabeth Sager, the body of Narcissa Whitman was the first to be laid in the grave and then one by one the other bodies were placed. Each time a body was lowered into the grave, there was a fresh outburst of sobs and weeping from the spectators. After all the bodies were in the grave, Father Brouillet read the Roman Catholic burial service. Years later, some of the survivors recalled that he used a strange language, Latin, which they could not understand.

Following the burial service, Stanfield began shoveling the earth back into the grave. It was no small task; Catherine wrote that it was night before he had finished his work. The grave, however, was too shallow and the layer of earth which covered the dead too thin; marauding wolves came that night and dug into the grave.

Spalding Escapes

In her account of the funeral service, Mrs. Saunders wrote: "Father Brouillet came back to the house to say a few words of encouragement. I offered him coffee and some food. He accepted the coffee, but refused the food, saying that he had some with him and that he must hurry away to intercept Rev. Spalding before he should reach the Mission."[108] By this time, Brouillet knew that the Indians were disappointed in not having found Spalding at Waiilatpu when the Whitmans were killed, as they had planned to kill him also. At considerable risk to himself, Brouillet decided to set out to warn Spalding. He had with him his interpreter. As the two left Waiilatpu, Edward,[109] one of the sons of Tiloukaikt, joined them. At first Brouillet was not concerned about Edward's presence but as they continued riding down the trail and Edward did not turn back,

Brouillet became fearful as he noticed that Edward was armed with a pistol. "I knew that the Indians were angry with all Americans," Brouillet wrote, "and more enraged against Mr. Spalding than any other. But what could I do in such a circumstance? I saw no remedy."[110]

After the three had ridden about three miles, the interpreter asked Edward for a smoke. Brouillet tells what then happened: "They prepared the calumet [Indian pipe], but when the moment came for lighting it, there was nothing to make fire. 'You have a pistol,' said the interpreter, 'fire it, and we will light.' This was done and then Edward, absent-mindedly, neglected to reload his pistol. A few minutes later, the three saw Spalding galloping towards them. "In a moment," Brouillet wrote, "he was at my side, taking me by the hand, and asking for news. 'Have you been to the Doctor's?' he inquired. 'Yes,' I replied. 'What news?' 'Sad news.' 'Is any person dead?' 'Yes, sir.'" Spalding was thinking of some of the sick children who might have died because of measles. "Who is dead?" he inquired. "Is it one of the Doctor's children?"

Brouillet hesitated to tell Spalding what had happened for fear that this would alert Edward and prompt him to shoot. Brouillet then spoke to the interpreter, perhaps in French as it appears that Spalding was unaware of what was being said, and requested him "to entreat the Indian, in my name, not to kill Mr. Spalding." The situation was most delicate as Brouillet explained: "I was waiting for his [i.e., Edward's] answer, and did not wish to relate the disaster to Mr. Spalding before getting it, for fear that he might, by his manner, discover [i.e., disclose] to the Indian what I had told him; for the least motion like flight would have cost him his life, and probably exposed mine also." Edward hesitated for a few moments to give an answer to Brouillet's entreaty and then replied: "…that he could not take it upon himself to save Mr. Spalding, but that he would go back and consult the other Indians; and so he started back immediately to his camp."

As soon as Edward left, Brouillet passed on to Spalding the dreadful news regarding what had happened at Waiilatpu, giving also an account of the funeral service he had so shortly before performed. 'The Indians have killed the Doctor!' cried Mr. Spalding, 'they will kill me also, if I go to the camp!' 'I fear it very much,' said I." In fear and consternation, Spalding asked: "What shall I do?" Again and again, he said: "Is it possible! Is it possible… they will certainly kill me." Brouillet told Spalding that the Cayuses had sent out war parties to Lapwai and to The Dalles to kill all Americans in the country. He advised Spalding to flee at once as a party of Cayuses would surely soon come when informed by Edward of Spalding's presence on the trail. The interpreter advised Spalding to take the trail that led to The Dalles; this became the basis for the report which reached Mrs. Spalding through a friendly Nez Perce on Sunday, December 5. Brouillet turned over to Spalding some food he happened to be carrying. Brouillet wrote that "Spalding was frightened and discouraged," and that as they parted, he wished him "a happy escape," and promised to pray for his safety. "In quitting him [i.e., upon leaving him]," wrote Brouillet, "I was so much terrified at the thought of the danger with which he was threatened, that I trembled in every limb, and could scarcely hold myself upon my horse."

Within twenty minutes after Spalding had left Brouillet and taken the trail that led towards The Dalles, three armed Cayuses rode up and demanded of the priest the whereabouts of Spalding. They became very angry when they learned that Spalding had fled and blamed Brouillet for aiding him in making his escape. Off they set in pursuit. Brouillet wrote: "They must inevitably have overtaken him, had not the approaching darkness of night and a heavy fog that happened to fall down prevented them from discovering his trail, and forced them to return."

After reviewing Brouillet's account of his meeting with Spalding, we can turn to Spalding's letters written on January 8 and 24 and March 16, 1848, in which he gave detailed descriptions of the ordeal he suffered in his travels back to Lapwai.[III] Instead of following the trail to The Dalles, as suggested by the interpreter, Spalding decided to try for Lapwai. Darkness came shortly after he left the priest and, as he wrote, "a dark fog opened its bosom to receive me." As has been stated, a half-moon did not rise until midnight.

Spalding described his experiences as follows: "I pushed my horse to the extent of his strength, through the night, keeping up a known stream [probably the Touchet]. Next day [Thursday, December 2] secreted myself in a ravine, and the next night kept up the same stream, till I came to a known trail, which the horse took and followed himself." At midnight, Spalding paused for a short rest. He was so worried about the fate of his family and about his own safety that he could not sleep. He mounted his horse and continued his travels. Hearing the sound of horses coming behind him, he "wheeled my horse to the right and lay flat upon him, hoping that in the thick darkness, they would pass without discovering me. But in a moment I found I was wheeling into them. I reined back instantly, and seized my horse by the nose, to prevent him from calling out." The Indians passed without seeing him.

In the early hours of Friday morning, Spalding, exhausted from riding and lack of sleep, stopped to rest. He neglected to hobble his horse and it got away, leaving him on foot in December weather about ninety miles from his home. His shoes, perhaps a gift from some missionary barrel, were so tight that they had to be discarded. He bound his leggings around his feet. The food he had received from Brouillet lasted only a day or so. Unfortunately, Spalding was still suffering from the knee injury received just before he and Whitman arrived at the Umatilla; this made walking difficult. His rain-soaked blankets became too heavy to be carried, so they were discarded along with his shoes. Fearful of being seen by hostile Indians, he remained in hiding all of Friday and that night continued his travels, walking about thirty miles. The same schedule was followed on Saturday.

Of the ordeal of those days and nights, he wrote: "Saturday night [December 4], I made 80 miles more. My feet suffered from the frozen ground. I avoided the places of encampment and forded the streams far from the trail, lest the Cayuse might be way-laying. I secreted myself on the Sabbath—and hunger, pain in my feet, and weakness were very great; I wanted sleep, but could get none, for the cold. From the moment I stopped traveling in the morning till I started at night, I shook to the center of every bone with cold." Spalding's caution saved his life, for sometime during Saturday or Sunday, the party of Indians from Joseph's band passed him on their way to Lapwai with murderous intent.

When darkness came on Sunday evening, Spalding resumed his painful trek. He came to Timothy's village at Alpowa, where he wanted to cross the Snake River and thus for safety's sake proceed up the north bank to its confluence with the Clearwater River. A cold rain was falling. He began searching in the darkness for Timothy's lodge. He hoped that if he could locate the right lodge, he would creep in and awaken his friend and through him learn "the fate of my family, the extent of the war, or murders, my own danger, obtain food, a blanket, and help over the river." Cautiously he crept through the encampment. He heard singing in one lodge where the Indians were having evening worship. Spalding crept close, hoping that he would hear Timothy's voice. He did not know that Mrs. Spalding had sent Timothy and Eagle to Waiilatpu to find out what had happened to Eliza. Since Spalding dared not make himself known to any other person but Timothy, he did not enter the lodge. Some dogs discovered his presence and broke out in a chorus of barking and snarling. Although he did not recognize the voice of the Indian who was praying, he was comforted by hearing him say that no one had been killed at Lapwai. "Oh, what an angel of mercy to the human family is hope!" wrote Spalding. He also learned that the Indians thought that he had been killed along with the Whitmans. Unable to find Timothy, Spalding decided to continue his journey during that night.

Finding a canoe, he crossed the Snake River and was able to arrive at the mouth of the Clearwater River before Monday morning. There he located another canoe and crossed to the south side, and by dawn was within five miles of Lapwai. For the first time during his flight, Spalding was cheered by warm rays of the sun. He was in such a weakened condition that he felt he dared not do anything else but stumble on his way. His feet were swollen and bleeding. Hunger gnawed within. Upon coming within sight of his home from the top of the hills which border the south bank of the Clearwater, he was dismayed to see a band of Indians about the mission premises, some of whom were engaged in looting. Spalding did not then know that his wife and family had been escorted to the Craig home.

Fearful of being discovered, Spalding concealed himself and waited until darkness came before trying to learn the fate of his family. Before evening on that December 6 clay, a friendly Nez Perce woman found him and told him that his family was sale. He was directed to the lodge of Luke, one of the faithful Nez Perce members of the Mission church, who with loving tenderness ministered to his needs. Spalding was soon restored to the company of his family, as he explained: "more dead than alive, from starvation, want of sleep, freezing, horrible swelled and mangled feet, having miraculously escaped..." The Spalding family remained with Craig until they were escorted by friendly Nez Perces to Fort Walla Walla during the closing days of December.

Several of Spalding contemporaries, including Walker and Eells, felt that the shock of the massacre and the terrible ordeal through which he had passed during his escape affected his mind.[112] Spalding's anti-

Catholic utterances and writings after the massacre became caustic and extravagant. When his wife died in January 1851, he even had the following inscribed on her tombstone: "She always felt that the Jesuit Missionaries were the leading cause of the massacre." [113] Spalding became obsessed with the idea that the Catholics were in league with the murderers. He even neglected to give due credit to Father Brouillet, who risked his life in order to give him the warning which permitted him to escape. A bitter controversy resulted, which extended over the remaining years of Spalding's life and was even carried on by his friends after his death [Appendix 4].

Events of December 5 to 8

Three of the children, who had been very sick with measles when the massacre began, died shortly thereafter. Louise Sager, age six, passed away early Sunday evening, December 5; Helen Mar Meek, eleven, died Wednesday, the 8th; and the Hays infant, Rapoleon, died on the 9th. Again, Joe Stanfield was the grave-digger. No one was present to read a burial service. It is possible that one or all of these three children would have survived, if Dr. Whitman had been alive to have cared for them.

After dark on Sunday evening, December 5, Daniel Young arrived at Waiilatpu from the sawmill to find out what had happened to his brother James, who had been sent to the mission with a load of lumber on the preceding Tuesday. Daniel had managed to pass undetected the Indian village near Waiilatpu where, unbeknown to him at the time, his brother had been killed. He went to the emigrant house, where Mrs. Saunders gave him the dreadful news of what had happened, including the death of his brother. She warned him to claim that he was an Englishman and not an American should he be questioned. Joe Stanfield also warned him about trying to return to the mill without the consent of Tiloukaikt.

Shortly after Daniel's arrival, Tiloukaikt came to the emigrant house and discovered Daniel's presence. Then a most curious thing happened: Tiloukaikt upbraided Daniel for traveling on Sunday and also "embraced the occasion to admonish the captives that they should not under any circumstances make shirts on the Lord's day." [114] He was referring to sewing that some of the Indians had demanded of the women. Tiloukaikt, responding to what appealed to him, was not concerned with inconsistencies. To him it was quite permissible to kill, but not to travel or sew on Sunday! Here is a reflection of the emphasis that the missionaries had placed on Sunday observance.

Although only a few days had passed since the Indians had killed Marsh at the mill, they had begun to feel the need for someone to grind their wheat and corn. Since Whitman had never taught any of the Indians to run the mill, they felt the need of a white man to do this. When Tiloukaikt learned that Daniel's father was a miller, he sent the young man back to the sawmill under the watchful eyes of three armed Cayuses to bring the two families there down to Waiilatpu. Tiloukaikt promised Mrs. Saunders that all those who were then alive would be saved and would be released in the spring. Thus a safe-conduct was promised to the Young and Smith families. Within a few days the Youngs, with their two grown sons, and the Smiths with their younger children, arrived at the mission and were quartered in the emigrant house.

Timothy and Eagle, the two Christian Nez Perces whom Mrs. Spalding had sent to Waiilatpu to get her daughter Eliza if possible, arrived at Waiilatpu sometime during the first part of the week of December 5. When Eliza saw Timothy, she wept for joy. He clasped the little girl in his arms and mingled his tears with hers. "Poor Eliza," he said, "don't cry, you will see your mother." [115] Catherine wrote: "The Indians refused to let Eliza go. The Indians [i.e., the Nez Perces] who had been sent after her laid plans to kidnap her at night but the Indians, suspecting this, said that if they did so, they would be pursued and the little girl killed, so they returned home without her." The Cayuses needed Eliza as an interpreter, as she was the only one among the captives who understood the native language.

Matilda remembered how Timothy went to see Helen Mar shortly before she died. She wrote: "Timothy... fell on his knees by the side of her bed, praying in his own language; when he arose, he pointed upward, indicating that the spirit had flown." [116] Even though Timothy and Eagle had to return to Lapwai without Eliza, they did carry back to Mrs. Spalding the comforting assurance that her daughter was well and that Tiloukaikt had assured them of the safety of all the women and children.

The massacre which had begun on Monday, November 29, 1847, ended with the killing of Crocket Bewley and Amos Sales on Wednesday, December 8.[117] Why this should have occurred after Tiloukaikt had told

Mrs. Saunders on the preceding Sunday that there would be no more killing is not certain. However, judging by the accounts of some of the survivors, it was a sadistic act by three young men—Edward (son of Tiloukaikt), Wai-e-cat [see reproductions of their portraits by Stanley in this volume], and Clokamas. Evidently Tiloukaikt had lost control over these young men from his band. Catherine gives the following account: "At the time of the massacre both were very sick and were spared by the Indians. They were so far recovered as to be able to sit up part of the time. The Indians told them they must take squaw wives and live among the Indians. Mr. Bewley would make no reply to these things; but Mr. Sales, who hated them bitterly, would swear at them and say that he would do no such thing; that he was going below to the valley when he got well."[118]

When Narcissa first arrived at Waiilatpu, she gave names of some of her brothers and sisters and other relatives to the native children. Tiloukaikt's son was called Edward after one of her brothers. Edward was the leader in this atrocity when the two sick men were murdered, as is seen in Elizabeth Sager's account: "One day Edward Tiloukaikt came in. He had taken a bed post and fixed it up as a war club. Eliza Spalding and I and some of the other children were in the room. Crocket Bewley and Amos Sales were lying in bed. They had the typhoid.[119] Edward Tiloukaikt raised his war club and hit Crocket Bewley on the head. We children screamed and ran out of the room. [Edward] Tiloukaikt came out and said, 'Come on back, you must stay in the room till we are finished.' We had to go back while the Indians beat Amos Sales and Crocket Bewley over their heads till they had killed them. When they had battered their heads for quite a while, they dragged them out into the yard. Next day Joe Stanfield... came with a wagon and yoke of oxen and took the bodies away and buried them."[120] Their deaths brought the total number of victims killed by the Cayuses to thirteen. To this number added the name of Peter Hall, who was drowned while trying to escape, thus bringing the total to fourteen. This number does not include the three children who died of measles during the month's captivity.

In a previous section of this chapter, entitled "The Conspirators Identified," William McBean at Fort Walla Walla listed eight Cayuses he believed had taken an active part in the massacre. Included in this list were the following three who were linked with the killing of the two sick men: "[#3] Tlocoomots said to have given his assistance in killing the sick... [#7] Tomsucky's son—a chip of the [old] block who is accused of assisting in the murder of Mr. Buly—sick at the time... [#8] Ex-yow-e-ah-nish, said to have dragged a sick man out of his bed whom he murdered with his axe." Since McBean made no mention of Edward as being one of the guilty parties, as claimed by Elizabeth Sager, it may be that E-yow-e-ah-nish was Edward's Indian name. [See pages 238–9.]

When the artist, John Mix Stanley, visited Waiilatpu during the first part of October 1847, he painted at least four portraits of Cayuse Indians, namely Tiloukaikt, Tamsucky, and a son of each of these chiefs. On the portrait of one of the young men, he wrote: "Shu Ma Hici or painted Shirt. Edward, son of Telocoit, Cayuse," and on the other, "Wai e cat, son of Tum[sucky], One that flies, Cayuse." Both of these portraits are reproduced as illustrations in this work. The picture of Edward shows a handsome fellow with a light complexion. His countenance is almost that of a white man. This agrees with the description that Catherine wrote of him: "His color was quite light, and he had a proud and noble bearing." [121]

SUMMARY OF THE FATE OF THE WAIILATPU RESIDENTS

The following table outlines the fate of the seventy-four people who were at Waiilatpu when the tragedy began on November 29, 1847:

	MEN	WOMEN	CHILDREN	TOTAL
Killed, including the drowning of Hall...	11	1	2	14
Died in captivity...	-	-	3	3
Escaped...	2	1	3	6
Released, three half-breed boys...	-	-	3	3
Adult half-breeds, Finley and Lewis...	2	-	-	2
Captives, including Stanfield...	5	8	34	47
TOTALS	20	10	45	75

The Canfield and Smith families were the only ones to come through the massacre without the loss of at least one member by violence, accident, disease, or neglect.

Chapter 22 Endnotes

[1] Pringle ms., p. 25, quoting Spalding's diary. Nancy Osborn Jacobs, however, in Waitsburg, Wash. *Times*, Feb. 2, 1934, states that her sister died on Nov. 16.

[2] Saunders ms., p. 7. See Chapter Twenty-One, fn. 64.

[3] Pringle ms., p. 25.

[4] Delaney, *A Survivor's Recollections*, p. 14.

[5] HBC Arch., D/5/21.

[6] Parker, *Journal*, p. 191.

[7] *O.H.Q.*, XXIX (1928):144, in article, "Indian Diseases as Aids to Pacific Northwest Settlement."

[8] Parker, *Journal*, p. 314.

[9] Drury, *Spalding and Smith*, pp. 129 & 207.

[10] Pringle ms., p. 25.

[11] Saunders ms., p. 7.

[12] Pringle ms., p. 25. Also in *Oregon American*, July 19, 1848.

[13] The lodges of both the Cayuses and Nez Perces constructed out of hides, bark, or reeds placed over a framework of poles were oblong in shape and often long enough to accommodate several families, each with its own fire for cooking.

[14] Pringle ms., p. 30.

[15] First published in *Oregon Spectator*, Dec. 10, 1847; republished in Cannon, *Waiilatpu*, pp. 135 ff., and in Gray, *Oregon*, pp. 519 ff.

[16] Brouillet, *House Document*, p. 27.

[17] Dart, Report to Commissioner of Indian Affairs, Sept. 4, 1851, in Records of the Oregon Superintendency of Indian Affairs, 1850–55.

[18] HBC Arch., D/5/21. Ogden and Douglas did not include in their total Peter Hall, who evidently was drowned in the Columbia River while trying to escape. He was not among those killed at Waiilatpu.

[19] *T.O.P.A.*, 1884, p. 34.

[20] See Chapter Eleven, "Meeting the Threat of Marauding Animals."

[21] Brouillet, *House Document*, pp. 22-3. This John Young is not to be confused with John, the son of Mr. and Mrs. Elam Young, who with his parents and brother arrived at Waiilatpu in the fall of 1847.

[22] See ante, fn. 15.

[23] Brouillet, *House Document*, p. 26.

[24] *T.O.P.A.*, 1893, p. 102.

[25] Hulbert, *O.P.*, VIII:260.

[26] *T.O.P.A.*, 1884, p. 35.

[27] Bancroft, *Oregon*, I:652.

[28] *W.C.Q.*, II (1898):3:37.

[29] Brouillet, *House Document*, p. 52. Brouillet, in a letter dated July 4, 1850, which was published in the July 15, 1850, issue of the *San Francisco Weekly Pacific News*, reported: "Five of the Indian murderers of Dr. Whitman and family, the only ones that

remained alive out of eleven who had been accused of having participated in the murder.

30 See Appendix 5.

31 Victor, *Early Indian Wars*, pp. 128 ff.

32 Records of the Oregon Superintendency of Indian Affairs, Letters Received, 1850, National Archives.

33 *T.O.P.A.*, 1893, pp. 97-8.

34 Father Ricard's journal, p. 76: "Reluctant at first to receive priests in his territory, he finally offered us, amicably enough, a piece of land…"

35 *Oregon American*, August 1848.

36 From undated ms. of Hilman F. Jones, a nephew of John Settle, Coll. W.S.H.S.

37 Pringle ms., p. 28.

38 *Ibid.*, p. 29.

39 *Ibid.*

40 Pringle ms., p. 29.

41 Spalding's letter to Dudley Allen of Kinsman, Ohio, March 16, 1848, found in the Philadelphia *Observer*, Oct. 28, 1848. Italics are the author's.

42 Clarke, *Pioneer Days*, II:568 ff., devoted a chapter to "Istachus, the Christianized Indian." His name is spelled Stickus, Stickas, and Sticcas. See also Records of the District Court, May 1850, Oregon State Archives, Salem; and Oregon Spectator, May 30, 1850.

43 Brouillet, *House Document*, p. 36.

44 Pringle ms., p. 30; Spalding, *Senate Document*, p. 26.

45 Testimony of Stickus given at the trial, Oregon City, May 1850. *Oregon Spectator*, May 30, 1850.

46 Pringle ms., quoting Spalding.

47 Catherine Sager's two accounts, one in the Pringle ms., and the other in Clarke, *Pioneer Days*, vary in some details. The quotation here given is a synthesis of the two.

48 Pringle ms., p. 32.

49 Both Coll. W. and Coll. O. claim to have the original tomahawk used to kill Dr. Whitman. See illustrations in Drury, *Whitman*, pp. 408-9.

50 When the bones of the victims were exhumed in 1897, at the 50th anniversary of the massacre, the skull of Dr. Whitman showed that he had received two blows from tomahawks. One cut out of the back of the skull a piece about the size of a dollar; the other cracked the skull on top. *Oregon Native Son*, I:63; Spalding, *Senate Document*, p. 27.

51 Bancroft, *Oregon*, I:659. Bancroft, however, does not give the source for this information.

52 Lockley, *Oregon Trail Blazers*, p. 355, quoting Elizabeth Sager.

53 See Chapter Twenty-One, fn. 29. The two Manson boys, John and Stephen, were present during the first day of the massacre and were then taken to Fort Walla Walla by Nicholas Finley. On July 29, 1884, John, then fifty years old, wrote his

recollections of what he had seen and heard at the time of the massacre. These are important since he and his brother knew the Indian language, thus he was able to report what he had heard. My attention was called to the Manson statement by Larry J. Waldon, Chief Interpreter of the Whitman Mission National Historic Site, in a letter dated July 1, 1972.

54 Clarke, *Pioneer Days*, XI:582. Probably quoting Catherine Sager.

55 Delaney, *A Survivor's Recollections*, p. 15. Helen Saunders Church in *W.C.Q.*, II (1898):4:21 also tells of the killing of Judge Saunders.

56 *T.O.P.A.*, 1903, p. 103.

57 Clarke, *op. cit.*, II:534.

58 Saunders ms., p. 8. Since she did not know the Indian by name, she identified him simply as being the one who later shot Mrs. Whitman.

59 *T.O.P.A.*, 1903, p. 189.

60 Lockley, *Oregon Trail Blazers*, p. 338.

61 Pringle ms., p. 32.

62 Lockley, *op. cit.*, p. 336; Spalding, *Senate Document*, p. 28.

63 *Oregon Spectator*, May 30, 1850, reported that "Isaiaasheluckes (Frank Escaloom)" confessed that he had shot Mrs. Whitman. Elizabeth and Matilda Sager claim that she was wounded in the left breast; Spalding and Catherine Sager, the right.

64 Clarke, *op. cit.*, II:532.

65 Hulbert, *O.P.*, VIII:262.

66 See Appendix 5, for a listing of articles by or about Nancy Osborn Jacobs.

67 Delaney, *A Survivor's Recollections*, p. 17.

68 Pringle ms., p. 35. Also, Eliza Spalding Warren in *Ladies Home Journal*, August 1913, p. 38.

69 Nancy Osborn Jacobs, Waitsburg, Wash., *Times*, Feb. 2, 1934; also *East Oregonian*, Pendleton, May 19, 1919.

70 *Oregon Spectator*, May 30, 1850.

71 The identity of the Indian who was willing to receive Narcissa is unknown. The fact that Narcissa was asked to travel ten miles before dark is an indication that the incident described occurred about 2:30 or 3:00 p.m. This is one of the few references to time in the contemporary accounts of the massacre.

72 Saunders ms., p. 11. Mrs. Saunders claimed that Narcissa "fainted at the sight of her husband lying dead before her."

73 From an interview with Elizabeth Sager Helm, *W.C.Q.*, I (1897):2:22.

74 Delaney, *A Survivor's Recollections*, p. 19.

75 The first Roman Catholic martyr, in what is now the Pacific Slope of the United States, was Padre Francisco Garcés, who was killed by Indians in 1781 at his mission across the Colorado River from what is now Yuma, Arizona.

76 Even though Five Crows had been appointed by Elijah White to be the Head Chief of the Cayuses, the head of each family group or band was often referred to as a chief.

77 Pringle ms., p. 35. Italics are the author's.

78 Spalding, *Senate Document*, p. 33.

[79] Pringle ms., p. 35. Delaney, *A Survivor's Recollections*, p. 20, gives a different account of the death of Kimball. Matilda claimed that Kimball started back to the house as soon as he had gotten the water and was then killed.

[80] Clarke, *Pioneer Days*, II:538, quoting Catherine.

[81] Pringle ms., p. 37.

[82] How Catherine learned these details is not known. Possibly she got the story from Joe Stanfield.

[83] Victor, *Early Indian Wars*, p. 128.

[84] Ricard, Journal, p. 6.

[85] McBean letter of March 12, 1866, published in the Walla Walla *Statesman*. Spalding, in a series of "lectures" published in this paper beginning February 9, 1866, made serious charges against McBean. McBean was answering these charges in this letter of March 12.

[86] Following Bushman's return to Fort Walla Walla, McBean on Nov. 30, 1847, wrote an account of what had happened at Waiilatpu to Ogden and Douglas at Fort Vancouver. Published in *Oregon Spectator*, Dec. 10, 1847; Victor, *Early Indian Wars*, pp. 128 ff.; and in Cannon, *Waiilatpu*, pp. 135 ff.

[87] Pringle ms., p. 54. Catherine states that Canfield rushed his family into the emigrant house. In the author's copy of her manuscript, she intimates that he fled to the blacksmith shop and then hid in the lumber stored over the rafters. This latter seems to be the more reasonable of the two accounts.

[88] Drury, *Spalding*, pp. 341-2, quoting from Spalding ms., Coll. W., dated Jan. 14, (1851?).

[89] Stanley to Walker and Eells, from Fort Walla Walla, Dec. 31, 1847, published in the Portland *Oregonian*, Aug. 30, 1885.

[90] *Ibid.*

[91] See ante, fn. 73 of this chapter.

[92] Philip Fox, once Director of Adler Planetarium, Chicago, in a letter to me dated Aug. 28, 1934, wrote: "...in the dates 30 November to 6 December 1847, the Moon was in the last quadrant of its journey, on November 30 rising about midnight as a Half Moon in the sky of course until dawn. Toward the end of this period, on December 6, the Moon would be an exceedingly small crescent, rising just before dawn."

[93] Spalding, *Senate Document*, p. 32, includes Osborn's account.

[94] Original letter in Coll. W. Copy in Hulbert, *O.P.*, VIII:257 ff.

[95] Bancroft, *Oregon*, I:661.

[96] Lockley, *Oregon Trail Blazers*, p. 357, quoting Nancy Osborn Jacobs.

[97] Brouillet, *House Document*, p. 54, quoting from a statement made by Stanley. McBean's letter of March 12, 1866 (see ante fn. 85), contains statements which do not agree with earlier accounts given by Osborn and Stanley.

[98] Nathan Kimball, "Recollections of a Survivor," *T.O.P.A.*, 1903, pp. 189-201. See also recollections of John Q. Young in *1964 Clark County History*, Fort Vancouver Historical Society, p. 30. The watch and some money Stanfield had taken from Mrs. Saunders were restored to her after the captives arrived in the Willamette Valley.

[99] Saunders ms., p. 12.

[100] See reproduction of Mrs. Spalding's painting of a "Protestant Ladder" in Drury, *F.W.W.*, I:219, where she depicted the twelve apostles wearing Prince Albert coats. Spalding valued this suit at $50.00 in his inventory of lost property compiled after the massacre. Drury, *Spalding and Smith*, p. 366.

[101] Pringle ms., p. 39. The pocket compass is now in Coll. W.

[102] Brouillet, *House Document*, p. 36. *The Pacific Northwesterner*, Fall 1970 contains article by Rev. Edward J. Kowrach, "Blackrobe Buried Whitmans," which gives a version of Brouillet's account somewhat different from that which appeared in Brouillet's *House Document*.

[103] Undoubtedly a reference to Tomahas, who was known even among the natives as "The Murderer" because he had killed an Indian.

[104] The late T. C. Elliott of Walla Walla informed me many years ago that he had examined the baptismal records of Father Brouillet without finding mention of these baptisms. This does not, however, mean that the children were not baptized.

[105] Brouillet, *House Document*, p. 37.

[106] Spalding, *Senate Document*, p. 33. Spalding was not alone in his reaction to the report of Brouillet baptizing the children, for the editor of the *Missionary Herald*, July 1848, p. 237, wrote: "It certainly seems very extraordinary that baptisms should have been administered to the children of the murderers in such circumstances."

[107] *W.C.Q.*, I (1897):2:24.

[108] Saunders ms., p. 14.

[109] See reproduction of portrait of Edward by Stanley in this volume.

[110] Brouillet, *House Document*, p. 88. Other quotations from Brouillet in this section are from this source.

[111] Spalding's letters of January 1848 are in Coll. A.; that of March 16, 1848, was published in the Philadelphia *Observer*, Oct. 28, 1848.

[112] Drury, *Spalding*, pp. 362 ff.

[113] *Ibid.*, p. 361. Walker to Greene, July 8, 1848, Coll. A: "Some doubtless attach too much blame to the Catholics. I am yet to be convinced that they had any direct agency in it... that they put the natives up to the deed, I do not believe." When Mrs. Spalding's remains were moved to the cemetery at Old Lapwai, now called Spalding, Idaho, in September 1913, the Presbyterian Church buried the original tombstone with the body and a new monument was erected over the graves of both the Spaldings.

[114] Cannon, *Waiilatpu*, p. 150.

[115] Warren, *Memoirs*, p. 30.

[116] Delaney, *A Survivor's Recollections*, p. 24.

[117] Saunders ms., p. 15. Pringle ms., p. 38, gives a different date, Dec. 10, and in another version, Catherine gives the 13th. Mrs. Saunders' date is to be preferred.

[118] Pringle ms., p. 38. See also, Delaney, *op. cit.*, p. 23.

[119] Lockley, *Oregon Trail Blazers*, pp. 340 ff. Elizabeth made this statement many years after the massacre occurred. There is no evidence that Dr. Whitman had sufficient knowledge of the disease that Bewley and Sales had to diagnose it as typhoid.

Lorinda Bewley called it "Camp fever" in her account. See ms. "Esther Among the Cayuses," Coll. O. Copy in Coll. Wn.

[120] Lockley, *Oregon Trail Blazers*, p. 340.

[121] Pringle ms., p. 43.

SHU-MA-HICI, OR PAINTED SHIRT
Portraits of two participants in the massacre: Shu-ma-hici and Wai-e-cat. Both were painted at Waiilatpu by John Mix Stanley, October 1847. Stanley's note indicates Shu-ma-hici was a son of Tiloukaikt; he was named Edward by Mrs. Whitman after her brother. Courtesy of the owner who prefers anonymity.

WAI-E-CAT, OR ONE THAT FLIES
Wai-e-cat by John Mix Stanley, Waiilatpu, October 1847. Stanley often portrayed
Indians with white features.. Courtesy of the owner who prefers anonymity.

[CHAPTER TWENTY-THREE]

CONGRESS ESTABLISHES OREGON AS A TERRITORY

When news of the massacre reached Fort Vancouver and Oregon City, the reaction was swift and effective. Chief Factors Ogden and Douglas of the Hudson's Bay Company were concerned with the necessity of securing the release of the captives; Governor George Abernethy and other officials of the Provisional Government of Oregon took steps to apprehend and punish the perpetrators of the crime.

Actions Taken by the Hudson's Bay Company

William McBean, in charge of Fort Walla Walla, first learned of the massacre on Tuesday morning, November 30, when Peter D. Hall staggered into the fort almost exhausted from his night's ordeal. McBean then wisely sent his interpreter, Bushman, to investigate. Bushman made the fifty-mile round trip to Waiilatpu and back in one day. He confirmed all that Hall had told and gave many more details.

In the meantime, Finley with the three half-breed boys had arrived at the fort. Finley delivered to McBean the letter that Mrs. Saunders had written which listed the names of those she believed had been killed. On the basis of this information, McBean wrote that Tuesday evening to the "Board of Management" at Fort Vancouver and reported what he had heard. He also repeated a rumor that Finley had brought to the effect that the Cayuses were planning to attack Fort Walla Walla. "Let them come!" wrote McBean, "if they will not listen to reason. Though I have only five men at the establishment [which number included two priests], I am prepared to give them a warm reception. The gates are closed day and night, and the bastions in readiness." [1]

McBean deputized Bushman to carry the letter to Fort Vancouver, since he could add his own testimony regarding the massacre to what had been written. Bushman left early on Wednesday morning, December 1, and made the first part of his journey on horseback to The Dalles, where he expected to get a canoe and then continue by water. Judging by circumstantial evidence, it appears that McBean gave Bushman strict orders not to say anything to Perrin Whitman or others at The Dalles regarding what had taken place at Waiilatpu. Evidently McBean was fearful that if the Cayuses should discover that he had written to Fort Vancouver, they would become angry and attack his fort.

Bushman arrived at The Dalles on the following Saturday morning where he found six Americans with Perrin Whitman. They were Mr. and Mrs. Alanson Hinman and their small child; Mr. and Mrs. William McKinney, an immigrant couple; and Dr. Henry Saffarans, who had but shortly before been appointed U.S. Indian Agent for The Dalles. Bushman was so nervous and so insistent on getting a canoe at once and pursuing his trip down the river that both Perrin and Hinman became somewhat apprehensive. Hinman asked if there had been some difficulty at Fort Walla Walla. Bushman replied by telling a falsehood. Hinman reported: "He said four Frenchman [i.e., the Company's employees] had died recently and he wished to get others to occupy their places." [2] A canoe was secured, and Hinman decided to accompany Bushman in order to get some medicine for the natives in the vicinity of Waskopum who had been stricken with measles.

When the two men were nearing the Cascades, about midway between The Dalles and Fort Vancouver, conscience-stricken Bushman confessed that he had lied; he then told the story of the "horrid massacre that took place at Waiilatpu" the preceding Monday. Hinman was aghast at the news, and at once was deeply concerned over the safety of those at The Dalles, including his wife and child. He upbraided Bushman for not warning them, but Bushman defended himself by saying that he was obeying McBean's order to say nothing.

Hinman and Bushman reached Fort Vancouver on Monday evening, December 6, just a week after the Whitman had been killed. Ogden and Douglas were stunned at the news the two men brought. McBean stated in his letter that he had heard that the Cayuses were sending war parties to the sawmill, to Lapwai, to Tshimakain, and to The Dalles to kill Americans in those places. When Douglas read that, he turned to Hinman and asked: "My God, Hinman why are you here?" The report that the Cayuses were planning to attack The Dalles was new to Hinman, and filled him with alarm. "Why was that Frenchman forbidden to tell me?" he cried. Douglas, seeking to calm his anxiety, replied: "You must remember that [that] man was in trying circumstances."

The next morning Douglas wrote to George Abernethy, a former Methodist missionary then serving as Governor of the Provisional Government of Oregon, informing him of the massacre. He enclosed a copy of McBean's letter, but the sentence referring to the intention of the Cayuses to send war parties to Lapwai and The Dalles to kill Americans in each of those places was deliberately omitted. Evidently, Douglas, knowing that publicity would be given to the letter, felt it best to edit McBean's letter so as not to alarm the Americans in the Willamette Valley unduly.[3]

On December 9, Douglas wrote to S. N. Castle, a member of the American Board's Mission in Hawaii, giving the details of the massacre, and included a copy of his letter of the 7th which he had sent to Governor Abernethy. Castle forwarded this letter to the editor of *The Friend*, a Honolulu paper, which published it in its March 1 issue. By an interesting coincidence, the ship which carried the letter from Douglas also carried a letter from Whitman, of unknown date, to Castle. In all probability this was the last letter Whitman wrote and, although the original is not known to be extant, Castle did make a quotation from it when he wrote to the editor of *The Friend* on February 2, 1848. Castle wrote: "By the same conveyance, we received a letter from Dr. Whitman informing us of the intention of the mission to erect a school house at his station for the children of the mission, *a meeting house for Indians*, and also to aid the Indians in erecting some permanent store houses, and requesting us some supplies for that purpose; *thus showing that to the last he was devising means for the benefit of those by whose hands he fell.*"[4]

Following the arrival of Hinman and Bushman at Fort Vancouver, Douglas and Ogden made immediate preparations to send a rescue party to Fort Walla Walla to secure, if possible, the release of the captives. Three boats under the command of Ogden left Vancouver on Tuesday, December 7. The expedition arrived at The Dalles on the 15th. Progress up the river was slow, partly because the heavy boats had to be carried over the portages, one being five miles long at the Cascades. The Ogden party reached Fort Walla Walla on the 19th. Ogden at once sought to communicate with the Cayuse chiefs. He realized the great importance of rescuing the captives before the Cayuses heard of any intention of the Provisional Government to send a punitive expedition into their country as Ogden knew it would.

When Douglas and Ogden wrote to Sir George Simpson in London on the following March 16 to report the massacre and the actions they had taken, they said that the primary purpose of sending the large company of employees to Fort Walla Walla was "for the protection of the Company's establishment." They also stated that it was then their hope "to rescue the surviving members of the unfortunate mission family, who remained in the hands of the Indians." [5] It may have been from fear of Simpson's disapproval of their actions that they put the material interests of the Company ahead of humanitarian considerations.

Cayuses Threaten to Kill Perrin Whitman

The report that McBean sent to Douglas and Ogden about the intention of the Cayuses to attack Waskopum proved to be true. About twenty minutes after Hinman and Bushman left The Dalles for Fort Vancouver, some of the local Indians crowded into Perrin Whitman's home. After sitting quietly for a time one asked: "Why are you not crying?" "Why should I be crying?" asked Perrin. "Because your father and mother [i.e., the Whitmans] are dead. All the Americans at Waiilatpu are dead; the Cayuses have killed them."

"How do you know?" Perrin anxiously inquired. "The Frenchman told us that he saw them lying dead about the doctor's house before he started." [6]

Dr. Saffarans, in a sworn statement made February 9, 1849, stated that Bushman was the first to tell the Indians at The Dalles about the massacre.[7] Although Bushman had been given strict orders not to tell the white people at The Dalles about the massacre, evidently he did not feel that such an order prevented him from communicating with the natives.

Perrin found it difficult to believe the report of the killings at Waiilatpu which had been relayed to him by the local Indians.[8] On December 12, more than a week after Bushman had called at The Dalles, a friendly Nez Perce arrived at Waskopum and confirmed the news of the massacre. Looking back on those terrifying days, Perrin recalled that the Nez Perce told him that the Cayuse chiefs had offered "one hundred horses... for my scalp."[9]

When the Indians at The Dalles heard rumors that the white people in the Willamette Valley planned to send soldiers into the upper Columbia River country, they fled to the mountains. Thus Perrin and those with him were left without any possible assistance from friendly natives.

After being warned by the Nez Perce Indian, Perrin and his companions made such preparations as they could to meet any attack. They all gathered in one house. Perrin, who was only seventeen years old, had the main responsibility as neither of the two men with him knew the Indian language. Moreover, one of the men was ill. "We fitted up some old flintlock guns," Perrin recalled, "and, armed with these and some axes and other weapons... determined to resist any attack the best we could. I stood at the doorway all night with an ax ready to hew down the first Indian that tried to enter. I knew an ax was longer than a tomahawk, and figured that I had the advantage."

At daybreak on the morning of the 13th, Perrin heard a party of Cayuses stealthily approaching the house. "With bated breath," he said, "I listened and heard murmurings." Fortunately, Perrin could understand what they were saying. "I heard the Indians say the white soldiers are coming. 'We must have the boy,' they said. 'He knows us all'... All hope left me. I awaited an attack in a terrible suspense. But again, just in time, some friendly Nez Perces galloped into view, and the Cayuses, guilty and suspicious, thought they were the volunteers. The attacking party fled, and this alone saved my life."

Later Perrin learned that the Cayuses had planned to call him out of the house on "a pretended truce," at which time he would have been killed. Perrin stated that he would "readily have fallen into the trap" in the hope of saving the others at Waskopum dependent on him.

To Perrin's great relief, Ogden and his party from Fort Vancouver arrived at The Dalles two days after this incident. With Ogden was Hinman. Ogden brought word that a company of volunteers was being raised in the Willamette Valley and that an advance contingent would soon be arriving. By this time it was clearly apparent to both Perrin and Hinman that the usefulness of Waskopum as a mission station had come to an abrupt end.[10] The very night of the day that Ogden and his party arrived at The Dalles, Perrin, the Hinmans, the McKinneys, and Dr. Saffarans left for the Willamette Valley. Perrin joined the Oregon Volunteers, being the youngest member of that punitive expedition, and was with a company which arrived at The Dalles in April 1848.[11]

Experiences of the Captives

Forty-seven men, women and children (including Stanfield) were captives of the Cayuses from the time the massacre began on November 29 to the day they arrived at Fort Walla Walla on Wednesday, December 29. Thus they lived through one month of terror before being rescued. During the first week of their captivity, their fate was undecided. Such hot-headed Indians as Tomahas, Tamsucky, and Frank Escaloom were in favor of killing all, even the women and children, but Tiloukaikt hesitated. When Mrs. Saunders and Beardy interceded with Tiloukaikt in behalf of the women and children, he then assured them that there would be no more killings. On Tuesday, McBean's interpreter, Bushman, arrived and told Tiloukaikt that the Hudson's Bay Company was shocked at what had happened. Bushman passed on McBean's stern warning that there should be no more killings.[12] No doubt Tiloukaikt was loath to incur the displeasure of the Company, as the Indians were dependent upon it for many supplies such as guns and ammunition for their hunts.

Stickus is known to have visited Waiilatpu shortly after the massacre, and it is safe to assume that he too registered his protest. When the Christian Nez Perces, Timothy and Eagle, arrived, they too protested.

Tiloukaikt, however, was unable to control some of the young men of his band. There was a generation gap even in that day. The murder of James Young on the day after Tiloukaikt had promised that there would be no more killings, was evidently done without the chief's knowledge or consent. The murder of the two sick men, Sales and Bewley, took place when Tiloukaikt was away and when his son, Edward, seemingly was in charge. At the time of the trial of the accused murderers in Oregon City in May 1850, Tiloukaikt was charged with complicity in the deaths of only Dr. Whitman and Judge Saunders. His participation in these cases is not clear for he may not have been the one who struck the fatal blows.

Years later, in her reminiscences, Catherine Sager wrote: "Old Teloukite was a man who intended to do right, as far as he knew... was ever after [the massacre] a heart-broken conscience-stricken man. I used to feel sorry for him as I saw him moving about, viewing the wreck of a once happy home."[13] Even though at least three of the girls were taken as wives by natives, the fact that forty-seven survived the month's captivity was due largely to the restraining influence of Chief Tiloukaikt.

Catherine and Mrs. Saunders have given us the best account of the experiences of the captives prior to their release. "They supplied us with an abundance of food, both meat and vegetables," wrote Catherine. "We were allowed to have all the sugar found in Dr. Whitman's house." Both the captives and the Indians dipped freely into the stores of supplies which Dr. Whitman had laid up to meet the needs of his large family and the immigrants through the winter of 1847-48. Stanfield, whom Mrs. Saunders called "a necessary evil," undoubtedly continued to perform such chores as milking the cows and getting wood and water for the comfort and survival of the captives. Catherine noted that often he did such things reluctantly.

During the first days of the captivity, the Indians often crowded into the rooms occupied by the women and children, sometimes lingering until late into the night. The women and children at first were fearful of going out-of-doors. Ten-year-old Eliza Spalding was in great demand as an interpreter. Of this Catherine wrote: "She had been born and brought up among the Indians, and could speak the language well. All day long she was here and there interpreting every silly thing the natives wished to say to the captives, sitting for hours at the mill in order to interpret for the men at work at the mill. The exposure, with anxiety for the fate of her father and mother, weighed on her till she gave out. Taking a fever, she lay very low for days."[14] She was still on her sick bed when Timothy and Eagle visited Waiilatpu in an effort to obtain her release.

The Cayuses found a quantity of calico and muslin in Whitman's storeroom. This they carried to the women and demanded that they sew shirts for them. They also set the women to work knitting socks. At least during the first days of the captivity, the women were also required to cook for the Indians. "The Indians commenced coming early [in the morning]," wrote Catherine, "and stayed until one or two at night. We had to give them their meals but they would not eat until we had first tasted it for fear of poison. They would sit down at the table and make us eat some from each dish." [15]

Catherine related an incident which throws light upon the constant danger the captives faced from the capricious and suspicious Cayuses. Because of the harassment suffered at the hands of some of the unruly young men of the tribe, Mrs. Saunders asked Beardy to stay with the women and children each evening until after the young men had returned to their lodges.

By this time Beardy was the most trusted Indian at Waiilatpu. In order to show her appreciation, Mrs. Saunders made him some peach pies from some dried peaches she had found in the Whitmans' storeroom. Evidently Whitman had secured this delicacy at Fort Vancouver at the time of his visit during the preceding summer. Beardy found the pies so delicious that he ate too heartily of them one day and as a result became violently ill.

Catherine wrote: "He vomited the peaches and thought it was blood, and came at once to the conclusion that he had been poisoned, and resolved to have us all put to death. As soon as he recovered, he made his decision known to his people. We were informed that they would kill us the next day. The Indians came armed and with dark brows. Taking my little sister in my arms, I quietly sat on the floor behind the stove determined to meet my fate with her in my arms." [16]

At that critical time, an Indian woman by the name of Katherine, the wife of a Hudson's Bay employee, arrived at Waiilatpu. Knowing some English, she quickly diagnosed the situation and told Beardy that there was nothing wrong except he had gorged himself on peach pies. After being convinced that he had no one to blame but himself, Beardy calmed down and later treated the whole incident as a huge joke. But at the time it was no joke for the captives. "We lived in constant fear of death," wrote Catherine. The Indian women, whose intercession had saved the captives from harm, brought the cheering news that Ellis, Head Chief of the Nez Perces, was coming in from the buffalo country, and would set them free.

Unknown to Catherine, however, Ellis and about sixty members of his band had died of measles, while in what is now western Montana, sometime before the massacre.[17] Moreover, Lawyer, who later became Head Chief of the Nez Perces, was also in the buffalo country. The absence of these two men left the Nez Perces without the leadership which might have effected the release of the captives sooner than was the case.

LORINDA BEWLEY RAPED

The old adage "to the victor belong the spoils" again proved to be true in the days following the outbreak of violence at Waiilatpu. From time immemorial, captors have ravished their women captives; so it is not surprising to read about the rape of at least three young women at Waiilatpu who were left without male protection. They were: Esther Lorinda Bewley,[18] age twenty-two; Susan Kimball, sixteen; and Mary Smith, fifteen. There may have been others, for Spalding made two references to girls being raped who were so young that "the knife had to be used."[19]

Lorinda's ordeal began the day before her brother, Crocket, was killed. Her attacker was Tamsucky, who is believed to have been the one who had tried about five years before to force his way into Narcissa's bedroom shortly after Marcus had left for the East. Regarding Lorinda's experiences, Catherine Sager wrote: "One evening an Indian came to the house and seemed to be looking for someone. We learned that it was Miss Bewley. She was sick with the ague, and was lying in bed. He went to the bed and began to fondle over her. She sprang up and sat down behind the stove. He sat down by her and tried to prevail upon her to be his wife. She told him that he had a wife, and that she would not have him. Finding that persuasion nor threats availed, he seized her and dragged her out of the house, and tried to place her upon his horse; he failed in this... He tried to stop her screams by placing his hand over her mouth. The contest lasted for some time, when, becoming enraged, he threw her with violence upon the ground. After perpetrating his hellish designs upon her, he ordered her to go to the house. The poor, heartbroken girl came in shaking with agitation."[20]

All this took place in the presence of witnesses and near the room where Lorinda's brother, Crocket, lay on his sick bed. "While the brute was thus maltreating his sister," wrote Catherine, "Mr. Bewley, unable to stand the screams, got up to go to her rescue. At our earnest request, we sent him back to bed." According to a deposition made by Lorinda in 1848: "The Indian abused me before his [i.e., her brother's] eyes, but he dared not raise his hand even if he had had the strength." [21] This incident took place the day before the two young men were killed. Just as the brother had heard the screams of his sister, had seen her being raped by Tamsucky, and was helpless to prevent the outrage, so the sister had to experience the agonizing ordeal of hearing the screams of her brother and Sales, unable to prevent their deaths. Catherine remembered that Lorinda "hid under a bed and gave vent to her grief."

Chief Five Crows, whose lodge was on the Umatilla River near that of his half-brother Young Chief, now enters the picture. As has been mentioned, Five Crows had been baptized by Spalding and received into the membership of the Mission church on June 16, 1843. He was the only Cayuse among the twenty-one natives received into the church during the mission period. Spalding had bestowed upon him the Biblical name, Hezekiah, which was spelled by Brouillet as Achekiak (Achekiah, Ackekaiah). Although Five Crows had no part in the Whitman massacre, he may have known what Tiloukaikt and his band were planning to do. If so, we have no evidence to indicate that he tried to prevent the killings. On the day after the deaths of Bewley and Sales, he sent a servant to Waiilatpu with horses to get Lorinda. Eliza Spalding noticed that one of the horses had belonged to her father and therefore came to the erroneous conclusion that he had been killed. When Lorinda learned of the intention of Five Crows to make her his wife, she went to Tiloukaikt and pled with him to allow her to stay at Waiilatpu with the other women, but he refused. "You will be safer at the camp of the chief," he said. "All the Indians will be glad to protect the squaw of Five Crows, but here you will become the property of all and I cannot help you. You will do well to many the great chief who wants a yellow haired wife."[22] At that time Five Crows had no wife. He is reported to have owned more than a thousand horses. Five Crows knew that many of the mountain men as well as the officers and employees of the Hudson's Bay Company had taken Indian wives. If white men could take Indian women for their wives, why should not an Indian take a white woman? In this instance, however, the importance difference lay in the fact that Lorinda Bewley did not want to be the wife of an Indian even if he were a rich and powerful chief.[23]

The Indian whom Five Crows had sent to get Lorinda insisted on starting back to the Umatilla on that same day, December 9, even though she was then sick with a fever. "There was no escape," wrote Catherine. "The poor girl had to go. We offered her all the comfort we could but what is comfort under such circumstances? We saw the weeping girl ride away."

Shortly after the two had left Waiilatpu, Tamsucky arrived with Joe Lewis and a team and wagon. Not having been able to abduct Lorinda earlier in that day by taking her away on horseback, he had come with a wagon. His plan was to bind her with a rope and put her in the wagon. "They ransacked the house well," wrote Catherine, "not believing our statement that she was gone."[24] The incident proved the correctness of Tiloukaikt's statement that if Lorinda had remained at Waiilatpu, she would have become "the common property of all."

Lorinda's experiences with Five Crows, although preferable to what she would have suffered at the hands of Tamsucky, were, nevertheless, deeply traumatic. Since she and the Indian servant left Waiilatpu too late in the afternoon to reach the Umatilla that day, they had to spend the night in the open. It was a cold, stormy night, with snow falling. They arrived at Five Crows' lodge before noon on the 10th. At first, Five Crows was kind. He carried her into his lodge and laid her upon a bed of robes and blankets. He built a fire and gave her food. Seeing her great unhappiness, he said that she could go to the "house of the white men... and at night he would come for her."[25]

In a second sworn statement, dated December 12, 1848, Lorinda said: "I obtained the privilege of going to the bishop's house before violation on the Umatilla, and *begged* and *cried to the bishop for protection* either at his house, or to be sent to Wallawalla. I told him I would do any work by night and day for him if he would protect me. *He said he would do all he could.*"[26] Lorinda stated that in the house at that time were Bishop Blanchet, Father Brouillet, two other priests, and three Frenchmen. When night came, Five Crows returned to the Bishop's house to get Lorinda. "I refused to go," Lorinda stated, "and he went away, apparently mad, *and the bishop told me I had better go*, as he might do us all an injury." On the Bishop's insistence, she was taken to the chief's lodge. When Five Crows saw the extent of her distress, he sent her back to the Bishop where she remained for that night and the following three days and nights. On Tuesday evening, December 14, Five Crows returned and demanded that she go with him. Lorinda stated: "*The bishop finally ordered me to go*; my answer was, I had rather die. After this, he still insisted on my going as the best thing I could do." [27] Father Brouillet said: "You must go, or he will come back and do us all an injury."

In Catherine's account of the incident, the details of which she had no doubt received from Lorinda, we may read: "She refused to go with him and he resorted to force. She held onto the table until her hands were skinned but what is the strength of a frail woman in the hands of a savage lustful man? She was taken to his lodge, and in the morning after *family prayers*; he sent her back to the Priest's house." Five Crows' attitude towards Lorinda alternated between gentleness and harshness. Likewise his conception of Christianity was filled with contradictions. While keeping up the ritual of family devotions, as taught by the missionaries, he, at the same time, indulged his lustful desires.

For two weeks, from December 14 until she was sent to Fort Walla Walla on the 28th, Lorinda spent the nights with Five Crows and the days in the house of the Bishop. Of this she said: "I would return early in the morning to the bishop's house, and be violently taken away at night. The bishop provided kindly for me while at his house."

Spalding, while glossing over the conduct of his only convert among the Cayuses, Five Crows, severely criticized the Catholic clergy for not protecting Lorinda.[28] It should be remembered, however, that the Bishop and his associates had to compromise their actions because of the threat of violence to themselves. In this respect, their situation paralleled that of McBean at Fort Walla Walla who hesitated to receive Osborn and his family.

Since Five Crows was a Protestant, the Bishop could make no appeal for mercy which was based on ecclesiastical authority. Moreover, Father Ricard at Fort Walla Walla had sent a messenger with an urgent warning to Bishop Blanchet: "that the lives of the priests were in danger... because the Vicar General [Father Brouillet] helped Mr. Spalding to escape."

Father Ricard also reported that the Cayuses had become so threatening, even towards the French Canadians in the employ of the

Hudson's Bay Company, that McBean had taken emergency measures at the fort to ward off a possible attack. The receipt of this warning at 4:30 on the morning of Monday, the 12th, no doubt accounted for the reluctance of the Bishop and his fellow clerics to do anything that might arouse the anger of Five Crows. Here is the explanation for those bitter words spoken by Father Brouillet to Lorinda: "You must go, or he will come back and do us all an injury."

Two Girls Taken as Wives

Emboldened by the apparent success of Tamsucky and Five Crows in their dealings with Lorinda Bewley, several of the young men from Tiloukaikt's camp cast lustful eyes on two teen-age girls, Mary Smith, age fifteen, and Susan Kimball, sixteen. Why sixteen-year-old Ellen Canfield was not involved is not known. She may have been ill at the time.

Mary Smith had so captured the attention of Edward, son of Tiloukaikt, that he had wanted her for his wife several weeks before the massacre took place. Mrs. Saunders wrote: "Edward had tried to buy Mary Smith when he had seen her at Umatilla when the [Smith] family was on their way to the Mission. She was a beautiful brunette and the young chief had offered five horses for her." [29]

According to Catherine, one of the chiefs [the implication is that he was Tamsucky] called a meeting of some of the young Indian men and the girl captives for the evening after Lorinda had been abducted. Through interpreters, including Nicholas Finley and Joe Stanfield, the chief pointed out the helpless condition of the young women; "that there were a lot of vagabond Indians who would be happy to introduce into their tepees a young woman;" that it was therefore best for each of the girls to select one of the young men for her husband and thus be protected. When the chief asked if they were willing, all answered with a firm "No."

Then followed another long harangue when the chief became increasingly threatening. Fresh in the minds of the girls was the memory of what had happened to Lorinda Bewley. When the chief threatened taking them by violence, Mary Smith and Susan Kimball consented. Catherine's account follows: "The chief told them they were wise now, and called on the young men that wanted white wives to come forward.

Two did so; one named Clark; the other Frank [Escaloom]; both influential and rich, and both able to speak some English. The girls were told to choose between these young men, when Mary Smith took Clark; and Susan Kimball, Frank... Miss Kimball wept all the time..." [30]

For some reason Clark, a son of Tiloukaikt, changed his mind. Then his brother, Edward, stepped forward and claimed Mary for his wife. Frank, who was to take Susan, was one who assisted in the killing of her father, a fact she must have known. Catherine wrote that Tiloukaikt was opposed to any of the Indians taking white wives, but by this time he had lost control over his son Edward, who was in various ways usurping his authority.

Among those present at the meeting were Mrs. Saunders and her daughter Helen. When Edward pointed to Helen and asked how old she was, Mrs. Saunders replied: "Eleven snows." Actually she was then fourteen years old. "Eleven snows, too young," said Edward and they let her go.

According to Mrs. Saunders, Susan Kimball, previous to the meeting with the Indians, had said that she would rather die than marry an Indian. "Of course," wrote Mrs. Saunders, "we all realized the enormity of the sacrifice, but we also knew that if the Indians once began to kill, they would spare no one. Mrs. Kimball said she would not insist upon life considering the terrible sacrifice her daughter would be called upon to make, but would leave the decision to the girl herself." [31]

Catherine wrote: "Mary was a brave girl. She took the young brave and when in his presence was cheerful, but in secret wept. Never was a young bridegroom prouder of his wife than Edward of this young girl. He strutted about with that consequential air so common with Indians. He would inquire, 'Where is my wife?' so as to cause everyone who heard him great amusement." [32]

According to Cannon, Edward wanted a marriage service. Mary's father was hesitant to give his consent but, after talking with Finley and Stanfield, was so cowed by what they said that he dared not object. Daniel Young, in his deposition of January 30, 1849, stated: "I told Mr. Smith, were I a father, I would never suffer that, so long as I had power to use an arm. His reply was, 'You don't know what you would do; I would not dare to say a word if they should take my own wife.'"

Cannon, in his *Waiilatpu*, published in 1915, without stating his source wrote that Mary gave herself freely to Edward because she loved him and that some form of a marriage ceremony was performed. He stated: "Sitting behind the stove, their arms encircling each other's waist, the Smith girl reading the Bible and Edward commenting on the same, was the manner in which these young lovers spent their evenings." After the service, the couple retired to an upper room in the emigrant house. And again from Cannon: "At the time of the ransom, when it came to the final parting, Edward was free to admit that the prospect of the girl's being happy with him after her people should have left the country was very remote and he willingly gave her up, both parting with an aching heart." [33]

This incredible story has been repeated in recent years by two writers. Thus the myths connected with the Whitman story continue to proliferate. Catherine tells a quite different story. According to her, after the captives had been taken to Fort Walla Walla, Edward came and asked McBean to let him see Mary. McBean then told the girl that Edward wanted to see her but she refused to see him. "Three times did Edward send for her," wrote Catherine, "requesting to see her, if but for a moment; but she would not comply. After they had left the Fort, Mr. McBean came in and laughingly told her that he thought her very hard hearted to treat that poor fellow so, remarking that he seemed heart broken, having wept freely. Mary told him that she did not care for his tears."

When Catherine wrote her reminiscences, she knew of the report being circulated that Mary was in love with Edward. She wrote in rebuttal: "I was a witness to the above, and would here refute a story that is going the rounds. It is as follows: Mary Smith was in love with the Indian as much as he was with her; that she did not want to leave him, and when we were embarking [at Fort Walla Walla], she stood on the bank with her lover, unable to make up her mind whether to go or stay. Mr. Ogden gave her five minutes to make up her mind; if she did not decide in that time, he would leave her. Mary stood still till just as the boat shoved off, when she kissed the Indian and jumped aboard... I know not what object the author of this tale has in view... I know the above story to be false and without the least foundation. At the time of our leaving the Fort, there was not a Cayuse Indian on the place... Being her constant companion,

I had opportunities of knowing her feelings on the subject. When not in the presence of the Indians, she wept over her disgrace, and would curse the author of it. It seems to me as though these poor girls suffered enough, without the foul language of calumny following them." [34]

With but one exception, the married women and widows were not molested during the month's captivity. Even before the massacre started, Joe Stanfield had cast lecherous eyes on the widow, Mrs. Hays. On the day after the Whitmans were killed, Joe told her that unless she was willing to be known as his wife, the women and children would be killed. "She consented to this in order to save the lives of the rest," wrote Catherine. "He then tried to persuade her to elope with him some night. This she steadily refused to do, asking him what would become of the others if she deserted them. He replied, 'Let them all go to hell.'" [35]

One night when Joe insisted on going to bed with her, Mrs. Hays, with the wisdom of Solomon, placed her four-year-old boy in between them.[36] According to Catherine, when Stanfield was finally convinced that she would not be his wife, he finally exclaimed that she could also go to hell.

Judging by the guarded comments of both Catherine and Mrs. Saunders, much that happened went unreported. Of this Catherine wrote: "In conclusion, I would like to say that I have endeavored to present things in their true light. What has been related in the foregoing pages, is for the most part what fell under my own observation. In giving a history, I have had to touch upon a delicate subject, —one that I have always avoided in conversation, namely, the treatment of the young women by the Indians. I have endeavored to present them in such a manner as to spare the feelings of those concerned. For this reason I have not related many things that would be interesting." [37]

Release of the Captives

On December 10, 1847, three days after being restored to his family, Spalding wrote to Bishop Blanchet, addressing him as "Reverend and Dear Friend." He begged for the Bishop's intercession with the Cayuse chiefs in behalf of the safety of the captives held at Waiilatpu. Naturally, Spalding was concerned for the welfare of his daughter Eliza. He wrote: "My object in writing principally is to give information through you, to the Cayuses, that it is our wish to have peace, that we do not wish the Americans to come from below to avenge the wrong; we hope the Cayuse and the Americans will be on friendly terms, that Americans will no more come in their country, unless they wish it... I know that you will do all in your power for the relief of the captives, women and children at Waiilatpu, that you will spare no pains to appease and quiet the Indians... Please send this, or copy, to Governor Abernethy. The Nez Perces held a meeting yesterday; they pledged themselves to protect us from the Cayuse if we would prevent the Americans from coming up to avenge the murders. This we have pledged to do, and for this we beg for the sake of our lives at this place and at Mr. Walker's [Tshimakain]. By all means keep quiet; send no war reports; nothing but proposals for peace." [38]

Spalding wrote as a frightened man, as indeed he had reason to be. When the Cayuses learned of the contents of this letter, they said that it was easy to see why he had written as he did because "he was in a hole." [39] After his rescue by Ogden, Spalding's attitude towards both the Bishop and the Cayuses made a complete about-face. The Bishop, whom he had called his "Dear Friend," became the object of bitter criticism along with members of his clergy.

Notwithstanding the assurances he had given the Nez Perces that he would do what he could to prevent the Americans from making war on the Cayuses, Spalding urged the Oregon Volunteers, whom he met at The Dalles on his way down the Columbia, to hasten and kill all the Cayuses except a few whom he named as worthy of being spared. "Let them be pursued with unrelenting hatred and hostility," he wrote, "until the life-blood has atoned for their infamous deeds." [40] Spalding may not be blamed for dissembling to the Indians when he, the members of his family, and those at Waiilatpu were in danger, yet the vehemence with which he advocated retaliation suggests the emotional reaction which came after being safely rescued.

The Indians Present Their Case

The enormity of the crimes committed by Tiloukaikt and members of his band at Waiilatpu was soon realized by the Cayuse chiefs who lived along the Umatilla River, and they became afraid. Even though they had not taken part in the massacre, they realized that in all probability the whole Cayuse nation would be subjected to a fearful retaliation at the hands of the Americans. On December 18, Chief Camaspelo, who was also known as Big Belly, called on Bishop Blanchet. According to Brouillet, Camaspelo told the Bishop: "...that he had disapproved of what had happened at Waiilatpu; that the young men had stolen his word." Camaspelo was fearful and discouraged. He even spoke of killing all his horses and "of leaving the country, as all the Indians expected to die." [41]

Camaspelo's visit followed by two days the receipt of Spalding's letter with its frantic appeal for the Bishop's intercession in behalf of peace. The Bishop felt that the time was opportune for a council to be held of all the Cayuse chiefs to see what steps should be taken. With Camaspelo's approval, messengers were sent to the different chiefs bidding them to assemble at St. Anne's Mission on Monday, December 20. At 10:00 a.m. on the appointed day, according to Brouillet's account of the meeting, all the great chiefs of the Cayuses, together with many sub-chiefs, crowded into Bishop Blanchet's house. Among those present were Tiloukaikt, Young Chief, Five Crows, and Camaspelo. With the Bishop were three of his clergy, including Father Brouillet, and their interpreter.

Blanchet, acting as chairman, opened the discussion by stating that the purpose of the gathering was to take counsel to see what could be done to prevent war. He passed on the substance of Spalding's letter, together with some proposals given verbally to him by two Nez Perces who had delivered the letter. These proposals were: "1. That Americans should not come to make war; 2. That they should send up two or three great men to make a treaty of peace; 3. That when these great men should arrive, all captives should be released; 4. That they would offer no offense to Americans before knowing the news from below [i.e., the Willamette Valley]." After presenting these proposals, the Bishop invited the chiefs to speak.

The meeting lasted for a full day and, according to Brouillet's account, the chiefs brought up all of their old grievances against the Americans. Here is the most reliable account of the reasons for the Whitman massacre from the Indians' point of view. After a brief speech by Camaspelo, who spoke in approval of the propositions, Tiloukaikt arose. He began by saying that "he was not a great speaker, and that his talk would not be long." He then launched into a detailed review of the history of the Cayuse nation "since the arrival of the whites in the country down to the present time." Brouillet noted that he spoke for two hours.

Since Brouillet did not know the Nez Perce language, he was unable to give a detailed report of all the grievances mentioned by Tiloukaikt, but enough was made clear to him through his interpreter to give him a fair appreciation of what was being said. According to Brouillet, Tiloukaikt referred to the death of the Nez Perce chief, called The Hat, who was with W. H. Gray when they were attacked by Sioux Indians in what is now western Nebraska on August 7, 1837, and to the death of Elijah Hedding, the son of a Walla Walla chief, Yellow Serpent, at Sutter's Fort in California in the fall of 1844.[42] Neither of these Indians was a Cayuse, yet Tiloukaikt referred to their deaths as a reason for complaint. In both cases, Tiloukaikt held the Americans to blame, as Gray was an American and Elijah Hedding was killed by an American. No doubt, Tiloukaikt also mentioned the death of Cayuse Halket, a nephew of Young Chief, at the Red River Mission in January 1837.

Some have advanced the "blood-feud" theory to explain the Indian code of conduct which demanded a life for a life. This was a matter of tribal honor. Such a theory would account for the killing of the eight immigrant men at Waiilatpu against whom the Cayuses held no personal grudges. Unfortunately for these victims, they were Americans and they happened to be at the scene of tragedy when the killings began. Although the members of Tiloukaikt's band harbored grudges against both Marcus and Narcissa Whitman, and possibly also against the two Sager boys and Andrew Rodgers, the existence of a racial feud may also have contributed to the decision of the Indians to kill these five. The fact that Tiloukaikt spoke of the deaths of The Hat and Elijah Hedding lends support to the theory of a blood-feud as one of the causes of the Whitman massacre.

Since Tiloukaikt spoke for about two hours, he must have mentioned many other complaints not recorded by Father Brouillet. No doubt he reviewed the issues discussed with Whitman in the fall of 1841 when he had demanded payment from Whitman for the use of the land. This Whitman had refused to give.[43] Undoubtedly, Whitman was accused of being too sympathetic to the immigrants who were crossing the Cayuse country each fall in ever increasing numbers. Tiloukaikt could have repeated the reports that such half-breeds as Joe Gray, Tom Hill, and Joe Lewis had given regarding the way the Americans had mistreated the

Indians in the States, and the probability of the Americans moving in to occupy Cayuse land and to take their horses. All of the fears and suspicions the Indians felt in regard to Americans came to a focus in their anger against the Whitmans.

Following Tiloukaikt, Five Crows and Young Chief spoke, and then Edward Tiloukaikt took the floor. He emphasized the terrible loss of life the Cayuses had suffered because of the introduction of the white man's diseases. Brouillet wrote: "He ...gave a touching picture of the afflicted families, in seeing borne to the grave a father, a mother, a brother, or a sister; spoke of a single member of a family who had been left to weep alone over all the rest who had disappeared." He repeated the accusation, first made by Joe Lewis, that Whitman and Spalding had plotted to poison the Indians in order to get their lands and their horses, and also the calumny that Rodgers, before he died, had admitted that this report was true.

After hours of discussion, the chiefs decided to ask Bishop Blanchet to draw up a "manifesto" to be sent to Governor Abernethy. This was to contain the four proposals suggested by the Nez Perces, which were supported in part by Spalding's letter. To these four, two more proposals were added. One stated that the Americans should "forget the lately committed murders, as the Cayuses will forget the murder of the son of the great chief of Walla Walla committed in California." The second new proposal, suggested perhaps by an ambiguous statement in Spalding's letter to the Bishop, stated: "They ask that Americans may not travel any more through their country, as their young men might do them harm." This called for the cessation of the annual Oregon emigration from the States which, of course, was an impossibility.

The Bishop wrote an introduction for the six-point manifesto in which he referred to the conviction held by the Indians that Whitman had actually been poisoning them. He mentioned the fact that six Cayuses had been buried on Sunday, November 28, and three more on the morning of the day the massacre began. In his concluding statement, the Bishop wrote: "They were led to believe that the whites had undertaken to kill them all, and that these were the motives which led them to kill the Americans." The document was signed by Tiloukaikt, Camaspelo, Young Chief, and Five Crows.[44]

Late in the afternoon or early that evening, a messenger arrived from Fort Walla Walla with the surprising news that Peter Skene Ogden had arrived at Fort Walla Walla and wanted to meet with the Cayuse chiefs and the Catholic clergy without delay.[45] This was a most surprising development for the Cayuse, as they had assumed that all negotiations for the release of the captives would be carried on with the Americans. Suddenly they were confronted with the fact that the Hudson's Bay Company had entered the picture. The manifesto so laboriously drawn up that day was now nullified. Some good results, however, came from the Monday meeting. The chiefs had come to an understanding that they should negotiate with the whites as a tribe and not as individuals. There was but one discordant note in their discussions. Five Crows had refused to give up Lorinda Bewley, even though all had entreated him to do so, including Bishop Blanchet.

None of the Catholic clergy had ventured to leave St. Anne Mission after Father Brouillet's return from Waiilatpu on December 1 because of fear of attack by members of Tiloukaikt's band. They had been warned that Brouillet's life was in danger because he had helped Spalding to escape. Having now been summoned to Fort Walla Walla, they ventured to make the trip and did so without incident.

Ogden Secures Release of the Captives

Fortunately for the captives, the responsibility of negotiating their release fell to the lot of white-haired Peter Skene Ogden. In all of Old Oregon there was no other person so well qualified, so highly regarded by the natives, and so strategically situated as he to induce the Cayuse to give up their hostages. He had the advantage of being able to speak to the Indians from a position of power, as they were dependent upon the Hudson's Bay Company for many of their supplies, especially guns and ammunition needed for their hunting expeditions. In exchange, the Company received their pelts or horses. Ogden was able to stop all such trading, a fact of which the Cayuse chiefs were fully aware. Here was an advantage which no American official enjoyed. Moreover, Ogden had a native wife and this constituted a bond of sympathy with the Cayuses. Ogden did not go to Fort Walla Walla to punish the Cayuses but to persuade them to release their captives. He did not take a single soldier with him, only sixteen boatmen. Realizing that the safety of nearly fifty men, women, and children at Waiilatpu was involved, and in addition those at Lapwai and Tshimakain, Ogden moved as rapidly as circumstances permitted to arrange for their deliverance.

The Cayuse chiefs, with the single exception of Five Crows, together with many of the younger men of the tribe, Bishop Blanchet and his clergy, and their interpreter assembled at Fort Walla Walla at 9:30 Thursday morning, December 23. Five Crows absented himself because he did not want to be persuaded to give up Lorinda.[46] Ogden opened the council by saying: "We have been among you for thirty years without the shedding of blood; we are traders, and of a different nation from the Americans; but recollect, we supply you with ammunition, not to kill Americans, who are of the same color, speak the same language, and worship the same God as ourselves, and whose cruel fate causes our hearts to bleed. Why do we make you chiefs, if you cannot control your young men?"[47]

Ogden pointed out that Dr. Whitman was not guilty of poisoning their people, as Indians all over Oregon were dying of measles and other diseases. Ogden asked: "How could he be responsible for the deaths of so many in such widely scattered places?" Ogden made it clear that he had not come to Walla Walla as a representative of the Americans in the Willamette Valley but rather as an official of the Hudson's Bay Company. He explained that he had left Fort Vancouver before the Americans in the Valley had been notified of the killings. "The company have nothing to do with your quarrel," he emphasized. "If you wish it, on my return I will see what can be done for you, but I do not promise to prevent war. Deliver me the prisoners to return to their friends, and I will pay you a ransom, that is all."

In the report of the negotiations sent to Sir George Simpson under date of March 12, 1848, Ogden stated that although the Cayuses had not altered "their usual friendly deportment towards the establishment, and expressed in very earnest language their desire to remain on friendly terms with the Company, [they] were not so tractable on the subject of restoring the American prisoners, whom they wished to retain as hostages for their own security." Since Ogden was unable to offer any assurances that the Americans would not seek revenge, it required "all his tact and great personal influence with them to procure the liberation of these unhappy captives, who would have been mercilessly butchered on the first commencement of hostilities."[48]

The discussion over the release of the captives and the amount of ransom to be paid continued late into the evening. The Cayuses kept demanding that Ogden give some assurance that the Americans would not make war against them, but this he said he could not give. Regarding this, Brouillet wrote: "He promised them only that he would speak in their favor."

Finally Ogden agreed to give a ransom consisting of "fifty blankets, fifty shirts, ten guns, ten fathoms of tobacco, ten handkerchiefs, and one hundred balls and powder,"[49] provided all the captives were brought to Fort Walla Walla within six days, i.e., by December 29. Ogden felt that he needed the interval of six days in order to get word to Spalding and to give time for those at Lapwai to arrive at the Fort.

No one could speak for Five Crows, but the chiefs who lived on the Umatilla promised to use their influence to obtain the release of Lorinda. Ogden was concerned about her rescue and emphasized that he would give no ransom until all the captives had been brought to the fort. Tiloukaikt promised to turn over twelve oxen and sixteen bags of coarse flour to provide food for the released captives on their way down the river to Fort Vancouver. Of course, such supplies would come from the property formerly owned by Dr. Whitman.

Some Nez Perces were also present at the December 23 meeting and, although they had not been involved in the Waiilatpu tragedy, they asked that a ransom be given to them for the safe delivery of the Spalding family, Mary Johnson, Horace Hart, W. D. Canfield, and Mr. Jackson. Ogden promised them "twelve blankets, twelve shirts, two guns, twelve handkerchiefs, five fathoms of tobacco, two hundred balls and powder, and some knives."

The items paid to the Cayuses and Nez Perces in ransom may have been limited to the stores on hand at Fort Walla Walla and possibly some supplies that Ogden had the foresight to take with him up the river. Ogden sent a special dispatch to Spalding on the evening of the 23rd reporting on the agreement reached with the natives and urging him to lose "no time in joining me." He warned Spalding against making any promises whatever to the natives. Ogden repeated his injunction for haste, and intimated that he might have to start for Fort Vancouver with the released captives from Waiilatpu before those from Lapwai could arrive. "Use all diligence possible to overtake us," he urged.

Spalding replied in a note dated December 25, which is evidence that Ogden's messenger had made the journey of about 140 miles to Lapwai in two days. Spalding wrote: "This people are unwilling that I should leave their country and I have promised to return and live with them provided the melancholy affair at Waiilatpu can be settled and the Nez Perces continue friendly to the whites." Just before sending his letter to Ogden, Spalding added a postscript: "I have just learned from the two [Nez Perces] who returned from [Walla Walla], that the Cayuses have resolved should they learn that the Americans purpose to come up to avenge the death of those who have been massacred, that they will immediately fall upon myself and family and all Americans in the country and kill all." In view of this alarming information, Spalding begged Ogden not to leave Walla Walla until those from Lapwai had arrived. Ogden sent word to Walker and Eells, who with their families had taken refuge in Fort Colville, to remain there until they could be rescued at some later date.

No Time to Lose

News of the arrival of Ogden at Fort Walla Walla had reached the Indians at Waiilatpu on Monday, December 20, the day that the meeting of the chiefs was being held at St. Anne's Mission. Although Mrs. Saunders was unaware of the cause, she remembered that the Indians became very excited and "were running about on horseback in every direction." The captives were not told of the December 23 meeting at Fort Walla Walla and did not know that they were to be released until a friendly Cayuse told Mrs. Saunders that "the big white chief" had come and that he was sure "we were not to be killed." Catherine has given us the following: "Christmas dawned upon us at last. Oh, how unlike any that had ever dawned before! Mrs. Saunders prepared a little treat for the children in her room, but we ate in secret when no Indians were about... We entertained little hope of ever leaving our prison house. We knew that as soon as the news reached the [Willamette] settlement, an army would be sent to our rescue. We also knew that this would be the signal for our death. Our captors had given us to understand that they expected the Americans would send an army to punish them, and their intention to kill us in such a case. It was, therefore, with alarm mingled with joy that we heard of the arrival of three boats at Walla Walla." [50]

Tiloukaikt probably returned from Fort Walla Walla, following his meeting with Ogden, on December 24. When some of the members of his band learned of the agreement reached with Ogden regarding the release of the captives, they strenuously objected. We may assume that they included Tamsucky, Tomahas, Frank Escaloom, and the chief's son, Edward. It is possible that some of these persons were at the Walla Walla meeting.

Sometime on Christmas day, Tiloukaikt told Mrs. Saunders that all could leave for the fort on Wednesday, the 29th. When she asked whether they could take their personal belongings, he replied: "Yes. Take all and heaps of food for a long journey." She interpreted this to mean that the released captives would be going down the Columbia River. In the few days interval before the 29th, when they could be leaving Waiilatpu, the five men among the captives had opportunity to butcher the seven oxen and to grind the sixteen bags of flour. Catherine searched through the debris on the floor of the main mission house where she found Dr. Whitman's original commission from the American Board dated February 17, 1835. This she took with some other items which later she presented to the museum at Whitman College.[51]

Mrs. Saunders tells of their departure from Waiilatpu: "So on December twenty-ninth, just one month after the massacre, we started on our way. We had finished loading before daylight and were traveling just as the sun rose." Five wagons were needed to carry their baggage, including their food supplies, and the women and children. The wagons pulled by horses soon took the lead, while those with the slow plodding oxen fell behind. Catherine wrote: "We had gone but a short distance when a squaw came out of her lodge nearby and told us to hurry, that the natives were going to kill us."

The wagon in which Mrs. Saunders and the Sager girls were riding, which was evidently at the rear of the caravan, reached the mouth of the Touchet River where it emptied into the Walla Walla River, at noon. They were then a little more than halfway to the fort. The day was cold and rainy. While fording the Touchet, those in the wagon got thoroughly drenched by the high water which washed over the sides of the wagon bed. After crossing the river, they stopped for refreshments. While still at the crossing, Tiloukaikt and Beardy rode up and warned them to keep moving. "Hurry, hurry," they said. "No camp, get to the fort." Now it was the experience of these two chiefs to become afraid of the rebellious young men of their own tribe. Beardy remained with the party and was especially helpful in urging the oxen on. "It rained all the afternoon," wrote Mrs. Saunders, "and the downpour still continued when we got to the Fort." [52]

Ogden met the Saunders party at the gate; it was then dark. "Thank God, Mrs. Saunders," he fervently exclaimed, "that you are all safe. I thought that you had been killed." They were quickly ushered into a large room where a fire was burning in a fireplace.

The Sager girls remembered Ogden as being a large, jovial man, whom they called "Uncle Pete." Also present was John Mix Stanley whose solicitude for the comfort of the Sager girls at the fort and while going down the river was never to be forgotten. Shortly after arriving at the fort, someone asked Catherine how long they had been held captives by the Indians. "I innocently replied," she wrote, "three or four months and was surprised to find that it had only been one month."

The released captives had a joyful reunion at the fort with the Osborn family and to their surprise found that Lorinda Bewley had arrived that afternoon. In a deposition dated December 12, 1848, Lorinda told her story: "On the 28th of December, in the morning, while I was at the Five Crows' lodge, an Indian rode up leading a large horse and handed me a note from Mr. Ogden, stating the joyful news that he had finally succeeded in redeeming all the unfortunate captives; that he had redeemed me. I had nothing to fear and nothing to do but to accompany the Indian as fast as I could, comfortably, to Walla Walla." [53] From contemporary sources we learn that the Indian who came to escort her to the fort was Camaspelo.[54] Lorinda's deposition continues: "I could hardly believe my eyes. I bowed upon my knees with a grateful heart, and thanked my Saviour for his great mercy to me. The Five Crows prepared tea and a good breakfast for me, and put a new blanket and buffalo robe upon the saddle to make it comfortable for me to ride and for sleeping at night, and a thick shawl around me, and assisted me on my horse, and bade me goodbye kindly and with much feeling, and gave me food for the journey." Evidently the note from Ogden, added to what Camaspelo had to say, convinced Five Crows that he had no choice but to let Lorinda go. This he did with surprising good grace.

Since a long ride of about fifty-five miles separated the lodge of Five

Crows from Fort Walla Walla, Camaspelo and Lorinda had to spend one night in the open. Lorinda stated that they camped on the Walla Walla River, a few miles below Waiilatpu. The night was cold and foggy and it began to rain in the morning. Camaspelo built a fire which he replenished during the night for her benefit. No one could have been kinder to her than he. After breakfast, the Indian spent a few minutes in his morning devotions, in which Lorinda joined, even though they spoke different languages in their prayers.

As they approached the gate of the fort, Ogden rushed out to meet them. Regarding this, Lorinda stated: "Mr. Ogden took me gently from the horse, as a father, and said, 'Thank God, I have got you safe at last... I feared they would never give you up.'" With all of the captives once held at Waiilatpu safely within the fort, Ogden paid the promised ransom to the Cayuses on Thursday, December 30. Mrs. Saunders wrote that the Indians "celebrated with a dance inside the fort yard." As Ogden was fearful as to what they might do to their former captives, he insisted on the women and children remaining in locked rooms with guards at the doors. "After the dance," wrote Mrs. Saunders, "the only Indians allowed in the fort were the old ones and those known to be friendly, and even these had to leave at sundown. A large band of Cayuses were camped just outside the fort, and this was the cause of no small anxiety to both Ogden and McBean.

The first detachment of Oregon Volunteers, recruited in the Willamette Valley and consisting of only ten men under the command of Major H. A. G. Lee, arrived at The Dalles on December 21.[55] Alanson Hinman returned to Waskopum with this party. Although Major Lee and his men were the first of the Volunteers to advance that far up the Columbia, their primary purpose was not punitive but rather to protect American mission property at The Dalles and to establish a base for future military operations against the Cayuses.

Exaggerated reports of the number of American soldiers at The Dalles were carried by Indians to Fort Walla Walla. This greatly excited the Cayuses. Fortunately for the safety of the captives at Waiilatpu, these reports arrived after they were safe within the palisades of Fort Walla Walla. Ogden would have been glad to leave for Fort Vancouver the day after the released captives had arrived at Walla Walla, but he felt constrained to wait for the Spalding party of nine who were to come from Lapwai.

Brouillet reported: "Divers rumors were in circulation among the Indians. It was said that an army had arrived at The Dalles, and they had come to avenge the murders. It was feared that these rumors might change the minds of the Indians, and cause them to retain the captives." Although Ogden, his men, and the former captives were within the walls of the fort, actually they were in a vulnerable situation, as the Indians could easily set fire to the palisades and burn down the fort.

Again and again the Cayuses asked Ogden if it were true that American soldiers were at The Dalles. Of this, Brouillet wrote: "Mr. Ogden told them he knew nothing about it, but that he did not believe it." Ogden was correct in assuming that the Americans would not send a punitive expedition into the Cayuse country before the captives were safely delivered into the Willamette Valley. Brouillet wrote that had the Americans attacked the Cayuses before the captives were in a safe place, such a step would have become "the signal for the general massacre of all those unfortunate beings." [56] No one appreciated the delicacy of the situation more fully than Ogden, who became increasingly anxious for the safe arrival of the Spalding party. He realized that there was no time to loose.

The Lapwai Mission Abandoned

After receiving Ogden's letter of December 23 late in the evening of the 25th, Spalding made immediate preparations to leave for Fort Walla Walla. Even though he and his wife had the help of Mary Johnson and the three men, Hart, Canfield, and Jackson—it took them two days to get ready to go. Food supplies for the journey of nearly 150 miles had to be packed. Personal belongings had to be selected and there were countless decisions that had to be made regarding which items were to be taken on pack animals to the fort and which were to be abandoned. The Spaldings had to face the difficulties involved in taking their three small children with them on horseback for such a long ride through wintry weather. Since it was raining during those days at Fort Walla Walla, it could well have been snowing at Lapwai. The children were a boy, eight years old, and two girls, aged three and one. No one can measure the depth of the emotions which stirred the hearts of both Henry and Eliza as they hastily prepared to abandon their home and leave their work among the Nez Perces where they had lived for eleven years and to go whither they knew not.

The inventory which Spalding later compiled of the property he was obliged to abandon at Lapwai gives eloquent evidence of the success of his work. A cluster of nine buildings were on the grounds: their story-and-a-half log cabin home which measured 30 x 20 feet; a schoolhouse, 20 x 16; a meeting house, 50 x 30; a printing shop, 28 x 16; and five other buildings used largely for storage purposes. There was a millrace one-third of a mile long with an enclosed gristmill. More than twenty acres were under cultivation and the fruit orchard contained more than two hundred trees, some of which were bearing. The livestock included 101 head of cattle, thirty-nine horses, and thirty-one hogs. Also listed were over six hundred bushels of wheat, corn, peas, and potatoes, and four hundred copies of the *Gospel of Matthew in Nez Perce*, five hundred copies of primers, and three hundred copies of a native hymn book. Spalding estimated the monetary value of the property abandoned to be more than $10,000.[57] This is a remarkable showing when it is remembered that Spalding received no salary from the Board [Appendix 2].

The evidence of the material prosperity of the Lapwai station reflects only indirectly the beneficial results which the Spaldings had achieved in their educational and religious activities for the natives. These achievements could never be catalogued or evaluated in financial terms. No Protestant missionaries in all of Old Oregon were as successful in their work of Christianizing and civilizing the natives as were Henry and Eliza Spalding. Then came the sad day, December 28, 1847, when all their work with the Nez Perces came to an abrupt end. They had to flee for fear of what might happen to them and to their children should the Oregon Volunteers bring war to the Cayuses.

When the Spalding party, consisting of six adults and three children, mounted their horses and guided their pack animals down the trail that led to Fort Walla Walla, they were joined by a company of forty armed Nez Perces who decided to escort them to make sure of their welfare and safety. No doubt Henry and Eliza remembered how, during the last week of November 1836, they had been escorted to the Lapwai Valley by a similar number of Nez Perces who were in that manner expressing their joy in having the missionary couple settle in their midst. Perhaps some of the Nez Perces who had been in the welcoming party were now guarding their departure. Perhaps also Spalding remembered that some of the Nez Perces had told him eleven years before: "The Nez

Perces do not have difficulties with the white men as the Cayuses do." As Spalding rode away, he resolved, God willing, to return.[58] William Craig, who had a Nez Perce wife and was living with the Indians, decided that he would for the time being remain in the Lapwai Valley.

When Ogden wrote to Spalding on December 23, he anticipated that Spalding would be able to arrive at the fort much sooner than proved to be the case. As each day passed and the Indians around the fort became more and more restless as they mulled over fresh rumors about the presence of American soldiers at The Dalles, Ogden became uneasy. Mrs. Saunders wrote that finally Ogden declared: "If the people from the Nez Perce Mission did not arrive by Saturday [January 1, 1848], he would not take the chances of staying any longer, but would start without them." On Saturday noon, an Indian, riding in advance of the Spalding caravan, reached the fort with the welcome news that the Lapwai party was approaching. "Great was the rejoicing," wrote Mrs. Saunders, when the Spaldings arrived. Canfield was reunited with his family and the Spaldings with their daughter Eliza. Catherine noted: "Mrs. Spalding found her daughter much changed from the healthy girl who had left her a month before. She was thin as a skeleton."

Catherine wrote of a different kind of welcome which Spalding might have received: "Early in the day Tamsucky came to the fort with his gun in his hand, evidently going to kill Mr. Spalding. Taking his stand by the side of the gate, he seemed to be waiting for Mr. Spalding to pass on. Mr. S. came right in to see his daughter, who stayed in the house. He kept his eyes on Tamsucky as he passed by. Seeing so many Nez Perces there armed, he [Tamsucky] became alarmed and left by the opposite gate."[59]

The ransom promised to the Nez Perces for the safe deliverance of the Spalding party was duly paid. Spalding listed the items in his inventory of the Lapwai property and valued them at $130.31. Writing to Simpson on March 12, 1848, Ogden reported the actions he had taken in paying the ransom to the Indians and directed that, should the Company not approve of this expenditure, "to avoid any remarks being made, let it at once be placed to my private account."[60] Spalding in a letter written to the American Board in 1851 stated: "I am not aware that the H.B. Co. have ever been indemnified by the Government of this Territory or the Home Government."[61] There is no evidence that the Hudson's Bay Company ever submitted any claim to any American authority for a reimbursement nor held Ogden liable for the modest cost of the goods given in ransom.

THE FINAL DELIVERANCE

As rumors of the presence of American soldiers at The Dalles continued to spread, the anger of the malcontents among the Cayuses increased. Looking back on those days, Ogden said that it was his firm conviction that "had not the women and children been given up, they undoubtedly would all have been murdered." [62] With the safe arrival of the Lapwai party, Ogden made immediate preparations to leave for Fort Vancouver the next morning. The urgency of the occasion was such that even the Spaldings seemingly made no objection to Sunday travel. In addition to the forty-seven, including Stanfield, arriving from Waiilatpu and the nine from Lapwai, there were eleven at the Fort who wanted to go down the river. This included the Osborn family of five, the artist Stanley, the two Manson boys, Bishop Blanchet, and two of his priests. The other members of the Catholic clergy decided to remain at Walla Walla with the hope of being able to return to one or both of their newly established missions. The combined parties seeking transportation to Fort Vancouver numbered sixty-seven, including fourteen men, eleven women, and forty-two children. With Ogden and his sixteen boatmen, this meant a grand total of eighty-four who had to be divided into three groups, one for each of the three boats. Much of the baggage which had been brought to Walla Walla from Waiilatpu and Lapwai had to be stored temporarily at the fort as the bateaux were not large enough to carry all this in addition to the passengers, necessary food supplies, bedding and camping equipment, and personal baggage.

A distressing decision had to be made regarding eight or nine-year-old David Malin Cortez, who had been under the Whitman's care ever since March 1842, when he was left as a forlorn and mistreated waif on their doorstep. No one of the refugee families wanted the responsibility of caring for him. According to Catherine, the priests recommended that the lad be left with McBean at Fort Walla Walla, since his father had been in the employ of the Company and his mother had been a native. Years later, when writing her reminiscences, Matilda recalled how, as the heavily laden bateaux shoved off for their voyage down the river, the lonely lad stood on the bank "crying as though his heart were breaking as his friends floated away from him."[63] No further reference has been found regarding what happened to him.

A few hours after the three boats had left, a party of about fifty armed Cayuses arrived at the fort with the demand that "Mr. Spalding be given up to be killed, as they had reliable news of American soldiers en route to their country." [64] By this time the Cayuses were convinced that Ogden had double-crossed them.

To offset the ill repute given the whole Cayuse tribe by the misdeeds of a few, the good deeds of such men as Stickus, Beardy, and Camaspelo should be remembered who, often at great personal risk, did what they could to ameliorate the lot of the white people. Many of the Cayuses, both men and women, whose names were unknown to the captives but who were anonymously referred to as "an Indian," rendered innumerable acts of kindness to the captives.

Many a flotilla of bateaux and canoes belonging to the Hudson's Bay Company had passed up and down the Columbia River, but never before had one carried such a precious cargo as that commanded by Chief Factor Ogden in January 1848. Catherine remembered how "the amiable man with an inexhaustible sense of fun... cheered the monotony of our journey with the reminiscences of his voyages up and down the river. He laughed a great deal about his large family, as he styled us." [65]

The voyage lasted from Sunday morning, January 2, to noon on the following Saturday, the 8th. Chief Factor James Douglas gave the party a warm welcome at Fort Vancouver. Catherine remembered that most of the refugees were given quarters near the river, while the Spaldings, the four Sager girls, and Lorinda Bewley were entertained in the Douglas home. Elizabeth Sager made such a favorable impression on Mrs. Douglas that she asked to keep her, but Ogden declared that it was his intention to deliver all the Americans into the hands of Governor Abernethy.

After spending the week-end at Fort Vancouver, the Americans were taken by boat to Portland. Since the captives had arrived in the lower Columbia country, the Oregon Volunteers, under the command of Colonel Cornelius Gilliam, were ordered to move up the river and into the Cayuse country to apprehend, if possible, the murderers. The first company of fifty men under Colonel Gilliam's personal command were on the wharf at Portland ready to leave for The Dalles at the time the boats arrived from Fort Vancouver. Also present to welcome the former captives were Governor Abernethy and Captain William Shaw; the latter being the one who had delivered the seven Sager orphans to the Whitman home in October 1844. Since Colonel Gilliam had also been a member of the 1844 Oregon emigration and had known the parents of the Sager children, he shared with Shaw a special interest in the twice-orphaned girls.

Elizabeth has given us the following description of their welcome to Portland: "As we pulled in toward the wharf at Portland, a lot of men on the wharf fired a salute. We children were terrified. We crawled under some canvass and tried to hide in the bottom of the boat. We thought they were trying to kill us." Seeing the terror of the children, Gilliam and Shaw hastened to comfort them. "They told us," wrote Elizabeth, "that they were firing the guns in our honor."[66]

The company of former captives began to separate at Portland as relatives and friends took them to their homes. The Spalding family the Sager girls, and Stanley first went with Governor Abernethy to Oregon City. There Stanley was received by Dr. McLoughlin, who was living in retirement and had become an American citizen. The others were entertained for several days in the Abernethy home. The Spaldings then moved to Tualatin Plains to be near their friends, the former independent missionaries, Mr. and Mrs. A. T. Smith. After a year or so on the Plains, the Spaldings moved to Calapooya, near Brownsville, Oregon, where Mrs. Spalding died on January 7, 1851.[67] Separate homes were found for each of the Sager girls. Their subsequent history is well told in Erwin N. Thompson's book, *Shallow Grave at Waiilatpu*.

Two of the children died after their arrival in the Willamette Valley, perhaps both as a result of lack of medical care during the captivity and the exposure suffered during their voyage down the Columbia River. Mention has already been made of the death of the four-year-old son of the Osborns. The second to die was the eleven-year-old girl, Mary Aim Bridger, who passed away sometime in the following March.[68] Where she had lived after her arrival in the Valley is not known. Her father, Jim Bridger, was then at Fort Bridger in the Rockies. The death of five children, three at Waiilatpu after the massacre began and two in the Valley, could well be counted as casualties of the massacre, thus bringing the total loss of life to nineteen.

CHAPTER TWENTY-THREE *Congress Establishes Oregon as a Territory*

The first to be arrested by authorities of the Provisional Government and charged with complicity in the massacre was Joe Stanfield, who had thrown in his lot with the Americans and had gone down to the Willamette Valley with them. Of him Catherine wrote: "On our arrival at Oregon City, Joe Stanfield was arrested on suspicion of taking part in the massacre, and brought to trial. On being taken by the sheriff, he attempted to conceal a watch which had belonged to Mr. Kimball and some money which had belonged to Mr. Hoffman.[69] Two of the widows testified that Joe had told them he knew of the plans of the Indians before he went after the beef [which was butchered on the morning the massacre began]. He was convicted and sentenced to be taken to General [sic] Gilliam in the Cayuse country to be dealt with as the General saw fit. Gilliam having died before he could reach him, Joe escaped punishment. Reports say that he died in the California gold mines in '49 or '50."[70]

Mrs. Saunders characterized Stanfield as "a French Canadian of a very common type." There is no doubt that he rendered much needed services to the captives during their month's detention. Since he was able to move among the Indians with impunity, he was able to get food, wood, and water for the captives. He helped Canfield escape. Possibly it was he who suggested that Mrs. Saunders write a letter to McBean which Finley carried to Fort Walla Walla. It was he who dug the graves and buried the dead. And finally he drove one of the ox teams which, yoked to a wagon, carried some of the captives with their belongings to Fort Walla Walla on the day of their deliverance. He was, as Mrs. Saunders described him, "a necessary evil."

Spalding's Letter of Appreciation

The Archives of the Hudson's Bay Company contain a letter of appreciation written by Spalding from Tualatin Plains on January 13, 1849, and addressed to Peter Skene Ogden whom he called "My Most Worthy Benefactor." Spalding wrote: "The date of this letter will call to your mind scenes of the liveliest interest, and does to mine, the occasion of the warmest gratitude to yourself, the honored agent in the hands of kind Heaven, in delivering myself & family & our fellow companions in suffering from the blood stained hands of ruthless, lawless savages, & placed us all in the arms of safety, the bosom of Christian society."

"I could not allow the anniversary day of our safe arrival at Oregon City to pass without doing myself the pleasure of repeating to you my warmest thanks for your prompt & philanthropic efforts in flying so speedily to our relief & for your judicious & successful efforts in rescuing us all from the perilous situation in the Indian country."[71] This is only a short quotation from Spalding's long and effusive letter of appreciation.

Discovery of Two Stanley Cayuse Portraits

The artist, John Mix Stanley, took a special interest in the four Sager girls during their voyage down the Columbia River. Catherine remembered: "When we camped at night, he gave me his guns to carry and taking my little sister would carry her to the camp and wrap us in his serape and kindle a fire for us. He also carried my sister for me when we made the portages." After their arrival at Fort Vancouver, Stanley bought some calico dress materials for each of the girls. "His care for us," wrote Catherine, "was a subject of much joking by Mr. Ogden." Matilda wrote of the visit that she and her sisters made on Dr. McLoughlin when they were in Oregon City: "Mr. Stanley had a room there and was painting portraits and he came to take us down to see his pictures. He wanted to paint my picture, but I was entirely too timid and would not let him."[72] Before leaving Oregon, Stanley painted pictures of Dr. McLoughlin, Dr. Forbes Barclay, and A. L. Lovejoy.[73]

As has been stated, Stanley painted the portraits of at least four Cayuses when he was at Waiilatpu during the first part of October 1847: Tiloukaikt; Tamsucky; Edward, son of Tiloukaikt; and Waie-cat, son of Tamsucky. We also knew from listings in one of his exhibition catalogues that he had two pictures entitled: "Massacre of Dr. Whitman's family at Waiilatpu Mission," and "Abduction of Miss Bewley from Dr. Whitman's Mission."[74]

It is possible that Stanley began work on these pictures during the weeks he was at Fort Walla Walla, getting details from McBean, Osborn, and others, and also drawing on his own recollections of his visit to Waiilatpu. Possibly, when Stanley took the Sager girls to see his pictures, he obtained further information from them as to some details he wished to include in his paintings.

After returning to the States, Stanley exhibited his Indian paintings in several cities including Washington, D.C., and Cincinnati, Ohio.

Catalogues describing his exhibit are extant for each of these places.[75] The annotations for the Cayuse portraits displayed in the Smithsonian Institution in Washington reflect information that Stanley had secured from the released captives. The legend for No. 120, listed below, contains some inaccuracies which may be excused when one remembers that he wrote the account several years after the massacre when both his notes and his memory were faulty. The annotations from the catalogue of the Smithsonian exhibit follow:

119. Te-lo-kikt, or Craw-fish walking forward. Principal Chief of the Cayuses, and one of the principal actors in the Whitman butchery at Wailetpu.

120. Shu-ma-hic-cie or Painted Shirt. [Edward] Son of Te-lo-kikt and one of the active murderers of the Mission family. After the massacre, this man was one who took a wife from the captive females, a young and beautiful girl of fourteen [Mary Smith, age 15]. In order to gain her quiet submission to his wishes, he threatened to take the life of her mother and younger sisters. Thus, in the power of Savages, in a new and wild country, remote from civilization and all hope of restraint, she yielded herself to one whose hands were yet wet with the blood of an elder brother. [An obvious reference to Crocket Bewley, who was not Mary's brother.]

121. Tum-suc-kee. The great ringleader and first instigator of the Whitman Massacre.

122. Waie-Cat. One that Flies. Cayuse Brave and son of Tum-suc-kee. This man, though young, was an active participator in the murder of Dr. Whitman and committed many atrocities upon the defenceless captives. He escaped the ignominious death which awaited those not more guilty than himself.[76]

A disastrous fire on the night of January 24, 1865, destroyed a part of the Smithsonian Institution including the room where the Stanley pictures were being displayed or stored. With the exception of five of his paintings, which happened to be in another part of the building, the whole Stanley collection then at the Smithsonian was lost including the portraits of Tiloukaikt, Tamsucky, and the pictures of the massacre and the abduction of Miss Bewley. This was an irreparable loss.

Now comes the story of an amazing discovery. The Stanley paintings of Shu-ma-hic-cie and Waie-cat have been found.[77] For years it had been assumed that all four of Stanley's portraits of Cayuse Indians had been lost in the Smithsonian fire. Now, however, it appears that Stanley had removed the portraits of the two young men sometime before the fire and that they, with perhaps some other of his works, remained in his possession until his death in 1872. Several efforts were made by Stanley, and later by his heirs, to interest the government in purchasing his paintings, but without success. We can surmise that these two Cayuse portraits passed from generation to generation, and perhaps from living room to attic, and then finally from attic to an antique store.

In the spring of 1968, a collector of antiques noticed two oil paintings of Indians, each measuring about 9 x 6½ inches, in an antique shop in upstate New York. Although not especially interested in Indian lore, he was sufficiently attracted by the paintings to buy them. Later he had opportunity to show them to a qualified authority on American Indians, who declared them to be original Stanley paintings. Although neither of the paintings was signed, positive identification was made on the basis of Stanley's handwritten inscriptions on each portrait and by a comparison of the legends on the pictures with the descriptions in the two known catalogues of Stanley exhibitions. The fortunate discoverer and owner of the two paintings wishes to remain anonymous at the time of this writing, but has graciously permitted colored reproductions to be used in this work.

In Pursuit of the Murderers

The Legislature of the Provisional Government of Oregon was in session in Oregon City, Wednesday, December 8, 1847, when the letter from Chief Factor Douglas, dated the 7th, arrived with the shocking news of the Whitman massacre. The legislators reacted immediately. Action was taken which called upon the governor to raise and equip an initial company of fifty riflemen to proceed as quickly as possible to The Dalles to protect American property and to establish a military base for future operations. On the 9th, the Legislature authorized the raising of a regiment "not to exceed 500 men" for the purpose of marching into the Cayuse country to apprehend, if possible, the murderers. Cornelius Gilliam was appointed Colonel-Commandant;

James Waters, Lieutenant-Colonel; and H. A. G. Lee, Major. Steps were taken to borrow money to pay for the expedition. The term of service for the Volunteers was ten months. These acts by the Legislature were tantamount to a declaration of war against the Cayuse nation. In reality, this marked the beginning of a series of Indian wars which troubled the Pacific Northwest for the following eleven years.

On December 14, the Legislature appointed Joel Palmer, Robert (also called "Doc") Newell, and Major H. A. G. Lee to serve as peace commissioners. On that date Ogden and his men were laboriously working their way up the Columbia to Fort Walla Walla and no one in the Willamette Valley knew the fate of the captives. The peace commissioners were directed to proceed "immediately to Walla Walla, and hold a council with the chiefs and principal men of the various tribes on the Columbia, to prevent, if possible, the coalition with the Cayuse tribe in the present difficulties."[78] Newell had first met Whitman at the 1835 Rendezvous; had accompanied him on his return trip to the Missouri frontier; and in 1840 had named a son after him.

Joe Meek Appointed Special Envoy

Jesse Applegate, who had traveled to Oregon with Whitman in 1843, suggested that a messenger be sent to Washington, and the Legislature gave this idea its immediate endorsement. First, however, an official "Memorial to Congress" had to be drawn up and adopted. For more than ten years, or ever since Lieut. Slacum had carried the first petition from Willamette Valley residents to Washington in 1837, repeated memorials had been sent to Washington praying for the extension of United States jurisdiction over Oregon. The time had come for another and a more urgent appeal.

The text of the memorial included the following: "Having called upon the government of the United States so often in vain, we have almost despaired of receiving its protection, yet we trust that our present situation, when fully laid before you, will at once satisfy your honorable body of the great necessity of extending the strong arm of guardianship and protection over this remote, but beautiful portion of the United States domain."

Reference was then made to the fact that eleven [sic] American citizens had been murdered by the Cayuse Indians, including "Dr. Marcus Whitman and his amiable wife." The memorial continues:

"Called upon to resent this outrage, we feel sensibly our weakness and inability to enter into a war with powerful Indian tribes. Such outrages can not, however, be suffered to pass unpunished... To repel the attacks of so formidable a foe, and protect our families from violence and rapine, will require more strength than we possess. We are deficient in many of the grand essentials of war, such as men, arms, and treasure; for them, our sole reliance is on the government of the United States; we have the right to expect your aid, and you are in justice bound to extend it."[79]

The Legislature selected one of its members, Joseph Meek, to be its special envoy to carry the memorial overland to Washington. This colorful ex-mountain man was an excellent choice. He had met the Whitmans for the first time at the 1836 Rendezvous. He had left his half-breed daughter, Helen Mar, with them in the fall of 1840 to be reared and educated. Of course he had no way of knowing at the time of his appointment that she had died of the measles. After moving to the Willamette Valley in 1840, Meek had become active in public affairs and held the office of sheriff in the Provisional Government. Moreover, Meek was a cousin by marriage of James Polk, then President of the United States. As will be seen, this served much to Meek's advantage after he arrived in Washington.

Colonel Gilliam set out for The Dalles with a company of Oregon Volunteers on January 8, 1848, the very day the released captives arrived in Portland. Traveling with Gilliam were Meek and his overland party of eight or nine men. On that same day, also, an incident occurred at The Dalles between some Indians and the small detachment of Volunteers under Major Lee's command. A band of Cayuses, together with some local Indians, succeeded in driving off about three hundred head of cattle which had been left at The Dalles by the immigrants of the preceding year. In the skirmish which resulted, the Americans succeeded in capturing about sixty head of horses from the Indians, a poor exchange for the cattle they lost. Three Indians were killed, and one wounded.[80] The first shots in the Cayuse War had been fired. On January 28, Colonel Gilliam arrived with his company of Volunteers. A few weeks later the remainder of the Volunteers reinforced the little company at The Dalles.

The Whitman Mission Burned

Following Gilliam's arrival, a detachment of the Volunteers pursued the Indian raiders in an effort to recover the stolen cattle. Several skirmishes took place between The Dalles and the Deschutes River early in February 1848 whereby some of the stolen animals were recovered. In retaliation for the theft, the soldiers burned some Indian lodges on the Deschutes River. As a direct result of this wanton act of destruction, the Cayuse Indians burned the mission buildings at Waiilatpu and also St. Anne's Mission on the Umatilla.

Included in Colonel Gilliam's regiment were seventeen-year-old Perrin Whitman; W. D. Canfield, one of the released captives; and half-breed Tom McKay who with John L. McLeod had escorted the Whitman-Spalding party from the Rendezvous of 1836 to Fort Walla Walla. McKay was serving in the Volunteers as a Captain, and a brother, Charles, had the rank of Lieutenant. With them was a company of French Canadians and half-breeds from the Willamette Valley. Their presence, and especially that of Tom McKay, was most disconcerting to the Cayuses, who never dreamed the half-breeds would take up arms against them.

Among the best first-hand accounts of the march of the Volunteers into the Cayuse country is Robert Newell's Memoranda. He tells of a skirmish which began on February 24 when the Volunteers were challenged by a band of about four hundred warriors which included Indians from several of the tribes from the upper Columbia River country. Newell made note of the fact that the Cayuses were divided, some not being in favor of making war. In his style, inimitable in both grammar and orthography, Newell wrote: "The murderers were verry eager for battle those not guilty kept off, except the Indians on the Columbia."[81]

We may assume that among the friendly Cayuses were Stickus, Beardy, and Camaspelo, while Tamsucky, Tomahas, Five Crows, and the younger men were among the hostiles.

A second skirmish took place on the 25th on the banks of the Umatilla River. During this engagement, two Cayuse chiefs, Gray Eagle and Five Crows, boastful of their prowess, rode within both shooting and shouting distance of the Americans and taunted them. Gray Eagle was a medicine man, well known to McKay, who had often boasted that he was immune to American bullets. He claimed that if he were shot by an American, "he would puke up the bullet." This boast was known to

Tom McKay. When Gray Eagle saw McKay among the Volunteers, he exclaimed: "There's Tom McKay: I will kill him." Before he could carry out his threat, McKay, who was a crack shot, fired at Gray Eagle, sending a ball through his head. As the medicine man tumbled from his horse, McKay said: "There, I've shot him above his pukin' spot." [82] About the time that Tom fired, his brother Charles McKay shot at Five Crows, hitting him in one of the arms, badly shattering a bone.

Perhaps the ease with which the Cayuses had killed ten American men (two beaten to death with clubs) and two boys at Waiilatpu had given them a false sense of their invincibility. They became boastful and some claimed that they could "beat the Americans to death with clubs." [83] Then came the skirmishes on February 24 and 25 which resulted in the death of eight and the wounding of five of their number. This shocked the Cayuses into a realization that the Americans could and would fight. Many of the temporary allies of the Cayuses fled. Being now divided and demoralized, the Cayuses ceased all forceful resistance to the advancing Volunteers.

After leaving the Umatilla, Colonel Gilliam first marched to Fort Walla Walla to get supplies, and then he and his men proceeded to Waiilatpu. On March 2, the little army camped within about two miles of the mission, perhaps near or at the place where Tiloukaikt had lived.

Eager to inspect the mission site, Gilliam with Newell and perhaps Perrin Whitman and Meek, together with two companies of soldiers, rode ahead that evening to Waiilatpu. They were shocked at the evidences of destruction and desolation which were spread before them.

Newell wrote: "The remains looked horible. Papers letters pieces of Books Iron and many other things lay around the premises waggon wheels and other property was put in the house before it was set on fire I got Some letters and many lay about in the water." [84] Perrin remembered that even some of the rail fences had been burned. Perhaps the rails had been piled inside the buildings to add to the intensity of the flames.

Archaeological evidence shows that some of the roofs were of dirt. When the rafters were burnt, the roofs collapsed, thus completing the ruin. Only the gaunt walls remained standing. Even the fruit trees in the orchard had been cut down. Only the unenclosed gristmill had escaped destruction. Here was a gift from the white man which the red man had come to appreciate.

Far more distressing than the scenes of material destruction was the discovery of the bones and other bodily remains of the massacre victims strewn about the premises. As has been stated, a day or so after the first ten victims had been buried, wolves dug up several of the bodies including those of the Whitmans. Joe Stanfield had then reburied the exhumed remains, but after the captives had left for Fort Walla Walla, the wolves again dug out the dead bodies. This was the gruesome sight which Gilliam and his party saw when they arrived at Waiilatpu.

After the full contingent of Volunteers arrived at Waiilatpu on the following day, a thorough search was made of the area, and the remains of the victims were collected. Catherine, who evidently secured her information from one or more of the Volunteers, wrote: "When the first of the volunteers reached there... they found the bones badly scattered. Some of Mrs. Whitman's hair was picked up... a mile from the grave."[85] Only five skulls of the ten bodies, once buried in the wide shallow grave, and a few bones were found. Among the skulls were those of both of the Whitmans. Perrin Whitman was able to identify his uncle's skull by the gold filling which was placed in one of his teeth while passing through St. Louis in May 1848. Since the skull of a woman has certain distinguishing characteristics not found on that of a man, it was easy to identify Narcissa's skull.

After Meek had arrived in Washington, D.C., Jonas Galusha Prentiss, one of Narcissa's brothers, wrote to him asking for information about the massacre. Meek, replying on July 8, 1843, commented as follows about the reburial: "I myself conducted the melancholy rites and a solemn one it was. The head of Mrs. W. was severed from her body and other portions of manes [possibly remains or her hair] scattered in various directions. The body of Dr. W., however was whole."[86]

Evidently the graves that Stanfield had dug after the first ten victims had been buried, including that of Helen Mar Meek, had not been molested by the wolves. The Volunteers dug a deeper grave and, after depositing such remains as they could find in it, covered them with an overturned wagon-box on which a mound of dirt was shoveled. Here the bones lay until the semicentennial of the massacre was observed in 1897, when the grave was reopened, the bones placed in a new sepulchre and covered with a marble slab.

Waiilatpu Becomes Fort Waters

The arrival of the Oregon Volunteers at Waiilatpu suddenly transformed what had once been a thriving mission station into a military outpost. According to Newell, Colonel Gilliam at once set his men to work tearing down the adobe walls of the burned-out mission buildings and using the bricks to erect "a wall 4 or 5 feet high around the Camp." This makeshift fortification was named Fort Waters after Lieutenant-Colonel James Waters who had been wounded in the skirmish on the Umatilla.

Even before the Volunteers had established Fort Waters, several contacts had been made with the natives by the peace commissioners for the surrender of the suspected culprits, but without results. Writing in his journal on March 9, Newell referred to another such meeting: "...we met Stickes one Nez perse and two Kiyuses with a flag. made us a proposition for a Council. After much talk the Col ordered the regiment to return to the fort. which order was obeyed, but with much dissatisfaction. Col Gillam offered to take Jo Lewis for five of the Murderers, but the Indians would not give up Tosucka [Tamsucky] or Towita [Tauitau or Young Chief]... We hear of many of the Keyuses separating from the Murderers." [87]

By this time, a serious difference of opinion had developed between Gilliam, representing the military, and Palmer, one of the peace commissioners, over the best policy to be pursued in apprehending the guilty Cayuses. Gilliam was willing to be content with the seizure of such ringleaders as Joe Lewis and let those less guilty go free. Palmer would not be satisfied until all of the guilty were captured.

Since the Americans had fragmentary and sometimes conflicting testimony as to just who the murderers were, it was difficult to determine who were to be apprehended.

On March 28, Gilliam left with some men for The Dalles to get supplies. That night he was accidentally killed while drawing a gun from a wagon. Waters succeeded him in command of the Volunteers. Joel Palmer, who was Superintendent of Indian Affairs as well as a peace commissioner, resigned his offices and left for the Willamette Valley. He was succeeded as Superintendent of Indian Affairs by Major H. A. G. Lee.

Several expeditions were sent out from Fort Waters in pursuit of the hostile Indians in the hope of capturing one or more of the murderers but always without success. Those being sought found refuge by fleeing to other tribes or hiding in the mountains. Pressure was laid upon the friendly Cayuses to aid in apprehending the murderers, and even generous rewards[88] were offered for delivering the guilty over to the Americans, but such methods were also fruitless. Once Stickus held Joe Lewis in his camp as a prisoner, but Lewis was rescued by some of his friends. This act of Stickus is evidence that some of the Cayuses may have begun to realize that the half-breed was a primary cause for their misfortunes.

Possibly hearing of the reward that the military authorities had offered for his capture, and being aware of the growing hostility towards him shown by some members of the Cayuse tribe, Joe Lewis decided that it was best for him to flee the country. He concocted a fanciful story about being able to persuade the Mormons, who had planted a colony in the Salt Lake Valley in 1847, to send sufficient troops to drive the Volunteers out of the country. Lewis succeeded in persuading three Cayuses, including Edward and Clark, sons of Tiloukaikt, to go with him on this errand. While in the vicinity of Fort Hall, he "cut their throats in the night," and then ran away with their horses and property.[89]

According to Perrin Whitman: "Angus McDonald, a Hudson's Bay Company clerk at Fort Hall, while en route to Wallula on his annual trip for supplies, came upon these Indians and recognized them." He carried the story of their fate to the Cayuse tribe. "It soon dawned upon them," Perrin stated, "that this was more of Joe Lewis's dastardly work."[90]

Lewis is reported to have settled in the Jocko Valley in the Flathead country, in what is now Montana, about forty-five miles due north of present-day Missoula.[91] There he was joined by Nicholas Finley, in whose lodge at Waiilatpu the conspirators had met to plan the killing of the Whitmans. Nicholas had a Flathead mother; this may have been the reason why he returned to that part of the country. The valley may have been named after Jocko Finley, once in charge of Spokane House, the father of Nicholas. Lewis is reported to have been killed in an attempted stagecoach robbery in 1862, nearly fifteen years after the Whitman massacre.[92]

Another factor which militated against the success of the military authorities in capturing the suspected murderers was the anger aroused against the Volunteers among even the friendly Cayuses because of the unrestrained way the soldiers stole the horses and cattle of the Indians.

They committed other atrocities also against the natives. After Anson Dart visited the Cayuse country in 1851, he reported: "While the Oregon troops were stationed at Waiilatpu, they were in constant practice of taking all the horses and cattle they could find belonging to the Cayuses; and using and disposing of them in various ways. The Chiefs of the Cayuses informed me that more than five hundred head of horses were taken from them during this war, for which they never have received the least compensation." [93] The friendly Cayuses, who had taken no part in the massacre or in the burning of the mission buildings, felt that it was most unjust to be treated as though they were as guilty as the murderers themselves. Even Perrin Whitman claimed that several of his horses, which had been left at Waiilatpu, had been taken by the soldiers for which he had been unable to receive any compensation.[94]

THE END OF THE OREGON MISSION OF THE AMERICAN BOARD

As has been stated, Stanley's Spokane Indian guide, Solomon, had arrived at Tshimakain on December 9 with Stanley's letter of the 2nd in which he told of his narrow escape and of the massacre.[95] The Walkers and the Eellses were shocked and grief-stricken. Naturally, their first concern was for their own safety. The Spokane Indians, living in the vicinity of Tshimakain, urged the missionaries to remain where they were and pledged their protection. Mary Walker wrote in her diary for December 17: "The Indians say that [i.e., the Cayuses] must kill them first before they can us." [96] When Chief Factor John Lee Lewes, then in charge of Fort Colville, heard of the massacre, he invited the missionaries to seek refuge in the fort.

The situation which the two families faced was complicated by the fact that Mary was expecting the birth of her sixth child at any time during the latter part of December. On the 9th of that month, she had written in her diary: "We were hoping to have Dr. Whitman to supper with us tonight." Instead that was the day that Solomon arrived with the news of the massacre. In view of the tense situation which had developed at Waiilatpu shortly before the tragedy, it is doubtful if Dr. Whitman would have felt free to go to Tshimakain at that time.

A son was born to the Walkers while they were still at Tshimakain on December 31. The presence of six Walker children, all under nine years of age, and the two Eells boys, six and four years old, made any lengthy travel on horseback in winter extremely difficult. Living with the Walkers at that time was a Mrs. Marquis who had gone out to Oregon with the 1847 emigration and who had accepted employment with the Walkers in October. The two families decided to stay where they were as long as their Indians remained friendly and there was no threat of danger from other tribes.

A potentially dangerous situation developed for the missionaries on or about March 8, when Nicholas Finley arrived from Fort Walla Walla to be with his two brothers who lived on the trail that connected Tshimakain with Fort Colville. Finley told the Spokane Indians that the Americans were planning "to make a grand sweep of the natives of the whole land," and that they intended to fight the Hudson's Bay Company as well. Nicholas had been with the Indians in the skirmishes which had taken place on the Umatilla on February 24 and 25. Elkanah Walker noted in his diary that Nicholas Finley "had come up to get his friends to go down & join the Cayuses." [97] If Walker had known the extent to which Nicholas had been involved in the Whitman massacre, he would have indicated more alarm than he did.

Reports of Nicholas' subversive agitations came to the attention of Lewes at Fort Colville, who felt it necessary to post guards day and night. Being concerned about the safety of the missionaries at Tshimakain, he again invited them to seek sanctuary in the fort. "We are most perplexed to know what to do," wrote Mary in her diary on February 12. "We fear to go, we fear to stay." A few days later the missionaries learned to their great relief that the Spokanes had refused to follow the advice of Nicholas Finley.

After trying for more than two months to carry on their normal activities, alternating between fear and hope, the missionaries decided that the uncertainties of their situation were such that it was prudent for them to move to Fort Colville. After leading ten or twelve pack animals with their personal belongings, the five adults and eight children started for the fort on March 15. Mary wrote that day in her diary: "We left home about noon. Perhaps to return no more." Had they remained until the 20th, the two couples would have rounded out nine full years of residence at Tshimakain. Although the men returned to the station several times during the following two months to do some spring planting, the departure for Fort Colville on the 15th marked the end of their missionary work among the Spokanes.

Because of the failure of the Volunteers to apprehend any of the suspected murderers and the fact that the enlistment period of the soldiers was coming to an end, Colonel Waters decided to evacuate all Americans living in the upper Columbia River country and then abandon Fort Waters. Since Tiloukaikt and some of his band were known to be in the Nez Perce country, Waters sent a detachment of soldiers to escort Craig to Fort Walla Walla. It may be assumed that Craig left his wife and their children with her people. Since the Nez Perces were friendly, he soon returned to his home.

Major Joseph Magone with a company of fifty-five soldiers was ordered to go to Tshimakain to escort the Walker-Eells party to safety. The soldiers arrived at the mission station on May 29 where they found Walker and Eells waiting for them. While the soldiers waited at Tshimakain, the two men hurried back to Fort Colville to get their families.

On June 1, the five adults and eight children left the fort for their long journey of over two hundred miles to Fort Waters and from there on down into the Willamette Valley. Undoubtedly Lewes accompanied them to Tshimakain, as Walker and Eells had made arrangements for him to get some of their belongings and when convenient ship them down the Columbia River. The mission party arrived at Tshimakain about 11:00 a.m., Saturday, June 3.

Hearing that their missionaries were about to leave them, all of the natives in the vicinity of Tshimakain gathered to express their sorrow on seeing them leave and to say good-by. Major Magone said that some of the Indians wept. Possessions which the missionaries were unable to take with them or have sent down the Columbia, were given to the natives. These included agricultural implements, tools, and some household goods.

No inventory was compiled for items left behind at Tshimakain, such as Spalding prepared for things destroyed, pillaged, or abandoned at Lapwai and Waiilatpu. Since the Walker and Eells families were not forced to abandon their station by the immediate threat of harm from hostile natives, there was no basis for a claim for compensatory payment from the government. With the closing of the stations at Lapwai and Tshimakain, it was not practicable to try to keep the work going among the Spokanes.

CHAPTER TWENTY-THREE *Congress Establishes Oregon as a Territory* 345

After completing the distribution of their belongings, the Walkers and the Eellses said farewell to Tshimakain, "the place of Springs"[98] and rode that afternoon with their military escort seven miles south to the Spokane River. Their departure from Tshimakain marked the end of the Oregon Mission of the American Board.

Out of deference to the scruples of the missionaries regarding Sunday travel, Major Magone kept his men in camp over the week-end. Since many Indians had followed their missionaries to the river, Walker and Eells conducted a worship service for them on Sunday. This was the last of innumerable services they had held for the natives.

No criteria are available to measure the results of the devoted services rendered by these two missionary couples to the Spokane Indians over nine years. Under their direction and encouragement, many of the natives had begun to cultivate the soil. The missionaries had promoted the raising of cattle. A school had been conducted, but without the degree of success which Spalding had achieved at Lapwai or Whitman at Waiilatpu. Walker had reduced the Spokane language to writing and had, with Spalding's help, printed a sixteen-page Spokane primer on the mission press at Lapwai in 1840. Moreover, Walker had translated the first four chapters of the Gospel of Matthew into Spokane (Flathead), but it was never published during the Mission period.[99] Although the two couples had lived among the Spokanes for nine years without the satisfaction of seeing a single convert received as a member of the Mission church, the Christian seed had been sown; in due time, as will be told, the results became apparent.

Major Magone with his soldiers and the mission party began their long march to Fort Waters on Monday morning, June 5, and arrived at their destination the following Saturday afternoon. The Walkers and the Eellses found their visit to Waiilatpu a sad and trying experience. The ruined buildings, deserted fields, and the great grave at the foot of the hill stood out in sharp contrast to what had been there.

Joseph Elkanah Walker, then only four years old, never forgot seeing his mother pick up some strands of Narcissa's golden hair and show them to Mrs. Eells.[100] Writing of their visit to Waiilatpu, Walker in a letter to Greene dated July 8, 1848, said that their visit was so painful that: "The shortest time was sufficient." Whereas the soldiers made camp at the military base established there, the missionary party could not bear the thought of spending a night in that ravaged spot; they moved down the Walla Walla River several miles before making camp. After being escorted to The Dalles by soldiers, the two families continued their way down the river by boat to the Willamette Valley, where they had to begin life anew.[101]

Realizing the futility of remaining any longer at Fort Waters in the hope of capturing the elusive murderers, Colonel Waters, disbanded the Volunteers on July 5 with the exception of fifty-five men who agreed to stay until September 15 in order to provide protection for the Oregon immigrants of that year. The hostile element within the Cayuse tribe had been so dispersed, and the others too eager to avoid any conflict with the Americans, that the immigrants experienced no difficulties while passing through the Cayuse country.

With the departure of the last soldiers from Fort Waters the desolation of the formerly prosperous mission station was complete. The adobe walls which had surrounded the military camp were gradually washed down by winter rains; the ryegrass crept back into the now uncultivated fields; and even the Indian camps which once had been in the vicinity were deserted. Only a small grove of locust trees, heaps of rubbish where buildings once stood, the outlines of the millpond and the irrigation ditches, perhaps some remnants of rail fences, and the graves in the cemetery remained as visible evidence of the fact that for eleven years Marcus and Narcissa Whitman had lived there.

Meek Carries News of the Massacre to Washington

On March 4, 1848, the day after the Volunteers established their camp at Waiilatpu, Joe Meek with nine companions began his long journey overland to Washington, D.C.[102] He was not only the special envoy of the Provisional Government of Oregon commissioned to carry its memorial to Congress, he was also to be the first person to reach the eastern states with the news of the Whitman massacre. Meek carried with him two letters from Spalding to Secretary Greene, dated January 8 and 24, giving details of the tragedy.[103] Undoubtedly he also carried letters from survivors of the massacre directed to their relatives telling what had happened to them at Waiilatpu. There was no person in Oregon so well qualified to report on the circumstances of the massacre as Meek.

Having spent several years in the mountains, he was well acquainted with the Indians. The Whitmans had been his friends to whom he had entrusted the rearing of a daughter. From interviews with the survivors and his visit to Waiilatpu at the time of the reburial of the remains of the victims, he had become well informed regarding the details of the tragedy.

A detachment of one hundred Volunteers escorted Meek and his party through the Cayuse country to the Blue Mountains. Since the season was early, Meek found travel exceedingly difficult at the higher elevations because of the deep snow. At times he and his men had to dismount and lead their horses. After arriving at St. Louis on May 17, Meek told a newspaper reporter: "We arrived at Fort Hall on the 25th of March, where we encountered a tremendous snow storm. At this place we crossed the Bear River—the snow very deep—our previsions all gone—and we were forced to eat our mules and horses."[104] The privations suffered are reminiscent of those of Whitman and Lovejoy in their journey over the Rockies in the late fall of 1848 and the following winter.

Meek, on his journey through the Rockies, met several of his old friends who had been with him in his fur trapping days. The Meek party stopped at Fort Bridger, where they met its proprietor, Jim Bridger. No doubt Meek told Bridger of the safe arrival in the Willamette Valley of his eleven-year-old daughter, Mary Ann. About the time these two former mountain men were together, Mary Ann died, but of course this was unknown to them.

When the Meek party was about 150 miles west of St. Joseph, Missouri, they met the first contingent of the Oregon emigration of that year, consisting of about 245 wagons.[105] Here is evidence that the news of the Whitman massacre did not reach the States early enough in 1848 to affect that year's emigration. Meek gave the emigrants the news of what had happened, and also assured them that it was safe for them to continue, as the hostile Cayuses had been scattered and the Volunteers were at Waiilatpu to insure safe-conduct through the country.

Meek and his companions arrived at St. Joseph on May 11, having traveled about 1,900 miles in sixty-six days, an average of about thirty miles a day. This was a remarkable record for that time of the year.

On May 18, the day after Meek arrived in St. Louis, the St. Louis

Republican devoted nearly a page to Meek's account of the Whitman massacre, the actions taken by the Provisional Government of Oregon, the rescue of the captives by the Hudson's Bay Company, and a brief summary of his travel experiences. This was the first newspaper account printed in the States of the massacre and of Meek's mission to Washington, D.C.

The news was quickly copied by other papers, and it seems evident that word of the massacre had reached eastern cities before Meek arrived in Washington on May 28.[106] Secretary Greene in Boston read about the death of the Whitmans on the 27th and immediately addressed a letter to the Commissioner of Indian Affairs in Washington requesting confirmation or denial of the report.[107] Greene received Spalding's letters carried east by Meek on June 5. That dated January 8 was published in the July issue of the *Missionary Herald*.

The Whitman Relatives Get the News

The reminiscences of the Rev. Joel Wakeman, to which references have been made in earlier chapters, contain an account of the reception of the news of the massacre by Narcissa's parents. In 1848 Wakeman was pastor of the Presbyterian Church at West Almond, New York, where one of Narcissa's brothers, Jonas Galusha Prentiss, owned a store. Judge and Mrs. Prentiss had moved there in the latter part of 1847 or the early part of 1848 and were living with their son. Wakeman wrote that when he read about the massacre in a newspaper, he hastened to the store to break the sad news to Jonas and his parents. Wakeman found Jonas and his father in the store and was about to tell them what he had read, when Mrs. Prentiss entered with her paper and said: "Marcus and Narcissa have been murdered by the Indians."[108]

On April 8, 1848, Spalding wrote a long letter to Narcissa's parents in which he gave a detailed account of the massacre.[109] He enclosed a lock of Narcissa's hair which had been found by one of the Volunteers at Waiilatpu.

Dr. Whitman's niece, Mary Alice Wisewell Caulkins, has given the following account of the reaction of members of her family: "His Mother received the news of the massacre with stony grief without tears, and sat alone for days without speaking, and his sister, Mrs. Wiswell, was made sick by the news... went out into the orchard and cried, until she could cry no more."[110] On the page in the Whitman family Bible which contains the record of births, marriages, and deaths, we find the following, possibly written by the grief-stricken mother:[111]

> Marcus Whitman was Killed by the Indians of Oregon together with his wife and several others.
>
> November 29th, 1847

Oregon Made a Territory

There is a direct connection between the deaths of Marcus and Narcissa Whitman and the final approval by Congress of the bill which made Old Oregon a territory of the United States. Ever since the boundary question had been settled with Great Britain in 1846, fixing the dividing line at the 49° parallel, the extension of United States jurisdiction over Oregon was inevitable. A number of troublesome political issues, such as those arising out of the Mexican War and the slavery problem, had postponed the final decision. It took a Whitman massacre to bring action.

When Meek arrived in Washington on May 28, he found that a fellow Oregonian, J. Quinn Thornton, who was a personal representative of Governor Abernethy, had preceded him by about two weeks. Thornton had sailed from Oregon for San Francisco on October 19, 1847. From there he had taken ship to Panama and, after crossing the Isthmus, caught another vessel for Boston, where he arrived on May 5. A week later he was in Washington.

Having left Oregon more than a month before the Whitman massacre, Thornton did not have the first-hand information of that event which Meek possessed. Moreover, Thornton had not been commissioned by the Legislature of the Provisional Government of Oregon to present its memorial, as had Meek. After Thornton arrived in Washington, he wrote out a petition which in effect begged the Government to extend its jurisdiction over Oregon. This he gave to Senator Thomas R. Benton of Missouri, who presented it to the Senate, but no action was taken.

Then came Joe Meek, who, because of his being a cousin of the wife of President Polk, had immediate access to the White House. Moreover, he had important information about an Indian uprising.

American citizens had been murdered. There was immediate need of government protection. On May 29, the day after Meek arrived in Washington, the President transmitted the memorial Meek had carried, together with other documents, to the two houses of Congress, with the recommendation that immediate favorable action be taken.

On June 29, Jonas G. Prentiss wrote to Meek while the latter was in Washington to ask for information about the massacre. Jonas asked: "Why did it happen?" Meek replied on July 8: "...the causes which led to the horrid perpetration, so far as I could glean information upon the subject, are briefly these: The Indian population for some time past had been suffering from various ills, and the measles finally breaking out among them, their discontent (swayed by superstitious motives), sought to fasten the cause upon something on which they could wreak their vengeance, while at the same time the sacrifice would offer the virtue of a remedy to put an end to their contagion. A Canadian [i.e., half-breed Joe Lewis] dwelling among them induced them to believe Dr. Whitman was the eyesore—that he, by his drugs and medicines, had created the pestilence in order to secure patients; and that, if himself and family were removed, the evil would be removed. Acting upon this advice—prompted by the worst species of vindictiveness and malice—a band of the tribe rode to the doctor's residence, and shot him as related..." [112]

As often as the Whitman story will be told, the question will be asked: Why did the massacre take place? The causes are many and complex and stretch back through the years to the fall of 1836 when the Whitmans first settled at Waiilatpu.

No person was better acquainted than Joe Meek with the many interlocking causes such as those which inevitably arise out of a conflict of cultures; the fears of the natives when they saw the repeated migrations of seemingly endless numbers of white men passing through their country; and the reports passed on by half-breeds about the way the Indians of the East had been treated by the white men. Yet, in this letter to Jonas G. Prentiss, Meek touched on none of these issues, but declared that the precipitating causes were the following: (a) the measles epidemic, (b) the superstitions of the natives, (c) and the false accusations of Joe Lewis who claimed that Whitman was poisoning the Indians.

The bill making Oregon a territory of the United States passed the House of Representatives on August 2, and the Senate gave its approval on the 13th. President Polk signed the bill the next day. Thus the hopes and aspirations of the American residents of Oregon were finally fulfilled.

Ever since Lieutenant Slacum had carried the first petition to Washington in 1837, the Americans in the Willamette Valley had worked for the extension of the jurisdiction of the United States over that land. Meek's visit to Washington brought the whole issue to a successful climax. Only five years earlier, Whitman had called on high government officials in behalf of Oregon but without success. The bill which he submitted to Congress in the fall of 1843 carried many provisions which were embodied in the Oregon Bill of 1848. To a remarkable degree, the prophetic words Whitman had spoken, when he and Spalding were riding through the rainy night of November 27 on their way to the Umatilla, had been fulfilled: "I believe my death will do as much for Oregon as my life can."

One of the best tributes ever paid to the memory of Marcus Whitman was that given by Peter H. Burnett, a member of the 1843 Oregon immigration and who served as the first Governor of the State of California, 1849-54. He wrote: "In my judgment he made greater sacrifices, endured more hardships, and encountered more perils for Oregon, than any other one man; and his services were more practically efficient than those of any other, except perhaps those of Senator Linn of Missouri. I say *perhaps*, because I am in doubt as to which of these two men did more in effect for Oregon." [113]

And now to return to the first paragraph of the first chapter of this book:

No seer could possibly have foretold a connection between a missionary meeting held in a small one-room country church at Wheeler, New York, on a raw November evening in 1834 and the action taken by Congress in August 1848 when Old Oregon became a territory of the United States. The fact that these two events were related is clearly evident from contemporary historical documents. The one who tied them together during that span of fourteen years was Dr. Marcus Whitman and this is the story of what happened.

CHAPTER 23 ENDNOTES

[1] Victor, *Early Indian Wars*, p. 129.

[2] Spalding, *Senate Document*, p. 40, quoting from a sworn statement made by Hinman April 9, 1849.

[3] Hinman, in his sworn statement, stated that Douglas edited McBean's letter when he made a copy for Abernethy. The revised letter together with accompanying correspondence was published in the *Oregon Spectator*, Dec. 10, 1847,

[4] Italics are the author's.

[5] HBC Arch., B/5/21.

[6] From an article about Perrin B. Whitman, *Spokane Spokesman-Review*, Dec. 26, 1895; reprinted in Washington Historian, II (1901):3:138 ff.

[7] Spalding, *Senate Document*, p. 38.

[8] *W.C.Q.*, II (1898):3:36.

[9] See ante, fn. 6.

[10] Chapter Twenty-One, "The Methodist give Waskopum to the American Board. Since Dr. Whitman had not completed payment for the property, the Methodists retained title. See article by Mrs. R. S. Shackelford, "The Methodist Mission Claim to the Dalles Town Site," *O.H.Q.*, XVI (1915):24 ff. Dr. Whitman had promised to give Perrin the western half of the Waskopum site.

[11] See fn. 8

[12] Marshall, *Acquisition of Oregon*, II:233 ff., gives the text of McBean's letter to the Walla Walla *Statesman*, March 12, 1866, in which McBean claimed that Bushman arrived at Waiilatpu on Tuesday, November 30, when he was able to prevent the massacre of the women and children. None of the survivors' accounts support this claim.

[13] Pringle scrapbook, Coll. W.

[14] Pringle ms., p. 40.

[15] *Ibid.*, p. 41.

[16] *Ibid.*, p. 45.

[17] Josephy, *The Nez Perce Indians*, p. 257.

[18] Information regarding Lorinda Bewley's experiences, in addition to that contained in the Pringle and Saunders mss., is found in a ms. by J. Elkanah Walker (son of Elkanah and Mary Walker) entitled "Esther Among the Cayuses," Coll. O., and an article, "Lorinda and Five Crows," Portland *Oregonian*, Sunday, May 23, 1948.

[19] Spalding, *Senate Document*, pp. 26 & 34.

[20] Clarke, *Pioneer Days*, II:540, quoting Catherine Sager. Also, Pringle ms., p. 41.

[21] Spalding, *Senate Document*, p. 35.

[22] Portland, *Oregonian*, May 23, 1948.

[23] The conduct of the Indians towards the women of the Oregon Mission was exemplary compared to that of white men toward Indian women.

[24] Pringle ms., p. 42.

[25] Spalding, *Senate Document*, p. 35. Other references to Lorinda's experiences with Five Crows are taken from this source, with the exceptions noted.

[26] Gray, *Oregon*, p. 497. This deposition, although given on the same day as that found in Spalding's Senate Document, differs in several particulars. Italics are in the original.

[27] Gray, *Oregon*, p. 498.

[28] In like manner, Brouillet in his House Document glosses over the account of Lorinda's experiences at the St. Anne Mission, condensing it to four lines.

[29] Saunders ms., p. 16.

[30] Pringle ms., pp. 42-3.

[31] Saunders ms., pp. 15-8.

[32] Pringle ms., p. 43.

[33] Cannon, *Waiilatpu*, pp. 156-7. The reprint of this book, brought out by Ye Galleon Press, Fairfield, Washington, 1969, contains in its introduction by Dr. Thomas E. Jessett a fictionized account of this supposed love affair. See also Fuller, *History of the Pacific Northwest*, p. 151.

[34] Pringle ms., p. 48.

[35] *Ibid.*, p. 39.

[36] Cannon, *Waiilatpu*, p. 139, gives the incredible story that it was Stanfield who suggested placing the little boy between him and Mrs. Hays when they were in bed together.

[37] Pringle ms., p. 51.

[38] *Oregon Spectator*, January 20, 1848, reprinted in works by Brouillet, Victor, and Marshall.

[39] Brouillet, *House Document*, p. 48.

[40] *Ibid.* Bancroft, *Oregon*, I:701 gives the *Oregon Spectator* for January 20, 1848, as the source of this quotation but an examination of this issue failed to find it.

[41] Brouillet, *House Document*, p. 43. Other references to Brouillet in this section have been taken from this work.

[42] See index of this volume for references to The Hat and Elijah Hedding.

[43] See sections dealing with confrontations with Tiloukaikt in Chapter Sixteen, and "Grounds for Uneasiness among the Indians," Chapter Twenty. No reference to any promise of payment for land allegedly made by Samuel Parker has been found in any of the writings of the Whitmans or Brouillet. Tiloukaikt in the fall of 1841 demanded pay for the use of the land, not for its occupancy by the mission.

[44] Published in the *Oregon Spectator*, January 20, 1848. If one or more of the chiefs had been unable to write their names, they could have signed by using the X sign beside their names which were inscribed by someone else.

[45] Circumstantial evidence in Brouillet's account of the meeting held on that December 20 indicates that the messenger arrived at St. Anne's Mission after the meeting with the chiefs had closed. However, Bishop Blanchet's journal states that the messenger arrived at 4:30 that morning. The entry for that day in the Bishop's journal appears to have been written some time later.

[46] Walker ms., "Esther Among the Cayuses," Coll. O., states: "Five Crows refused to come, and said that Esther [i.e., Lorinda] wished to remain with him; but one of the priests... told Mr. Ogden that she did nothing but cry day and night."

[47] A copy of Ogden's speech to the Cayuses appeared in the *Oregon Spectator*, January 20, 1848, together with the correspondence that Ogden had with Spalding.

⁴⁸ HBC Arch., D/5/21. See also Drury, "Whitman Material in the Hudson's Bay Company Archives," *P.N.Q.*, XXXIII (1942), 59 ff.

⁴⁹ Brouillet, *House Document*, p. 47. Brouillet's list of ransom items differs somewhat from that given in *Oregon Spectator*, January 20, 1848. Twisted strands of tobacco were measured, thus the reference to "fathoms of tobacco."

⁵⁰ Pringle ms., p.46.

⁵¹ *W.C.Q.*, II (Dec. 1898):4:32.

⁵² Saunders ms., p. 18.

⁵³ Spalding, *Senate Document*, p. 36.

⁵⁴ Lorinda called the Indian "Big Belly." Walker ms., "Esther Among the Cayuses" identifies him as Camaspelo. Contemporary references to him indicate that he was friendly to the white people.

⁵⁵ Gray, *Oregon*, p. 549, quoting Lee's letter of December 26, 1847. This corrects the statement in Josephy, *The Nez Perce Indians*, p. 264, that Lee had "an advance group of some fifty volunteers" with him when he arrived at The Dalles.

⁵⁶ Brouillet, *House Document*, p. 48.

⁵⁷ See Drury, Spalding and Smith, pp. 539 ff., for list of inventory items which Spalding compiled under date of October 2, 1849. Although Spalding mentioned two spinning wheels, sheep shears, and a loom, he neglected to mention sheep. This was either an oversight or possibly the sheep were driven later to The Dalles and turned over to Perrin Whitman.

⁵⁸ For an account of Spalding's later life with the Nez Perces, see Drury, *Spalding*, and his *A Tepee in His Front Yard*.

⁵⁹ Pringle ms., p. 48.

⁶⁰ HBC Arch., D/21. Also P.N.Q., XXXIII (1942):60.

⁶¹ Spalding ms., Coll. W. Published in part in the *Missionary Herald*, 1851, p. 248.

⁶² *Oregon Spectator*, January 20, 1848; Bancroft, *Oregon*, I:696.

⁶³ Delaney, *A Survivor's Recollections*, p. 26.

⁶⁴ Victor, *Early Indian Wars*, p. 120; Bancroft, *Oregon*, I:696.

⁶⁵ Pringle ms., p. 49.

⁶⁶ Lockley, *Oregon Trail Blazers*, p. 342.

⁶⁷ According to a letter written by Mrs. Cushing Eells, March 28, 1851, now in Coll. W., Spalding was convinced that his wife's death was caused by the strain and exposure suffered during the days following the Whitman massacre. In 1853 Spalding married Rachel Smith, a sister of Mrs. J. S. Griffin. The Griffins were one of the independent missionary couples who went out to Oregon in 1839.

⁶⁸ Spalding, in the inventory he prepared of property lost or abandoned at Waiilatpu, included the following: "Expenses for Board & Physician for Mary Ann till her death. $33.00." Richardson, *The Whitman Mission*, p. 155.

⁶⁹ Nathan Kimball's "Recollections" verify the story of the theft of his father's watch and that it was found in the culprit's possession at Oregon City, and then returned to Mrs. Kimball. *T.O.P.A.*, 1903, p. 193. J. Q. A. Young says the watch belonged to Mrs. Hays. His memory of the incident was probably at fault. *Clark County History*, Vancouver, Washington, V (1964), p. 30.

[70] Pringle ms., p. 50.

[71] HBC Arch., B/223/c.

[72] Delaney, *A Survivor's Recollections*, p. 26.

[73] The present location of Dr. McLoughlin's portrait, if still extant, is unknown. The Barclay portrait is in the Barclay House, Oregon City, and the Lovejoy picture is in the Provincial Library, Victoria, B.C.

[74] *Portraits of North American Indians Deposited with the Smithsonian Institution*, 1852, Washington, D.C. A copy is in Huntington Library, San Marino, California.

[75] *Catalogue of Pictures in Stanley & Dickerman's North American Indian Portrait Gallery*, Cincinnati, 1846 [sic]. The date is an evident anachronism. A copy of this catalogue is in the New York City Public Library.

[76] Waie-cat may have been the only one of the fourteen Cayuse conspirators who escaped being apprehended or being killed during the Cayuse War. Robert H. Ruby and John A. Brown, *The Cayuse Indians* (University of Oklahoma Press, 1972, p. 208), mention Waie-cat as one of the Cayuse Chiefs who took part in the Yakima War of 1855.

[77] There is some variation in the spelling of the names of Shu-ma-hic-cie and Waie-cat on the Stanley portraits and in the catalogues mentioned in fn. 74 & 75.

[78] Victor, *Early Indian Wars*, p. 152.

[79] *Oregon Spectator*, December 27, 1847.

[80] Bancroft, *Oregon*, I:703 ff.

[81] *Robert Newell's Memoranda*, edited by Dorothy O. Johanson, Champoeg Press, 1959, pp. 109 ff.

[82] Victor, *op. cit.*, p. 175, and J. E. Walker ms., "Esther Among the Cayuses," Coll. O. A variation in the account of this incident is found in an article by Judge C. E. Wolverton in *T.O.P.A.*, 1898, p. 68: "The mad chieftain derisively taunted the American leader: 'I can swallow all your bullets.' Whereupon McKay replied: 'I will give you one too high to swallow,' and straightway shot Grey Eagle in the forehead."

[83] Victor, *op. cit.*, p. 175.

[84] Newell, *op. cit.*, p. 110.

[85] Pringle scrapbook, Coll. W. Several museums in the Pacific Northwest have locks of Narcissa's hair, including Coll. O.

[86] Original Meek letter is at the Whitman Mission National Historic Site.

[87] Newell, *op. cit.*, p. 112.

[88] Victor, *op. cit.*, pp. 212 ff. Generous rewards were offered for the capture of Tiloukaikt, Tamsucky, Tomahas, Joe Lewis, and Edward. Lesser rewards were offered for the capture of others.

[89] Portland, *Catholic Sentinel*, July-August, 1872, p. 7.

[90] From interview with Perrin Whitman, Portland *Oregonian*, December 1, 1897.

[91] *Frontier*, XI (November 1903), fn. p. 16, from article by Paul C. Phillips and W. S. Lewis, "The Oregon Mission as shown in the Walker Letters, 1839-1851."

[92] Royal R. Arnold, *Indian Wars of Idaho*, Caldwell, Idaho, 1932, p. 101.

[93] Report of Anson Dart, 1851, Records of Oregon Superintendency of Indian Affairs, National Archives, Washington, D.C.

[94] From clipping giving an interview with Perrin Whitman, *Spokesman Review*, probably July 16, 1893. Clipping in Coll. S.W.S.H.S.

[95] See section, "Artist Stanley's Narrow Escape," Chapter Twenty-Two.

[96] Drury, *F.W.W.*, II:326.

[97] *Ibid.*, II:335, fn. 19.

[98] The mission site at Tshimakain is now in private hands. A copious spring still flows back of the farmhouse where the Walker home once stood. A very old lilac bush and some rail fences (the latter across the road from the present farmhouse), which may date back to the mission period, are on the premises.

[99] Drury, *Walker*, pp. 270 ff. published Walker's translation of these four chapters for the first time. David C. Wynecoop, *Children of the Sun*, Wellpinit, Washington, 1969, p. 69, reprinted Chapter Two.

[100] Drury, *Walker*, p. 219. J. E. Walker, ms., Coll. Wn.

[101] Drury, *Walker*, pp. 222 ff., gives a brief review of the experiences of the Walker and Eells families in the Willamette Valley. Mary Walker died on Dec. 5, 1897, being in her eighty-seventh year. She was the last person to die of the six couples who once belonged to the Oregon Mission.

[102] Bancroft, *Oregon*, I:717, and Victor, *Early Indian Wars*, pp. 180 ff., give the names of those in Meek's party. Several who started dropped out along the way while others joined the group.

[103] Spalding's letters to Greene, in Coll. A., bear the postmark of St. Joseph, Mo., but without a date. Both letters were published in Mowry, *Marcus Whitman*, pp. 300 ff.

[104] St. Louis *Republican*, May 18, 1848.

[105] *Ibid.*

[106] The full-page article about Meek, which first appeared in the St. Louis *Republican*, was reprinted in the Boston *Cultivator* (exact date unknown as the clipping in Coll. W. is undated, probably the first part of June). The Weston, Missouri, *Herald*, May 19, 1848, also carried the story, as did the Columbia, Missouri, *Statesman*, of the same date.

[107] Original Greene letter in files of the Old Indian Bureau, National Archives.

[108] Prattsburg, N.Y., *News*, Jan. 27, 1898.

[109] Original in Coll. W. Published in *T.O.P.A.*, 1893, p. 93 ff.

[110] Caulkins ms., Coll. Wn.

[111] The original Whitman family Bible is in Coll. W. A picture of the page with the reference to the death of Marcus is in Drury, *Whitman*, p. 412.

[112] The Sunday, Oct. 30, 1966, issue of the *Los Angeles Times* carried an article by Dan Thrapp about my researches and writings. This came to the attention of Warren Prentiss, a great-nephew of Narcissa Whitman, who resides at Palos Verdes Peninsula, Calif. Among family items he had was this original letter of Joe Meek to his grandfather, Jonas C. Prentiss. See ante, fn. 86.

[113] *W.C.Q.*, II (1898):1:32.

[CHAPTER TWENTY-FOUR]

EPILOGUE

Following the signing of the Oregon Bill on August 14, 1848, General Joseph Lane, who had distinguished himself in the Mexican War, was appointed governor of the new territory. Joe Meek was made United States Marshal. Lane accompanied Meek on his return trip to Oregon. The two took the southern route through Santa Fe on their way to San Francisco and thence went by sea to Portland. They arrived at Oregon City on March 2, 1849. The next day Governor Lane in an official proclamation declared that the Territorial Government of Oregon was then established and that "the laws of the United States extended over and were declared to be in force in said territory."[1]

THE APPREHENSION OF FIVE OF THE ALLEGED MURDERERS

The defeat of the Indians in the skirmish with the Volunteers, which took place on the Umatilla on February 24 and 25, 1848, convinced such chiefs as Stickus, Camaspelo, and even Young Chief, that it was folly to fight the Americans. Thereafter they refused to join with Tiloukaikt and other hostile-minded Cayuses in any armed clash with the Americans except, perhaps, when trying to protect their herds of cattle and horses. Following the safe passage of the 1848 Oregon immigration through the Cayuse country, the last of the Volunteers at Fort Waters left for their homes in the Willamette Valley. For more than a year after their departure, nothing was done by American authorities to apprehend the alleged murderers. The mission site lay abandoned until about 1853, when three stockmen made it their headquarters. They left in the fall of 1855, shortly before the second Cayuse war began.[2]

Although Governor Lane realized that one of his first official obligations was to capture those guilty of the Whitman massacre, he knew that he would have to wait until a contingent of United States troops had arrived in Oregon. The first military unit to go to Oregon over the Oregon Trail was a regiment of Mounted Riflemen.[3] This regiment, which had taken part in the Mexican War, left Fort Leavenworth, Kansas, on May 10, 1849. It consisted of about six hundred men, thirty-one officers, and a few women and children. The long caravan, including seven hundred horses, twelve hundred mules, and 175 wagons, made its way westward slowly. Two military posts were established en route—one at Fort Laramie and the other near old Fort Hall. Thus was fulfilled one of the recommendations that Whitman had made in his proposed Oregon bill of 1843.

With the arrival of the government troops at Oregon City in October, Governor Lane was prepared to use force to secure the cooperation of the friendly elements in the Cayuse and neighboring tribes in apprehending the alleged murderers. No doubt the passage of the Mounted Riflemen through their country in the fall of 1849 gave the Cayuses impressive evidence of the military might which could be used against them. Another factor which weakened any spirit of resistance to the Americans that may have existed among certain elements with the Cayuse tribe, was the tragic loss of life during the measles epidemic which continued into the spring of 1848. According to Archbishop F. N. Blanchet of Oregon City: "197 of them had succumbed to the epidemic."[4] When Indian Agent Anson Dart visited the Walla Walla country in June 1851, he learned that the Cayuses, including women and children, then numbered only 126.[5]

During the two years following the Whitman massacre, the once proud Cayuse nation lost the prestige it once enjoyed among the tribes of the upper Columbia River country. Not only were they reduced in numbers, they also suffered a loss of much of their wealth. Hundreds of their horses and cattle had been taken by the Volunteers. Many including especially Tiloukaikt and his band, had been obliged to leave their farms. Having been persuaded by Dr. Whitman to turn to agriculture, they had by the fall of 1847 become dependent on their farms for much of their food. Thus when obliged to flee to avoid capture during the first part of the Cayuse War, they were ill prepared to find sustenance elsewhere. Their ill fortune was further aggravated by the reluctance of the Hudson's Bay Company, under pressure from American authorities, to sell guns and ammunition to the Cayuses, especially to the hostiles. This was a serious blow, for arms were needed for hunting as well as for defense.

After being convinced that it was to their best interest to cooperate with American authorities in apprehending the alleged murderers, Young Chief with sixty Cayuses, Timothy with twenty Nez Perces, and a Walla Walla chief with five of his men, joined forces in December 1849 to capture Tiloukaikt and others whom the American authorities wanted. When Tiloukaikt and his men heard of what was being contemplated, they fled with their families, and such livestock as they had, into the Blue Mountains.

Two letters from McBean to Lane,[6] dated January 6 and February 7, 1850, give a summary of what took place. When Tiloukaikt and his band realized that the attacking party was approaching, they barricaded themselves the best they could in the deep snow which then covered the higher elevations of the Blue Mountains. The cold was intense and the attackers and the attacked alike were poorly clad and ill provisioned for the confrontation.

At the beginning of the skirmish, Young Chief and his party succeeded in capturing all of the livestock belonging to Tiloukaikt and his band. McBean, in the first of his letters stated that: "two principal Murderers, Tomsucky & Shumkain[7] were shot" in the first day of the fighting. Only one of the assailants was wounded, which may indicate that Tiloukaikt and his men lacked both guns and ammunition. Four of the alleged murderers were taken prisoners: Waie-cat, Kia-ma-sump-kin, Clokamas, and Frank Escaloom.[8] After besieging Tiloukaikt and his band for two days, the attackers withdrew taking with them, at Tiloukaikt's request, the women and children. Young Chief took the prisoners to his camp but, for lack of a proper place to keep them in confinement, they soon escaped and rejoined Tiloukaikt.

For a few more weeks, Tiloukaikt and his band remained free but their situation became increasingly desperate with the passing of time. They found it necessary to come down from the mountains. McBean, in his letter of February 7th, wrote: "The Murderers, whom we supposed to be far [away], are near the Cayuse Camp—starvation prevented them making their escape & forced some of them to surrender themselves to the Young Chief. I had a visit from him recently & he told me that he fully expects to decoy the whole of them into his camp for the purpose of giving them up to be punished." McBean strongly recommended to Lane that "no time should be lost" in sending soldiers into the Cayuse country to apprehend the murderers before they should try to flee again. Lane replied by saying that if the Cayuse tribe did not give up the guilty parties by June, he would "make war on them." [9] Faced with this ultimatum, Young Chief agreed to deliver the accused to Lane at The Dalles during the first part of May.

The grim hand of necessity had been laid on Tiloukaikt. Faced with the threat of war on the whole Cayuse tribe by an overwhelming superior military force, which would have resulted in the suffering of many innocent people; after two years of wandering and having already lost ten of his band including his two sons and Tamsucky;[10] robbed of most if not all of his cattle and horses; driven from his fields and faced with starvation; being short on guns and ammunition; and finally learning that Young Chief was in favor of delivering him and some of his associates over to the Americans, Tiloukaikt had no alternative but to surrender.

Young Chief demanded that the following four go with Tiloukaikt: Tomahas, Clokamas, Ish-ish-kais-kais (Frank Escaloom), and Kia-ma-sump-kin. It is not known why some others, such as Waie-cat who had been listed by McBean as having taken part in the massacre, were not included. The very fact that Young Chief surrendered these five was used at the time of their trial as evidence of their guilt.

The five were given some vague promise of immunity from punishment by Young Chief who told them that they were being asked to go to the Willamette Valley to tell what they knew about the massacre. This may have been open deception on the part of Young Chief or possibly a ruse on the part of the Americans. Tiloukaikt said: "When I left my people, the Young Chief told me to come down and talk with the big white chief, and tell him who it was that did kill Dr. Whitman and others." Kia-ma-sump-kin explained his presence: "Our chief told me to come down and tell all about it... I was sent by my chief to declare who the guilty persons were, the white chief would then shake hands with me; the Young Chief would come after me, we would have a good heart." Clokamas said: "Our chief told us to come down and tell who the murderers were." And Tomahas echoed the same sentiment: "Our chief told us to come and see the White chief and tell him all about it. The white chief would then tell us all what was right and what was wrong, and learn us [how] to live when we returned home."[11]

This vague promise of immunity, the fear of American reprisals, and the realities of their starving condition provide sufficient explanation for the voluntary surrender of the five accused Cayuses to the American authorities. When Tiloukaikt as later asked why he allowed himself to be taken prisoner, he is reported to have replied: "Did not your missionaries tell us that Christ died to save his people? So die we, to save our people."[12]

The five prisoners were escorted to The Dalles by Young Chief and many warriors of the Cayuse tribe.[13] There Governor Lane met them during the first week of May and then took the five men to Oregon city and turned them over to the care of Joe Meek who, as United States marshal, was responsible for their incarceration. Since a number of Cayuses also went to Oregon City, the authorities were apprehensive of an attempt being made to rescue the prisoners. The five were shackled and put in a building on Rock Island, also known as Abernethy Island, in the Willamette River just above the falls, and guarded by twenty soldiers from the regiment of Mounted Riflemen.

THE TRIAL OF THE FIVE CAYUSES

The dispatch with which the United States District Court, seated at Oregon City, Clackamas County, Oregon Territory, conducted the trial of the five accused Cayuses stands out in sharp contrast to the slower pace of present-day procedures. Only fifteen days elapsed between May 9, when the grand jury met, and the 24th, when the death sentence by hanging was pronounced.

The presiding judge was O. C. Pratt and the district attorney, Amory Holbrook.[14] Evidently the court made every effort to conduct a fair and impartial trial. Three able men were appointed to serve as defence counsels: Territorial Secretary K. Pritchett, Major Robert B. Reynolds, and Captain Thomas Claiburne. Contemporary records do not indicate whether any of the three had any legal training. The Cayuse tribe offered to give fifty horses as a retainer fee to the defense counsels, but whether they were actually given is not known. Lane in a letter dated November 29, 1879, stated that Pritchett was paid $500 by the United States Government for his services.[15]

The grand jury met on May 9 and heard testimony from several of the survivors of the massacre, who were unanimous in identifying all five of the accused as being at Waiilatpu at the time of the tragedy. On May 15, the grand jury summoned eight Cayuses to appear before them including Stickus, Young Chief, and Camaspelo. On May 21, an indictment for murder was issued against each of the five prisoners. The trial began on Wednesday morning, May 22. Twenty-two prospective jurors were challenged and excused in an effort on the part of the defense to exclude all older Oregon citizens and any who might have felt embittered against the Indians. From two to three hundred spectators crowded into the courtroom each day to listen to the proceedings.

Witnesses for the prosecution included the three girls—Eliza Spalding, Catherine and Elizabeth Sager—and several adults such as Mrs. Eliza Hall, Mrs. Lorinda Bewley Chapman, Josiah Osborn, and W. D. Canfield. More than sixty years later, Eliza Spalding (then Mrs. A. J. Warren), looking back on her experiences as a witness at the trial, said: "It was trying on the nerves, and I think I was nearly as frightened in the courtroom as I was while held prisoner. The lawyers asked such questions about the massacre and the Indians looked so threatening that altogether it was a most unpleasant experience." [16]

The defense counsels argued that at the time of the massacre, the laws of the United States had not been extended over the area occupied by the Cayuse tribe. In reply, the court ruled that by an Act of Congress of 1844, all the territory west of the Mississippi River was "embraced within and declared to be Indian Territory; and as such, subject to the laws regulating intercourse with the Indians." The defense then asked for a change of venue because the five accused felt that the attitude of the residents of Oregon City was so hostile they could not receive a fair and impartial trial in that city. In the petition drawn up for this purpose, each of the five, being illiterate, made an "X" mark opposite his name written at the end of the document. The petition was denied by the court.

Finally, the defense sought to lessen the degree of guilt by showing that Whitman had been warned repeatedly of the danger he faced by remaining at Waiilatpu because of the practice of the Cayuses to kill their own medicine men when one of their patients died. Both Dr. McLoughlin and Spalding were summoned to testify that such warnings had been given. Stickus also testified that he had told Dr. Whitman "to be careful for the bad Indians would kill him." The court refused to admit the relevance of such testimony.

Since the records of the trial, now on file in the Oregon State Archives at Salem, do not give a verbatim report of the testimony of the individual witnesses for the prosecution, we are unable to determine the specific crime with which each of the accused was charged. After only two days of hearings, the case went to the jury.

The judge, in his charge to the jury, stated that the Cayuse nation, which had voluntarily surrendered the five prisoners, knew best "who were the perpetrators of the massacre." After deliberating for only one hour and fifteen minutes on Friday afternoon, May 24, the jury returned a verdict of guilty against each of the five. The judge then sentenced the five to be hanged at 2:00 p.m. on Monday, June 8, 1850. Although Judge Pratt did not quote from the code of laws which Indian Agent Elijah White induced the Nez Perces and Cayuses to accept in 1842, the sentence he pronounced reflects Article 1 of that code: "Whoever wilfully takes life shall be hung." Eliza Spalding remembered that the five prisoners, when informed of the sentence, "grew very much excited... and said that they wouldn't mind being shot, but to die by the rope was to die as a dog and not as a man."

GUILTY OR INNOCENT

As soon as the trial was over, a division of opinion arose among the residents of Oregon City regarding the guilt or innocence of each of the condemned Indians. Evidently the majority approved the sentence. Their opinion was strengthened by a news item which appeared in the May 30 issue of the *Oregon Spectator* under the heading "Cayuses Have Confessed." The reporter wrote: "We are informed that Telokite now admits that he did strike Dr. Whitman with his hatchet, as testified by Mrs. Hall,[17]—Tomahas, or The Murderer, admits that he shot Dr. Whitman. Isiasheluckas [Ish-ish-kais-kais or Frank Escaloom] confesses to have shot Mrs. Whitman,—and Clokamas, the smallest one of the five, admits that he assisted in dispatching young [Francis] Sager. But Kiamasumkin says he was present but did not participate in the massacre."

Prior to this newspaper report which contained the alleged confessions of four of the five prisoners, several in the Oregon City community were convinced that all five were innocent and that the real culprits were among the ten Cayuses who had already been killed. Among these ten were Tamsucky and the two sons of Tiloukaikt, Edward and Clark. Among those who held these views was Territorial Secretary K. Pritchett, who had been one of the three defense counsels.

Following the trial, Governor Lane was called to southern Oregon and northern California to settle some difficulties with the Rogue River Indians. During his absence from Oregon City, Pritchett as Territorial Secretary, became Acting Governor. Taking advantage of this situation, some people, who believed in the innocence of the five condemned men, circulated a petition which called upon the Acting Governor to grant a reprieve and free them. Although Pritchett was eager to do this, he was fearful of possible legal complications, especially if Lane were still in Oregon at the time set for the execution. So nothing was done.[18]

Among those who believed in the innocence of the five condemned Indians were Sergeant Henry R. Crawford and Corporal Robert D. Mahon of the Mounted Riflemen Regiment who were a part of the detachment of soldiers set to guard the prisoners. From their close associations with the five Cayuses during their confinement on the island, the two soldiers found themselves in full agreement with the petition that had been presented to Acting Governor Pritchett. It also seems evident that Crawford and Mahon, who may have been Roman Catholics, wanted to correct some calumnious statements that Spalding had published in the *Oregon American and Evangelical Unionist*, which claimed that the massacre "had been committed at the instigation of the priests."[19]

The two soldiers interviewed the five Cayuses on Sunday, June 2, and again at 11:80 a.m. on Monday shortly before they were taken to the gallows. From the notes taken at these interviews, a paper was written entitled "Important declaration made June 2d and 3d, 1850" which the two men signed.[20] The manuscript copy contains about 1,200 words on two legal-size pages, with five paragraphs, one for each of the condemned men. Each claimed that he was innocent of murder. Tiloukaikt placed the blame for the deaths of the Whitmans and others at Waiilatpu on the ten members of his band who were already dead, implicating Tamsucky especially. Tiloukaikt said: "I am innocent of the crime of which I am charged; those who committed it are dead, some killed, some died. There were ten, two were my sons... Tamsucky, before the massacre, came to my lodge. He told me they were going to hold a council to kill Dr. Whitman. I told them not to do so, that it was bad... I had told Tamsucky over and over, to let them alone. My talk was nothing. I shut my mouth... The Priest tells me I must die tomorrow. I know not for what. They tell me that I have made a confession to the Marshall[21] that I struck Dr. Whitman. It is false. I never did such a thing. He was my friend, how could I kill my friend: You ask me if the priest did not encourage the people to kill Dr. Whitman? I answer, no, no." During the interview with Crawford and Mahon late Monday morning, Tiloukaikt said: "I am innocent but my heart is weak since I have been in chains, but since I must die, I forgive them all."

Kia-ma-sump-kin stated: "I was up the river at the time of the massacre, and did not arrive until the next day... I was not present at the murder nor was I any way concerned with it. I am innocent—it hurts me to talk about dying for nothing... I never made any declaration to any one that I was guilty." Kia-ma-sump-kin admitted that he was at Waiilatpu after the first day of the massacre, but added: "There were plenty of Indians all about." He argued that if his guilt were based solely on being at Waiilatpu at the time of the killings, then all who were there were equally guilty.

Clokamas said: "I was there at the time. I lived there, but I had no hand in the murder. I saw them when they were killed, but did not touch or strike any one. I looked on. There were plenty of Indians... There were ten... they are killed. They say I am guilty, but it is not so. I am innocent... I must die by being hung by the neck... I have no reason to die for nothing... I never confessed to the Marshall that I was guilty, or to any other person. I am innocent. The priest did not tell us to do what the Indians have done."

The shortest statement came from Ish-ish-kais-kais who said: "I say the same as the others. The murderers are killed, some by the whites, some by the Cayuses... They were ten in number... The priest did not tell us to do this." Tomahas said: "I did not know that I came here to die... My heart cries my brother [i.e., Tamsucky] was guilty, but he is dead. I am innocent. I know I am going to die for things I am not guilty of, but I forgive them. I love all men now. My hope, the Priest tells me, is in Christ."

The most telling argument in support of Kia-ma-sump-kin's claim of innocence is the fact that not one of the nineteen extant eyewitness accounts of the massacre and the subsequent captivity mentioned him as having taken part in the killing of any one of the victims. Nor was he so accused at the Oregon City trial according to the extant records. He was not listed as one of the culprits in McBean's letter to the Hudson's Bay Company of November 30, 1847. However, when the Americans advertised rewards for the apprehension of thirteen of the alleged murderers, "Quia-ma-shou-skin" was included in the list.[22] Also, McBean in his letter to Lane of January 6, 1850, claimed that Kia-ma-sump-kin was the one who "shot Dr. Whitman's lady." Such reports, evidently received from Indian sources, may have been the reason why Governor Lane insisted that Kia-ma-sump-kin be one of the five to be surrendered at The Dalles in May 1850. In the opinion of the author of this book, Kia-ma-sump-kin was innocent.

The evidence against the other four who were found guilty is much more convincing. The first to accuse Tiloukaikt and Tomahas of being ringleaders in the massacre was William McBean, who listed them with others in his letter of November 30, 1847. With but few exceptions, this initial list of suspected culprits proved to be accurate. In the list of thirteen Cayuses for whom the Oregon Volunteers offered rewards, in addition to that of Kia-ma-sump-kin, occur the names of Tiloukaikt Tomahas, and Frank Escaloom. Clokamas does not appear in this list except, possibly, under a different Indian name.

Two years after the massacre, McBean was able to compile a more detailed list of the alleged murderers which he gave in his letter of January 6, 1850, to Governor Lane. During this interval, McBean had been able to secure further information regarding the culprits from such Cayuse chiefs as Stickus, Camaspelo, and Young Chief.

In this letter to Lane, McBean claimed that Tiloukaikt had killed Judge Saunders; Tomahas had murdered Dr. Whitman; Clokamas "had given his assistance in killing the sick" [i.e., Bewley and Sales]; and Ish-ish-kais-kais had killed "some of Doctor's household." Confirmation of each of these accusations has been found in the eyewitness accounts of the massacre, references to which have been given. The evidence presented during the Oregon City trial was such as to make inevitable the verdict rendered against these four. In the opinion of the author, these four were guilty as charged. Their protestations of innocence were the cries of desperation when faced with the imminence of death by hanging. Catherine Sager, in her reminiscences, stated: "Old Teloukite was a man who intended to do right, as far as he knew... The other four were as bad men as ever lived. I knew them well for three years. If ever men deserved to hang, they did." [23]

BAPTISM AND EXECUTION

According to the *Catholic Sentinel* of April 20, 1872: "The sentence condemning the prisoners to lose their lives was no sooner pronounced against them, than they immediately thought of saving their souls by looking to a minister to prepare them for death." Archbishop Francis Norbert Blanchet, a brother of Bishop A. M. A. Blanchet, who founded St. Anne Mission on the Umatilla River, responded. Of this he wrote: "The archbishop went to see them without delay, and continued to go twice a day to teach them and prepare them for baptism and death." [24] Spalding also called on the condemned men, who refused to see him.

"On the eve of their death," wrote Blanchet, "the old chief Kilo Kite and his four companions made a declaration of innocence." After the execution, duplicate copies were made of the document and a copy given to the Archbishop.[25] Although the latter, in his account of administering the sacraments of baptism and confirmation to the five, made no comment as to whether he believed their protestations of innocence, it seems evident that he considered them spiritually prepared for the sacraments.

At nine o'clock on Monday morning, June, the day of the execution,

Archbishop Blanchet and Father F. Veyret conducted low mass for the Indians in their private quarters. After the mass, the archbishop baptized each of the five, giving to each a Bible name. Tiloukaikt was named Andrew; Tomahas, Peter; Ish-ish-kais-kais, John; Clokamas, Paul; and Kia-ma-sump-kin, James.[26] After the baptism, the five were confirmed and thus became members of the Roman Catholic Church.

The gallows had been constructed on the east bank of the Willamette River near the island where the five had been held prisoners and two or three blocks to the southwest of Dr. McLoughlin's house, which then stood on Main Street.[27] The two priests accompanied the doomed men to the scaffold where Joe Meek, as United States marshal, was waiting. The priests ascended to the scaffold platform with their converts.

According to an article in the *Catholic Sentinel* signed "An Observer" [possibly Father Veyret]: "Words of consolation and encouragement were addressed to them by the Archbishop, who recited the prayer for the dying. When their hands were about to be bound, the old chief, Tilokite, refused to submit with great energy; but at the sight of the image of our crucified Saviour, he instantly submitted to the humiliation and kept profoundly silent."

Hundreds of curious people thronged Oregon City that day to witness the gruesome event. The Cayuses, however, who had attended the trial, had fled the city upon learning the fate pronounced on the five, "struck with consternation and fear, and with hearts full of grief."[28] Possibly Young Chief and the others who had cooperated with him in apprehending and surrendering the five to the Americans never anticipated such a humiliating and terrible end.

Promptly at 2:00 p.m., Meek cut a rope with his tomahawk. Five trapdoors dropped open; five bodies jerked from the ends of taut ropes; and the souls of Andrew, Peter, John, Paul, and James entered the next world. About a half hour later, after being pronounced dead, the five bodies were cut down and taken to the edge of modern-day Kelly Field, about one mile distant on the north edge of Oregon City. The place where the bodies were buried is believed to have been on what is now market road No. 20, about one-half mile east of Abernethy Bridge on Oregon State highway, No. 160. No marker was placed to indicate the location of the grave.[29]

The *Oregon Spectator* for June 27, 1850, carried the following newsstory under the caption: "Execution of the Cayuse Indians."

The five Indians, whose trial and condemnation we recorded in our last paper, were hung on the 3rd inst., according to the sentence of the court. The execution was witnessed by a large concourse of people. The chief (Telokite) pled earnestly to be shot, as hanging, in his view, was not only an ignominious fate, but not in exact accordance with the true principle of retributive justice. Hanging, however, was the requirement of the law, and hang they did. Some of them died almost without a struggle, others seemed to suffer more, and one showed signs of life after hanging fourteen minutes. They were attended on the scaffold by the Arch Bishop of the Catholic Church, who administered to them the rites and consolations of that church appropriate to such occasions. This closes another act in the sad and horrible tragedy.

A FINANCIAL REVIEW

No biography of the Whitmans would be complete without a review of the financial problems involved in the founding and the support of the Oregon Mission of the American Board. Many of the personality difficulties which arose within the Mission stemmed from the straitened condition of the Board's treasury.

A good example is seen in Parker's refusal to hire a man to help with the packing when he and Whitman made their exploring trip to the Rockies in the summer of 1835. The sharpest letter Whitman ever wrote to the Board was that of May 10, 1839, when he answered the charges that Parker had made regarding what Parker thought were the excessive costs of the Oregon Mission.

Another example is found in Gray's determination to save money for the Board by buying only two 8 x 10 tents for the four newly-wedded couples to use on their westward trek in 1838 rather than four smaller tents. Smith reminded Secretary Greene that he had been assured before leaving his home that he and his bride would have their own tent.

The American Board was always facing financial problems throughout the eleven-year period, 1836–47, of its Oregon Mission.

For one thing, foreign missions, which then included work with the American Indians since they spoke non-English languages, was still comparatively new in American Protestantism. Although the American Board was founded in 1810, its promotional techniques within its chief supporting denominations, the Congregational and the Presbyterian, were still weak by the time its Oregon Mission was established. Giving was largely on an individual basis; however, by the 1830s, many churches were contributing to the Board, and the women's missionary societies within local churches, such as "Female Cent Society," "Female Benevolence Society," and "Female Missionary Association," were increasing in number. To promote its missionary projects, the Board relied heavily on its field agents, some of whom served voluntarily or on a part-time salaried basis, and in its official publication, the *Missionary Herald*.

An examination of the list of givers, which was published monthly in the *Herald*, shows that during the years 1834–48, most of the donations were for sums under $100.00; many were less than $10.00; and even gifts of fifty cents were acknowledged. The Board had no endowment and was the recipient of only a few bequests.

During 1811, the first full year after its founding, the Board reported receipts of less than $1,000.00. During the twenty year period, ending in 1831, more than $101,000.00 had been received. In 1836, when the Whitman-Spalding party went to Oregon, receipts had risen to $176,232.15, but expenditures were $210,407.54. The accumulated deficit then amounted to more than $38,000.00. During 1837, the deficit increased by another $2,500.00 even though the receipts rose to over $252,000.00. By that time the Board had 360 missionaries under appointment in what is now continental United States and in foreign lands. Its most flourishing mission was that in the Hawaiian Islands. A financial depression, felt throughout the nation in 1837, alarmed the Board. Notices were sent to all its missionaries warning them that the Board would have to reduce its allocations. The whole Oregon Mission was limited to an annual expenditure of only $1,000.00.[30] This suggested limitation, however, was never actually enforced.

The total cost of the Oregon Mission to the American Board from the time Samuel Parker went to St. Louis in 1834 to the payment of the last drafts drawn on the Board by the surviving members of the Mission in 1851 was $38,833.39 [Appendix 2]. This sum can be divided into three parts. First came the cost of the exploring tours, the travel expenses of the two mission parties sent out in 1836 and 1838, and the initial cost of establishing the three stations at Waiilatpu, Lapwai, and Tshimakain.

The total expenditures for the founding years, 1834–38 inclusive, came to $10,686.27, or nearly one-fourth of the total for the eleven-year period. The missionaries were supposed to be self-supporting as far as possible; hence the initial costs included the purchase of farm and home equipment, and livestock The cost of goods delivered in Oregon, after making the long voyage around South America, was about double the original price. This was true of items shipped by the Board and also of goods purchased directly from the Hudson's Bay Company's store at Vancouver.

The second category of expenses covered the period 1839–48 inclusive, when the Board spent $22,099.38 to support no fewer than eight adults, and sometimes thirteen, in three, and for a short time in four, different stations. This means an average annual cost of about $2,200.00. During the ten years, 1837–47, inclusive, seventeen children were born to Mission families. Although the Board made no provision for hired help to relieve the missionaries of some menial tasks, occasionally they incurred such expenses and charged them to the Board.

The third category of expenses covered the years 1849–51 inclusive, when the Board was closing its Oregon Mission and resettling the surviving families in the Willamette Valley. The expenditure for these years amounted to $6,047.64.

The financial reports of the Board did not always include the value of gifts sent direct to Oregon by churches or individual donors. The missionaries often mentioned in their letters the receipt of missionary barrels which would contain clothing, books, and incidental items. We know that some of Whitman's relatives and the church at Rushville sent plows to the Oregon Mission, and there is evidence that Whitman spent some of his personal funds for such items. Such gifts as molasses, sugar, and money came from the Hawaiian converts of the American Board's Mission in Hawaii.

If the financial reports of the Board suggest that it was parsimonious in its support of its Oregon Mission, the fault was in its policy of trying to do too much with too little. The zeal of the Board to evangelize the world led it to undertake more projects than it could adequately support.

Among the Board's contributors were many who gave sacrificially even though their gifts were small. But those who gave the most were the missionaries themselves who, through these years under review, not only served without a salary but also without the promise of furloughs, educational benefits for their children, or retirement allowances.

The basic weakness of the Board's policy to encourage its missionaries in Oregon to make their work as self-supporting as possible was that too much time and energy had to be spent on secular activities. Whitman and his three ordained associates were so occupied with their fanning responsibilities that they were unable to make the best use of their specialized training for their main objective of Christianizing the natives. Under such circumstances, we marvel that the Whitmans and the Spaldings were able to do as much as they did for the material, educational, and spiritual benefit of the Indians.

THE WAIILATPU INVENTORY

The inventory which Spalding compiled in 1849 of property lost, stolen, or destroyed at Waiilatpu because of the massacre is of more historical significance than merely being a catalog of such items.[31] The facts revealed in this document pay tribute to Whitman's business ability. He was not only the doctor for the Mission and a lay preacher for the Indians, he was also a good administrator and a hard worker. H. K. W. Perkins, in his letter to Jane Prentiss of October 19, 1849, stressed this point by writing: "He was always at work" [Appendix 6]. Beginning in the spring of 1837 with limited equipment, and at first with untrained assistants, Whitman had succeeded by the fall of 1847 in bringing thirty acres under cultivation, all fenced and part of it ditched for irrigation. Spalding, in his Waiilatpu inventory, valued this at $413.90 which represented the cost of labor in splitting rails for fences and in digging ditches. Clearing the land of the head-high, tough ryegrass, which gave the station its name, "Waiilatpu," must have been a laborious task. Spalding also listed an orchard with "75 apple trees, a few bearing," and a nursery of "apple & peach trees tame currents, hops, locusts (trees)," all valued at $280.00.

The inventory tells much about Whitman's agricultural activities. His equipment included: "1 Harrow, 1 Cultivator, 1 Threshing Machine, 1 Corn Sheller, 1 Fanning Mill, and 2 large Prairie Plows," with a total value of $205.00. The threshing machine, corn sheller, and fanning mill were the supplies that Whitman got at The Dalles in September 1847. Until he got these machines, all of his wheat had to be flailed and then winnowed by hand. Spalding also listed twenty-three cast plows value at $24.00 each and forty-two plows without the wooden parts at $18.00 each. These plows were on hand to be traded or sold to the Indians. Included in the inventory were four wagons, one priced at $100.00; twelve ox yokes; I set of harness; and a variety of farm tools such as axes, hand sickles, hoes, spades, saws, and saddles. The blacksmith shop equipment included 1,000 pounds of iron and 300 pounds of nails. Spalding listed a "coal house" in connection with the blacksmith shop. The question arises: where did Whitman get coal? It may be that this came from a place near Lapwai where Spalding had discovered an outcropping of low grade lignite.[32] Or it may be that the reference was to charcoal which might have been locally made.

The list of Whitman's livestock with their values follows:

100 Milch Cows at $16 each	$ 1600.00	2 Broke Horses at $30	60.00
80 young cattle at $5 each	400.00	6 Unbroke at $12	72.00
11 Yoke of oxen at $50	550.00	30 mares & Colts at $12	360.00
80 Calves at $4 each	320.00	80 Sheep at $3	240.00
8 beef cattle at $20	160.00	12 Bucks Southdown	
8 broke Horses	160.00	imported	60.00

The total of 290 head of cattle (a yoke of oxen representing two head), valued at $3,030.00, represents a remarkable increase over the small beginning of five or seven cows which Whitman had kept out of the small herd which he and Spalding had driven across the country in 1836. In addition to the natural increase of his herd during eleven years, Whitman had received some cattle by trading horses and supplies with the Oregon immigrants while they were passing through the Cayuse country. The Waiilatpu inventory listed forty-six head of horses, at least ten of which were broken to harness, valued at $652.00, and ninety-two sheep at $300.00.

According to Anson Dart's report to the Bureau of Indian Affairs in Washington, D.C., in the fall of 1851, Perrin Whitman returned to Waiilatpu sometime following the compilation of the Waiilatpu inventory and was able to recover some of the sheep that Whitman and Spalding had owned. These he drove to the Willamette Valley. None of the Indians seemed to appreciate the value of sheep. Although some Whitman letters contain references to hogs and poultry at Waiilatpu, none were listed in this inventory. This was undoubtedly an oversight on Spalding's part. When the Oregon Volunteers were at Waiilatpu in March 1848, Newell noted in his journal that they killed "a fat swine." [33]

Spalding also listed the following: "300 Bush[els] wheat [$]300.00; 60 Bush corn... 75.00; 250 Bush potatoes 125.00; 20 Bush Onions... 60.00." He made no mention of peas, but Whitman had some because the Volunteers found a supply at the mission site when they arrived in March.[34] Spalding also neglected to mention other vegetables such as squash, turnips, beans, etc., which were no doubt a part of Whitman's annual harvest. Included in the inventory were the following items, some of which had been imported from the Hawaiian Islands: "8 bush salt... 24.00; 4 sacks sugar (120) lbs 20 cts... 24.00; 1 Keg molasses... 12.00." The mention of a "Cheese Press" in the inventory, valued at $48.00, indicates that the Whitmans were able to add cheese to their tables. The animals which could have been butchered and these stores of grain and vegetables would have provided sufficient food for all seventy-five people who were expecting to spend the winter of 1847–48 at Waiilatpu.

In the list of buildings, Spalding mentioned the sawmill in the Blue Mountains as being "well made, quick stroke, heavy dam across a furious stream, Bull [i.e., large] Wheel... $4,000.00" and the adjacent log cabin valued at $100.00. In the list of buildings at Waiilatpu, he mentioned: "1 Flour Mill (without mill house), Stones good size and quality... heavy dam & large pond with race... 2,000.00."

The main T-shaped house was described in considerable detail, room by room, with references to number of doors, windows, chimneys, cupboards, and type of wall and roof construction. This detailed inventory will be of inestimable value should it ever be possible to build a replica of the house at some future time. Spalding estimated the total cost at $1,834.91, which would have included such items as hardware, paint, window shashes, etc. and perhaps labor.

Other buildings listed in the inventory include a blacksmith shop, a "Corn & wheat house," an "Out kitchen with Store room above 20 x 24," and a "Wood house, 20 x 12, not finished." Strange to say, Spalding made no mention of the emigrant house which was large enough to accommodate thirty people at the time of the massacre.

Anson Dart, in his report of October 1851 to the Commissioners of Indian Affairs in Washington, D.C., stated that many of the values that Spalding gave in his Waiilatpu inventory were "very much too high."[35] Dart claimed that the gristmill was "a very small affair... and would not have cost in the States three hundred Dollars." He also felt that the value placed on the sawmill was "equally too high." It is possible that Dart, who was a relative newcomer to Oregon when he wrote his report, did not give sufficient consideration to Oregon's inflated prices. On the other hand, Spalding's failure to list some property such as the emigrant house, offsets to some extent Dart's accusation of inflated prices.

GLIMPSES INTO THE WHITMAN HOME

The Waiilatpu inventory not only bears tribute to Whitman's ability as a good business man, it also throws much light on the nature of the home life of the Whitman family. Although the inventory that Spalding prepared for the Waiilatpu station is less detailed than that for Lapwai, enough information is given to indicate that the Whitman home was furnished with only the barest necessities. Under the heading of "Furniture" are the following items with values indicated:

2 settees $18, 2 settees $8	26.00	1 Table, 6 legs	20.00
2 settees $12, with 2 cushions	36.00	1 Table 4 legs	18.00
2 Rocking Chairs	10.00	1 Table end with drawers	6.00
12 Common chairs	18.00	2 Stands with drawers	6.00
2 bed steads with cords	18.00	2 stands wash	6.50
5 bed steads	15.00	2 Clothes Press	24.00
3 feather beds	60.00	2 Clocks	17.00
7 straw ticks	14.00	2 Looking Glass	5.50

All the furniture was homemade. A rocking chair was a special luxury as is suggested by the following entry in Elkanah Walker's diary for April 8, 1841: "We now have one chair, the first that we ever had. It is a rocking chair & it is really good to get into it."[36] The beds had no mattresses or springs, hence a feather bed was doubly appreciated. Narcissa had been able to get enough feathers, probably from wildfowl, while at Fort Vancouver in the fall of 1836, to make her first feather bed. The fact that Spalding valued these at $20.00 each indicates their scarcity. The straw ticks, which were poor substitutes for feather beds, were sometimes filled with corn husks instead of wheat straw. Possibly the two cushions were also filled with feathers.

Under the heading: "Bedding for at least 20 persons," Spalding itemized: "30 quilts, blankets & comfortables... 150.00; 12 sheets Wool & Linen... 36.00; 40 sheets Cotton... 42.00; 16 Pillows... 16.00." Since the Whitman household, after 1843, usually numbered fourteen or more, the supply was barely sufficient for their needs, especially in cold winter weather. All washing of clothes was by hand in tubs. Spalding listed two washtubs at $2.00 each. Although he included soap and "2 sad irons" [i.e., solid flat-irons] in his Lapwai inventory, Spalding failed to list such items at Waiilatpu.

A prized possession of the Whitmans was a cookstove worth $45.00. They also had two "Box Stoves" or heating stoves, $68.00; two spinning wheels and attachments, $20.00; 200 pounds of wool, $100.00; a grindstone, $12.00; and an assortment of "Table Furniture including Tin, handware [sic] & Crockery" at $18.00. Spalding listed a loom at Lapwai, but none at Waiilatpu. The schoolroom contained a blackboard, and also writing desks and benches which must have been crude because they were listed at only $6.00. Also in the schoolroom were "Mitchels Map of the U.S.A... 15.00; Tracy's Map of the World... 3.00." As has been stated, Catherine Sager remembered that one of the Cayuse Indians used one of the maps as a saddle blanket. The inventory also included mention of several large kettles, two pairs of andirons, one bellows, several trunks or chests, and a library worth $100.00.

Whitman's medical library, listed separately from the family collection, was valued at $80.00. His medicines were valued at $189.00. A "Full & Complete" case of surgical instruments was listed at $100.00, with an imperfect set, $15.00, and a "Pocket case with medical bags," $20.00. Spalding also mentioned a museum cabinet which contained geological specimens, shells, and Indian curiosities, valued at $50.00; and a shipment of goods which had but recently arrived from Boston and had not been distributed, $1,500.00.

Dr. Whitman's clothing included a "superfine" coat worth $45.00, and a "silk velvet vest... 8.00." Whitman may have brought these items with him from the East when he returned in 1843. All other articles of clothing belonging to him were valued at $325.00. Mrs. Whitman's clothing was listed at $200.00 and that of the Sager children and Perrin, $280.00. The fact that Spalding included in the Waiilatpu inventory two brass locks priced at $4.00 each and six cheaper locks at $1.00 each, as well as the mention that certain doors were equipped with bolts, shows that the Whitmans had found it prudent to keep some of their storerooms and private quarters locked.

Spalding included in his Lapwai inventory a number of items not given in that for Waiilatpu such as candles, soap, a churn, cowbells, and even a lamp and a lantern. Where Spalding was able to get oil for the last two items is not known. It is reasonable to believe that Whitman also had such articles. Neither of the two inventories mentioned guns, although Spalding listed one-half keg of powder at Lapwai. The Waiilatpu inventory did not include mention of the personal belongings of any of the immigrants. No doubt many of their possessions had to be abandoned. What happened, we wonder, to the violin that Andrew Rodgers played to Narcissa's great enjoyment?[37] Were there no pictures for the walls, curtains for the windows, or rugs for the floors?

According to Spalding's figures, the Waiilatpu inventory, including the value of $7,000.00 placed on the two mills and the "40,000 feet of sawed lumber," totaled $22,221.26. The details given in this inventory regarding the plain furnishings of their home, their modest wardrobes, and their simple fare illuminate the primitive conditions under which the Whitmans lived. The claims that the American Board made to the United States Government for property lost or destroyed at Waiilatpu and Lapwai, based on Spalding's inventories, were never honored. The Methodists were more fortunate in their claim for compensation for their mission site at The Dalles which the government had taken for a military post. Since the American Board had never completed payment for the site, the Methodist title remained valid. In June 1860 Congress authorized the payment of $20,000.00 to the Methodists for the property, which included title to 353 acres.

Monuments, Memorials, and Anniversary Observances

The fame of the Whitmans has grown with the passing of the years. It can now be stated without fear of contradiction that no Protestant missionaries in the history of the United States have been honored by so many monuments and memorials as Marcus and Narcissa Whitman.

Whitman College

The best known of all monuments erected to perpetuate the Whitman memory is Whitman College at Walla Walla, Washington. After his return from his eastern journey in the fall of 1843, Whitman dreamed of seeing a college established in the vicinity of Waiilatpu which he believed would be the center of a thriving American settlement. In his letter of May 31, 1844, addressed to the Rev. A. B. Smith then serving in the Hawaiian Islands under the American Board, Whitman wrote: "Could I have staid home longer, I should have tried to have raised the means of establishing some Academies & Colleges, but I trust to influence others to do so." In his letter of October 25 of that year to Secretary Greene, Whitman wrote: "This is a place most advantageous for the commencement of what may soon be an Academy & College, both on account of its fine & healthy climate & of its eligible situation."

In Whitman's last letter to the Board, dated October 18, 1847, he begged it to do what it could to promote the emigration of a colony of Christian laymen and ministers who would settle in the interior of Oregon. Whitman was hoping that such a colony would make its homes in the vicinity of Waiilatpu. Regarding the possible migration of ministers to Oregon, he wrote: "One or more ought to be with the intent to found a College." The proximity of two Catholic missions to Waiilatpu caused Whitman to reconsider the location of his proposed college. Having begun negotiations for acquiring the former Methodist property at The Dalles, Whitman in his last letter to Greene favored that as a possible location. He wrote: "I know of no place so eligible as at the Dalls close by our station. Here a salubrious climate & near proximity to market & the main settlement will be secured."

When the Cayuse chiefs met with Bishop Blanchet at St. Anne's Mission on December 20, 1847, to discuss peace proposals which could be submitted to the American authorities, they asked for the cessation of immigrant travel through their country. However, the Whitman massacre, instead of discouraging the coming of the Americans, actually promoted the opening of the upper Columbia River country for settlement. This must have been to the Indians a disturbing reversal of their expectations.

Following the Cayuse War and the hanging of the five condemned Indians at Oregon City in June 1850, settlers began drifting into the Walla Walla Valley to take up land. Settlement of the interior of Old Oregon was temporarily slowed during the early 1850s by continued Indian unrest. Old Fort Walla Walla was abandoned in 1855 and the name transferred to a new site about six miles east of Waiilatpu where Colonel George Wright established a military post. Here the present city of Walla Walla arose. Washington Territory was created in 1853; Oregon became a State in 1859 with the present boundaries.

Although Whitman seems to have been the first to dream of establishing an academy or college in the vicinity of Waiilatpu, Cushing Eells was the one who made the dream come true. Hearing of the influx of settlers in the Walla Walla Valley, Eells decided in 1859 to lay claim to 640 acres of land which included the Whitman mission site in order to prevent it from falling into the hands of others. Dreaming of the possibility of establishing an academy [or seminary, which was the term commonly used in that generation for such an institution] at Waiilatpu to be named after his martyred friend, Marcus Whitman, Eells applied to the Legislature of Washington Territory for a charter. This was granted on December 20, 1859, when Whitman Seminary became a legal reality even though it had no buildings or students at that time.

At first Eells planned to build his seminary on the mission site at Waiilatpu. In order to secure title to the land as a homestead, he had to make some material improvements and fulfill certain residential requirements. A log cabin was erected in the summer of 1860 at Waiilatpu and Eells moved his family there two years later.

With nearby Walla Walla growing rapidly, Eells saw the wisdom of establishing his seminary in that place. After much effort and personal sacrifice, he succeeded in raising enough money to erect a building on a site in Walla Walla which is now a part of the campus of Whitman College. The Seminary, which began as a private elementary school, opened its doors to classes in 1866. Later a secondary course of study was made available and, after a few years, the school was known as Whitman Academy.

After sixteen difficult years, being always faced with the problem of finances, the Academy came under the sponsorship of the Congregational Education Society in 1882. The name was then changed to Whitman College with the former academy being continued until 1912 as a part of the college. The first classes in Whitman College began on September 4, 1882, which would have been Whitman's eightieth birthday, had he lived that long. A women's dormitory erected in 1925 was called Narcissa Prentiss Hall. Today Whitman College ranks as one of the best private colleges in the United States. Its library and archives contain a prime collection of source materials—letters, diaries, and other memorabilia—dealing with the Whitmans and the whole Oregon Mission of the American Board.

THE WHITMAN MONUMENT AT WAIILATPU

A second monument erected to honor the Whitmans is a granite shaft which crowns the hill at Waiilatpu. This is eighteen feet high, two feet square at its base, and tapers to the top. The shaft stands on a pedestal about nine feet high with the name Whitman carved on one side. The idea for the erection of such a monument at Waiilatpu originated with W. H. Gray. During the last years of his life, while living in Portland, Oregon, Gray zealously solicited funds for this project and succeeded in raising about $800.00 before he died on February 16, 1893. For several years nothing was done to complete the project. Then the Whitman Monument Association was formed in March 1897, largely by residents of Walla Walla, to fulfill Gray's dream. The approach of the semicentennial of the massacre in November of that year injected a feeling of urgency into the project. The Monument Association soon secured title to eight acres which included the original mission cemetery, with the great grave containing the remains of the victims of the massacre, and the hill, over one hundred feet high, which rises near it.[38] Plans were made not only for the erection of the granite shaft but also for the placing of a memorial slab of Vermont marble over the great grave. The total cost of land and memorial stones came to about $2,500.00.

Under the joint sponsorship of the Monument Association and Whitman College, elaborate plans were made for the semicentennial observance of the massacre on Monday and Tuesday, November 29 and 30, 1897. The monument and the memorial slab for the grave were to have been dedicated, but unfortunately the stones did not arrive in time. Nevertheless, the ceremonies were held as planned. The opening event was a public meeting in the Opera House of Walla Walla on Monday evening; it was "packed with the greatest crowd ever gathered under one roof in that City." [39]

Only eight of the seventeen survivors who were then alive were able to attend.[40] They were the three older Sager sisters—Catherine, Elizabeth, and Matilda; the three Kimball sisters—Susan, Sarah, and Mina; and Nancy Osborn, all of whom were married; and Byron S. Kimball. Perrin Whitman, who was ill at the time in his home in Lewiston, Idaho, sent greetings by his grandson, Marcus Whitman Barnett. Only one of the original band of thirteen missionaries of the Oregon Mission of the American Board was still alive, Mrs. Elkanah Walker. She passed away at her home in Forest Grove, Oregon, on December 4, 1897, just a few days after the semicentennial was observed.[41]

A large crowd made a pilgrimage to Waiilatpu on Tuesday morning by train. Among those who took part in the ceremonies either at the Opera House or at the grave were the Rev. Samuel Greene[42] of Seattle, a son of Secretary David Greene, and the Rev. L. H. Hallock, D.D., undoubtedly a descendant of the Rev. Moses Hallock under whom Whitman had studied as a boy in the school at Plainfield, Massachusetts. Catherine Sager Pringle also spoke at the services held at Waiilatpu. According to one report, her "short speech... moved many to tears." [43]

After the granite and marble stones arrived, the remains of the victims were placed in a large metal casket and reburied on January 29, 1898, in the same place where they had been laid by the Oregon Volunteers in March 1848.[44] Over this was placed the polished marble slab, which measured 11' x 5½' x 4", and on which were inscribed the names of the fourteen who had lost their lives during the massacre. Several years later, the bodies of William and Mary Gray, which had been buried at Astoria, Oregon, were exhumed and brought to Waiilatpu where they were reburied near the great grave. Appropriate memorial services were held there on November 1, 1916. A tall monument was erected over the Gray grave and the site enclosed with an iron fence.

The Mystery of the Skulls

When the remains of the massacre victims were exhumed on October 22, 1897, only five skulls and a few bones were found under the overturned wagon box which had been placed there by the Oregon Volunteers in March 1848. The skull of Dr. Whitman was easily identified by the gold filling in a "posterior molar tooth on the left side." Since there was only one woman's skull among the five, this was identified as being that of Narcissa. The amazing fact was then discovered that both skulls had been sawed in two, probably by one of Dr. Whitman's surgical saws. A contemporary newspaper account stated: "The skull [of Dr. Whitman] had been mutilated by being cut in two, the cut commencing at the nasal bones and extending back to the seat of the back wound. Marks of the saw are well defined on each side of the saw incision, where the instrument evidently slipped in the hands of the operator. The skull had not been separated by this cut, which seems to have been made for some other definite purpose than of opening the skull. The sawing was done unskillfully, probably when the body was lying on the ground face upward." [45]

Among those who examined the severed skulls was Matilda Sager Delaney who wrote: "A man's skull showed two tomahawk cuts. I asked Dr. Penrose to hold the skull, which was in two parts, together... Both his and Mrs. Whitman's had been cut in two." [46] Matilda thought that perhaps the mutilation had been done by the Indians, but Catherine, in a letter to Dr. Penrose dated December 14, 1898, wrote: "I wish to inform you that I have found out about the sawing of Dr. Whitman's and his wife's skulls. It was done Monday night, Nov. 29, by Joe Lewis." [47] Of the various theories advanced to explain the mystery of the severed skulls, this seems to be the most reasonable. We know that the half-breed Joe Lewis harbored deep grudges against both Marcus and Narcissa and that he played a leading role in plotting their deaths. Perhaps he found some sadistic satisfaction in using one of the doctor's own saws in this act of mutilation.

The Whitman-Spalding Centennial, 1936

The approach of the centennial of the arrival in Old Oregon of the members of the Whitman-Spalding mission party stimulated a tremendous amount of interest in both church and secular circles. The Presbyterian Church, U.S.A., was especially active in promoting centennial observances. The General Assembly of this denomination held a commemorative service at its annual meeting in Syracuse, New York, in May 1936. Following the Assembly, special exercises were held at Rushville and Prattsburg, New York, on June 4. Hundreds of churches throughout the country also remembered the occasion.[48]

Such communities as Lewiston, Idaho, and Walla Walla, Washington, staged elaborate celebrations which continued in each community over several days. The celebration at Lewiston, emphasizing the Spalding story, was held May 8–10, while that at Walla Walla took place on August 13–16, honoring the Whitmans. The United States Post Office Department issued a special Oregon commemorative stamp although the names of Whitman and Spalding did not appear on it.[49] The State of Idaho created the Spalding State Park in 1936, which included the old mission site at the first Lapwai. This in 1965 became a part of the Nez Perce National Historical Park.

WHITMAN LITERATURE

Following the death of the Rev. Myron Eells in 1907, the old theory of Whitman riding to Washington to save Oregon for the United States was kept alive largely in ecclesiastical circles by unhistorically-minded authors of Sunday school literature and mission study books. Ministers, more interested in good illustration than in being accurate, repeated the legend. These authors and ministers accepted Nixon's *How Marcus Whitman Saved Oregon* as their final authority. It took years before the basic conclusions of such scholars as Edward G. Bourne and William I. Marshall were able to penetrate into ecclesiastical circles [Appendix 4]. Whitman lost none of the honor due him by being deprived of these legends. Rather, a new appraisal of his life and work, based upon documented facts, serves to increase his fame.

The observance of the Whitman-Spalding centennial in 1936 inspired an outburst of literary activity on the subject of the Whitmans. Following the publication of the author's *Henry Harmon Spalding* in 1936 and his *Marcus Whitman, M.D.* in 1937, at least eight "historical novels" or "fictionalized biographies" of the Whitmans appeared. In some instances the authors of these books were so adroit in romanticizing history that the reader is often unable to discern where fact ends and fancy begins. Often historical events are distorted and individuals grossly misrepresented for the sake of a plot. By such means erroneous impressions are again spread abroad.[50] Some fictionalized biographies, however, can be recommended. Jeanette Eaton's book for girls, *Narcissa Whitman, Pioneer of Oregon* (1941), and Nard Jones' *The Great Command* (1959), have rendered a real service in visualizing Marcus and Narcissa Whitman as living human beings.

Among the tributes paid to the Whitmans are several of a musical nature. A four-act opera, The *Cost of Empire*, sometimes called *Narcissa*, by Mary Carr Moore and her mother Sarah Pratt Carr,[51] was first presented in Spokane, Washington, in 1911, and then in such other cities as Seattle, San Francisco, and Chicago. More than thirty years later, the opera was revived and presented March 16 and 17, 1945, in the Philharmonic Auditorium of Los Angeles, and in several of the larger churches of California. The *Hymnal* of the Presbyterian Church, U.S.A., in its 1933 edition and its many subsequent reprintings, contains a hymn, "Braving the Wilds all Unexplored," which emphasized the pioneer theme. The words were by the late Dr. Robert Freeman, then pastor of the Pasadena Presbyterian Church, and the music by the late Dr. William F. Merrill, then pastor of the Brick Presbyterian Church, New York City. The tune was called "Marcus Whitman."

In addition to such books and musical items mentioned above, the observance of the Whitman-Spalding centennial in 1936 inspired the writing of many pamphlets, magazine articles, songs, and dramatizations,[52] all adding to the fame of the Whitmans.

OTHER MEMORIALS

During the observance of the centennial, attention was directed to the old Prentiss house in Prattsburg where Narcissa spent her girlhood. The house was in a dilapidated condition and in danger of being razed. Financed by contributions from interested individuals and church groups, the house was purchased and restored to its original condition.[53] It is now a retirement home for a Presbyterian minister and his wife. A room in the United Presbyterian Church in Prattsburg has been named the Narcissa Prentiss Hall.

Among the many features of the National Presbyterian Church, Washington, D.C., is a series of commemorative plaques placed to honor American leaders of the Calvinistic tradition. Among these is one dedicated to Marcus Whitman.

In 1928 two bronze plaques were placed on the grounds of the Prattsburg school, once the Franklin Academy, in memory of Henry Harmon Spalding and Narcissa Prentiss Whitman, both of whom had studied there. New York State Highway No. 53, connecting Kanona with Prattsburg, has been designated by the Highway Department of the State as the Whitman-Spalding Highway with appropriate markers at either end. The road connecting Prattsburg with Naples is called the Narcissa Prentiss Highway, and that between Penn Yan and Rushville, the Marcus Whitman Highway. A change of routing of a road going through Wheeler, New York, where Samuel Parker first interested Whitman in Oregon, requiring the razing of the original building in which Whitman had his medical office in 1832-35. Members of the Geneva Presbytery dismantled the building in May 1959 and moved the salvageable materials to the Presbytery's camp for young people, called Camp Whitman, near Dresden, New York. Lack of funds has delayed the reerection of the building.

A bronze plaque honoring Dr. Whitman is on a boulder near the side of the office building in Wheeler, and another is on a fifteen-ton boulder located in front of the Congregational Church at Rushville. A monument honoring Whitman and Parker, dedicated May 12, 1935, stands before the First Presbyterian Church of Ithaca, New York.

The Marcus Whitman Central School was erected at Rushville in 1971 on a site bordering the cemetery which contains the graves of Whitman's parents. There is a Marcus Whitman Junior High School in Seattle. No doubt there are other schools, especially in the Pacific Northwest, which bear the Whitman name or those of other members of the Oregon Mission.[54] A Marcus Whitman D.A.R. chapter is in Everett, Washington, a Narcissa Whitman chapter in Yakima, and an Alice (Clarissa) Whitman chapter in Lewiston, Idaho. A Marcus Whitman Historical Society Museum is in Gorham, New York.

The Whitmans have been memorialized many times in stained glass windows in churches and chapels throughout the nation. The oldest known is in the Plymouth Church of the Pilgrims, Brooklyn, New York, placed there before the Whitman-Saved-Oregon story was discredited. It pictures Whitman standing before President John Tyler and Daniel Webster. An inscription reads: "In grateful recognition of the man who saved Oregon to the nation."

Whitman memorial windows are to be found in St. John's Episcopal Cathedral, Spokane, Washington;[55] Pasadena Presbyterian Church, Pasadena, California;[56] Stewart Memorial Chapel, San Francisco Theological Seminary, San Anselmo, California;[57] and in United Presbyterian Churches in Springfield, Illinois, and in Wallingford, Pennsylvania. Rooms or halls named after one or both of the Whitmans are in Presbyterian churches in Pocatello, Idaho, in Camp Hill, Pennsylvania, and in Menlo Park, California. The capitol building of the State of Oregon has a large mural depicting the arrival of the Whitman-Spalding party at Fort Vancouver in September 1836 when they were greeted by Dr. John McLoughlin and others at the fort. Most of these memorials have been erected or placed since the observance of the Whitman-Spalding centennial in 1936.

Two large geographical areas bear the Whitman name: the Wallowa-Whitman National Forest in northeastern Oregon, and Whitman County in southeastern Washington. The latter with an area of 2,166 square miles is larger than the State of Delaware and twice as large as Rhode Island. As has been mentioned, there is a Whitman Park at Grand Junction, Colorado, with a monument which draws attention to the fact that Whitman swam the Colorado River at that place in the winter of 1842–43 while on his journey to the East.

Several monuments or road signs are to be found along the route of the old Oregon Trail. Mention has been made of the monument which has been erected at the summit of South Pass in the Rockies to honor Narcissa Whitman and Eliza Spalding, who rode through the Pass on July 4, 1836. A road sign at the site of the 1836 Rendezvous proclaims the fact that these two women were the first white women to cross what is now Wyoming and also the first to go over the Oregon Trail. Typical of the markers along the present-day highway which more or less parallels the Oregon Trail is that at Hagerman, Idaho, which carries the following inscription:

> COMMEMORATING THE MEMORY OF
> MARCUS WHITMAN
> PIONEER MISSIONARY WHO IN 1836
> BROUGHT THE FIRST WAGON OVER THE TRAPPERS PATH
> THAT AFTERWARDS BECAME THE OREGON TRAIL

Perhaps the most unusual memorial to honor the Whitmans was the naming of Liberty ships after each of them during World War II—SS Marcus Whitman, which was torpedoed and sunk on November 9, 1942, and the SS Narcissa Whitman, which was sold for scrap July 28, 1961.[58] Both the Whitmans and the Spaldings are to be memorialized in the Museum of Westward Expansion planned for the Jefferson National Expansion Memorial in St. Louis, Missouri, when the necessary funds are available.

A striking evidence of the great esteem in which Marcus Whitman was held by those of his generation is the fact that six baby boys were named after him during his lifetime. His sister married Henry F. Wisewell and they became the parents of a son born on May 23, 1838, whom they called Marcus Whitman. A cousin of Whitman's, Abner C. Bates living at Chester, Ohio, named a son after him, born on April 26, 1840. Two boys born in the Old Oregon country were named after Whitman. The first was the half-breed son of Robert Newell, born on April 17, 1840, and the second was the son born to Elkanah and Mary Walker on March 16, 1842. The fifth namesake was Marcus Whitman Saunders born May 8, 1846, at Rushville, and the sixth was a son of one of Narcissa's brothers, Jonas Galusha Prentiss, born sometime late in 1846. After Whitman's death, a number of boys were named after him including a son of Perrin Whitman. At least two members of the Whitman family, in collateral branches, bear the name of Marcus Whitman in this generation. A grandson of Henry Harmon Spalding who was a son of Henry Hart Spalding bears the name of Marcus Whitman Spalding, who, at the time of this writing, lives in Olympia, Washington.

WHITMAN MISSION NATIONAL HISTORIC SITE

As the Whitman-Spalding centennial of 1936 drew near, many public-spirited citizens of Walla Walla initiated efforts to acquire more land at the mission site and to persuade the National Park Service of the United States Department of the Interior to make it a National Monument, In 1936 the Whitman Centennial Corporation secured title to 37½ acres, which included the site of the original mission buildings, and which adjoined the eight acres the Whitman Monument Association had secured in 1897. Before the National Park Service could accept the land, certain legal technicalities had to be cleared as the title was clouded;[59] this took three years. Finally on January 20, 1940, the two tracts consisting of about forty-five acres were donated to the Government and the Whitman National Monument was officially established. In 1961 the Park Service secured another forty-three acres, bringing the total to ninety-eight acres, and the name was changed to the Whitman Mission National Historical Site.

A Visitor's Center, containing administration offices, museum space and a lecture hall, was dedicated on June 6, 1964. Trained archaeologists have conducted extensive excavations of the various building sites and many artifacts have been discovered. The foundations of the main buildings have been outlined with bands of cement; an apple orchard has been planted near where the original trees stood; the mill pond and some of the irrigation ditches have been restored; and a self-guiding trail to the principle points of interest has been laid out. Clumps of ryegrass are still growing on the site. The improved facilities have been attracting an ever increasing number of visitors; over 105,000 were expected in 1972.

THE WHITMAN STATUES

Marcus Whitman has been twice honored by statues erected in his memory. The first, sculptured by Alexander S. Calder, shows Whitman in frontier dress standing by a wheel. It is said that Calder used Perrin Whitman, who resembled his uncle, as a model. The nine-foot terracotta statue, together with twelve others, was set on a ledge of the facade of Witherspoon Building in Philadelphia. This building, dedicated on October 24, 1896, houses the headquarters of the United Presbyterian Church, U.S.A. When the Presbyterian Historical Society moved into its new building at 425 Lombard Street, Philadelphia, six statues which had adorned the Witherspoon Building, including the Whitman statue, were moved in 1961 to the new site and placed at ground level. The Whitman statue is to the right of the main entrance.

The second Whitman statue is in Statuary Hall of the Capitol in Washington, D.C. By law each state is permitted to place the statues of two of its most distinguished sons or daughters in this Hall. By 1950 all but seven states had at least one statue there; among the states not represented was Washington. The Business and Professional Women's Clubs of Washington at their annual convention in 1948 adopted the project of placing a statue of Marcus Whitman in our nation's hall of fame. Since no composite statue was permitted in the Hall, no plans could be made to include Narcissa in this memorial. Mrs. Goldie Rehberg of Walla Walla was made chairman of the committee commissioned to achieve the goal. The first step necessary was to obtain the approval of the State Legislature in the selection of Marcus Whitman. Senate Bill No. 32 was introduced in the 1948–49 session. It not only designated Whitman to receive this honor but also provided an appropriation to cover all necessary costs. Opposition developed from some unidentified people who remembered the old Whitman-Saved-Oregon legends. A postcard, signed only by the "Good Government League" and sent to all of the 145 legislators, bore the following message:

Senate Bill No. 32 is Bad — Very Bad!

Its authors and sponsors may be well meaning, but uninformed. The Marcus Whitman legend is 90% fictitious. It is one of our historical fables like William Tell, Romulus and Remus, Robin Hood, Washington's prayer at Valley Forge, and his cherry tree.

Did Whitman's trip save Oregon? It DID NOT! Should he have a monument? If he should, there are hundreds of other citizens of Washington more entitled to be thus honored. Don't vote a memorial which will make Washington State the laughing stock of the nation.

As a result of the opposition, the sponsors of the bill decided that it would be wise not to ask for an appropriation to cover the cost of the statue but to raise this by popular subscription. Thus amended, the Bill passed the Legislature by an almost unanimous vote and the Governor signed it on March 10, 1949. Subsequently the Marcus Whitman Foundation was organized and incorporated, with headquarters at Walla Walla. A campaign was launched for the necessary funds and after several years' efforts, over $27,000.00 was raised, one-third of which came from sources in Whitman County. Thousands of schoolchildren, church groups, civic clubs, and individuals contributed. "During the years I worked on the project," wrote Mrs. Rehberg to the author, "it seemed like an endless and thankless job, and many times I was on the verge of giving up. Then to my thinking would come thoughts of the courage the Whitmans had, and I would go on with more determination."[60]

The Foundation selected Dr. Avard Fairbanks, a sculptor of national reputation, then Dean of the School of Fine Arts of the University of Utah, to make a bronze statue of Dr. Whitman. Fairbanks sought to portray Whitman as being an alert, professional-looking man, full of energy and vitality. Whitman is represented as wearing a buckskin suit with a beaver-skin hat, thus stressing the fact that he was a frontiersman. Under his right arm is a large Bible, reminiscent of the story of the four Nez Perces who journeyed to St. Louis in 1831 looking for missionaries and the white man's Bible. In his left hand, Whitman clutches a pair of saddlebags. These were copied from those which Whitman had used when practising medicine at Wheeler, New York, before leaving with Parker on their exploring tour of 1835.[61] In the back of Whitman's statue, rising to his waist, is a representation of the ryegrass from which his mission station, Waiilatpu, got its name.

The finished statue, eight feet high, rests upon a block of Washington granite, and then upon a marble pedestal about three feet high and four feet square. On the pedestal is engraved a paraphrased quotation from Whitman's letter of November 5, 1846, to his brother-in-law, the Rev. Lyman P. Judson: "My plans require time and distance."[62] The pedestal also carries the following inscription: "Citizens of the State of Washington express their gratitude to this pioneer and medical missionary." A picture of the statue is included as an illustration in this volume.

The Whitman statue was dedicated on May 22, 1953, while placed temporarily in the rotunda of the Capitol. Mrs. Rehberg and Dr. Fairbanks were present and each spoke briefly. The dedication address was delivered by an Associate Justice of the United States Supreme Court, the Honorable William O. Douglas, an alumnus of Whitman College. The Vice-President of the United States, Richard Nixon, was also present and made a few remarks. A unique item in the dedication program was the singing by a soloist of the hymn, "Yes, my native land, I love thee," which had been sung at the wedding of Marcus and Narcissa at Angelica, New York, on February 18, 1836. The descendants of a collateral branch of the Whitman family, a father and a son, each with the name of Marcus Whitman, unveiled the statue.[63]

How deeply significant are the three symbols used in these two statues: the wheel, the Bible, and the saddlebags. Each refers to a major aspect of Whitman's work in Old Oregon. The wheel suggests the services he rendered in opening the Old Oregon country; the Bible reminds us that Whitman's primary concern was that of taking Christianity to the Oregon Indians; and the saddlebags symbolize his faithfulness as a doctor in ministering to natives and whites alike. Monuments and memorials such as parks, educational institutions, roadside markers, stained glass windows, rooms or halls in church buildings, murals, and statues are to be found in the following ten states and the District of Columbia: New York, Pennsylvania, Illinois, Wyoming, Colorado, Idaho, Washington, California, Oregon, and one planned for Missouri. No other Protestant missionary in the history of the United States, whether serving in the homeland or abroad, has been so widely remembered in literature, monuments, and memorials, as Dr. Marcus Whitman.

THE CONTINUING FIRST PRESBYTERIAN CHURCH OF OREGON

The First Presbyterian Church of Oregon was not dissolved by the massacre as has been claimed.[64] Even though its elder, Dr. Whitman, was killed, and its pastor, the Rev. H. H. Spalding, was obliged to leave his mission station, the Christian faith was sufficiently viable among the Nez Perce and Cayuses to continue without pastoral oversight until Spalding's return to the Nez Perces in the fall of 1871.

None of the twenty-one native members of the church took part in the Waiilatpu tragedy. Although Five Crows, the only Cayuse who had joined the church, did not take part in the massacre, he did play, by white man's standards, a dishonorable role in the abduction of Lorinda Bewley.

By native standards, however, he may well have considered himself to have acted within his rights. Only three members of the church were killed—the two Whitmans and Andrew Rodgers. Judging by the observations of several white men who had contacts with the Cayuses and the Nez Perces during the years 1847–71, many of the members of these two tribes remained faithful in maintaining their daily devotions and in observing Sunday, as they had been taught by their missionaries. Thus the Christian faith was continued.

Spalding returned to the Nez Perces in the fall of 1871 as an appointee of the Presbyterian Board of Foreign Missions, he took with him the original record book of the mission church in which was written the names of his converts.⁶⁵ The Nez Perces welcomed their old missionary with enthusiasm. The fact that he could speak their language was like a magnet, drawing great crowds to him. Old age and gray hair, added to the memory of his eleven-year residence at Lapwai, gave Spalding a prestige with the natives never before so enjoyed.

He found a few of the original members of the First Presbyterian Church of Oregon still alive, including Timothy and Jude. Ignoring the rules of Presbyterian polity, he arbitrarily appointed these to be his elders. On November 12, 1871, after being back at Lapwai for less than three weeks, Spalding baptized and received into the church twenty-one men and twenty-three women. No longer was he inhibited as formerly by the caution and restraint of colleagues. He made no effort to give his converts a thorough indoctrination into the teachings of John Calvin. Instead he received all who came who professed repentance and claimed that they believed in Christ.

Heading the list of those baptized on November 12 were Lawyer and Tackensuatis, the latter of whom was christened Samuel. These were the two Nez Perces who had ridden out from the Rendezvous in the Summer of 1836 to meet the incoming Whitman-Spalding party. Following his earlier practice, Spalding bestowed Bible names on his converts at the time of their baptism. With the passing of the years, these Christian names became surnames. Running out of Bible names, Spalding gave some of his converts the family names of friends in New York State; these names also continue among the Nez Perces. Once Spalding gave the names Henry and Eliza Spalding to a couple he baptized.

In the fall of 1872, Spalding rode down into the Cayuse country, no doubt stopping to see the old mission site at Waiilatpu. The Eells couple had sold their holdings the previous June and had moved to Snohomish, Washington. A stranger, Charles Moore, then occupied the land. We can only imagine the memories which surged through his mind, if indeed he visited Waiilatpu, as he rode down the trail that he and Whitman had traveled in late November 1847. On September 27, Spalding with the Methodist minister, the Rev. H. H. Hines, met with some Cayuses at "Wild Horse," a creek which empties into the Umatilla River just above Pendleton. Eight adults and children were baptized there that day. The fact that Wild Horse Creek was near the place where Stickus had his camp back in 1847 suggests the possibility that these converts were once members or descendants of his band. Evidently by this time, Stickus was dead. After making inquiry as to the fate of Five Crows, Spalding wrote after his name in the record book of the church: "Now dead, 1872."

On March 27, 1873, Spokane Garry wrote to Spalding and invited him to visit Spokane "to baptize his people and marry them according to laws."[66] Spokane Garry, who had been baptized at the Red River Mission school on June 24, 1827, never gave the missionaries at Tshimakain his sympathetic support in their work.[67] This failure was a serious obstacle in the endeavors of Walker and Eells to evangelize the Spokanes. Now, twenty-five years after the work at Tshimakain had been abandoned, Garry had a change of attitude. In response to his invitation, Spalding spent the summer of 1873 among the Spokanes and baptized 253 adults and eighty-one children.[68] Walker and Eells had planted the Christian seed; Spalding had gathered in the harvest.

Spalding claimed in the record book of the church that, during the revival which began with his return to the Nez Perces in the fall of 1871, he had baptized over a thousand Nez Perces, Cayuses, and Spokanes. Some of his critics accused him of baptizing some people twice. The fact that Spalding wrote the baptismal names of his converts in the record book of the Mission Church is evidence that he did not consider it to have been dissolved by the massacre. He was still pastor of the First Presbyterian Church of Oregon. At a meeting of the Presbytery of Oregon, held at Lapwai on May 10, 1873, the Nez Perce field was divided into two parishes, one at Kamiah and the other at Lapwai. Later four other Presbyterian churches were organized among the Nez Perces, two among the Spokanes, and one on the Umatilla Reservation for the Cayuses and Walla Wallas.[69]

I Baptize You, Marcus Whitman

With Spalding, when he returned to the Nez Perce field in the fall of 1871, was the Rev. Henry T. Cowley who opened a school for the Indians at Kamiah. In the late spring of 1874, Cowley with his family moved to Spokane where he assumed responsibility for the Presbyterian mission work among the Spokane Indians.[70] His place at Kamiah was taken by the Rev. Samuel N. D. Martin, also an appointee of the Presbyterian Board of Foreign Missions.

Spalding received an injury while cutting wood at his home in Kamiah in November 1873. His health gradually failed during the following months. A few weeks before he was taken to Lapwai in July 1874, where he died on the following August 3, an incident took place about which both Cowley and Martin have given details. A Cayuse chief by the name of Umhawalish and his wife rode some 210 miles from the Umatilla Indian Reservation near present-day Pendleton, Oregon, to Kamiah, arriving there about May 1, in order to be baptized by Spalding. Cowley wrote: "Umhawalish... was one of the early pupils of the Martyr Whitman," and Martin noted: "He is a friend of Dr. Whitman, whose memory he holds in the highest veneration, & also Father [sic] Spalding, who has known him for nearly 40 years." [71]

The baptismal service was held in Spalding's home on Monday, May 11. Spalding was so infirm that he had to be held up in bed so that he could apply the baptismal water to the head of the kneeling Cayuse chief. As he did so, he said: "I baptize you Marcus Whitman,[72] in the name of the Father, the Son, and the Holy Ghost." This was Spalding's final tribute to his martyred co-worker.

Those present knew that Spalding intended to give the baptismal name of Narcissa Whitman to the wife of the chief. When she stepped forward to receive the sacrament, Spalding, perhaps overcome with emotion as a flood of memories surged through his mind, found himself unable to proceed with the service. Was he overwhelmed by memories of his love for Narcissa when they attended the same church and school in Prattsburg? And by memories of eleven years of association in the Oregon Mission, some bitter, some sweet, mingled with the remembrance of her tragic death at the time of the massacre?

Being both physically and emotionally exhausted, Spalding directed Cowley and Martin to take the woman into the nearby First Presbyterian Church of Kamiah[73] and for one of them to administer the sacrament. The group withdrew from the sick room. In the church one of the ministers baptized the Cayuse woman with the words: "I baptize you Narcissa Whitman."

The death-bed baptism of the Cayuse chief by Spalding to whom he gave the name of Marcus Whitman, and his instruction that the chief's wife be christened Narcissa Whitman was not only the last final tribute that the veteran missionary paid to the Whitmans, it was also tantamount to throwing out a challenge to the Christian Cayuses to "carry on."

So it was that another Marcus and another Narcissa Whitman lived among the Cayuses.[74]

CHAPTER 24 ENDNOTES

[1] Bancroft, *Oregon*, I:780.

[2] *P.N.Q.*, XL (1949):297. Following the departure of the stockmen, the site lay unoccupied until 1859 when Cushing Eells filed a claim for 640 acres which included the mission site. See following section on "Whitman College."

[3] See Raymond W. Settle (ed.), *The March of the Mounted Riflemen*, Arthur Clark Co., Glendale, Calif., 1940, for an account of this regiment.

[4] Francis Norbert Blanchet, *Historical Sketches of the Catholic Church in Oregon*, Portland, 1876, p. 165.

[5] Report of Anson Dart, October 20, 1851. Records of the Oregon Superintendency of Indian Affairs, National Archives.

[6] Records of Oregon Superintendency, Letters Received, 1850, National Archives, Copy in Coll. E.W.S.H.S.

[7] Shumkain is not mentioned by any of the eyewitnesses of the massacre, but this is not strange as the survivors, for the most part, were unacquainted with the names of the Indians involved.

[8] See Chapter Twenty-Two, "The Conspirators Identified."

[9] Letter from Joseph Lane, Nov. 29, 1879, in Portland *Oregonian*. Undated clipping in Coll. E.W.S.H.S.

[10] From "Important Declaration made June 2nd and 3d, 1850," Coll. O. Published in Portland *Catholic Sentinel*, April 27, 1872.

[11] *Ibid.*

[12] Victor, *Early Indian Wars*, p. 249.

[13] Lane letter, see ante, fn. 9.

[14] The original records of the trial are in the State Archives, Salem, Oregon. See also Oregon *Spectator*, May 30, 1850, and Portland Sunday *Oregonian*, Sept. 24, 1933. All references to the trial in this section, unless otherwise noted, are from these sources.

[15] See ante, fn. 9.

[16] Article about Eliza Spalding Warren, "First Woman Born in the West," *Ladies' Home Journal*, August 1913, p. 40.

[17] Catherine Sager later claimed that Mrs. Hall's testimony was in error. See Chapter Twenty-Two, "The Attack Out-of-doors." The person who was being attacked by Tiloukaikt, whom Mrs. Hall thought to be Dr. Whitman, was actually Judge Saunders.

[18] Portland *Catholic Sentinel*, April 20, 1872.

[19] See Appendix 3 for an account of Spalding's anti-Catholic charges.

[20] See ante, fn. 10.

[21] A reference to Joe Meek who, evidently, was responsible for the news item which appeared in the *Oregon Spectator* of May 30, 1850.

[22] Victor, *Early Indian Wars*, p. 212. The rewards offered for the apprehension of Tiloukaikt, Tomahas, Tamsucky, Joe Lewis, and Edward were twice those offered for the other eight, which included Frank Escaloom and "Quiamashouskin" (or Kia-ma-sump-kin).

[23] Pringle scrapbook Coll. W.

[24] Blanchet, *Historical Sketches* (see ante, fn. 4), p. 181, fn. 4.

[25] See ante, fn. 10.

[26] Register of the Roman Catholic Church of St. John the Evangelist, Oregon City, p. 11. Information supplied by kindness of Mrs. Harriet D. Munnick of West Linn, Ore.

[27] Portland *Catholic Sentinel*, April 20, 1872. The McLoughlin house was moved in 1909 up Singer Hill to the park that Dr. McLoughlin had given to Oregon City.

[28] Portland Sunday *Oregonian*, September 24, 1933, p. 3.

[29] Information about the probable location of the grave was supplied by Mrs. Munnick.

[30] See circular from American Board to Spalding, Coll. W.

[31] The inventory was "Sworn to & Subscribed" by Spalding and Perrin Whitman on Sept. 1, 1849. Original in Coll. A. Copy in Richardson, *The Whitman Mission*, p. 149 ff.

[32] Drury, *Spalding and Smith*, p. 249. The late Carrol E. Brock of Orofino, Idaho, in a letter to me dated May 20, 1970, stated that a lignite outcropping was about two miles east of Old Lapwai near Arrow junction on the north side of the Clearwater River.

[33] *Robert Newell's Memoranda*, pp. 111-112.

[34] *Ibid.* Newell mentions finding a supply of both potatoes and peas at the mission site when the Volunteers arrived.

[35] Dart's report on mission claims of Oct. 20, 1851. Oregon Superintendency of Indian Affairs, 1850–55, National Archives.

[36] Drury, *F.W.W.*, II:210, fn. 26.

[37] See Chapter Twenty, "Rodgers Studies for the Ministry."

[38] Richardson, *The Whitman Mission*, gives a good account of the various owners of Waiilatpu following the massacre. Eells sold his claim in 1872. Myron Eells stated in his *Marcus Whitman*, p. 296, that the Monument Association paid $30.00 an acre for the site. Other reports state that the eight acres were donated by Mr. and Mrs. Sweagle.

[39] Eells, *Marcus Whitman*, p. 297. See also W.C.Q., I (1897):4 for an account of the semicentennial observances.

[40] The last of the survivors to die was Mrs. Gertrude Hall Denny, who passed away in Portland, Oregon, on August 5, 1933. She was then about 96 years old. Mrs. Denny was the wife of Judge Owen N. Denny, who served in several diplomatic posts in the Orient. While U.S. Consul General at Shanghai, he became interested in the Chinese ring-necked pheasant and in 1882 and 1884 introduced the bird into Washington and Oregon. From there, it has spread over much of the United States.

[41] The author had the privilege of knowing Sam Walker, the youngest son of Elkanah and Mary Walker, who with his wife lived in the old Walker home at Forest Grove, Oregon. See Drury, *Walker*, p. 253 ff., for an account of a visit paid on Sam Walker in the summer of 1939 when he turned over an apple box full of books, letters, and other source material pertaining to the Oregon Mission. These are now in Coll. Wn.

[42] Another son of David Greene also became a resident of the State of Washington. He was Robert S. Greene who became Chief Justice of Washington Territory in 1879.

[43] *W.C.Q.*, I (Dec. 1897):4:30.

[44] Correcting a statement in Drury, *Whitman*, p. 425, that the grave site was changed when the remains were reburied in 1897. Dr. Stephen B. L. Penrose, for many years President of Whitman College and who was active in the semicentennial activities, told me that the reburial was in the same place as that selected by the Oregon Volunteers.

[45] From undated clipping in the Pringle scrapbook, Coll. W.

[46] Delaney, *A Survivor's Recollections*, p. 45.

[47] From copy of original letter supplied by Mrs. H. W. Platz of Seattle, Wash, a granddaughter of Catherine Pringle.

[48] Presbyterian churches observing the centennial were asked to take a collection for the restoration of the Presbyterian (Indian) Church at Spalding, Idaho. Some $10,000.00 were received for this purpose.

[49] Drury, *Whitman*, p. 427. Those interested in the issuance of this commemorative stamp requested that the names of Whitman and Spalding be on the stamp, but this request was denied.

[50] See Drury, "Marcus Whitman, M.D.," in *Journal of the Presbyterian Historical Society*, XXXI (Dec. 1953):205 ff., for a discussion of some of the erroneous impressions of the Whitmans given by fiction writers.

[51] Published by the Stuff Printing Concern, Seattle, Wash. (1917). Mary Carr Moore is listed as the author of the libretto for the opera, and her mother, Sarah Pratt Carr, as composer of the music. The words are in a stilted Victorian style. Copy in Coll. W.

[52] *The Balled of Waiilatpu*, with words and music by Borghild Nelson, copyrighted in 1965, is a good example of these songs; and *Waiilatpu* by Wm. Kelley, Adams Publishing Co., Chicago, 1952, is an example of a dramatization.

[53] The late Dr. Arthur H. Limouze, then a secretary of the Presbyterian Board of National Missions, was largely responsible for the purchase and restoration of the Prentiss home.

[54] A Junior High School at College Place, about three miles east of Waiilatpu, has been called the John Sager School.

[55] Cushing Eells and Elkanah Walker are also memorialized by stained glass windows in this cathedral.

[56] The Whitman window in the chapel of this church portrays him carrying a rifle. Being a pacifist by conviction, Whitman is not known ever to have used a gun except to kill an animal for food.

[57] Separate windows in this chapel are dedicated to each of the Whitmans and to each of the Spaldings. Dedication took place in May 1955.

[58] See Drury, "Floating Memorials," *Army and Navy Chaplain*, Jan-Feb., 1946.

[59] A good description of the difficulties involved in clearing the title is in Richardson, *The Whitman Mission*, pp. 138 ff.

[60] From letter to the author, August 21, 1953.

[61] Original saddlebags are in the Presbyterian Historical Society, Philadelphia.

[62] Whitman was writing to Judson about the latter's acceptance of the Seventh-day Adventist belief in the imminent second coming of Christ which nullified any effort to make plans for the future. Whitman actually wrote: "For to my mind all my work & plans involved time & distance & required confidence in the stability of God's government."

[63] See *Acceptance of the Statue of Marcus Whitman, 83d Congress, 2d Session, Senate Document, No. 167*, Government Printing Office, Washington, D.C., for a full account of the program with text of speeches given. Two with whom Whitman had close associations during those history-making years, 1836–47, have also been honored by statues in the nation's Hall of Fame. They are Jason Lee and John McLoughlin, both selected by the Legislature of the State of Oregon.

[64] For more than thirty years a note was carried in the annual *Minutes of the General Assembly* (Presbyterian) under the listing of the churches of the Presbytery of Walla Walla that the church had been dissolved by the massacre. The wording has been changed to read: "Following the massacre of November 29, 1847 (the Waiilatpu church) merged into the Nez Perce churches."

[65] The original volume is now in the Presbyterian Historical Society, Philadelphia. An account of Spalding's activities in the great revival of 1871-73 is in Drury, *A Tepee in His Front Yard*.

[66] Original letter in Coll. W.

[67] Spokane Garry was a polygamist. This may have been one reason why he did not cooperate with the American Board missionaries. See fn. 45, Chapter One.

[68] Drury, *Spalding*, pp. 409 ff.

[69] Today four Presbyterian churches among the Nez Perces, one among the Spokanes, and one on the Umatilla Reservation remain active. The latter, known as the Tutuilla Church, near present-day Pendleton, Oregon, was organized June 17, 1882, with twenty-six charter members. In 1971 this church reported having forty-two members who represented several tribes on the Umatilla Reservation. Sister M. Florita, for many years associated with the St. Andrews School at Pendleton, in a letter to me dated March 3, 1971, stated that there were then only "17 fullblooded Cayuses, 7... Walla Wallas, and 10... Umatillas" living. The Umatilla Reservation was established in 1855 with the dwindling Cayuse tribe as one of the confederated tribes.

[70] Drury, *A Tepee in His Front Yard*, tells about Cowley's missionary activities with the Nez Perces and Spokanes.

[71] See fn. 11, Chapter Thirteen. The account of the baptism of Chief Umhawalish, *Minutes of the Synod of Washington*, 1906, p. 301, quotes Martin's account of the event.

[72] The Whitman name was also introduced among the Nez Perces but at a later date. Silas Whitman, a fullblooded Nez Perce, was ordained to the Presbyterian ministry in 1888.

[73] The building still used by the First Presbyterian (Indian) Church of Kamiah was erected by the U.S. Government in 1873 and is the oldest existing Protestant church building in Idaho.

[74] According to information supplied by the Rev. Robert C. Hall, Pendleton, Oregon, the Cayuse Indians, christened Marcus and Narcissa Whitman, were charter members of the Tutuilla Presbyterian Church. See fn. ante, No. 69. Today visitors to the church's cemetery may see the tombstones of Marcus and Narcissa Whitman.

WHITMAN MISSION NATIONAL HISTORIC SITE
Looking southwest from the monument. The Whitman home was located near the three larger trees at upper right. The mill pond and an irrigation ditch paralleling the fence have been restored. In the distance are some of the Blue Mountains.
Courtesy, Whitman Mission National Historic Site.

THE GREAT GRAVE AT WAIILATPU
The large flat stone covers the remains of the thirteen victims of the massacre. One other, Peter D. Hall, fled unobserved by the Indians, but is supposed to have drowned en route to Fort Vancouver. The shaft marks the graves of Mr. and Mrs. Gray whose bodies were moved here from Astoria in 1916. Courtesy, Whitman Mission National Historic Site.

GREAT GRAVE DEDICATION, 1897
The Great Grave dedication ceremony, occurring on the 50th Anniversary of the Whitman's deaths was attended by approximately 3,000 people. A speech was given by Catherine Sager Pringle (5th woman from left), one of the surviving Sager children. Courtesy, Whitman Mission National Historic Site.

THREE OF THE SAGER SISTERS
A photo of the three witnesses of the Whitman massacre taken at its fiftieth anniversary at Walla Walla in November 1897. From left: Catherine Sager Pringle, Elizabeth Sager Helm, and Matilda Sager Delaney. Courtesy, Sadie Collins Armin, Catherine's granddaughter.

WHITMAN MONUMENT AT WAIILATPU
On the knoll northeast of the Whitman homesite, where it was placed in 1897 at the fiftieth observance of the massacre. The view is to the east, toward the Blue Mountains, and in the direction of the Whitman's sawmill, some twenty-two miles distant. Courtesy, Whitman Mission National Historic Site.

THE MARCUS WHITMAN STATUE BY AVARD FAIRBANKS
Representing the State of Washington, Capitol Building, Washington, D.C. In frontier costume, with Bible and saddlebags to symbolize the missionary doctor. The saddlebags used by Whitman before going to Oregon are now in the Presbyterian Historical Society, Philadelphia. Below the statue is the inscription, from Marcus Whitman's letter of November 5, 1846: "My plans require time and distance." Courtesy, Whitman Mission National Historic Site.

I think I have now, by God's help, discharged my obligation in writing this large work. Let those who think I have said too little, or those who think I have said too much, forgive me; and let those who think I have said just enough join me in giving thanks to God. Amen.

    Last paragraph of Saint Augustine's *City of God*.

APPENDICES

Appendix I

Index of the Letters of Marcus and Narcissa Whitman

Three hundred and two Whitman letters, written during the years 1827–47 inclusive, have been consulted in the writing of this work. This is an amazing number to survive the vicissitudes of 125 or more years, especially when the majority of the extant letters were kept for decades by individuals rather than by some organization, such as the American Board. Of the total, 176 were written by Marcus and 126 by Narcissa.

The following index of the Whitman letters, first used in my *Marcus Whitman, M.D.*, has been compiled in order to give something of the history of each letter and to provide a quick reference in the text to any letter quoted or consulted. When such a reference is made, the number of the letter will be given in brackets. By checking the number in the following index, one can learn the place where the letter was written; the person or persons to whom it was addressed; the date of writing; the present location of the original if known; and the name of at least one publication in which it appeared if published. The letters of Mrs. Whitman are indicated by underlining the dates of writing.

I had access to 222 Whitman letters when writing my *Marcus Whitman, M.D.*, which appeared in 1937. Since that time, eighty more Whitman letters have been located or made available to me. Sixteen of this number were located in libraries, in private hands, or reprinted in publications. The other sixty-four were held by a dealer in Western Americana in 1935 who was unwilling to let me examine them. He said: "If you use them, the bloom is off the peach." Later these letters became part of the Coe Collection, now in the Beinecke Rare Book and Manuscript Library of Yale University, where I have had the privilege of examining them. Most of the letters in this collection were written by Dr. Whitman to Elkanah Walker, and dealt largely with mission business. In addition to the Whitman letters in the Coe Collection, Yale University library previously had ten Whitman letters which were once in the Oregon Historical Society. These had been published in the 1891 and 1893 issues of the *Transactions of the Oregon Pioneer Association*.

The 302 letters here listed do not include twelve letters which Dr. Whitman sent to Henry Hill, Treasurer of the American Board or one which Mrs. Whitman sent to Hill. These dealt with financial matters.

Eight libraries hold 245 Whitman letters of the 302 here catalogued. The following abbreviations will be used to indicate the collections of the different libraries which own three or more of these letters. The figures in parenthesis indicate the extent of their holdings. Each of the libraries here listed have kindly granted me permission to use these letters.

    Coll. A (65)—A.B.C.F.M., on file in Houghton Library, Harvard University

    Coll. B (9)—Bancroft Library, University of California, Berkeley

    Coll. H (6)—Hawaiian Mission Children's Society, Honolulu, Hawaii

    Coll. O (56)—Oregon Historical Society, Portland, Oregon

    Coll. W (14)—Whitman College, Walla Walla, Washington

    Coll. Wn (3)—Washington State University, Pullman

    Coll. WSHS (17)—Washington State Historical Society, Tacoma

    Coll. Y (75)—Yale University, New Haven, Connecticut

Nineteen original letters are held by other libraries or are privately owned. Thirty-seven letters are known only in copies or in some published form. The following is the key used to designate the person or persons to whom the letters were addressed:

    1—Secretaries of the A.B.C.F.M., usually the Rev. David Greene

    2—Members of Dr. Whitman's family

    3—Members of Mrs. Whitman's family

    4—Rev. or Mrs. Samuel Parker

    5—Rev, or Mrs. Elkanah Walker

    5a—"Walker & Eells," or "Dear Brethren"

    6—Rev, or Mrs. H. K. W. Perkins, Methodist missionaries at The Dalles

    7—Mr. or Mrs. H. B. Brewer, Methodist missionaries

Names in parenthesis before the numbers "2" or "3" refer to individual members of the families of Dr. or Mrs. Whitman. Example—"Jane," mentioned in listing of letter No. 21, was a sister of Narcissa's. Other names mentioned can be identified by checking the index. The numbering of the 222 letters, listed in Appendix I of my *Marcus Whitman, M.D.*, has been retained; the additional eighty letters have been inserted in their proper chronological sequence with letters from the alphabet added to the number immediately preceding. The retention of the old numbering is intended to accommodate those who, in their writings, have referred to a Whitman letter by the number used in my earlier work. All letters not previously listed are easily identified by noticing the numbers which are followed by a letter from the alphabet.

Other abbreviations used in this index include the following: Ft. Van.—Fort Vancouver; Ft. W.W.—Fort Walla Walla; and Waii.—Waiilatpu. See "Acknowledgments, Sources, and Abbreviations" for other abbreviations used.

No.	Place of Writing	To Whom	Date	Present Location; Published in; Notes
			—1827—	
1	Rushville, N.Y.	Pratt	Sept. 11	Wn
			—1828—	
2	"	"	Feb. 5	Presby. Hist. Soc., Phila.
			—1834—	
3	Wheeler, N.Y.	I	June 3	A; Hulbert, O.P., V:258
4	"	I	June 27	A; " :262
5	Rushville, N.Y.	I	Dec. 2	A; " :269
			—1835—	
6	Wheeler, N.Y.	I	Feb. 2	A; " :281
7	Amity, N.Y.	I	Feb. 23	A; " VI:281
8	Liberty, Mo.	Narcissa	Apr. 30	Mowry, Whitman, 56; Hulbert, VI:142
9	"	I	May 13	A; Hulbert, VI:144
10	?	Mrs. Hull	undated	Mowry, 65
11	Whitman diary	I	May 14–Oct. 26	A & B; Hulbert, VI:146
12	Bellevue	Narcissa	June 21	Mowry, 58; Hulbert. VI:148
13	St. Louis, Mo.	I	Nov. 7	A; Hulbert, VI:167
14	Rushville, N.Y.	I	Dec. 17	A; " :171
15	Cohocton, N.Y.	I	Dec. 28	A; " :173
			—1836—	
16	Rushville, N.Y.	I	Jan. 6	A; " :179
17	"	I	Jan. 29	A; " :183
17a	"	Harley Lord	Feb. 6	W in Parker ms.
18	"	I	Feb. 15	A; Hulbert, VI:186
19	"	I	Mar. 3	A; " :193
20	Steamboat Siam	(mother) 3	Mar. 15	O; Drury, F.W.W., I:40
21	Steamboat Chariton	(Jane) 3	Mar. 31	O: " :44
22	Leavenworth		May 5	A; Hulbert, VI:200
23	Platte River	(Harriet) 3	June 3	O; Drury, F.W.W., I:50
24	"	(parents) 3	June 4	O; T.O.P.A., 1893. 109;O.H.Q. XXXVIII (1937), 209
25	"	(") 2	June 6	B
26	"	(Augustus) 2	June 27	B; Drury, F.W.W., I:55
27	Rendezvous, Green R.	4	July 15	Priv. owned; O.H.Q., XXXIX (1938), 219
28	Rendezvous	I	July 16	A; Hulbert, VI:204
29	Mrs. Whitman diary	2 & 3	July 18–Oct. 22	B, W, WSHS; Drury, F.W.W., I:71 & other publications

No.	Place of Writing	To Whom	Date	Present Location; Published in; Notes
30	Ft. W.W.	1	Sept. 5	A; Hulbert, VI:212
31	Ft. Van.	4	Sept. 18	W in Parker ms; Hulbert, VI:229
31a	"	Hiram Bingham	Sept. 19	H; joint letter with Spalding & Gray
32	Ft. W.W.	4	Oct. 8	W in Parker ms; Hulbert, VI:233
33	"	(mother) 2	Oct. 13	B; Drury, F.W.W., I:72; copied for her parents on Oct. 20, in ibid., 72
34	Ft. Van.	(Oren & Nancy) 2	Oct. 24	Wn copy; Naples, N.Y., Record, Oct. 1 1913; Penn Yan, N.Y., Chronicle Express, Jan. 8, 1936
35	"	4	Oct. 24	W in Parker ms; Hulbert, VI:236
36	"	4	Oct. 25	" " ; " :240
37	"	Rev. L. Hull	Oct. 25	" " ; " :242
38	"	3	Nov. 1	W copy; Drury, F.W.W., I:112
39	Ft. W.W.	(mother) 3	Dec. 5	O; " ; " :119
			—1837—	
40	Waii.	(parents) 3	Mar. 30	O; T.O.P.A., 1891, 90; Hulbert, VI:267
41	"	(parents) 3	May 2	O; " " , 93; " :269
42	"	1	May 5	A; Hulbert, VI:278
42a	Waii.	Mrs. G.P. Judd	Sept. 1	partial pubn. in Hawaiian Spectator, I (1838), 325, 332, 375
42b	"	Jason & Daniel Lee	Sept. 28	Priv. owned; copy in W
42c	"	L. Chamberlain	Oct. 7	H
42d	"	L. Chamberlain	Oct. 16	H
			—1838—	
42e	"	F.W. Ewing	Feb. 20	Brigham Young Univ., Provo
43	"	1	Mar. 12	A; Hulbert, VI:291
44	"	(parents)	Mar. 14	Y; T.O.P.A., 1891, 97
45	Columbia River	1	Mar. 17	Hulbert, VI:301; joint letter with Spalding
46	Waii.	(parents) 3	Apr. 11	Y; in part in T.O.P.A., 1891, 101ff.
46a	"	F.W. Ewing	Apr. 17	Brigham Young Univ., Provo
47	"	1	Apr. 21	A; Hulbert, VI:302; joint letter with Spalding
48	"	1	May 8	A; Hulbert, VI:311
49	"	1	May 15	A; " :302; joint letter with Spalding

No.	Place of Writing	To Whom	Date	Present Location; Published in; Notes
49a	Waii.	Rev. & Mrs. Judson	May 15	Priv. owned; O.H.Q., XLVII (1946), 31
50	"	6	July 4	O; T.O.P.A., 1893, 110
50a	"	5a	Aug. 22	Y
50b	"	5a	Aug. 28	Y
51	"	(Jane) 3	Sept. 18	Y; T.O.P.A., 1891, 106
52	"	(Mary Ann) 3	Sept. 25	O; " ", 109
53	"	(father) 3	Sept. 28	T.O.P.A., 1891, 113
54	"	(Judson) 3	Sept. 29	W; Hulbert, VI:319
55	"	4	Oct. 3	T.O.P.A., 1891, 116
56	"	1	Oct. 5	A; Hulbert, VI:316
57	"	1	Oct. 20	A; " :325
58	"	L. Chaimberlain	Oct. 30	H; " :131
59	"	6	Nov. 5	O; T.O.P.A., 1893, 112
			—1839—	
59a	"	5a	Jan. 29	Y
60	"	6	Feb. 18	O; T.O.P.A., 1893, 114
61	"	6	Mar. 23	O; " ", 116
62	"	1	May 10	A; Hulbert, VI:139
63	"	(Jane) 3	May 17	O; T.O.P.A., 1893, 118
64	"	6	June 25	O; " ", 123
64a	"	5	June 30	Y
65	"	6	July 26	T.O.P.A., 1893, 126
66	"	5	July 29	Y
67	"	(father) 3	Sept. 30	T.O.P.A., 1891, 120
67a	"	5	Oct. 8	Y
68	"	(mother) 3	Oct. 9	T.O.P.A., 1891, 120
68a	"	5	Oct. 15	Y
69	"	L. Chamberlain	Oct. 17	H; Hulbert, VII:153
70	"	1	Oct. 22	A; " :155
71	"	W.H. Gray	Nov. 30	A; " :165 & 169
72	"	5	Dec. 3	Y; Frontier Mag., Nov. 1930, 74
72a	"	5	Dec. 27	Y

No.	Place of Writing	To Whom	Date	Present Location; Published in; Notes
			—1840—	
73	Waii.	6	Jan. 1	O; T.O.P.A., 1893, 127
73a	"	5a	Mar. 7(?)	Y
74	"	1	Mar. 27	A; Hulbert, VII:172
75	"	(father) 3	Apr. 30	O; T.O.P.A., 1891, 130
76	"	(mother) 3	May 2	O; " ", 133
76a	"	5a	June 12	Y
77	"	1	July 6	A; Hulbert, VII:177
77a	"	5	July 25	Y
78	"	(mother) 3	Oct. 9	O; T.O.P.A., 1893, 133
79	"	(father) 3	Oct. 10	Y; " ", 128
80	"	1	Oct. 15	A; Hulbert, VII:182
81	"	(Harriet) 3	Oct. 20	T.O.P.A., 1893, 137
82	"	(father) 3	Oct. 21	O
83	"	1	Oct. 29	A; Hulbert, VII:195
83a	"	5	Nov. 18	Y
83b	"	5	Dec. 7	Y
			—1841—	
83c	"	5	Jan. 2	Y
83d	"	5	Jan. 19	Y
83e	"	5	Jan. 21	Y
84	"	6	Mar. 2	O; T.O.P.A., 1893, 139
85	"	5	Oct. 29	W; Hulbert, VII:213
86	"	1	Mar. 28	A; " :217
86a	"	5	Apr. 19	Y
87	"	5	Apr. 29	W
87a	"	5	May 8	Y
87b	"	7	May 10	O.H.Q., XLVII (1926), 29
87c	"	5	May 11	Y
87d	Ft. W.W.	5	May 12	Y
88	"	5	May 12	O copy
89	Waii.	(Augustus) 2	May 24	W copy
90	"	Dr. Bryant	May 24	Hulbert, VII: 222

No.	Place of Writing	To Whom	Date	Present Location; Published in; Notes
91	Waii.	(Edward)	May 30	O; T.O.P.A., 1893, 140
92	"	1	July 13	A; Hulbert, VII: 225
93	"	(Samuel) 3	Aug. 9	Priv. owned
93a	"	5	Sept. 16	Rosenbach Found., Phila.
94	"	5	Sept. 20	W; Hulbert, VII: 230
95	"	Arch McKinlay	Sept. 30	Priv. owned; Hulbert, VII: 230
96	"	(Jane) 3	Oct. 1	O; T.O.P.A., 1891, 138
97	"	(parents) 3	Oct. 6	O; " ", 145
98	"	7	Oct. 12	WSHS
98a	"	5	Oct. 21	Y
99	"	1	Oct. 22	A; Hulbert, VII: 234
99a	"	5	Nov. 6	Y
99a	"	7	Nov. 10	Priv. owned; O.H.Q., XLVIII (1947), 30
100	"	1	Nov. 11	A; Hulbert, VII: 236
101	"	(father) 3	Nov. 18	O; T.O.P.A., 1891, 154
			—1842—	
102	"	5	Jan. 24	Y; Frontier Mag., Nov. 1930, 75
102a	"	5	Jan. 24	Y
103	"	7	Feb. 1	WSHS
104	"	(Jane) 3	Feb. 2	T.O.P.A., 1891, 140
104a	"	5	Feb. 5	Y
105	"	(Jane & Ed) 3	Mar. 1	Y; T.O.P.A., 1891, 143
106	"	7	Mar. 25	WSHS
106a	"	Mrs. Daniel Lee	Mar. 25	San Francisco Theol. Sem.; Jour. of Presby. History, Dec. 1953
106b	"	5	Mar. 26	Y
107	"	7	Mar. 30	WSHS
107a	"	5	Apr. 14	Y
108	"	1	May 12	A; Hulbert, VII:263, Joint letter with Gray
109	Waii.	(Jane) 3	May 17	O; T.O.P.A., 1891, 143
110	"	5	June 13	Y
111	"	Maria Pambrum	July 7	Wn; Hulbert, VII:265
112	"	7	July 9	WSHS

No.	Place of Writing	To Whom	Date	Present Location; Published in; Notes
113	Waii.	7	July 22	O; T.O.P.A., 1893, 154
114	"	4	July 25	O; Hulbert, VII:267
114a	"	L. Chamberlain	July 25	H
115	"	Rev. & Mrs. A.S. Allen	Aug. 23	O; T.O.P.A., 1893, 162; letter incomplete
116	"	(Jane & Ed)	Sept. 29	O; T.O.P.A., 1893, 165
117	"	(parents) 3	Sept. 30	O; " " , 167
118	"	Marcus W.	Oct. 4	O; " " , 162
119	Ft. W.W.	Marcus W.	Oct. 22	Y; " " , 167
119a	Waskopum	5	Nov. 5	Y
120	Waii.	5	Dec. 18	Wn; Hulbert, VII:271
			—1843—	
121	Waskopum	(parents) 3	Feb. 7	O; T.O.P.A., 1891, 170
122	"	Marcus W.	Mar. 4	A; Hulbert, VII:273
123	"	(Harriet) 3	Mar. 11	O; T.O.P.A., 1893, 154
124	"	(Augustus) 2	Mar. 14	Priv. owned; Hulbert, VII:284
125	"	Marcus W.	Mar. 29	A; " " :289
126	Waii.	(Jonas Galusha) 3	Mar. 31	T.O.P.A., 1893, 158
127	Boston, Mass.	1	Apr. 4	A; O.H.Q., XXII (1921), 357
128	"	1	Apr. 7	A; Hulbert, VII:294
129	"	U.S. Ind. Bur.	Apr. 8	Ind. Bur. Archives; Hulbert, VII:302
129a	Ft. W.W.	5	Apr. 11	Y
130	"	(Jonas Galusha) 3	Apr. 14	O; T.O.P.A., 1893, 160
131	St. Louis, Mo.	1	May 12	A; Hulbert, VII:303
132	Waskopum	Marcus W.	May 18	A; " :305
133	Shawnee Mission	(Ed) 3	May 27	O; T.O.P.A., 1891, 177
134	" "	(mother) 2	May 27	B; Hulbert, VII:312
135	" "	(Jonas G.) 2	May 28	T.O.P.A., 1891, 178: Hulbert, VII:316
136	" "	1	May 30	A; Hulbert, VII:319
137	Ft. Van.	6	June 8	O; T.O.P.A., 1893, 169
134	"	5	June 27	W; Hulbert, VII:311
139	"	(Jane) 3	July 11	O; T.O.P.A., 1893, 53
140	Black Hills	1	July 20	A; Hulbert, VII:322

No.	Place of Writing	To Whom	Date	Present Location; Published in; Notes
141	Ft. George	(parents) 3	Aug. 11	Y; T.O.P.A., 1893, 156
141a	"	Geo. Abernethy	Oct. 31	Whitman Mission Nat. Hist. Site
142	Ft. W.W.	1	Nov. 1	A; Hulbert, VII:325
142a	Waii.	5	Nov. 14	Y
142b	"	5	Nov. 17	Y
143	"	(?) Hon. J.M. Porter	Dec. ?	Archives, U.S. War Dept., No. 424052 see Appendix 7

—1844—

No.	Place of Writing	To Whom	Date	Present Location; Published in; Notes
144	Waii.	7	Jan. 29	WSHS
145	"	7	Jan. 30	O; T.O.P.A., 1893, 170
146	"	6	Jan. 31	O; " " , 173
146a	"	5	Feb. 5	Y
146b	"	Rev. H. Clark	Mar. 4	State Library, Salem, Oreg.
147	"	7	Mar. 5	WSHS
147a	"	5	Mar. 6	Y
147b	"	5a	Apr. 4	Y
148	"	1	Apr. 8	A; Hulbert, VIII:81
149	"	(father) 3	Apr. 12	O; T.O.P.A., 1893, 56
150	"	7	Apr. 24	O; " " , 175
151	"	7	Apr. 25	WSHS
152	Waii.	(parents) 3	May. 16	Hulbert, VIII:97
153	"	1	May 18	A; " :100
154	"	Mrs. Porter	May 18	T.O.P.A., 1893, 176
155	"	(Clarissa) 3	May 20	" " , 179
156	"	(mother) 2	May 20	B; Hulbert, VIII:105; from Marcus and Narcissa
157	"	(Augustus) 2	May 21	B; Hulbert, VIII:108; incomplete
157a	"	7	May 25	WSHS
158	"	Mrs. Leslie	May 28	W copy
159	"	Rev. & Mrs. A. F. Waller	May 31	O
159a	"	Rev. A. B. Smith	May 31	Y; Drury, F.W.W., III:286
159b	"	5a	July 15	Y
159c	"	5	July 15	Y

No.	Place of Writing	To Whom	Date	Present Location; Published in; Notes
160	Waii.	1	July 22	A; Hulbert, VIII:110
161	"	7	July 29	WSHS
162	"	7	Aug. 5	O; T.O.P.A., 1893, 181
163	"	7	Oct. 9	Y; " " , 66
164	"	1	Oct. 25	A; Hulbert, VIII:119
164a	"	5	Nov. 11	Y
165	"	7	Nov. 27	WSHS
165a	" (?)	5	undated	Y
			—1845—	
165b	"	5	Jan. 27	Y
166	"	7	Feb. 20	O; T.O.P.A., 1893, 182
167	"	Mrs. Leslie	Feb. 20	W copy
167a	"	5a	Mar. 5	Y
168	"	1	Apr. 8	A; Hulbert, VIII:126
169	"	(Henry) 2	Apr. 8	Priv. owned
170	"	(father) 3	Apr. 8	T.O.P.A., 1893, 68
171	"	(parents) 3	Apr. 8	" " , 70
172	"	7	May 19	" " , 184
173	"	7	May 20	A; Hulbert, VIII:141
174	Ft. Van.	(H.F. Wisewell) 3	June 29	W; " :146; W.C.Q., II 4:26
175	"	1	June 30	A; " :149
175a	Waii.	5a	July 15	Y
176	"	7	Aug. 9	T.O.P.A., 1893, 184
177	"	7	Sept. 20	WSHS
178	"	5	Sept. 29	W; Hulbert, VIII:153
179	"	1	Oct. 26	A; " :154
179a	"	5	Oct. 29	Y
180	"	1	Nov. 1	A
180a	"	5	Nov. 16	Y
181	"	5	Nov. 20	Hulbert, VIII:158
181a	"	5	Nov. 20	Y
181b	"	5a	Nov. 25	Y
182	"	7	Nov. 27	WSHS

No.	Place of Writing	To Whom	Date	Present Location; Published in; Notes
183	Waii	7	Nov. 28	T.O.P.A., 1893, 187
183a	"	5	Dec. 3	Y
			—1846—	
183b	"	5a	Feb. 3	Y
183c	"	5	Feb. 3	Y
184	"	7	Feb. 6	Y
184a	"	5	Feb. 16	Y
185	"	5	Feb. 23	O copy
186	"	(Edward) 3	Apr. 2	O; T.O.P.A., 1893, 188
187	"	(Jane) 3	Apr. 2	O; " " , 191
188	"	7	Apr. 7	WSHS
189	"	(Mother) 3	Apr. 9	O; T.O.P.A., 1893, 71
190	"	(father) 3	Apr. 10	O; " " , 75
191	"	7	Apr. 13	A; Hulbert, VIII:168; in Perrin Whitman handwriting
192	"	(Harriet) 3	Apr. 13	O; T.O.P.A., 1893, 79
193			Apr. 16	Mother's Mag., XIV (1846), 279; O.H.Q., XXXIX (1938), 119
194	"	1	May 15	A; Hulbert, VIII:179
195	"	(Ed & Jane) 3	May 15	O; T.O.P.A., 1893, 194
195a	"	5	May 19	Y
195b	"	5	June 3	Y
195c	"	5	June 3	Y
195d	"	5	June 22	Y
195f	"	5	June 22	Y
196	"	7	July 17	O; T.O.P.A., 1893, 196
197	"	7	July 20	WSHS
198	"	Mrs. Osborn	Aug. 29	Huntington Library, San Marino, Calif.
199	"	Rev. A.F. Waller	Sept. 7	Hulbert, VIII:182
200	"	1	Sept. 8	A; " :183
201	"	5	Sept. 9	Y; " :187
202	"	(Bro. & Sis.) 3	Sept. 11	O; T.O.P.A., 1893, 87
202a	"	5	Sept. 11	Y
202b	"	5	Sept. 29	Y

No.	Place of Writing	To Whom	Date	Present Location; Published in; Notes
203	Waii	Mrs. Gilbert	Oct. 15	W
204	"	7	Oct. 19	O copy
205	"	Mrs. Spalding	Nov. 2	W; Hulbert, VIII:189
206	"	(Clarissa) 3	Nov. 3	T.O.P.A., 1893, 88
207	"	(mother) 3	Nov. 3	O copy
208	"	1	Nov. 3	A; Hulbert, VIII:193
209	"	(Rev. L.P. Judsen) 3	Nov. 5	A; " :197; with note by Narcissa
209a	"	5	Nov. 6	Y
209b	"	6	Nov. 6	Y
210	"	7	Dec. 7	Q; Hulbert, VIII:208
			—1847—	
211	"	Mrs. A.T. Smith	Feb. 8	W; " :212
211a	"	5	Mar. 30	Y
212	Ft. Van.	1	Apr. 1	A; " :215
213	Waii.	(Jane) 3	Apr. 16	O; T.O.P.A., 1893, 205
214	"	Mrs. Gilbert	May. 3	B
214a	"	5	May 17	Y
215	"	1	May 19	A; Hulbert, VIII:221
216	"	Spalding	May 20	W; " :225
217	"	(mother) 3	July 4	O; T.O.P.A., 1893, 208
217a	"	5	July 13	Y
217b	"	5a	July 15	Y
217c	"	5	July 26	Y
218	"	1	Aug. 3	A; Hulbert, VIII:226
219	Waskopum	1	Sept. 13	A; " :231
220	Waii.	(Jane) 3	Oct. 12	O; T.O.P.A., 1893, 216
221	"	U.S. Secy. War	Oct. 16	A; Hulbert, VIII:237; with note to Secy. Greene
222	"	1	Oct. 18	A; Hulbert, VIII:243

Appendix 2

Financial Reports of the American Board

I. *Initial Costs Involved in Explorations and Founding of the Mission*

1834 (135) Expenses of Rev. Samuel Parker, Rev. John Dunbar, and Samuel Allis, Jr., on an exploring tour to the Indians west of the State of Missouri. $471.01

1835 (121) Expenses of Rev. Samuel Parker and Dr. Marcus Whitman on an exploring tour to the Rockies 710.63

Services of Rev. S. Parker, including traveling expenses 510.79

1836 (121) Expenses of Rev. Samuel Parker on an exploring tour to Indian tribes in the Oregon Territory................ 250.00

Expenses Messrs. Whitman, Spalding & Gray.............. 3,743.04

1837 (132) Expenses of Rev. Samuel Parker and family 785.25

1838 (147) Oregon Mission, Drafts, etc. 605.87

Expenses in part of Mr. Parker's family. 50.00

Outfit and expenses of Messrs. Gray, Walker, Eells, and Smith, and their wives including funds for their traveling expenses to the Oregon Territory, and various purchases 3,559.68

Total $10,686.27

II. *Expenses Incurred in Maintaining the Oregon Mission, 1839–48 Inclusive*

1839 (159) Drafts, purchases, &c. 1,392.70
1840 (201) Drafts, purchases, &c. 4,886.14
1841 (203) Remittances, drafts, &c. 3,783.07
1842 (215) Drafts, &c. 259.18
1843 (193) Drafts, purchases, etc. 3,043.33
1844 (239) Drafts, purchases, &c. 3,568.38
1845 (213) Drafts, purchases, &c. 1,822.62
1846 (233) Drafts, purchases, &c. 2,285.20
1847 (203) Purchases, &c. 584.39
1848 (281) Drafts and purchases. 474.37

Total $22,099.38

III. *Costs Involved in Closing the Oregon Mission*

1849 (228) Drafts & purchases 3,605.17
1850 (203) Drafts & purchases 2,143.65
1851 (168) Drafts, &c. 298.82
Total $6,047.74

Grand Total $38,833.39

The above figures, giving the annual expenditures of the American Board for its Oregon Mission, have been taken from its *Annual Reports* for the fiscal years ending August 31. Pagination is given in parentheses. A summary of expenses incurred by Dr. Whitman for his station at Waiilatpu is given in Drury, *Marcus Whitman, M.D.*, p. 442. See also section, "A Financial Review," in Chapter Twenty-Four above. The above classification of the expenses under three categories is the author's.

Because of delays in the mails, costs listed for one year often include expenses of the previous year. The expenses incurred after the Whitman massacre of November 1847 include costs involved in moving the Spaldings, the Eells, and the Walker families to the Willamette Valley and helping them get settled.

Appendix 3

The Evolution of the Whitman-Saved-Oregon Story

The author wishes to draw a clear distinction between his interpretation of Whitman's contribution to the opening of Old Oregon to American settlement and the consequent influence that this had on the settlement of the boundary question with Great Britain, and the rejected Whitman-Saved-Oregon story which was so zealously promulgated by Spalding, Gray, Myron Eells, and others a century ago.

Some of the points of the Spalding version of the Whitman-Saved-Oregon story were true. Whitman did visit Washington in the early spring of 1843 where he had interviews with high government officials. He was active in promoting emigration to Old Oregon and was influential in leading the first great covered wagon train with about a thousand people across the Snake River desert and over the Blue Mountains in 1843. Whitman was active in trying to persuade the government to protect all emigrants on their way to Oregon and to extend its jurisdiction over that territory.

Spalding's theory was essentially false in that he made claims which historically were not true. For instance, he claimed that Whitman arrived in Washington in the spring of 1843 in time to intercede with President Tyler and Secretary of State Daniel Webster and to prevent them from signing a treaty with Great Britain which would have traded off United States rights in Old Oregon for a codfishery off the coasts of Newfoundland.[1] Thus Whitman saved Oregon!

Actually no such proposal was then being considered. It is possible that Spalding heard rumors that such might happen from Dr. White when he returned to Oregon in the fall of 1843 as a sub-Indian Agent. A number of apocryphal stories and legends about Whitman were spread abroad by Spalding, some of which became a part of the Whitman-Saved-Oregon story.

The Background of the Whitman-Saved-Oregon Story

The Whitman-Saved-Oregon story evolved slowly. There was no deliberate conspiracy on the part of Spalding and Gray to formulate it, and then join in foisting it upon a gullible public. Each was sincere in what he said or wrote, even though some of their statements were erroneous, biased, or distorted. Spalding was the chief offender.

As explained in Chapter Sixteen of this book, one of the main reasons why Whitman decided so suddenly to go East in the fall of 1842 was to persuade the American Board to rescind its disastrous order of February 1842 which called for the closing of the Waiilatpu and Lapwai stations and the dismissal of Spalding. Naturally Spalding hesitated to speak or write about the dissensions within the Oregon Mission in which he was a central figure and which resulted in his dismissal. Instead, Spalding concentrated on the political interests of Whitman. Gray was inclined to accept Spalding's statements without questioning their accuracy, sometimes adding his own prejudicial embellishments.[2]

An important factor in the evolution of this theory which must be kept in mind, was Spalding's bitter anti-Catholic feeling. This can be traced back to his early life in western rural New York State where he had had no direct contacts with Roman Catholics. Anti-Catholic prejudices were common in the communities where all members of the Oregon Mission had been born and reared. The Pope was commonly referred to as "the Man of Sin"; the adoration of the Virgin Mary was idolatry; and the mass, an abomination. When Roman Catholic missionaries entered Oregon and began to seek converts among the tribes where the Protestants were at work, the latter were resentful and alarmed. If Spalding had known that the Hudson's Bay Company was subsidizing the Catholic missionaries in the Willamette Valley, he would have shouted this news abroad as proof of his suspicions that the Catholics were conspiring with the Company to gain control of Old Oregon.

Even though Father J. B. A. Brouillet had risked his life when he warned Spalding of the massacre when the latter was approaching Waiilatpu on November 30, 1847, thus permitting him to escape, Spalding had no feeling of gratitude, but turned in bitter criticism on Brouillet. When Spalding learned that Brouillet had baptized some of the children of the Cayuses, when they were seriously ill with measles and about to die, he accused Brouillet of being in league with the murderers. To Spalding, who was evidently uninformed regarding Roman Catholic teachings on the importance of baptism for the salvation of souls, Brouillet's acts were incomprehensible.

Spalding became obsessed with the idea that the Catholic priests, in their desire to gain possession of the Whitman mission property and to drive the Protestant missionaries out of that part of the country, had incited the Cayuse Indians to perform their horrible deed. When Mrs. Spalding died on January 7, 1851, Spalding included the following in the inscription carved on her tombstone: "She always felt that the Jesuit missionaries were the leading cause of the massacre." [3] The most charitable explanation of this unreasonable and unchristian attitude of Spalding is that the terrible experiences through which he passed when trying to escape unsettled his mind.

THE RELIGIOUS QUARREL BREAKS INTO PRINT

With Spalding's consent, the Rev. J. S. Griffin obtained the use of the old mission press, which was at The Dalles at the time of the massacre, and between June 1848 and May 1849 published eight numbers of his *Oregon American and Evangelical Unionist*. Griffin was as fanatical in his anti-Catholic views as was Spalding. The latter wrote seven articles, which Griffin published, in which Spalding made serious accusations against the Catholics; for instance, the following taken from the June 21, 1848, issue: "It is said that the Catholics took part in the murders and in the distribution of the plundered goods... It is said that they actually placed the seal of their bloody approbation upon the bloody deed, by baptizing the children of the murderers."

The publication of Spalding's articles seems not to have aroused much public interest in what appeared to be nothing more than a religious quarrel. The one person who was moved to write a rebuttal was Father Brouillet; after reading several of Spalding's tirades, he wrote a reply in the fall of 1848. Father Brouillet collected a number of testimonials from Oregon residents to disprove many of Spalding's slanderous allegations.

In the introduction to his defense, Brouillet wrote: "But a certain gentleman, moved on by religious fanaticism, and ashamed of owing his life and that of his family and friends to some priests, began to insinuate false suspicions about the true causes of the disaster, proceeded, by degrees, to make more open accusations, and finally declared publicly that the bishop of Walla Walla and his clergy were the first cause and great movers of all the evil. That gentleman is the Rev. H. H. Spalding, whose life had been saved from the Indians by a priest, at the peril of his own." [4]

After writing his defense, Father Brouillet waited five years before he found an opportunity to have it published. It finally appeared in 1853 in several issues of the *New-York Freeman's Journal*, a Catholic publication, under the title: "Protestantism in Oregon. Account of the Murder of Dr. Whitman, and the ungrateful calumnies of H. H. Spalding, Protestant Missionary." On the whole, Father Brouillet wrote in a much more restrained manner than Spading, yet at times he was as biting in his criticisms of Spalding as Spalding had been of him. Some of the testimonials which Father Brouillet included in his articles are of doubtful value in resolving the contradictions in the controversy. Brouillet's articles appeared as a pamphlet in June 1853.

The publication of Spalding's articles in the Oregon American in 1848–49, and of Brouillet's articles in the *New-York Freeman's Journal* in 1853, marked the beginning of an acrimonious debate, which continued for decades in government publications, books, pamphlets, and innumerable articles in religious and secular papers and magazines.

The Browne Government Document Appears

Perhaps the controversy would have died with the appearance of Brouillet's pamphlet in 1858 had not a fortuitous incident suddenly given it national recognition. The Commissioner for Indian Affairs in the Department of the Interior sent J. Ross Browne in 1857 to investigate the causes of the Indian wars which plagued Washington and Oregon Territories after the Whitman massacre. Browne, in his report submitted in January 1858, referred to Spalding's claim that the massacre "was done with the knowledge and connivance of the Catholic missionaries." He attached a copy of Brouillet's pamphlet to his report, which contained a refutation of Spalding's charges.

"A perusal of the pamphlet," wrote Browne, "will abundantly show the bitterness of feeling existing between the different sects, and its evil effects upon the Indians. It will readily be seen that, as little dependence can be placed upon the statements by one side as by the other, and that, instead of christianizing the Indians, these different sects were engaged in quarrels among each other, thereby showing a very bad example to the races with whom they chose to reside." [5] How strange that a theological quarrel, which had originated more than three hundred years earlier in Europe, should have been transplanted to the Indian tribes of Oregon to rend them apart.

Browne's thirteen-page report might well have become just another forgotten government document had it not been published with Brouillet's fifty-two page pamphlet as *Executive Document, No. 38, House of Representatives, 35th Congress, 1st Session, 1858*.[6] As could be expected, neither Spalding nor any of his friends were readers of the *Congressional Record*; hence he was unaware of the publication of the Brouillet pamphlet for about ten years. The story of what then happened follows.

Spalding Prepares His Reply

Following the appearance of his articles dealing with the causes of the Whitman massacre which appeared in the *Oregon American* in 1848 and 1849, Spalding continued to speak and write against the Catholics as opportunities afforded. The first detailed account of his Whitman-Saved-Oregon story is to be found in a series of eleven "lectures" which he wrote for the San Francisco *Pacific* beginning with the May 23, 1865, issue. The *Pacific* was a New-School Presbyterian-Congregational weekly publication which served the churches of those denominations on the Pacific Slope; thus it was the best medium available for the dissemination of his views. A second series of Spalding articles, covering much of the same ground but giving some amplifications to the Whitman-Saved-Oregon story, appeared in the Walla Walla *Statesman* in February and April 1866, and a third series in the Albany, Oregon, *States Rights Democrat* between November 17, 1866, and January 18, 1868.

In these articles, Spalding turned history into propaganda. Much that he said was true. In some instances, he was guilty of giving only half-truths. For instance, he never referred to the difficulties within the Mission which resulted in the Board's disastrous order of February 1842. Through all of his writings ran his bitter anti-Catholic prejudices. He magnified Whitman's role on the national scene, making claims for him that Whitman never made for himself. These writings are far different from the diary he kept while living at Lapwai, which remains a reliable historical document.

Sometime during the early months of 1868, a copy of Browne's report of 1858, with Brouillet's article on "Protestantism in Oregon," came to Spalding's attention. His anger was immediately aroused, not only by what he considered to be the false and slanderous accusations of Brouillet against him and his former associates, but also by the fact that the inclusion of Brouillet's pamphlet in a government document implied an official endorsement of the views therein expressed. Spalding claimed that Browne was a Catholic and this was the reason why he included the Brouillet article. Calling upon the worst epithet in his vocabulary, Spalding stigmatized Browne as a "Jesuit" Actually Browne was a Protestant, although not an active church member.[7] In rebuttal, Browne claimed that the inclusion of the Brouillet pamphlet was not intentional. It had been done without his knowledge or consent.

Following his discovery of the Browne report, Spalding had a consuming desire to obtain a vindication by having his side of the controversy published in some official Congressional document. He began assembling his material. He turned first to his published lectures and took certain passages, especially those which embodied his Whitman-Saved-Oregon theory. He then turned to Brouillet's article and picked out a number of passages which he felt were false, misleading, or slanderous. These he took to such prominent citizens of the Willamette Valley as A. L. Lovejoy, Dr. Henry Saffarans, Alanson Hinman, H. A. G. Lee, William Geiger, Jr., George Abernethy, Robert Newell, and Joel Palmer (each of whom figures in the Whitman story), and asked for their endorsement of his views. This they gave.

Spalding then turned to several ecclesiastical bodies, representing the Presbyterian, Congregational, Baptist, Methodist, and Christian Churches of Oregon, and secured from each resolutions which denounced the Brouillet article and which extolled the work of the missionaries belonging to the Oregon Mission of the American Board, especially that of the martyred Whitmans. Most of the leading Protestant clergymen of the Willamette Valley signed one or more of these resolutions.

Thus armed with a hodge-podge but impressive collection of documents, Spalding sailed from Portland on October 27, 1870, for San Francisco. He then had to go by river steamer to Sacramento before he could take the train over the newly constructed transcontinental route for the East. As his train rolled across the plains of the Missouri River

Valley, no doubt Spalding remembered how he, his wife, Gray, and the Whitmans had made their way westward in 1836. He had lived to see the fulfillment of the prophecy he had made regarding the possibility of building a railroad over the Rockies to the Pacific Ocean. A. B. Smith had scoffed at the idea, calling it "visionary" and stating that: "a man... must be strongly beside himself to make such a remark." [8]

THE NEZ PERCE'S "LAMENT"

While passing through Chicago on his way East, Spalding called on the Rev. S. L. Humphrey, editor of the Chicago *Advance*, a religious publication. Humphrey in the December 1, 1870, issue of his paper published an account of his interview with Spalding under the caption, "An Evening with an Old Missionary." In one of Spalding's articles which appeared in the Walla Walla *Statesman* on February 16, 1866, he attributed an eloquent speech to one of the surviving Nez Perces, who went to St. Louis in the fall of 1831, given just before he and his companion were to leave in the spring of 1832 to return to their homeland. This speech has often been called "the Indian's lament." In this first version of the lament, the chief made reference to *"the Book of God."* Spalding claimed that he got the text of the speech from a man who was in an adjoining room when the chief spoke and had written down what he had heard.

Notice, now, the account as given to editor Humphrey: "...the Flatheads and Nez Perces had determined to send four of their number into 'the Rising Sun' for 'that *Book of Heaven*.' They had got word of the Bible and a Saviour in some way from the Iroquois. These four dusky wise men, one of them a chief, who has thus dimly 'seen His star in the east,' made their way to St. Louis." There they met General Clark, who, Spalding claimed, was a "romanist." [9] Humphrey's account continues: "How utterly he failed to meet their wants is revealed in the sad words with which they departed: 'I came to you'—and the survivor repeated the words years afterward to Mr. Spalding—'with one eye partly opened; I go back with both eyes closed and both arms broken. My people sent me to obtain that *Book of Heaven*. You took me where your women dance as we do not allow ours to dance, and the Book was not there. You took me where I saw men worship God with candles; and the Book was not there. I am now to return without it, and my people will die in darkness.'" [10]

This apocryphal speech reflected Spalding's puritanical views regarding dancing, the theater, and the use of candles in Catholic worship. No Oregon Indian could ever have made such a speech.

The final version of the lament appeared in print thirty-nine years after the words were reported to have been spoken! There is no evidence that Spalding ever met either of the two survivors, whose portraits were painted by George Catlin when they were passengers aboard a river steamer that ascended the Missouri River in the spring of 1832.[11] There is good evidence to indicate that neither of the survivors ever returned to their homeland but had died long before Spalding had settled at Lapwai.[12]

Spalding was so pleased with the account of his interview with Humphrey, which was published in the Chicago *Advance*, that he included it in the collection of documents which he intended to present to some Congressional committee for publication. This account of the visit of the four Nez Perces to St. Louis, with the apocryphal lament, was given wide publicity, especially in Protestant church circles. Spalding was more eloquent than accurate. He did what many do. He fictionalized history for propaganda purposes.

THE SPALDING GOVERNMENT DOCUMENT

After leaving Chicago, Spalding went to Prattsburg where he visited old friends and familiar scenes. He then went to New York City where he solicited the support of the Hon. William E. Dodge, who had once been a Vice President of the American Board, in his project to get his collection of documents published by the government. Dodge, perhaps more than any other person, was largely responsible for Spalding's success in Washington. After visiting Boston, Spalding went to Washington where he arrived on January 5, 1871. Armed with a letter of introduction from Dodge, Spalding met Senator H. W. Corbett of Oregon. Through the Senator's influence, Spalding was given a hearing before the Senate Committee on Indian Affairs on January 25.

Just before he was to appear, Spalding wrote a hasty note to Rachel, his second wife, which reveals his anxiety: "Dearest Wife, may God help your husband. In 5 minutes... appear before the Senate... my case... this infamous outrage is corrected." The original letter has been mutilated, possibly by mice, so that the complete text is not available, but enough remains to give the meaning.

On February 9, Spading wrote another note to his wife: "Glory to God. Bless His Holy Name. Victory complete. The Senate has just ordered by a unanimous vote my manifesto printed and committed to Committee on Indian Affairs."[13]

Spalding's collection of documents appeared in the *Congressional Record* and was then reprinted as an eighty-one page pamphlet under the title *Executive Document, No. 37, U.S. Senate, 41ˢᵗ Congress, 3d Session*. The first edition contained 1,500 copies. Spalding was jubilant. He felt that he had been completely vindicated. Brouillet had been answered. Spalding's account of Protestantism in Old Oregon, with his Whitman-Saved-Oregon story, had been given the stamp of Congressional approval. A second edition consisting of 2,500 copies appeared in January 1903. Spalding's *Senate Document* together with Brouillet's *House Document* are prime sources for the history of both Roman Catholic and Protestant missionary work in Old Oregon.

Appendix 3 Endnotes

1. Spalding, *Senate Document*, p. 22. Bourne, *Essays in Historical Criticism*, p. 82, quotes from a letter of Daniel Webster, August 23, 1842: "The only question of magnitude about which I did not negotiate with Lord Ashburton is the question respecting the fisheries."

2. Gray claimed that he never heard of the Board's order of February 1842 which called for his dismissal. See circular 8, reprint from *Daily and Weekly Astorian*, p. 5, no date, probably sometime during 1883–85. Circular in Coll. W. The same amazing denial was made by Gray in the Portland *Oregonian*, Feb. 1, 1885. Gray stated: "Of this object (i.e. the Board's order) I have no personal knowledge of its being talked about at the time." See also Marshall, *Acquisition of Oregon*, II:138, and ante, Chap. 16, fn. 8.

3. Drury, *Spalding*, p. 361.

4. Brouillet, *House Document*, p. 14.

5. Brouillet, *op. cit.*, p. 3.

6. A fine account of the history of this document by George N. Belknap appeared in *Papers of the Bibliographic Society of America*, Vol. 55, 4th Quarter, 1961, pp. 319 ff. Reprinted as a pamphlet.

7. Spalding, *Senate Document*, p. 64. On the same page, Spalding erroneously referred to Brouillet as being a Jesuit. Belknap, op. cit., p. 332, fn. 27.

8. Drury, *Spalding and Smith*, pp. 159 & 235.

9. Marshall, *Acquisition of Oregon*, II:17, claims that Clark was not a Roman Catholic, and that he was a Mason and was buried by that fraternity.

10. Spalding, *Senate Document*, p. 8. Italics are in the original. See also Chapter One, "Nez Perce Delegation to St. Louis." Also, *W.H.Q.*, II (1907):195 ff., for article by C. T. Johnson (pseudonym for T. C. Elliot), "The Evolution of a Lament."

11. Catlin's paintings of the two survivors are in the Smithsonian Institution, Washington, D.C. Reproduced as illustrations in Drury, *Spalding*, p. 83.

12. McBeth, *The Nez Perces Since Lewis and Clark*, p. 31, gives the Nez Perce tradition regarding the fate of the two survivors.

13. Original letters are in Coll. O.

Appendix 4

The Literature of the Whitman Controversy

An extensive literature has grown out of the Whitman-Saved-Oregon controversy. The October 1908 issue of the *Washington Historical Quarterly* carried an article, "A Contribution towards a Bibliography of Marcus Whitman" by Charles W. Smith, the late librarian of the University of Washington at Seattle. It took fifty-nine pages to carry the list of titles, with annotations, of books, pamphlets, magazine articles, and manuscripts bearing on the subject.

Following the publication of Spalding's *Senate Document* in 1872, Brouillet issued a rebuttal which appeared in the Portland *Catholic Sentinel* and in the St. Louis *Catholic World*, both in 1872. Again Brouillet accused Spalding of deliberate falsification.

Controversy was renewed in the 1880s, with a new generation of writers appearing on the scene, The Rev. Myron Eells, a son of Cushing Eells, published his *Indian Missions* in 1882, in which he endorsed the Whitman-Saved-Oregon story. Beginning with the December 1882 issue of the New York *Observer*, a series of articles by the Rev. William Barrows repeated some of the main points of the Whitman legend as told by Spalding. In his *Oregon, The Struggle for Possession*,[1] Barrows included much of the material which had appeared in his magazine articles. Barrows also wrote an article on Oregon for the 1884 edition of the *Encyclopedia Britannica*, where again he endorsed the Whitman story. By this time the Whitman-Saved-Oregon story was so widely accepted that it was included without question in a number of history textbooks for public schools. Later, Edward Bourne, one of the first critics of the legend, wrote: "Never were confiding scholars and a more confiding public so taken in... The propagation of the legend of Marcus Whitman after the publication of Barrows' *Oregon* is simply amazing."[2]

Among the first to cast doubt upon the authenticity of the Whitman legend was Mrs. Frances Fuller Victor who, together with the Hon. Elwood Evans, collaborated with H. H. Bancroft in the writing of his two-volume *History of Oregon*, published in San Francisco in 1886. Mrs. Victor had accepted the Whitman legend when she wrote her *River of the West*, which appeared in 1870. Soon afterwards she changed her mind. Elwood Evans also at first had believed the story and had contributed a testimonial to Spalding's *Senate Document*, but he too came to disbelieve the legend.

Recognizing the growing doubt about the Whitman-Saved-Oregon-Story, Myron Eells in 1883 published a pamphlet, *Marcus Whitman, M.D., Proofs of His Work in Saving Oregon to the United States and in Promoting the immigration of 1843*. Eells was more moderate than Spalding in his claims, but was able to set forth considerable evidence that Whitman did much to promote the Oregon emigration of that year. The publication of this pamphlet sparked a controversy which was carried on through the columns of the Portland *Oregonian* during the late fall of 1884 and the following winter. On one side were Mrs. Victor and Elwood Evans, and on the other, Myron Eells, W. H. Gray, and E. C. Ross. The articles of the last three men were reprinted in pamphlet form in Portland in 1885 under the title *The Whitman Controversy*.[3]

The decade beginning 1890 produced two biographies of Marcus Whitman, both written by ministers who were adherents of the Whitman legend. The first, *The Story of Marcus Whitman*, by the Rev. J. G. Craighead, appeared in 1895. In June of the same year, the Rev. O. W. Nixon published his *How Marcus Whitman Saved Oregon*. Both works are unscholarly, for both authors accepted without question all the main points of Spalding's Whitman-Saved-Oregon story.

In a letter dated March 8, 1898, Nixon explained to a friend: "In fact, it was with great difficulty I snatched the Mo. of April, 1895, to write the Book, & was too busy when it was issued to ever read a line of proof, or many errors of the earlier editions would have been corrected."[4] The book was written to be a campaign document to help raise funds for Whitman College.[5] It ran through five editions and became the most widely distributed and most popular book on Whitman of that generation—and yet it was written in only one month! Since Nixon's book got into so many public and church school libraries, it is still being quoted as authoritative by uncritical readers.

The publication of the Craighead and Nixon books inspired another flurry of articles in the *Oregonian* in which Myron Eells, then the foremost defender of the Whitman legend, again figured. The observances of the semicentennial of the Whitman massacre in the fall of 1897 served as another occasion to publicize the legend. A number of articles on various aspects of the Whitman story, many of which are of real historical value, appeared in the Whitman College Quarterly beginning in January 1897.

The peak of Whitman's reputation, based on Spalding's and Gray's Whitman-Saved-Oregon theory came in 1899 when his name was considered for inclusion in New York University's Hall of Fame. Edward Gaylord Bourne, Professor of History at Yale University, wrote: "Fifty-two years later [i.e., after the massacre], in the most careful appraisal of human achievement in America that has ever been made... Marcus Whitman received nineteen out of a possible ninety-eight votes to be ranked as one of the fifty greatest Americans." This score put Whitman ahead of such well-known national figures as John Charles Frémont and George Rogers Clark. Bourne added: "History will be sought in vain for a more extraordinary growth of fame after death."[6]

WHITMAN LEGEND DISCREDITED

The decade beginning in 1900 brought a sharp reaction to the Whitman-Saved-Oregon story. Two men, Prof. Bourne and William I. Marshall, Principal of a school in Chicago, independently reached the conclusion at about the same time that the story was based largely upon myth and legend and was without historical foundation.

Bourne and Marshall met at the meeting of the American Historical Association held in Detroit, December 27–29, 1900, when Bourne read his paper, "The Legend of Marcus Whitman." Although he had not studied the subject as long as Marshall, Bourne anticipated him in the publication of his findings. Bourne's paper appeared in the January 1901 issue of the *American Historical Review*, and, revised and enlarged, in his *Essays in Historical Criticism* in the same year. Bourne's paper was also included in a volume, *Essays in Criticism*, used extensively in historical research course in colleges and universities. Marshall, who had assembled a mass of detailed information, was unable to publish his findings for lack of funds before he died on October 30, 1906. His two-volume *Acquisition of Oregon*, appeared posthumously in Seattle in 1911.

Together, Bourne and Marshall demolished the Whitman legend although it took several decades before the conclusions of their researches became known and accepted by the general public. Bourne is more restrained than Marshall, who was, at times, vitriolic in his criticisms.

One result of the writings of these two was that Whitman's fame plummeted. Unfortunately the real achievements of Dr. Whitman suffered the fate of the legendary Whitman, and for years little new was written about him.

Among the last works to appear before Whitman's eclipse began were two new biographies. The first was William A. Mowry's *Marcus Whitman*, which appeared in 1901. Mowry, unaware of the researches done by Bourne and Marshall, accepted the legendary views of Whitman. His book was an improvement over Nixon's as he gave some important new material. Myron Eells, who had become acquainted with the findings of both Borne and Marshall, modified some of his earlier views and became more objective in his writings. His *Marcus Whitman* was published in 1909, two years after his death.

The celebration of the Whitman-Spalding centennial in 1936 awakened new interest in the Whitman story and inspired the publication of many books, magazine articles, pamphlets, etc.[7] By this time no one arose to defend the old Whitman-Saved-Oregon story although a few echoes of the old controversy were still heard. As has been stated in a preceding chapter, when the effort was made in 1948 to get the Washington State Legislature to appropriate money for the erection of a statue honoring Dr. Whitman in Statuary Hall of the Capitol in Washington, D.C., some opponents of the measure circulated the legislators claiming: "The Marcus Whitman legend is 90% fictitious. It is one of our historical fables..." This was true. Today no reputable scholar claims that the primary reason for Whitman's famous ride East was to prevent the government trading off Oregon for some fishing rights off the Newfoundland coast. Spalding's Whitman-Saved-Oregon story is completely discredited and rejected.

On the basis of new documented evidence, not available or known to earlier writers on Whitman, we are now able to reappraise objectively the real contributions made by Whitman towards the extension of United States jurisdiction over the Old Oregon territory.

APPENDIX 4 ENDNOTES

[1] This was one of the American Commonwealth series edited by Horace E. Scudder. Check index of this work for reference to Barrows, who was a boy in the home of Dr. Edward Hale, the dentist in St. Louis, in the spring of 1843 when he saw Dr. Whitman.

[2] Bourne, *Essays in Historical Criticism*, p. 41.

[3] A copy of this rare item is in the Library of Congress.

[4] Nixon to S. W. Pratt, Coll. Wn.

[5] *W.C.Q.*, I (1897):1:21.

[6] Bourne, *op. cit.*, p. 4.

[7] See Chapter Twenty-Four, "Whitman Literature."

APPENDIX 5

ACCOUNTS OF THE MASSACRE AND THE CAPTIVITY

The following list of eyewitness and contemporary accounts of the massacre and the subsequent captivity of the survivors does not include the testimony of the witnesses given at the trial of the five Cayuses accused of the murder of the Whitmans and others, a brief review of which appeared in the May 30, 1850, issue of the *Oregon Spectator*. It should be noted that most of the accounts listed below were written many years after the massacre had occurred. The recollections of those who were children at the time no doubt reflect much that was told to them during the years following the events described. The recollections of the two Manson boys did not come to the author's attention until June 1972. They knew the Indian language but were taken to Fort Walla Walla the day after the massacre began. Thus their knowledge of what happened was limited. Ten-year-old Eliza Spalding was the only one of the captives who understood and spoke Nez Perce.

EYEWITNESS ACCOUNTS BY ADULTS

1. Lorinda Bewley, deposition, December 12, 1848; Gray, *Oregon*, pp. 486-9, 501; Spalding, *Senate Document*, pp. 34-7.
2. Mr. and Mrs. W. D. Canfield gave an account of their experiences to Dr. E. F. Elinwood, who wrote two articles which appeared in the May and June 1886, issues of the (Presbyterian) *Foreign Missionary*. These articles were reprinted the same year as a pamphlet under the title: *Marcus Whitman and the Settlement of Oregon*.
3. Josiah Osborn wrote a letter on April 7, 1848, to "Dear Brother and Sister" which is the earliest known account of the massacre by a survivor. First published in the Oquawka, Illinois, *Spectator*, August 23, 1848; republished in Spalding, *Senate Document*, pp. 31-3; Warren, *Memoirs*, pp. 126-8; Hulbert, *O.P.*, VIII:257; and Walla Walla *Union*, August 12, 1936.
4. Mary Saunders, pamphlet, *The Whitman Massacre*, Oakland, Calif., 1916. Only known copy is in the Library of Congress. Typewritten copies are in Colls. B. & E.W.S.H.S.

5. Daniel Young, deposition, Jan. 20,1849; Gray, *Oregon*, pp. 474-9.
6. Elam Young, deposition, January 20, 1849; *ibid.*, pp. 482-5.
7. John Young. See "Life Sketches of J. Q. A. Young" written about 1880, and published in Fort Vancouver Historical Society, *Clark County History*, V (1964): pp. 24-32.

Eyewitness Accounts by those who were children at the time. Ages indicated in parentheses.

8. Oscar F. Canfield (9), Portland *Oregonian*, July 21, 1894; Lewiston *Tribune*, Jan. 1, 1908; *W.H.Q.*, VIII:250 ff.
9. Mary Marsh Cason (11), interview given R. J. Hendricks, Oregon *Statesman*, Nov. 6-10, 1936; Walla Walla *Union*, August 12, 1936; *Reminiscences of Pioneer Life in Washington*, "Saw Massacre from Window," I (1937), Olympia, Wash.
10. Helen Saunders Church (14), "The Massacre at Whitman Mission," *W.C.Q.*, II (1898): pp. 21-26.
11. Matilda Sager Delaney (8), pamphlet, *A Survivor's Recollections of the Whitman Massacre*, Spokane, Wash. (1920); Lockley, *Oregon Trail Blazers*, pp. 344-51.
12. Gertrude Hall Denny (10), *Oregon Native Son*, June 1899; Portland *Oregonian*, July 21, 1894.
13. Elizabeth Sager Helm (10), *W.C.Q.*, I (April 1897): pp. 17-28; Lockley, *op. cit.*, pp. 120 ff; *T.O.P.A.*, 1896, pp. 120 ff; letter dated Jan. 17, 1885, to Frederick Sager, Paradise City, Iowa, published in several newspapers including the Portland *Oregonian*, October 30, 1932, and the Ogden, Utah, *Examiner*, summer 1934; letter of March 3, 1913, to Dr. James Wightman, Yates County *Chronicle*, Yenn Yan, N.Y., March 18, 1914.
14. Nancy Osborn Jacobs (9), paper read at Walla Walla, May 29, 1912, printed in Waitsburg *Times*, Feb. 2, 1934, copy Coll. W; Lockley, *op. cit.*, pp. 351-63; interview in Pendleton, Oregon, *East Oregonian*, May 19, 1919.
15. Nathan Kimball, Jr. (12), "Recollections of the Whitman Massacre," T.O.P.A., 1903, pp. 189-95.
16. John D. (13) and Stephen Manson (11), statements made at Vancouver, B.C., July 29, 1884. Copy at Whitman Mission National Historic Site.

17. Susan Kimball Munson (6), short statement in Cannon, *Waiilatpu*, pp. 157-8.
18. Catherine Sager Pringle (13), Clarke, *Pioneer Days*, II: 528-44; *O.H.Q.*, XXXVII (1936):354-60, giving letter written Dec. 21, 1854; manuscript, "Account of Overland Journey to Oregon in 1844; Life at the Whitman Mission; the Whitman Massacre," Huntington Library, San Marino, California, and in many libraries of the Pacific Northwest.
19. Eliza Spalding Warren (10), *Ladies Home Journal*, Aug. 1913, pp. 14 ff, "The First White Woman Born in the West;" *Memoirs of the West*, pp. 22-32; Walla Walla Union, August 12, 1936.

SOME CONTEMPORARY ACCOUNTS.

20. Most Rev. A. M. A. Blanchet, Bishop of Walla Walla, journal in Archdiocesan Archives, Seattle.
21. Rev. J. B. A. Brouillet, letter to Colonel Cornelius Gilliam, Fort Walla Walla, March 2, 1848, in Brouillet, *House Document*, pp. 35 ff.
22. James Douglas from Fort Vancouver to S. N. Castle, Dec. 9, 1847, published in The Friend, Honolulu, March 1, 1848.
23. William McBean, Fort Nez Perces (i.e., Walla Walla), November 30, 1847, report to the "Board of Management of the H.B.C." in Victor, *Early Indian Wars of Oregon*, pp. 128 ff; Cannon, *Waiilatpu*, pp. 135-7; *Oregon Spectator*, Dec. 10, 1847.
24. H. H. Spalding to Bishop of Walla Walla from Clear Water, Dec. 10, 1847, Victor, *op. cit.*, pp. 112-3; to American Board from Fort Vancouver, Jan. 8, 1848, Coll. A., printed in Marshall, *Acquisition of Oregon*, II: 200 ff; letter to editor *Oregon Spectator* from Oregon City, February 8, 1848, reprinted in Marshall, op. cit., II: 228 ff; letter to parents of Narcissa Whitman from Oregon City, April 6, 1848, *T.O.P.A.*, 1898, pp. 93 ff; letter to Dudley Allen, Kinsman, Ohio, March 14, 1848, in Philadelphia *Observer*, October 28, 1848.

Note: A collection of clippings from periodicals listed above is in Coll. E.W.S.H.S.

Appendix 6

Letter from H. K. W. Perkins to Jane Prentiss

While gathering material for my *Marcus Whitman, M.D.*, which appeared in 1937, I found in the archives of Whitman College a copy of an unpublished letter written by the Rev. Henry Kirk White Perkins from Hallowell, Maine, on October 19, 1849, to Miss Jane Prentiss, West Almond, New York. A notation on the copy states: "Copied by M. Eells from Original." Myron Eells wrote on very thin paper; this makes his writing most difficult to read. Recognizing the importance of this letter, I included it as an appendix in my earlier book, and it is here reprinted. All words italicized were underlined in the copy that Eells had made.

Perkins was one of the most capable and conscientious of all members of the Methodist Mission in Oregon and, therefore, his comments must be taken seriously. A good indication of his character is to be found in the firm stand he took against certain members of his Mission, including A. F. Waller and Jason Lee, in the dispute over title to some valuable property at Oregon City. Perkins maintained that Dr. McLoughlin had prior claim and expressed shame over the actions of some of his brethren in taking the property under dispute. (See Perkins letters, Coll. W.S.H.S.)

Evidently Jane Prentiss had returned to her parental home from Illinois after hearing of the death of her sister and brother-in-law. Knowing that Narcissa had spent the winter of 1842–43 at Waskopum, where the Perkins and Brewer families were stationed, and learning that Mr. Perkins was in the East, Jane wrote to him asking for the causes of the massacre. Perkins was handicapped in his ability to make an accurate and balanced appraisal of the causes which moved the Indians to murder, as he had not met the Whitmans during the first several years they were in Oregon. Hence Perkins was unable to judge the importance of the work the Whitmans had done for the natives during these earlier years of their residence at Waiilatpu. Moreover, Perkins had never visited Waiilatpu after he became acquainted with Marcus and Narcissa and was not, therefore, able to base his judgments on first-hand observations.

Perkins first met Narcissa in the fall of 1842 after she was obliged to leave Waiilatpu following the departure of her husband for the East, and when she was received at Waskopum as a guest by the Methodist families living there. Narcissa was ill at that time and remained so throughout the following year. In June 1843, she went to Fort Vancouver where she remained for two months under the care of Dr. Forbes Barclay, the Company's physician. Then, after a brief visit with friends in the Willamette Valley, Narcissa returned to Waskopum to await her husband who arrived in October to take her back to Waiilatpu. Still sick and depressed in spirits, Narcissa dreaded returning to the loneliness and isolation of their mission station. [See, "Adapted to a Different Destiny," Chapter Seventeen; and "Narcissa, Sick and Discouraged," Chapter Twenty.] Perkins' penetrating analysis of Narcissa's attitude towards the natives was naturally colored by her physical and mental condition during the time he had contact with her. Therefore, allowances should be made for his rather severe judgments. He did not see her at work among the Cayuses during the first six years of her residence at Waiilatpu, nor did he meet her after she regained her health following her return to the mission station. It is true that, with an enlarged household, Narcissa was unable to do much, if anything, for the natives in the school or in other activities after her return.

The contacts that Perkins had with Dr. Whitman were also limited. The two first met in October 1838 when Marcus paused briefly at Waskopum on his way down the Columbia to Fort Vancouver for supplies. On several subsequent occasions, Whitman had opportunity to visit Waskopum. We have no evidence that Perkins ever visited Waiilatpu where he could have observed Whitman at work. Therefore Perkins was obliged to base his judgments regarding Whitman's adaptability as a missionary to the Indians on these brief meetings and on the observations of others.

On the whole, Perkins made an excellent appraisal of Whitman's characteristics. The main weakness of his appraisal is that he failed to indicate the full impact of the measles epidemic as a primary cause for the massacre. He glided over this factor. One can well ask: Would there have been a massacre, admitting all that Perkins had to say about the inadaptability of the Whitmans to their missionary responsibilities, if there had been no measles epidemic? In the author's opinion, the answer is "No." Perkins also fails to mention that the malcontents in the Cayuse tribe were relatively few; it is estimated that only fourteen took part in the massacre. Contemporary evidence shows that a majority within the tribe, including such chiefs as Stickus, Camaspelo, Young Chief, and Five Crows, refused to join with the conspirators. While it is true, as Perkins pointed out, that Whitman believed the Indians were a doomed race and that the white men would inherit the land, Perkins was mistaken in claiming that white settlers were taking land in the Walla Walla Valley before the massacre.

Actually, Whitman was spending more time with the natives than with the immigrants during those last five years at Waiilatpu. The passing of the immigrant wagon trains through the Cayuse country took about two months. The immigrants who found it necessary to winter at Waiilatpu left for the Willamette Valley as soon as possible in the spring. Whitman had no need to minister to any white people during the seed-time and harvest months of the year. He then was able to give all possible help to the natives. Today, because we have access to Whitman's letters which were not available to Perkins, we know more of what Whitman was doing for the Indians and what he planned to do than did Perkins. The coming of the annual immigrations meant no diminution of Whitman's efforts to help the natives.

Although the analysis of the characteristics of both of the Whitmans is penetrating and most helpful in an understanding of their situation, yet the main assumption that Perkins makes regarding their failures, as being a primary cause for the massacre, is inadequate. The reasons for the massacre, as has been stated, were many and complex. Perkins mentions some contributory factors but does not emphasize the major cause, which was the devastating effects of the measles epidemic.

A praiseworthy characteristic of the Perkins letter is his endeavor to give the Indians' side of the story. So far as the author is aware, this is the first time that this was attempted. The letter, minus a few unimportant eliminations, follows.

Dear Sister:

Yours of Aug. 29 was recd. in due time but owing to a press of business & absence in Boston of late, I have not had time to attend to your request concerning your dear sisters letters until today.

You write that Mrs. Whitman was a dear Sister of yours. She was a dear sister of ours also. The acquaintance we formed with her was very intimate. For several months during her husband's last visit to the U. States, she was a member of our family. The circumstances that induced her to spend so long a season with us, I presume you must be familiar with as she kept up a constant correspondence, I believe, with her friends in the United States. If so you will recollect that even then, her situation among the natives at Waiilatpu was far from being *safe*. The truth is, Miss Prentiss, your lamented sister was far from happy in the situation she had chosen to occupy.

She no doubt felt a strong desire for the salvation of the Indian race & perhaps it might have been said of her: "She hath done what she could," but if I may be allowed the liberty of expressing my opinion, I should say, unhesitatingly that both herself & husband were out of their proper sphere. They were not adapted to their work. They could not possibly interest & gain the affections of the natives. I knew for a long time before the tragedy that closed their final career that many of the natives around them looked upon them suspiciously. Though they *feared* the Doctor, they did not *love* him. They did not love your sister. They could appreciate neither the one nor the other.

The Doctor, I presume, you knew familiarly. And k*nowing him* as *I knew him* you would not need to be told that an Oregon Indian & he could never get along well together. It was "the last place," to use a familiar phrase, that he ought to have occupied. And first, I need hardly tell you, he cared for no man under heaven,—perfectly fearless & independent. Secondly, he could never stop to *parley*. It was always *yes* or *no*. In the 3d place, he had no sense of *etiquette* or personal dignity—manners, I mean. 4. And in the fourth place, *he was always at work*.

Now I need not tell you that he & an Indian would ever agree. How could they? What would such a man have in common with an Indian? How could they symbolize with each other? In connection with some other man, perhaps, Sister Whitman would have done better. Perhaps she would have been more familiar—

sympathizing—open hearted. That she felt a deep interest in the welfare of the natives, no one who was at all acquainted with her could doubt. But the affection was manifested under false views of Indian character. Her carriage towards them was always considered *haughty*. It was the common remark among them that Mrs. Whitman was "very proud."

Now I do not really suppose that this was the case or that she ever suspected that she conveyed such an impression. But so the natives always spoke of it. Sister Whitman partook a good deal of her husband's independent spirit. She doubtless supposed also that it was necessary to maintain considerable *reserve*.

What contributed still more, I presume, to increase the distance between her & the natives was her *ill health & increasing nervousness*. Her constitution was a good deal impaired, toward the close of her labors & she could not in reality bear much. Her hopes of success also, were very much weakened and melancholy musings occupied her more than at her first setting out in missionary life.

I wish I could tell you just how it was. And yet I cannot do it, without seeming somewhat severely to reflect upon the Doctor. Again, I am afraid that you will never get at the real truth in the case if I do not tell you. The published accounts of that melancholy catastrophe which cut short so many lives, are all one sided. They fail almost entirely to account for the proceedings of the natives. I will briefly state a few things which ought to be kept in view with the whole affair.

And first, Dr. Whitman in pursuing his missionary labors never so identified himself with the natives as to make their interests *paramount*. He looked upon them as an inferior race & doomed at no distant day to give place to a settlement of enterprising Americans. With an eye to this, he laid his plans & acted. His American feelings even while engaged in his missionary toils, were unfortunately suffered to predominate. Indeed it might almost be doubted whether he felt half the interest in the natives that he did in the *prospective* white population. He wanted to see the country settled. The beautiful valley of the Walla Walla, he wanted to see teeming with a busy, bustling white population. Where were scattered a few Indian huts, he wanted to see thrifty farm houses. Where stalked abroad a few broken-down Indian horses, cropping the rich grasses of the surrounding plain, he wanted to see grazing the cow, the ox, & the sheep of a happy Yankee community. With his eye bent on this, he was willing meantime to do what he could incidentally, for the poor, weak, feeble doomed Oregonians.

And now, Miss Prentiss, what would be the natural result? Why, what every sensible man must have seen. *Jealousy on the part of the natives*. And in meeting death in the way that he did, it might be said with more truth that he died a martyr to the progress of American civilization than to the cause of Missions.

Had Dr. Whitman given himself up wholly to the interests of the natives, with all his natural unfitness for the place he occupied, he no doubt would have been *safe*, safe as anywhere in Christendom.

(2) It has been said that the natives are dying very rapidly & that Dr. Whitman was suspected as the cause of their rapid decrease. No doubt this suspicion might operate to some extent but then why seek their vengeance on the poor unsuspecting white settlers? The fact was the natives identified the Doctor with the whites. While they were rapidly coming in year by year & occupying their rich lands, they looked upon the Doctor as at the head of the concern. They saw him entering no protest—making no remonstance, but rather aiding & abetting—planning & directing, & all the family of course including Mrs. W. concurring apparently in their displaceance [sic]. What would they do? They would do what they did do—"strike for their altars & their fires." They wanted their lands, their *homes*, the *graves of their fathers*, their *rich hunting grounds* & *horse ranges*. They did not look upon the man or men who would connive at the usurpation of all these as their real friends. They looked upon the Doctor & wife as not missionaries to them but to the Americans. With these brief statements of facts, I need not add another word explanatory. You see everything at a glance. The result would have hardly been otherwise than it was.

In your letter you remarked that I doubtless have recollections of her (Mrs. W.) which, if expressed, would greatly interest her acquaintance & friends. Yes, Miss Prentiss, I have recollections of her,—interesting recollections which I shall always cherish. But they are not recollections of her as a *missionary* but as a *woman*. Mrs. Whitman was not adapted to savage but *civilized* life. She would have done honor to her sex in a polished & exalted sphere, but never in the low drudgery of Indian toil. The natives esteemed her as proud, haughty, as *far above them*. No doubt she really seemed so. It was her *misfortune*, not her *fault*. She was adapted to a different destiny. She wanted something exalted—communion with *mind*. She longed for society, *refined society*. She was intellectually & by association fitted to do good only in such a sphere. She should have been differently situated. I think her stay with us, including her visit to the Willamette, the pleasantest portion of her Oregon life. She saw considerable company & really seemed to *enjoy it*. She had leisure also for reading & writing, which she also seemed always to enjoy. She loved company, society, excitement & ought always to have enjoyed it. The self-denial that took her away from it was suicidal. Perhaps, however, more good was accomplished by it than could have been accomplished by pursuing a different course. Certain it is that we needed such minds to keep us in love with civilized life, to remind us occasionally of *home*. As for myself, I could as easily have become an Indian as not. I completely sympathized with them in all their plans & feelings. I could gladly have made the wigwam my home for life if duty had called. But it was not so with Mrs. W. She had nothing apparently with them in common. She kept in her own original sphere to the last. She was not a *missionary* but a *woman*, an American highly gifted, polished American lady. And such she died.

I desire with you her death may be sanctified to the cause of God. I think it more likely to be when the truth in the case is really known. I sympathize with you. I sympathized with her. I would that with her it might have been otherwise. But so it was. May we ever be found in our lot & place that when the Master calls for us, we may be found waiting.

Yours truly,

H. K. Perkins

Appendix 7

Whitman's Proposed Bill for Oregon

The Records of the War Department, File No. 424052, National Archives, Washington, D.C., contain an undated letter of Dr. Whitman's together with his proposed bill for the protection of Oregon-bound emigrants. Both were evidently written shortly after his return to Waiilatpu in the fall of 1843 On the back of the letter is the notation which indicates date of receipt: "Marcus Whitman. Enc[losed] synopsis of a bill, with his views in reference to import[ance] of the Oregon Territory. June 22 `44."

Both the letter and the bill also contain a notation that each was copied by the Rev. J. G. Craighead on November 27, 1891. The first printing of these two documents appeared in the *Transactions of the Oregon Pioneer Association*, 1891 (but published in 1893). Craighead included a copy of the letter in his *The Story of Marcus Whitman*, 1895. Nixon in his *How Marcus Whitman Saved Oregon*, 1895, included both documents, as did Mowry in his *Marcus Whitman*, 1905. Each of these printings contain some minor inaccuracies. The following is my transcription. The proposed bill is in Mrs. Whitman's handwriting.

To the Hon. James M. Porter, Secretary at War

Sir: In compliance with the request you did me the honor to make last winter while at Washington,[1] I herewith transmit you the synopsis of a Bill which if it could be adopted, would, according to my experience and observation, prove highly conducive to the best interests of the United States generally; to Oregon where I have resided for more than seven years as a missionary; and to the Indian Tribes that inhabit the intermediate country.

The Government will doubtless [by] now for the first time be apprised, through you and by means of this communication, of the immense immigration of families to Oregon which has taken place this year. I have since our interview been instrumental in piloting across the route described in the accompanying Bill, and which is the only eligible wagon road, no less than [— —]² families consisting of one thousand persons of both sexes with their waggons, amounting in all to more than one hundred and twenty, 698 oxen and 973 loose cattle.

The emigrants are from different states but principally from Missouri, Arkansas, Illinois and New York. The majority of them are farmers, lured by the prospects of Government bounty in lands, by the reported fertility of the soil, and by the desire to be first among those who are planning our institutions on the Pacific coast. Among them also are artisans of every trade, comprising with farmers the very best material for a new Colony. As pioneers these people have undergone incredible hardships and having now safely passed the Blue Mountain range with their waggons and effects³ have established a durable road from Missouri to Oregon which will serve to mark permanently the route for larger numbers each succeding year; while they have practicably demonstrated that waggons drawn by horses or oxen can cross the Rocky Mountains to the Columbia River contrary to all the sinister assertions of those who pretended it to be impossible.

In their slow progress these persons have encountered, as in all former instances and as all succeding emigrants must if this or some similar Bill be not passed by Congress, the continual fear of Indian aggression, the actual loss through them of horses, cattle, and other property, and the great labour of transporting an adequate amount of provision for so long a journey. The Bill herewith proposed would in a great measure lessen these inconveniences by the establishment of Posts, which, while they possessed power to keep the Indians in check, thus doing away [with] the constant Military vigilance on the part of the traveler by day and night, would be able to furnish in transit with fresh supplies of provisions, diminishing the original burdens of the emigrants and finding thus a ready and profitable market for their produce—a market that would in my opinion more than suffice to defray all the current expenses of such Posts.

The present party are supposed to have expended no less than two thousand dollars at Laramie and Bridger Forts and as much more at Fort Hall and Fort Boisie, two of the Hudson Bay Companies Stations. These are at present the only shopping places in a journey of twenty two hundred miles and the only places where additional supplies can be obtained even at the enormous rates of charge called Mountain prices (i.e.) Fifty Dollars the hundred for flour and fifty dollars the hundred for coffee, the same for sugar & powder &c.

Many cases of sickness and some deaths took place among those who accomplished the journey this season owing in a great measure to the uninterrupted use of meat, salt and fresh, with flour which constituted the chief articles of food they are able to convey in their waggons, and this would be obviated by the vegetable productions which the Posts in contemplation could very profitably afford them. Those who rely upon hunting as an auxiliary support are at present unable to have their arms repaired when out of order; horses and oxen become tender footed and require to be shod on this long journey sometimes repeatedly, and the waggons repaired in a variety of ways. I mention these as valuable incidents to the proposed measure, as it will also be found to tend in many other incidental ways to benefit the migrating population of the United States choosing to take this direction and on these accounts as well as for the immediate use of the Posts themselves, they ought to be provided with the necessary shops and mechanicks which would at the same time exhibit the several branches of civilized art to the Indians.

The outlay in the first instance need be but trifling. Forts like those of the Hudson Bay Company, surrounded by walls enclosing all the buildings and constructed almost entirely of adoby or sundried bricks with stone foundations only, can be easily & cheaply erected. There are very eligible places for as many of them as the Government will find necessary at suitable distances, not further than one or two hundred miles apart at the main crossing of the principal streams that now form impediments to the journey and consequently well supplied with water, having alluvial bottomlands of a rich quality and generally well wooded.

If I might be allowed to suggest the best sites for said Posts, my personal knowledge and observation enable me to recommend—First, the main crossing of the Kansas River where a Ferry would be very convenient to the traveller and profitable to the station having it in charge; next, and about eighty miles distant, the crossing of Blue River where in times of unusual freshet, a Ferry would be in like manner usefull; next, and distant from one hundred to one hundred and fifty miles from the last mentioned, the Little Blue or Republican fork of the Kansas; next, and from sixty to one hundred miles distant from the last mentioned, the point of intersection of the Platt river; next, and from one hundred to one hundred and fifty miles distant from the last mentioned, the crossing of the South Fork of Platt river: next, and about one hundred and eighty or two hundred miles distant from the last mentioned, Horseshoe Creek which is about forty miles west of Laramie's Fork in the Black hills. Here is a fine creek for Mills & irrigation, good land for cultivation; fine pasturage, Timber & Stone for building. Other locations may be had along the Platt & Sweetwater, on the Green River or Black's or Ham's Fork on the Bear River near the great Soda Springs, near Fort Hall & at suitable places down to the Columbia. These localities are all of the best description, so situated as to hold a ready intercourse with the Indians in their passage to and from the ordinary Buffalo hunting grounds and in themselves so well situated in all other respects as to be desirable to private enterprise if the usual advantage of trade existed. Any of the farms above indicated would be deemed extremly valuable in the States.

The Government cannot long overlook the importance of superintending the Savages that endanger this line of travel and that are not yet in treaty with it. Some of these are allready well known to be led by desperate white men and Mongrels who form banditti in the most difficult passes and are at all times ready to cut off some lagging emigrant in the rear of the party or some adventurous one who may proceed a few miles in advance, or at night to make a descent upon the sleeping camp and carry away or kill horses and cattle. This is the case even now in the commencement of our western emigration and when it comes to be more generally known that large quantities of valuable property and considerable sums of money are yearly carried over this desolate region, it is to be feared that an organized Banditti will be instituted.

The Posts in contemplation would effectually counteract this. For that purpose they need not nor ought not to be military establishments. The Trading posts in this country have never been of such a character and yet with very few men in them have for years kept the surrounding Indians in the most pacifick disposition so that the traveler feels secure from molestation upon approach(ing) Fort Laramie, Bridger's Fort, Fort Hall, &c &c. The same can be obtained without any considerable expenditure by the Government while by investing the officers in charge with competent authority, all evil disposed white men, refugees from justice or discharged vagabonds from the trading Posts might be easily removed from among the Indians and sent to the appropriate States for Trial.

The Hudson Bay Company's system of rewards among the savages would soon enable the Posts to root out these desparadoes. A direct and friendly intercourse with all the Tribes even to the Pacific might be thus maintained; the Government would become more intimately acquainted with them and they with the Government, and instead of sending to the State Courts a manifestly guilty Indian to be arraigned before a distant tribunal (and) acquitted for the want of testimony by the technicalities of Lawyers and of Laws unknown to them and sent back into this wilderness loaded with presents as an inducement to further crime, the Posts should be enabled to execute summary justice as if the criminal had been already condemned by his Tribe because the Tribe will be sure to deliver up none but the party whom they know to be guilty. They will in that way receive the trial of their peers and secure within themselves to all intents and purposes if not tecnically the trial by jury, yet the spirit of that trial. There are many powers which ought to reside in some person on this extended route for the convenience and even necessity of the publick.

In this the emigrants and the people of Oregon are no more interested that the resident inhabitants of the States. At present no person is authorized to administer an oath or legally attest a fact from the western line of Missouri to the Pacific. The emigrant cannot dispose of his property, although an opportunity ever so advantageous to him should occur after he passes the western border of Missouri. No one can here make legal demand and protest of a promissory note or Bill of Exchange. No one can secure the valuable testimony of a Mountaineer or of an emigrating witness after he has entered this at present lawless country. Causes do exist and will continually arise in which the private rights of citizens are, and will be, seriously prejudiced by such an utter absence of legal authority. A contraband trade from Mexico, the introduction from that country of liquors to be sold among the Indians west of the Kansas river is already carried on with the mountain trappers and very soon the teas, silks, nankins,[4] spices, camphor and opium of the East Indies will find their way duty free through Oregon across the mountains and into the States unless custom house Officers along this line find an interest in intercepting them.

Your familiarity with the Government policy, duties and interest render it unnecessary for me to more than hint at the several objects intended by the enclosed Bill and any enlargement to its adoption would be quite superfluous, if not impertinent. The very existence of such a system as the one above recommended suggest the ability of Post Office and Mail arrangements which it is the wish of all who now live in Oregon to have granted to them; and I need only add that contracts for this purpose will be readily taken at reasonable rates for transporting the mail across from Missouri to the mouth of the Columbia in forty days with fresh horses at each of the contemplated Posts. The ruling policy proposed regards the Indians as the police of the country, who are to be relied upon to keep the peace, not only for themselves but to repel lawless white men and prevent Banditti, under the salutary guidance of the Superintendants of the several Posts, aided by a well directed system of bounty to induce the punishment of crime. It will be only after a failure of these means to procure the delivery or punishment of violent, lawless and savage acts of aggression that a band or Tribe should be regarded as conspirators against the peace, or punished accordingly by force of Arms.

Hoping that these suggestions may meet your approbation and conduce to the future interests of our growing Colony, I have the honor to be, Hon. Sir, Your Obt. Servant, Marcus Whitman.

THE PROPOSED BILL

Title of the proposed Act

A Bill to promote safe intercourse with the Territory of Oregon; to suppress violent acts of aggression on the part of certain Indian Tribes west of the Indian Territory Necho [as the Indian Country was sometimes called]; better protect the revenue, for the transportation of mail and for other purposes.

Synopsis of the Act.

Section 1   Be it enacted by the Senate and House of Representatives of the United States of America in Congress assembled that from and after the passage of this act, there shall be established at suitable distances and in convenient and proper places to be selected by the President a chain of agricultural Posts or Farming Stations extending at intervals from the present most usual crossing of the Kansas river west of the western boundary of the State of Missouri, thence ascending the Platte river on its southern border, thence through the valley of the Sweetwater river to Fort Hall, and thence to the settlements of the Willamette in the Territory of Oregon. Which said Posts shall have for their object to set examples of civilized industry to the several Indian Tribes; to keep them in proper subjection to the laws of the United States; to suppress violent and lawless acts along the said line of frontier; to facilitate the passage of Troops and munitions of war and out of the said Territory of Oregon; and the transportation of the mail as here after provided.

Sec. 2   And be it further enacted that there shall reside at each of the said Posts one Superintendent having charge thereof with full power to carry into effect the provisions of this act, subject always to such instructions as the President may impose. One Deputy Superintendent to act in like manner in case of the death, removal or absence of the Superintendent and such other artificers and labourers not exceeding twenty in number as the said superintendent may deem necessary for the conduct and safety of the said Post, all of whom shall be subject to his appointment and liable to his removal.

Sec. 3   And be it further enacted that it shall be the duty of the President to cause to be erected at each of the said Posts suitable buildings for the purpose herein contemplated, to wit; One main Dwelling House, one Store House, one Black Smiths and gun smiths Shop and one Carpenters Shop with such and so many other buildings for storing the products and supplies of the said Post as he may from time to time deem expedient. To supply the same with all necessary implements of mechanical art and agricultural labor incident thereto and with all such other articles as he may judge requisite and proper for the safety, defence, and comfort thereof.

To cause the said Post in his discretion to be visited by detachments of the Troops stationed on the western frontier; to suppress through the said Post the sale of munitions of war to the Indian Tribes in case of hostilities and annually to lay before Congress at its general session full returns verified by the oaths of the said several superintendents, of the several acts by them performed and of the condition of the said Posts with the income & expenditures growing out of the same respectively.

Sec. 4   And be it further enacted that the said superintendents shall be appointed by the Presidents by and with the advice and consent of the Senate for the term of four years with a salary of two thousand dollars[5] payable out of any monies in the treasury not otherwise appropriated, that they shall respectively take an oath before the district judge of the United States for the western district of Missouri, faithfully to discharge the duties imposed on them in and by the provisions of this act and give a bond to the President of the United States and to his successors in office and assigns with sufficient security to be approved by the said judge in at least the penalty of twenty five thousand dollars to indemnify the President, his successor or assigns for any unlawful acts by them performed, or injuries committed by virtue of theft offices, which said bonds may be at any time assigned for prosecution against the said respective superintendents and theft sureties upon application to the said judge at the instance of the United States District Attorney or of any private party aggrieved.

Sec. 5   And be it further enacted that it shall be the duty of the said Superintendents to cause the soil adjacent to the said posts in extent not exceeding six hundred and forty acres to [be] cultivated in a farmerlike manner and to produce thereon such articles of culture as in their judgment shall be deemed the most profitable and available for the maintenance of said posts, for the supply of troops and other government agents which may from time to time resort thereto, and to render the products aforesaid adequate to defraying all the expenses of labor in and about the said posts, and the salary of the said deputy superintendent without resort to the treasury of the United States, remitting to the Secretary of the Treasury yearly a sworn statement of the same with the surplus monies if any there shall be.

Sec. 6   And be it further enacted that the said several Superintendents of posts shall, ex officio, be superintendents of Indian affairs west of the Indian Territory Necho, subordinate to and under the full control and supervision of the Commissioner General of Indian affairs at Washington. That they shall by virtue of their offices be conservators of the peace with full powers to the extent hereinafter prescribed in all cases of crimes and misdemeanors, whether committed by citizens of the United States or by Indians within the frontier line aforesaid. That they shall have power to administer oaths to be valid in the several courts of the U. States; to perpetuate testimony to be used in the said courts; to take acknowledgement of deeds and other specialties in writing; to take the probate of wills and Testaments executed upon the said frontier and of which the testators shall have died in transit between the state of Missouri and the Territory of Oregon; to do and certify all notarial acts, and to perform the ceremony of marriage with as legal effect as if the said several acts above enumerated had been performed by the magistrates of any of the States having power to perform the same.

That they shall have power to arrest and remove from the line aforesaid all disorderly white persons and all persons inciting the Indians to hostilities and to surrender up all fugitives from justice upon the requisition of the Governor of any of the states, that they shall have power to demand of the several tribes within the said frontier line the surrender of any Indian or Indians committing acts in contravention of the laws of the United States, and in case of such surrender, to inflict punishment thereon according to the tenor and effect of the said laws without further trial, presuming such offending Indian or Indians to have received the trial and condemnation of the tribe to which he or they may belong; to intercept and cease [seize] all articles of contraband trade whether introduced into their jurisdiction in violation of the acts imposing duties on imports or of the acts to regulate trade and intercourse with the several Indian Tribes; to transmit the same to the Marshal of the western district of Missouri together with the proofs necessary for the confiscation thereof and in every such case the superintendent shall be entitled to and receive one half the sale value of the said confiscated articles and the other half be disposed of as in like cases arising under the existing Revenue laws.

Sec. 7   And be it further enacted that the several superintendents shall have and keep at their respective Posts, seals of office for the legal authentication of theft public acts herein enumerated, and that the said seals shall have as a device, the spread Eagle with the words "U.S. Superintendency of the Frontier" engraved thereon.

Sec. 8   And be it further enacted that the said superintendents shall be entitled in addition to the salary herein before granted to the following prerequisites and fees of office, to wit: For the acknowledgement of all deeds and other written specialties, the sum of one dollar; for the administration of all oaths, twenty five cents; for the authentication of all copies of written instruments, one dollar; for the perpetuation of all testimony to be used in the United States courts, by the folio, fifty cents; for the probate of all wills and Testaments by the folio, fifty cents; for all other writing done by the folio, fifty cents; for solemnizing marriages, two dollars, including the certificate to be given to the parties; for the surrender of fugitives from justice, in addition to the necessary costs and expenses of arrest and detention which shall be verified to the demanding Governor by the affidavit of the Superintendent, ten dollars.

Sec. 9   And be it further enacted, that the said Superintendents shall by virtue of their offices be Post Masters at the several stations for which they are appointed and as such shall be required to facilitate the transportation of the mail in its transit to and from the Territory of Oregon and the nearest Postoffice within the State of Missouri, subject to all the regulations of the Post Office Department and with all the immunities and privileges of the Post masters in the several States except that no additional compensation shall be allowed them for such services and it is hereby made the duty of the Postmaster General to cause proposals to be issued for the transportation of the mail along the line of said Posts to and from the said Territory within six months after the passage of this act.

Sec. 10   And be it further enacted that the sum of (—) thousand dollars be and the same is hereby appropriated out of any monies in the treasury not otherwise appropriated, for the purposes of carrying into effect the several provisions of this act.

APPENDIX 7 ENDNOTES

[1] Here is clear evidence that Whitman was in Washington, D.C., early in 1843.

[2] Two words have been scratched out in the original document. Craighead wrote in "three hundred" which figure was accepted by Nixon and Mowry.

[3] This indicates that Whitman was writing some time about the middle of October 1843.

[4] Nankeen was a buff-colored Chinese cotton fabric.

[5] Mowry in his transcription substituted "hundred" for "thousand" evidently thinking that Whitman could not possibly have meant so large a salary to be allowed the Superintendents.

BIBLIOGRAPHY

BIBLIOGRAPHY

The following list of books consulted in the preparation of this work does not include items listed in "Accounts of the Massacre and the Captivity," Appendix 5, or of sources consulted only once or twice when bibliographic data are given in endnotes. See listing of frequently quoted periodicals under "Abbreviations." Periodicals quoted only once or twice will be mentioned only in endnotes. See also references to manuscript sources under "Acknowledgments."

Allen, Miss A. J. *Ten Years in Oregon; Travels and Adventures of Doctor E. White and Lady West of the Rocky Mountains.* Ithaca, N.Y., 1848.

Bagley, C. B. *Early Catholic Missions in Oregon.* Seattle, 1932. (Contains Brouillet's pamphlet of 1848).

Bancroft, H. H. *History of Oregon*, 2 vols. San Francisco, 1886–1888.

Barrows, William. *Oregon.* Boston, 1884.

Bourne, E. H. *Essays in Historical Criticism.* New York, 1901.

Brosnan, Cornelius J. *Jason Lee, Prophet of the New Oregon.* New York, 1932.

Brouillet, J. B. A. *Authentic Account of the Murder of Dr. Whitman.* Oregon, 1869, included in Executive Document, No. 38, House of Representatives, 35th Congress, 1st Session. 1858. (Cited in endnotes as *House Document.*)

Burnett, Peter. *Recollections of an Old Pioneer.* New York, 1880.

Cannon, Miles. *Waiilatpu.* Boise, 1915. (Reprinted by Ye Galleon Press, Fairfield, Washington, 1969.)

Clarke, S. A. *Pioneer Days of Oregon History*, 2 vols. Portland, 1905.

Delaney, Matilda Sager. A *Survivor's Recollections of the Whitman Massacre.* Spokane, Washington, 1920.

De Smet, Pierre Jean. *Letters and Sketches.* Philadelphia, 1843.

Drury, Clifford M. *Henry Harmon Spalding, Pioneer of Old Oregon.* Caldwell, Idaho, 1936.

———. *Marcus Whitman, M.D., Pioneer and Martyr.* Caldwell, 1937.

———. *Elkanah and Mary Walker, Pioneers Among the Spokanes.* Caldwell, 1940.

———. *A Tepee in His Front Yard.* Portland, 1949.

———. *Diaries and Letters of Spalding and Smith Relating to the Nez Perce Mission, 1838–1842.* Glendale, California, 1958.

———. *First White Women Over the Rockies,* 3 vols. Glendale, 1963–1966.

Eells, Myron. *Marcus Whitman, Proofs of His work in Saving Oregon,* (Pamphlet). Portland, 1883.

———. *Marcus Whitman, Pathfinder and Patriot.* Seattle, 1909.

Gray, William H. *History of Oregon.* Portland, 1870.

Hafen, LeRoy R. *The Mountain Men and the Fur Trade of the Far West,* 10 vols. Glendale, California, 1965–1972.

Hines, Gustavus. *Wild Life in Oregon.* New York, n.d. Also published as *A Voyage Round the World with a History of the Oregon Mission,* Buffalo, 1850.

Hulbert, A. B., and Dorothy P. *Overland to the Pacific,* 8 vols. Denver, 1932–1941. Vols. VI-VIII are subtitled *Marcus Whitman, Crusader.* (Cited in endnotes as Hulbert, O.P.)

Johansen, Dorothy O., ed. *Robert Newell's Memoranda.* Portland, 1959.

Josephy, Alvin M., Jr. *The Nez Perce Indians and the Opening of the Northwest.* New Haven, 1965.

Kane, Paul. *Wanderings of an Artist* (1859). Toronto, 1925.

Lee, Daniel, and J. H. Frost. *Ten Years in Oregon.* New York, 1844.

Lockley, Fred. *Oregon Trail Blazers.* New York, 1929.

Marshall, W. I. *Acquisition of Oregon,* 2 vols. Seattle, 1911.

McBeth, Kate C. *The Nez Perces since Lewis and Clark.* New York, 1908.

McLoughlin, John. *The Letters of, from Fort Vancouver to the Governor and Committee* [of the Hudson's Bay Company], Second Series, 1839–1844. Edited by E. E. Rich. Champlain Society, Toronto, 1943.

Merk, Frederick, ed. *Fur Trade and Empire: George Simpson's Journal.* Cambridge, 1931.

Minutes of the Synod of Washington, (Presbyterian). Seattle, 1906. (Includes the Minutes of the First Presbyterian Church of Oregon.)

Mowry, William A. *Marcus Whitman.* New York, 1901.

Nixon, Oliver W. *How Marcus Whitman Saved Oregon.* Chicago, 1896.

Parker, Samuel. *Journal of an Exploring Tour Beyond the Rocky Mountains.* Ithaca, N.Y., 1838. (Subsequent editions appeared in 1840, 1842, 1844, and 1846, with varying pagination. That used in this work is from the 1846 edition.)

Richardson, Marvin M. *The Whitman Mission*. Walla Walla, Washington, 1940.

Saunders, Mrs. Mary. *The Whitman Massacre, A True Story by a Survivor.* Oakland, California, 1916. (The only known copy is in the Library of Congress.)

Simpson, George. *An Overland Journey Round the World.* Philadelphia, 1847.

Spalding, Henry H. *Executive Document, No. 37, U.S. Senate, 41 Congress, 3rd Session.* 1871. (Cited in endnotes as Senate Document.)

Thompson, Erwin N. *Shallow Grave at Waiilatpu: The Sagers' West.* Portland, 1969.

Victor, Frances Fuller. *The Early Indian Wars of Oregon.* Salem, Oregon, 1894.

INDEX TO THE TWO VOLUMES

Index to the Two Volumes

Numbers followed by an asterisk (*) indicate important sections of the text which bear on the listed subjects. In addition to commonly-used abbreviations, the following are also used: ABCFM — American Board of Commissioners for Foreign Missions; Cong. — Congregational; Meth. — Methodist; Presby. — Presbyterian or Presbytery; R.C. — Roman Catholic; Ft. Van. — Fort Vancouver; Ft. W.W. — Fort Walla Walla; HBC – Hudson's Bay Company; Waii. – Waiilatpu; Tsh. – Tshimakian; Will. Vall. – Willamette Valley. Mrs. Marcus Whitman is referred to as Narcissa, and Mrs. Henry Spalding as Eliza,

Abernethy, Gov. George: i, 326; ii, 16; entertains Narcissa, 24; 105; learns of massacre, 301 ff.; welcomes former captives, 331 ff.; 350

Adams, Thomas (Indian): i, 315, 322, 326

Adobe buildings: i, 250, 293*, 362

Agriculture at Waii: i, 256*, 264, 275*, 362, 452, 458*, 509; Whites impressions, ii, 21, 136*; fall 1846, 181 ff.; tools, 376

Ais, John (Nez Perce): i, 137, 141, 153, 165, 183, 206, 213, 258

Alcom, Rowena Lung: i, 431n

Allen, Mrs. Orville R: i, 161

Alphabet, Nez Perce: i, 389-90

Alpowa (Timothy's camp): i, 290

American Bible Society: i, 4, 6; ii, 173n

ABCFM: i, xiii, 5 ff., 25, 28, 54, 77, 78, 87 ff., 89, 103, 112, 144 ff.; Hawaiian mission, 232; Oregon mission, 241*, 258, 276; in debt, 316, 337, 346; missionaries apprehensive, 469; drastic order, 499*; end of Oregon Mission, ii, 343*; basic weakness, 376; correspondence files, 416; financial reports, 373*, 429*; see also Greene, David; Prudential Committee.

American Colonization Society: i, 6

American Colony, Will. Vall: i, 316, 320, 361, 481; population, 484; 528; see also Oregon colonization

American Fur Co: i, 30, 77, 85, 113, 119, 128 ff., 176, 184 ff., 192, 209, 346, 349, 405, 424; last caravan, 441

American Heritage: i, 158

American Historical Review: ii, 443

American Home Miss. Soc: i, 38n; 33

American Philosophical Soc: i, xv

Ames, Edward R: ii, 49; interviews Whitman, 76

Amity (N.Y.): i, 33, 77, 86, 100, 104, 139

Ammunition: i, 444; ii, 381; see also guns

Amon Carter Museum: ii, 221n

Angelica (N.Y.): i, 139, 149 ff., 160
Anniversaries: ii, 382*, of massacre, 385 ff.; arrival in Ore., 386*
Animal husbandry: beginnings, i, 279; see also cattle, hogs, horses, sheep
Anti-R.C. sentiment: i, 174, 361; Spalding's, ii, 286, 432 ff.
Apashwahaikt or Looking Glass: see Meoway
Applegate, Jesse: ii, 78n; praises Whitman, 179, 336
Applegate, Lindsay: ii, 41 ff., 179
Applegate cut-off: ii, 179
Apple trees: see trees
Aps (Cayuse Indian): i, 532; ii, 1
Archaeological findings at Waii: i, 253, 305n, 318, 364; ii, 339
Arkansas River: ii, 36 ff.
Arsenic: ii, 235; see also poison
Artists: Mrs. Orville R. Allen, i, 161; Paul Kane, ii, 192*, 194*; Drury Haight, 196; John Mix Stanley, 197*
Ash Hollow (Nebr.): i, 342, 356; claim on Govt, ii, 55
Ashburton-Webster Treaty: i, 515, 524; ii, 40, 45, 95; see also Webster
Ashfteld (Mass.): i, 7
Astor, John Jacob: i, 128, 310
Astoria (Ore.): i, 12, 310; see also Ft. George
Athabasca Pass (Canadian): i, 241
Atkinson, Rev. George H: i, 207, 536n

Babcock, Dr. Ira: ii, 105
Baker Bishop Osmon C: i, 18
Balloon line to Oregon: i, 411
Bancroft, H.H: i, 308, 313, 325, 483, 484, 536n; ii, 36;
appraisal of McBean, 275
Bancroft Library: i, xiii; ii, 416
Bangs, Dr. Nathan: i, 323-4
Bannock Indians: i, 129
Baptisms: i, 13; by R.C., 288, 291, 340, 509; few Protestants, 408; theology of, 408; 469; ii, 116, 139; by Brouil-let, 294 ff.; criticized by Spalding, 279; of condemned men, 371 ff.; hundreds by Spalding, 396; Indian couples named after missionaries, ii, 398
Barclay, Dr. Forbes: i, 460; ii, 23 ff.; cares for Narcissa, 105; painting, 333n
Barclay, Wade C: i, 36
Barley: i, 226
Barnes, Rev. Albert: sermons, ii, 183
Barnett, Marcus Whitman: ii, 385
Barrows, Rev. Wm: meets Whitman in St. Louis, ii, 39 ff.; 441
Bath Presby: i, 157, 341
Beardsley, Rev. Wm: i, 529
Beardy, Cayuse Chief: ii, 263 ff.; ill, 306; helps captives. 323
Beaver, Rev. Herbert: i, 225, 227; disgruntled, 228; Narcissa's comments, 247, 376
Beaver trade: i, 127, 129
Bedding: in Whitman home, ii, 380; see also feather beds
Beecher, Rev. Lyman: i, 156, 173, 176, 345; ii, 43
Beef: first butchered at Wait., i, 502; price, ii, 152; 246
Beers, Alanson: i, 395n
Belknap, George M: i, 476n; ii, 440n
Bellevue (Nebr.): i, 117, 120, 122-3, 138, 185 ff.
Belmont (N.Y.): i, 32

Benevolent giving: methods, **i**, 365 ff.
Bent, George: **ii**, 37
Bent's Fort: **ii**, 36 ff.
Benton, Sen. Thomas H: **ii**, 73, 350
Berens, Joseph Jr: **i**, 15
Berries, wild: **ii**, 159, 162
Bewley, Crockett: **ii**, 218-9, 241, 249, 266; massacre victim, 287 ff.; 334
Bewley, Esther Lorinda: **ii**, 218-9; sick, 250; 256, 261 ff.; raped, 307*; her testimony, 309; 319; rescued, 324; witness, 366, 447
Bewley, John W: and wife, **ii**, 218-9
Bible names for natives: **i**, 265; **ii**, 396
Bibles: distribution at Rendezvous, **i**, 206 ff.; gift to Whitman from De Smet, 527; Whitman's family, **ii**, 350 ff.
Big Belly: *see* Camaspelo
Big Head, Spokane Chief: *see* Cornelius
Big Ignace, Flathead Chief: **i**, 256; killed at Ash Hollow, 342
Bill, Oregon: Whitman's, **ii**, 46; 92; Whitman's Memorial. 210*; 245; 459*
Billington, Ray: **i**, 24, 197n
Bingham, Rev. Hiram: **i**, 197n, 234n, 232, 281
Birnie, James: **ii**, 25
Bitter Root River Valley: **i**, 425
Blackfeet Indians: **i**, 131
Blacksmith shop: **i**, 318; at Lapwai, 353; cost, 382; at Wait., 480; equipment from Lapwai, 498; **ii**, 220, 377, 378
Blain, Rev. Wilson: **ii**, 154
Blair. A.M: **i**, 411
Blanchet, Rt. Rev. A.M.A: **i**, 303, 394n; at Ft. W.W., **ii**, 200-2; meets Whitman, 202; negotiates with Cayuses, 205*, 207, 241-3, 246; receives Lorinda Bewley, 309 ff.; calls Indian council, 316 ff.; 329, 362, 449
Blanchet, Rt. Rev. Francois Norbert: **i**, 358 ff.; 394n., 483, 507; **ii**, 201, baptizes condemned Cayuses, 371 ff.
Blanchet, Rev. Francis Xavier: **i**, 394n
Blanchet, Rev. George: **i**, 394n
Bleeding as a remedy: **i**, 76; **ii**, 111
Blood Feud theory: **ii**, 230, 317 ff.
Bloody Chief, Nez Perce: **ii**, 13
Blue Mountains: **i**, 220, 252, 302; crossed by emigrants, **ii**, 85; 123, 147
Boarding school for natives: suggested, **ii**, 144, 150; 157
Books: **i**, 187, 336, 388; at Wait.. 380
Boone, A.G: **ii**, 38
Boston (Mass.): Whitman to, **i**, 529; **ii**, 43, 50*
"Boston Men": Indian term, **ii**, 174n; Stanley denies, 272
Boundary: *see* Oregon boundary
Bourne, Prof. E.G: **ii**, 387, 440n, 443*
Bowden, Mrs. Edmund: **i**, 169,n, 537n; **ii**, 221n
Boyers, C.W: **ii**, 38, 74
Brackett, Rev. Joseph: **i**, 67
Breckenridge, W.D: **i**, 304n; meets Whitman, 474
Brewer, Henry B: **i**, 323; at Waskopum, **ii**, 7, 105, 123, 185; leaves Waskopum, 192
Brewer, Mrs, H.B: writes Narcissa, **ii**, 141
Bridger, Jim: **i**, 131, 294, 348, 456
Bridger, Mary Ann: **i**, 456; **ii**, 129, 250-1, 261, dies, 331

Brock, Carrol E: **ii**, 401n
Brooks, Wm. (Indian boy): **i**, 315
Broom corn: **i**, 257
Brosnan, Cornelius J: **i**, 308, 331n; **ii**, 59n
Brouillet, Rev. J.B.A: **ii**, 169, 206-7, 219, 238, 233, 243, 247; to Waii. after massacre, 279*; conducts burial service, 280; warns Spalding, 281; re. Lorinda Bewley, 309; at Indian council, 316 ff.; life in danger, 319; 326, 433 ff.; 449
Brouillet's *House Document:* **ii**, 175n, 222n, 290-91n, 355n, 356n, 433-34*, 440n
Brown, John (of Harper's Ferry): **i**, 53
Brown, John A: **ii**, 357n
Browne, J. Ross: **ii**, 434*
Brown's Hole: **ii**, 32
Bryant, Dr. Ira: **i**, 47, 60 ff., 283, 285, 462-3
Bryant, Wm. Cullen: **i**, 49, 53 ff., 60
Buffalo: **i**, 122 ff., 125 ff., 143, 184, 190 ff.; chips, 191; dried meat, 213; tongues, 190, 334
Buffalo (N.Y.): **ii**, 69 ff.
Bullard, Artemas: **i**, 157
Burnett, Peter H: **ii**, 74 ff., 80, 82, 83; defends Whitman, 89, 352
Burnt River: **i**, 219
Bushman (interpreter): investigates massacre, **ii**, 268 ff., 299; sent to Ft. Van., 274 ff., 299 ff.

Cabanne, Jean Pierre: **i**, 138
Calder, Alex. S: **ii**, 392
Calhoun, Sen. John C: **i**, 485, 487
Calomel: **i**, 178
California: **i**, 441; emigrants to, 480; **ii**, 83, 147
Camas plant: **i**, 261

Camaspelo, Cayuse Chief (Big Belly): **ii**, 316 ff.; escorts Lorinda Bewley to Ft. W.W., 324; 361; witness, 366, 371
Camp meeting: at Tualatin Plains **ii**, 24
Canandaigua (N.Y.): **i**, 44; **ii**, 46, 63
Candles: dipping, **i**, 368; at Wait., 381
Canfield, Oscar: **ii**, 448
Canfield, W.D: **ii**, 218, 220, 249; escapes, 269*; with Volunteers, 338; witness, 366, 447
Cannon, Miles: **ii**, 4, 312-13, 355n
Cannon balls: left by Fremont, **ii**, 110
Canoe travel: **i**, 291, 387, 449; Mrs. Smith uses, 459; **ii**, 300
Cape Horn: **i**. 26, 27, 145, 205, 281, 456, 501; **ii**, 6
Capendel, Mrs: at Ft. Van., **i**, 225
Captives after massacre: experiences, **ii**, 304*; released, 314*, 319*; ransomed, 321, 323 ff.; trip down Columbia, 329 ff.; accounts of, 447*
Carding machine for wool: **i**, 48; **ii**, 156
Carr, Sarah Pratt: music composer, **ii**, 388
Carson, Kit: **i**, 137
Carter, David: **i**, 326
Carver, Jonathan: **i**, 50 ff.
Cason, Mary Marsh: **ii**, 448
Caspar (Wyo.): **i**, 127, 192
Cass, Hon. Lewis: **i**, 175
Castle, S.N. (Honolulu): **ii**, 301
Catholic: Cathedral, St. Louis, **i**, 17, 173; *see also* Roman Catholic
Catholic "Ladder": *see* "Ladder"
Catholic Standard: **ii**, 357n, 371, 441

Catlin, George: **i,** 17, 172; illus. by, 40; **ii.** 438
Cats: **i,** 254; not fed, **ii,** 264
Cattle drive from Calif: **i,** 280, 311 ff.
Cattle taken to Ore: **i,** 26, 143, 182 ff., 188, 189, 213, 222-23, 347; **ii,** 42 ff., 78, 236; at Ft. Van: **i,** 227; herd divided, 249; desired by natives, 256 ff.; HBC herds, 310 ff; given to Indians: **ii,** 55, 96, 363; at Lapwai, 327; at Waii., 377 ff.
Caulkins, Mrs. Mary Alice Wisewell (Whitman's niece): **i,** 141; tells of sorrow of Whitman's mother, **ii,** 349
Cayuse Halket: **i,** 15; death, 16; 247, 260, 263, 286, 507; **ii,** 165, 317
Cayuse Indians: **i,** xvii, 129, 206-08, 215, 242, 259; semi-nomadic, 260, 473; period of change, 261*, begin agriculture, 261, 264, 275-76; three chiefs, 263*: interest in Whitman baby, 265; land ownership, 278; schools, 286; religious services, 286 ff.; Lee's opinion, 299; filthy habits, 415; make progress, 430; Christian standards difficult, 453*; resent white men, 471; census in 1841, 473; quarrelsome, 473; threaten Whitman, 488*; aroused by half-breeds, 488*; suspicious of laws, **ii,** 14 ff.; of Whitman, 15; of Dr. White, 15; restless, 17*; accept laws, 21*, 22*; cultural conflicts with whites, 101; reactions to emigrants, 116 ff.; attack emigrants, 148, 209; grievances, 164 ff.; Kane's comments, 192; war party to Calif., 199; B.C., 207 ff.; dying tribe, 232*; census, 232 ff.; measles epidemic, 232 ff.; conspirators, 238*; some weeping, 263 ff.; threaten Stanley, 272; loot Waii., 278; try to kill Perrin, 302; present their case, 315*; manifesto, 318; fearful of Americans, 325; search for Spalding, 330; begin Cayuse War, 336-39; burn Waii., 338; tribe divided, 338, 341; flee to mountains, 342; friendly Cayuses alienated, 347; tribe dispersed, 362-63; sufferings of, 363 ff.; on trial, 365 ff.; executed, 371
Cayuse Pitt: **i,** 15 ff., 260; death, 506*
Cayuse War, 1848: **ii,** 337*
Caxton Printers: **i,** xiii
Cellar or basement: **i,** 251, 365
Cemetery at Waii: **i,** 250, 388; **ii,** great grave, 268; illus., 405; burial of victims, 281, 286, 288; bodies dug up by wolves, 340, 348; reburial, 385
Chamberlain, Rev. Levi: **i,** 282, 536n
Champoeg (Ore.): **i,** 310, 359, 484; **ii,** 102
Cheese: Narcissa makes, **i,** 471; cheese press, **ii,** 378
Cherokee Indian Mission: **i,** 258
Chester (Ohio): **i,** 112
Chickens at Waii: **i,** 222, 227, 285; hen house, 481; **ii,** 378
Chinaware at Wait: **i,** 318
Chinese pheasants: in U.S., **ii** 401n
Cholera: **i,** 74*, 118 ff., 120*
Chouteau, Pierre, Jr: **ii,** 38
Christian Advocate and Journal: **i,** 9 ff., 18-19, 28, 32, 134, 224, 266, 324
Christian observances by Ore. Indians: **i,** 20-21, 22, 139, 244, 259-60

Christmas: non-observance, **i**, 176; observed by Meth., **ii**, 16; by captives, 322
Church, Mrs. Helen Saunders, **ii**, 448
Church Missionary Society: **i**, 10 ff., 22-3
Churches: *see* denominational names
Cincinnati (Ohio): i. 155 ff., 172, 345; **ii**, 42 ff., 70
Civilization of Indians: necessity of, **i**, 261 ff., 275 ff.; **ii**, 156, 181, 219
Civilize or evangelize: **i**, 262; Smith opposed to civilizing natives, 374; issues debated, 439; **ii**, 156
"Civis": describes Whitman, **ii**, 51
Clairburne, Capt. Thomas: defense counsel in Cayuse trial, **ii**, 366
Clam shells burned for lime: **i**, 415
Clapp, B: **ii**, 38
Clark, son of Tibukaikt: **ii**, 240; killed by Joe Lewis, 342
Clark, Rev. Harvey: **i**, 423; to Kamiah, 447, 459; to Will. Vail., 460
Clark, Gen. Wm: **i**, 9 ff., 17 ff., 18-9, 24, 32; not R.C., 437
Clearwater Mission: *see* Lapwai
Clearwater River: **i**, 230, 242, 244
Clocks in Whitman home: **ii**, 264, 379
Clokamas: **ii**, 240; helped in massacre, 258, 288; taken prisoner, 363 ff.; confesses, 368; declares innocence, 369; baptized, hanged, 372
Coal house at Waii: **ii**, 377
Cochran, Rev. Wm: **i**, 11 ff., 246, 392n, 429
Cod-fishery: not traded for Oregon, **ii**, 45, 431

Coeur d'Alene Indians: **i**, 15
Coffee: **i**, 228; **ii**, 162
College: Whitman's dream, **ii**, 119, 215; suggested location at The Dalles, 382; *see also* Whitman College
College of Physicians & Surgeons: *see* Fairfield Medical College
Colorado River: **ii**, 32; Whitman swam, 33*
Columbia Maternal Assoc: **i**, 353*; **ii**, 172n
Columbia River: **i**, 19 ff., 27, 50, 128, 218 ff., 241; suggested as Oregon boundary, 307, 486, 518; **ii**, 25, 95, 146
Colvile, Andrew: **i**, 11, 35n; illus., 39
Commissioner of Indian Affairs: claim for Gray's loss, **ii**, 55, 349
Communion silver and service: **i**, 164, 291, 409, 469; **ii**, 21
Compass: of Whitman, **ii**, 2, 279
Compo, Charles: **i**, 132, 135, 223, 245, 259, 295, 339 ff.; baptized, 340; 356, 406 ff.; **ii**, 139
"Concert" of prayer: **i**, 98
Cone, Anson Sterling: visits Waii., **i**, 179
Congregational Church: Plainfield, Mass., **i**, 51 ff.; Rushville, N.Y., 58 ff., 67, 166, 277; Prattsburg, N.Y., **i**, 94; Oregon City, 476n; **ii**, 64; memorial, 389
Conner, James: **i**, 350, 356; joins church, 409; suspended, 410; excommunicated, **ii**, 139*
Conspirators of Whitman massacre: **ii**, 238*, 288, 368
Continental Divide: **i**, 27, 124, 193 ff.; crossed by Whitman, **ii**, 35*; illus. **i**, 182
Converts: **i**, 340, 370* **ii**,

21, 23, 114; *see also* Presby. Church, First
Cook, Mr: ii, 497-8, 505
Cook, Grover: kills Hedding, ii, 144
Coonc, Elizabeth Ann: ii, 210
Corbett, Hon. H.W: ii, 438
Corn: i, 257, 362, 452, 472; ii, 378
Corn sheller: ii, 197, 376
Cornelius, Spokane Chief: ii, 357, 377
Cortez, David Malin (half-breed boy): left at Waii., i, 503*; *see also* Malin
Cosmopolitan: article on Sagers, ii, 130
Cowley, Rev. Henry T: ii, 397-98
Cowlitz River: i, 312; portage, 327, 329, 358 ff., 481
Coyotes: i, 284; *see also* wolves
Craig, Wm: i, 441 ff.; ii, 233, 236; receives Lapwai refugees, 270 ff.; 328; escorted to Ft. W.W., 345
Craighead, Rev. J.G: ii, 442
Crawford, Medorem: to Oreg., i, 516, 519
Cuba (N.Y.): i, 103, 106; ii, 63, 67
Cultural conflict for Indians: i, 464; ii, 101, 117 ff.
Cummings, Sarah J: describes Indian attack, ii. 148, 150
Cummington (Mass.): i, 46 ff.
Cupidity of Indians: i, 470 ff.; Simp-son's judgment, 495; aroused by half-breeds, ii, 120
Cushing, Hon. Caleb: i, 324
Customs of Indians: described, ii, 55
Cut Lip, Cayuse Chief: *see* Umtippe

Dagosta, Andy: i, xv; map by, 397

Dalles: *see* The Dalles
Daniel (Wyo.): i, 128
Danville (Ill.): i, 112; ii, 65
Dart, Dr. Anson: ii, 234, 362, 377, 379
D.A.R. Chapters: ii, honoring Whitmans, 34, 389
Davis, Rev. Wm. J., S.J: i, xv, 394n; ii, 222n
Dayton (Wash.): i, 289
Deformed Indian heads: i, 19, 25, 224, 265-66, 331n; illus., 42
Degen, Dr. Theophilus: ii, 173 ff.
Delaney, Mrs. Matilda Sager: i, 162; ii, 448; illus., 407; *see also* Sager
Delaware Indians: in Ore., ii, 120; at Kamiah, 151; Joe Lewis, 218
Demers, Father Modeste: i, 358-9, 427, 507; baptizes chiefs, 508; ii, 201
Denny, Gertrude Hall: ii, 401n, 448; *see also* Hall, Peter
Dentist: ii, 70; *see also* Hale, Edward
Deschutes River: ii, 148
Deutsch, Herman: i, xv
Dibble, Rev. S: i, 326
Discord in Oreg. Mission: i, 230, 334*, 349, 365, 373*, 377 ff., 417*, 468, 496*, 511*
Diseases: *see* cholera; measles; scarlet fever; smallpox; typhoid
Dishes, crockery: i, 183, 318
Disoway, Gabriel P: i, 9, 18, 19, 24, 42
Distances: i, 201, 246; Whitman's on professional calls, 292; overland, 390; Wait, to Ft. Hall, ii. 31
Dix, Mary Augusta: i, 165; *see also* Gray, Mrs- W.H.
Dodd, Lawrence L: i, xvi
Dodge, Col. Henry: i, 138

Dodge; Hon. Wm. E: **ii**, 438
Dog: **i**, 254; of Indians, 284; 385; of trapper, 532; **ii**, 11-12, eaten, 35
Dorion, Baptiste: **ii**, 9, 14-15 ff., 17
Dorion, Madame: **i**, 302*
Dorion, Pierre: **i**, 302
Dougherty, Maj. John: **i**, 31, 117, 186, 262
Douglas, Sir James: **i**, 177, 225, 321 ff., 329, 350, 358, 487; **ii**, 95-6; succeeds McLoughlin, 171; 234; learns of massacre, 299 ff.; 302, 449
Douglas, Hon. Wm. O: **ii**, 394
Drayton, Joseph: visits Waii., **i**, 472; describes R.C. activities, 507
Drinking & Drunkness: **i**, 92, 95, 116, 129 ff.
Drips, Andrew: **i**, 126
Drury, Clifford M: *Marcus Whitman, M.D.*, **i**, xix, 320, 384; **ii**, 387, 415n, 430
Duel at 1835 Rendezvous: **i**, 137
Dunbar, Rev. John: **i**, 30, 81, 85, 117, 138, 166n, 187, 258, 273
Dye, Eva Emory: **i**, 35n, 100

Eagle, Nez Perce Chief: **i**, 445; **ii**, 270, 285, 304
East, John W: **ii**, 108
Eastern Wash. State Hist. Soc: **i**, xiii; **ii**, 175n, 449
Eaton, Jeanette: *Narcissa Whitman*, **ii**, 388
Ebberts, G.W: **i**, 147n
Eddy, Rev. Chauncey: **i**, 82, 151, 181, 269n
Edinburgh Review: re. emigration, **i**, 486
Edward (Shuma-hici) son of Tilou-kaikt: **i**, 287; **ii**, 98, 203, 240, 259; tries to kill Spalding, 281; helps kill Bewley and Sales, 288; 305, 311; takes Mary Smith to wife, 312 ff.; at Indian council, 318; killed by Joe Lewis, 342; illus, 296
Edwards, Philip L: **i**, 26, 313-14; *Emigrants Guide*, **ii**, 72
Eells, Rev. Cushing: **i**, 343*; selects Tsh., 356*; house burned, 457; summons Whitman, **ii**, 87; 187; files Wait. claim, 400n; founds Whitman College, 383; *see also* Walker and Eells; Tshimakain
Eells, Mrs. Cushing (Myra): **i**, 343; ill, 390; Edwin born, 471; Myron born, **ii**, 87
Eells, Rev. Myron: **i**, 156, 195; write about Whitman, **ii**, 41; 59n, 387, 442 ff., 444
Elkhom River: **i**, 125, 187
Ellice, Edward: **i**, 15; illus., 39
Elliott, T.C: **i**, 235n; **ii**, 294n, 440n
Ellis (Euice) Nez Perce Chief: **i**, 15 ff., 256, 301, 342; opposed R.C., 429; 445, 507; **ii**, 4; made High Chief, 13*, 21 ff.; meets with Cayuses, 22; 151, 158, 167; dies, 307
Elm Grove (Kan.): **ii**, 74, 75
Emigrant House, Waii: **i**, 463, 480; **ii**, 220; shelters captives, 266
Emigration: *see* Oregon emigration
Ermatinger, Francis: **i**, 255, 264, 349, 380, 405, 441, 455-6
Escalante, Fray Velez de: **ii**, 32
Escaloom, Frank: *see* Ish-ish-kais-kais
Evangelization of natives: first efforts, **i**, 258, 287; services at Lapwai, 369*; first converts, 408; Spalding success, **ii**, 21; *see also* religious meetings

Evans, Hon. Elwood: **ii**, 59n; denies Whitman went to Wash., 441
Expenses for Oregon Mission: **i**, 31; 111, 136, 166, 182, 231 ff., 335*, 347, 382, 467; **ii**, 56, 132, 133; summary, 373 ff., 429*
Eyewitness accounts of massacre: **ii**, 239, 250; Appendix, 447 ff.
E-you-e-ah-nish: *see* Edward
Eyres, Miles: **ii**, 42, 73; drowned, 85, 106

Fairbanks, Dr. Avard: **ii**, 394; illus., 409
Fairfield Medical College: **i**, 62 ff., 298, 322, 342, 347, 481
Farnham, Thomas J: **i**, 410*; **ii**, 32, 61
Fay, O.P: **i**, 100
Feather beds: **i**, 247, 249; **ii**, 379-80
Feathercap: *see* Tamsucky
Federal Hollow (N.Y.): **i**, 46
Fences: need for, **i**, 458, 464; **ii**, 134, 151, 181; burned, 339
Fenn, John: **ii**, 210
"Fifty-Four Forty or Fight": **i**, 484; **ii**, 146
Figueroa, Gov. Jose: **i**, 308
Financial matters: **i**, 232, 271, 335*; **ii**, 373*, 429*; *see also* expenses; payment; subsidy
Finlayson, Chief Factor: **i**, 330
Finley, Joco: **ii**, 342
Finley, Joseph: **ii**, 153; dies, 154
Finley, Nicholas: **ii**, 218-20, 236 ff., 249, 291n, 258, 268, 299; flees to Mont., 342 ff.; visits Spokane, 344
First white women over Rockies: **i**, xviii, 1, 171*, 193-4, 208-10, 226 ff., 327
Fitzpatrick, Thomas: **i**, 126, 138, 186 ff., 189, 192, 209

Five Crows, Cayuse Chief (Hezeldah): **i**, 497-8 ff.; **ii**. 10, 17; high chief, 22; joins church, 23; described by Simpson, 114; 202, 238, 243, 246 ff.; abducts Lorinda, 308 ff.; at Indian council, 316; surrenders Lorinda, 324; wounded, 338; listed as dead, 397
Flathead Indians: **i**, 9 ff., 17, 19, 23 ff., 26, 132, 206
Flathead station: **i**, 352; *see* Tshimakain
Flattened heads: *see* deformed
Fleas: **i**, 224; *see also* lice
Flogging: *see* whipping
Flour: **i**, 318; **ii**, 152; unbolted, 162
Flowers: Narcissa's love for, **ii**, 161
Fontenelle, Lucian: **i**, 18, 23, 113 ff., 120 ff., 126 ff., 130, 132, 138 ff., 143, 209
Food: **i**, 184, 190, 254*; for emigrants, **ii**, 80; prices at Ft. Laramie, 80; at Ft. Hall, 82; from Lapwai, 109; *see also* berries; flour; grape; horse meat; peas; pork; potatoes; sugar; molasses; vegetables; wheat
Foisy, Medora G: **ii**, 136
Forsyth, John, Sec. of State: **i**, 309
Fort Boise: **i**, 156, 217 ff.; **ii**, 85
Fort Bridger: **ii**, 82, 348
Fort Camosun (Victoria): **ii**, 171
Fort Colville: **i**, 13 ff., 20, 22, 241, 367; **ii**, 183, 198; refuge for missionaries, 345
Fort George (Astoria): **i**, 12 ff., 310; **ii**, Narcissa visits, 25
Fort Hall: **i**, 27, 210, 214, 349; **ii**, 22, 31-2; arrival of emigration, 82*
Fort Laramie: **i**, 123, 126, 138,

144, 192, 346; arrival of emigration, **ii**, 80
Fort Leavenworth: **i**, 117, 138, 184 ff.
Fort Nez Perce (Walla Walla): **i**, 119, 220
Fort Nisqually: **i**, 486
Fort Okanogan: **i**, 241; **ii**, 198
Fort Uncompahgre: **ii**, 32
Fort Vancouver: **i**, 12, 133, 225; women at, 226*; gardens, orchards, 226; illus., 237; Narcissa to, **ii**, 23; moved to Vancouver Is., 94
Fort Victoria: established, **ii**, 94
Fort Walla Walla: **i**, 21, 27, 220; gardens at, 221; 241 ff., 248; burned, 482; 494; Whitman visits, 531; Narcissa to, **ii**, 4, 104; 199, 242; Hall to, 267 ff.; Stanley at, 272; Ogden at, 302, 319 ff.; captives arrive, 324 ff.; captives leave, 329 ff.; abandoned, 383
Fort Waters (Waiilatpu): **ii**, 341*, 347
Franklin Academy (Prattsburg): **i**, 99 ff., 154; memorials at, **ii**, 389
Freemasonry: **i**, 95
Fremont, John C: **ii**, 73, visits Waii., 110; leaves howitzers, 172n, 443
French Canadians: in Ore., **i**, 311, 315, 359 ff.; Red River colony, 482; oppose provis. govt, 483; some vote with Americans, **ii**, 102; in Mission church, 115
French Prairie (Will. Vall.): **i**, 27; R.C. church, 359
Frost, Rev. Joseph: **i**, 18
Fur trade: **i**, 13, 127*; end, 425, 455; traders, 40; *see also* rendezvous
Furniture: **i**. 254, 293, 408, 414; **ii**, 151; in Whitman home, 379 ff.

Gambling: among natives, **ii**, 157
Gantt, Capt. John: with emigration, **ii**, 75, 78
Garces, Padre Francisco: **ii**, first R.C. martyr on Pacific Coast, 292n
Garden at Waii: **i**, 472; **ii**, 161
Garry, Nicholas: **i**, 10 ff.; illus., 39
Garth, Thomas R: archaeologist, **i**, 332n, 364
Gary, Rev. George: successor to J. Lee, **i**, 526; **ii**, 76, 104; gives Waskopum to ABCFM, 185 ff.
Geiger, Wm. Jr: **i**, 149, 390, 404; at Waii., **ii**, 8, 18, 44, 51, 86, 182; defends Whitman, 89-90; leaves Waii., 103
Gilbert, Newton: **i**, 61; calls on Whitman, **ii**, 123
Gilliam, Col, Cornelius: **ii**, 126; commands Volunteers, 330 ff.; 332, 335; to The Dalles, 337 ff.; visits Waii., 339; differs with commissioners, 341; killed, 341
Gilliland, Isaac: **ii**, 217, 220, 249; massacre victim, 254
Gilmore, S.M: **ii**, 80
Glenday, Mr: **ii**, 211, 223 fn,
Goats: **i**, 222, 227
Goodyear, Miles: **i**, 184, 188, 209, 215; **ii**, 32
Gospel of Matthew: in Nez Perce, **i**, 498; **ii**, 135; inventory, 327; in Flat-head, **ii**, 346
Granaries at Waii: **i**, 481
Grand Junction (Colo.): Whitman crossing, **ii**, 33*; Whitman park, 34, 390
Grande Ronde Valley: **i**, 219 ff; **ii**, 148
Grant, Capt, Richard: **ii**, 31-2, 82; confronts Whitman, 83*;

comments on emigration, 209, 219
Grape vines: **i**, 278
Gray, Asa: **i**, 63
Gray Eagle, Cayuse Chief: killed, **ii**, 339
Gray, Joe, half-breed Iroquois: **i**, 488-90, 494
Gray, Wm. Henry: **i**, 45, 64, 119, 134, 155, 162-3, 166; life, 180*; 184; illus., 200; 204, 221, 227, 230; 236 fn., 243, 245, 249; returns to States, 255*, 284, 271, 317; brings reenforcement, 341*; Ash Hollow fight, 342, 346; called "Dr.", 347; unpopular, 352; at Lapwai, 376, 380; demands his station, 401; rejected by HBC, 402; critical of Spalding, 419, 438; explores, 420; desires station at Shimnap, 452, 468; assists Eells, 457; builds emigrant house, 483; practices medicine, 481; fanciful reason for Whitman's ride, 483; at Waii., 491; dismissed by ABCFM, 500; resigns from Mission, 520*; leaves Waii., 532; to Will. Vail., **ii**, 1; loss at Ash Hollow, 55; 234, 317, 373, 384; buried at Waii., 385; promotes Whitman-Saved-Oregon story, 431n
Gray, Mrs. W.H. (Mary): **i**, married, 343 ff.; pregnant, 354; dau. born, 426; 505; as teacher, 453; diary, 519; buried at Waii., **ii**, 385
Great Britain: see Oregon boundary
Greek lexicon: relic of massacre, **ii**, 154-5
Greeley, Horace: **ii**, 32; receives Whitman, 48-9; 64
Green, Capt. Henry: **i**, 46, 58

Green River: **i**, 128, 203; **ii**, 33
Greene, Rev. David: **i**, 29 ff., 81 ff., 103, 142 ff., 150 ff., 158, 174; instructions to Whitman, 176 ff.; 180 ff.; 298, 319 ff.; letters to Ore., 337*; critical of expenses, 377; drastic order, 499*; meets Whitman, **ii**, 51 ff.; order revoked, 53*; opposes aid to emigrants, 133; last letter to Whitman, 215*; learns of massacre, 347, 349
Greene, Judge Robert S: **ii**, 402n
Greene, Rev. Samuel: **ii**, 385
Griffin, Rev. John S: **i**, 168n; arrives in Ore., 404*; fails to establish mission, 422*; surly, 452; **ii**, 356n, 433
Griffin, Mrs. Desire: **i**, 407
Gristmill: at Ft. Van., **i**, 227; requested for Lapwai, 318, 353; millstones, 375; at Waii., 412, 454, 472; at Lapwai, 497; at Waii. burned, **ii**, 8; replaced, 113; 3rd at Waii., 134, 163, 378
Gunnison River: **ii**, 34
Guns and ammunition: **i**, 183, 319; none in inventories, **ii**, 381

Hafen, LeRoy R: **i**, 147n
Haight, Rev. Drury: **i**, xv; illus. by, frontispieces
Haines, Francis: **i**, 34n
Hale, Dr. Edward (dentist): Whitman a guest, **ii**, 39*; fills tooth, 70
Hale, Horatio (philologist): **i**, 476n
Half-breeds: agitation by, **i**, 488*; children in Whitman home, 503; **ii**, 107; 120, 143 ff.; *see also* Gray, Joe; Hill; Lewis
Halket, John: **i**, 15

INDEX *Index to the Two Volumes* 489

Hall, Edwin O: **i**, arrives at Ft. Van. with printing press, 380 ff., 387, 390, 406, 419; returns to Honolulu, 437; criticizes Spalding, 439

Hall, Mrs. E.O: invalid, **i**, 381; dau. born, 406

Hall, Gertrude: *see* Denny

Hall, Peter D: arrives at Waii., **ii**, 217, 220, 249; escapes massacre, 266 ff.; drowned, 267 ff.; McBean's account questioned, 275; wife Eliza as witness, 366-7

Hall, Rev. Robert G: **ii**, 403n

Hallock, Rev. L.H: **ii**, 385

Hallock, Rev. Moses: **i**, 52*

Ham's Fork: **i**, 27, 129 Harness: **i**, 459

Harper, J. Russell: **ii**, 193n, 221n

Harris, Black (or Moses): **ii**, 32

Harrison, Benjamin: **i**, 10 ff., 15, 229; 248; illus., 39

Harrison, Pres. Wm. Henry: **i**, 484

Hart, Eliza: *see* Spalding, Mrs. H.H.

Hart, Horace: **ii**, 179, 270, 326

Hart, Capt. Levi: **i**, 155-6, 404

Harvard University Library: **ii**, 416

Hastings, Lansford W: **i**, 517

Hat: *see* The Hat

Hatfield, Gov. Mark O: **ii**, 131

Hawaiian Mission: **i**, 59, 282, 380; aids Oregon Mission, 282, 336, 381; **ii**, 378; Children's Soc., **i**, xiii; **ii**, 416

Hawaiian workmen: **i**, 232, 250, 255, 282-3, 295, 336, 382; see also Maki; and Jack

Hays, Mrs. Rebecca: arrives at Waii., **ii**, 217-8, 220; infant dies, 286; Stanfield desires her, 314

Haystack prayer meeting: **i**, 7 ff., 54

Hebard, Prof. Grace R: **i**, 195

Hedding, Elijah (Walla Walla Indian): killed in Calif., **ii**, 143-4, 150; remembered, 155-6, 165, 199, 317

Helm, Mrs. Elizabeth Sager: **ii**, 407; 448; see also Sager

Henry, Matthew: **i**, 388 ff.

Heron, Chief Trader Francis: **i**, 15 ff., 20, 22

Hill, Tom (half-breed): **i**, 489; **ii**, 120-21, 143, 145, 165; visits Whitman, 167*

Hinds, John (Black): **i**, 209, 243; died, 250; 295

Hines, Rev. Gustavus: **ii**, 19; interpreter for White, 21-22; at camp meeting, 25; 221n

Hines, Rev. H.H: **ii**, 396

Hines, Rev. Harvey K: **i**, 325

Hinman, Alanson: **i**, 163; **ii**, 58n; hired as Waii. teacher, 124; 131, 138; baptized, 139-40; gets press, 189 ff.; to Waskopum, 190, 197; hears of massacre, 300-01, 302

Hobson, John: **ii**, 42, 73, 106; daughters, Emma and Ann, 113, 140, 162

Hoes for Indians: **i**, 261, 276, 318; *see also* plows

Hoffman, Jacob: **ii**, 218, 220, 249; massacre victim, 253

Hogs: **i**, 222, 281*; butchered, 502; at Lapwai, **ii**, 327; at Waii., 378

Hohots Ilppilp (Red Grizzly Bear), Nez Perce Chief: **ii**, 10

Holbrook, Attorney Amory: **ii**, 366

Holidays observed: **ii**, 16

Holland Patent (N.Y.): **i**, 155 ff.

Holmes, Kenneth L: **i**, 331n

Horse meat: **i**, 254, 267, 279, 411, 502; **ii**, 155

Horses: for 1836 trip, **i**, 182-3, 279, 342; Lapwai inventory, 325; at Waii., 369 ff.

490   *Marcus and Narcissa Whitman and the Opening of Old Oregon* INDEX

Horticulture: beginnings, i, 278*
Hostility of natives: i, 437, 443*; ii, 101, 148, 163
Hotchkin, Rev. James J: i, 4 ff., 32, 82, 93 ff., 153
Housel, Mrs. Eliza Ann: ii, 64
Howard (N.Y.): i, 159, 164, 345
Howe, Charlotte: i, 109
Howell, John Ewing: ii, 149
Hudson's Bay Co: i, xiii, 10 ff.; illus. of officials 39; 21, 22, 27, 119, 127-9, 177, 210 ff., 211 ff.; did not sell cattle 223, 269n; 279, 310-11; sells supplies, 232 ff.; 296; approves flogging, 301; re. boundary, 307*, 312*; criticized by Kelley, 309 ff.; suspicious of Methodists, 321 ff., 327*; free passage to R.C. missionaries, 358; subsidizes R.C., 360-61*; sends Red River colony to Ore. 481*, 360-61; rejects Dr. White, 517-8; refuses to help White, ii, 9 ff.; reaction to 1843 emigration, 94-5*, 102*; informed of massacre, 266*; take action, 299*; secures release of captives, 319
HBC Archives: i, xiii, xix
HBC Express: i, 23, 34, 241-2, 246; carries mail, 499
Hulbert, A.B. & Dorothy: *Overland to the Pacific*, i, 320
Hull, Rev. Leverett: i, 149, 164, 246
Hull, Sarah (Indian girl): i, 265, 294; dies, 334
Humphrey, Rev. S. L: ii, 437 ff.
Hunt.WilsonP: i, 310
Huntington Library and Art Gallery: i, xiv
Hussey, John A: i, 533n
Hymns in native tongue: i, 384, 395, 413

Iatin (Cayuse Indian); i, demands payment for land, 488
Idaho: *see* Lapwai; Old Ore.
Independence Rock: i, 127, 193
Indian census: i, 314; ii, 232n; in 1971, 403n
Indian goods for trading: i, 183, 318
Indian labor: undependable, i, 232, 454, 490
Indian languages: i, 16
Indian names: ii, 239
Indian rubber: i, 183, 249
Indians: *see* tribal names; trouble with, at Lapwai, i, 444*, ii, 6; at Kamiah, i, 445*; at Waii., 488*; 491*, 493*; Young Chief confrontation, II, 164-5*
Iroquois Indians in Ore: i, 17, 248, 424, 488; ii, 33
Irrigation: i, 243, 464, 473
Irving, Washington: i, 302
Ish-ish-hol-hoats-hoats: *see* Lawyer
Ish-ish-kais-kais (Frank Escaloom): i, 490; shoots Saunders, ii, 253; kills Gilliland, 254; shoots Narcissa, 256; kills Kimball, 265; 304; takes Susan Kimball to wife, 312; taken prisoner, 363 ff.; confesses, 364; declares innocence, 368; baptized, named John, and executed, 372 ff.
Ithaca (N.Y.): i, 8, 29, 84, 141, 165-7, 343; memorials at, 380

Jack or John (Hawaiian): i, 366; ii, 2-3 ff., 9
Jackson, Mr: with Spalding, ii, 241, 326
Jackson, Pros. Andrew: i, 309
Jacobs, Mrs. Nancy Osbom: *see* Osbom

James, Old, Nez Perce Chief: **i**, 443; **ii**, 121-22, 184
Jason, Nez Perce: **ii**, 114
Jefferson Nat. Meml., St. Louis: **i**, 173
Jessett, Rev. Thomas E: **i**, 35n, 23; **ii**, 355n
Jesuits: **i**, 25, 424; **ii**, 158, 223n, 436, 440n
Jocko Valley (Mont.): **ii**, 342
Johansen, Prof. Dorothy O: on boundary, **i**, 535n; **ii**, 357n
Johnson, D.G: **i**, 390
Johnson, Elvira (Mrs. H.K.W. Perkins): **i**, 314, 394n
Johnson, Mary: **ii**, 161; works for Narcissa, 182; to Lapwai, 218, 326
Jones, Rev. David T: **i**, 11 ff., 14, 22, 246, 306n
Jones, Nard: *Great Command*, **ii**, 388
Joseph, Old, Nez Perce Chief: **i**, 245, 370; joins church, 409; farms at Lapwai, 444; wife joins church, **ii**, 21; 114; his band loots Lapwai, 271
Joseph, Young, Nez Perce Chief: **i**, 370; baptized, 410
Josephy, Alvin, Jr: **i**, 35n, 36n, 37n, 234n, 269n. 392n, 393n, 476n; **ii**, 222n
Joset, Father Joseph: **ii**, 136
Judd, Mrs. G.P. (Honolulu): **i**, 266
Judson, Rev. Adoniram: **i**, 6n
Judson, Rev. Lyman: **i**, 180, 253; **ii**, 68; becomes Adventist, 68-9; Whitman's letter to, 394

Kamehameha, King: aids Ore. Mission, **i**, 336
Kamiah (Ida.): **i**, 20, 374 ff.; station at, 402; trouble at, 444 ff.; teacher sent to, **ii**, 151; 397-8; Presby. Church, 397 ff.; 403n; *see also* Smith, A.B.
Kamloops (Brit. Col.): **i**, 14
Kane, Paul: **i**, 161 ff., 365; illus., 433; visits Wait., **ii**, 192*; sketches of Whitmans, 194*; illus., 224-7
Kansut, Nez Perce Chief: baptized by R.C., **i**, 508
Ka-ou-pu, or Paul: Nez Perce with flattened head, illus., **i**, 42
Kelley, Hall Jackson: **i**, 308-9, 313
Kentuc, Nez Perce Indian: **i**, 135, 204 ff., 215, 370
Kettle Falls Indians: **i**, 15
Kia-ma-sump-kin: conspirator, **ii**, 240; prisoner, 363 ff., denies guilt, 369-70; baptized, named James, executed, 372 ff.
Kickapoo Indian Mission: **i**, 186
Kimball, Byron S: **ii**, 385
Kimball, Rev. Milton: **i**, 174
Kimball, Nathan: **ii**, 217, 220, 249; wounded, 253-4, 256 ff., 260; massacre victim, 264 ff.; watch recovered, 342
Kimball, Nathan Jr: **ii**, 254-5, 278n, 356n, 448
Kimball, Susan: raped, **ii**, 307; Escaloom takes to wife, 311; weeps, 312; rejects Edwards, 312 ff.; at 1897 observance, 385; *see also* Munson
Kone, Rev. W.W: **i**, 526
Kooskooske (Clearwater) River: **i**, 231, 268n
Kootenai Indians: **i**, 13, 15
Kootenai Pelly: **i**, 14 ff.; death, 16; 22 ff., 137
Kowrach, Rev. Edward J: **i**, xv; **ii**, 294n

Lachme (Canada): HBC hdqs., **i**, 128
"Ladder": R.C.. **i**, 508;

Protestant, 508; ii, 203; 294n
Ladies Home Journal: description of Whitman, ii, 59n
Lake Pend Oreille: i, 21
Lamps & lanterns: ii, 381
Land: ownership, i, 263, 278, 444, 458, 488; ii, 122, 206; for mission sites: at Wait., i, 136, 305n; payment for, 208, 263
Lane, Gov. Joseph: ii, 239; receives prisoners, 365; 368
Lane Theological Seminary: i, 155
Language problems: i, 258, 266, 285, 371, 389, 450; instruction, ii, 157
Languages, Indian: i, 268n, 352, 390; *see also* Nez Perce language
Lapwai Creek: i, 244, 333; Valley, 443
Lapwai Mission: i, 230*, 243-4, 333; founded, 249; buildings, millrace, 369*; 370, 376; ordered closed, 500; described by White, ii, 10; abandoned, 326 ff.; inventory, 381; Presby. church, 397 ff.
Larison, John: i, 441 ff.
Larkin, Thomas O: i, 270n
Lash: use of, i, 300*; *see also* whipping
Lausanne (ship): i, 314; chartered, 324*; 447-8; arrives in Ore., 479; 485
Laws, Nez Perces: i, 301; ii, 9*, Cayuses reject, 17; ineffective, 102, 144
Laws, white man's: without, "hell on earth" i, 496, ii, 245; White's code, 10 ff., Cayuses suspicious, 15
Lawyer, Nez Perce Chief: i, 20 ff., 21 ff.; son Corbett, 23; 204 ff.; teaches language, 375; argues with R.C. priest, 428-9; 445; ii, 114, 307; baptized, 346
Le Claire, Deacon (R.C.): ii, 207
Lee, Rev. Daniel: i, 18, 26, 300, 313, 341; ii, at Waskopum, 7; leaves Ore., 25
Lee, Rev. Jason: i, xviii, 37n, 26-7*, 29 ff., 33, 133, 198n, 287, 296 ff.; visits Whitman & Spalding, 299 ff.; views on colonization, 302-3*; receives Slacum, 310; Cattle Co., 311 ff.; leaves for N.Y., 314*; carries memorial, 315; visits Waii., 315; in N.Y., 323; successful, 326 ff.; remarries, 328; on *Lausanne*, 328; arouses suspicions of HBC, 329; 348, 448; memorial to Congress, 465; 485; govt. subsidy, 516; dismayed by White's return, 517; dismissed, 526; camp meeting, ii, 25-6; recalled, 49; dismissal, 104; exonerated, 104; statue, 403n, 451
Lee, Maj. H.A.G: of Ore. Volunteers, ii, 325, 336; Supt. of Indian Affairs, 341
Lennox, David: ii, 45
Lenox, Edward: ii, 82, 90
Leslie, Rev. David: i, 314; dau. marries Rogers, 462
Lewes, John Lee (Chief Trader): at Ft. Colville, ii, 343; receives missionaries, 344-5
Lewis, Joe (half-breed & archvillain): i, 489; ii, 195, 218-20; poisoning accusation, 236 ff.; 241, 246, 257 ff.; kills Francis Sager, 258; loots buildings, 278; 309, 341; capture and

escape, 342; kills Edward and Clark, 342; flees to Mont., killed, 342; mutilated skulls of Whitmans, 386
Lewis & Clark: explorers, **i**, 24, 289, 310, 312; **ii**, 10
Lewiston (Ida.): **i**, 244, 290; **ii**, 33, observes centennial, 387
Liberty (Mo.): **i**, 26, 111, 118, 178 ff., 184-5, 346
Liberty ships: named for Whitmans: **ii**, 391
Library: of mission, **i**, 392n
Lice, body: **i**, 503; **ii**, 160
Life preservers, rubber: **i**, 183
Limouze, Rev, Arthur H: **i**, 304 fn,; **ii**, 402n
Lincoln, Abraham: **i**, 46
Linn, Senator Lewis F: **i**, 194, 324, 465, 515 ff.; **ii**, 40-41, 47, 352
Liquor trade among Indians: **i**, 129 ff.; **ii**, 139, 464; *see also* drinking
Littlejohn, Phil B: **i**, 423; to Will. Vail., 456, 469; returns to Waii., **ii**, 8, 103; son drowns, 16 ff.; child born, 108; to Will. Vall., 113; returns to States, 212
Lobelia & Cayenne pepper: **i**, 178
Locks at Waii: **ii**, 381
Locust trees at Waii: **i**, 256, 481; **ii**, 347; *see also* trees
Looking Glass, Nez Perce Chief: **i**, 475n; *see also* Meoway
Loom at Lapwai: **i**, 283; **ii**, 380
Loomis, Calvin: **i**, 51
Loomis, Mrs. (mother of Marcus): **i**, 50, 141; urged to become Christian, **ii**, 63; learns of death of Marcus, 349; *see also* Whitman, Mrs. Beza
Loomis, Elisha: **i**, 59, 285
Looney, Jesse: at Wait., **ii**, 108; dies, 113
Loriot (ship): **i**. 309, 311
Loup River: **i**, 125, 188
Lovejoy, Asa: with 1842 emigration, **i**, 524 ff.; accounts of Whitmans ride, 525, 530; leaves Waii. with Whitman, **ii**, 31 ff.; describes trials, 32 ff.; parts with Whitman, 38; claims Whitman saw Pres. Tyler, 44 ff.; joins 1843 emigration, 80
Lovejoy, Elijah: **i**, 177 ff.
Luke, Nez Perce Indian: **ii**, 114

M'Allister, Rev. A: **i**, 25
McBean, Wm. (HBC trader at Ft. W.W.): **ii**, 178, 199, 201; comments on measles, 233-36; identifies conspirators, 239-40, 288; unfriendly to Hall, learns of massacre, 267; informs Ft. Van., 269; cool to Stanley and Osborn, 272, 274 ff.; fearful of attack, 299; sends Bushman to Ft. Van., 300 ff.; writes Lane, 363, 370 ff.; 449
McClane, J.B: **ii**, 90
McDonald, Angus: **ii**, 342
McDonald, Archibald: at Ft. Colville, **i**, 334, 357; wife, 334, 355
McKay, Alexander: **i**, 225
McKay, Charles: **ii**, 338; wounds Five Crows, 339
McKay, Margaret: **i**, 294, 386
McKay, Thomas: **i**, 27, 210 ff., 217, 225, 294 ff.; sends sons East to school, 296; sons return, 516; **ii**, 3-4, 9; approves code of laws, 12, 17, 203-4; characterized by Simpson, 204; baptized Catholic, 204; with Ore. Volunteers, 338; kills Gray Eagle, 339
McKee, Ruth Karr: **i**, 431n

McKinlay, Archibald: at Ft. W.W., **i**, 470, 488, 491-2; warns Cayuses, 494*; comments on Whitman, 531 fn,; escorts Narcissa to W.W., **ii**, 3; with White, 12; 17, 19; leaves Ft. W.W., 178; 235, 238
McKinlay, Mrs. A: **i**, 355; **ii**, 112
McKinney, Wm: at Waskopum, **ii**, 300
McLeod, John L: **i**, 210 ff., 212 ff., 219 ff., 223, 248, 254, 296
McLoughlin, Dr. John: **i**, 11 ff.; 133, 210, 225*; trouble with Rev. Beaver, 229; provides supplies, 231 ff., 246 ff., at Ft. W.W., 298*; approves whipping, 301, 331n; 310; in London, 327; sympathetic to R.C., 359 ff., 402; opposes Provisional Govt., 484 ff., 485; baptized, 509; marriage, 509; disturbed by White's return, 517; **ii**, 19, 24; re-emigration, 88; moves to Vancouver Island, 94; supports Provisional Govt., 102 ff.; warns Whitman, 145; retires, 171; 178, 211, 333; witness, 367; house in Ore. City, 372
McLoughlin, Mrs. John (Margaret): **i**, 225 ff., 247, 509; Lee baptizes, 359
McLoughlin, Maria: **i**, 227
McNary Dam: **i**, 221
McWhorter, L.V: **ii**, 28n
Magone, Maj. Joseph: escorts Tsh. missionaries to Ft. Waters, **ii**, 345-6
Mahon, Corp. Robert D: takes deposition from Cayuses, **ii**, 368 ff.
Mails, transmission of: **i**, 80, 144, 173, 253, 298; received by Whitmans, 335*, 416*; long delays, 499; Narcissa longs for, **ii**, 8; proposal for Pony Express, 47, 211; no mail for three years, 158
Maki, Joseph: **i**, 283, 295 ff., 340; dies, 423; wife Maria, 283, 441
Malheur River: **i**, 219; **ii**, 147
Malin, Rev. David: **i**, 108n, 504
Malin, David Cortes: **i**, 503*; **ii**, 5, 87; taken to Ft. W.W., 257, 329
Manson, Donald: **ii**, 212, 222n
Manson boys, John & Stephen: at Waii., **ii**, 198, 212; recollection of massacre, 252; 291n; taken to Ft. W.W., 257-8, 329, 448
Maps: **i**, 201, 397
Marriages, White to Native: **i**, 375
Marsh, Mary: *see* Cason
Marsh, Walter: **ii**, 217, 220, 220; massacre victim, 249
Marshall, W.I. (author, *Acquisition of Oregon*): **i**, 320, 449; **ii**, 43, 59n, 169, 387, 443*
Martin, Rev. Samuel N.D: **ii**, 397
Massacre: *see* Whitman massacre
May, Rev. Samuel W: **i**, 106
May Dacre (ship): **i**, 27
Measles: introduction of, **ii**, 199*; among Indians, 199; use of sweat baths, 200; epidemic, 231*; 241, 318, 362
Medical practice: training, **i**, 57 ff., 67 ff.; early, 71 ff.; medicines, 183; of Whitman, 272*; **ii**, 251; instruments, 380; *see also* bleeding; calomel; quinine
Medicine men, Indian: *see* "Te-wats"
Meek, Helen Mar: **i**, 441-2; **ii**, 23, 128; sick, 248; 256; among captives, 266; dies, 286

Meek, Joe L: **i,** 132, 205-6, 294, 441; **ii,** 24; converted, 25; 32; envoy to Wash., 336*; writes to J. G. Prentiss, 340 ff., 351; carries word of massacre to East, 347*; arrives St. Louis, 351; cousin of wife of Pres. Polk, 350; appt. Marshal, 361; receives Cayuse prisoners, 365, 369; at execution, 372

Meek, Stephen H.L: cut-off of, **ii,** 147

Melons: **i,** 222, 226, 472; **ii,** 162; emetic injected into, 234-5

Memorials to Congress: **i,** 484; first, 311, 359; second, 314, 321, 360, 465; third, 360; **ii,** of 1847, 336, 351

Meoway or Meiqay: **i,** 445, 506; **ii,** 13

Merrill, Rev. Joseph: **i,** 58, 59

Merrill, Rev. Moses: **i,** 114, 117 ff

Methodist Missionary Soc: **i,** 24 ff., 27, 308 ff., 313; re. govt. subsidy, 321*; Simpson fearful, 328; in Will. Vail., 177, 263, 281, 299, 310, 313, 321; reenforcement, 323*; Lausanne chartered, 325*; proposed transfer of Mission to Meth., 446 ff.; ABCFM suggestion, 499; Lee dismissed, 526; **ii,** 49; Gary to close out work, 76; Waskopum to ABCFM, 185*; see also Lausanne; Lee, Jason

Mevway, Mungo: **i,** 294, 339; reports assault on Narcissa, **ii,** 3 ff.

Mexican War: **ii,** 155

Middlefield (Mass.): **i,** 8, 28 ff.

Mill Creek at Waii: **i,** 243; **ii,** 134

Miller, Wm. (Adventist): **ii,** 68 ff.

Mills, Samuel J: **i,** 7 ff.

Millstones: **i,** 375, 454; at Waii., **ii,** 134

Mission meetings: Sept. 1838, **i,** 341 ff., 351*; Feb. 1939, 375*; Sept. 1839, 401; July 1840, 420*; May 1841, 457, 466*; May 1842, 509*, 511*; Sept. 1842, 482, 518*; May 1845, **ii,** 138*; June 1847, 188 ff.

Missionaries, independent: **i,** 404*; Greene warns, 407*; 2nd party, 423*; all at Waii., 425, 452; Greene advises, 426; goods burned, 482

Missionary barrels: **i,** 336

Missionary Herald: **i,** 101, 109n, 113, 193, 344, 374, 419; account of massacre, **ii,** 349, 374

Missionary methods: **i,** xvii, 261 ff., 271 ff., 278; Smith critical, 401; debated, 438

Missionary qualifications: **i,** 152; no medical examination, 167

Moccasins: worn by children, **ii,** 162

Molasses: from Hawaii, **i,** 381; **ii,** 378

Moody, Robert E: **i,** xv; 56n, 61, 70n; **ii,** 97n

Monuments and memorials to Whitman: **ii,** 382*, 384*, 388*, 392*; illus., 409

Moore, Charles: **ii,** 396

Moore, Mary C: Cost of Empire, **ii,** 388 ff.

Morgan, Dale: **ii,** 98n

Morisette, Rev. A.L, S.J: **ii,** 222n

Mormons: **i,** 112

Morrow, Mrs. Honore Willsie: re. Sager myth, **ii,** 130*

Mother's Magazine: **i,** 355

Mosquitoes & flies: **i,** 216

Mt. Hood: **i,** 220; **ii,** 88

Mt. St. Helens: **i,** 220

Mountain men: **i**, 129, 206-7, 443
Mounted Riflemen: **ii**, 362, 365, 368
Mowry, Rev. Wm: **i**, 107; **ii**, 444
Mules: **i**, 182-3, 223, 257, 279; eaten, **ii**, 35; left at Waii, by Fremont, 110
Munger, Asahel: draws floor plan, **i**, 364; 404*; insane, 455; suicide, 456; 495
Munger, Mrs: **i**, 408, 455
Mungo: *see* Mevway Munnick, Mrs. Harriet: **ii**, 174n
Munson, Susan Kimball: **ii**, 449
Murderers, Whitman massacre: pursuit of, **ii**. 335*; apprehended, 361*; trial, 365*; found guilty, 367*; baptized, executed, 371*
Music: in Whitman home, **ii**, 161; with Andrew Rodgers, 183

Naples (N.Y.): **ii**, 64
National Archives (Wash., D.C.): **i**, xiv
Nesmith, Judge J.W: **ii**, 73, 74-5; describes Whitman, 79; 84, 130; 145
New Caledonia: **i**, 128
New York City: Whitman in, **ii**, 48*
New York Freemans Journal: **ii**, 434 ff.
New York, state: **i**, 48 ff., 71 ff., 90 ff., 153 ff.; **ii**, 389
New York Univ. Hall of Fame: **ii**, 443
Newell, Marcus Whitman: **i**, 441
Newell, Robert ("Doc"): **i**, 138, 425, 445; **ii**, 212; appointed Commissioner, 336; *Memoranda,* 338; visits Waii., 339; meets with Cayuses, 341
Nez Perce books: primer, **i**, 438; *see also* printing press
Nez Perce "Delegation" to St. Louis: **i**, 8-9 ff., 17*; illus., 40, 42; 20 ff., 23 ff., 132, 136; **ii**, 437*
Nez Perce Indians: **i**, xvii, 129 ff., 132, 135, 206 ff., 215, 242, 245 ff.; escort Spaldings to Lapwai, 249 ff.; in transition, 261*; friendly, 291; Lee's opinion, 300; blame Gray, 356 ff.; revival, 373; adopt laws, **ii**, 9*; census, 232; protect Mrs. Spalding, 270; warn Perrin, 303; peace proposals, 318; demand ransom, 321; escort Spaldings to Ft. W.W., 327; "Lament," 437*
Nez Perce language: **i**, 16, 258-9, 285, 438; dictionary, grammar, 476n, 499; *see also* alphabet, gospel
Nez Perce Nat. Hist. Park: **i**, 370; **ii**, 387
Nichols, B.F: **i**, 163; **ii**, 89, 173n
Nixon, Rev. Oliver: **i**, 162, 195, 536n; **ii**, 387, 442
Nixon, Pres. Richard M: **ii**, 394
No-Horns-On-His-Head: illus., **i**, 40
Norling, Ernest Ralph: **i**, 163
North West Company: **i**, 35n, 128, 232

Oats: **i**, 226
Oberlin (Ohio): **i**, 404
Ogden, Peter Skene: **i**, 470; Chief Factor, Ft. Van., **ii**, 171, 203, 234; hears of massacre, 299; leaves for Ft. W.W., 302 ff., 319; secures release of captives, 319-22; summons Spalding, 321-3*; fearful of attack, 324-5 ff., 328; departs for Ft. Van.,

329; letter from Spalding, 332*
Old Oregon: definition, i, 34n; see also opening of
Oliphant, Orin J: i, 34n, 35n, 15
Omaha Indians: i, 31
Onions: ii, 378
Opening of Old Oregon: i, xviii, 211, 219, 328, 424; wagons over Blue Mts., 440; success of emigration, ii, 85*, 88*; results of Whitman's ride, 91*, 93
Orchard at Waii: i, 481; see also trees
Oregon American: ii, 291n, 433 ff.
Oregon Bill: ii, 352; signed, 361
Oregon boundary: i, xviii, 211, 298, 307*, 312, 315 ff., 325, 394n, 465, 484*, 515 ff., 524, 528 ff.; ii, 40, 45, 94 ff.; effects of Amer. emigration, 145*, 170*, 350
Oregon City: ii, 25, 178, 365; place of trial and execution, 372
Oregon colonization: i, 308 ff,; need for, 313-4; Lee's plan, 324; 484*; Whitman submits plan, ii, 54; 63; his continuing hope, 122, 215
Oregon emigration: i, 316, 320, 443, 485*, 522*; ii, 214; of 1840, i, 328; of 1841, 480, 487, 489; 1842, 487, 516*; 1843, 194, ii, 25, 40*, 61*, 71*, 74*, 77*, 83*, 85*, 88*, 90*, Whitman's appraisal, 91, 101*, 108*, results, 170 ff.; of 1844, 95, 122*, 131*; 1845, 95, 147*, 149 ff.; 1846, 179*; 1847, 209*, 211, 216*; 1848, 348; Indians urge cessation, 318; *see also* Linn; opening; Whitman's concern: ii, 40*;

requests protection, 46 ff.; promotes Christian colony, 54; 214; his Bill, 459 ff.
Oregon Historical Society: i, xiv, 108n; ii, 28n; has mission press, 221; Whitman letters, 415
Oregon Institute (Meth.): hires Gray, i, 514; Hinman serves, ii, 189
Oregon Mission, ABCFM: limits expenses, i, 337; action to forestall order, 513*; peace within, ii, 101 ff.; end, 209, 343*; finances, 373 ff.; *see also* ABCFM; Whitman; Spalding
Oregon Pioneer Assn., *Trans:* i, xiv
Oregon Provisional Emigration Soc: i, 327 ff., 486
Oregon Provisional Govt: i, 316, 326, 360, 484; ii. 102, 170; weak, 245; action against Cayuses, 335; ended, 361
Oregon Spectator: i, 194; ii, 175n, 292n, 293n, 354n, 355n, 355n, 355n, 357n, 400n, 400; describes execution, 373
Oregon Territory: established, i, xviii; ii, 350; U.S. jurisdiction over, 91*, 361
Oregon Trail: illus., i, 201; 193 ff.; distances, 208, 242 ff., 245; wagons across Ida., 442; one-way road, 456; Waii. an outpost, 523 ff.; proposal to guard, ii, 46 ff.; cut-off, 147, 149, 179
Oregon Volunteers: recruited, ii, 304, 315; to The Dalles, 325, 327 ff.; seek murderers, 330 ff.; in pursuit, 335*; offer rewards, 342n;

vandalism against natives, 342; disbanded, 347, 361
Oregonian and Indians Advocate: **i,** 327
Osage Indians: Spalding appt. to, **i,** 157
Osborn, Josiah: **ii,** 151, 213, 219, 237, 257; flight of, 273*; rescued, 275 ff.; death of children, 277; witness, 366, 447
Osborn, Nancy: **ii,** 151, 219 ff., 231; account of escape, 257 ff.; 262 ff, 273*; at 1897 observance, 385, 448
Otis, Judge James: **ii,** 69
Oto Indians: **i,** 31; Agency, 184 ff.
Oxen: preferable to horses, **ii,** 97n; sore feet, 147

Pacific (San Francisco): **ii,** 435 ff.
Pacific Hist. Quarterly; Review; Northwest Quarterly: **i,** xiv
Packard, Col. John: **i,** 51, 112
Page, Rev. David: **i,** 59
Palladino, Rev. L.B: **i,** 432n
Palmer, Miss Emeline: **i,** 142, 166; married to Allis, 184
Palmer, Joel: visits Waii., **ii,** 155; appt. Commissioner, 336; differs with Gilliam, 341; resigns, 341
Palouse River: **i,** 376, 379; **ii,** 192, 196
Pambrun, Maria: **i,** 250, 269n, 254, 294; engaged to Rogers, 461*, 466*; **ii,** 114
Pambrun, Pierre: **i,** 21, 221, 227, 233, 242, 253, 260; abused by Indians, 445, 461; death, 462; builds house for Young Chief, 471
Pambrun, Mrs: **i,** 222, 254, 264, 335
Pandosy, Father: at Ft. W.W., **ii,** 267
Paris, Rev. John D: **i,** 437

Parker, Henry: **i,** 8
Parker, Rev. Samuel: **i,** 5, 7*, illus., 43; 28*, 45, 74, 81 ff., 102 ff., 107; differs with Whitman, 113*, 119 ff., 123 ff.; prophesied railroad, 127; 131; exploring tour, 132*, 137; wife, 141; 204, 207, 223, 231, 243, 260, 338, 343, 370; Whitman answers charges, 381*; **ii,** 61, 65, 373
Parker, Dr. Samuel J: **i,** 7, 103, 146n; 141, 165
Parrish, Rev. Josiah L: **i,** 325; **ii,** 88
Passports to Oregon: **i,** 174; **ii,** 9
Patterson, Mrs. Isaac Lee: **i,** 61
Pawnee Indians: **i,** 31, 118, 187, 189, 273; Mission, 30, 125, 258
Payette, Francis: **ii,** 85
Payment for mission sites: **i,** 208, 263; at Kamiah, 444; at Lapwai, 470; 488, 490; refused by Whitman, **ii,** 317; *see also* land
Peabody Museum, Harvard Univ: **ii,** 225
Peas: **i,** 257, 277, 452; **ii,** 378
Pelly, John Henry: **i,** 14
Pend Oreille Indians: **i,** 15
Pendleton (Ore.): **i,** 471; **ii,** 149
Penrose, Dr. Stephen B.L: **i,** 268n; **ii,** 402n, 386
Perkins, Rev. H.K.W: **i,** 48, 162, 314, 416, 496; receives Narcissa, **ii,** 7*, 18, 21; 25; writes to Jane Prentiss, 26, 451 ff.; 107, 118, 230
Perkins, Joel: takes Francis Sager to Will. Vall., **ii,** 140
Pettibone, Rev. Ira: re. Gray, **i,** 181
Peu-peu-mox-mox: *see* Yellow Serpent
Pickering, John: on orthography, **i,** 390

Pictures: used in teaching Indians, i, 507 ff.; see also "Ladder"
Pierre's Hole Battle: i, 131, 133
Pigeons: i, 222, 227
Pilcher, Maj. Joshua: ii, 55
Pitt, Thomas: i, 15
Pittsburgh (Pa.): i, 167
Plainfield (Mass.): i, 49-52
Platte River: i, 123, 127, 184; forded, 187; 190; ii, 78
Platz, Mrs. H.W. (Celista): i, xvi; ii, 402n
Plows: i, 262, 276, 300, 319, 439; demand for, 458; sent by Rushville, 463; ii, 136, 376
Pocatetello (Ida.): i, 27, 214; see Ft. Hall
Poison: for wolves, i, 284; ii, 234 ff.
Political developments: i, 465*; see also Oregon Boundary
Polk, Pres. James K: ii, 146, 337; sends Meek's memorial to Congress, 350; signs Oregon Bill, 352
Polygamy: ii, 115 ff., 186
Pony Express: Whitman's proposal, ii, 47, 211
Popo Agie River: i, 348
Population, Will. Vall: i, 394n, 483; see also American Colony
Pork: prices, ii, 152
Portages on Columbia River: i, 223, 233
Porter, Hon. James M: Whitman meets, ii, 43; 46 ff., 92; writes to, 459*
Potatoes: i, 222, 226, 257, 278, 299, 362, 452, 472; ii, 89, 110; price, 152; 246, 378
Powder River: i, 219; ii, 148
Powell, Rev. Oliver S: i, 86, 102, 104-6, 151
Pratt, Carlton: i, 61
Pratt, Capt. Joel: i, 90, 93; Jared, 93

Pratt, Jonathan, Jr: i, 61 ff., 65 ff.; ii, 44
Pratt, Judge O.C: at trial, ii, 366
Pratt, Rev. S.W: i, 34n, 48; 108n, 94
Prattsburg (N.Y.): i, 77, 90 ff.; church life, 93 ff.; 154 ff., 158-9; observes centennial, ii, 387; Prentiss house, 389
Prayer meetings: male priority, i, 366
Prentiss, Judge Stephen: i, 32, 77; ancestry, 90 ff.; 95; moves to Amity, 101; to Angelica, 149; made elder, 149; 164, 178; to Cuba, ii, 63; home, i, 91, 98, ii, 349
Prentiss, Mrs. Stephen (Clarissa): i, 32, 90, 93 ff.; ii, hears of death of Narcissa, 316

Prentiss Children
Prentiss, Clarissa: i, 91; marries, ii, 67
Prentiss, Edward Warren: i, 91; Cayuse boy named after him, 287; 502, 505; ii, 39, 70, 212
Prentiss, Harriet: i, 91, 100, 191, 384; marries, ii, 67
Prentiss, Harvey: i, 90, 97
Prentiss, Jane Abigail: i, 77, 91; letter from Narcissa, 371 ff.; 502, 529; writes to Perkins, ii, 26; Whitman calls on, 70*; marriage suggested, 182; urged to migrate, 212 ff.; letter from Perkins, 451*
Prentiss, Jonas Galusha: i, 91, 326, 451, 503; ii, 42, 67, 340 ff.; learns of death of Whitmans, 349; writes to Meek, 351
Prentiss, Mary Ann: i, 91; marries Lyman Judson, 180
Prentiss, Narcissa: i, 4*, 31 ff.;

engaged, 86; early life, 90 ff.; church life, 96*; singer, 97; education, 99*; rejects Spalding, 100*; teaches school, 100*; applies to ABCFM, 101*; engaged, 103*; appointed, 105*; Marcus returns, 139 ff.; marriage, 149*; *see also* Whitman, Narcissa

Prentiss, Stephen: **i**, 91, 97
Prentiss, Warren: **ii**, 358n

"Presbygational churches": **i**, 58, 94
Presbyterian Church: **i**, 58; New School, 87n; 94, 392n; **ii**, 386
Presbyterian Church, Associate: **ii**, 153
Presbyterian Church, First of Ore: organized, **i**, 339*; 370; native members, 408, 498; **ii**, 21, 23, 114*; Finley and Rodgers join, 153-4; continuing, 395*; members killed in massacre, 395; record book, 403n
Presbyterian Churches, in Ore: among Nez Perces and Spokanes, at Kamiah and Lapwai, Ida., **ii**, 397 ff.; Umatilla Reservation, 397
Presbyterian Churches, of N.Y: of Wheeler, **i**, 74; Prattsburg, 93 ff.; Angelica, 149; Utica, 181
Presbyterian Historical Society: **i**, xiv; **ii**, 173n, 392; 403n
Printing press: **i**, 59, 353; to Lapwai, 377, 380 ff.; **ii**, 15, 135; taken to The Dalles, 189
Pritchett, K: defense counsel at trial, **ii**, 366, 368 ff.
Pringle, Mrs. Catherine Sager: **i**, xvi, 97; **ii**, illus., 407; 449; *see also* Sager, Catherine

Privacy, lack of: **i**, 366, 415
Protestant Churches: respond to Nez Perce appeal, **i**, 24*
Protestant colony in Ore: **i**, 107, 485, 523; Whitmans hope, **ii**, 56, 76, 208; *see also* reenforcement
Provost, J.B: U.S. Commissioner, **i**, 310
Prudential Committee, ABCFM: **i**, 28 ff., 31, 81-3, 107, 151; appoint Gray, 182; 439, 450; meets Feb. 1842, 499 ff.; dismisses Spalding, 502, 513; **ii**, 51, hears Whitman, 53*
Puget Sound: **i**, 312, 315, 485; **ii**, 170
Puget Sound Agricultural Co: **i**, 327, 483
Pugh, Mrs: assists Narcissa, **ii**, 182

Quarrels: **i**, 230; *see also* discord
Quincy (Ill.): **i**, 424; **ii**, 70
Quinine: Narcissa takes, **ii**, 5

Rae, W.G: **i**, 119
Railroad: over Rockies, **i**, 127; across Panama, 335; Whitman travels by, **ii**, 63 ff., Spalding crosses country, 436
Ransom paid by HBC: to Cayuses, **ii**, 321; to Nez Perces, 328
Raped, girls by Indians: **ii**, 307
Readers Digest: article in, **ii**, 131
Reconciliation and Rededication: **i**, 388
Red River Colony: at Winnipeg, **i**, 10; sent to Ore., 481*, 487
Red River Mission School: **i**, 10 ff., 15 ff.; illus., 41; 36n, 22, 246, 506-7; **ii**, 165
Reenforcement to Ore. Mission: **i**, 341*; personnel, 343*; arrives at Wait., 350;

Whitman pleas for help, 438; regrets asking, 527 ff.
Reenforcement of 220 requested: i, 315*; Whitman's involvement, 320*, 527; 348, 523; only a dream, ii, 54, 77
Rehberg, Mrs. Goldie: ii, 393-4
Religion: primitive beliefs of natives, i, 454; ii, 29n
Religious meetings for natives: i, 285, 299, 385, 413; at Lapwai, 369*; 498; described by Hastings, 511; Spalding's success, ii, 21; Whitman's summary, 53-4, 111, 157; see also evangelization
Religious rivalry: i, 427*; ii, 112, 120, 142
Religious training: white children: ii, 160
Rendezvous, fur: of 1831, i, 18, 128; 1834, 27, 129; 1835, 33*, 127 ff.; 1836, 205*; 1838, 348 ff.; 1840, 424, 441
Rennet, calves: for cheese, i, 471
Rewards offered for capture of murderers: ii, 357n, 400n
Reynolds, Maj. Robert B: defense counsel at trial, ii, 366
Ricard, Father Pascal: ii, 201 ff., 203; 291n, 267, 310
Rice, William H.: i, 437
Richard, Nez Perce: see Tack-i-too-tis
Richards, Deacon James: i, 53; sons, James Jr. & William, 53-4
Richards, Walter Alden: i, xvi
Richardson, Marvin M: ii, 401n, 401n
River Indians (Columbia): accepts code of laws, i, 507; ii, 20
Roberts, Rev. Wm: ii, 189
Robidoux, Antoine: ii, 32

Rocking chair: ii, 379
Rocky Mountain Fur Co: i, 18
Rodgers, Andrew: ii, 152*; studies for ministry, 154*; 159 ff., 182, 236, 241, 249; wounded, 254-6; massacre victim, 260 ff.
Rogers, Cornelius: i, 198n, 345, 356; leaves Mission, 459*; engaged to Maria Pambrun, 461*; marries Sarah Leslie, 462; drowned, 462; criticizes Spalding, 466; transferred to Tsh., 500; interpreter, ii, 9-10; drowned, 16
Roman Catholic Archdiocesan Archives: i, xiv
R.C. missionaries: i, 247, 263*, 358; subsidized by HBC, 360*; brought complications, 361, 427*; at Ft. W.W., 482; activities, 507; Whitman seeks to counteract, 525*; de Smet's plans, 527; ii, 71, 76; plan stations near Waii, 142, 158; begin stations, 200*; meet Whitman, 202*; negotiate with Cayuses, 205*; appraisal, 208*; 276
R.C. priests for Will. Vall: i, 358, 483
Roof, sod: i, 251, 365; emigrant house, 480; plans for board roof, ii, 151
Rosati, Bishop Joseph: i, 18-9
Rose, Isaac P: i, 207
Ross, Alexander: i, 13
Ross.John E: ii, 210
Rotten Belly: see Tack-en-sua-tis
Rousseau, Father: ii, 207
Royal Ontario Museum, Toronto: ii, 193-4
Ruby, Dr. Robert H: ii, 357n
Rudd, Rev. George: i, 77, 83, 98
Rushville (N.Y.): i, 47, 67, 165, 458; sends plows, 463; Whitman returns, ii, 63*;

observes centennial, 387; Whitman Memorial School, 389
Russell, Burwell W: ii, 222n
Russell, Osborne: i, 207
Rye grass, place of (Wait-): i, 243; ii, 347, 376
Rynearson, Jacob: to Kamiah, ii, 151 ff

Sabbath observance: by natives, i, 21; 51, 95, 117, 123, 141, 172, 176, 192, 259; 377; Whitman observes, ii, 31, 37; 159; Mrs. Spalding refuses to flee, 271; Tiloukaikt inconsistent, 286
Saddlebags: Whitman's, ii, 394
Saffarans, Dr, Henry: at Waskopum, ii, 300, 302-4
Sagebrush: i, 216
Sager, Henry: ii, 125*; dies on trail, 126; property, 129-30
Sager, Mrs. Henry (Naomi): ii, 125 ff.; birth of dau., 126; dies, 127

Sager Children

Sager, Catherine: ii, 125; breaks leg, 126; describes Waii., 128; Narcissa, 128; life at Waii., 137*; reminiscences, 160*; comments on food, 162; feast for Tom Hill, 168 ff.; re. Joe Lewis, 218-9; measles epidemic, 233; re. Stickus, 246; account of massacre, 248 ff., 252-3, 255 ff.; terror indoors, 256*; heroine, 264 ff.; night of terror, 269*; account of Canfield, 278 ff.; describes looting, 281; burial of victims, 305; re. Tiloukaikt, 371, 305; captivity, 307 ff.; rape of Lorinda, 307 ff.; defends Susan Kimball, 313 ff.; Christmas observed, 322; Stanley's concern for, 333; witness at trial, 366; at 1897 observance, 385; re. Whitman's skull, 386; illus., 407; *see also* Pringle
Sager, Elizabeth: ii, 125; reminiscences, 161, 248 ff.; 291n, 253-4, 262, 266; 294n, 331; witness, 366; at 1897 observance, 385; *see also* Helm, Mrs.
Sager, Francis: ii, 125, 128; rebels, 138; runs away, 140*; returns, 141, 248-9, 257; massacre victim, 258
Sager, Hannah Louise: ii, 125, 248, 256, 266; dies during captivity, 286
Sager, Henrietta: born on trail, ii, 126; arrived at Wait., 129; 256, 266
Sager, John: ii, 125; weeps, 128; 141, 248-51; wounded, 252; massacre victim, 258, 262; John Sager School, 402n
Sager, Matilda: ii, 125; life at Waii., 137; describes Narcissa, 195; comments on Kane, 196; 212, 231, 254; describes massacre, 257; at 1897 observance, 385; re. Whitman skull, 386; illus., 407; *see also* Delaney

Sager myth: ii, 130*
Sager orphans: taken to Waii., ii, 128*, 129-30, at Waii., 137*; baptized, 139
St. Anne Mission: ii, 202; established 207*, 243; council at, 316; burned, 338
St. Anne (Ontario): i, 66
St. Louis (Mo.): i, 17 ff., 113 ff., 128, 138, 424; ii, 38-41, 70 ff.
St. Louis *Republican*: account of massacre, ii, 348-9 ff.
St. Mary's Mission (Mont.): i, 17, 526

St. Rose Mission: site, **ii**, 201*, 209, 241
Sakiaph, Cayuse Chief: believed to be Tamsucky, **i**, 490, 493
Salary for missionaries: **i**, 166, 336
Salem (Ore.): **i**, 308
Sales, Amos: **ii**, 218, 220, 249, 266; massacre victim, 287 ff.
Salmon: **i**, 216, 228, 260; Falls, **ii**, 85
Salt: **i**, 281
Salt Lake Basin: **ii**, 32
San Francicso Theological Sem: **i**, xiv
San Juan Mountains: **ii**, 35, 49
San Leandro (Cal.): **ii**, 155
San Polls Harrison (Indian boy): **i**, 15
San Foil Indians: **i**, 16
Sandwich Islands: *see* Hawaiian
Santa Fe: **ii**, 32
Satterlee, Dr. Benedict: **i**, 151, 166, 185
Satterlee, Mrs. B: ill, **i**, 166; died, 185
Saunders, Helen: see Church, Mrs.
Saunders, Judge L.W: arrives Waii., **ii**, 217; helps write Memorial, 217; teaches school, 249, 252 ff., massacre victim, 253; beheaded, 254
Saunders, Mrs. L.W, (Mary): her pamphlet, **ii**, 217, 220, 231, 249, 254; intercedes, 258 ff.; writes McBean, 268; describes looting, 278; heroine of captivity, 280; 299; describes captivity, 305 ff.; re. rescue, 322 ff.; 447
Saunders, Persia: **i**, 66-7
Sawmill: need for, **i**, 464; at Waii., 472; erection, **ii**, 134*, dam completed, 151; 181; cabin at, 220, 378; *see also* whipsawing

Scalping knives: **i**, 319
Scarlet fever: of Spaldings, **ii**, 86 ff,; of Walker, 111
Schools: at Ft. Van., **i**, 228; at Waii. for whites, **ii**, 110, 124, 131, 138, 152, 182, 190, 214; taught by Judge Saunders, 217, 231, 249, 252; experiences at, 257 ff.
Schools for Indians: **i**, 285*, 413; **ii**, 112; none in 1845, 135; criticized by Young Chief, 165; at Lapwai, 114, 184
Scott, Leslie M: **ii**, 232
Secret Service Fund: **i**, 315, 325; **ii**, 67
Seeds: **i**, 183, 256
Sehon, Rev. E.W: **i**, 25
Settle, John: warns Whitman, **ii**, 242
Settling the Indians: **i**, 464; **ii**, 181 ff.; *see also* agriculture; civilize
Seymour, Sir George F: **ii**, 96
Shaffner, Mrs. Helen L: **i**, 395n
Shaw, Wm: **ii**, 126 ff.; takes Sager orphans to Waii., 126*, 129; greets children at Portland, 331
Shawnee Mission: **ii**, 67 ff., 76; Indians in Oregon, 120
Sheep: at Ft. Van., **i**, 227, 232, 281*, 339; none overland in 1843, **ii**, 42; 156; at Waii., 377 ff,
Shepard, Cyrus: **i**, 26, 313, 394n
Shimnap: proposed for station, **i**, 420, 452, 457; idea abandoned, 468; site of St. Rose Mission, 468
Shoes: ordered, **i**, 318
Shortess, Robert: **i**, 411
Shoshone or Snake Indians: **i**, 129
Shults, Harold: **i**, 34n
Shuma-hici (Cayuse): **ii**, 198,

240; portrait by Stanley, 296, 289, 333*; *see also* Edward
Shumkain, Cayuse Indian: killed, ii, 363
Shunar: duels Kit Carson, i, 137
Side-saddles: i, 124, 135, 144, 183, 211, 216, 247, 289, 346
Simpson, Sir George: i, 11 ff., 14 ff., 312; meets Lee, 327 ff.; writes McLoughlin, 328; reports subsidy to priests, 360; re. Red River colony, 481; re. Will. Vall., 483; suspicious of Lee, 485; journey around world, 486 ff.; advocates River as boundary, 486; 517; distrusts Americans, ii, 45, 94*; describes Five Crows, 114; re. McKay, 204
Sinclair, James: i, 481
Sioux Indians: attack Gray's party, i, 342
Skulls of Whitmans: identified, ii, 340; mutilated, 386*
Slacum, Lt. Wm. A: visits Oregon, i, 308*, 311, 313, 320; meets Lee, 323; influences Wilkes exped., 472; sees Puget Sound value, 485; ii, 170; 352
Slavery: Negro, i, 53; Whitman not abolitionist, 471; Indian, ii, 172n
Smallpox epidemic: ii, 232
Smet, Pierre Jean de, S.J: i, 17, 424*, 429; at Rendezvous, 526; meets Whitman, 527; Whitman comments re. book of, ii, 71, 76*, 142
Smith, Alvin T: i, 423, 427; leaves for Will. Vall., 456; ii, 331
Smith, Mrs. AT. (Desire): i, 405
Smith, Rev. Asa B: i, 20, 87n, 145, 204, 268n, 258; critical of Whitman, Spalding, 284; his appointment, 344*; 347 ff., 352, 366-8; unhappy, 373*; threatens to leave, 377*; 376 ff.; goes to Kamiah, 379 ff.; hardships, 389; language student, 389; trouble-maker, 401; critical of Spalding, 419 ff., 439*, 449*; trouble with Indiana 445*; leaves Mission, 459*; to Honolulu, 460; re. cupidity of Indians, 470; dismissed, 500, 518; describes chiefs, ii, 13; Whitman writes to, 119; 185; takes Indian census, 232
Smith, Mrs. A.B. (Sarah): i, 343 ff; describes Whitman house, 363; poor health, 380; writes about missionaries, 407; sick, 440; terrified, 445; taken down river in canoe, 459
Smith, Jedediah: i, 21
Smith, Mr. & Mrs. Joseph: ii, 217, 220; move from sawmill to Waii., 287
Smith, Mary: ii, 220; raped, 307; 311; fictionized account, 313*; reference by Stanley, 334
Smith, Rachel (2nd Mrs- H. H. Spalding): i, 153; ii, 438
Smith, Rev. Samuel: i, 164
Smith, Sidney: i, 411
Smith, Thomas: ii, 42
Smithsonian Institution: Stanley's paintings, i, 40; ii, 334; 440n
Smoke house at Waii: i, 481, 502
Snake River: i, 209, 215 ff, 217 ff.
Soap making: i, 268; ii, 381
Soda Springs (Ida.): i, 214; ii, 32
Solomon, Spokane Indian: i, 358; ii, 111; Stanley's guide,

271; carries news of massacre, 273; 275; 343

South Pass: **i**, 27, 127 ff.; illus., 201; 192-6, 241, 349, **ii**, 31, 126, 390

Spalding, Rev. Henry Harmon: **i**, xvii, 4, 45, 71, 94, 98 ff.; rejected by Narcissa, 100; 140; 150*; life, 153*; appt. by ABCFM, 156; wagon, 156; characterized, 157; ordained, 157; remarks about Narcissa, 158*, 160, 417 ff., 421, 467; decides for Ore., 158; calls on Prentiss, 160; 172; receives passport, 174; journey, 184 ff.; arrives Ft. W.W., 223; at Ft. Van., 230 ff,; decides on separate station, 231; selects Lapwai, 243*; to Ft. Van. for supplies, 248 ff.; equipment, 249; dau. Eliza born, 289*; whipping Indians, 300*; requests reenforcement, 315*; moves to Clearwater River, 333; defends costs, 338; organizes Mission Church, 339*; potato crop, 362; success with Nez Perces, 369*; Whitman with, 370*; criticized by Smith, 374 ff.; married white to Indian, 376; printing press to Lapwai, 381; translates hymns, 395n; funeral for Alice Clarissa, 387; receives Griffings, 406; criticized, 419*, 421*, 438*, 467; trouble with Indians, 444*; called to Kamiah, 446; opposed selling to Meth., 447*; claimed unbalanced, 449; Whitman objects to natives as church members, 498 ff.; dismissed by Board, 499 ff.; order received, 518*;

Vol. **ii**: life threatened, 6; approves laws of Nez Perces, 9*; White visits Lapwai, 21*; beginning of Whitman-Saved-Oregon story, 45; suspicious of R.C. missionaries, 76*; ill, 86; successful missionary, 114*; prints Gospel in Nez Perce, 135*; trouble with Old James, 184; poisoning accusation, 236 ff.; illus., 241; ride to Umatilla, 243*; parts with Whitman, 248; with Brouillet, 279 ff.; escapes Cayuses, 281*; anti-Catholic obsession, 285-6; appeals to Bishop, 314; urges retaliation, 315; leaves for Ft. W.W., 322*, 326*; appraisal, 327; in Will. Vail., 331 ff.; remarries, 356n; letter of appreciation to Ogden, 332*; witness, 367; returns to Nez Perces, 395; baptizes many, 396 ff.; injured and ill, 398; Whitman names to Cayuse couple, 398; dies, 398; letters to wife, 438, 449

Spalding, Mrs. H.H. (Eliza): **i**, xvii, 45; stillborn babe, 140; 150 ff.; life, 155*; description, 155; 157, 172; anti-Catholic, 174; ill, 186, 459, 467; 190-6, 205 ff.; 216, 222, 245 ff.; has dau., 289*; son, 403; advises husband, 421; harassed at school, 444; teaches Indian women to spin, 509; insulted by Indians, **ii**, 6 ff.; ill, 7; 26; has scarlet fever, 86; brother arrives, 179; dau. born, 182; her "ladder," 222n; learns of massacre, 270 ff.; tombstone, 286; dies, 331

Spalding, Eliza (dau.): born, **i**, 289; ill, 390; at Waii. school, **ii**, 131, 152; spoke Nez Perce, 162, 239, 241; 258;

Timothy tries to rescue, 287; interpreter, 305; effects of captivity, 328; witness, 366; *see also* Warren
Spalding, Henry Hart (son): born, i, 431n; baptized, 409
Spalding, Marcus Whitman (grandson): ii, 391
Spalding, Henry and Eliza (Nez Perce Indians): ii, 396
Spalding (Ida.): church at, ii, 402n
Spalding State Park: *see* Nez Perce Park
Spalding's *Senate Document:* ii, 39, 223n, 291n, 291n, 292n, 294n, 354n, 354n, 354n, 354n, 440*, 438*; *see also* Whitman-Saved-Oregon
Spanish Trail: ii, 32
Spectacles: i, 73; for Narcissa, 451; 503; ii, 2; poor eyesight, 7
Spencer, Hon. J.C: i, 17, 424, 514; ii, 44, 47
Spin & weave: i, 509; by Nez Perce women; spinning wheels, 283; ii, 151, 380
Spokane Berens: i, 15; death, 16; son of Chief Cornelius, 357
Spokane Falls (Wash.): i, 255; 471
Spokane Garry: i, 14 ff., 35n, 16, 19*, 22 ff.; illus., 42; 137, 204, 301, 356; opposed R.C., 429; 507; ii, 186; invites Spalding to baptize, 397
Spokane House: i, 13
Spokane Indians: i, 13, 16; promise protection, ii, 343; mourn departure of missionaries, 345; mission work resumed, 397
Spokane Mission: *see* Tshimakain
Squash: ii, 152, 246
Stanfield, Joseph: hired by Whitman, ii, 180; 218, 249, 257, 260, 266; digs grave for victims, 268; 281, 288; joins in looting, 278; "a necessary evil," 305; desires Mrs. Hays, 314; arrested, 332; flees to Calif., 332; re-buried bodies, 340
Stanley, John Mix: i, xv, 287, 431n; visits Waii., ii, 197; Tsh., 198*; narrow escape, 271; reports massacre to Walker & Eells, 273; helps Osborn, 276; helps Sager girls, 324, 331; illus., 296; discovery of paintings, 333*
Statuary Hall (Wash., B.C.): ii, 69
Steamboats: *Majestic,* i, 173; *Chariton,* 178; *Diana* 180, 184, 282; *Junius,* 172; *May Dacre,* 27; *Tliaddeus,* 59
Stephen, Nez Perce: ii, 114
Stewart, Sir Wm. Drummond: i, 133
Stickus, Cayuse Chief: i, 274*; ii, 82; guides emigration, 85-6; 238; warns Whitman, 246*, 304; meets with Newell, 341; captures Joe Lewis, 342; 361; witness, 366, 371; dead, 397
Stoves: i, 227, 253, 318; at Ft. W.W., ii, 5; Indians destroy, 278, 380
Strong, Rev. Henry P: i, 78 ff., 83; ii, 64
Strong, James Clark: ii, 64
Suapies" (Americans): i, 204, 234n
Subsidy from HBC for R.C: i, 360*, 483, 487; unknown to Whitman, 528
Subsidy from U.S. Govt: for Meth. Mission, i, 313, 315, 321*; 325; 361, 487; for emigration, 516
Sugar: from Hawaii, i, 381; price, ii, 152; 378
Sugargrove (Penna.): i, 65 ff.

Sunday: *see* Sabbath

Superstitions, Indian: *see* "Te-wats"

Supplies: from HBC, **i**, 231 ff.; request for, 318*; bill, 336, 347; Spalding sends to Ft. Hall, **ii**, 82; emigrants' demands, 103, 112-3, 122, 131; loss of sales, 149*; Osborn's account book, 152*; sold by Indians, 116; trade for cattle, 123, 136; fewer calls in 1846, 179; Whitman refuses to sell to R.C., 205; none at The Dalles, 214

Sutter, John A: **i**, 350-1; Fort, **ii**, 144, 155, 199

Sweat baths, Indian: **ii**, 200, 233

Sweetwater River: **i**, 127, 193

Tack-en-sua-tis, Nez Perce Chief (Rotten Belly): **i**, 133 ff., 204, 209 ff., 215, 244 ff., 249, 370, baptized by R.C., 508; Spalding baptizes, **ii**, 396

Tack-i-too-tis, Richard (Nez Perce): **i**, 136, 141, 165, 183, 234n, 206, 258-9, 266, 508

Talbot, Theodore, **ii**, 75

Tallow: **i**, 502

Tamsucky, Cayuse Chief (Sakiaph or Feathercap): **i**, 288, 490 ff., 531; accused of assault on Narcissa, **ii**, 4; son, Waie-cat, 8; emotional, 8; savage countenance, 21; 149, 198, 237, 240, 246, 260, 304; rapes Lorinda Bewley, 307; 309, 311; threatens Spalding, 328; painting by Stanley, 334; 341; killed, 363; accused, 369

Taiutau or Tawatoe: *see* Young Chief

Taos (New Mex.): **ii**, 32, 36*

Temoni, Samuel (Nez Perce): **i**, 184

Tents: **i**, 183; for 1838 party, 347; for Whitmans on Tucannon, 369 *

Teutakas, Nez Perce Chief: *see* Joseph

"Te-wats," Indian medicine men: **i**, 273 ff., 506; **ii**, 142; Whitman, a white te-wat, 237*; killed, 56, 277

Thaddeus (ship): to Hawaii **i**, 59

Thanatopsis: re. Ore., **i**, 50

The Dalles: **i**, 233; Indians accept code of laws, **ii**, 20; Narcissa at, 104, 123, 140, 149, 197, 200; Bushman at, 300; Indians flee, 303; skirmish with Cayuses, 338; Whitman recommends site for college, 215, 382; *see* Waskopum

The Hat (Nez Perce Indian): **i**, 256, 342 ff.; killed, 356; **ii**, 317

Thing, Capt. Joseph: **i**, 214

Thompson, Albert W: **i**, xvi

Thompson, David: **i**, 21

Thompson, Erwin N: **ii**, 58 fn, 173n, 221n, 331

Thompson, Lucy: Jason Lee wife, **i**, 326

Thomson, Samuel: founder of medical cult, **i**, 178; Thomsonianism, 272

Thornhollow (Ore.): **i**, 471; **ii**, 246

Thomton, J. Quinn: in Wash., **ii**, 350

Thrapp, Dan: **ii**, 358n

Threshing machine: **i**, 454; **ii**, 197, 376

Thunder Strikes: *see* James, Old

Tiloukaikt, Cayuse Chief: **i**, 263, 287, 416, 451*, 489*; confronts Whitman, 489*, 491*, 531; **ii**, 149; portrait by Stanley, 221n, 194, 333; illus., 226; negotiates with

R.C., 205*, 238 ff.; 240; warriors of, die, 249; attacks Whitman, 252 ff.; 258, 264, 279; lost control of young men, 287, 304; protects captives, 304; conscience-stricken, 305; 312; at Indian council, 315*; escorts captives to Ft. W.W., 323; flees, 345, 361; surrenders, 363 ff.; confesses, 368; declares innocence, 369; Catherine's comments, 371; baptized, hanged, 372

Timothy, Nez Perce Chief (Timosa): i, 245, 290, 372 ff.; joins church, wife baptized, 409; portrait, 431n; farms at Lapwai, 444; ii, 122; wife Joins church, 21; tries to rescue Eliza, 270, 284; fails, 287, 304-5; pursues murderers, 363 ff.

Tobacco: i, 233, 454, 152; price, ii, 152; 356n

Toilets: i, 305 fn,

Toledo (Wash.): i, 327

Tolmie, Dr. Wm. Frazer: i, 225; writes re. te-wats, ii, 238

Tomahas, Cayuse Chief: i, 490, 494; ii, 149, 163; Kane's comments, 193; portrait, 194, 225; conspirator, 220; kills Whitman, 252; attacks Saunders, 254; 279, 304; taken prisoner, 365; confesses, 368; declares innocence, 370; baptized, hanged, 372

Tomahawk: ii, 252

Toupin, John: marries Mme. Dorion, i, 303

Townsend, John K: i, 129, 221, 225

Trading with the Indians: difficulties of, i, 444

Trappers, American: i, 21, 203 ff.; see also beaver trade

Travel experiences: i, 122*; 171*; from Narcissa's letters, 177*, 212*; outfit, 182*; on march, 187*; South Pass, 192*; at Rendezvous, 205*; Ft. Boise to Ft. Van., 219*; from Wait. to Lapwai, 289; travel with sheep, 339; in canoe, 447; Spalding's ride, ii, 6; Whitman's ride, 31 ff.; dust on trail, 126

Treaty of Joint Occupation, 1818: i, xvii, 174, 297, 307*, 311, 465, 485, 487, 518; ii, 9, 41, 94; see also Oregon boundary

Trees, fruit fit nut: at Ft. Van., i, 226; Narcissa takes sprouts to Waii., 256; locust, chestnut, butternut, walnut, 256; beginnings in horticulture, 278*; apple trees cut down, ii, 339; inventory at Waii., 376; at Lapwai, 376

Trial of murderers: court records, ii, 240; 246, 365*; guilty verdict, 367*

Tshimakain: i, 355; site selected, 356*; no converts, 408; limited possibilities, ii, 185; abandoned, 345 ff.

Tualatin Plains: camp meeting, ii, 24

Tucannon River: i, 290; Whitmans camp, 369*

Turkeys: i, 222, 227, 285

Tutuilla Presby. Church: ii, 403n

Tyler, Pres. John: i, 424, 464, 514, 515; ii, 44 ff., 45, 431

Typhoid fever: ii, 288

Uinta Basin: ii, 32-3

Umatilla Indians: i, 242

Umatilla Reservation: ii, 403n

Umatilla River: i, 220, 274, 471; ii, 149, 197, 246

Umhawalish, Cayuse Chief:

baptized, named Marcus Whitman, **ii**, 398; wife named Narcissa, 398; graves, 403n
Umtippe, Cayuse Chief (Cut Lip): **i**, 243, 263, 267, 273 ff., 287 if., 299, 395n; died, 451
Uncompahgre River: **ii**, 35
United States jurisdiction over Oregon: Whitman's interest in, **i**, 523, 528; **ii**, 91*; Whitman's boasts, 93 ff.; his claim, 214; prophesy about his death, 245; 352; *see also* Ore. Territory
U.S. War Dept: **i**, 173, 174
Ute Indians: **i**, 129

Vancouver Island: Ft. Van. moved to, **ii**, 94; awarded to Great Britain, 170
Vegetables: **i**, 210, 222; at Ft. Van., 226; at Waii., 257, 362; prices, **ii**, 152; 378
Veyret, Father F: **ii**, 372
Victor, Frances Fuller: **i**, 205; **ii**, 59n; doubted Whitman legend, 441-2
Victoria (B.C.): **ii**, 158
Violin: Eells, **i**, 511; Rodgers, **ii**, 153, 381
Voorhees, Mrs. Dudley: **i**, 70n
Wagon, Spalding's: first across Ida., **i**, 156 ff., 185, 188, 206, 209 ff.; reduced to cart, 214; 217-8; left at Ft. Boise, 218; opened part of Oregon Trail, 440; seen at Ft. Boise, **ii**, 85
Wagons: over Rockies, **i**, 135, 140, 142*, 192*; over Blue Mts., 440*; at Waii., 442; Whitman recommends emigrant wagons, **ii**, 73 ff.; wagon road to Columbia, 92; in Waii. inventory, 377
Wagons with emigrations: **i**, 346; left at Ft. Hall, 480;

516*; **ii**, 72, 83*, 85*, 88
Waie-cat, Cayuse, son of Tamsucky: accused of burning gristmill, **ii**, 8; portrait by Stanley, 198, 297, 289; among conspirators, 240; helps kill Bewley and Sales, 288; picture discovered, 333-4; escapes capture, 357n, 363-4
Waiilatpu (Whitman's Mission): outpost on Ore. Trail, **i**, xviii, 244, 523-4; site selected, 241*; meaning of name, 243; illus., 245, 287; begin housekeeping, 252*; Indian ownership, 305n; visitors at, 302; strategic location, 410, 479; described, 411, 472; life at, 463; ordered closed, 500, 518; called "the dark spot," **ii**, 26; refuge for immigrants, 103; crowded, 216*; roll-call, eve of massacre, 219*; looted, 278*; desolate, 347; Eells buys claim, 400n; described in inventory, 376 ff.; illus., 405, 408
Waiilatpu buildings: 1st house, **i**, 250*, 267, 285, 293*, 362; illus., 434; torn down, 480; 2nd house, 364*, 414*; whitewashed, 415; emigrant house, 463; blacksmith shop and other buildings, 480*; schoolroom added, **ii**, 109; for missionary wives, 190; Indians prevent building, 205; burned, 338*; ruins, 339 ff.; inventory, 379; *see also* gristmill; sawmill
Waite, Dr. F.C: **i**, 70n, 63, 70n, 87n, 76, 146n
Wakeman, Rev. Joel: **i**, 75, 92-4, 98 ff., 100, 161; **ii**, 349
Waldo, Daniel: critic of Whitman, **ii**, 90

Waldo, Rev. Levi Fay: **i**, 92, 95, 97, 100, 161; **ii**, 194
Waldo, Peter: Whitman critic, **ii**, 77, 80
Waldron, Larry J: re. millstones, **ii**, 173n, 292n
Walker, Courtney M: **i**, 26
Walker, Deward E: **i**, 268n
Walker, Rev. Elkanah: **i**, 230, 343, 351*; selects Tsh. site, 356*; to Lapwai, 363; chews tobacco, 367; 379; opposes selling to Meth., 448, 451; at mission meeting, 466*; describes meeting, 512; meets de Smet, 527; ill with scarlet fever, **ii**, 111; tutors Rodgers, 154; rejects moving to Waskopum, 188 ff.; portrait by Stanley, 198; leaves Tsh., 345; translates part of Gospels into Flathead, 346; letters from Whitman, 415; *see also* Tshimakain
Walker, Mrs. Elkanah (Mary): **i**, 292, 343; comments re. R.C., 361; re. discord, 366 ff.; children born, 368-9, 416, 502; comments re, mission meeting, 512; re: Whitman's ride, 523; children born, **ii**, 112, 158, 343; learns of massacre, 343 ff.; at Waii., 346; died, 358n, 385

Walker Children
Walker, Abigail: born, **i**, 416; portrait by Stanley, **ii**, 198
Walker, Cyrus: born at Wait., **i**, 369; to school, **ii**, 152
Walker, Jeremiah, **ii**, 158
Walker, Joseph Elkanah: **ii**, 112, 346
Walker, Sam: **i**, 392n, 393n

Walker and Eells: interview with Whitman, **i**, 378; Narcissa begs forgiveness, 458; at 1841 meeting, 466*; Board's order of Feb. 1842, 501; at Waii., 1842, 511 ff.; learns of fateful order, 519 ff.; 522, 529; to Waii., 1845, **ii**, 138*; winter 1846-7, 183; abandonment of Tsh. considered, 185; no converts at Tsh., 186; shocked by massacre, 343; move to Ft. Colville, 344 ff.; escorted to Ft. Waters, 345; appraisal, 346; visit Waii., 346; to Will. Vall., 347
Walker, Joel P: **i**, 426, 441 ff.
Walker, Wm: **i**, 9, 18, 19, 23-4
Walla Walla (Wash.): **ii**, 134, 382 ff.; observes centennial, 387
Walla Walla Indians: **i**, 420, 490; accept code of laws, **ii**, 22; attack immigrants, 148; party to Calif., 199-201; census, 403n
Walla Walla River: **i**, 220 ff., 250, 252; **ii**, 134
Walla Walla *Statesman*: **ii**, 435 ff.
Walla Walla Valley: settlement, **ii**, 383 ff.
Waller, Rev. Alvin F: **ii**, 24; leaves Waskopum, 185; 191, 451
Wallowa Valley: **i**, 410
Wap-tash-tak-mahl (Feathercap): *see* Tamsucky
War, Diplomacy, or Emigration: **i**, 484*
Warren, Mrs. Eliza: *see* Spalding, Eliza
Washing clothes: on trail, **i**, 192, 218, 368; at Waii., **ii**, 160 ff., 380
Washington (D.C.): **i**, 529; **ii**, 42*, 48
Washington state: *see* Old Ore.
Washington Historical Quarterly: **i**, xiv, 195

Washington State Historical Soc: **i, xiv; ii,** 416

Washington State University (Pullman): **i, xiv; ii,** 416

Waskopum (The Dalles): station started, **i,** 314; Narcissa at, **ii,** 8, 26; picture mentioned, 28n; winter at, 15; given to ABCFM, **ii,** 185*; Perrin and Hinman move to, 191*, 197; lives threatened, 302 ff.; end of mission, 304; *see also* The Dalles

Watch: owned by Saunders, stolen by Stanfield, **ii,** 278; recovered, 356n

Waters, Lt. Col. James: **ii,** 336; Ft. Waters established, 341*; commands Volunteers, 341, 347; sends for Tsh, missionaries, 345

Webster, Daniel: **i,** 515; Webster-Ash-burton Treaty, **ii,** 40; met Whitman, 44, 431; *see also* Ashburton-Webster Treaty

Weed, Dr. George L: Whitman called, **ii,** 42 ff.; dress described, 43; return visit, 70

West, Rev. John: **i,** 10 ff.

West Almond (N.Y.): **ii,** 67

Westport (Mo.): **ii,** 36 ff., 71-4

Western Reserve College: **i,** 71 ff., 154

Wheat: at Ft. Van., **i,** 226; at Waii., 257, 362, 452, 472; supply burned, **ii,** 8*, 89, 378

Wheaton, Mrs. W. Merle: **i,** 70n

Wheeler (N.Y.): **i,** 23, 58, 83 ff., 93, 150 ff.

Whipping of Indians: **i,** 300*; common practice in Calif., by U.S. Navy, bv HBC, 302; practiced by Indians, 490; penalty for breaking laws, **ii,** 11; Indians resist, 20

Whipsawing logs: **i,** 250, 364, 414; **ii,** 134

White, Dr. Elijah: **i,** 16, 302, 313; returns to States, appointed Indian agent, 448; carries Board's order to Ore., 501, 514; with emigration, 514*; arrival in Ore., 517; meets Whitman, 524; describes assault on Narcissa, **ii,** 3; goes to Waii. and Lapwai, 9; impressions of Narcissa, 9; gives code of laws to Nez Perces, 10 ff.; insists on office of High Chief, 13; reaction of HBC, 19, 94*; returns to Waii., 19*; Cayuses accept laws, 22; tells Whitman about treaties, 40; 44, 46; critical of Lee, 49; accuses Whitman of high prices, 88; Whitman critical, 102, 104, 105; confronted by Whitman, 141; 143; returns to States, 147; blamed by Whitman, 149

Whitewashing of house: **i,** 373

Whitman, Dr. Marcus: portrait, **i,** frontis.; introductory summary, xvii ff.; volunteers for Ore., 3*, 31*; ancestry, early years, 45 ff.; to Plainfield, Mass., 51*; religious experience, 54 ff.; medical training, 57*; riding with Dr. Bryant, 60*; life, 1826-31, 64*; in Canada, 66 ff.; receives M.D. degree, 89; three years at Wheeler, 71*; rejected by ABCFM, 77; poor health, 79 ff.; commissioned by ABCFM, 81*; leaves for Rockies, 84; engaged to Narcissa, 86

1st journey to Rockies, **i,** 111*; commissioned, 112*; differences with Parker, 113*; hostility of men of caravan, 115*; journal, 117*; treats cholera victims, 120*; over Rockies, 122*; at

512 *Marcus and Narcissa Whitman and the Opening of Old Oregon* INDEX

Rendezvous, 127*; operates on Bridger, 131*; buckskin dress, 131; separates from Parker, 132*; return journey with Indian boys, 136*; advocates use of wagons, 142*; married, 149*; search for associates, 150*; finds Spalding, 158 ff.; personal appearance, 161*; wedding, 163*; final instructions, 176*; to Liberty, Mo., 178*; buys outfit, 182*; on march, 184*, 187*; at South Pass, 192*; to Ft. Van., 203*; at Rendezvous, 205*; struggle with wagon, 217 ff.; over Blue Mts., 220 ff.; at Ft. Van., 225*, 230*

Waiilatpu selected, i, 242*; first house, 250*, 293*; food supplies, 254*; beginnings of agriculture, 256*; evangelization, 258*; birth of Alice, 264*; versatile doctor, 271*; medical practice, 272*; farms, 275*; animal husbandry, 279-80*; educational activities, 285*; household, 294*; Lee and Dr. McLoughlin visit, 298-300*; requests workers, 315*, 319*; financial report, 335*; reenforcement arrives, 341*; second house, 362*; language study with Nez Perces, 369*; dissension in Mission, 373*; answers Parker, 382 ff.; death of Alice, 383*; independent missionaries arrive, 404*, 423*; difficulties with Spalding, 417*, 468*; difficulties with R.C., 427*; first immigrants arrive, 1840, 440*; trouble with Indians, 443*; called to Kamiah, 445; opposes selling to Meth., 449*; ill health, 451 ff.; letter to Bryant, 462*; described by Drayton, 472*; arrival of Red River colony, 481 ff., life threatened, 488*; confrontations with Tiloukaikt, 489-93*; Board's order of Feb. 1842, 499*; Mission meeting Sept. 1842, 518*; decides to go to Boston, 520 ff.; motives, 521*; leaves for Wash., 529

Vol. ii: Leaves for East with Lovejoy, 31; swam Colorado River, 33; crossed Continental Divide, 35*; Taos to St. Louis, 36*; promotes Ore. emigration, 40*; in Washington, 42*; buckskin dress, 43, 49, 51 ff., 64; synopsis of Bill, 46*, 459; in New York, 48*; in Boston, 50*; order revoked, 53*; silhouette of, 53; plans for future of Mission, 53*; returns to Rushville, 63*; gets Perrin Whitman, 65*; last farewells, 66*; "My plans Require Time and Distance," 68*; westward, 69*; advice to emigrants, 71*; with emigration, 74*, 77*, 79*; arrival at Ft. Hall, and confronts Grant, 82*, 83*; wagon road opened, 85*; accused of exhorbitant prices, 88*; results of ride, 91*; meets Lee, 104; escorts Narcissa to Waii., 104 ff.

Immigrants at Waii., ii, 108 ff., 150*, 219*; foot injured, 111; believes white men to inherit land, 118 ff.; dreams of establishing college, 1844, 119; receives Sager orphans, 125 ff.; their guardian, 130, 141; confrontation with White, 141; anxiety, 142*; life threatened, 145; saves immigrants from Indians,

148*; considers leaving Waii., 163*; confrontation with Young Chief, 164*; success of immigration, 170*; receives Waskopum from Meth., 185*; sketch by Kane, 192*, 194*, 227; meets with R.C. priests, 202 ff.; memor-izes Congress, 210*; last letters, 212*; crowded Waii., 216*;

Measles epidemic, ii, 231*; accused of poisoning Indians, 234*; white te-wat, 237; warned of tragedy, 242*, 246*; prophecy of death, 245; parts with Spalding, 248; wounded, 251*; dies, 262; burial, 281; unfulfilled plans, 301; prophecy fulfilled, 352; Waii. inventory, 376*; clothing, medical instruments, 381; reburial, 385; skull identified, 386; name used for Cayuse baptism, 398

Whitman, Mrs. Marcus (Narcissa): (see Prentiss, for life before marriage): i, xvii; personal appearance, 161; marriage, 163*; travel letters, 171 ff.; anti-Catholic, 174; letters, 177*, 189 ff., 504*; diary, 212*; soliloquy to trunk, 216; at Ft Van., 225*, 226*; singing, 228; return to Ft W.W., 246*; arrival at Waii., 252*; Alice Clarissa born, 264*; aids sick Stickus, 274*; first trip to Lapwai, 289 ff.; alone at Waii, 334, 530*; Columbia Maternal Assoc., 353*; discord in home, 365*; objects to Walker chewing tobacco, 367; "down to the river to cry," 368; camping on Tucannon, 369*; objects to leaving Wait., 379 ff.; illus., 398; critical of Spalding, 417*; poor eyesight, 451, 503; receives half-breed girls, 441, 456; threatened by Indians, 493; "Among a people of no law," 495*; lonely, 503; receives David Malin, 503*;

Vol II: Portrait, frontis.; attempted assault, 2*; ill, 4, 7; to Waskopum, 7*, 15*; under doctor's care, Ft Van., 24; in Will. Vall., 25 ff.; Marcus returns, 26; "Adapted to a different destiny," 26*; dreads returning to Waii., 26; letters to Marcus, 81*; sick, discouraged, 104*; crowded home, 108*; limited food supplies, 109; arrival of Sager orphans, 125*; prayers, 173n; Sagers describe home life, 137*; sings with Rodgers, 153*; yearns for relatives, 158*; picnic for children, 161 ff.; bathing in river, 161; improved health, 181; Kane sketch, 194*; 227; low-necked dress, 195; last letters, 212*; last day, 248*; wounded, 256; death, 260*; burial, 281; her remains, skull, hair, 340; wardrobe, 381; memorial building, 384; reburial, 386; name used for Cayuse baptism, 398

Whitman family
(relationship to Marcus and Narcissa noted in parenthesis):
Alice (niece): see Wisewell
Alice Clarissa (dau.): birth, i, 264*; 291 ff.; illus., 398; death, 384*; grave, ii, 129
Augustus (bro.): i, 46, 61, 141, 166, 191, 277, 458, 463
Beza (father): i, 46 ff., 48, 58
Mrs. Beza (Alice) (mother): i, 46-7, 58; see also Loomis, Mrs.

Deborah (niece): **i**, 141
Freedom (uncle): **i**, 49, 112
Freeman (cousin): **ii**, 70
Henry (bro.): **i**, 47, 61
John (ancestor): **i**, 45
Perrin B. (nephew): **i**, 112, 235n, 486; **ii**, 63, 65*, 75, 84 ff.; sees Spalding's wagon, 98n; arrives at Waii., 103; called "good boy," 113; comments re. sawmill, 173n; learns language, 157; to Waskopum, 190 ff., 197, 238; 300 ff.; life threatened, 302; with Volunteers, 338; back at Waii., 339 ff.; identifies Marcus skull, 340; Volunteers take horses, 343; rescues sheep, 377
Samuel (grandfather): **i**, 49, 112
Samuel (bro.): **i**, 47, 59; **ii**, 65

Whitman, Rev. Silas (Nez Perce minister): **ii**, 403n
Whitman Academy: **ii**, 384
Whitman College: **i**, xiv, 161; **ii**, 382*, 416; *Quarterly*, **i**, xiv; **ii**, 443
Whitman controversy: literature, **ii**, 441*
Whitman County (Wash.): **ii**, 390
Whitman household: **i**, 294; home life described, 502; **ii**, 108, 131; Sager children in, 137*, 160*; Narcissa describes, 182; 219
Whitman letters: **i**, xix, 61, 89, 108n, 106, 171, 212, 246, 257 ff., 272, 299; given to Ore. Hist. Soc., 384; last letters, **ii**, 212*; 415* ff.
Whitman literature: **ii**, 387*, 431*, 441*
Whitman massacre: list of victims, **ii**, 219; day of, 248* ff.; Whitman skulls opened, 291n; attack outdoors, 252*; indoors, 255*; first reports, 269; HBC investigates, 266; victims buried, 281, 288, 340; summary of, 289; eyewitness accounts, 447 ff.
Whitman massacre, causes: te-wats superstitions, **i**, 273 ff., 473, **ii**, 142, 237*, 351; location of Waii., **i**, 444; poisoning wolves, 284, **ii**, 234; immigrations, **i**, 444, **ii**, 165, 317; culture conflicts, **i**, 443, **ii**, 118, 229; land ownership, **i**, 445, 488, **ii**, 205, 317-8 ff.; alleged poisoning of Indians, 166, 318, 351; Whitman sympathetic to immigrants, 101, 230 ff.; blood feud theory, 230, 317 ff.; half-breed agitation, 166, 317; lies of Lewis, 218*; measles, precipitating cause, 165, 199, 231*, 233, 318, 351; *see also* murderers
Whitman memorials: *see* monuments
Whitman Mission National Historic Site: **i**, xvi, 351, 364, **ii**, 155, 391*; illus., 404-6, 408-9
Whitman Monument Assoc: **ii**, 384, 391
Whitman National Monument: **ii**, 392
Whitman namesakes: **i**, 138, 441, 502; **ii**, 64, 391 ff.
Whitman-Saved-Oregon Story: **i**, 482-3, 523; **ii**, 39 ff., 45, 49, 83, 387 ff.; evolution of, 431*; theory discredited, 443*; lingering echoes, 393 ff., 444
Whitman Seminary: chartered, **ii**, 383
Whitman-Spalding Centennial: **ii**, 386

Whitman's Ride: **i**, 482, 529; causes, 521*, 528*; Narcissa's comments, 530; **ii**, Board explains, 56; appraisal, 90*; Whitman's comments, 180

Wild Horse Creek: **ii**, 396
Wilkes, Lt. Charles: exploring expedition, **i**, 465*, 472, 486
Wilkes, George: **ii**, 74, 83
Willamette: River, **i**, 128; Valley, 133; Falls, **ii**, 16; *see also* population
Willamette Cattle Co: **i**, 310
Willard, Miss Emma: **i**, 100
Wilkins, Caleb: **i**, 441
Williams, Rev. Joseph: visits Waii.. **i**, 480, 510
Williams, Richard: mountain man married by Spalding, **i**, 375
Williams College (Mass.): **i**, 7 ff., 28, 53
Willoughby, Dr. Westel: **i**, 62 ff, 72
Wind River (Wyo.): **i**, 348; Mts., 129
Window glass: **i**, 253, 415
Winter, 1846-47: severity, **ii**, 181, 183*
Wisewell, Mrs. Alice Whitman (niece): **i**, 47, 50; **ii**, 59n, 349
Wisner, B.B: **i**, 78, 84, 109n
Wolves: **i**, 284; poisoned, **ii**, 235, 281; dig up bodies, 340
Women: restricted privileges, **i**, 352; no prayers in presence of men, 366; invited to Mission meeting, 512
Woodbridge, Ross: **i**, xvi, 108n, 169n, 537n; **ii**, 194*, 221n
Wool industry: **i**, 48, 283; **ii**, 156, 380
Wright, Col. George: **ii**, 383 ff.
Wyandot Indians: **i**, 9 ff.
Wyeth, Nathaniel: **i**, 26 ff., 133, 210

Yakima River: **ii**, 201
Yale University: Beinecke Coll., **i**, xiv; Coe Coll., 166; **ii**, 415-6
Yellow Serpent (Peu-peu-mox-mox): **ii**, 19, 22; son killed, 143 ff.; **ii**, 201, 222n, 241
Young Chief (Tauitau or Tawatoe), Cayuse Chief: **i**, 247, 263; becomes Catholic; house for him, 471; 496; confrontation with Whitman, **ii**, 164*; 110; house becomes St. Anne Mission, 201, 205, 208; negotiates with Catholics, 205*; at Indian council, 316 ff.; house burned, 338; cooperates with Volunteers, 361; attacks Tiloukaikt, 363; surrenders culprits, 364 ff.; witness, 366, 371; flees Oregon City, 372
Young, Mr. and Mrs. Elam: **ii**, 217, 220, 448; operate mill at Waii., 287
Young, Daniel: **ii**, 217, 220, 448
Young, Ewing: **i**, 308
Young, F.Y: **i**, 315
Young, James: **ii**, 217; victim, 269
Young, John: **ii**, 217, 220; at Waii., 235; 293n, 448
Youth's Companion: **i**, 355

www.ingramcontent.com/pod-product-compliance
Lightning Source LLC
Chambersburg PA
CBHW022054150426
43195CB00008B/138